Map Legend

BOUNDARIES

▬ ▪ ▬ ▪ ▬ ▪ ▬	.... International Boundary
▬ ▪ ▬ ▪ ▬ ▪ ▬	.... Internal Boundary
++++++++++++++	.... National Park or Reserve
─ ─ ─ ─ ─ ─ ─ ─ ─	.... The Equator
·················	.... The Tropics

SYMBOLS

◉ NATIONAL	.... National Capital
● PROVINCIAL	.... Provincial or State Capital
● Major	.... Major Town
● Minor	.... Minor Town
■	.... Places to Stay
▼	.... Places to Eat
✉	.... Post Office
✈	.... Airport
i	.... Tourist Information
⬤	.... Bus Station or Terminal
66	.... Highway Route Number
☾ ✝ 🕌 ⛪	...... Mosque, Church, Cathedral
∴	.... Temple or Ruin
✚	.... Hospital
☼	.... Lookout
⚑	.... Camping Area
⌐	.... Picnic Area
⌂	.... Hut
▲	.... Mountain or Hill
═╪═	.... Gate
┄━┄	.... Railway Station
═══	.... Road Bridge
┅┿┅	.... Railway Bridge
⇒ ⇐	.... Road Tunnel
⟶⟶ ⟵⟵	.... Railway Tunnel
⌇⌇⌇	.... Escarpment or Cliff
⌣	.... Pass

ROUTES

───────	.... Major Road or Highway
─ ─ ─ ─ ─ ─	.... Unsealed Major Road
───────	.... Minor Road
─ ─ ─ ─ ─	..... Unsealed Road or Track
═══════	.... City Street
+++++++++++	.... Railway
━━●━━	.... Subway
─ ─ ─ ─ ─	.... Walking Track
─ ─ ─ ─ ─	.... Ferry Route
+++++++++	.... Cable Car or Chair Lift

HYDROGRAPHIC FEATURES

	.... River or Creek
	.... Intermittent Stream
	.... Lake, Intermittent Lake
	.... Coast Line
	.... Spring
	.... Waterfall
	.... Swamp
	.... Salt Lake or Reef
	.... Glacier

OTHER FEATURES

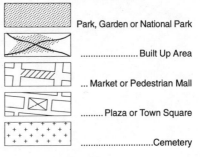

Park, Garden or National Park

.... Built Up Area

... Market or Pedestrian Mall

.... Plaza or Town Square

.... Cemetery

Note: not all symbols displayed above appear in this book

Kenya

a travel survival kit

Hugh Finlay
Geoff Crowther

Kenya – a travel survival kit

2nd edition

Published by
  Lonely Planet Publications
  Head Office: PO Box 617, Hawthorn, Vic 3122, Australia
  Branches: PO Box 2001A, Berkeley, CA 94702, USA
                12 Barley Mow Passage, Chiswick, London W4 4PH, UK
                71 bis rue Cardinal Lemoine, 75005 Paris, France

Printed by
  Singapore National Printers Ltd, Singapore

Photographs by
  Rona Abbott (RA), Geoff Crowther (GC), David Else (DE), Hugh Finlay (HF),
  George Pavlu (GP), Mark Savage (MS), Debra Tan (DT), Tony Wheeler (TW)

  Front cover: Kikuyu dancer, The Image Bank (MS)
  Back cover: Giant lobelia (DE)

  Safari Guide illustrations by Matt King

First Published
  February 1991

This Edition
  February 1994

Although the authors and publisher have tried to make the information as accurate as possible, they accept no responsibility for any loss, injury or inconvenience sustained by any person using this book.

National Library of Australia Cataloguing in Publication Data

Crowther, Geoff, 1944
    Kenya – a travel survival kit.

    2nd ed.
    Includes index.
    ISBN 0 86442 202 4.

    1. Kenya – Guidebooks.
    I. Finlay, Hugh II. Title. (Series: Lonely Planet travel survival kit).

916.762044

text © Hugh Finlay 1994
maps © Lonely Planet 1994
photos © photographers as indicated 1994
climate charts compiled from information supplied by Patrick J Tyson, © Patrick J Tyson 1994

Hugh Finlay

After deciding there must be more to life than a career in civil engineering, Hugh first took off around Australia in the mid '70s, working at everything from spray painting to diamond prospecting, before hitting the overland trail. Since joining Lonely Planet in 1985, Hugh has written *Jordan & Syria – a travel survival kit*, co-authored *Morocco, Algeria & Tunisia*, and has contributed to other Lonely Planet guides including *Africa on a shoestring* and *India*.

Hugh lives in central Victoria, Australia, with Linda and daughters Ella and Vera.

Geoff Crowther

Born in Yorkshire, England, Geoff took to his heels early on in search of the miraculous, taking a break from a degree in biochemistry. The lure of the unknown took him to Kabul, Kathmandu and Lamu in the days before the overland bus companies began digging up the dirt along the tracks of Africa.

In 1977, he wrote his first guide for Lonely Planet – *Africa on the cheap*. He has also written *South America on a shoestring*, travel survival kits to *Korea & Taiwan*, *Korea* and *East Africa* and has co-authored guides to *India, Malaysia, Singapore & Brunei* and *Morocco, Algeria & Tunisia*.

He still spends at least six months overseas each year, these days often accompanied by his Korean wife, Hyung Poon, and his son, Ashley Choson. The trio live in a Korean temple-style house in northern New South Wales, Australia.

When not travelling or sweating over a hot computer, Geoff devotes his time to landscaping, playing guitar, dreaming up impossible schemes, arguing with everyone in sight, pursuing noxious weeds and brewing Davidson's plum wine. To his credit, he remains generally *compos mentis*.

From the Authors

Without listing them in any order of preference, Geoff would like to sincerely thank the following people for their friendship, help, encouragement, hospitality and constructive criticism:

George Pavlu of Brisbane, Australia, who I took with me on my previous trip to East Africa and who hasn't been able to stay away from the place ever since (bless you Wangui but you missed out; Norwegian millionaires don't make it). George contributed to the research, maintained his usual highly explosive degree of humour (most of the time), and amazed all and sundry by his prodigious consumption of Tusker lager. A professional photographer and film scriptwriter, he has continued to introduce me to facets of Kenya about which I might otherwise have remained ignorant. More power to your elbow, my friend.

Malcolm Gascoigne of Yare Safaris, Nairobi, Kenya, who enthusiastically met me at Nairobi airport on arrival with a Tusker lager and never let up until the day I left. Malcolm's humour was contagious, he helped me with facts and figures which I wouldn't have had access to otherwise, and his consumption of Tusker lager was at least the equal of George's. I also have to thank him for introducing me to my first ever Maralal International Camel Derby.

Alice Njoki Chege, a Kikuyu from Kiambu, who not only helped me out of sticky situations (and, sometimes, into them) but contributed enormously to the research with a speed and thoroughness which would have left me for dead. She also introduced me to life on the 'wrong side of the tracks' where all you meet are smiling children's faces, tenacity and extreme hardship. Alice showed me a Kenya which I would probably never have seen without her help. Good luck with your studies.

Ian North, formerly of Kumuka (an overland company) who first greeted me with the words, 'I used to hate you', but subsequently became one of my best friends, gave me his house for a month, and helped me in so many other ways. Good luck with your negotiations, mate!

Don Cornes and Margaret, a Kiwi and Kikuyu (respectively) from Nairobi, both of whom injected sense into nonsense when nothing else prevailed. What's also not generally known is that he makes the best spaghetti bolognaise in Nairobi (invitation only) and that he has a very discerning eye for African art – real art. Don's place is awash with *the best*.

Philip Jackson (and Purity – or was it Catherine? – only time will tell), a bearded, bespectacled, Yorkshire tyke and ex-overland safari driver who never let up on the jokes and who now runs a safari/travel agency (in between Tusker lagers) in Nairobi. Philip, you don't need growth hormone.

Alex McCafferty, Australian balloon pilot at Fig Tree Lodge, who gave me a free flight over Masai Mara – my first ever. What an experience!

Mem Bourke, an ebullient Kiwi based in Nairobi with Kumuka, who took me to Masai Mara after the Maralal Camel Derby (where she won the cup for 'Best Lady'). Keep riding those camels, Mem!

Aidan Flannery, former Africa representative for the *Observer* and the *Guardian* and now an advertising manager based in Nairobi, for his astute analysis of political trends, his good humour and for looking after excess research material whilst I was in Tanzania. Even after a crate of White Cap, his BBC delivery would have David Attenborough green with envy.

Jane and Julia Barnley of Sirikwa Safaris, Kitale, for their superb hospitality whilst I was in that area.

Paul 'Sliderule' Marsh and Kikuyu Jackie of Nairobi (for whom I was best man at their wedding). Shame on you, Paul, you couldn't even pronounce Jackie's Kikuyu names at the ceremony but then you never were circumcised! I trust your marriage will be as tumultuous as expected.

Brian Mitchell, technical officer at the British High Commission in Nairobi, who drove me through to Kampala. We couldn't believe it when we discovered that we were born only half a km from each other in the same town (Todmorden) yet had never met.

And all the regulars at Buffalo Bill's and The Pub – 'Welsh' Gareth, 'Kenyan' Kevin, 'Maori' Kevin, big Don Fergie, Sonny, Alex plus many of those mentioned above, and that inimitable and boisterous trio, Margaret Zemei, 'Cutie' and Gladys, who were the

originators of that now famous Nairobi saying: 'Just imagine! No problem! Even you!'

As well as many of those already mentioned by Geoff, Hugh would like to thank Paul Cameron at the Australian High Commission for his efforts to revive Hugh's laptop, which suffered a major breakdown in Nairobi.

From the Publisher

This edition of Kenya was edited at the Lonely Planet office in Melbourne by Miriam Cannell. Richard Stewart handled the mapping, illustrations, design and layout, and Margaret Jung designed the cover. Thanks to Frith Pike for proofreading, and to Ian Foletta and Rob Rachowiecki for help with editing the Safari Guide. Thanks also to Matt King for the Safari Guide illustrations and to Greg Herriman for the Safari Guide design.

Finally, thanks to all those travellers who took the time and effort to write to us with suggestions and comments; their names appear on page 327.

Warning & Request

Things change – prices go up, schedules change, good places go bad and bad places go bankrupt – nothing stays the same. So if you find things better or worse, recently opened or long since closed, please write and tell us and help make the next edition better.

Your letters will be used to help update future editions and, where possible, important changes will also be included in a Stop Press section in reprints.

We greatly appreciate all information that is sent to us by travellers. Back at Lonely Planet we employ a hard-working readers' letters team to sort through the many letters we receive. The best ones will be rewarded with a free copy of the next edition or another Lonely Planet guide if you prefer. We give away lots of books, but, unfortunately, not every letter/postcard receives one.

Contents

Introduction

In past centuries the main visitors to Kenya were the Arab traders who plied their dhows along the eastern coast of Africa. These days it's tourists and adventurers who come to Kenya in large numbers – currently around one million annually – and little wonder as it has an amazing variety of attractions.

For many people Kenya means wildlife and in this field alone it is one of the best places in Africa. Millions of wildebeest on their annual migration, and equally large numbers of pink flamingos massing on the shores of the rift valley soda lakes are breathtaking sights. For sheer majesty it's hard to beat the sight of a herd of elephants crossing the plains with Africa's most famous mountain, the evocative snowcapped Kilimanjaro, rising in the background. Kenya is also the

heart of safari country and a trip through a few of Kenya's spectacular reserves is a memorable experience.

If relaxation is on your mind then head for the coast. Mombasa is a town with a history, and from here any of the superb picture-postcard beaches are easily accessible. But without doubt the highlight of the coast is the island of Lamu, where the Arab influence is evident and the pace of life definitely a few steps behind the rest of the country – the perfect place to unwind for a week, or two...

Those people seeking more energetic pursuits will find no shortage of challenges – Kenya has some excellent mountains to climb, especially the popular Mt Kenya with its unusual alpine flora, and the much less visited Mt Elgon in the west on the Ugandan border. Organised camel treks through the semidesert north of the country also attract a steady stream of hardy souls.

The heart of this relatively prosperous country is the bustling capital, Nairobi, a friendly, modern and efficient city where things work and business can be taken care of in a snap – a far cry from so many other African countries where even simple things like a telephone call can be a major exercise. Added to this is the fact that Kenya has excellent air connections with Europe, Asia and elsewhere in Africa, making it the ideal place for a short visit, or the starting or finishing point for a longer sojourn in Africa. Either way it's a great place – don't miss it.

Facts about the Country

HISTORY
The Birthplace of Humanity
The rift valley which runs through the centre of Kenya has been established as the 'cradle of mankind' as a result of the now famous digs of the Leakey family in Olduvai Gorge (Tanzania) and around Lake Turkana (Kenya). Their discoveries of several hominoid skulls, one of which is estimated to be 2½ million years old, have radically altered the accepted theories on the origin of humans.

Before the East African digs, the generally accepted theory was that the ancestors of modern humans were of two different species: the ape-like *Australopithecus africanus* and the *Australopithecus robustus*. It was believed one of these died out while the other gave rise to *Homo sapiens*. The Leakey discoveries suggested that there was a third contemporary species, *Homo habilis*, and that it was this one which gave rise to modern humans while both the Australopithecus species died out, leaving no descendants.

Early Tribes
This area of Africa has a large diversity of peoples – Kenya is home to almost every major language stock in Africa. Even Khoisan, the 'click' language spoken by the Bushmen and Hottentots in southern Africa, has its representatives, although these days they are only a tiny community close to the Tana River near the coast. This diversity is clear evidence that Kenya has been a major migratory pathway over the centuries.

The first wave of immigrants were the tall, nomadic, Cushitic-speaking people from Ethiopia who began to move south around 2000 BCE. They were pastoralists and depended on good grazing land for their cattle and goats, so when the climate began to change and the area around Lake Turkana became more arid, they were forced to resume their migration south. They were to reach as far as central Tanzania.

A second group of pastoralists, the Eastern Cushitics, followed them around 1000 BCE and occupied much of central Kenya. The rest of the ancestors of the country's medley of tribes arrived from all over Africa between 500 BCE and 500 CE, though there was still much movement and rivalry for land right up to the beginning of the 20th century. Even today it hasn't ended completely. The Bantu-speaking people (such as the Gusii, Kikuyu, Akamba and Meru) arrived from West Africa, while the Nilotic speakers (such as the Maasai, Luo, Samburu and Turkana) came from the Nile Valley in southern Sudan.

Arab Traders
While migrations were going on in the interior, Muslims from the Arabian peninsula and Shirazis from Persia (now Iran) began to visit the East African coast from the 8th century CE onwards. They came to trade, convert and settle, rather than conquer as they had done in North Africa and Spain. Their dhows would head down on the north-east monsoon bringing glassware, ironware, textiles, wheat and wine and return with ivory, slaves, tortoiseshell and rhino horn.

This trade soon extended right across the Indian Ocean to India and beyond. (Even China entered the fray at one point early in the 15th century, with a fleet of 62 ships and an escort of some 37,000 men, after the king of Malindi had sent the Chinese emperor a gift of a giraffe!) Many of the traders stayed to settle and intermarry with the Africans. As a result, a string of relatively affluent and Islamic-influenced coastal towns sprang up along the East African coast from Somalia to Mozambique, acting as entrepôts for the cross-Indian Ocean trade. Though there was naturally rivalry between these towns from time to time, up until the 16th century life was relatively peaceful. All this was to be rudely shattered with the arrival of the Portuguese.

Portuguese Invaders

While the Spanish Crown was busy backing expeditions to the Americas, the Portuguese were determined to circumvent the Ottoman Turks' grip on trade with the Far East, particularly the trade in spices which were worth more than their weight in gold in Europe. Throughout the 15th century, the Portuguese had been exploring further and further down the western coast of Africa until, in 1498, they finally rounded the Cape of Good Hope and headed up the east coast under the command of Vasco da Gama.

They were given a hostile reception both at Sofala on the Mozambique coast and at Mombasa but were lucky to find a friendly sultan at Malindi who provided them with a pilot who knew the route to India. Da Gama was back again with another expedition in 1502, after selling the first expedition's cargo of spices in Portugal and earning a small fortune.

The main Portuguese onslaught began with Dom Francisco de Almeida's armada of 23 ships and some 1500 men in 1505. Sofala was burned to the ground and looted, Kilwa was occupied and garrisoned, and Mombasa was taken after a naval bombardment and fierce street fighting. Mombasa was sacked again by Nuña da Cunha in 1528. The Arab monopoly of Indian Ocean trade had been broken. Though the Ottoman Turks attempted to wrest it back from the Portuguese in 1585 and again in 1589, they were unsuccessful.

After the original onslaught, there followed two centuries of harsh colonial rule. Tribute was demanded and levies were imposed on all non-Portuguese ships visiting the coastal towns. Severe retribution was the reward for the slightest offence. Economic exploitation came hand in hand with a drive to convert the local population to Catholicism but they never had much success at this, and whenever they abandoned an outpost, those who had been 'converted' reverted to Islam. Mombasa came to be the principle Portuguese outpost following the construction of Fort Jesus there in 1593.

The Portuguese task was made easier since they were able to play one sultan off against another, but their grip over the East African coast was always tenuous since their outposts had to be supplied from Goa in India, where the viceroy had his headquarters. Delays were inevitable. The colonial bureaucracy also became moribund because of the sale of offices to the highest bidder. And, in the final analysis, Portugal was too small a country with insufficient resources to effectively hold onto a worldwide empire.

The beginning of the end came in 1698 when Fort Jesus fell to the Arabs after a siege lasting 33 months. By 1720, the Portuguese had packed up and left the Kenyan coast for good.

Omani Dynasties

The Arabs were to remain in control of the East African coast until the arrival of the British and Germans in the late 19th century. The depredations of the Portuguese period, however, had exacted a heavy price and the constant quarrelling among the Arab governors who succeeded them led to a decline in the trade and prosperity which the East African coast had once enjoyed. Political and economic recovery had to wait until the beginning of the 19th century.

Throughout the 18th century, Omani dynasties from the Persian Gulf entrenched themselves along the East African coast. They were nominally under the control of the Sultan of Oman but this control was largely ineffective until Seyyid Said came to the Omani throne in 1805. The Omanis had built up a relatively powerful navy during the latter part of the 18th century and Seyyid Said decided to use this to bring the East African dynasties into line. In 1822 he sent an army to subdue Mombasa, Paté and Pemba, which were then ruled by the Mazrui clan.

The Mazruis appealed to Britain for help, which it provided the following year in the form of two warships on a survey mission. The commander of one of these ships,

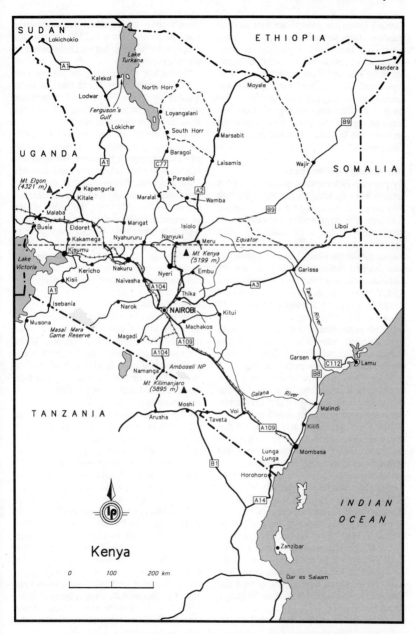

Kenya

Captain Owen, decided to act first and ask questions later, so the British flag was raised over Fort Jesus and a protectorate was declared. A small garrison was left in charge, but three years later the British government repudiated the protectorate and the flag was hauled down. Seyyid Said reasserted his control the following year, garrisoned Fort Jesus and began to lay out clove plantations on Zanzibar. In 1832 he moved his court to Zanzibar.

19th-Century Colonialism

By the mid-19th century, several European nations were showing an interest in the East African coast, including the British and the Germans. The British were interested in the suppression of the slave trade and when Seyyid Said moved to Zanzibar they set up a consulate at his court. Later an agreement was reached between the British and the Germans as to their spheres of interest in East Africa. Part of the deal was that the Sultan of Zanzibar would be allowed to retain a 16 km-wide strip of the Kenyan coastline under a British protectorate. It remained as such right up until independence when the last Sultan of Zanzibar, Seyyid Khalifa, ceded the territory to the new government.

Since it was occupied by the Maasai pastoralists, the Kenyan interior, particularly the rift valley and the Aberdare highlands, remained impregnable to outsiders until the 1880s. Their reputation as a proud warrior tribe had been sufficient to deter Arab slavers and traders and European missionaries and explorers up to that date. But with the rest of Africa being combed by European explorers, Kenya's turn was soon to follow.

Notable early explorers who lived to tell the tale were Gustav Fischer (a German whose party was virtually annihilated by Maasai at Hell's Gate on Lake Naivasha in 1882), Joseph Thomson (a Scot who reached Lake Victoria via the rift valley lakes and the Aberdares in 1883), and Count Teleki von Szek (an Austrian who explored the Lake Turkana region and Mt Kenya in 1887). James Hannington, an Anglican bishop who set out in 1885 to set up a diocese in Uganda,

wasn't quite so fortunate. He discovered Lake Bogoria (known as Lake Hannington during colonial days) but was killed when he reached the Nile.

By the late 19th century, the Maasai were considerably weakened and their numbers reduced by years of civil war between two opposing factions, the Ilmaasai and the Iloikop. The dispute was about which of the two were the true descendants of Olmasinta, the legendary founder of the tribe. Rinderpest (a cattle disease), cholera, smallpox and famine had also taken their toll between 1880 and 1892. Because of this, the British were able to negotiate a treaty with Olonana (known as Lenana today), the *laibon* (chief, or spiritual leader) of the Maasai. Armed with this treaty, the British were able to construct the Mombasa-Uganda railway through the heart of the Maasai grazing lands. The approximate halfway point of this railway is where Nairobi stands today.

White Settlement

With the railway completed and the headquarters of the colonial administration moved from Mombasa to Nairobi, White settlers began to move into the fertile highlands north of Nairobi in search of farming lands. Their interests naturally clashed with those of the Maasai, prompting the colonial authorities to pressure Olonana into restricting the Maasai to two reserves, one on either side of the new railway. Though this was a blow to Maasai independence, worse was to follow since the White settlers soon wanted the northern reserve as well. In 1910-11 those Maasai who lived there were forced to trek south, despite Olonana's objections.

Though it's probably true that it was the Maasai who had the greatest amount of land taken from them by the White settlers, the Kikuyu, a Bantu agricultural tribe which occupied the highlands around the western side of Mt Kenya, also suffered. The Kikuyu came to nurse a particular grievance about the alienation of land by White settlers later on in the 20th century. (See African Nationalism later in this chapter.) Many of the numerically larger tribes such as the Luo and

Luyha and the tribes of the north-east were hardly affected, if at all.

White settlement in the early years of the 20th century was led by Lord Delamere, a pugnacious gentleman farmer from Cheshire, England. Since he was not familiar with the land, its pests and its wildlife, his first ventures – into sheep farming and, later, wheat growing – were disastrous. By 1912, however, following the move to the highlands, Delamere and his followers had put the colony onto a more realistic economic footing by establishing mixed agricultural farms. Other European settlers established coffee plantations about the same time, including Karen von Blixen and her hunter husband, Bror. Her memoirs are to be found in the book *Out of Africa*, which has also been made into a very successful film.

WW I interrupted White settlement of Kenya for four years during which some two-thirds of the 3000 White settlers formed impromptu cavalry units and went off in search of Germans in neighbouring Tanganyika, leaving their wives behind to manage the farms. They were not entirely successful but they did eventually manage to drive the German forces into Central Africa with assistance from Jan Smut's South African units. However, Vorbeck's intrepid unit of 155 Germans and 3000 Africans remained undefeated when the armistice was signed in November 1918. Under the Treaty of Versailles, Germany lost Tanganyika and the British were given a mandate by the League of Nations to control the territory.

Settlement of Kenya resumed after the war under a scheme where veterans of the European campaign were offered land in the highlands, either at rock-bottom prices or on long-term loans. The effect of this was to raise the White settler population to around 9000 by 1920. By the 1950s it had reached 80,000.

African Nationalism
While all this was going on, more and more Kikuyu were migrating to Nairobi or being drawn into the colonial economy in one way or another. They weren't at all happy about the alienation of their land and this led to the formation of a number of associations whose principle concern was the return of land to the Kikuyu.

One of the early leaders of the Kikuyu political associations was Harry Thuku. Shortly after he was arrested for his activities by the colonial authorities in March 1922, a crowd of Africans gathered outside the Nairobi Central Police Station where he was being held. Reports differ as to what happened next but by the time the police had stopped shooting, between 21 and 100 people had been killed. Thuku was eventually exiled to Kisimayo and was only finally released from jail in 1930 after he had agreed to cooperate with the colonial authorities. His cooperation cost him his leadership of the Kikuyu movement since he was thenceforth regarded as something of a collaborator. This early Sharpeville led to the

Jomo Kenyatta

politicisation of the Kikuyu and was the start of a sustained campaign for political, social and economic rights. (Sharpeville refers to the notorious massacre by police of unarmed Black demonstrators in 1960 in the town of the same name in South Africa. It signalled the beginning of the ANC's armed struggle against the apartheid regime.)

While Harry Thuku's star was on the wane, that of another member of the tribe was on the rise. His name was Johnstone Kamau, later changed to Jomo Kenyatta, who was to become independent Kenya's first president. Kenyatta was born in 1892 in the highlands north of Nairobi, the son of a peasant farmer. He spent the early years of his life as a shepherd tending his fathers' flocks. When he was in his teens he ran away to a nearby Church of Scotland mission school where he picked up an education.

At the age of 29 he moved to Nairobi. He worked there as a court interpreter and water-meter reader but his real skills lay elsewhere – as an orator. He soon became the propaganda secretary of the East Africa Association which had been set up to campaign for land reform, better wages, education and medical facilities for Africans. At this time, Africans were barred from hotels and restaurants and were only considered for the most menial jobs within the colonial administration. Although it was official British government policy to favour African interests over those of the settlers in the event of conflicts, this was often ignored in practice because of the dominance of Lord Delamere's lobby in the Whites-only legislative council which had been formed after the protectorate became a colony. Recognising this, Kenyatta soon moved to the more outspoken Kikuyu Central Association as its secretary-general.

Shortly afterwards, in 1929, with money supplied by Indians with communist connections, he sailed for London to plead the Kikuyu case with the British colonial secretary. Though the colonial secretary declined to meet him, Kenyatta teamed up with a group called the League Against Imperialism which took him to Moscow and Berlin and then back again to Nairobi. He returned to London the following year and remained there for the next 15 years. He spent his time perfecting his oratory with Trafalgar Square crowds, studying revolutionary tactics in Moscow, visiting cooperative farms in Scandinavia and building up the Pan-African Federation with Hastings Banda (who later became the president of Malawi) and Kwame Nkrumah (who later became the president of Ghana). By the time he returned to Kenya in 1946, he was the recognised leader of the Kenyan liberation movement.

During WW II, the Belgian, British, French and Italian governments all recruited African troops to fight. The overall effect on Africans (as well as soldiers from other colonised peoples) was a realisation that the Europeans were not omnipotent. They could be defeated or, at the least, forced to come to terms with African aspirations for the same benefits and opportunities as their European overlords. Africans had also been trained in the use of arms. When the war ended, therefore, the returning soldiers were in no mood to accept the status quo and began to actively campaign for change.

The main African political organisation involved in the confrontation with the colonial authorities was the Kenya African Union (KAU), first headed by Harry Thuku and then by James Gichuru who himself stood down in favour of Kenyatta on the latter's return from Britain. The Kikuyu Central Association had been banned in 1940 along with many other similar organisations.

Mau Mau Rebellion

As the demands of the KAU became more and more strident and the colonial authorities less and less willing to make concessions, oath-taking ceremonies began to spread among various tribes like the Kikuyu, Maasai and Luo. Some of these secret oaths bound the participants to kill Europeans and their African collaborators. The Mau Mau was one such secret political society which bonded its members, willingly or otherwise, to the organisation via oathing ceremonies. Formed in 1952, it consisted mainly of

Kikuyu tribespeople, and its aim was to drive White settlers out of Kenya.

The first blow was struck early in 1953 with the killing of a White farmer's entire herd of cattle. This was followed, a few weeks later, by the massacre of 21 Kikuyu loyal to the colonial government. The Mau Mau rebellion had started. The government declared an emergency and began to herd the tribespeople into 'protected villages' surrounded by barbed wire and booby-trapped trenches which they were forbidden to leave during the hours of darkness. Some 20,000 Kikuyu 'home guards' were recruited to assist British army units brought in to put down the rebellion and to help police the 'protected villages'. By the time it came to an end in 1956 with the defeat of the Mau Mau, the death toll stood at over 13,500 Africans – Mau Mau guerrillas, civilians and troops – and just over 100 Europeans, only 37 of whom were settlers. In the process, an additional 20,000 Kikuyu had been thrown into detention camps.

Only a month after the rebellion started, Kenyatta and several other KAU leaders were arrested and put on trial as the alleged leaders of the Mau Mau. It's very doubtful that Kenyatta had any influence over the Mau Mau commanders, let alone that he was one of their leaders, but he was, nevertheless, sentenced to seven years' jail in the remote Turkana region after a trial lasting five months. He was released in 1959 but was immediately sent to Lodwar under house arrest.

The rebellion shook the settlers to the roots and gave rise to a number of White political parties with opposing demands, ranging from partition of the country between Blacks and Whites to the transfer of power to a democratically elected African government. It should have been obvious to anyone with eyes to see that the latter view would have to prevail in the end, but it wasn't adopted as official policy until the Lancaster House Conference in London in 1960. The rebellion did lead, however, to an exodus of White settlers who packed their bags and headed off to Rhodesia, South Africa and Australia. At the conference, independence was scheduled for December 1963 and the British government agreed to provide the new Kenyan government with US$100 million in grants and loans so that it would be able to buy out European farmers in the highlands and restore the land to the tribes from whom it had been taken.

In the meantime a division occurred in the ranks of the KAU between those who wanted a unitary form of government with firm centralised control in Nairobi and the others who favoured a federal set-up in order to avoid Kikuyu domination. The former renamed their party the Kenya African National Union (KANU) and the latter split off under the leadership of Ronald Ngala to become the Kenya African Democratic Union (KADU). Many of the White settlers, who had come to accept the inevitable, supported the KADU.

Kenyatta was released from house arrest in mid-1961 and assumed the presidency of the KANU. Despite his long period of incarceration by the colonial authorities, he appeared to harbour no resentment against the Whites and indeed set out to reassure the settlers that they would have a future in the country when independence came. At a packed meeting of settlers in Nakuru Town Hall in August 1963, he asked them to stay, saying that the country needed experience and that he didn't care where it came from. He assured them of the encouragement and protection of the new government and appealed for harmony, saying that he wanted to show the rest of the world that different racial groups were capable of living and working together. It did the trick. Kenyatta's speech transformed him, in the eyes of the settlers, from the feared and reviled spiritual leader of the Mau Mau into the venerable *mzee* (respected elder) of the post-independence years.

Most of the White settler farms have been bought out by the government over the years and the land divided up into small subsistence plots which support 15 to 20 people. This may well have appeased the pressure for land redistribution in a country with the world's highest birth rate but it has led to a serious decline in agricultural production (and therefore a diminishing tax base for the government) and has threatened to damage the region's delicate ecology. By 1980, Kenya was forced to import half its grain needs whereas in 1975 it was self-sufficient in these. The government is keen to halt the break-up of the 100-odd settler farms which remain but the prospects of being able to do this in a land-hungry nation are not good.

Independence

The two parties, KANU and KADU, formed a coalition government in 1962, but after the May 1963 elections, KANU and Kenyatta came to power. Independence came on 12 December 1963 with Kenyatta as the first president. He was to rule Kenya until his death in 1978. Under Kenyatta's presidency, Kenya developed into one of Africa's most stable and prosperous nations. Unlike many other newly independent countries, there was no long string of coups and counter-coups, military holocausts, power-crazy dictators and secessionist movements. It wasn't all plain sailing but he left the country in a much better state than he found it and, although there were excesses, they were minor by African standards. By the time he died, there were enough Kenyans with a stake in their country's continued progress to ensure a relatively smooth succession to the presidency. Violence and instability would have benefited few people. Kenyatta's main failings were that he was excessively biased in favour of his own tribe and that he often regarded honest criticism as tantamount to treason.

Control of the government and large sectors of the economy still remain in the hands of the Kikuyu, to the social and financial detriment of other ethnic groups. Corruption in high places remains a problem and once prompted J M Kariuki, a former Mau Mau fighter and later an assistant minister in the government, to remark that Kenya had become a nation of '10 millionaires and 10 million beggars'. There are indeed great disparities in wealth. Many destitute squat-

ters and unemployed people, especially in Nairobi, have little hope of ever finding employment – but this is hardly a problem peculiar to Kenya.

In 1964, Kenya effectively became a one-party state following the voluntary dissolution of the opposition KADU party. With it died the party's policy of regionalism and the two-chamber legislature became the single-chamber legislative assembly. However, when Oginga Odinga, a Luo, was purged from the KANU hierarchy in 1966 over allegations that he was plotting against the government, he resigned from the vice-presidency and formed his own opposition party, the Kenya People's Union. The party was later banned and Odinga was jailed. He was released when he agreed to rejoin KANU, but was imprisoned again in 1969 on spurious charges. After his release in 1971 he was banned from running for public office until 1977.

Similarly, Tom Mboya, an intelligent young Luo who was widely regarded as future presidential material, was murdered by a Kikuyu gunman in 1969. The ambitious Mboya was feared by influential Kikuyu who felt that he might have designs on succeeding Kenyatta as president. J M Kariuki, a very popular Kikuyu who spoke out stridently and often about the new Black elite and their corrupt practices, met a similar fate. He was assassinated in 1975. Other politicians who opposed Kenyatta – however mildly – found themselves arrested and held for long periods, often without trial.

The 1980s

Kenyatta was succeeded by Daniel arap Moi, a member of the Tugen tribe and regarded by Kikuyu power brokers as a suitable front man for their interests. Lacking the charisma of Kenyatta and the cult following which he enjoyed, Moi was even less willing to brook criticism of his regime and his early years were marked by the arrest of dissidents, the disbanding of tribal societies and the frequent closure of universities. There were allegations of conspiracies to overthrow the government whose details were often so labyrinthine they could have come straight out of a modern spy novel. Whether these conspiracies were real or just a convenient façade to justify Moi's consolidation of power is hard to tell since names and details were rarely released.

What certainly was real was the attempted coup by the Kenyan air force in August 1982. It was put down by forces loyal to the government but, by the time it was over, about 120 people had been killed and there was widespread looting of the major shopping areas. Twelve ringleaders were subsequently sentenced to death and 900 others received jail sentences. The entire Kenyan air force was disbanded and replaced by a new unit. Since then, other alleged conspiracies have come to light but, again, the details are rarely made known. The most publicised of these clandestine opposition groups was Mwakenya which supposedly centred around a number of lecturers at Nairobi University along with the exiled novelist and playwright, Ngugi wa Thiong'o. Certainly Ngugi has made his opposition to the Kenyan government quite plain but there's little evidence to support the claim that he was a leading light behind the movement.

President Moi was re-elected in March 1987 in an election which was most notable for the controversial voting system used. Candidates could only run in the secret ballot election after gaining a set percentage of the vote in a preliminary election whereby voters queued behind the candidate of their choice. If the candidate gained more than 70% of the queue vote, they were automatically elected and did not have to take part in the secret ballot election. The outcome was that at least 45 constituencies had no secret ballot as the candidate who had received over 70% of the turnout in the queue vote was automatically elected (it didn't matter that in one case the turnout was less than 9% of registered voters). In other constituencies, the number of candidates was significantly reduced because the nominees failed to win sufficient support at the preliminary election.

After the election, Moi expanded his cabinet to 33 ministers – many on the basis of political patronage – and, as a result, the government's (and therefore Moi's) position seemed totally secure. With the fall of a couple of outspoken politicians in the 1987 elections (amid allegations of vote rigging) it seemed unlikely that parliamentary opposition to Moi on major issues in the immediate future would be anything more than a whisper. Perhaps more significantly, changes to the constitution were rushed through parliament unopposed in late 1987 which gave Moi increased presidential powers, including the right to dismiss senior judges and public servants without redress. The independence of the judiciary had been a much-admired cornerstone of the Kenyan political system ever since independence and the changes were viewed with alarm by many sections of society.

From this point on there ceased to be any effective political opposition within the parliamentary system and the party further strengthened its hold by augmenting the ranks of the KANU Youth Wing who essentially served as pro-government vigilantes. They were frequently unleashed to disrupt demonstrations, harass opposition figures and maintain a climate of intimidation amongst those who might have similar thoughts. Many opposition political leaders were detained without trial during this period.

Yet the government was unable to silence various leaders of the Christian churches (especially the bishops of the Anglican church) who increasingly turned their sermons into political speeches. They were supported by an outspoken critic of government nepotism, Professor Wangui Mathai, the leader of the Green movement. All of them were vilified by both the president and various ministers and there were calls for their removal and even arrest on charges of sedition. Mathai probably suffered most when she was thrown out of her modest offices on University Way and forced to endure a public character assassination blitz whose script could have been put together from the trash scrawled on toilet walls.

But times were changing. Multiparty politics was sweeping Africa and Kenya was not to escape.

The 1990s

With the collapse of Communism in Eastern Europe and the break-up of the Soviet Union, the West's attention was abruptly refocused. No longer was it necessary to prop up corrupt African regimes which grabbed Western aid for all it was worth and pocketed the lion's share of the proceeds in the name of containing Communism. All that was finished.

The Kenyan government quickly found itself under intense pressure from the donor countries to introduce a multiparty system and to name a date for elections if aid were to be maintained. Though it prevaricated for a while, the government, faced with a foreign debt of some US$9 billion, a downturn in the economy, and determined grass-roots opposition in the form of FORD (Forum for the Restoration of Democracy), was forced to capitulate. To drive the point home, aid was suspended by virtually all Western countries in early 1992.

Suddenly, everyone was talking politics everywhere and anywhere and there emerged a clear consensus that FORD would sweep to victory in any election assuming it could keep its act together and that the elections were reasonably 'free and fair'. Unfortunately, the opposition shot itself in the foot in the lead-up to the elections. The principle players were Oginga Odinga, Kenneth Matiba, and Mwai Kibaki. Originally all members of FORD, but unable to stomach the idea of anyone but themselves being the new president, they split the party into three – FORD-Kenya (Oginga Odinga), FORD-Asili (Kenneth Matiba), and the Democratic Party or DP (Mwai Kibaki). From that point on, they had no chance.

In the meantime, Moi, no doubt, watched with glee. But he did more than that. According to the IMF/World Bank, he authorised the printing of KSh 9 billion (over US$250 million), unsupported by foreign currency/gold reserves, which was used to line the pockets of his supporters and blatantly buy votes for the ruling party (KANU). In the lead-up to the elections, the newspapers were full of pictures and stories of *wananchi* (peasants and workers) lining up to collect their KSh 500, a KANU-emblazoned T-shirt and a cap. Moi knew that full stomachs bought votes even if the economy collapsed shortly after the elections. Which it virtually did.

He also played the tribal card for all it was worth in his home area, allowing the Kalenjin to wreak havoc amongst Kikuyu settlers in the area whilst at the same time denying any complicity with police lack of action. Hundreds were killed and injured in these tribal clashes and thousands left homeless and destitute. Hardly anything has been done since to rehabilitate these people. The violence succeeded in driving Kikuyu (who were clearly not going to vote for KANU) from Kalenjin areas (Moi's home ground).

Another blatant ploy was to postpone the election until the final week of December and to ensure that it fell on a normal working day. Had it not finally been declared a public holiday about a week in advance, thousands of registered voters, particularly in the Nairobi area, would have been unable to travel back to the place where they were registered in order to vote. Moi was aware that he had little support in the Nairobi area and amongst the Kikuyu as the elections results were to show.

To curry the favour of the donor nations, international observers were brought in to monitor a cross section of the polling stations and to decide whether the elections had been 'free and fair'. As far as the voting itself went, the elections were fair to a greater rather than a lesser degree, though the various opposition parties predictably denied this. The trouble was, the observers were flown in only days before the election and, by then, the dirty deeds had been done. Moi and KANU swept to victory yet with only one-third of the total vote. Clearly, the opposition would have won if they had presented a united front but vanity and ambition got in the way.

The Future

Once the new Kenyan parliament gets down to serious business instead of staging walk-outs and trading insults (and even fisticuffs), the government will have a much harder job ahead of it. No longer will it be able to do just what it pleases. Outstanding issues which need urgent attention are corruption, the economy and resolution of the chaos in the currency market.

It's perhaps unfair to hammer a fledgling democracy in this way – how long did it take the Europeans and North Americans to get their systems stabilised and how much bloodshed did it involve? – but it's the '90s and the world is a smaller place. What cannot be excused is Moi's cynical sabotage of the economy in the pursuit of continued political power. This has affected everyone and those at the bottom of the economic scale most. Inflation is now rampant and prices are escalating daily, yet wages have remained the same. No doubt things will stabilise before too long since, after all, Kenya does have a diverse economy, but that may not be before major social upheaval.

And it's not just the economy which the government has to deal with but the continuing population expansion of around 4% per annum (one of the highest in the world) which is going to see Kenya's population grow from its present 22 or 23 million to around 37 or 38 million by the end of the century. This is already putting intense strain on health and educational facilities and is likely to result in increasing social, economic and political turmoil. Of the estimated 400,000 school leavers who come onto the job market each year, only around 30,000 manage to find formal jobs. Or, put another way, of the labour pool of some seven million, there are only about one million formal wage-paying jobs. By the end of the century, it's estimated that the labour pool will double.

This is an enormous problem, the solution to which is not at all obvious. The International Monetary Fund (IMF), from which Kenya was seeking loan support, prescribed the usual 'structural adjustment programme' (SAP) which included the sacking of some 45,000 civil servants. To most Kenyans, this was a dangerous and counterproductive measure since, on average, each wage earner in Kenya supports five people. The measure, if carried out, would therefore have directly affected a quarter of a million people. Indirectly, it would have affected the livelihoods of millions more since those affected by the cuts would have been forced to curtail their spending to the very bare essentials.

It seemed obvious to all those on the Kenyan side of the negotiating table that the IMF's SAP was designed not to create jobs but to push unemployment to an unacceptably high level, wipe out small business and put most products out of the reach of the average family. It would also clearly not wipe out corruption but increase it since, as those still in a job would find it harder and harder to make ends meet, the only solution would be to demand higher bribes for any service rendered. A corollary of this for those thrown out of work, their dependants and others who found themselves destitute, would have been a marked increase in crime, particularly robbery and theft. The effects of hard economic times are already plainly visible especially in Nairobi where there has been a vast increase in child beggars, on the one hand, and muggings by teenagers and young men, on the other.

Fortunately, to Kenya's credit, the IMF was thrown out in March 1993. It was a brave move in many ways, but the consequences may be just as traumatic. Most bilateral and multilateral aid is linked to IMF/World Bank approval of a country's economic policies. Without that approval, aid from the USA and Europe may not be resumed. The move incited a hot debate in the country's press about the pros and cons of aid. Some suggested it was a foolhardy decision which would bring further hardship and see Kenya marginalised; others suggested it was about time Kenya stopped relying so heavily on foreign aid and got its own act together. There are merits to both arguments but, when the dust has settled, the problems which led to Kenya's current turmoil will still be there and will have to be constructively addressed. ∎

Vanity and ambition also resurfaced shortly after the elections as several MPs, unable to stomach the prospect of life on the opposition benches, cynically defected to the KANU and were welcomed with glee. Loyalty to the voters who had elected them on an opposition ticket was apparently of no concern to these MPs.

Since then, Moi has continued to rule in much the same fashion as before and the opposition has so far disgraced itself in far-cical public conflicts over who should be the opposition leader. This was finally resolved with the choice of Kenneth Matiba – leader of FORD-Asili, the party which gathered the majority of the opposition votes.

GEOGRAPHY

Kenya straddles the equator and covers an area of some 583,000 sq km which includes around 13,600 sq km of inland water in the form of part of Lake Victoria. It's bounded in the north by the arid bushlands and deserts of Ethiopia and Sudan, to the east by Somalia and the Indian Ocean, to the west by Uganda and Lake Victoria, and to the south by Tanzania.

The country can be roughly divided into four main zones: the coastal belt, the rift valley and central highlands, western Kenya and northern and eastern Kenya.

Coastal Belt

This area covers some 480 km of Indian Ocean littoral including coral reefs and beaches, the Lamu archipelago, the Tana River estuary (Kenya's principal river) and a narrow, low-lying and relatively fertile strip suitable for agriculture. Beyond this, the land rises fairly steeply towards the central plateau and gives way to bushland and scrub desert.

Rift Valley & Central Highlands

These regions form the backbone of the country and it's here that Kenya is at its most spectacular scenically. The lake-studded rift valley runs the whole length of the country from Lake Turkana to Lake Magadi and is peppered with the cones of extinct volcanoes. It's bounded on the eastern side by the thickly forested slopes of the Aberdare Mountains and, further to the east, by the massif of Mt Kenya – Africa's second-highest mountain at 5199 metres. This is the most fertile area of the country and the lower slopes of the mountains are intensively cultivated. Nairobi, the capital, sits at the southern end of the central highlands.

Western Kenya

The west of the country consists of an undu-lating plateau stretching from the Sudanese border to Tanzania in the south. The northern part, particularly around the shores of Lake Victoria, is fertile, well watered and intensively cultivated and it's here that Mt Elgon (Kenya's second-highest mountain at 4321 metres) is situated. Further south the land gradually merges into scrub and savannah and is suitable only for cattle grazing but it's here that Kenya's largest and most popular wildlife sanctuaries are situated – Masai Mara, Amboseli and Tsavo. To the south of Amboseli rises the spectacular massif of Mt Kilimanjaro – Africa's highest mountain.

Northern & Eastern Kenya

These two regions cover a vast mountainous area of bushland, scrub and desert where rainfall is sparse and where the land is suitable only for cattle grazing. It's this area, however, where Kenya is at its wildest and most untouched by the modern world.

CLIMATE

Because of Kenya's diverse geography, temperature, rainfall and humidity vary widely but there are effectively four zones about which generalisations can be made.

The undulating plateau of western Kenya is generally hot and fairly humid with rainfall spread throughout the year though most of it falls in the evenings. The highest falls are usually during April when a maximum of 200 mm may be recorded, whilst the lowest falls are in January with an average of 40 mm. Temperatures range from a minimum of 14 or 18°C to a maximum of 30 to 34°C.

The central highlands and rift valley enjoy perhaps the most agreeable climate in the country though there's quite a variation between the hot and relatively dry floor of the central rift valley and the snow-covered peaks of Mt Kenya. Rainfall varies from a minimum of 20 mm in July to 200 mm in April and falls essentially in two seasons – March to May (the 'long rains') and October to December (the 'short rains'). The Aberdares and Mt Kenya are the country's main water-catchment areas and falls of up to 3000 mm per year are often recorded.

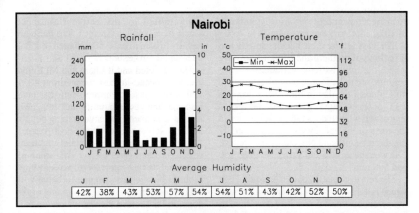

Nairobi

Rainfall

Temperature

Average Humidity

J	F	M	A	M	J	J	A	S	O	N	D
42%	38%	43%	53%	57%	54%	54%	51%	43%	42%	52%	50%

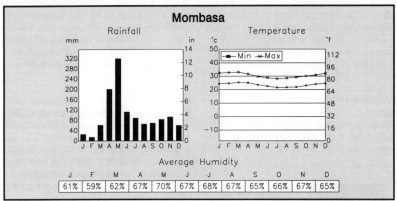

Mombasa

Rainfall

Temperature

Average Humidity

J	F	M	A	M	J	J	A	S	O	N	D
61%	59%	62%	67%	70%	67%	68%	67%	65%	66%	67%	65%

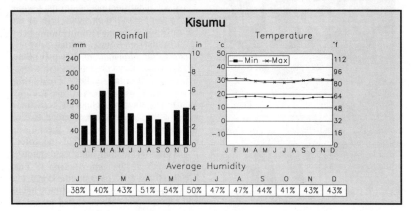

Kisumu

Rainfall

Temperature

Average Humidity

J	F	M	A	M	J	J	A	S	O	N	D
38%	40%	43%	51%	54%	50%	47%	47%	44%	41%	43%	43%

Average temperatures vary from a minimum of 10 or 14°C to a maximum of 22 to 26°C.

The vast semiarid bushlands, deserts and lava flows of northern and eastern Kenya are where the most extreme variations of temperature are to be found, ranging from up to 40°C during the day in the deserts down to 20°C or less at night. Rainfall in this area is sparse and when it does fall it often comes in the form of violent storms. July is generally the driest month and November the wettest. The average annual fall varies between 250 and 500 mm.

The fourth climatic zone is the coastal belt which is hot and humid all year round though tempered by coastal sea breezes. Rainfall ranges from a minimum of 20 mm in February to a maximum of 300 mm in May. The average annual fall is between 1000 mm and 1250 mm. Average temperatures vary little throughout the year ranging from a minimum of 22°C to maximum of 30°C.

FLORA & FAUNA
Flora

With its range of physiographic regions, Kenya has a corresponding diversity in its flora. The vast plains of the south are characterised by distinctive flat-topped acacia trees, and interspersed with these are equally distinctive bottle-shaped baobab trees and thorn bushes.

On the slopes of Mt Elgon and Mt Kenya the flora changes with altitude. Above about 1000 metres it is thick evergreen temperate forest which continues to around 2000 metres and then gives way to a belt of bamboo forest up to about 3000 metres. Above this height is mountain moorland which is characterised by the amazing groundsel tree *(Dendrosencio)* with its huge cabbage-like flowers, and giant lobelias with long spikes. In the semidesert plains of the north and north-east the vegetation cover is unremarkable, yet very characteristic – thorn bushes seem to go on forever. In the northern coastal areas mangroves are prolific and the trees are cut for export, mainly to the Middle East for use as scaffolding; mangrove wood is termite resistant and is in high demand.

Fauna

Kenya has such a dazzling array of wildlife that game-viewing in the national parks is one of the main attractions of a visit to this country. All of the 'big five' (lion, buffalo, elephant, leopard and rhino) can be seen in at least two of the major parks, and there's a huge variety of other less famous but no less impressive animals.

To aid identification of animals while you're game-spotting on safari, refer to the Safari Guide at the back of this book. For a full treatment of Kenya's animals, *A Field Guide to the Mammals of Africa* (Collins, 1988) has excellent colour plates to aid identification as does the smaller *A Field Guide to the Larger Mammals of Africa* (Collins, 1986). The main trouble with both these books is the relatively poor index (which lists many animals only by their Latin names) and the placement of the colour plates often far from the actual description of the animals in question. *Animals of East Africa* (Hodder & Stoughton, 1960) has good descriptive notes of the animals' habits and appearance, but the sketches are not the

greatest and the notes on distribution are out of date.

The birdlife is equally varied and includes ostriches, vultures, eagles, a wide variety of water birds such as flamingos, storks, pelicans, herons, ibis and cormorants, and others such as the yellow weaver birds which you'll see everywhere. The best reference source for twitchers is *A Field Guide to the Birds of East Africa* by John G Williams. It is widely available in Kenya.

NATIONAL PARKS & GAME RESERVES

Kenya's national parks and game reserves rate among the best in Africa. Obviously the tremendous variety of birds and mammals is the main attraction, and the more popular parks such as Masai Mara Game Reserve and Amboseli National Park see huge numbers of visitors – from the budget campers to the hundreds-of-dollars-a-day Hilton hoppers. In the peak season (from January to February) on a game drive, you can observe at close quarters the daily habits of the prolific Nissan Urvan. Other smaller parks, such as Saiwa Swamp National Park, near Kitale in the country's western highlands, would be lucky to see a handful of visitors a day at any time of year.

In addition to the protection of wildlife, some parks have been created to preserve the landscape itself, and these too can be exciting and rewarding places to visit – places such as Mt Kenya, Mt Elgon, Hell's Gate, Mt Longonot and the Kakamega Forest are all worth investigating.

Marine life is also in abundance and the marine national parks of Malindi and Watamu off the central coast both offer excellent diving possibilities. Shimoni and Wasini islands in the extreme south offer even better opportunities but are much less accessible and developed.

What probably helps to make Kenyan parks such a draw card for the budget traveller is that the competition among safari companies for the traveller's dollar is so fierce that a safari of at least a few days is within the reach of the vast majority of travellers. For those at the other end of the scale

the competition is equally brisk and there are lodges and tented camps within the major parks which have superb facilities and are a real experience – if you can afford them.

Information

Entry Fees The entry fees to all national parks and to Masai Mara Game Reserve is US$12 per person per day for nonresidents (US$1.50 for residents) plus US$1.50 for a car. Camping costs US$3.20 per person per night for nonresidents, and US$0.80 for residents. Children's entry fees are US$1.35 for nonresidents (US$0.55 for residents) and camping fees US$1.20/0.80. Entry fees to game reserves other than Masai Mara vary because they are administered by local county councils but to be on the safe side it's best to assume they are the same as for national parks. If you find them less, consider it a bonus.

The latest word from the Kenya Wildlife Service is that the above fees are due to rise soon but the exact figures have not yet been agreed on.

Maps If you are driving your own vehicle it's a good idea to equip yourself with maps of the parks before you set out. The best are all published by the Survey of Kenya and obtainable either from the Public Map Office or bookshops in Nairobi. The ones you will need are SK 87 *Amboseli National Park*, SK 86 *Masai Mara Game Reserve*, SK 82 *Tsavo East National Park* and SK 78 *Tsavo West National Park.*

Accommodation

Camping out in the bush is, of course, the authentic way of going about a safari. There's nothing quite like having just a sheet of canvas between you and what you would normally see only on the residents' side of a zoo. Full-on contact with the bush, its potential dangers and rewards is surely what you are looking for. Anything more luxurious than this is going to dilute the experience and remove the immediacy of it all.

It's true there are some beautifully conceived and constructed game lodges and, if

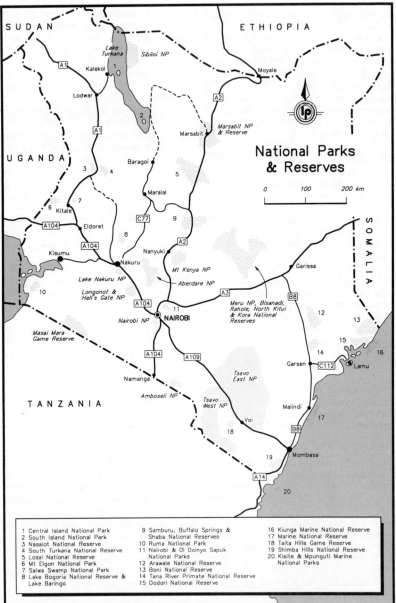

National Parks & Reserves

0   100   200 km

1 Central Island National Park
2 South Island National Park
3 Nasalot National Reserve
4 South Turkana National Reserve
5 Losai National Reserve
6 Mt Elgon National Park
7 Saiwa Swamp National Park
8 Lake Bogoria National Reserve & Lake Baringo
9 Samburu, Buffalo Springs & Shaba National Reserves
10 Ruma National Park
11 Nairobi & Ol Doinyo Sapuk National Parks
12 Arawale National Reserve
13 Boni National Reserve
14 Tana River Primate National Reserve
15 Dodori National Reserve
16 Kiunga Marine National Reserve
17 Marine National Reserve
18 Taita Hills Game Reserve
19 Shimba Hills National Reserve
20 Kisite & Mpunguti Marine National Parks

Animal Spotting

In the parks and reserves you'll be spending a lot of time craning necks and keeping watchful eyes out for the animals and birds you've come so far to see. There are a few telltale signs, as well as a few things you can do to maximise your chances. Most of them are just common sense but it's amazing the number of people who go belting around noisily expecting everything to come to them:

• Drive slowly and, where possible, quietly, keeping eyes trained not only on the ground ahead but also to the side and in the branches above.
• Go in search in the early morning or the late afternoon, although in the more popular parks such as Amboseli and Masai Mara the animals are actually changing their normal hunting habits to fit in with the tourists, so at midday, when most people are safely back in their lodges stuffing their faces, the carnivores are out hunting in the hope that they may be able to do the same thing – in peace.
• Vultures circling are not necessarily an indication of a kill below, but if they are gathering in trees and seem to be waiting you can reasonably assume they are waiting their turn on the carcass.
• In wooded country, agitated and noisy monkeys or baboons are often a sign that there's a big cat (probably a leopard) around. ■

Minimising Your Impact

In their quest for the perfect photo opportunity some drivers do some crazy things. Again, a healthy dose of common sense goes a long way, but too many drivers are under too much pressure to please their clients with little regard for the effects on the wildlife.

• Never get too close to the animals and back off if they are getting edgy or nervous. On a safari I was on, a female cheetah (with cub) became extremely agitated when she was totally surrounded and hemmed in by a dozen minibuses, all full of excited visitors trying to get their 'shot'. She reacted by dropping the cub and bolting.
• Never get out of your vehicle, except at designated points where this is permitted. The animals may look tame and harmless enough but this is not a zoo – the animals are wild and you should treat them as such.
• Animals always have the right of way. Don't follow predators as they move off – you try stalking something when you've got half a dozen minibuses in tow.
• Keep to the tracks. One of the biggest dangers in the parks today is land degradation from too many vehicles crisscrossing the countryside. Amboseli's choking dust is largely a result of this. Likewise, Masai Mara in November 1992 looked, from the air, as though the East African Rally had been run entirely in the park. There were tyre tracks literally everywhere and they were clearly acting as drainage channels for the rain. If that continues, there won't be much grassland left.
• Don't light fires except at camp sites, and dispose of cigarettes with care.
• Don't litter the parks and camp sites. Unfortunately the worst offenders are often the safari drivers and cooks who toss everything and anything out the window, and leave camp sites littered with all manner of crap. It won't do any harm to point out to them the consequences of what they're doing, or clean it up yourself. ■

Wildlife Conservation

As Kenya relies so heavily on tourism for income, and because it's the animals which people have chiefly come to see, the government has placed a high priority on wildlife conservation and the eradication of poaching. To this end it has appointed Richard Leakey, grandson of Louis Leakey, head of the Kenya Wildlife Service, and he has not been afraid to stick his neck out and get things done. Poaching patrols are now much more efficient, extremely stiff penalties for poaching are now in effect, and the estimated 500 of the service's Land Rovers which had been left to rot due to lack of maintenance are gradually being refurbished and pressed into service. It was Leakey who recommended that President Moi should take a high-profile stance on Kenya's anti-ivory policy and burn the stockpile of confiscated ivory in 1989. This action got good press coverage abroad but was widely criticised at home by people who thought that the ivory should have been sold and the money (estimated at around US$3 million) put to good use.

It's a moot point since although the tourist industry brings in some US$400 million a year, the budget for the national parks was, until very recently, only a tiny fraction of this amount and depended heavily for its anti-poaching measures on gifts from Western governments and environmental groups.

you have the money, it's probably worth spending a night or two at one or another of them though it's probably true to say they are mainly for those who prefer to keep the bush at arm's length and a glass of ice-cold beer within arm's reach. Or for those who are simply on a package tour or short holiday and prefer creature comforts and predictability to the rigours of camping.

Certainly the way in which some game lodges attract wildlife to their door is somewhat contrived. Hanging up shanks of meat in a tree which a 'resident' leopard comes to feed off 10 minutes later – despite the spotlights – is hardly the essence of Africa. You

might as well feed your domestic cat at home and suck on a cold beer. It's only fair to add, on the other hand, that not all game lodges go in for this sort of circus.

Getting There & Away

Since you are not allowed to walk in the national parks (with the exception of Hell's Gate, Saiwa Swamp and certain designated areas within Nakuru) you will have to hitch a ride with other tourists, hire a vehicle or join an organised tour.

Hitching is really only feasible if the people you get a ride with are going to be camping. Since this requires some consider-

Yet, despite the risks, poaching still goes on and has virtually become a war between the Kenyan government and the poachers who turn to robbing tourists when denied elephants and rhino. And it's easy to see the reasons for poaching. There is big money in ivory and rhino horn and as long as the Taiwanese government and various Arab governments – notably the two Yemens, Oman and Kuwait – refuse to ban their importation, the slaughter of Kenya's wildlife is likely to continue. A kg of ivory is worth about US$300 wholesale and rhino horn is US$2000 a kg (or up to US$30,000 for a single horn). In the Middle East, rhino horn is prized for dagger handles whilst in China and Korea, in powdered form, it's a supposed aphrodisiac.

Although poaching has been going on for many years, it took on a new dimension in 1972 as a result of the drought in north-eastern Africa which rendered some 250,000 Somali pastoralists destitute as their sheep, goats and camels died by the million. Many drifted south armed with weapons ranging from bows and arrows to WW II guns and found poaching to be a suitable antidote to poverty. Meanwhile, corruption in the Kenya Wildlife Service deepened, with officials taking bribes in return for turning a blind eye to the poachers' activities. By 1976, it was plain that the number of elephants being slaughtered by poachers far exceeded those dying as a result of drought and deforestation and it was estimated that there were over 1300 poachers operating within Tsavo National Park alone.

Worse was yet to come. In 1978, waves of Somalis hungry for ivory and rhino horn and encouraged by official corruption swept across the border and into the national parks, only this time they came with modern automatic weapons issued to them by the Somali government during the 1977 war with Ethiopia. They killed everything in their path including any Kenyan tribal poachers they came across. By the end of the decade, some 104,000 elephants (about 62% of the total) and virtually the entire rhino population had been slaughtered.

There was little improvement during the early '80s despite the setting up of anti-poaching patrols armed with modern weapons, high-speed vehicles and orders to shoot on sight. Part of the reason was the patrols' reluctance to engage the Somalis who have a reputation for toughness and uncompromising violence. By 1989, however, following George Adamson's murder by poachers in the Kora National Reserve and attacks on tourists in other national parks, the Kenyan government signalled its determination to seriously address the problem. Following Leakey's appointment, corrupt wildlife officials were sacked and the anti-poaching units beefed up, to the extent that 200 US-trained paramilitary personnel were deployed in 1990 on shoot-to-kill patrols.

The measures have had a large degree of success though it appears that some poachers, denied ivory, are turning to robbing tourists. A few tourists have actually been shot dead and others seriously injured but the numbers are very small – less than 10 so far. Put in the context of the huge numbers of tourists who visit Kenya (around 800,000 to a million each year), that's still a pretty good safety record and it's only fair to add that some areas are worse than others. Masai Mara, Amboseli and Samburu are considered safe, for example, whereas parts of Tsavo East and Meru are more dubious. ■

able preparation in terms of food, drink and equipment, people with their own cars are naturally reluctant to pick up hitchhikers. If they intend to stay at the lodges then you have the problem of how to get from the lodge to the camp site at the end of the day. Lodges and camp sites are often a long way apart and driving in the parks is not allowed between 7 pm and dawn. You'll then have the problem of transport the following day for game drives and again when you want to leave. All in all, it can be very problematical and probably not worth the effort.

Most travellers opt for organised safaris. There are scores of companies offering safaris and they cater for all pockets and tastes. The cheaper ones involve camping and a degree of self-sufficiency (including erecting your own tent, helping with the catering) and are for people who don't expect much in the way of comfort but do want an authentic experience in the African bush.

For a full description of safari possibilities, costs and company addresses, etc see the Organised Safaris section in the Getting Around chapter.

The alternative to an organised safari is to get a group together and rent a vehicle. If you're looking for other people to join you on a safari using a rented vehicle then check out the notice boards at the youth hostel and Mrs Roche's in Nairobi. As with safaris, a full description of costs and conditions for vehicle hire can be found in the Getting Around chapter.

GOVERNMENT

Kenya is a multiparty state with the Kenya African National Union (KANU) being the ruling party. The major opposition parties (in order of numbers of seats held) are FORD-Asili, FORD-Kenya, and the Democratic Party (DP). The government consists of the president, who holds executive power, and a single legislative assembly of 188 members, 176 of whom are elected, the rest being nominated by the president. There's a high degree of political patronage.

The judiciary were, until 1987, independent of government pressure and free to interpret both the constitution and the laws passed by the legislative assembly. In that year, however, parliament rushed through a bill giving the president the right to dismiss judges without recourse to a tribunal, thus effectively silencing them as a source of opposition. The measure was viewed with dismay by many sectors of Kenyan society and has yet to be repealed.

As far as the independence and freedom of action of government ministers is concerned, it would be fair to say that it's very limited. Indeed, it would not be inappropriate to slightly misquote Louis XIV's classic statement: 'L'état? C'est Moi!'

ECONOMY

The cornerstone of Kenya's capitalist economy is agriculture which employs around 80% of the population, contributes some 31% to the GDP, and accounts for over 50% of the country's export earnings. The principal food crops are maize, sorghum, cassava, beans and fruit while the main cash crops are coffee, tea, cotton, sisal, pyrethrum and tobacco. The bulk of the food crops are grown by subsistence farmers on small plots of land whereas most of the cash crops originate from large, privately owned plantations employing contract labour though there's a

significant input from smaller growers. Coffee and tea are the largest of the agricultural export earners with annual production being around 120,000 tonnes and 160,000 tonnes respectively.

While such figures might be a healthy sign for the country's balance of payments, there's a great deal of discontent among the small farmers and labourers who are paid a pittance for the tea and coffee which they produce or pick. In 1989-90, the country witnessed riots over this paltry sum. The dispute was handled badly by the Kenya Tea Development Authority (KTDA) and, although several heads rolled and price increases were promised, it was all too little too late. Small growers regularly wait up to a year and more to be paid. The situation is similar in the coffee sector and exacerbated by internationally imposed quotas which limit Kenya's ability to dispose of its stockpile. Coffee exports amounted to about 40% of export earnings in 1987.

On the other hand, tourism has replaced coffee as the country's largest export earner, although arrivals dropped off markedly in 1992 due to the tribal clashes in western Kenya and the uncertainty which accompanied the elections held in late December. Estimates of the downturn in tourism ranged from 50 to 70% and, although some sources disputed these figures, there were clearly far less tourists in Kenya in 1992 than there were in previous years. Hopefully things will improve now that the uncertainty which surrounded the first multiparty election has passed. There are also concerns that the continued depletion of the wildlife in Kenya's game parks through poaching may lead to a fall-off, with Tanzania becoming the preferred destination.

In addition to agriculture and tourism, Kenya has a relatively well developed industrial base which accounts for some 15% of GDP, though the bulk of this industry is concentrated around Nairobi and Mombasa. The principal manufactures include processed food, beer, vehicles and accessories, construction materials, engineering, textiles, glass and chemicals. Initially, this sector of the economy was developed with import substitution in mind but the bias has now changed in favour of joint-venture, export-oriented industries as a result of the increasing deficit in the balance of payments and IMF loan conditions. (The IMF have since returned after being thrown out in March 1993.) Kenya's external debt of around US$9 billion is still considered to be low but the most worrying thing is the proportion of the country's foreign exchange earnings which go into servicing foreign debt – currently around 35%.

Mining is a relatively small contributor to GNP and centred around the extraction of soda and fluorspar for export. There are other minerals, which include silver, gold, lead and limestone, but these have yet to be developed commercially.

Kenya's major export trading partners are the UK (17%), Germany (11.5%), Uganda (about 9%), the USA (about 7%) and the Netherlands (6.5%).

Some 75% of domestic energy requirements are imported, mainly in the form of oil from Saudi Arabia, but geothermal projects are being developed and there are four hydroelectric plants in operation along the Tana River and the recently completed hydroelectric plant in the Turkwel Gorge.

Kenya's major sources of imports are Saudi Arabia (18.5%), the UK (about 14%), Japan (10%), Germany (8%) and the USA (5.5%).

POPULATION & PEOPLE

Kenya's population stands at around 25 million and is made up almost entirely of Africans with small (although influential) minorities of Asians (about 80,000), Arabs (about 40,000) and Europeans (about 40,000). The population growth rate of 3.8% is one of the highest in the world and is putting great strain on the country's ability to expand economically and to provide reasonable educational facilities and other urban services. It has also resulted in tremendous pressure to increase the area of land under cultivation or for grazing with its associated environmental problems.

Africans

There are more than 70 tribal groups among the Africans, although the distinctions between many of them are already blurred and are becoming more so as Western cultural values become more ingrained. Traditional values are also disintegrating as more and more people move to the larger towns, family and tribal groups become scattered and the tribal elders gradually die off.

Yet even though the average African may have outwardly drifted away from tribal traditions, tribe is still the single most important part of a person's identity. When two Africans meet and introduce themselves they will almost always say right at the outset what tribe they are from. Although nominally Christian for the most part, a surprising number of people still practice traditional customs. Some of the more inhumane customs, such as cliterodectomy (female circumcision), were outlawed by the British, usually with the aid of the local missionaries, but circumcision still remains the principal rite of passage from childhood to adulthood for boys.

Maasai warrior

The most important distinguishing feature between the tribes is language. The majority of Kenya's Africans fall into one of two major groups: the Bantu speakers and the Nilotic speakers. The Bantu people arrived in East Africa in waves from West Africa over a period of time from around 500 BCE. Among the Bantu the largest tribal groups are the Kikuyu, Meru, Gusii, Embu, Akamba, Luyha and Mijikenda.

The Nilotic speakers migrated to the area from the Nile Valley some time earlier but then had to make room for the migrations of Bantu-speaking people. Nilotic speaking groups include the Maasai, Turkana, Samburu, Pokot, Luo and Kalenjin. Together these tribal groups account for more than 90% of the total African population in Kenya. The Kikuyu and the Luo are by far the most numerous groups, and between them hold practically all the positions of power and influence in the country.

A third language grouping, and in fact the first migrants into the country, are the Cushitic speakers who occupy the north-east of the country and include such tribes as the El-Molo, Somali, Rendille and the Galla.

On the coast, Swahili is the name given to the local people who, while having various tribal ancestries, have in common the fact that they have been mixing, trading and intermarrying both among themselves and with overseas immigrants for hundreds of years.

Asians

The economically important Asian minority is made up largely of people of Indian descent whose ancestors originated from the western state of Gujarat and from the Punjab. Unlike the situation in Uganda, sensibility prevailed and the Asians here were not thrown into exile, largely because their influence was too great. (Uganda is still trying to get its economy back on track.)

India's connections with East Africa go back centuries to the days when hundreds of dhows used to make the trip between the west coast of India or the Persian Gulf and the coastal towns of East Africa every year.

In those days, however, the Indians came as traders and only a very few stayed to settle. This all changed with the building of the Mombasa-Uganda railway at the turn of the century. In order to construct it, the British colonial authorities brought in some 32,000 indentured labourers from Gujarat and Punjab. When their contracts expired many of them decided to stay and set up businesses. Their numbers were augmented after WW II with the encouragement of the British.

Since they were an industrious and economically aggressive community they quickly ended up controlling large parts of the economies of Kenya, Tanzania and Uganda as merchants, artisans and financiers. Not only that, but they kept very much to themselves, regarding the Africans as culturally inferior and lazy. Few gave their active support to the Black nationalist movements in the run-up to independence despite being urged to do so by Nehru, India's prime minister. And when independence came, like many of the White settlers, they were very hesitant to accept local citizenship, preferring to wait and see what would happen. To the Africans, therefore, it seemed they were not willing to throw their lot in with the newly independent nations and were there simply as exploiters.

As is well known, Uganda's Idi Amin used this suspicion and resentment as a convenient ruse to enrich himself and his cronies. Uganda's economy collapsed shortly afterwards since Amin's henchmen were incapable of running the industries and businesses which the Asians had been forced to leave.

Asians have fared somewhat better in Tanzania though nationalisation of many of their concerns has considerably reduced their control over the economy. It is in Kenya that they have fared best of all. Here they have a virtual stranglehold over the service sector (smaller hotels, restaurants, bars, road transport and the tourist trade), the textile trade, book publishing and selling, and they are very important in the construction business.

For a time in the 1970s it seemed that there

was little future for them in Africa. Governments were under heavy pressure to 'Africanise' their economies and job markets. Even in Kenya thousands of shops owned by Asians who had not taken out Kenyan nationality were confiscated in the early 1970s and Asians were forbidden to trade in the rural areas. Those days appear to have passed and African attitudes towards them have mellowed. What seemed like a widespread demand that they should go 'home' has been quietly dropped and the Asians are there to stay. The lesson of what happened to the economy of Uganda when the Asians were thrown out is one reason for this.

Refugees & the Dispossessed

Kenya, being a relatively stable country with opportunities to make a living or at least working the tourists for hand-outs, is a natural magnet for refugees from strife-torn neighbouring countries. Nairobi and Mombasa and, to a lesser degree, the coastal resort towns, are the favoured destinations. You'll come across plenty of these people on your travels and it's relatively easy for them to remain anonymous if they can make enough money to stay off the streets.

There's nothing remarkable about this – it happens all over the world. What is remarkable in Kenya is the number of unattached teenage and early-20s mothers – many of them Kenyan but also quite a lot from Uganda, Sudan, Ethiopia and even Rwanda. With the break-up of many traditional communities as a result of colonial policies that

were designed to bring people into the money economy, and the continuation of this system under post-colonial regimes, there has been large-scale movement of people to urban areas. Most arrive with nothing and are forced to live in overcrowded shantytowns (some 60% of Nairobi's population lives in these places) with little hope of anything resembling a steady job with reasonable pay. As a result, all the facets of urban alienation can be found in these places with drunkenness, theft and rape (particularly of schoolgirls) being fairly commonplace. But this isn't confined to the major urban areas. It appears to be fairly widespread everywhere outside of traditional tribal areas.

As far as the girls are concerned, once they become pregnant they're expelled from school (in other words, it's the end of their educational prospects) and, as likely as not, rejected by their families, too. In 1986, the number of young girls who found themselves in this position (according to official figures) was 11,000 and it's been rising steadily ever since. The options for those to whom this happens are extremely limited. A few shelters do exist (usually run by Christian organisations) but it's only the lucky few who get in. For the rest, it's very poorly paid domestic work or the flesh market.

Laws regarding the responsibilities of paternity in Kenya either don't exist or are hardly ever enforced – it's definitely a man's world – and establishment Kenyan society remains tight-lipped about the problem. What it remains even more tight-lipped about is the practice of well-to-do Kenyan

Sisal Baskets

Sisal baskets, or *kiondos*, are probably the most distinctive Kenyan souvenir and are now popular and widely available in the West. They are still an excellent buy here and the range is staggering – take a look in the market in Nairobi (although buying here is expensive). They come in a variety of sizes, colours and configurations with many different straps and closures. Expect to pay around KSh 100 for a basic one up to around KSh 300 for a large one with a leather 'neck'. Some of the finer ones have the bark of the baobab tree woven into them and this bumps up the price considerably.

Fabrics & Batik

Kangas and *kikois* are the local sarongs and they serve many useful purposes.

Kangas are colourful prints on thin cotton, and each bears a Swahili proverb and are always sold in pairs – one to wrap around your waist and one to carry your baby with on your back – though you can buy just one if you prefer. Biashara St in Mombasa is the kanga centre in Kenya, and here you'll pay upwards of KSh 200 for a pair, depending on quality.

Kikois are made of a thicker cotton and just have stripes. They are originally from Lamu and this is still the best place to buy them, though the kanga shops in Mombasa also stock them. These days they are also made into travellers' clothes in Lamu.

Batik cloth is another good buy and there's a tremendous range, although the good prints are not cheap. The cheapest are printed on cotton and you can expect to pay around KSh 400 for one measuring a metre square, although the price also varies depending on the artist. Batiks printed on silk are of superior quality and prices are generally in the thousands rather than the hundreds of shillings.

Soapstone

Soapstone carvings from Kisii in the west of Kenya are the main offering. The soft, lightly coloured soapstone is carved into dozens of different shapes – from ashtrays to elephants. The best place for buying Kisii soapstone carvings is not in Kisii, as you might expect, but in Kisumu on Lake Victoria. The only problem is that it's extremely heavy and a kg or two of dead weight in your rucksack is not something to be taken lightly.

families recruiting little girls from the bush as domestic servants. Those recruited are even more circumspect.

Though clothed and fed and, if lucky, paid a pittance which varies between US$1 and US$16 a month, these children work on average 15 to 17 hours a day with no days off. Some get no pay at all with just food and clothing provided in lieu of salary. The reason their parents push them into this, apart from the wages which they expect to recoup, is the hope that their children will acquire a

Makonde

Makonde carvings, which are made from ebony, a very black and very heavy wood, are the best pieces of woodcarving and also the most expensive. This genre of carving had its origins in the highlands on either side of the Ruvuma River in southern Tanzania but, because of its popularity, has been copied by other carvers all over East Africa. Done with inspiration, attention to detail, and an appreciation of the life force which motivates its imagery, it's a superbly unique art form matched nowhere else in the world. Unfortunately, too many imitators create inferior products. It's not the fact that much of what is passed off as ebony is lighter (and cheaper) wood blackened with Kiwi boot polish that degrades it, but the quality of the carving which is often slap-dash. A quality piece of makonde carving is always superbly finished.

Maybe you don't care too much about this. Perhaps you like what you imagine to be the slightly rough quality of 'ethnic art'. But, if you do, you're not buying makonde. You're buying repro rubbish.

Before you buy any of this type of carving, do the rounds of the expensive craft shops in Nairobi and see what it ought to look like. Better still, buy it in Tanzania where it's much cheaper anyway. And, when you've seen the real thing, don't become too obsessed with ebony. There are some excellent Kenyan carvers even if they do it on local hardwoods and employ Kiwi boot polish as the finish.

Basically, there are two forms of this art – the traditional and the modern – and they're instantly distinguishable. The modern stuff is pure Modigliani, though the carvers have doubtless never heard of the man or seen any of his works.

The best pieces are to be found in the expensive craft shops and were probably made in Tanzania, but you shouldn't pass up the opportunity of having a good look at what is hawked around the bars of Nairobi. Some of it is good; most of it is rubbish. If you're interested, heavy bargaining is the name of the game. ∎

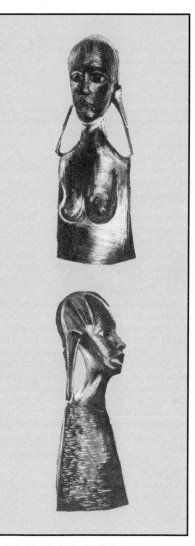

training and education of sorts. The reality is often quite different. These girls are often raped by either the man of the house or his sons and thrown out when they become pregnant. Like their more fortunate counterparts who did actually go to school before being expelled, these girls, as likely as not, join the flesh market.

Whatever you may think of prostitution, it's a hard life in Kenya. Minimal rentals, even in rough areas of Nairobi, are around US$50 a month. In better areas it's much more. Add on decent clothes and footwear and medical attention when necessary, that's a lot of money to be made even to make ends meet – let alone save anything. It's not surprising, therefore, that those who do manage to get their heads above water go for the bars and discos frequented by expatriate workers and tourists since it's more lucrative and there is the vague possibility of marriage or, at least, a long-term friendship. Even so, it's not that easy. Ever since the advent of AIDS, there's been a profound reluctance to tempt fate, and prostitutes now carry condoms out of economic necessity as well as to protect themselves from infection.

It isn't just pregnant young girls who find themselves dispossessed of course. The conditions under which young boys have to work in the coffee, sisal and rice plantations are equally onerous and many find their way onto the streets of Nairobi (so-called 'parking boys') and Mombasa along with other jobless adult males.

Blaming the government for this state of affairs is all too easy for those from rich Western countries but is, to a large degree, unfair. Because of Kenya's high birth rate and the limited amount of funds available, the government is already flat out keeping pace with the demand for schools, hospitals and other social services, the transport infrastructure, and paying interest on its foreign loans. Given this, it's unlikely that much can be done in the foreseeable future for those who fall under the category of the dispossessed.

RELIGION

It's probably true to say that most Kenyans outside the coastal and eastern provinces are Christians of one sort or another whilst most of those on the coast and in the eastern part of the country are Muslim. Muslims make up some 30% of the population. In the more remote tribal areas you'll find a mixture of Muslims, Christians and those who follow their ancestral tribal beliefs.

As a result of intense missionary activity from colonial times to the present, just about every Christian sect is represented in Kenya, from Lutherans to Catholics to Seventh Day Adventists and Wesleyans. The success which all these sects have enjoyed would be quite mind-boggling if it were not for the fact that they have always judiciously combined Jesus with education and medicine – two commodities in short supply until recently in Kenya. Indeed, there are still many remote areas of Kenya where the only place you can get an education or medical help is at a mission station and there's no doubt that those who volunteer to staff them are dedicated people.

On the other hand, the situation is often not as simple as it might at first appear. As with Catholicism in Central and South America which found it necessary to incorporate native deities and saints into the Roman Catholic pantheon in order to placate local sensibilities, African Christianity is frequently syncretic. This is especially so where a tribe has strong ancestral beliefs. There are also many pure home-grown African Christian sects which owe no allegiance to any of the major Western cults. The only thing they have in common is the Bible though their interpretation of it is often radically different. It's worth checking out a few churches whilst you're in Kenya if only to get an understanding of where the religion is headed and even if you can't understand the language which is being used, you'll certainly be captivated by what only Africans can do with such beauty and precision – unaccompanied choral singing.

The upsurge of home-grown Christian sects has much to do with cultural resurgence, the continuing struggle against neocolonialism, and the alienation brought about by migration to urban centres far from tribal homelands in search of work. Some of these sects are distinctly radical and viewed with alarm by the government. The Tent of the Living God, for instance, was denounced by the president as being anti-Christ and three of its leaders were arrested at a gathering in Eastleigh, Nairobi, in late January 1990. The charges against them were thrown out of court the following week and the men released, but the government's action was perhaps an indicator of how it intends to deal with such perceived threats to the status quo in the future.

It isn't just the radical sects which worry the government, however. During the agitation for the introduction of a multiparty political system, even mainstream church leaders took to criticising the government from the relative safety of their pulpits. Many were denounced and some came so close to the bone that they were accused of treason and there were calls for their arrest, although none were actually arrested.

As far as Islam is concerned, most Muslims belong to the Sunni branch of the faith and, as a result, the Sunni communities have been able to attract substantial Saudi Arabian funding for schools and hospitals along the coast and elsewhere.

Only a small minority belong to the Shia branch of Islam and most are to be found among the Asian community. On the other hand, Shiites have been coming to East Africa from all over the eastern Islamic world for centuries, partially to escape persecution but mainly for trading purposes. They didn't come here to convert souls, and there was a high degree of cooperation between the schismatic sects and the Sunnis which is why there's a total absence of Shiite customs in Swahili culture today.

Among the Asian community, there are representatives of virtually all Shiite sects but the most influential are the Ismailis – followers of the Aga Khan. As with all Ismailis, they represent a very liberal version of Islam and are perhaps the only branch of the faith which is strongly committed to the education of women at all levels and their participation in commerce and business. It's obvious that the sect has prospered well in Kenya, going by all the schools and hospitals dedicated to the Aga Khan which you will come across in most urban centres.

Hinduism, as is the case in India, remains a self-contained religion which concerns only those born into it. You'll come across a considerable number of temples in the larger urban areas where most of those of Indian origin live. There are literally scores of different sects of Hinduism to be found in Kenya which are too numerous to mention here but many are economically quite influential.

For a superb and very detailed account of each and every Asian-derived sect of both Islam and Hinduism see *Through Open Doors – A View of Asian Cultures in Kenya* (Kenway Publications, Nairobi, 1989), by Cynthia Salvadori. This is a large-format, hardback book with many illustrations, and is on sale in most of Nairobi's bookshops. It's one of the best researched and readable books I've ever come across.

LANGUAGE
English and Swahili (correctly known as Kiswahili) are the official languages and are taught in schools throughout Kenya, but there are many other major tribal languages which include Kikuyu, Luo, Kikamba, Maasai and Samburu as well as a plethora of minor tribal languages. Most urban Kenyans and even tribal people involved in the tourist industry speak English so you shouldn't experience too many problems making yourself understood. Italian and German are also spoken by many Kenyans but usually only among those associated with the tourist trade on the coast.

It's extremely useful, however, to have a working knowledge of Swahili, especially outside of urban areas and in remote parts of the country since this will open doors and enable you to communicate with people who don't speak English. It's also the most common language which speakers of different tribal languages use to communicate with each other. Even tribespeople who haven't been to school will usually be able to speak *some* Swahili. If you're planning on visiting Tanzania then you'll find it extremely useful as it's now the official language there (though English is still used extensively).

Another language you'll come across in Kenya, which is spoken almost exclusively by the younger members of society, is Sheng. Essentially a patois, it's a fairly recent development and, like Swahili, is still evolving. It's composed of a mixture of Swahili and

English along with a fair sprinkling of Hindi, Gujarati, Kikuyu and several other Kenyan tribal languages. It originated in the colonial days as a result of the employment of African nannies by Whites to look after their children.

Unless you can speak reasonable Swahili, you probably won't realise it's being spoken since it does sound quite similar to Swahili. One of the keys to know that it's being spoken is in the initial greeting between friends. The greeting will be, 'Sassa!' The response to this can be, 'Besht', 'Mambo' or 'Fit' (pronounced almost like 'feet'). There is then an option to continue in Sheng or any other mutually intelligible language.

The *Swahili Phrasebook* by Robert Leonard is available in the Lonely Planet language survival kit series.

Pronunciation
Swahili vowels are pronounced as follows:

a	as the 'a' in 'father'
e	as the 'e' in 'better'
i	as the 'ee' sound in 'bee'
o	as the 'a' in 'law'
u	as the 'oo' in 'too'

Double vowels, or any two vowels together, are pronounced as two separate syllables. Thus *saa* (time/hour) is pronounced 'sa-a', and *yai* (egg) is pronounced 'ya-i'. There are no diphthongs as in English.

One thing you should know about pronunciation in Kenya is that the majority of Kikuyu are incapable of pronouncing the letter 'r' (much like the Japanese and Koreans). It comes out as 'l'. This can lead to some hilarious pronunciations of certain words in English. Even the Kikuyu laugh at this and one joke which a Kikuyu speaker related to me was to ask me how I thought a Kikuyu would pronounce the following: 'Red lolly on the road.' I'll leave you to work it out. I have a similar joke with my Japanese friend when I ask him to pronounce, 'Are the rafters on the roof?' In Kenya, you'll hear the most common example in bars when a Kikuyu orders a 'Pilsner'. However acute your hearing, there's no-doubt it comes out as 'Prisoner'!

General Rules
Swahili relies heavily on prefixes; adjectives change prefix according to the number and class of the noun. Thus *mzuri, wazuri, vizuri* and *kizuri* are different forms of the word 'good'.

Verbs use a pronoun prefix:

I	*ni*
you	*u*
he/she	*a*
we	*tu*
you	*m*
they	*wa*

and a tense prefix:

present	*na*
past	*li*
future	*ta*
infinitive	*ku*

giving you:

We are going to Moshi.
  Tunakwenda Moshi.
Shall I take a picture?
  Nitapiga picha?
Juma spoke much.
  Juma alisema sana.

Some Useful Words & Phrases
hello*
  jambo or *salama*
welcome
  karibu
How are you?
  Habari?
I'm fine, thanks.
  Mzuri.
Goodbye.
  Kwaheri.
yes
  ndiyo
no
  hapana
Thank you.
  Asante.

Thanks very much.
  Asante sana.
What's your name?
  Unaitwa nani?
It is...
  ninaitwa...
How was the journey?
  Habari ya safari?
how much/how many?
  ngapi?
where?
  wapi?
money
  pesa
today
  leo
tomorrow
  kesho
guesthouse
  nyumba ya wageni
toilet
  choo
eat
  kula
sleep
  lala
want
  taka
come from
  toka
there is
  kuna
there isn't
  hakuna
White people
  wazungu
White person
  mzungu

* There is also a respectful greeting used for elders: *shikamoo*. The reply is *marahaba*.

Food
food
  chakula
rice
  mchele or *wali*

bananas
  ndizi
bread
  mkate
vegetables
  mboga
salt
  chumvi
meat
  nyama
beef
  ng'ombe
goat
  mbuzi
chicken
  kuku
fish
  samaki
egg(s)
  (ma)yai
milk
  maziwa
water
  maji or *mai*

Numbers

½	*nusu*
1	*moja*
2	*mbili*
3	*tatu*
4	*nne*
5	*tano*
6	*sita*
7	*saba*
8	*nane*
9	*tisa*
10	*kumi*
11	*kumi na moja*
20	*ishirini*
30	*thelathini*
40	*arobaini*
50	*hamsini*
60	*sitini*
70	*sabini*
80	*themanini*
90	*tisini*
100	*mia*

Facts for the Visitor

VISAS & EMBASSIES

Visas are required by all except nationals of Commonwealth countries (excluding nationals of Australia, New Zealand and Sri Lanka and British passport holders of Indian, Pakistani and Bangladeshi origin), Denmark, Ethiopia, Germany, the Republic of Ireland, Italy, Norway, Spain, Sweden, Turkey and Uruguay. Those who don't need visas are issued a Visitor's Pass on entry which is valid for a stay of up to six months. Three months is the average, but it depends what you ask for.

If you enter Kenya through a land border no-one will ever ask you for an onward ticket or 'sufficient funds'. This isn't always the case if you enter by air. A lot depends on what you look like, whether you're male or female, what you write on your immigration card and which immigration officer you deal with. If it's fairly obvious that you aren't intending to stay and work then you'll generally be given the benefit of the doubt. Put yourself in a strong position before you arrive: look smart, and write the name of an expensive hotel on your immigration card in the appropriate section.

Single women have occasionally been told that 'sufficient funds' in the absence of an onward ticket were suspect 'because women lose money easily'! Perhaps the appropriate rejoinder should be that 'men spend money faster'. To balance these experiences, it should be said that we've never heard of anyone being refused entry to Kenya even if, as a last resort, they've had to buy a refundable onward ticket.

So long as your visa remains valid you can visit either Tanzania or Uganda and return without having to apply for another visa. This does not apply to visiting any other countries. There is, however, a charge at the border for doing this – usually about US$4.

Kenyan Embassies

Visas can be obtained from the following Kenyan diplomatic representatives in:

Australia
  QBE Bldg, 33 Ainslie Ave, Canberra, ACT 2601 (☎ (062) 474788)
Belgium
  1-5 Avenue de la Joyeuse, 1040 Brussels (☎ (02) 230-3065)
Canada
  415 Laurier Ave, Ottawa, Ontario, KIN 6R4 (☎ (613) 563-1773)
Egypt
  20 Boulos Hanna St, PO Box 362, Dokki, Cairo (☎ 704455)
Ethiopia
  Fikre Miriam Rd, Hiher 16 Kebelle 01, PO Box 3301, Addis Ababa (☎ 180033)
France
  3 Rue Cimaros, 75116 Paris (☎ 4553-3500)
Germany
  Villichgasse 17, 5300 Bonn-Bad Godesburg 2, Micael Plaza, (☎ (0228) 356042)
India
  E-66 Vasant Marg, 110057 New Delhi (☎ 672280)
Italy
  Icilio No 14, 00153 Rome (☎ 578-1192)
Japan
  24-20 Nishi-Azobu 3-Chome, Minato-Ku, Tokyo (☎ (03) 479-4006)
Netherlands
  Koninginnegracht 102, 2514 A1, The Hague (☎ (070)504215)
Nigeria
  52 Queens Drive, Ikoyi, PO Box 6464, Lagos (☎ 682768)
Pakistan
  Sector G-6/3, House 8, St 88, PO Box 2097, Islamabad (☎ 811243)
Rwanda
  UN Toit A Toi Bldg, Rue Kadyiro, PO Box 1215, Kigali (☎ 72774)
  Open Monday to Friday from 8.30 am to noon and 2 to 4.30 pm; US$10, two photos, same-day issue for applications before 11.30 am, otherwise 24 hours. No onward tickets or minimum funds required.
Somalia
  Km 4 Via Mecca, PO Box 618, Mogadishu (☎ 80857)
Sudan
  Street 3 Amarat, PO Box 8242, Khartoum (☎ 43758)
Sweden
  Birger Jarlsgatan 37, 2tr, 10395 Stockholm (☎ (08) 218300)

Tanzania
NIC Investment House, Samora Ave, PO Box 5231, Dar es Salaam (☎ 46362/6)
Open Monday to Friday from 8 am to 3 pm, from 9 am for visa applications; US$10, two photographs, 24 hours.

Uganda
Plot No 60, Kira Rd, PO Box 5220, Kampala (☎ 231861)
Open Monday to Friday from 8.30 am to 12.30 pm and 2 to 4.30 pm; US$10, two photos, same-day issue for applications before noon.

UK
45 Portland Place, London W1N 4AS (☎ (071) 636-2371)

USA
2249 R St NW, Washington DC 20008 (☎ (202) 387-6101)
424 Madison Ave, New York, NY 10017 (☎ (212) 486-1300)

Zaïre
5002 Ave de l'Onganda, BP 9667, Gombe, Kinshasa (☎ 30117)

Zambia
Harambee House, 5207 United Nations Ave, PO Box 50298, Lusaka (☎ 212531)

Zimbabwe
95 Park Lane, PO Box 4069, Harare (☎ 792901)

Where there is no Kenyan embassy or high commission, visas can be obtained from the British embassy or high commission.

The cost of visas generally increases with the distance from Kenya, though not by a great deal. In Africa, they generally cost US$10 (sometimes payable in local currency if the exchange rate is stable). Two photos (sometimes three) are required but you normally do not have to show an onward ticket or a letter from a travel agent confirming that you have booked one. Visas remain valid for a period of three months from the date of issue. Apply well in advance for your visa especially if doing it my mail – they can take up to two weeks in some countries (eg Australia). Kenyan visa applications are simpler and less time-consuming in Rwanda, Tanzania and Uganda, and payment is accepted in local currency (see the earlier list for details).

Visas are also available on arrival at Jomo Kenyatta International Airport in Nairobi for US$10.

Visa Extensions

Visas can be renewed in Nairobi at the immigration office (☎ (02) 332110), Nyayo House (ground floor), on the corner of Kenyatta Ave and Uhuru Highway; at the office in Mombasa (☎ (011) 311745), or at immigration on the 1st floor of Reinsurance Plaza, corner of Jomo Kenyatta Highway and Oginga Odinga Rd during normal office hours. A three-month single-entry visa costs US$10 and a 12-month multiple-entry visa US$50 (except in Kisumu where a visa can be renewed for three months free of charge). You must pay in foreign currency. No onward tickets or 'sufficient funds' are demanded (except in Kisumu where they may ask to see an onward ticket but won't refuse you if you don't have one). Remember that you don't need a re-entry visa if you're only going to visit Tanzania or Uganda *as long as your visa remains valid*. Staff at the immigration offices are generally friendly and helpful.

Foreign Embassies in Kenya

Since Nairobi is a common gateway city to East Africa and the city centre is easy to get around, many travellers spend some time here picking up visas for other countries which they intend to visit. If you are going to do this you need to plan ahead because some embassies only accept visa applications in the mornings, others only on certain days of the week. Some take 24 hours to issue, others 48 hours. Some visas (Sudan, for instance) may have to be referred to the country's capital city, but this is rare.

Burundi The embassy is currently not issuing visas and will tell you to get one on arrival at the border.

Egypt The embassy is open Monday to Friday from 9 am to 12.30 pm. The cost of a one month, single-entry visa varies depending on your nationality. For the USA and Denmark it's US$10.70, for Canada it's US$44 and for the UK it's US$57. For all others it's US$15.60. One photo is required plus you need to show an onward ticket and vaccination certificates for yellow fever and cholera. Visas take 48 hours to issue and you can collect them in the afternoons only from 2 to 3.30 pm.

Ethiopia The embassy is open Monday to Friday from 9 to 11 am and 2.30 to 4 pm. One-month visas cost US$6.85, require one photo and take 48 hours to issue. You must show an onward ticket when applying for the visa.

Madagascar The embassy is open Monday to Friday from 8.30 am to 1 pm and 2 to 5 pm but visa applications are only accepted between 9 am and noon. Visas cost US$11.40, require four photos and are issued in 24 hours.

Malawi The high commission is open Monday to Friday from 9 am to 12.30 and 2 to 4.30 pm. Visas require two photos, cost US$17.15 and are issued in 48 hours.

Rwanda The embassy is open Monday to Friday from 9 am to noon and 2 to 5 pm. One-month visas cost US$5.70, require two photos and take 48 hours to issue. On the application form you will be asked the date you want to enter Rwanda. Think carefully about this as the visa will run from then.

Sudan The embassy is open Monday to Friday from 8.30 am to noon (closed Wednesday). Visas are difficult to get because of the civil war and all applications have to be referred to Khartoum. An onward ticket is necessary so get one of these before you apply.

Tanzania The high commission is open Monday to Friday from 8.30 am to 12.30 pm and 2 to 5 pm but visa applications are only accepted between 9 am and noon. The cost of a visa depends on your nationality and ranges from US$6.85 to US$42.85. Canadians pay the most followed by Belgians, Dutch, Italians, Spanish, Swiss and Japanese. Americans, Germans, French and Israelis pay least. Two photos are required and visas are issued in 48 hours (two weeks for Israelis).

Uganda The high commission is open Monday to Friday from 9.30 am to noon and 2 to 4 pm. Single-entry visas cost US$20 for British and Irish nationals and US$25 for all others (US$40/50 respectively for double-entry visas), two photos are required and visas are issued in 24 hours.

Zaïre The embassy is open Monday to Friday from 8.30 am to 12.45 pm and 2 to 5 pm. Visa fees are the same for all nationalities. A single-entry/double-entry visa costs US$75/120 for one month; US$135/180 for two months, US$200/225 for three months US$270/360 for six months. One-way transit visas (three days) are also available for US$45. Four photos are required and a letter of introduction from your own embassy. The visas take 24 hours to issue.

Zambia The high commission is open Monday to Friday from 8.30 am to 12.30 pm and 2 to 4.30 pm. Visas cost US$8.60, require three photos and take 48 hours.

Francophone Countries The French Embassy issues visas for French-speaking countries which don't have embassies in Nairobi, such as Chad and the Central African Republic.

MONEY
The unit of currency is the Kenyan shilling (KSh), which is made up of 100 cents. Notes in circulation are KSh 500, 200, 100, 50, 20 and 10; coins are KSh 5 (seven-sided) and KSh 1, and 50, 10 and 5 cents.

Treat the following exchange rates as a guide only. The Kenyan shilling continues to depreciate (see the Demise of the Kenyan Shilling section), so prices in this book are quoted in US dollars to retain some semblance of reality. As of October 1993 the rates were:

US$1	=	KSh 120
UK£1	=	KSh 180
1FF	=	KSh 20
DM1	=	KSh 75
A$1	=	KSh 80

Import and export of local currency is allowed up to KSh 100 and, when you leave the country, customs officials may ask you if you are carrying any. If you say you are not that's generally the end of the matter. If you're only leaving the country for a short while and intend to return via the same border and don't want to convert all your Kenyan shillings into another currency, you can leave any excess at a border post against a receipt and pick it up again when you get back, but who could be bothered?

When leaving via Nairobi airport it's possible to reconvert any amount of Kenyan shillings to hard currency as long as you have the bank receipts to cover the amount. This is only possible at the airport, and not only is the exchange rate a little low but they charge KSh 100 commission. This facility is obviously meant for those who are leaving the country and have excess shillings (which you can't legally export) but they don't ask to see your air ticket at the time so presumably anyone could do this.

It is sometimes still possible to cash US dollar travellers' cheques at banks in Kenya and get US dollars cash for them, but it's difficult. Who wants Kenyan currency under

---

The Demise of the Kenyan Shilling

Throughout the 1970s, 1980s and early 1990s, the Kenyan shilling was East Africa's most stable currency and there was little difference between the official rate of exchange and the parallel (black) market. This all changed in late 1992 when the government, strapped for dollars (and other 'hard' currencies), authorised banks to pay a premium for the exchange of 'hard' currencies into Kenyan shillings – known as the Forex-C. This meant that anyone with dollars (cash or cheques) could walk into a bank, request the premium, and, so long as they changed a minimum of US$500, get whatever was the free-market rate of exchange (which fluctuated between KSh 47 and KSh 51) as opposed to the official rate of exchange of around KSh 35.

The idea was to encourage those with dollars to keep their money in the country and re-invest it and, to this end, those with businesses which received dollar payments, were allowed to keep 50% of their earnings in dollar accounts (known as 'retention accounts'). The measure didn't quite achieve what it had intended to do since speculators began to buy up hard currency wherever they could find it thus driving the shilling down and forcing up the price of imports. Within weeks, the price of just about everything doubled (if you were paying for it in local currency).

Then, in November 1992, the whole scheme was abruptly cancelled when the central bank was unable to honour Forex-C certificates (ie the premium which the banks had paid) due to a lack of 'hard' currency (vehemently denied by the central bank, naturally, but obvious to all concerned).

What happened next was beyond belief. Pressured into multiparty elections (which took place at the end of December 1992) and determined to win, the government flooded the currency market with what was estimated to be KSh 9 billion unsupported by reserves, most of which went into buying votes.

As a result, the currency took a dive and was devalued to US$1 = KSh 46 in January 1993. Concurrently, the black market roared ahead while the major banks prevaricated about what to do.

Enter the IMF and the World Bank which demanded (among other things) that if Kenya's debts were to be rescheduled and a major loan package put in place, then the government would have to withdraw from circulation the KSh 9 billion. The government threw them out but not necessarily over this issue (see the History section in the Facts about the Country chapter for more details). At the same time, dollar retention accounts were cancelled and the central bank demanded that those holding dollars in such accounts sell them to the central bank at the official exchange rate (US$1 = KSh 46) within 48 hours.

There was panic on the currency market and the Kenyan shilling took another plunge but, although the official exchange rate remained at KSh 46 to the US dollar, the international banks (eg Barclays, Grindlays, IBN, etc) began trading at KSh 67 to the dollar, which is very close to the black-market rate of around KSh 72.

At the time of writing, the Kenyan shilling continues to depreciate and probably will not stabilise until late 1993 when it is predicted it will hit US$1 = KSh 150 or thereabouts. ■

the present circumstances? Barclays and certain other banks will quote a rate for selling dollars (between 3 and 5% higher than the buying rate) but, although you can watch someone right in front of you cashing dollars, they won't sell them back to you. Overcome this hurdle by doing a deal with people who want to sell dollars before they reach the counter.

Naturally, if they won't sell you cash dollars for Kenyan shillings, they're not going to sell you cash dollars for travellers' cheques. Things may change, but, for the present, this is one of your few options.

It may be possible to get cash dollars if you make a withdrawal against your home account using a Visa card at Barclays Bank. So long as you don't want more than US$150 to US$200 per day it takes about 20 minutes but, if you want more, then it has to be referred to your home country and this takes longer.

Your last options are the black market and the casino on Uhuru Highway just below the National Museum. At the latter you can change your travellers' cheques to gambling chips then, after pretending you've been gambling for a while, go back to the cashier and change the chips back to cash dollars.

Bank Charges

Travellers' cheques attract a 1% commission at some banks but none at others. Barclays is probably the best bank to change cheques at since there's hardly any red tape and the transaction takes just a few minutes, though other international banks are just as good.

Banking hours are Monday to Friday from 8 or 9 am to 2 pm and on the first and last Saturdays of the month from 9 to 11 am.

Black Market

Because of the unrealistic official exchange rate and the virtual impossibility of buying dollars from the banks, there is a black market for hard currency in Nairobi (cash or travellers' cheques) and you can get up to 20% above the rate at which the banks are trading. The places to do this are generally well-known among travellers who have been

in Nairobi for a little while, so make enquiries.

Transferring Money

Kenya is a good place to have funds transferred to. It generally takes only a few days. You can collect your money entirely in US dollars travellers' cheques but the money is transferred first into Kenyan shillings then back into dollars.

If you have a Visa or American Express card, you can do the same thing directly by going to Barclays or Express Kenya, respectively.

Costs

Despite the chaos on the currency market and spiralling inflation which has seen the price of almost everything double (in Kenyan shilling terms) since the beginning of 1993, prices in US dollar terms have remained fairly stable.

Prices in this book have been quoted in US dollars on the basis of US$1 = KSh 46 (the official exchange rate) but the international banks are trading at a much higher rate (US$1 = KSh 120) so, if you have hard currency, everything costs considerably less. Bear this in mind when considering costs.

The cost of budget accommodation in Kenya is very reasonable so long as you're happy with communal showers and toilets. Clean sheets are invariably provided and sometimes you'll also get soap and a towel. For this you're looking at US$3 a single and US$5 a double and up. It can be slightly cheaper on the coast, especially at Lamu. If you want your own bathroom, costs rise to from around US$5 a single and US$7 a double. Again, it can be slightly cheaper on the coast but more expensive in Nairobi.

There are plenty of small cafés in every town, usually in a certain area. They cater to local people and you can get a traditional meal for around US$1 to US$2. Often the food isn't up to much but sometimes it can be excellent. For a little more, the Indian restaurants are great value. Some offer all-you-can-eat lunches for around US$3. They're not only tasty but you won't need to eat for the rest of the day either. A splurge at a better class restaurant is going to set you back between US$8 and US$15.

The price of beer and soft drinks depends entirely on where you buy them. They're obviously cheapest bought from a supermarket (around US$0.33 for a beer assuming an exchange rate of US$1 = KSh 46). Using this as a benchmark figure, you would be paying around 60% more for them in a basic bar, slightly more than double in a better class bar or restaurant, and up to eight times as much in a five-star hotel!

Public transport is very reasonable and the trains are excellent value. To travel from one end of Kenya to the other (Mombasa to Malaba) on the train in 2nd class is going to cost you about US$38. In 3rd class it's less than half that. Buses are priced about halfway between the 3rd and 2nd-class train fares.

The thing that is going to cost you most in Kenya is safaris. A safari for three nights and four days, for instance, with companies which cater for budget travellers is priced around US$180; seven days costs around US$385. This includes transport, food, hire of tents, national park entry fees, camping fees and the wages of the guides and cooks. In other words, more or less everything except a few drinks and tips.

Car hire is even more expensive and is probably out of reach of most budget travellers. A 4WD Suzuki costs from US$650 to US$900 per week with unlimited mileage; petrol is extra. If you don't want 4WD then a small car, such as a Nissan Sunny, costs around US$420 per week.

Tipping

With such an active tourist industry, Kenya is a country where tipping is expected. Obviously there's no need to tip in the very basic African eateries or hotels, on *matatus* (local minibuses) or when using other public transport. In better restaurants 5 to 10% of the bill is the usual amount, although in these a service charge of 10% will often have been included on the bill (though it's debatable whether the employees ever get it).

If you take a safari then it's also expected that you tip your driver, guide and cook. The majority of employees in this industry earn low wages so it's suggested you be as generous as you feel able to. Around US$1.50 per day per employee is about the right amount. This is the cost per person, and how much you give obviously depends on whether they have worked well to make your safari enjoyable.

WHEN TO GO

There are a number of factors to take into account when considering what time of year to visit Kenya. The main tourist season is January and February, as the weather at this time of year is generally considered to be the best – hot and dry. It's also when you'll find the largest concentrations of birdlife on the rift valley lakes, and the animals in the game parks tend to congregate more around the watercourses as other sources dry up, making them easier to spot.

From June to September could be called the 'shoulder season' as the weather is still dry and it's the time of that visual extravaganza – the annual wildebeest migration into the Masai Mara Game Reserve from the Serengeti.

During the long rains (from March to May) and the short rains (from October to December) things are much quieter – places tend to be less full and accommodation prices come down. The rains generally don't affect your ability to get around and see things (although Amboseli National Park can be flooded out), it's just that you may well get rained on, especially in the late afternoon. This is especially so in the highlands and the west of the country.

WHAT TO BRING

Bring the minimum. One thing that many travellers in Kenya find once they actually get there is that they have far too much gear. This is not only an uncomfortable inconvenience, it also means that instead of taking back some special reminders of Kenya you'll be taking back the same extra pullover and jeans that you set off with. Unless it's absolutely essential, *leave it at home!*

A rucksack (backpack) is far more practical than an overnight bag, and is essential if you plan to climb Mt Kenya or do any amount of walking. It is worth buying a good quality bag right at the start – African travel soon sorts out the good stuff from the junk, and if it's the latter you've opted for you'll be cursing it the whole way.

What type of pack you buy is largely a matter of personal preference. I find that the travel packs with the straps which zip into a compartment in the back are excellent. Although expensive, they are a compromise solution to a number of different problems; however, they are not really suited for specialised activities such as climbing or serious walking. Of the other types of packs, internal frame ones seem to be the best as they have less protuberances and straps to catch on things.

A day pack is a worthwhile item, if only for keeping your camera dry and out of the incredible dust which seems to permeate every crack and crevice when you're on safari. For those reasons and for security, it needs to be one which zips shut. Quite a few travellers use the local *kiondos* (woven baskets) which are fine if they suit your purpose.

A sleeping bag is more or less essential if you are travelling overland beyond Kenya or planning to climb mountains, but in the country itself there are enough hotels for you not to need one. On the other hand, carrying a sleeping bag and closed-cell foam mat does give you a greater degree of flexibility and means that if you take a safari you know you'll have adequate gear. Sleeping bags are the one thing which all camping safari companies require you to provide.

There's always much discussion about the pros and cons of carrying a tent, and basically it boils down to what sort of travelling you want to do, and how much weight you're prepared to carry. As with a sleeping bag, a tent is not necessary if you're just travelling from town to town, but carrying your own portable shelter opens up a whole stack of exciting possibilities. The same applies to carrying a stove and cooking gear, so give some careful thought to what you want to do, and how. On the other hand, the full range of camping equipment can be hired from various places in Nairobi (principally Atul's on Biashara St) and from certain hotels elsewhere in the country (principally the Naro Moru River Lodge on the western side of Mt Kenya).

Quite a few travellers carry a mosquito net, and with the risk of malaria there is no doubt that this is not a bad idea. Personally I have found that with judicious use of insect repellent and mosquito coils, I was never unduly discomfited. On the topic of insect repellent, bring a good supply and make sure that whatever you bring has as the active ingredient NN-diethyl-m-toluamide, commonly known as DEET. This has been found to be the most effective against mosquitoes. Brands which have this include Mijex and Rid. Mosquito coils are what the locals use (when they use anything at all, that is) to keep the mozzies at bay, and local brands such as Doom are available in even the smallest stores.

Clothes need to be both practical and take into account local sensibilities. Although Kenya straddles the equator, the large variations in altitude lead to equally large variations in climate. The coast is hot and steamy year-round, while Nairobi and the western highlands get decidedly cool in the evenings in July and August, so you need to carry one decent warm pullover as well as warm-weather gear. A windproof and waterproof jacket also comes in handy, particularly during the rainy seasons. Most travellers seem to get around in T-shirts and shorts which is fine in most areas, but you should be more circumspect on the Muslim-dominated coast, particularly in Lamu. Here women should wear tops that keep the shoulders covered and skirts or pants which reach at least to the knees. Shorts on men are likewise not particularly appreciated. Civil servants and embassy staff, likewise, do not appreciate scantily dressed travellers and will treat you with disdain.

Overlooked by many people but absolutely indispensable is a good pair of sunglasses. The amount of glare you experience in the bright tropical light is not only uncomfortable but can damage your eyes. A hat which shades your face and neck is also well worth considering. A water bottle is well worth any slight inconvenience it may cause. It needs to be unbreakable, have a good seal, and hold at least one litre.

Also important are little things which can make life just that little bit more comfortable: a Swiss Army knife, a small sewing kit (including a few metres of fishing line and a large needle for emergency rucksack surgery), a 10-metre length of light nylon cord for a washing line along with a handful of clothes pegs, and half a tennis ball makes a good fits-all washbasin plug.

Most toiletries – soap, shaving cream, shampoo, toothpaste, toilet paper, tampons – are available throughout the country.

The one thing that you're really going to appreciate in Kenya is a pair of binoculars, whether they be pocket ones or larger field binoculars. When out in the game parks you can put them to constant use and they are essential for identifying the dozens of species of mammals and birds that you'll come across. If you don't plan on going to the game parks they are are still handy just for the scenery, or perhaps for trying to spot that potential lift coming over the horizon when you're stuck out in the north somewhere...

TOURIST OFFICES

Considering the extent to which the country relies on tourism, there's not much available in the way of printed information, and it's incredible to think that there's not even a tourist office in Nairobi! There are a couple of free pamphlets which go some way towards filling the gap. They are the monthly *Kenya Tourist Guide* (☎ 226206 in Nairobi) published by Rank Communications Inc, and the quarterly *What's On* (☎ 221222 in Nairobi) put out by Nation Newspapers. Both contain articles on subjects of tourist interest plus listings of hotels, restaurants,

airlines, embassies, banks, safari and car-hire companies, train and boat schedules, and a considerable amount of advertising (which is why they're free). You can pick them up at the larger hotels and at travel agencies.

The fortnightly *Tourist's Kenya* (☎ 33-7169 in Nairobi) put out by Savers Cards Ltd, hasn't been produced since March 1992, but the staff are still in the office on the 1st floor of Union Towers, Moi Ave, keeping the information on their computers up to date, so they may go back into production soon.

The only tourist offices in the country are the ones in Mombasa on Moi Ave (☎ 31-1231) and in Malindi on Lamu Rd.

The Ministry of Tourism maintains several overseas offices including:

France
    Kenya Tourist Office, 5 Rue Volney, Paris 75002 (☎ 260-6688)
Germany
    Kenya Tourist Office, Hochstrasse 53, 6 Frankfurt A M (☎ 282552)
Sweden
    Kenya Tourist Office, Birger Jarlsgatan 37, 11145 Stockholm (☎ (08) 218300)
Switzerland
    Kenya Tourist Office, Bleicherweg 30, CH- 8039 Zurich (☎ 202-2244)
UK
    Kenya Tourist Office, 25 Brook's Mews (off Davies St) Mayfair, London (☎ (071) 355-3144)
USA
    Kenya Tourist Office, 9100 Wilshire Blvd, Doheney Plaza Suite 111, Beverly Hills CA 90121 (☎ (213) 274-6634)
    Kenya Tourist Office, 424 Madison Ave, New York, NY 10017 (☎ (212) 486-1300)

BUSINESS HOURS & HOLIDAYS

Government offices are open Monday to Friday from 8 or 8.30 am to 1 pm, and 2 to 5 pm. Some private businesses are also open on Saturday mornings from around 8.30 am to 12.30 pm.

Banking hours are Monday to Friday from 9 am to 2 pm. Banks are also open on the first and last Saturday of the month from 9 to 11 am.

Nairobi and Mombasa both have branches of Barclays Bank which stay open until 4.30

or 5 pm Monday to Saturday. The branch at Nairobi airport is open 24 hours.

Outside normal banking hours you may be able to change at one of the five-star tourist hotels, although many are reluctant to help unless you're a guest, and their exchange rates are poor anyway.

Public Holidays
January
New Year's Day
March-April
Good Friday
Easter Monday
Id al Fitr (end of Ramadan, 1994-95)
1 May
Labour Day
1 June
Madaraka Day
20 October
Kenyatta Day
12 December
Independence Day
25 December
Christmas Day
26 December
Boxing Day

POST & TELECOMMUNICATIONS
The Kenyan postal system is very reliable. Letters sent from Kenya rarely go astray but do take up to two weeks to reach Australia or the USA. Incoming letters to Kenya take around a week to reach Nairobi.

Parcels or books sent by surface mail take up to 4½ months to arrive – but they do get there. I can vouch for this – I've sent plenty of stuff this way.

Postal Rates
The airmail rates in US$ for items posted from Kenya are:

Item	Africa	Europe	USA & Australia
letter	$0.20	$0.30	$0.40
postcard	$0.10	$0.20	$0.28
aerogram	$0.20	$0.20	$0.23

Sending Mail
Kenya is a good place from which to send home parcels of goodies, or excess gear. In the main post office in Nairobi you'll always see at least a couple of people busily taping and wrapping boxes to send home. You have to take the parcel *unwrapped* to be inspected by customs at the post office not later than 3.30 pm. You then wrap and send it. The whole process is very simple and, apart from wrapping the parcel, takes only a few minutes.

There's usually no-one selling wrapping material outside the post office in Nairobi so you need to bring along your own cardboard, paper, tape and string. The cheapest place to get this stuff is the supermarket on Koinange St between Kenyatta Ave and Standard St. Otherwise go to Biba on Kenyatta Ave at the junction with Muindi Mbingu St. Cardboard boxes are usually available free of charge or for a few shillings at supermarkets.

Receiving Mail Letters can be sent care of poste restante in any town. Virtually every traveller uses Nairobi as a mail drop and so the amount of mail in poste restante here is amazing. The vast majority of it finds its way into the correct pigeonholes though there's

naturally the occasional mistake. Most of the mistakes are entirely the fault of the letter writer. Make sure you write the addressee's name in block capitals and underline the surname. (I can only admire the ingenuity of the postal staff in sorting out poste restante letters into the correct pile after seeing the way that some people address letters!) If you're not getting expected letters, try looking under all possible initials including 'M' (for M, Mr, Mrs, Ms, if you're an English or French speaker), 'S' (for Señor, Señora, etc, if you're a Spanish or Portuguese speaker), etc.

Some travellers use the American Express Clients Mail Service and this can be a useful alternative to poste restante. Officially you are supposed to have an Amex card or be using their travellers' cheques to avail yourself of this service but no check of this is made at the office in Nairobi. The postal addresses in Nairobi and Mombasa are:

American Express Clients Mail Service
    Express Kenya Ltd, PO Box 40433, Nairobi
Express Kenya
    PO Box 90631, Mombasa

The Nairobi office is in Bruce House on Standard St (☎ (02) 334722), while the Mombasa office is on Nkrumah Rd (☎ (011) 312461).

There's also a set-up called Africa Travel Centre that has offices in London, Sydney and Nairobi which offers mail-holding services (and baggage storage). You can have your mail reliably held or forwarded by the centre for a small fee. It also provides a fax service. The addresses are:

London
    4 Medway Court, Leigh St, London WC1 9QX
    (fax (071) 383-7512)
Sydney
    12th Floor, 456 Kent St, Sydney 2000 (fax (02) 267-3047)
Nairobi
    PO Box 63006, 1st Floor, Union Towers, Moi Ave, Nairobi (fax (2) 213445)

Telephone

The phone system works reasonably well, although it can take a number of attempts to get an international connection depending on the time of day.

International Calls International calls are easy to make from Nairobi, Mombasa and Kisumu where you can either go through the operator or dial yourself on a private line. Phonecards used to be available at the Nairobi Extelcoms office and at the Kenyatta Conference Centre in denominations of KSh 200, 400 and 1000 but the supply of them is erratic and you usually have to go through the operator.

If phonecards are still available, there's one card phone in Nairobi at the main post office, and another in the Extelcoms office on Haile Selassie Ave. There are also two in the lobby of the Kenyatta Conference Centre and these are by far the best to use as there's little background noise there. Mombasa, Malindi, Lamu and Kisumu each have one cardphone at the main post office.

Operator-connected calls are also easy to make. The Extelcoms office in Nairobi is open from 8 am to midnight. Again, the Kenyatta Conference Centre is the best place to ring from as there's an international call office in the lobby and this is much quieter and less frantic than the Extelcoms office. It is only open until 6 pm, however.

In other towns, calls can be made from the post office, although there may be some delay in getting through to the international operator in Nairobi.

It's possible to make reverse-charge (collect) calls to the UK, Europe and the USA, but not to Australia. The cost of international calls to any of these destinations from Kenya when going through the operator is US$20 for three minutes.

Calls put through a hotel operator from your room will be loaded at between 25 and 50% so check what they're going to charge you before you make the call.

Local Calls Local and long-distance (STD) calls are also quite straightforward. There are public phone boxes in every town and these all seem to work. The only problem is that there aren't enough of them, especially in Nairobi where you'll find a queue of four or five people at each box. Local calls cost KSh 2, while STD rates vary depending on the distance. Call boxes accept only KSh 1 and KSh 5 coins. When making an local call, make sure you put a KSh 1 coin into the machine first (regardless of what you insert after that). If you don't, you may have problems.

Calls to Tanzania and Uganda are only STD calls, not international.

The STD area codes for the main towns and cities in Kenya are as follows:

Busia	03362
Diani Beach	01261
Eldoret	0321
Embu	0161
Garissa	0131
Isiolo	0165
Kakamega	0331
Kericho	0361
Kilifi	0125
Kisii	0381
Kisumu	035
Kitale	0325
Lamu	0121
Lodwar	0393
Malindi	0123
Maralal	03681
Marsabit	0183
Meru	0164
Mombasa	011
Nairobi	02
Naivasha	0311
Nakuru	037
Nanyuki	0176
Nyahururu	0365
Nyeri	0171
Thika	0151
Voi	0147
Watamu	0122

TIME

Time in Kenya is GMT/UTC plus three hours all year round.

One thing that must be borne in mind is that Swahili time is six hours out of kilter with the way we tell the time, so that noon and midnight are 6 o'clock *(saa sitta)* Swahili time, and 7 am and 7 pm are 1 o'clock *(saa moja)*. Just add or subtract six hours from the time you are told and hope-

fully from the context you'll be able to work out whether the person is talking about am or pm! You don't come across this all that often unless you speak Swahili but you still need to be prepared for it – I met one person who missed the one daily bus from a particular town on two consecutive days because he was at the station six hours late.

ELECTRICITY

Kenya uses the 240 V system. The power supply is usually reliable and uninterrupted in most places though Nairobi has been having problems lately. Power sockets are of the three-square-pin variety as used in the UK, although some older buildings have round-pin sockets. Bring a universal adapter if a power supply is important to you.

BOOKS

You can walk into any decent bookshop in Europe, America or Australasia and find countless books on Western and Eastern history, culture, politics, economics, religion/philosophy, craft and anything else you care to name. Finding the same thing for Africa is somewhat more difficult except in specialist bookshops. Things are improving, however, but so far only in the large-format, hardback, photo-essay genre. What you will be hard-pressed to find is a good selection of novels, plays and biographies by contemporary African authors, many of them published by the African branches of major Western publishing houses. Heinemann's African Writers Series offers a major collection of such works but they're generally only available in large African cities. In East Africa, the bookshops of Nairobi carry an excellent selection but the choice is considerably more limited in Tanzania and Uganda. In Western countries, they're to be found only in specialist bookshops.

General Books

There are some excellent but quite expensive photo-essay hardbacks which you may prefer to look for in a library. They include *Journey though Kenya* (Bodley Head, 1982), by Mohammed Amin, Duncan Willets &

Brian Tetley. There is a companion volume entitled *Journey through Tanzania* by the same authors and publisher.

Other colourful books on the region include *Africa Adorned* (Collins, 1984) by Angela Fisher; *Ivory Crisis* (Chatto & Windus, 1983) by Ian Parker & Mohammed Amin; *Isak Dinesen's Africa* (Bantam Books, 1985) by various authors; *Africa: A History of a Continent* (Weidenfield & Nicolson, 1966) by Basil Davidson; and *Through Open Doors: A View of Asian Cultures in Kenya* (Kenway Publications, Nairobi, 1983) by Cynthia Salvador. Salvadori also co-authored with Andrew Fedders *Peoples & Cultures of Kenya* (Transafrica, Nairobi, 1989).

In addition to the above, there has recently been a flurry of large-format, hardback books on the various tribal societies of Kenya, especially the Maasai and Samburu, which you'll see in the bookshops of Nairobi and Mombasa.

History, Politics & Economics

There are numerous books on the history of Africa which include *The Penguin Atlas of African History* (Penguin, 1980) by Colin McEvedy, *A Short History of Africa* (Penguin, 1962) by Roland Oliver & J D Fage, and *The Story of Africa* (Mitchell Beazley/Channel Four, 1984) by Basil Davidson. Also excellent reading is *The Africans – A Triple Heritage* (Guild Publishing, 1986) by Ali A Mazrui, which was published in conjunction with a BBC TV series of the same name.

For the origins and development of the coastal Swahili culture and how it has been affected by the arrival of the Portuguese in the Indian Ocean, the standard work is *The Portuguese Period in East Africa* (East African Literature Bureau, 1961) by Justus Strandes. For a radical African viewpoint of the effects of colonialism in general, Walter Rodney's *How Europe Underdeveloped Africa* (Bogle L'Ouverture, 1976) is well worth a read.

Worthwhile contemporary accounts include the extremely readable but rather discouraging *The Africans* (Vintage Books/Random Books, 1984) by David Lamb. Or there's *The Making of Contemporary Africa* (Indiana, 1984) by Bill Freund, and *A Year in the Death of Africa* (Paladin, 1986) by Peter Gill. On contemporary Kenyan politics, it's well worth reading Oginga Odinga's *Not Yet Uhuru* (Heinemann) and *Detained – A Prison Writer's Diary* (Heinemann, 1981) by Ngugi wa Thiong'o, for a radically different view from that put out by the Kenyatta and Moi regimes.

Not exclusively about Africa but very relevant to bilateral and multilateral aid issues, is the *Lords of Poverty* (Mandarin, London, 1991) by Graham Hancock, an exposé of the bungling and waste perpetrated by the UN, IMF, World Bank and others.

The *Africa Review* (NTC Publishing Group, UK) an annual production by World of Information, offers an overview of the politics and economics of every African country as well as detailed facts and figures. It's well balanced and researched and makes no attempt to curry favours with any particular regime.

Travellers' & Other Accounts

Dian Fossey's research with the mountain gorillas of Rwanda is recounted in her book *Gorillas in the Mist* (Penguin, 1983). *The White Nile* (Penguin, 1973) by Alan Moorehead is a superbly evocative account of the exploration of the upper Nile and the rivalry between the European powers.

Journey to the Jade Sea (Paladin, 1974) by John Hillaby, recounts this prolific travel writer's epic trek to Lake Turkana in northern Kenya in the days before the safari trucks began pounding up the dirt in this part of Kenya. Other books to look for include *Initiation* (Penguin, 1985) by J S Fontaine, *A Bend in the River* (Penguin, 1979) by V S Naipaul and *Travels in the Congo* (Penguin, 1927) by André Gide.

Two women's accounts of life in East Africa earlier this century have been recent best sellers. *Out of Africa* by Karen Blixen (Isak Dinesen) is published by Penguin books and has also been made into a hugely popular movie. *West with the Night* (North Point Press) by Beryl Markham has also been a major best seller.

African Fiction

Heinemann's African Writers Series probably has the greatest range of contemporary African authors. There's a list of their writers on the first page of each of their books. Two of Kenya's best authors are Ngugi wa Thiong'o and Meja Mwangi whose books are a good introduction to what's happening in East African literature at present. Ngugi is uncompromisingly (but somewhat dogmatically) radical and his harrowing criticism of the neocolonialist politics of the Kenyan establishment landed him in jail for a year, lost him his job at Nairobi University and forced him into exile. His books, on the other hand, are surprisingly not banned in Kenya even though he was considered a dangerously subversive thorn in the side of the government. Meja Mwangi sticks more to social issues and urban dislocation but has a brilliant sense of humour which threads its way right through his books.

Titles worth reading by Ngugi wa Thiong'o include *Petals of Blood* (1977), *A Grain of Wheat* (1967), *Devil on the Cross* and *Weep Not Child*. Titles by Meja Mwangi include *Going Down River Road, Kill me Quick* (1974) and *Carcass for Hounds* (1974). All these titles are published by Heinemann.

For a hilarious but at times poignant account of the higher education system and its relationship with the political system you probably can't beat *The People's Bachelor* (East Africa Publishing House, Nairobi, 1972) by Austin Bukenya. Though set at Makerere University in Kampala, Uganda, shortly after independence, its theme is relevant to virtually all British ex-colonies. Another author whose books are well known even outside Africa is Chinua Achebe. Although Achebe is a Nigerian and his material is drawn from his experiences in that country, many of the themes and issues are relevant to contemporary East Africa. His most famous title is *Things Fall Apart* (Heinemann, 1958). *Ant Hills of the Savannah*, a much more recent publication, is also well worth reading.

Another Nigerian author who writes about similar themes is Elechi Amadi. Try his *The Concubine* (Heinemann, 1968).

For writing by women in Africa try *Unwinding Threads* (Heinemann, 1983), a collection of short stories by many different authors from all over the continent.

Travel Guides

Africa on a shoestring (Lonely Planet, 1992), by Geoff Crowther, covers more than 50 African countries, concentrating on practical information for budget travellers. His *East Africa – a travel survival kit* (Lonely Planet, 1993) covers this area in considerably more detail.

Insight Kenya (APA Productions, 1985), edited by Mohammed Amin & John Eames, is another of the popular APA guidebook series with many excellent photographs and a lively text. It concentrates more on the country's history, its peoples, cultures, sights and wildlife rather than on practical information and is a good book to read either before you go or whilst you're there.

Guide to Mt Kenya & Kilimanjaro (Mountain Club of Kenya, Nairobi, 1981), edited by Iain Allan, has been written and added to over the years by dedicated enthusiasts, but is mainly directed at skilled climbers and mountaineers. It contains information on the rock and ice routes, but also has some (very dated) trail descriptions, maps, photographs, descriptions of fauna, flora, climate and geology, even mountain medicine.

More recent practical guides to East Africa which would be excellent companions to the one you are reading are those by David Else. His *Trekking in East Africa* (Lonely Planet, 1993) covers a selection of treks and expeditions in the mountains and wilderness areas of Kenya, Tanzania, Uganda and Malawi, and has plenty of advice and general information about trekking in this part of the world. The *Camping Guide to Kenya* (Bradt Publications, 1990) covers every camp site in Kenya – the cities, national parks and mountain areas – and contains information and advice for campers and backpackers venturing off the main routes into the more remote areas of Kenya. *Mountain Walking in Kenya* (Robertson-McCarta, 1991) covers a selection of walking routes through the mountain and highland regions of Kenya including everything from easy strolls around Lake Naivasha to longer hikes on Mt Kenya. There's an equipment guide as well as accurate maps and colour photographs.

Flora & Fauna Guides

A Field Guide to the Larger Mammals of Africa (Collins, 1986) by Jean Dorst & Pierre Dandelot, together with *A Field Guide to the Birds of East Africa* (Collins, 1963) by J G Williams & N Arlott, should suffice for most people's purposes in the national parks and wildlife reserves.

MAPS

Largely as a result of the prosperous tourism industry, there's a wide range of maps available, although many are just made to look pretty and have very little practical use.

One of the best maps of the region is the Hallwag map *Kenya & Tanzania* which also covers Uganda, Rwanda, Burundi and eastern Zaïre. Covering a similar area, but not as well, is Hildebrand's travel map of *East Africa*. The Michelin maps are usually pretty reliable but the only one which takes in this area (No 155, Southern Africa) covers too wide an area to give enough detail.

The *Tourist Map of Kenya*, printed and published in Kenya, gives good detail and there are a few similar ones.

Macmillan publishes a series of maps to the game parks and these are not bad value at US$3.50 each.

The Public Map Office next to the Kenyatta Conference Centre in Nairobi has a stock of government survey maps covering the whole country. The most popular ones (Mt Kenya, Mt Elgon and those covering the game parks) are often out of stock but it's worth getting hold of these maps if possible.

The only trouble with maps published by the Survey of Kenya other than those available in the bookshops is that they're not available to the general public without official authorisation. This is hard to get and takes time so, if you're a tourist with limited time, you can forget it. Even people with credentials, such as Kenyan residents of the Mountain Club of Kenya (MCK), have great difficulty or find it simply impossible to get hold of detailed maps of the country.

MEDIA
Newspapers & Magazines

Tabloid newspapers are printed in both English and Swahili. Of the three English-language papers, the best is the *Daily Nation*, which has a surprising amount of both local and overseas coverage, and is well worth reading on a daily basis if you want to get a feel for what's happening in the country. It has the best cartoons, doesn't shirk from criticising the government and exposing corruption, but balances this with a similar attitude towards the opposition parties. The others are the *Kenya Times* (the KANU party rag) and the *Standard*.

There is also a surprising range of locally produced magazines in both English and Swahili. Principal among these is the *Weekly Review* which is the Kenyan equivalent of Time/Newsweek. Radicals berate this magazine as being a tool of government propaganda but it does, nevertheless, discuss issues in much greater detail than any of the daily newspapers and it's well worth a read. There are plenty of other weekly and monthly magazines, some of them sufficiently critical of the government to occasionally prompt their seizure by the police, and others which are largely titillative such as *True Love* (the 'Dear Claire.....' agony column is often hilarious) and the less silly *Drum*.

Foreign newspapers (up to a week old) in English, French, Italian and German are readily available in Nairobi and Mombasa but vary greatly in price depending on where you buy them. They're expensive at the pavement newsstand next to the New

Stanley Hotel in Nairobi, but you can buy the same papers from a man who lays them out on the pavement at the junction of Kaunda and Kimathi Sts much more cheaply.

Current affairs magazines such as *Time, Newsweek, New African* and *South* are also widely available at a controlled price which is printed on the front cover. New Africa is the best of the bunch if you're looking for detailed coverage of African affairs and events. It's published monthly.

Radio & TV

The Kenyan Broadcasting Corporation (KBC) has radio transmissions in English, Swahili and more specialised languages such as Hindi and African languages.

The BBC World Service transmits to East Africa on short wave around 12 hours a day and has programmes in English and Swahili. The *Daily Nation* prints the programme each day. Although frequencies change from time to time, the main ones to try if you have a short-wave radio include: 21470, 17885 and 15420 kHz.

There are two TV channels – KBC and KTN. The latter is better except that it no longer produces its own independent news programmes but takes them from KBC. Many programmes are imported from Europe, the USA and Australia.

FILM & PHOTOGRAPHY
Film

Film is widely available, especially in Nairobi and on the coast, and the price compares fairly well with what you'd pay at home. You'll need plenty of it – Kenya has heaps to photograph, and anyone with a camera inevitably gets very shutter-happy in the game parks looking for that 'perfect' shot.

It's wise to bring films of varying ASA. If you're using a zoom or long focal length camera (recommended) you're going to need film of at least 200 ASA to give you enough light, especially as the best photo opportunities are early and late in the day when the light is not as bright as the middle daylight hours. Higher speed film also makes it pos-

sible to take photos with a higher shutter speed, which is important when you're trying to photograph moving animals at the same time as being bumped around inside a minibus.

Some of the lodges have salt licks which the animals are attracted to at night, so with 800, 1600 or higher ASA film, non-flash photos are a possibility.

You'll find Kodak and Fuji 64, 100, 200 and 400 ASA slide film readily available in Nairobi and Mombasa, but 800 ASA is virtually impossible to find. The same is true for colour-negative film. Agfa film is also very difficult to find. As an indication of price, 36-exposure slide film in Nairobi costs US$9.60 (64 ASA), US$11.30 (100 ASA), US$13.60 (200 ASA), and US$15.70 (400 ASA). Colour-print film (36 exposures) costs US$6.70 (100 ASA), US$7.70 (200 ASA), and US$9.60 (400 ASA). B&W print film costs less than colour-print film.

Cameras & Lenses

For serious wildlife photography a SLR (single lens reflex) camera which can take long focal length lenses is necessary. If all you have is a little generic 'snapomatic' you may as well leave it behind. Although they are becoming more sophisticated these days, the maximum focal length is around 110 mm – still too small for getting decent shots.

Zoom lenses are best for wildlife photography as you can frame your shot easily to get the best composition. This is important as the animals are constantly and often quickly on the move. The 70 to 210 mm zoom lenses are popular and the 200 mm is really the minimum you need to get good close-up shots. The only problem with zoom lenses is that with all the glass (lenses) inside them they absorb about 1½ 'f' stops of light, which is where the 200 and 400 ASA film starts to become useful.

Telephoto (fixed focal length) lenses give better results than zoom lenses but you're limited by having to carry a separate lens for every focal length. A 400 or 500 mm lens brings the action right up close, but again you need the 200 or 400 ASA film to make the most of them. You certainly need a 400 or 500 mm lens if you're keen on photographing birdlife.

Another option is to carry a 2x teleconverter, which is a small adapter which fits between the lens and the camera body, and doubles the focal length of your lens, so a 200 mm lens becomes 400 mm. These are a good cheap way of getting the long focal length without having to buy expensive lenses. They do, however, have a couple of disadvantages. The first is that, like the larger lenses themselves, a teleconverter uses about 1½ 'f' stops of light. Another disadvantage is that, depending on the camera and lens, teleconverters can make it extremely difficult to focus quickly and precisely, which is an important consideration when both you and the animals are on the move.

When using long lenses a tripod can be extremely useful, and with anything greater than about 300 mm it's a necessity. The problem here is that in the confined space of the hatch of a minibus (assuming you'll be taking an organised safari) it is impossible to set up the tripod, especially when you are sharing the confined space with at least three or four other people. Miniature tripods are available and these are useful for setting up on the roof of the van, although you can also rest the lens itself on the roof, provided that the van engine is switched off to kill any vibration.

Whatever combination of camera, lenses and accessories you decide to carry, make sure they are kept in a decent bag which will protect them from the elements, the dust, and the knocks they are bound to receive. It's also vital to make sure that your travel insurance policy includes your camera gear if it gets stolen.

Camera Hire & Repair

If you don't have the inclination or the resources to buy expensive equipment but still want some decent pictures of your safari, it is possible to hire SLR cameras and lenses in Nairobi. The best place to do this from is Expo Camera Centre (☎ 221797), Jubilee Exchange, Mama Ngina St, which is run by Mo Hussein, a very friendly and helpful man. Its busy here everyday of the working week both with local businesses and tourists so you know it must be reliable and that the prices are competitive.

Expo also has a well-equipped repair shop where you can leave an ailing camera to be repaired with confidence. They do an excellent job but they're not cheap (neither is anyone else).

Selling Cameras

With the high duty placed on imported goods, you may be surprised to find that your old used camera is worth quite a bit in Kenya. Obviously the better the condition of the camera, the more it will be worth. There are a few camera shops in Nairobi which deal in second-hand equipment, so check them out. Bear in mind, however, that you'll most probably be paid in Kenyan shillings, so if it's at the end of your stay you'll need to have enough bank exchange certificates to reconvert the shillings to hard currency at the airport.

Film Processing

There are plenty of one-hour film-processing labs in Nairobi, and at least one in all other major towns. They can handle any film speeds. The cost is reasonable and the results just as good as what you'd get back home. Three good places to have this done are Expo Camera Centre, Camera Experts and the lab next to the Coffee House, all on Mama Ngina St. The lab also has a wide variety of film for sale.

Photographing People

As is the case in any country where you are a tourist, this is a subject which has to be approached with some sensitivity. People such as the Maasai and the Samburu have had so many rubbernecks pointing cameras at them for so many years that they are utterly sick to death of it – with good reason. There are even signs up in Namanga and Amboseli saying that it is prohibited to take photos of the Maasai. This doesn't mean that you can't, but just that you'll have to pay for it. Much as you may find this abhorrent, it is nevertheless an aspect of the tourism industry you'll just have to accept – put yourself in their position and try to think what you'd do.

It is of course possible to take pictures of people with zoom lenses but, most of the time, what's the point? By paying or giving some sort of gift, you'll not only get a better picture by using a smaller lens but you'll have some interaction with your subject. You might even get an invitation to see the family (and possibly photograph them).

HEALTH

Kenya is a fairly healthy country to visit. Malaria is endemic and you need to take precautions against chloroquine-resistant strains. Chloroquine-based malaria tablets are available over the counter even in tiny stores out in the country. Locally manufactured Maloprim is also available, in Nairobi at least, and at a fraction of the cost you'll pay at home.

Tap water throughout the country is safe to drink but water obtained from other sources, especially wells and bores, should be treated with suspicion.

Travel health depends on your predeparture preparations, your day-to-day health care while travelling and how you handle any medical problem or emergency that does develop. While the list of potential dangers can seem quite frightening, with a little luck, some basic precautions and adequate information, few travellers experience more than mild upset stomachs.

Travel Health Guides

Two useful books are *The Traveller's Health Guide* (Lascelles, London) by Dr A C Turner, and *Preservation of Personal Health in Warm Climates* published by the Ross Institute of Tropical Hygiene, Keppel St, London WC1. Another helpful book on health is David Werner's *Where There is No Doctor: a village health care handbook* (Macmillan Press, London). *Travel with Children* (Lonely Planet Publications, Hawthorn), by Maureen Wheeler, includes basic advice on travel health for younger children.

Predeparture Preparations

Medical Insurance Get some! You may never need it, but if you do you'll be very glad to have it. Medical treatment in East Africa is not free and public hospitals are often very crowded. Don't expect the same quality of medical treatment in an East African public hospital as you get back home either. There are many different travel-insurance policies available and any travel agency will be able to recommend one.

Before you choose one collect several different policies and read through them for an hour or two, as the cost of a policy and the sort of cover offered can vary considerably. Many policies are pitched at the family package-tour market and are not really appropriate for a long spell in Africa under your own steam. Usually, medical insurance comes in a package which includes baggage insurance and life insurance, etc. You need to read through the baggage section carefully as many policies put a ceiling on how much they are prepared to pay for individual items which are lost or stolen. Check the small print:

• Some policies specifically exclude 'dangerous activities' which can include scuba diving, motorcycling, even trekking. If such activities are on your agenda you don't want that sort of policy.
• You may prefer a policy which pays doctors or hospitals direct rather than you having to pay on the spot and claim later. If you have to claim later make sure you keep all documentation. Some policies ask you to call back (reverse charges) to a centre in your home country where an immediate assessment of your problem is made.
• Check if the policy covers ambulances or an emergency flight home. If you have to stretch out you will need two seats and somebody has to pay for them!

Medical Kit A small, straightforward medical kit is a wise thing to carry. A possible kit list includes:

• Aspirin or Panadol – for pain or fever
• Antihistamine (such as Benadryl) – useful as a decongestant for colds, allergies, to ease the itch from insect bites or stings or to help prevent motion sickness
• Antibiotics – useful if you're travelling well off the

beaten track, but they must be prescribed and you should carry the prescription with you*

• Kaolin preparation (Pepto-Bismol), Imodium or Lomotil – for stomach upsets

• Dehydration mixture – for treatment of severe diarrhoea, this is particularly important if travelling with children

• Antiseptic, mercurochrome and antibiotic powder or similar 'dry' spray – for cuts and grazes

• Calamine lotion – to ease irritation from bites or stings

• Bandages and Band-aids – for minor injuries

• Scissors, tweezers and a thermometer (note that mercury thermometers are prohibited by airlines)

• Insect repellent, sunscreen, suntan lotion, chap stick and water-purification tablets

* Ideally antibiotics should be administered only under medical supervision and should never be taken indiscriminately. Overuse of antibiotics can weaken your body's ability to deal with infections naturally and can reduce the drug's efficacy on a future occasion. Take only the recommended dose at the prescribed intervals and continue using the antibiotic for the prescribed period, even if the illness seems to be cured earlier. Antibiotics are quite specific to the infections they can treat; stop immediately if there are any serious reactions and don't use it at all if you are unsure if you have the correct one.

Prescriptions & Medications Make sure you're healthy before you start travelling. If you are embarking on a long trip make sure your teeth are OK; dentists are few and far between in Africa and treatment is expensive.

If you wear glasses take a spare pair and your prescription. Losing your glasses can be a real problem, although in Nairobi you can get new spectacles made up quickly, cheaply and competently.

In East Africa, medicines which you would normally need a prescription for in your own country are available over the counter (if they have them) at either a chemist (pharmacist) or a dispensary and the price will be much cheaper than what you would pay in the West. You need, however, to check the expiry date as it may have passed. It's also possible that drugs which are no longer recommended in the West (or have even been banned) are still being dispensed in East Africa, so make sure you know what medicine you require.

Immunisations Before you're allowed to enter most African countries you must have a valid International Health Certificate as proof that you're not the carrier of some new and exotic plague. The essential vaccinations are yellow fever (valid for 10 years) and cholera (valid for six months). While it is generally agreed that cholera vaccinations are a waste of time, many African countries (including Kenya) still require that you have a cholera jab. Good vaccination centres in the West will still stamp your card for you without giving you the shot. In addition, you're strongly advised to be vaccinated against typhoid (valid for three years), tetanus (valid for 10 years), tuberculosis (valid for life) and polio (valid for 10 years).

Gamma globulin shots are also available for protection against infectious hepatitis (type A) but they are ineffective against serum hepatitis (type B). Protection lasts three to six months. There is also a vaccine for type A which provides 100% protection for 12 months (a course of two injections) or for 10 years (with a third, booster, injection), though it is quite expensive. There is a vaccine available for type B but it's only recommended for individuals at high risk. It's also expensive, and the series of three injections takes six months to complete.

You need to plan ahead for these vaccinations, as they cannot all be given at once and typhoid requires a second injection about two or three weeks after the first. Cholera and typhoid jabs usually leave you with a stiff and sore arm for two days afterwards. The other injections generally don't have any effect. Tetanus requires a course of three injections.

If your vaccination card expires whilst you're away, there are a number of medical centres in Kenya where you can have booster vaccinations. There's usually a small fee for these but sometimes they are free.

Avoid turning up at borders with expired vaccination cards, as officials may insist on your having the relevant injection before they will let you in and the same needle may be used on a whole host of people.

Your local physician can arrange a course

of injections for you, or in most large cities there are vaccination centres (including the following) which you can find in the telephone book:

Belgium
Ministère de la Santé Publique et de la Famille, Cité Administrative de l'État, Quartier de l'Esplanade, 1000 Brussels
Centre Médical du Ministère des Affaires Etrangères, 9 Rue Brederode, 1000 Brussels
France
Direction Départementale d'Action Sanitaire et Sociale, 57 Blvd de Sevastopol, 75001 Paris (☎ 4508-9690)
Institut Pasteur, 25 Rue du Docteur Roux, 75015 Paris (☎ 4566-5800)
Holland
Any GGD office or the Academical Medical Centre, Amsterdam
Switzerland
L'Institut d'Hygiène, 2 Quai du Cheval Blanc, 1200 Geneva (☎ (022) 438075)
UK
Hospital for Tropical Diseases, 4 St Pancras Way, London, NW1. Injections here are free but the hospital is often booked up about a month ahead (☎ (071) 387-4411).
West London Designated Vaccination Centre, 53 Great Cumberland Place, London W1. No appointment is necessary, and the fees vary depending on the vaccine (☎ (071) 262-6456).
British Airways Immunisation Centre, Victoria Terminal, Buckingham Palace Rd, London, SW1. Try to book a few days in advance, or you might have to wait around for a few hours before they can fit you in (☎ (071) 834-2323).
British Airways Medical Centre, Speedbird House, Heathrow Airport, Hounslow, Middlesex (☎ (081) 759-5511).

General Health

The main things which are likely to affect your general health while you're abroad are diet and climate. Stomach upsets are the most likely problem but the majority of these upsets will be relatively minor. Don't become paranoid – trying the local food is part of the experience of travel after all.

Water Avoid drinking unboiled water anywhere it's not chlorinated, unless you're taking it from a mountain spring. Unboiled water is a major source of diarrhoea and hepatitis, as are salads that have been washed in contaminated water and unpeeled fruit that has been handled by someone with one of these infections.

Avoiding contaminated water is easier said than done, especially in the desert, and it may be that you'll have to drink water regardless of where it came from. This is part of travelling and there is no way you can eliminate all risks. Carrying a water bottle and a supply of water-purifying tablets is one way around this. Halazone, Potable Aqua and Sterotabs are all good for purifying water but they have little or no effect against amoebas or hepatitis virus. For this you need a 2% tincture of iodine – five drops per litre in clear water and 10 drops per litre in cloudy water. Wait 30 minutes and it's safe to drink.

In hot climates you sweat a great deal and lose a lot of water and salt. Make sure you drink sufficient liquid and have enough salt in your food to make good the losses (a teaspoon of salt per day is generally sufficient). If you don't make good the losses, you run the risk of suffering from heat exhaustion and cramps.

Food & Nutrition Cheap food from cafés and street stalls tends to be overcooked, very starchy (mainly maize and millet) and lacking in protein, vitamins and calcium. Supplement your diet with milk or yoghurt (where it's available and pasteurised) and fresh fruit or vitamin/mineral tablets. Avoid untreated milk and milk products. Peel all fruit. Read up on dietary requirements before you set off. And watch out for grit in rice and bread – a hard bite on the wrong thing can lead to a cracked tooth.

Rest Adjustment to the outlook, habits and social customs of different people can take a lot out of you. Many travellers suffer from some degree of culture shock. This is particularly true if you fly direct from your own country to an African city. Under these conditions, heat can aggravate petty irritations which would pass unnoticed in a more temperate climate. Exhausting all-night, all-day bus journeys over bad roads don't help if you're feeling this way. Try to take things at a slower pace, and make sure you get enough sleep.

Hygiene Many health problems can be avoided by taking care of yourself. Wash your hands frequently – it's quite easy to contaminate your own food. Clean your teeth with purified water rather than straight from the tap. Avoid climatic extremes: keep out of the sun when it's hot, dress warmly when it's cold.

Hot, dry air will make your hair brittle, so oil it often with, say, refined coconut oil. Take great care of cuts, grazes and skin infections otherwise they tend to persist and get worse. Clean them well with antiseptic or mercurochrome. If they're weeping, bandage them up since open sores attract flies. Change bandages daily and use an antibiotic powder if necessary.

Avoid potential diseases by dressing sensibly. You can get worm infections through walking barefoot, or severe cuts from coral or sea urchin spines by walking over coral without foot protection. You can avoid insect bites by covering bare skin when insects are around, by screening windows or beds or by using insect repellents. Seek local advice: if you're told the water is unsafe due to jellyfish, crocodiles or bilharzia, don't go in it. In situations where there is no information, discretion is the better part of valour.

Medical Problems & Treatment

The list of medical problems might seem long and off-putting, but isn't meant to be. Most travellers arrive healthy and leave even healthier. If you do pick up something, however, it's useful to know what to do.

Self-diagnosis and treatment can be risky, so wherever possible seek qualified help. Although we do give treatment dosages in this section, they are for emergency use only. Medical advice should be sought before administering any drugs.

An embassy or consulate can usually recommend a good place to go for such advice. So can five-star hotels, although they often recommend doctors with five-star prices. (This is when that medical insurance really

> **Vital Signs**
> A normal body temperature is 98.6°F or 37°C; more than 2°C higher is a 'high' fever. A normal adult pulse rate is 60 to 80 per minute (children 80 to 100, babies 100 to 140). You should know how to take a temperature and a pulse rate. As a general rule the pulse increases about 20 beats per minute for each °C rise in fever.
>
> Respiration (breathing) rate is also an indicator of illness. Count the number of breaths per minute: between 12 and 20 is normal for adults and older children (up to 30 for younger children, 40 for babies). People with a high fever or serious respiratory illness (like pneumonia) breathe more quickly than normal. More than 40 shallow breaths a minute usually means pneumonia. ■

comes in useful!) In some areas of Kenya, standards of medical attention are so low that for some ailments the best advice is to get on a plane to Nairobi.

Prickly Heat

A temporary but troublesome skin condition which affects many people from temperate climates is prickly heat. Many tiny blisters form on one or more parts of your body – usually where the skin is thickest, such as your hands. They are sweat droplets which are trapped under your skin because your pores aren't large enough or haven't opened up sufficiently to cope with the greater volume of sweat. Anything which promotes sweating – exercise, tea, coffee, alcohol – makes it worse. Keep your skin aired and dry, reduce clothing to a loose-fitting minimum and keep out of direct sunlight. Calamine lotion or zinc oxide-based talcum powder helps to soothe the skin. Apart from that, there isn't much else you can do. The problem is one of acclimatisation and shouldn't persist for more than a few days.

Heat Stroke

This serious, sometimes fatal, condition can occur if the body's heat-regulating mechanism breaks down and the body temperature rises to dangerous levels. Long, continuous periods of exposure to high temperature can leave you vulnerable to heat stroke. You should avoid excessive alcohol or strenuous activity when you first arrive in a hot climate.

The symptoms of heat stroke are feeling unwell, not sweating very much or at all and a high body temperature (from 39 to 41°C). Where sweating has ceased the skin becomes flushed and red. Severe, throbbing headaches and lack of coordination will also occur, and the sufferer may be confused or aggressive. Eventually the victim will become delirious or convulse. Hospitalisation is essential, but meanwhile get patients out of the sun, remove their clothing, cover them with a wet sheet or towel and then fan continually. Be careful not to cool them down too rapidly; if they start to shiver, their core temperature will rise still further rather than decrease.

Fungal Infections

Hot weather fungal infections are most likely to occur on the scalp, between the toes or fingers (athlete's foot), in the groin (jock itch or crotch rot) and on the body (ringworm). You get ringworm (which is a fungal infection, not a worm) from infected animals or by walking on damp areas, like shower floors.

To prevent fungal infections wear loose, comfortable clothes, avoid artificial fibres, wash frequently and dry yourself carefully. If you do get an infection, wash the infected area daily with a disinfectant or medicated soap and water, and rinse and dry well. Apply an antifungal powder like the widely available Tinaderm. Try to expose the infected area to air or sunlight as much as possible and wash all towels and underwear in hot water as well as changing them often.

Tropical Ulcers

These are sores which often start from some insignificant scratch or blister which doesn't seem to heal up. They often get worse and spread to other areas of the body and they can be quite painful. If you keep clean and look after any sores which you get on your arms, feet and legs (from poorly fitting shoes, cuts and scrapes, or from excessive scratching of insect bites) then it's unlikely you will be troubled by them. If you do develop sores which won't clear up then you need to hit the antibiotics quickly. Don't let them spread.

Altitude Sickness

Acute Mountain Sickness or AMS occurs at high altitude and can be fatal. The lack of oxygen at high altitudes affects most people to some extent. Take it easy at first, increase your liquid intake and eat well. Even with acclimatisation you may still have trouble adjusting – headaches, nausea, dizziness, a dry cough, insomnia, breathlessness and loss of appetite are all signs to heed. If you reach a high altitude by trekking, acclimatisation takes place gradually and you are less likely to be affected than if you fly straight there.

Mild altitude problems will generally abate after a day or so but if the symptoms persist or become worse the only treatment is to descend – even 500 metres can help. Breathlessness, a dry, irritative cough (which may progress to the production of pink, frothy sputum), severe headache, loss of appetite, nausea, and sometimes vomiting are all danger signs. Increasing tiredness, confusion, and lack of coordination and balance are real danger signs. Any of these symptoms individually, even just a persistent headache, can be a warning.

There is no hard and fast rule as to how high is too high: AMS has been fatal at altitudes of 3000 metres, although 3500 to 4500 metres is the usual range. It is always wise to sleep at a lower altitude than the greatest height reached during the day.

Motion Sickness

Eating lightly before and during a trip will reduce the chances of motion sickness. If you are prone to motion sickness try to find a place that minimises disturbance – near the wing on aircraft, close to midships on boats, near the centre on buses. Fresh air usually helps, reading or cigarette smoke doesn't. Commercial antimotion-sickness preparations, which can cause drowsiness, have to be taken before the trip commences; when you're feeling sick it's too late. Ginger is a natural preventative of motion sickness and is available in capsule form.

Diarrhoea

Sooner or later most travellers get diarrhoea, so you may as well accept the inevitable. You can't really expect to travel halfway around the world without succumbing to diarrhoea at least once or twice, but it doesn't always mean that you've caught a bug. Depending on how much travelling you've done and what your gut is used to, it can be merely the result of a change of food. If you've spent all your life living on food out of sterilised, plastic-wrapped packets and tins from the local supermarket, you're going to have a hard time until you adjust.

If and when you get a gut infection, avoid rushing off to the chemist and filling yourself with antibiotics. It's a harsh way to treat your system and you can build up a tolerance to them with overuse. Try to starve the bugs out first. Eat nothing and rest. Avoid travelling. Drink plenty of fluids. Have your tea with a little sugar and no milk. Diarrhoea will dehydrate you and may result in painful muscular cramps in your guts. The cramps are due to a poor salt balance in your blood, so take a small amount of salt with your tea. If you can find it, tincture of opium (known as 'paregoric' and often mixed with kaolin – a stronger version of milk of magnesia) will relieve the pain of cramps. Something else you may come across, called RD Sol, also helps to maintain a correct salt balance and so prevent cramps. It's a mixture of common salt, sodium bicarbonate, potassium chloride and dextrose. Two days of this regime should clear you out.

If you simply can't hack starving, keep to a *light* diet of curd, yoghurt, toast, dry biscuits, rice and tea. Stay away from butter, milk, sugar, cakes and fruit.

If starving doesn't work or you really have to move on and can't rest for a couple of days, try Pesulin (or Pesulin-O which is the same but with the addition of a tincture of opium). The dosage is two teaspoons four times daily for five days. Or try Lomotil –

the dosage is two tablets three times daily for two days. Avoid overuse of Lomotil.

If you have no luck with either of these, change to antibiotics or see a doctor. There are many different varieties of antibiotics and you almost need to be a biochemist to know what the differences between them are. They include tetracycline, chlorostep, typhstrep, sulphatriad, streptomagma and thiazole. If possible, have a word with the chemist about their differences. Overuse will do you more harm than good but you must complete the course otherwise the infection may return and then you'll have even more difficulty getting rid of it.

Giardia

Giardia is prevalent in tropical climates and is characterised by swelling of the stomach, pale-coloured faeces, diarrhoea and, after a while, depression and sometimes nausea. Many doctors recommend Flagyl (metronidazole) – seven 250 mg doses over a three-day period should clear up the symptoms, repeated a week later if not. Flagyl, however, has many side effects and some doctors prefer to treat giardia with Tinaba (tinadozole). Two grams taken all at once normally knocks it right out but if not you can repeat the dosage for up to three days.

Dysentery

Dysentery is, unfortunately, quite prevalent in some places. It's characterised by diarrhoea containing blood and lots of mucus, and painful gut cramps. There are two types. Bacillary dysentery is short, sharp and nasty but rarely persistent – it's the most common variety. Amoebic dysentery is, as its name suggests, caused by amoebic parasites. This variety is much more difficult to treat and often persistent.

Bacillic dysentery comes on suddenly and lays you out with fever, nausea, painful cramps and diarrhoea but, because it's caused by bacteria, it responds well to antibiotics. Amoebic dysentery builds up more slowly and is more dangerous. You cannot starve it out and if it's untreated it will get worse and permanently damage your intestines. If you see blood in your faeces persistently over two or three days, seek medical attention as soon as possible.

Flagyl is the most commonly prescribed drug for amoebic dysentery. The dosage is six tablets per day for five to seven days. Flagyl is both an antibiotic and an antiparasitic. It is also used for the treatment of giardia and trichomoniasis. Flagyl should not be taken by pregnant women. If you get bacillic dysentery, the best thing for slowing down intestinal movements is codeine phosphate (30 mg tablets – take two once every four hours). It's much more effective than Lomotil or Imodium and cheaper. Treatment for bacillic dysentery consists of a course of tetracycline or bactrim (antibiotics).

Hepatitis

Hepatitis is a liver disease caused by a virus. There are basically two types – infectious hepatitis (known as type A) and serum hepatitis (known as type B). The one you're most likely to contract is type A. It's very contagious and you pick it up by drinking water, eating food or using cutlery or crockery that's been contaminated by an infected person. Foods to avoid are salads (unless you know they have been washed thoroughly in purified water) and unpeeled fruit that may have been handled by someone with dirty hands. It's also possible to pick it up by sharing a towel or toothbrush with an infected person.

An estimated 10% of the population of the Third World are healthy carriers of type B but the only ways you can contract this form are by having unprotected sex with an infected person or by being injected with a needle which has previously been used on an infected person.

Symptoms of type A appear 15 to 50 days after infection (generally around 25 days) and consist of fever, loss of appetite, nausea, depression, complete lack of energy and pains around the base of your rib cage. Your skin will turn progressively yellow and the whites of your eyes yellow to orange. The easiest way to monitor the situation is to watch the colour of your eyes and urine. If

you have hepatitis, the colour of your urine will be deep orange no matter how much liquid you've drunk. If you haven't drunk much liquid and/or you're sweating a lot, don't jump to conclusions. Check it out by drinking a lot of liquid all at once. If the urine is still orange then you'd better start making plans to go somewhere you won't mind convalescing for a few weeks. Sometimes the disease lasts only a few weeks and you only get a few really bad days, but it can last for months. If it does get really bad, cash in that medical insurance you took out and fly back home.

There is no cure as such for hepatitis except rest and good food. Diets high in B vitamins are said to help. Fat-free diets have gone out of medical fashion, but you may find that grease and oil make you feel nauseous. Seeking medical attention is probably a waste of time and money, though you are going to need a medical certificate for your insurance company if you decide to fly home. There's nothing doctors can do for you that you can't do for yourself other than run tests that will tell you how bad it is. Most people don't need telling; they can feel it! Wipe alcohol and cigarettes right off the slate. They'll not only make you feel much worse, but alcohol and nicotine can do permanent damage to a sick liver.

To avoid these problems, think seriously about getting that gamma globulin vaccination. There is also a vaccine available for hepatitis A (brand name Harvix) which provides protection for 12 months, or for 10 years if you choose to have a booster injection as well. There is also a very effective vaccine against hepatitis B, given as a course of three injections over a six-month period, which is an option for those who know their travel plans well in advance of their trip. The course offers protection for about five years.

Typhoid

Typhoid fever is another gut infection that travels the faecal-oral route – ie contaminated water and food are responsible. Typhoid is very infectious and vaccination against it is not totally effective. It is one of the most dangerous infections so medical help must be sought.

In its early stages typhoid resembles many other illnesses: sufferers may feel like they have a bad cold or flu on the way, as early symptoms are a headache, a sore throat, and a fever which rises a little each day until it is around 40°C or more. The victim's pulse is often slow relative to the degree of fever present and gets slower as the fever rises – unlike a normal fever where the pulse increases. There may also be vomiting, diarrhoea or constipation.

In the second week the high fever and slow pulse continue and a few pink spots may appear on the body; trembling, delirium, weakness, weight loss and dehydration are other symptoms. If there are no further complications, the fever and other symptoms will slowly go during the third week. However you must get medical help before this because pneumonia (acute infection of the lungs) or peritonitis (burst appendix) are common complications.

The fever should be treated by keeping the victim cool and dehydration should also be watched for. Chloramphenicol is the recommended antibiotic but there are fewer side affects with ampicillin. The adult dosage is two 250 mg capsules, four times a day. Children aged between eight and 12 years should have half the adult dose; younger children should have one-third the adult dose.

Patients who are allergic to penicillin should not be given ampicillin.

Worms

These parasites are most common in rural, tropical areas and a stool test when you return home is not a bad idea. Worms can be present on unwashed vegetables or in undercooked meat and you can pick them up through your skin by walking bare foot. Infestations may not show up for some time, and although they are generally not serious, if left untreated they can cause severe health problems. A stool test is necessary to pinpoint the problem and medication is often available over the counter.

Tetanus

This potentially fatal disease is found in undeveloped tropical areas. It is difficult to treat but is preventable with immunisation. Tetanus occurs when a wound becomes infected by a germ which lives in the faeces of animals or people, so clean all cuts, punctures or animal bites. Tetanus is known as lockjaw, and the first symptom may be discomfort in swallowing, or stiffening of the jaw and neck; this is followed by painful convulsions of the jaw and body.

Rabies

Rabies is found in many countries and is caused by a bite or scratch by an infected animal. Dogs are a noted carrier. Any bite, scratch or even lick from a mammal should be cleaned immediately and thoroughly. Scrub with soap and running water, and then clean with an alcohol solution. If there is any possibility that the animal is infected medical help should be sought immediately. Even if the animal is not rabid, all bites should be treated seriously as they can become infected or can result in tetanus. A rabies vaccination is now available and should be considered if you are in a high-risk category – eg if you intend to explore caves (bat bites could be dangerous) or work with animals.

Meningococcal Meningitis

Sub-Saharan Africa is considered the 'meningitis belt' and the meningitis season falls at the time most people would be attempting the overland trip across the Sahara – the northern winter before the rains come.

This very serious disease attacks the brain and can be fatal. A scattered, blotchy rash, fever, severe headache, sensitivity to light and neck stiffness which prevents forward bending of the head are the first symptoms. Death can occur within a few hours, so immediate treatment is important.

Treatment is large doses of penicillin given intravenously, or, if that is not possible, intramuscularly (ie in the buttocks). Vaccination offers good protection for over a year, but you should also check for reports of current epidemics.

Tuberculosis

Although this disease is widespread in many developing countries, it is not a serious risk to travellers. Young children are more susceptible than adults and vaccination is a sensible precaution for children aged under 12 travelling in endemic areas. TB is commonly spread by coughing or by unpasteurised dairy products from infected cows. Milk that has been boiled is safe to drink; the souring of milk to make yoghurt or cheese also kills the bacilli.

Bilharzia

This is caused by blood flukes (minute worms) which live in the veins of the bladder or the large intestine. The eggs which the adult worms produce are discharged in urine or faeces. If they reach water, they hatch out and enter the bodies of a certain species of freshwater snail where they multiply for four or more weeks and are then discharged into the surrounding water. If they are to live, they must find and invade the body of a human being where they develop, mate and then make their way to the veins of their choice. Here they start to lay eggs and the cycle repeats itself. The snail favours shallow water near the shores of lakes and streams and they are more abundant in water which is polluted by human excrement. They particularly like reedy areas. Generally speaking, moving water contains less risk than stagnant water but you can never tell.

Bilharzia is quite a common disease in Africa so stay out of rivers and lakes. If you drink water from any of these places, boil it or sterilise it with chlorine tablets. The disease is painful and causes persistent and cumulative damage by repeated deposits of eggs. If you suspect you have it, seek medical advice as soon as possible – look for blood in your urine or faeces that isn't associated with diarrhoea. The only body of water in Africa which is largely free of bilharzia is Lake Malawi, so keep out of Lake Victoria. As the intermediate hosts (snails) live only in fresh water, there's no risk of catching bilharzia in the sea.

Sexually Transmitted Diseases

Sexual contact with an infected sexual partner spreads these diseases. While abstinence is the only 100% preventative, using condoms is also effective. Gonorrhoea and syphilis are the most common of these diseases; sores, blisters or rashes around the genitals, discharges or pain when urinating are common symptoms. Symptoms may be less marked or not observed at all in women. Syphilis symptoms eventually disappear completely but the disease continues and can cause severe problems in later years. The treatment of gonorrhoea and syphilis is by antibiotics.

There are numerous other sexually transmitted diseases, for most of which effective treatment is available. However, there is no cure for herpes and there is also currently no cure for HIV/AIDS. HIV/AIDS is rampant in Uganda, less so in Kenya and Tanzania but still a serious problem and on the increase. The latest figures put the number of carriers of the HIV virus (the virus that causes HIV/AIDS) at one in 12. Most of those who have it are not aware of the fact, and hospitals (if they ever get to them) are likely to diagnose their symptoms as something more mundane. The obvious way to pick up the HIV virus is to have sex with someone who has the disease. The obvious way to avoid it is to be celibate. Not everyone can do this so if you do have sex make sure you cut the risk as far as you can by using condoms. You are still a long way from 100% safe if you do this but the message has definitely got through and most sexually active Africans living in urban areas carry condoms.

There are two other ways you can pick up the HIV virus. The first is if you need a blood transfusion. Blood donors in Kenya are rarely screened for HIV/AIDS and if you receive blood from an infected donor you will be exposed to the virus. Your options are probably limited if you get into the sort of strife which requires a transfusion. It is also possible to pick up the virus if you are

Mt Kenya's Unusual Alpine Flora

As in other alpine areas of the tropics such as the Andes, the Himalayas, Borneo and on neighbouring Mt Kilimanjaro, there are a number of unusual plant species to be found on the upper slopes of Mt Kenya. Some of these are so characteristic as to be one of the major features of the area. The most prominent are the giant lobelia and the giant groundsel.

The giant lobelia are unmistakable with their unbranched treelike stems topped by a wild looking mop of thick, hairy leaves which, depending on the species, grow to a height of between two and nine metres. The hairs are an adaptation to the severe climate which the plants experience at these altitudes. The stems, nevertheless, remain largely non-woody. Like other lobelia species, the giants have blue to purple flowers borne in clusters on long, terminal spikes which project above the foliage. However, unlike the smaller annual species, giant lobelias flower only once in their lifetime.

There are three giant species found in Kenya. In the wetter forests between 1200 and 2700 metres high, the most usual is *Lobelia gibberoa* which grows up to a height of nine metres. The other two, *Lobelia aberdarica* and *Lobelia telekii*, which grow to a height of two metres, are found between 2100 and 3400 metres, though some hardy individuals grow even as high up as 4600 metres. ■

Giant lobelia & giant groundsel (MS)

Jewellery & Tribal Souvenirs

Most of the jewellery on sale is of tribal origin, although very little of it is the genuine article. The colourful Maasai beaded jewellery is the most striking and the most popular, and items include long earrings and the sets of three 'collars', all made with brightly coloured beads.

Other Maasai items include the decorated *calabash* – dried gourds used to store a mixture of blood and milk which is then left to ferment for a few days before it is drunk. Before the mixture is placed in the gourd, specific grasses are burnt inside it, and the soot deposit imparts a certain flavour and aids in fermentation. As you might imagine, these gourds often smell a bit, but are quite strikingly decorated with Maasai beads. Spears and shields are also popular although these are all made specifically for the tourist trade these days.

One of the best places to pick up Maasai souvenirs is at Namanga on the Tanzanian border. This is where all the minibuses headed for Amboseli pass through and stop for a few minutes, so prices are outrageous. However, with some persistent bargaining you can reduce the prices to realistic levels. They know as well as you that the prices they ask are ridiculous, but there are plenty of well heeled tourists passing through here who have more money than sense. For instance, the starting price for earrings is KSh 100 per pair, but they are quite happy to sell them for KSh 10; similarly I expressed an interest in a calabash and was quoted KSh 500 – and eventually paid KSh 35!

All this stuff is bought cheaper out in the bush away from the tourist circuits but buying still demands judicious haggling. ■

Maasai jewellery (HF)

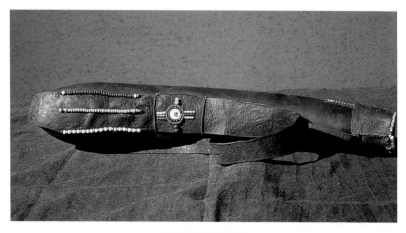

Maasai calabash (HF)

injected with an unsterilised needle. If you do have an injection in Kenya try to ensure the needle is either new or properly sterilised.

Malaria

Malaria is caused by a blood parasite which is spread by certain species of night-flying mosquito (anopheles). Only the female insects spread the disease but you can contract it through a single bite from an insect carrying the parasite. Start on a course of antimalarial drugs before you set off and keep it up as you travel.

The drugs are fairly cheap in some places but horrendously expensive in others – the USA and Scandinavia in particular. There are basically two types: proguanil (brand name Paludrine in the USA) which you take daily, and chloroquine (brand name Aralen in the USA) which you take once or twice per week (depending on its strength). Both are marketed under various trade names. In Kenya the parasite is beginning to acquire immunity to some of the drugs, so you will need to take Maloprim in addition to chloroquine, or mefloquine (brand name Larium in the USA). You would be very unlucky to contract malaria if you are taking one or more of these drugs but they are not a 100% guarantee.

Having said that, it's fair to say that many expatriates working in East Africa for long periods of time prefer not to take prophylactics but to treat the disease if and when it occurs. The reasoning behind this is that the prophylactic drugs can have serious side-effects, specifically to the liver and eyes, when taken continuously over a long period of time. I've experienced this myself. These people prefer insect repellants, mosquito nets and screening. So did I for six months – and didn't get malaria.

If you do develop malarial symptoms – high fever, severe headaches, shivering, liver pains and aching joints – and are not within reach of medical advice, the treatment is one single dose of four tablets (600 mg) of chloroquine followed by two tablets (300 mg) six hours later and two tablets on each

following day. As an alternative (or in chloroquine-resistant areas) take a single dose of three tablets of Fansidar, or two tablets of Larium followed by two more 12 hours later.

Other than the malaria hazard, mosquito bites can be troublesome and although it's probably useless to say this, *don't scratch the bites*. If you do, and they don't heal quickly, there's a chance of them becoming infected with something else. You'll come across people in Africa pockmarked with angry sores which started out as insignificant mosquito bites – the owners couldn't resist the urge to scratch them. Don't join them. Will-power works wonders, as does antihistamine cream. To keep the mosquitoes off at night, use an insect repellent or sleep under a fan. Mosquitoes don't like swift-moving currents of air and will stay on the walls of the room in these circumstances.

There is not yet a vaccination against malaria, so take those pills.

Trypanosomiasis (Sleeping Sickness)

This is another disease transmitted by biting insects, in this case by the tsetse fly. Like malaria, it's caused by minute parasites which live in the blood. The risk of infection is very small and confined to areas which are only a fraction of the total area inhabited by the tsetse fly. The flies are only found south of the Sahara but the disease is responsible for the absence of horses and cattle from large tracts of central Africa, particularly central and eastern Tanzania.

The fly is about twice the size of a common housefly and recognisable from the scissor-like way it folds its wings while at rest. The disease is characterised by irregular fevers, abscesses, local oedema (puffy swellings caused by excess water retained in body tissues), inflammation of the glands and physical and mental lethargy. It responds well to treatment.

Yellow Fever

Yellow fever is endemic in much of Africa. Get that vaccination before you set off and you won't have to worry about it.

Cuts & Scratches

Skin punctures can easily become infected in hot climates and may be difficult to heal. Treat any cut with an antiseptic solution and mercurochrome. Where possible avoid bandages and Band-aids, which can keep wounds wet. Coral cuts are notoriously slow to heal, as the coral injects a weak venom into the wound. Avoid coral cuts by wearing shoes when walking on reefs, and clean any cut thoroughly.

Bites & Stings

Bee and wasp stings are usually painful rather than dangerous. Calamine lotion will give relief, or ice packs will reduce the pain and swelling. There are some spiders with dangerous bites but antivenenes are usually available. Scorpion stings are notoriously painful and in Mexico can actually be fatal. Scorpions often shelter in shoes or clothing.

There are various fish and other sea creatures which can sting or bite dangerously (eg jellyfish, stone fish on coral reefs) or which are dangerous to eat. Again, local advice is the best suggestion.

Snakes

To minimise your chances of being bitten always wear boots, socks and long trousers when walking through undergrowth where snakes may be present. Don't put your hands into holes and crevices, and be careful when collecting firewood.

Snake bites do not cause instantaneous death and antivenenes are usually available. Keep the victim calm and still, wrap the bitten limb tightly, as you would for a sprained ankle, and then attach a splint to immobilise it. Then seek medical help, if possible with the dead snake for identification. Don't attempt to catch the snake if there is even a remote possibility of being bitten again. Tourniquets and sucking out the poison are now comprehensively discredited.

Fleas, Lice & Bedbugs

Unwanted passengers you're likely to come across are fleas, lice and bedbugs. There isn't a lot you can do about fleas. They vary considerably in numbers from one season to another; some places have a lot, others none at all. The less money you pay for a bed or a meal, the more likely you are to encounter fleas.

You can generally avoid lice by washing yourself and your clothes frequently. You're most likely to pick them up in crowded places like buses and trains, but you might also get them by staying in very cheap hotels. You'll occasionally meet tribespeople whose hair is so matted and so unwashed that it's literally crawling with lice. However, it takes a while for lice to get stuck into you so you should get a companion to have a look through your hair about once a week to see if you've acquired any eggs. They are always laid near the base of the hairs. If you find any, you can either pick them out one by one (very laborious) or blitz them with insecticide shampoo like Lorexane or Suleo. We've had letters from people who have doused their hair in petrol or DDT. You're certainly guaranteed total wipeout this way, but it does seem mildly hysterical!

With luck you won't come across bedbugs too often. These evil little bastards live in the crevices of walls and the framework of beds where they hide during the day. They look like lice but they move like greased lightning once you become aware of their presence and switch on the light to see what's happening. Look for telltale bloodstains on the walls near beds in budget hotels. If you see them, find another hotel.

Jiggers are nasty small fleas *(Tunga penetrans)* which burrow under the skin of the feet (usually under the toe nails) to lay their eggs! After incubation the eggs hatch out and you'll have enough fleas to start a circus! The best preventative is to avoid walking around barefoot.

Women's Health

Gynaecological Problems Poor diet, lowered resistance due to the use of antibiotics for stomach upsets and even contraceptive pills can lead to vaginal infections when travelling in hot climates.

Keeping the genital area clean, and wearing skirts or loose-fitting trousers and cotton underwear will help to prevent infections.

Yeast infections, characterised by a rash, itch and discharge, can be treated with a vinegar or even lemon-juice douche or with yoghurt. Nystatin suppositories are the usual medical prescription to thrush. Trichomoniasis is a more serious infection; symptoms are a discharge and a burning sensation when urinating. Male sexual partners must also be treated, and if a vinegar-water douche is not effective, medical attention should be sought. Flagyl is the prescribed drug.

Pregnancy Most miscarriages occur during the first three months of pregnancy, so this is the most risky time to travel. The last three months should also be spent within reasonable distance of good medical care, as quite serious problems can develop at this time. Pregnant women should avoid all unnecessary medication, but vaccinations and malarial prophylactics should still be taken where possible. Additional care should be taken to prevent illness and particular attention should be paid to diet and nutrition.

WOMEN TRAVELLERS

Sexual harassment of women is far less prevalent in Kenya than in many countries though essentially this relates only to White women. If you're Black and walking the streets alone after 7 pm, there's a very good chance you'll be arrested, accused of being a whore and pressured into bribing your way out. KSh 200 is the usual amount. Refuse to pay and you could well spend the night in a cell at the central police station, be taken to court the following morning and fined KSh 1000. According to the people I've met to whom this has happened, you break no ice protesting your innocence even if you're married and your husband happens to be back at a hotel room or elsewhere. It can even happen if you're a Black woman in the company of a White man. The obvious way around this is to take taxis at night if you're going anywhere.

White women come under the category of 'tourists' and enjoy a somewhat dubious though privileged status. If you're a white woman, you may get the occasional hassle but it's rarely persistent if treated with the cold shoulder. There are certain areas in Nairobi where you wouldn't want to walk alone at night, but that applies equally to men, though usually for different reasons.

DANGERS & ANNOYANCES
Theft

Travelling in Kenya is basically trouble-free but you definitely do need to keep your wits about you. The time when you face the biggest risk is within the first couple of days of arriving in the country. The people who make a living by relieving people of their possessions can often spot new arrivals by their uncertain movements and general unfamiliarity with the place. This is particularly true in Nairobi, and in fact the number of people who get their passports and money knocked off on the No 34 public bus in from the airport is amazing. The thieves use the 'instant crowd' technique, you'll find yourself jostled and before you know it your bag or money-belt strap has been slashed. Personally, I wouldn't use this bus for quids and, instead, take the Kenya Airways minibus, or even a taxi and get into Nairobi with my valuables intact.

Never leave your gear unattended anywhere as chances are it won't be there when you get back, no matter how short a time you are away. In hotel rooms your gear is generally safe but use your common sense – in some places (particularly the real cheapies/brothels) the door locks are purely cosmetic. In Nairobi the danger of theft of your possessions from your hotel room has to be weighed against the risk of having them ripped off on the street. If your hotel and room is secure, it's probably safer to leave valuables there. If you are going out raging at night, only carry as much money as you're likely to need, and leave everything else in your hotel. If your hotel has safety deposit boxes, leave your valuables there.

The place to carry your passport, money and other precious documents is in a pouch against your skin, either around your waist or your neck. Neither method is foolproof but both give a good measure of security and make it much harder to lose things. Leather pouches are far more comfortable to have against your skin than synthetic ones, and the moisture from perspiration is far less likely to turn your precious documents into a soggy pulp.

Small pouches and other wallets worn on the outside of your clothes are like flashing beacons to a thief as are the ubiquitous money belts, yet they continue to be immensely popular. Personally, I wouldn't step out of the hotel with one strapped to my waist. Advertise your valuables, and someone will be watching you. Day packs, especially in Nairobi, instantly classify you as a tourist (and probably one who hasn't been around too long). Elsewhere, they're not quite such a beacon. Minimise the risk by wearing them on your front rather than your back.

If you are the victim of a snatch theft, think twice before yelling 'Thief!' Nairobi people hate thieves, pursue them with a vengeance and, if they can catch them, mete out instant, brutal and often lethal punishment on the spot. One or more thieves lose their lives everyday in Nairobi for this. The police may intervene, but not always.

Confidence Tricks

In Nairobi the chances are you'll come across people who play on the emotions and gullibility of foreigners. People with tales about being 'refugees', usually from South Africa (but it could be anywhere with a political problem), can sound very convincing as they draw you into their net but they all end up asking for money. If you do give any, expect to be 'arrested' by 'plain-clothes police', complete with fake ID cards, who then extract a 'fine' from you on the basis that 'it's illegal to give money to foreigners'. It's actually only illegal to give them foreign currency. Stories such as this abound and the number of travellers who get taken in – sometimes to the tune of hundreds of dollars

– is legend. The best policy is to ignore all such requests for money even though by doing this you'll occasionally be turning down what is a genuine request for help.

Another trick in Nairobi is the envelope full of money which gets dropped on the footpath in front of you. The idea is that, as you are reaching to pick it up, someone else (the accomplice of the person who dropped it) grabs it and then suggests to you that, as you both found it, you should go somewhere and share your 'good luck'. If you go along the only thing that will be shared is your money in a side alley somewhere.

Another tried and tested con trick is what appears to be a school student who approaches you with a photocopied sponsorship form headed by the name of a school. He tells you his school needs funds to buy equipment and can you give a donation? Look at the form and you'll find the names of two or three wonderfully philanthropic people (usually from the USA, Germany or the UK) who have apparently donated vast amounts of Kenyan shillings to this worthy cause. If you fall for this then you need your head examined. If the person proves persistent, just ask him to go along with you to a telephone so you can confirm that the request is genuine and that the person is a registered student at the school in question.

The story changes each week. Whatever works gets pumped for all it's worth.

In Nakuru they don't lack ingenuity either. A trick that has been popular for years involves tourists with cars. Locals splash oil on your wheels, then tell you that your wheel bearings, differential or something else had failed, and then direct you to a nearby garage where their friends will 'fix' the problem – for a substantial fee. We've even had reports of oil being splashed on the back wheels and then the driver being told that the rear differential had failed even though the car was front wheel drive! Another vehicle trick is that people on the side of the road will gesticulate wildly to you as you are driving along, indicating that your front wheels are wobbling. Chances are that if you stop you'll be relieved of your valuables.

Mugging

Foreigners (and even experienced expatriates) do occasionally get mugged, but if you're sensible the chances of it happening to you are extremely small. There are certain places in Nairobi and on the coast where it's not recommended to walk at night, but other than that it's just a matter of common sense: don't go out drinking in the nightclubs or bars carrying your valuables and then go rolling home down the street; don't wear your wealth, or you become a very tempting target. Leave valuable jewellery at home, keep cameras out of sight and don't pull out wads of money to pay for something. Always have enough small change for everyday transactions handy and keep the rest concealed. Take a cue from the taxi drivers of Nairobi who stash their money in at least half a dozen places on their body and in various articles of clothing.

Lastly, be wary on crowded matatus. It's not the ragamuffins you should watch but those who appear to be well dressed and on their way home from work. Plenty of these people work the matatus and you, as a tourist, are just one of their targets. Kenyans get hit, too.

And, if you do get mugged, don't listen to anyone who swears blind that he/she can get back what you've lost because they know 'the scene'. You'll end up several hours later being told a sob story or simply never see the person again.

WORK

With the economic downturn in Kenya, it's difficult for foreigners to find jobs, but by no means impossible. The most likely areas in which employment might be found are in the safari business, teaching, advertising and journalism but, except for teaching, it's unlikely you'll see them advertised and the only way you'll find out about them is to spend a lot of time getting to know resident expatriates. You will also need to be able to prove that you have the relevant qualifications and/or experience in the field. Basically the rule of thumb is that if an African can do the job there's no need to hire a *mzungu* (White person).

The most fruitful area in which to look for work, given that you've had some experience and have the relevant skills, is the 'disaster industry'. Nairobi is awash with UN and other aid agencies servicing the famines in Somalia and southern Sudan and the refugee camps along the Kenyan border with those countries. But remember that the work is tough, often dangerous and the pay low. To find such work you would, again, have to spend a lot of time getting to know the expatriates involved in this.

Freelance work in the fields of journalism, literature and the film industry is also possible but, if you get involved in this, make sure you have a cast-iron contract for the work which you do. Too many people neglect to do this, go ahead on a kiss and a promise, don't get paid and/or see their work ripped-off or shelved and end up tearing their hair out.

Work permits and resident visas are not the easiest of things to arrange either. A prospective employer may be able to arrange them relatively painlessly but, usually, you would find yourself spending a lot of money (US$300 minimum) and time at Nyayo House (immigration).

ACTIVITIES

Diving & Snorkelling

Malindi, Watamu, Shimoni and Wasini Island are the spots for scuba diving, the latter two being preferred. At Watamu, diving is from a boat not far offshore. A typical anchor dive is made at 12 to 15 metres depth. Visibility is often only fair and in fact Kenyan diving visibility has a poor reputation due to the plankton in the water. There are, however, usually plenty of fish in the water even if the coral is not that spectacular. A typical dive costs US$30. For more information contact the Dive Shop at the Driftwood Club in Malindi, or the Ocean Sports Hotel at Watamu. Possibilities at Shimoni and Wasini Island in the extreme south are covered in The Coast chapter.

Windsurfing

Most of the resort hotels south and north of Mombasa have sailboards for hire, and the conditions are ideal – the waters are protected by the offshore reefs and the winds are usually reasonably strong and constant. The going rate at most places seems to be about US$3 per hour, more if you need instruction.

Beaches

One of the great attractions of Kenya is the superb beaches which line the coast. Many travellers find themselves staying much longer than they anticipated. This is real picture postcard stuff – coconut palms, dazzling white sand and clear blue water. The only problem is that for the most part the resort hotels have a virtual monopoly on accommodation, although there are a couple of budget options both south and north of Mombasa.

The beach at Diani is one of the best although it's lined solidly with resort hotels. Tiwi Beach, between Diani and Mombasa, is much more low key and you can camp right on the beach at the Twiga Lodge. There are similar possibilities north of Mombasa, although at certain times of year seaweed accumulates on the beach in huge quantities. Lamu doesn't suffer this problem and has some of the best beaches on the coast.

Caving

For information on this adventurous activity contact the Cave Exploration Group of East Africa, PO Box 47583, Nairobi.

Desert Grandeur

There's the opportunity to experience this on either side of Lake Turkana and for a considerable distance south of there on the eastern side of the lake. For most travellers, this is one of the highlights of their trip to Kenya.

On the western side, access to the lake is easy with a bitumen road all the way from Kitale, and there's at least one bus and often a matatu or two every day in each direction. If you're heading up this way then don't miss the opportunity of exploring the Cherangani Hills east of the Kitale to Lodwar road using the Marich Pass Field Studies Centre as your base. Either side offers many challenging possibilities. The Turkana, Samburu and Rendille tribespeople are also fascinating and, like the Maasai, have hung on to their traditional ways. It's certainly an area which you shouldn't miss at any cost.

Climbing & Walking

Mt Kenya is the obvious one, but other promising and relatively unexplored territory includes Mt Elgon on the Uganda border, the Cherangani Hills north of Kitale, the Matthews Range and Ndoto Mountains north of Isiolo, and even the Ngong Hills close to Nairobi. For more information refer to the relevant chapters in this book or contact the Mountaineering Club of Kenya (MCK) at its clubhouse at Wilson Airport (meetings every Tuesday at 8.30 pm – visitors welcome), or at its Nairobi address (☎ (02) 501747), PO Box 45741, Nairobi.

Gliding

The Gliding Club of Kenya has its headquarters in Mweiga near Nyeri in the Aberdares, and there are flights every day except Monday. For more information contact the Gliding Club of Kenya (☎ (0171) 2748), PO Box 926, Nyeri.

Ballooning

Balloon safaris in the game parks are an absolutely superb way of seeing the savannah plains and of course the animals, but without the intrusion of vehicles and dozens of other tourists doing the same thing. The most popular of these trips is that in the Masai Mara Game Reserve. The hot-air balloons depart daily from both Keekorok Lodge and the Fig Tree Lodge just after dawn and return around mid-morning. The flight includes a champagne breakfast on the plains. The cost is US$300. Bookings can be made through Adventures Aloft (☎ (2) 220592), Eagle House, Kimathi St, PO Box 40683, Nairobi; the Fig Tree Lodge; Block Hotels (☎ (02) 335807), PO Box 47557, Nairobi; or directly at Keekorok Lodge.

There's another outfit which offers balloon trips in Taita Hills Game Reserve. Bookings for this can be made through the Hilton International (☎ (02) 334000), PO Box 30624, Nairobi.

Fishing

The Kenya Fisheries Department operates a number of fishing camps in various parts of the country. They are really only an option if you have your own transport as the sites are off the main roads. Before you head off you need to get a fishing licence from the Fisheries Department. Advance bookings are not taken so it's just a matter of turning up at the site. For full details of the exact locations of the camps, see the Fisheries Department in Nairobi; the office is near the National Museum.

White-Water Rafting

Rafting is still in its infancy in Kenya, perhaps because of the limited possibilities – there are only two major rivers in Kenya, the Athi/Galana and Tana. The Tana flows through relatively flat country so it's sluggish and unsuitable for rafting. The Athi/Galana, on the other hand, has substantial rapids, chutes and waterfalls. The only outfit which can fix you up with a trip down this river is operated by Mark Savage (☎ 521590), PO Box 44827, Nairobi. He has two units of the Avon Ranger 3 river rafts.

A day trip from Nairobi consists of putting in just above Sagana on the Athi River and finishing about four km above the Masinga Dam. The trip starts with about two km of mild rapids followed by six km of smooth water and then two km of Grade 4-plus rapids without a breather and another two km of the same grade but with a few calm stretches for bailing out. This is followed by portage around a waterfall and a further 13 km of smooth water to the take-out point.

There's also an exciting three-day trip available from Yatta Gap on the Athi down to Tsavo Safari Camp (74 km).

ACCOMMODATION

Kenya has a good range of accommodation from the very basic US$2-a-night budget hotels to luxury tented camps in the national parks for up to US$500 a night!

Camping

There are enough opportunities for camping that it is worth considering bringing a tent. It is also possible to hire camping equipment in Nairobi and elsewhere but it's not the sort of lightweight gear you could carry without a vehicle.

There are camp sites in just about every national park and game reserve and these are usually very basic. There'll be a toilet block with a couple of pit toilets, and usually a water tap, but very little else. Private sites are few and far between but where they do exist they offer more in the way of facilities. Often it's possible to camp in the grounds of a hotel but this is obviously not an option in the bigger towns where space is limited.

Camping out in the bush is also possible though you would be advised to ask permission first. On the coast this is not advisable and sleeping on the beaches would be just asking for trouble.

Just in case you thought that the tented camps in the game parks might be a cheap option – forget it. They are luxury camps with all the facilities laid on, and high prices. The 'tents' barely justify the name – they usually just have canvas or mosquito netting for walls, but otherwise have a roof and bathroom. High, shoulder and low-season pricing policies apply equally to these places as they do to the top-end hotels.

Youth Hostels
The only youth hostels affiliated with the International Youth Hostels Federation (IYHF) are in Nairobi and Malindi. If you like youth hostels, they are fine. At US$2.40 for a dorm bed they are not so cheap but, as usual, they are good places to meet people. There are other places which call themselves 'youth hostels' but are not members of the federation. Some are good, others less so.

Hotels
Real bottom-end hotels (known everywhere as boardings & lodgings – hotels are often only restaurants) are generally brothels first and hotels second. This in itself is not a problem as long as you don't mind the noise, disruption and general atmosphere. Most places don't mind renting out rooms all night, although in some you get distinctly strange looks when they discover that not only do you want the room for the whole night, but that you want to spend it alone! These places are also not all that clean – you'll have to ask for clean sheets, and the shared bathrooms smell – and the rooms are often claustrophobic cells. On the other hand, you do occasionally come across cheap places which are clean and pleasant places to stay, so don't dismiss them totally; there's usually at least one cheap boarding & lodging in each town. On the plus side, they are cheap – around US$2.50/3.50 for a single/double room.

Things improve dramatically if you have a dollar or two more to spend, although there are always exceptions. For around US$4.50/6 a single/double, you will get a clean room with private bath (soap and towel supplied). These places often have a restaurant and bar (usually noisy). The only real advantages you get over the cheap places are your own bathroom and toilet and a degree of security.

Those who prefer a mid-range hotel are well catered for. If you're willing to spend US$8 to US$15 a night then you can expect all the basic comforts and sometimes even touches of luxury such as your own shower and toilet with hot water, towels, soap and toilet paper; clean sheets and beds; a table and chair; and often a telephone and room service.

At the top end of the market, accommodation ranges from better than the average mid-range to the five-star international chain hotels which provide the lot with prices to match. These start at around US$20/30 for a single/double and head up from there. Some of these places are old colonial buildings with bags of atmosphere, but most are modern and vary from characterless to the luxurious. The resort hotels on the coast and the lodges in the game parks also fall into this category, although some of the latter are superb places to stay if you can afford it – having animals come to drink at the salt lick in front of your lodge as you sit on the verandah sipping a cool drink is just great, but pleasures such as this can set you back up to US$100 per person for full board, depending on the season.

If you intend to stay in any of the top-range hotels, it's important to know that the price depends on the season. The high season generally runs from 16 December to 31 March and from 1 July to 31 August. The shoulder season is from 1 September to 15 December and the low season from 1 April to 30 June. There's generally also an additional supplement over the Christmas and New Year periods.

FOOD

For the main part, Kenyan cuisine consists largely of stodge filler with beans or a (tough) meat sauce and is really just survival food for the locals – maximum filling-up potential at minimum cost. It is still possible to eat cheaply and well although the lack of variety becomes tedious after a while. People with carnivorous habits are far better served by the local food than vegetarians.

The most basic local eateries (often known as *hotelis*) hardly warrant being called restaurants. These places usually have a limited menu and are open only for lunch – the main meal of the day. If you're on a tight budget you'll find yourself eating in these places most of the time. However, if you have the resources, even in the smaller towns it's usually possible to find a restaurant that offers more variety and better food at a higher price. Often these places are connected with the mid-range and top-end hotels.

Preparing your own food is a viable option if you are camping and carrying cooking gear. Every town has a market and there's usually an excellent range of fresh produce available.

Fast food has taken off in a big way and virtually every town has a place which serves food that rates high in grease and low in price. Fried chips with lashings of lurid tomato sauce are a basic filler, but sausages, eggs, fish and chicken are also popular. In Nairobi there are literally dozens of these places, and they can be handy places to pick up a snack.

The only place where any sort of distinctive African cuisine (other than *nyama choma* or barbecued goat's meat) has developed is on the coast where the Swahili dishes reflect the history of contact with the Arabs and other Indian Ocean traders – coconut and spices are used heavily and the results are generally excellent.

As might be expected with the large number of Asians in Kenya, there are also large numbers of Indian restaurants. In addition, many hotels are owned by Indians and the choice of food available on their menus reflects this. If you like this cuisine, you'll have no problems even in the smaller towns though most of these restaurants are confined to Nairobi and Mombasa.

Vegetarians are not well catered for. Away from the two main cities there are virtually no vegetarian dishes to accompany the starch. Beans are going to figure prominently in any vegetarian's culinary encounters in Kenya! Buying fresh fruit and vegetables in the market can help relieve the tedium.

Snacks

Sambusas are probably the most common

Nyama Choma

If you had to name a national dish in Kenya, nyama choma (barbecued goat's meat) would probably be it. In recent years it has become almost a fetish amongst Africans and expatriates alike and, to cater for the demand, hundreds of places have opened up offering just that. Sometimes it's good; sometimes it's tough as old leather. What you get is what you choose from a refrigerated selection of various cuts which you buy by the kg. Once it's barbecued, it's brought to your table by a waiter and sliced into bite-sized pieces along with a vegetable mash (often *matoke*, which is plantains and maize). It's not a cheap option but not expensive either.

The trouble with nyama choma, if you've ever had any culinary experience, is that in no way does it resemble (except in the most expensive establishments) anything similar to marinated and seasoned barbecued meat. Most of the time, you'll take years off the life of your teeth chewing it and end up spending more time with a tooth pick than you spent eating. Marination and the use of herbs, let alone basting, have yet to reach Kenya.

Nevertheless, the Kenyan middle class regard an invitation to nyama choma (and copious quantities of Tusker lager) as a special night out. So don't let me put you off – try it! Maybe this is how Africans keep their beautiful, healthy teeth. ■

snack and are obvious descendants of the Indian samosa. They are deep-fried pastry triangles stuffed with spiced mince meat. Occasionally you come across sambusas with vegetable fillings, but this is usually only in the Indian restaurants. If you can find them freshly made and still warm, sambusas can be excellent. However, more often by the time you get them they are at least several hours old, are cold and have gone limp and greasy from the oil saturation.

Another item that fits into the pure starch category is that curious beast known as the *mandazi*. It's a semisweet, flat doughnut and, once again, when they're fresh they can be very good. They are usually cooked and eaten at breakfast time – often dunked in tea. Should you decide to eat one later in the day, chances are it will be stale and hard.

Something that you don't come across very often but which makes an excellent snack meal is *mkate mayai* (literally 'bread-eggs'). This was originally an Arab dish and is now found in countries as far ranging as Kenya and Singapore. Basically it's a wheat dough which is spread into a thin pancake, filled with minced meat and raw egg and then folded into a neat parcel and fried on a hot-plate. The Iqbal Hotel in Nairobi is a good place to try this snack.

Seemingly on every second street corner someone is trying to make a few bob selling corn cobs roasted on a wire grille over a bed of hot coals. You pay only a couple of shillings for these. Another street-corner snack is deep-fried yams, eaten hot with a squeeze of lemon juice and a sprinkling of chilli powder.

Main Dishes
Basically it's meat, meat and more meat, accompanied by starch of some sort. The meat is usually in a stew with perhaps some potato or other vegetables thrown in, and is often as tough as an old boot. Beef, goat and mutton are the most commonly eaten meats.

The starch comes in three major forms: potatoes, rice and *ugali*. The last of these is maize meal which is cooked up into a thick porridge until it sets hard. It's then served up in flat bricks. It's incredibly stodgy, almost totally devoid of any flavour and tends to sit on the stomach like a royal corgi, but most Kenyans swear by it. It's certainly the equivalent of mashed potato for the Poms or sticky rice for the Chinese and Koreans but it certainly isn't a culinary orgasm. Freshly cooked it's palatable; when stale, just about inedible. Naturally, you must try it at least once and some travellers actually get to like it, but don't hold your breath! The only thing it has going for it is that it's cheap.

Cooked red kidney beans are always an alternative to meat and are widely available in local eateries.

Roast chicken and steak are popular dishes in the more up-market restaurants of the bigger towns. Food in this sort of place differs little from what you might get at home.

Menus, where they exist in the cheaper places, are usually just a chalked list on a board on the wall. In better restaurants they are usually just in English.

The following food list gives some of the main words you are likely to come across when trying to decipher Swahili menus or buy food in the market.

Useful Words

boiled	*chemka*
bread	*mkate*
butter	*siagi*
cup	*kikombe*
curry	*mchuzi*
egg(s)	*yai (mayai)*
food	*chakula*
fork	*uma*
fried	*kaanga*
glass	*glasi*
hot/cold	*moto/baridi*
hot (spicy)	*hoho*
Indian bread	*chapati*
knife	*kisu*
napkin	*kitambaa*
pepper	*pilipili*
plate	*sahani*
raw	*mbichi*
ripe	*mbivu*
roast	*choma*

table	*mesa*
teaspoon	*kijiko*
salt	*chumvi*
sauce	*mchuzi*
soup	*supu*
sugar	*sukari*
sweet	*tamu*
yoghurt	*maziwalala*

Vegetables & Grains

aubergine	*biringani*
cabbage	*kabichi*
capsicum	*pilipili baridi*
carrots	*karoti*
cassava	*muhogo*
garlic	*vitunguu saumu*
kidney beans	*maharagwe*
lettuce	*salad*
maize-meal porridge	*ugali*
mashed plantains &	
maize	*matoke*
onions	*vitunguu*
plantains	*ndzi*
potatoes	*viazi*
rice	*wali*
spinach	*sukuma wiki*
boiled spinach	*sukuma wiki*
tomatoes	*nyana*
vegetables	*mboga*
vegetable stew	*mboga*

Meat & Fish

beef	*nyama ya ngombe*
kebabs	*mushkaki*
meat	*nyama*
meat stew	*karanga*
mutton, goat	*nyama ya mbuzi*
pork	*nyama ya nguruwe*
steak	*steki*
crab	*kaa*
fish	*samaki*
lobster	*kamba*
squid	*ngisi*

Fruit

This is where Kenya really excels. Because of the country's varied climate, there's an excellent array of fruits. The tropical ones are especially good. Depending on the place and the season you can buy mangoes, papaya, pineapple, watermelon, oranges, guavas, custard apples, bananas (many varieties) and coconuts. Prices are cheap and the quality very high.

bananas	*ndizi*
coconut (green)	*dafu*
coconut (ripe)	*nazi*
custard apples	*stafeli*
dates	*tende*
fruit	*matunda*
grapefruits	*madanzi*
guava	*pera*
limes	*ndimu*
mangoes	*maembe*
oranges	*machungwa*
papayas	*paipai*
passionfruit	*pasheni*
pineapples	*mananasi*
sugar cane	*miwa*
watermelon	*tikiti*

DRINKS
Nonalcoholic Drinks

Tea & Coffee Despite the fact that Kenya grows some of the finest tea and coffee in the world, getting a decent cup of either can be difficult.

Tea *(chai)* is the national obsession and is drunk in large quantities. It bears little resemblance to what you might be used to but as long as you look on it as just a different hot drink and not actually tea it can be quite good. Be warned that it is generally very milky and horrendously sweet. Chai is made the same way in Kenya as it is in India: all the ingredients (tea, milk and masses of sugar) are put into cold water and the whole lot is brought to the boil and stewed. Finding a good honest cup of tea is virtually impossible outside the fancy restaurants. For tea without milk ask for *chai kavu*.

Coffee is similarly disappointing. Instant coffee is what is generally used, and in small quantities, so, once again, you're looking at a sweet milky concoction which is not quite what you might be expecting. However, as each cup is individually made it's somewhat easier to order one tailored to your own liking.

Soft Drinks All the old favourites are here, including Coke, Pepsi and Fanta, and they go under the generic term of soda. As with beer, prices vary depending on where you buy. In most places you pay around US$0.25 per bottle but in the more exclusive places you can pay up to US$1 though a more usual price would be US$0.75. There are no such predictable prices for freshly squeezed fruit juices which range from US$0.50 to US$2 per glass.

Alcohol

Beer Kenya has a thriving local brewing industry and formidable quantities of beer are consumed. It's probably true to say that beer is the most widely available manufactured product in the country. Go to just a tiny group of *dukas* (local stores) by the side of the road somewhere and chances are one of them will either be a bar, or it will stock beer. Sure, it won't be cold, but then even in the most up-market places beer is available both chilled and warm. 'Why warm?' you might ask as your face wrinkles in horror! The answer is because most Africans appear to prefer it that way. I've certainly never seen them drink cold White Cap though you'll occasionally see an African drinking cold Pilsner or Premium.

The beer names are White Cap, Tusker and Pilsner (all manufactured by Kenya Breweries Ltd) and they're sold in 500 ml bottles. They are basically the same product with different labels (though there is a discernible difference in taste) but most people end up sticking to just one brand. The same company manufactures export-quality 300 ml beers – Export and Premium respectively – and these are slightly stronger and more expensive. Guinness is also available but tastes and looks nothing like the genuine Irish article (or even the bastardised but similar variety sold outside of the Emerald Isle in the West and Hong Kong).

Lastly, Kenya Breweries have also brought out a draught version of Tusker which is very good but only available in a few places. Check the price before ordering – in some places it's cheaper than the bottled

variety; in others it costs more (sometimes considerably more).

Beers are cheapest bought from a supermarket where a 500 ml bottle will cost you around US$0.50. Bought from a normal bar, you are looking at US$0.60 to US$0.90. Bought at a bar in a five-star hotel it can cost you up to US$3. This would be exceptional but, as there are no price controls on beer – bars and hotels can charge what they like.

Wine Kenya has a fledgeling wine industry and the Lake Naivasha colombard wines are said to be quite good. This is something that cannot be said about the most commonly encountered Kenyan wine – papaya wine. It tastes foul and even the smell is unbearable.

On the other hand, you can get cheap imported European and even Australian wine by the glass for around US$2 in Nairobi restaurants. This is expensive when compared to the price of beer but is actually not too bad.

Local Brews Although it is strictly illegal to brew or distil liquor this doesn't stop it going on. *Pombe* is the local beer and is usually a fermented brew made with bananas or millet and sugar. You may get the chance to sample it here and there and it shouldn't do you any harm. The same cannot be said for the distilled drinks, known locally as *chang'a*, as these are often very effective poisons – inefficient/amateur distilling techniques ensure various percentages of methyl alcohol creep into the brew. They'll blind you if you're lucky; kill you if you're not. Leave it alone!

THINGS TO BUY

Kenya is an excellent place for souvenirs, although much of the cheap stuff available is just pure junk mass-produced by hand for the tourist trade. Look carefully at what's available before parting with your money.

Nairobi and Mombasa are the main centres but many of the items come from the various regions, so it's often possible to pick

Elephant Hair Bracelets
On the streets of Nairobi you'll undoubtedly be approached by hawkers trying to sell you 'elephant hair' bracelets. Despite all the protestations to the contrary, these bracelets are made from reed grass (which is then covered in boot polish), from slivers of cow horn, or simply from plastic. You can safely assume that none of them are the real McCoy. ∎

up the same at source, although you then have the problem of transporting it.

The best buys include *makonde* carvings, sometimes made from ebony (but often softer woods stained with boot polish), kiondos (woven sisal baskets), jewellery and tribal souvenirs, including colourful Maasai beaded jewellery, the decorated *calabash* (dried gourds) and spears and shields. There are also batiks, local sarongs *(kangas* and *kikois)*, soapstone carvings from Kisii in the west of Kenya, and paintings.

It's possible to pick up something which will look good in your living room back home without spending a fortune but, these days, something of genuine quality and artistry is going to cost real money because there are a lot of skilful artists around who produce works of genuine art (as opposed to tourist tat) and know that there are quite a few tourists around who are very discerning and will pay big bucks for quality. This particularly applies to makonde carvings, jewellery and paintings. In some cases, you can be talking about thousands of US dollars.

If you're interested in quality artwork, spend time doing the rounds of the shops and galleries which deal in it.

Getting There & Away

Unless you are travelling overland, flying is just about the only – and the most convenient – way of getting to Kenya. Nairobi is the main hub for flights and the route on which you are most likely to get a relatively cheap ticket, but it's worth checking out cheap charter flights to Mombasa from Europe too.

Buying an ordinary economy-class ticket is not the most economical way to go, but it does give you maximum flexibility and the ticket is valid for 12 months.

Students and those under 26 (under 29 in the USA) can often get discounted tickets so it's worth checking first with a student travel bureau (such as STA Travel) to see if there is anything on offer. Another option is an advance purchase ticket which is usually between 30 and 40% cheaper than the full economy fare, but has restrictions. You must purchase your ticket at least 21 days in advance (sometimes more) and you must stay away for a minimum period (usually 14 days) and return within 180 days (sometimes less). The main disadvantage is that stopovers are not allowed and if you have to change your dates of travel or destination then there will be extra charges to pay. Standby fares are another possibility. Some airlines will let you travel at the last minute if there are seats available just before departure. These tickets cost less than the economy fare but are usually not as cheap as the advance purchase fares.

Of all the options, however, the cheapest way to go is via the so-called 'bucket shops'. These are travel agencies which sell discounted tickets. Airlines only sell a certain percentage of their tickets through bucket shops so the availability of seats can vary widely, particularly in the high season. You have to be flexible with these tickets, although if the agents are sold out for one flight they can generally offer you something similar in the near future.

Most of the bucket shops are reputable organisations, but be careful as there is always the occasional fly-by-night operator who sets up shop, takes your money for a bargain-basement ticket and then either disappears or issues you with an invalid or unusable ticket. Check carefully what you are buying before you hand over money. Having said this, I must add that I've used bucket shops for years and been handed the most weird and wonderful tickets. For example, tickets issued in East Berlin but bought in London for a flight from London to Malaysia with stopovers in New Delhi, Bangkok and Kuala Lumpur. They've all been sweet.

Bucket shops generally advertise in newspapers and magazines and there's a lot of competition and different routes available so it's best to telephone first and then rush round if they have what you want. In Europe, the market for these sort of tickets to American and Asian destinations has been well developed over many years, but little has been available to African destinations south of the Sahara until fairly recently. Fares are now becoming more flexible, and Nairobi is one of a handful of destinations that has plenty of options.

AIR

To/From North America

In the USA, the best way to find cheap flights is by checking the Sunday travel sections in the major newspapers such as the *Los Angeles Times* or *San Francisco Examiner-Chronicle* on the west coast, and the *New York Times* on the east coast. The student travel bureaus are also worth trying – STA Travel or Council Travel.

North America is a relative newcomer to the bucket-shop traditions of Europe and Asia so ticket availability and the restrictions attached to them need to be weighed against what is on offer on the more normal advance purchase or full economy fares.

Return tickets to Nairobi from New York (Air France) cost US$1340 in the low season

(1 November to 14 December, 16 January to 24 March and 11-14 April), and US$1525 in the high season (15 December to 15 January, 25 March to 10 April, 15 June to 30 September). From Los Angeles a return ticket costs US$1525 in the low season and US$1832 in the high season. Note that these fares are for students aged up to 29 years.

If you shop around, it's possible to get one-way tickets from New York to Nairobi for as little as US$599 in the low season, and return tickets for US$1099 also in the low season.

From Canada, Air France offers flights from Toronto to Nairobi for US$1340 in the low season and US$1697 in the high season.

It may well be cheaper in the long run to fly first to London from the east coast of the USA using Virgin Atlantic (from around US$140 one way or US$270 return in the low season), or stand-by on the other airlines for a little more, and then buy a bucket shop ticket from there to Kenya with or without stopovers. But you must do your homework to be sure of this. All the main magazines which specialise in bucket shop advertisements in London will mail you copies so you can study current prices before you decide on a course of action.

To/From Europe

You can find bucket shops by the dozen in London, Paris, Amsterdam, Brussels, Frankfurt and a few other places too. In London, there are several newspapers with lots of bucket shop ads which will give you a good idea of current fares, as well as specialist magazines catering entirely to the travel industry.

Trailfinder is a magazine put out three times a year by Trailfinders at 46 Earls Court Rd, London W8 6EJ (☎ (071) 938-3366), and 194 Kensington High St, London W8 (☎ (071) 937-5400). It's free if you pick it up in London but if you want it mailed it costs UK£8 for three issues in the UK or Eire, and UK£12 or US$20 for four issues elsewhere in the world including airmail postage. Trailfinders can fix you up with all your ticketing requirements for anywhere in the world as well as providing information on insurance, immunisation and books. Trailfinders has been in business for years and can be highly recommended. All the staff are experienced travellers so they speak your language. It's open Monday to Saturday from 9 am to 6 pm (7 pm on Thursdays). There are branch offices at 194 Kensington High St, London W8 7RG (☎ (071) 938-3939), 58 Deansgate, Manchester M3 2FF (☎ (061) 839-6969), and 2 McLellan Galleries, Sauchiehall St, Glasgow G2 3EH (☎ (041) 353-2224).

Africa Travel Now is a quarterly newspaper put out by the Africa Travel Centre (☎ (071) 387-1211), 4 Medway Court, Leigh St, London WC1H 9QX. It's free and, as its name indicates, it specialises entirely in travel to and around Africa. It contains an excellent run-down of discount flights to most major cities in Africa as well as details on safaris which you can book in advance if you care to. Office hours are Monday to Friday from 9.30 am to 5.30 pm and on Saturdays from 10 am to 2 pm. As with Trailfinders, the Africa Travel Centre is highly recommended.

Time Out (☎ (071) 836-4411), Tower House, Southampton St, London WC2E 7HD, is London's weekly entertainment guide and it's available from all bookshops and newsagents. Subscription enquiries should be addressed to Time Out Subs, Unit 8 Grove Ash, Bletchley, Milton Keynes MK1 1BZ, UK.

The price of airline tickets from London to Nairobi advertised in the above magazines is around UK£220 one way and UK£385 return. The corresponding fares to Dar es Salaam are UK£264 one way and UK£451 return. The airlines used are generally Aeroflot and other Eastern European and Middle Eastern airlines but this isn't always the case. Both Trailfinders and Africa Travel Centre can also fix you up with multistopover tickets which include Nairobi and other African destinations on them. Also check out Africa Travel System (☎ (071) 602-5091) at 6 North End Parade, London W14 0SJ, which specialises in airline tickets to Africa.

If you plan to head further east or to Australasia after Africa, Africa Travel System can arrange a ticket at a price comparable to anything you'll be offered at the bucket shops in Nairobi.

There is no advantage in buying a one-way ticket to Nairobi and then another one-way ticket back to Europe from there. You'll end up paying more than if you bought a return ticket in the first place. You may also run foul of immigration on arrival in Kenya without an onward ticket and be forced to buy one on the spot – an expensive exercise in lack of forethought.

A round-the-world (RTW) ticket is another economical option if you have the time, but only very few of these include African stopovers and hardly any include Nairobi. Johannesburg is the most common African stopover. For example, a London, Johannesburg, Perth, Sydney, San Francisco, Orlando, Washington, London ticket costs around UK£811.

Don't take advertised fares as gospel truth. To comply with truth in advertising laws, UK companies must be able to offer *some* tickets at their cheapest quoted price but they might only have one or two of them each week. If you are not one of the lucky ones, you may find yourself looking at tickets which cost up to UK£50 more (one way or return). The best thing to do, therefore, is to start looking into tickets well before your intended departure date so you have a very good idea what is available.

Remember that discounted tickets cannot generally be paid for with a credit card. You must pay with cash or with a bank cheque.

To/From Asia

You may safely assume that flying is the only feasible way of getting between the Indian subcontinent and Kenya. There are plenty of flights between East Africa and Bombay due to the large Indian population in Kenya. There are bucket shops of a sort in New Delhi, Bombay and Calcutta and most of the discounted tickets will be with Air India. In New Delhi I'd recommend Tripsout Travel, 72/7 Tolstoy Lane behind the Government of India Tourist Office, Janpath.

Typical fares from Bombay to Nairobi are around US$312 return with either Ethiopian Airlines, Kenya Airways or Pakistan International Airlines (PIA) via Karachi.

In Nairobi there are a lot of bucket shops offering tickets to Karachi, Islamabad, New Delhi, Bombay and Calcutta. Most of these will be with Air India or PIA.

To/From Australasia

There are no longer tight constraints on ticket discounting in Australia, and fares are continuing to fall, but for Australians and New Zealanders there are still very few route options to Africa. The only direct connections are the weekly Qantas flight from Sydney to Perth and Harare (Zimbabwe) which costs A$1760 return from Perth (A$1999 from Melbourne or Sydney) in the low season (16 January to 15 February) and A$2200 from Perth (A$2500 from Sydney or Melbourne) in the high season (1 December to 15 January), and South African Airways' flight from Perth to Johannesburg. A return ticket from Sydney or Melbourne to Johannesburg costs the same as that to Harare; ie around A$1999 in the low season and A$2500 in the high season.

Another option between Australia and Africa is the weekly Air Mauritius flight from Perth to Mauritius, from where there are twice-weekly flights to Nairobi. The fare is A$2000 from Sydney or Melbourne, and you can have a stopover in Mauritius if you wish. For about A$300 more, you can use another carrier from Melbourne, Sydney or Brisbane to Singapore and hook up with Air Mauritius there. Other cheap options include going via Bombay with Air India, or via Karachi with PIA. The price on either of these routes from Sydney or Melbourne is around A$2600.

It obviously makes sense for Australasians to think in terms of a RTW ticket or an Australia/New Zealand to Europe round-trip ticket with stopovers in Asia and Africa. It shouldn't be too much trouble for a travel agency to put together a ticket which includes various Asian stopovers plus a Nairobi stopover. Having Nairobi added to such a ticket bumps up the price a little and you may have to go through several travel agencies before you get satisfaction as many of them know very little about deals via Africa.

It's probably best to start your search for a ticket by looking in the travel section of the Saturday issue of either the *Sydney Morning Herald* or the *Age* and by visiting a student travel bureau. It's also worth writing or telephoning for a copy of *Airfares Guide* from The Travel Specialists (☎ (02) 262-3555), 62 Clarence St, Sydney, NSW 2000. It has been published for a number of years now and will give you a very good idea of what's available.

To/From Ethiopia
Both Ethiopian Airlines and Kenya Airways operate regular direct flights between Nairobi and Addis Ababa.

To/From Somalia
Somali Airlines is defunct and Kenya Airways no longer flies there. There are, on the other hand, plenty of UN and other aid agency aircraft which fly between Mombasa and Mogadishu. If you're interested in getting there, talk to aid workers in Mombasa or Nairobi. I found it was very easy to get a (free) lift there and back.

To/From Sudan
Kenya Airways and Sudan Airways operate direct flights between Khartoum and Nairobi.

To/From Tanzania
The cheapest regular flights from Tanzania to Kenya are between Dar es Salaam and Nairobi on Kenya Airways. A one-way full economy fare is US$123 (but you can find tickets for as little as US$110) though you must add the US$20 departure tax to these prices. There are also flights between Zanzibar and Mombasa (US$45). However, as these are very popular, you'll need to book at least two weeks ahead if you want to be

sure of getting a seat. You can forget about Air Tanzania for the present because, although they schedule a Dar es Salaam to Nairobi flight, they have only one jet in their 'fleet' of just two planes and it's fully occupied servicing the Tanzanian domestic routes.

There are also two private companies based in Zanzibar with six and eight-seater propeller planes which occasionally fly between Zanzibar and Mombasa or Nairobi. They are Air Zanzibar (☎ (054) 32512), 302 Kenyatta Rd, Shangani, Zanzibar; and Zan Air (☎ (054) 33670), Malindi, Zanzibar. The price of flights to Mombasa are the same as on Kenya Airways but to Nairobi a ticket costs US$100. To find out if the companies are operating, contact their offices in Zanzibar or keep an eye on the notice boards at Africa House Hotel or the Fisherman Restaurant. Neither company has offices in Mombasa or Nairobi.

LAND
To/From Ethiopia
Since the change of regime in Ethiopia, land borders are once again open. The only problem is transport. There are buses from Isiolo to Marsabit and Moyale (the border town) but from there transport is problematical. Hitching may be your only option and traffic is sparse until you get further into Ethiopia.

To/From Somalia
There's no way you can get overland from Kenya to Somalia at present (unless you're part of a refugee aid convoy). Even if you attempted it, the Kenyan police or the army would turn you back. Moreover, the entire border area is infested with well-armed Somali *shifta* (bandits) making any attempt to cross it a dangerous and foolhardy venture.

To/From Sudan
As with Somalia, there's no way you can get overland between Kenya and Sudan at present. The furthest north you're going to get is Lokichokio, and you'll be lucky to get

that far unless you're with a refugee aid convoy.

To/From Tanzania

Dar es Salaam to Mombasa There are a number of bus companies (such as Coast, Cat and Tawfiq) which do the run from Dar es Salaam to Mombasa via Tanga and vice versa, though usually only once a week in either direction. The trip takes anything from 16 to 24 hours (eight to 12 hours from Tanga). The border crossing at Lunga Lunga (Kenya) and Horohoro (Tanzania) is quite straightforward but it takes as long as four hours to clear all 50 or so people through both posts. The fare from Dar es Salaam to Mombasa is TSh 3000. The Cat bus office in Dar es Salaam is on Msimbazi St close to the Kariakoo Market and the Caltex station.

If you're going to take one of these buses it's worth considering doing the journey partly by train. It's much more comfortable, and costs only about TSh 300 more to take the overnight train 1st class from Dar es Salaam to Tanga. From Tanga, you can pick up one of the buses running between Dar es Salaam and Mombasa at around 8 am; however there's a chance you may have difficulty getting on. The trip from Tanga to Mombasa costs TSh 700.

You can also do the journey the hard way. From Tanga to the Tanzanian border post at Horohoro there are a couple of buses per day (TSh 400) along the rough single-lane dirt road. From Horohoro it's a six-km walk to the Kenyan border post at Lunga Lunga and there's very little traffic so hitching is difficult. Once through the Kenyan border post, however, there are frequent matatus for the one-hour journey to Mombasa.

Arusha/Moshi to Nairobi These days the trip between Nairobi and Arusha or Moshi is a breeze. The trip takes five hours and getting through customs and immigration is no problem. There are at least three companies with direct buses/minibuses operating on a daily basis. The most expensive of them is the DHL Shuttle (run by the international courier company of the same name) which leaves Nairobi daily at 8.30 am from the Norfolk Hotel, and from Arusha at 2 pm from the Novotel Mt Meru. The fare from Nairobi is US$17. Advance booking is advisable, and this can be done at DHL, 8th Floor, Town House, Kaunda St, Nairobi (☎ (02) 212804). In Arusha, the DHL office is in the foyer of the Novotel Mt Meru.

A similar shuttle service is operated by Tayler's Travel, Tubman Rd, Nairobi (☎ (02) 335365), and Swahili St, Arusha (☎ 3488).

Much cheaper is the Arusha Express, which operates full-sized buses and has its office in amongst the cluster of bus companies down Accra Rd in Nairobi. In Arusha, the office is at the bus station. Buses leave Nairobi daily except Wednesday at 8.30 am and the fare is US$5.70.

It's also easy, but less convenient, to do this journey in stages, and since the Kenyan and Tanzanian border posts are next to each other at Namanga, there's no long walk involved. There are frequent matatus and share-taxis from Arusha to Namanga every day which go when full and cost TSh 700 to TSh 1300 (negotiable). The taxis normally take about 1½ hours, though there are a number of kamikaze drivers who are totally crazy and will get you there in just one hour. From the Kenyan side of the border there are frequent matatus and share-taxis which go when full and cost US$2.85 and US$4.30 respectively. The journey by taxi takes about two hours, and by matatu about three hours. Both have their depot outside the petrol station on Ronald Ngala St close to the junction with River Rd.

Moshi to Voi The crossing between Moshi and Voi via Taveta is also reliable as far as transport goes (buses, matatus and share-taxis). A matatu between Taveta and Voi (along a bumpy road) takes 2½ hours and costs US$2.60. There's also a train which takes five hours and costs the same.

Musoma to Kisii It's much more difficult to cross the border between Musoma and Kisii via Isebania in the north as there are no matatus or buses which go all the way to the border so you're looking at hiring a taxi or hitching. Hitching is difficult as there's very little traffic. On the other hand, this is one of the routes through to Zaïre which overland trucks use so you may be lucky and get a lift all the way, but trucks don't come through that often.

To/From Uganda

The two main border posts which most overland travellers use are Malaba and Busia with Malaba being by far the most commonly used.

Kampala to Nairobi via Malaba Akamba operates direct buses between Kampala and Nairobi daily which cost USh 15,000, depart at 3 pm, and arrive the following morning. Its office in Kampala is on Dewinton St.

Doing the journey in stages, there are frequent matatus until the late afternoon between Kampala (USh 2500, three hours) or Jinja (USh 1500, two hours) and Malaba. There are also frequent matatus in either direction between Tororo and Malaba (Uganda) which cost USh 250 and take less than one hour. The road has recently been resurfaced and is excellent, although it does mean that the drivers can get up to terrifying speeds. Luckily, there's not much traffic on this road except close to Kampala.

There's also a train from Kampala to Tororo but it only runs three times a week and is diabolically slow. The fare is USh 1950 (3rd class only).

The Ugandan and Kenyan border posts are about one km from each other at Malaba and you will have to walk.

There are trains from Malaba to Nairobi via Eldoret and Nakuru on Wednesdays, Saturdays and Sundays at 4 pm, arriving in Nairobi the next day at 9.30 am. The fares are US$22 in 1st class, US$12.50 in 2nd class and US$4.75 in 3rd class. The trains do not connect with the Ugandan system.

If you don't want to take the train, there are daily buses by different companies between Malaba and Nairobi which depart at around 7.30 pm arriving at about 5.30 am the next day. The fare is US$5.40. If you prefer

to travel by day there are plenty of matatus between Bungoma and Malaba which take about 45 minutes. If you stay in Bungoma overnight there are plenty of cheap hotels to choose from. From Bungoma there are several daily buses to Nairobi which leave at about 8 am and arrive about 5 pm the same day.

The other main entry point into Kenya from Uganda is via Busia further south. There are frequent matatus between Jinja and Busia and between Busia and Kisumu. This border is more convenient to get across because the Ugandan and Kenyan border posts are right next to each other.

SEA

To/From Asia

There are no longer any passenger ships from India or Pakistan to Kenya. Don't believe any rumours that there are such ships. There are about four or five dhows which do the journey from Zanzibar and Mombasa to Karachi and Bombay each year via Somalia, South Yemen and Oman, but they are extremely difficult to locate and even more difficult to get onto. The days of the dhows were numbered decades ago and those you find in Mombasa harbour will only be plying between Lamu, Mombasa, Pemba and Zanzibar.

To/From Tanzania

It's possible to go by dhow between Zanzibar, Pemba and Mombasa plus there's a catamaran, the MV *Flying Horse*, which does the Dar es Salaam to Mombasa run via Zanzibar once a week in either direction (on Mondays from Mombasa). For full details, refer to to the Mombasa section in The Coast chapter.

There are no steamer services which connect Kenya with Tanzania on Lake Victoria.

LEAVING KENYA

Nairobi is the best city in East Africa (and perhaps in the whole of Africa) to pick up cheap airline tickets for international flights. There is a lot of competition between travel agencies so most of them lean over backwards to give you whatever discounts they can. They are the equivalent of bucket shops in Europe. Only a few of the airlines sell discounted tickets through these agencies and none of them sell them directly from their own offices. The most common discounters are Aeroflot, Air India, EgyptAir, Olympic Airways, Pakistan International Airlines (PIA) and Sudan Airways and most of the cheap tickets available are for flights to Europe, although there are others to India, Pakistan and Singapore and sometimes to Madagascar, Mauritius and Réunion.

Except on Kenya Airways, all airline tickets must be paid for in hard currency (cash, travellers' cheques or credit card).

The cheapest flight from Nairobi to London costs US$350 (US$330 to Frankfurt or Rome) one way with Sudan Airways. The flight leaves once weekly on Sunday and goes via Addis Ababa, Khartoum and Frankfurt (making it quite a long haul if your destination is London). Kenya Airways flies Nairobi to London nonstop for US$450 return – this is a good deal if you want a return ticket. British Airways also flies Nairobi to London nonstop but the price of an economy-class ticket is US$867 one way.

The cheapest flight from Nairobi to New York costs US$595 one way with Saudia. The flight leaves once weekly on Monday. Remember there's no alcohol aboard Saudia flights. The next cheapest to New York is US$947 one way with Gulf Air. A regular economy-class ticket costs US$1113 one way.

The cheapest flight from Nairobi to Bombay (India) costs US$265 one way with PIA and goes via Karachi. The fare to Karachi with the same airline costs US$230. If Delhi is your destination then the same airline will take you there for US$305 but Gulf Air will do Nairobi to Delhi for US$288. Regular economy-class tickets to Karachi, Bombay and Delhi are US$291, US$312 and US$383 respectively.

The cheapest tickets from Nairobi to Bangkok and Singapore are US$455 and US$527 one way, respectively, on Gulf Air which flies twice a week on Thursdays and Saturdays via Bahrain. The regular economy-class tickets on this sector cost US$569 and US$658.

Between Nairobi and Sydney/Melbourne, the cheapest fare is US$907 one way and US$1400 return with Gulf Air. The flights leave twice a week on Thursdays and Saturdays and go via Bahrain and Singapore. A regular economy-class ticket to Sydney or Melbourne is US$1133 one way.

Between Nairobi and Hong Kong, the cheapest fare is US$496 one way, again with Gulf Air. An economy-class fare on this route is US$699.

The cheapest flight between Nairobi and Johannesburg costs US$300 one way on Olympic Airways although Air Malawi is presently offering a return ticket for the same price. How long this will last remains to be seen. A regular economy-class ticket to Johannesburg costs US$372 one way.

Other discounted fares within Africa include the Kenya Airways twice-weekly flight from Nairobi to Kigali (Rwanda) or Bujumbura (Burundi) for US$163 one way (US$326 return). Kenya Airways also offers a 21-day return excursion ticket for US$229, and flies from Nairobi to the Seychelles for US$300 return.

A list of recommended travel agencies can be found in the Nairobi chapter.

Departure Tax

The airport departure tax for international flights is US$20. You must pay this in foreign currency (cash); travellers' cheques and Kenyan shillings are not accepted. Kenyan shillings can be reconverted into US dollars at the airport on presentation of a bank receipt proving you have already changed sufficient hard currency into Kenyan shillings.

Getting Around

AIR
Kenya Airways
Kenya Airways, the national carrier, connects the main cities of Nairobi, Mombasa, Kisumu and Malindi. It's advisable to book in advance and essential to reconfirm 48 hours before departure if you're coming from either Malindi or Kisumu and have to connect with an international flight from either Nairobi or Mombasa airports. Otherwise you may well find that your seat has been reallocated. The flight schedules and fares can be found in the respective city chapters.

Private Airlines
There are also a number of private airlines operating light aircraft which connect the main cities with smaller towns and certain national parks. The airlines are Air Kenya Aviation (☎ (02) 501421), Prestige Air Services (☎ (02) 501211), and Eagle Aviation, and they all operate out of Nairobi's Wilson Airport and Mombasa's Moi Airport.

These airlines connect Nairobi with Mombasa, Kisumu, Nanyuki, Nyeri, Malindi, Lamu and the national parks/reserves of Amboseli, Masai Mara and Samburu. Their services to Eldoret and Turkana are temporarily suspended. Flight schedules can be found under the relevant sections.

BUS
Kenya has a network of regular buses, matatus (normally minibuses), share-taxis and normal private taxis. The cheapest form of transport is by bus, followed by matatu, share-taxi (Peugeot services) and lastly private taxi (expensive). There's not a great deal of difference in journey times between normal buses and matatus, but there's a huge difference in safety.

Bus fares are generally about halfway between what you would pay on the railways in 2nd class but journey times are quicker.

Unlike the trains, which usually travel at night, many buses travel during the day so you may prefer to take a bus if you want to see the countryside. All the bus companies are privately owned but some of them run better buses than others. Coastline Safari, Goldline, Tana River Bus Company, Malindi Bus and Garissa Express are about the best of the bunch. Akamba Bus Service has the most comprehensive network, but its buses are older.

Some Kenyan towns have what you might call a 'bus station', although this is often nothing more than a dirt patch. In others each bus company will have its own terminus though these are often close to each other. There are exceptions and these are indicated on the street maps. Matatu and share-taxi ranks sometimes use the same stations as buses but this isn't always the case, especially in Nairobi.

Nairobi also has the local KBS public buses which run within and around Nairobi.

MATATU
The way that most local people travel is by vehicles known as matatus. (The name comes from 'three', because when matatus first started running it cost three coins to travel.) These can be anything from small, dilapidated Peugeot 504 pick-ups with a cab on the back, to shiny, brightly painted 20-seat minibuses complete with mega-decibel stereos, as found in Nairobi. Most matatu drivers are under a lot of pressure from their owners to maximise profits so they tend to drive recklessly and overload their vehicles. They also put in long working days. Stories about matatu smashes and overturnings in which many people are killed or injured can be found almost daily in the newspapers. Of course, many travellers use them and, in some cases, there is no alternative, but if there is (such as a bus or train) then take that in preference. The Mombasa to Nairobi road is notorious for smashes.

Overcrowding, on the other hand, isn't confined to matatus. I once counted 136 people getting off a Malindi to Mombasa bus at Kilifi excluding the driver and his mate.

As in most East African countries, you can always find a matatu which is going to the next town or further afield so long as it's not too late in the day. Simply ask around among the drivers at the park. Matatus leave when full and the fares are fixed. It's unlikely you will be asked for more money than the other passengers.

TRAIN

Kenyan trains are a very popular form of travel, despite the fact that the rolling stock, tracks and other essential works have been allowed to deteriorate. The trains generally run on time and are considerably safer than travelling by bus or matatu.

The main railway line runs from Mombasa to Malaba on the Kenya-Uganda border via Voi, Nairobi, Nakuru and Eldoret with branch lines from Nakuru to Kisumu, Nairobi to Nanyuki, Voi to Taveta and Eldoret to Kitale. There are no passenger services on the Nairobi to Nanyuki or Eldoret to Kitale branches. Although the Kenyan tracks are contiguous with both the Tanzanian and Ugandan systems, there are no international services at present. (See the Nairobi chapter for fare details.)

Classes

First class consists of two-berth compart-ments with a washbasin, drinking water, a wardrobe and a drinks service. There's a lockable door between one compartment and the adjacent one so, if there are four of you travelling together, you can make one com-partment out of two, if you wish. They're usually very clean. What you cannot do is lock the door of your compartment from the outside when you go for dinner.

Second class consists of four-berth com-partments with a washbasin and drinking water supply. Third class is seats only. All the compartments have fans. Sexes are separated in 1st and 2nd class unless you book the whole compartment. Third class can get a little wearing on the nerves on long journeys especially if you are travelling overnight, (most journeys are overnight). Second class is more than adequate in this respect and 1st class is definitely a touch of luxury as far as budget travel goes.

Reservations

You must book in advance for both 1st and 2nd class (two to three days is usually enough) otherwise you'll probably find that there are no berths available and you'll have to go 3rd class. Visa credit cards are accepted for railway bookings. If you're in Malindi and planning on taking the train from Mombasa to Nairobi, bookings can be made with travel agencies and major hotels in Malindi, or by calling the station yourself. Compartment and berth numbers are posted up about 30 minutes prior to departure.

Matatus
Matatus are not just transport. They are Kenya's contribution to world culture. These gaudily painted minibuses, featuring 200-decibel stereo systems pumping out disco beat at bone-con-duction level have a crew of three: the driver, who normally hasn't slept for three days, keeping himself going by chewing *miraa* shoots, a bush which contains a natural amphetamine; the conductor, who extracts fares from reluctant passengers; and the tout, a veritable Daddy Cool whose aerial gymnastics on the outside of the minibus ought to be an Olympic event. The tout performs these antics to attract customers.

All Nairobi matatus are individually named and the most popular ones on the Eastleigh run are 'Public Enemy', 'Defending Champion', 'Get in & Die', 'Florida 2000', 'You Move with the Best', and 'You Die Like the Rest'. Driving standards and the frequency of fatal accidents justify these names, yet despite this, matatus are still the preferred mode of local transport. ■

Meals & Bedding

Most trains have a dining car which has dinner and two sittings of breakfast. Meals on the trains used to be quite an experience with plentiful and cheap four-course meals served on starched white linen by smartly dressed waiters. Sadly, these days the meals are neither cheap nor special, and the level of service is generally poor.

All meals must be booked and paid for at the time of purchasing your ticket. Breakfast is US$3.60, lunch or dinner US$6. Cold beers are available at all times.

Bedding is available in 1st and 2nd class, and this too must be booked and paid for when you buy your ticket. A bed roll, which consists of sheets, blankets and pillow, costs US$2.85, and a mattress is available for an extra US$1.70.

CAR & 4WD

If you are bringing your own vehicle to Kenya you should get a free three-month permit at the border on entry, so long as you have a valid *carnet de passage* for it. If you don't have a carnet you should be able to get a free one-week permit at the border on entry after which you must get an 'authorisation permit for a foreign private vehicle' at Nyayo House, Kenyatta Ave, Nairobi, which costs a few dollars but a lot of time queuing. Before you do this, however, get in touch with the Automobile Association of Kenya which is in the Hurlingham shopping centre (signposted) in Nairobi.

When you are driving your own vehicle there are certain routes in north-east Kenya where you must obtain police permission before setting out. This is just a formality but there will be a roadblock to enforce this. The main stretch where this applies is between Isiolo and Marsabit where all transport must travel in convoy at a particular time of day unless you're turning off to go somewhere else (such as Samburu National Park, Wamba or Maralal).

Foreign registered vehicles are not allowed into Kenyan game parks and reserves, which is a major inconvenience if you are travelling this way.

Road Conditions

Kenyan roads in the south-western part of the country – west of a line drawn through Malindi, Isiolo and Kitale – are excellent. In fact they're some of the best in Africa, though sections of the Nairobi to Mombasa road sometimes get badly potholed before resurfacing. North and north-east of this line and in the national parks the roads are all gravel, usually in a reasonable state of repair though there are long sections of corrugated gravel in some parts. Driving on these, at the necessary speed to avoid wrecking a vehicle, can be agony on your kidneys after several hours, especially if you're on a bus which has had a double set of unyielding springs fitted to it. Naturally, there are washouts on some of these gravel roads during the rainy seasons and, under these circumstances, journey times can be considerably longer. Naturally, if a bridge gets washed out, you'll either have to turn back or wait.

Right up in the north on the eastern side of Lake Turkana, especially in the Kaisut and Chalbi deserts, you can make good headway in the dry season and the roads (which would be better described as tracks) are often surprisingly smooth and in good condition. This is certainly true of the road from Wamba to North Horr via Parsaloi, Baragoi, South Horr and Loyangalani, except for the *luggas* (dry riverbeds) between Wamba and Parsaloi for which you'll need 4WD.

After rain, however, it's another story, particularly on the flat parts of the deserts. They turn into treacherous seas of mud, often as much as a metre deep in places. Only a complete fool would attempt to drive in these circumstances without 4WD, sand ladders, adequate jacking equipment, shovels, a tow rope or wire, drinking water and spare metal jerry cans of fuel. This is particularly true of the stretches of track between North Horr and Maikona and on any of the tracks leading off the Marsabit to Isiolo road to South Horr.

To get out of the mud, if you're really stuck, you're going to be entirely dependent on the small number of vehicles which *may* pass by and *may* stop and help (they won't want to get stuck either), or on a passing herd of camels. It's going to cost you money either way. Not only that, but you can sometimes drive for hours only to find that it's impossible to cross a river, which may not even exist in the dry season, and have to drive all the way back again. Fuel is very difficult to find in this region and is usually only available at mission stations for up to three times what you would pay for it in Nairobi – and they'll only sell you a limited amount. Make adequate preparations if you are driving your own vehicle.

Car & 4WD Rental

Hiring a vehicle to tour Kenya (or at least the national parks) is a relatively expensive way of seeing the country but it does give you freedom of movement and is sometimes the only way of getting to the more remote parts of the country. On the other hand, if you're sharing costs, it's quite a feasible option.

There are a number of factors to take into consideration before deciding what type of vehicle to take and which company to go through, and there's no real substitute for sitting down with pen and paper and working out as near as possible what the total cost will be. To do this you'll need as many hire-charge leaflets as you can get hold of and a distances table.

The other major consideration is what type of vehicle is going to be suitable to enable you to get where you want to go. At times other than the rainy season, a 2WD vehicle may be perfectly adequate in some parts of the country including Masai Mara Game Reserve, Amboseli and Tsavo national parks (at least on the main access routes of the latter), but it won't get you to the east side of Lake Turkana and would restrict your movements in the Aberdare and Meru national parks and the Buffalo Springs and Samburu game reserves. Most companies also have a policy of insisting that you take a 4WD vehicle if you're going upcountry and off the beaten track.

Rental Costs This is something of a minefield since the daily/weekly base rates vary quite a lot as do the km (mileage) charges.

What initially looks cheap often works out just as expensive as anything else.

To give you some idea of average costs, the base rates for a 2WD saloon car are between US$20 and US$30 per day plus around US$0.30 per km (often with a minimum charge of 100 km) plus insurance of between US$11 and US$20 per day. All-inclusive daily charges with unlimited km are around US$90 per day for one day, with a sliding scale dropping to around US$60 per day if you take the car for one week or more. Limited-km weekly rates start at around US$260 (Payless) for 500 km, and head up to US$375 for 1200 km.

In the next category, an average small 4WD vehicle such as a Suzuki Sierra costs between US$30 and US$45 per day plus insurance plus around US$0.30 to US$0.45 per km. On a daily unlimited-km basis it costs around US$120 (with a minimum of four days), while a weekly limited-km rental costs around US$350 (500 km) or around US$575 (1200 km). Unlimited weekly rental will cost you around US$650 to US$900.

In the highest category – a 4WD Isuzu Trooper or Mitsubishi Pajero, for instance – daily rates vary between US$51 (Habib's) and US$75 (Avis) plus insurance and mileage of around US$0.55 to US$0.70 per km. All-inclusive limited km rates are around US$650 with 500 km and US$1050 with 1200 km. Unlimited weekly rental rates are around US$1300 to US$1500.

Minimum Mileage Conditions Some of the so-called 'unlimited' km rates are not quite that. Some have a ceiling of 1200 to 1400 km per week free after which you pay the excess at the normal km rate. Some companies also offer the option of 500 km or 1200 to 1400 km per week free of charge with corresponding lower or higher base rates. If you are renting on a daily basis, some companies have a 100-km minimum charge, regardless of whether you travel this far or not. If you're not planning on going too far then it may be more economical to opt for the lower free km rate.

Insurance The only way to cover yourself against damage to the hire vehicle and other property is to take out Collision Damage Waiver (CDW) insurance. The thing to really look out for here is the excess payable by you in the event of a collision. With the larger and generally more reputable companies (Avis, Hertz, Europcar, Central, among others) it's generally US$30, but with others (Glory, Market, Payless, Habib's, among others) it's as high as US$750, and this is over and above the US$10 to US$30 or so you pay per day for insurance in the first place! Some companies are less than forthcoming about what your liability is, so make sure you know exactly what the conditions of the rental are – getting hit for US$750 when you think you are insured can come as a rude shock. The reason companies do this is that their own insurance premiums are lower if the customer is liable for a higher amount. Windscreens and tyres are not covered by insurance with any company. If you are renting on an 'unlimited km' basis, CDW is usually included in the charge, but make absolutely sure of this.

The cost of CDW insurance ranges from around US$10 per day for a small car up to US$30 for a large 4WD. Theft insurance is also available from some companies for around US$5 per day.

Deposits There's a wide variation in the deposits charged on hired vehicles. It's usually the estimated total hire charges (base rate and km) plus whatever the excess on the CDW is (from US$30 to US$750, depending on the company). No deposit is necessary if you are paying by credit card.

Drivers' Licences & Minimum Age An international driver's licence or your own national driving licence is standard. Some companies stipulate a minimum age of 23 years but with others it is 25. There are occasionally stipulations about endorsements on licences (clean licences preferred) and that you must have been driving for at least two years.

Maintenance Although it's not always the case, it's probably true to say that the more you pay for a vehicle, the better condition it will be in. It's worth paying attention to this, especially if you're planning on going a long way. It doesn't necessarily mean that all the cheaper companies neglect maintenance but, as our feedback mail indicates, some certainly do.

The other factor related to maintenance is what the company will do for you (if anything) in the event of a major breakdown. The major companies *may* deliver you a replacement vehicle and make arrangements for recovery of the other vehicke, but with most companies you'll be entirely responsible for getting the vehicle fixed and back on the road. Only when you return it will you be refunded and you'll need receipts to prove what you spent.

Equipment Some companies provide you with adequate tools to tackle breakdowns, others with just sufficient to change a tyre. If you have mechanical skills, it's worth enquiring about what tools are provided. The only company which includes a full complement of camping equipment in their 4WD hire charges is Habib's. With other companies you'll have to hire this separately.

One-Way Rates If you want to hire a vehicle in one place and drop it off in another there will be additional charges to pay. These vary depending on the vehicle, the company and the pick-up and drop-off locations but range from around US$30 (Mombasa to Malindi) and US$100 (Nairobi to Mombasa).

Driving to Tanzania Only the larger (and more expensive) companies cater for this and there are additional charges. Briefly, these are US$28.50 for insurance and US$71.50 for documentation (both payable to the hire company) plus US$100 for Tanzanian road tax (payable to Tanzanian customs on entry).

Rental Agencies At the top end of the market are two companies:

Avis
      Koinange St, Nairobi (☎ (02) 336794)
      Moi Ave, Mombasa (☎ (011) 223048)
      Sitawi House, Malindi (☎ (0123) 20513)
      Two Fishes Hotel, Diani Beach (☎ (0127) 2101)
      Jomo Kenyatta International Airport, Nairobi
      (☎ (02) 822186)
Hertz
      Muindi Mbingu St, Nairobi (☎ (02) 331960)
      Moi Ave, Mombasa (☎ (011) 316333)
      Blue Dolphin Hotel, Malindi (☎ (0123) 20069)

In much the same league but considerably less expensive on weekly rates is Europcar at Bruce House, Standard St, Nairobi (☎ (02) 334722), and also in the Times building, Nkrumah Rd, Mombasa (☎ (011) 226198). It also has branch offices at Jomo Kenyatta International Airport in Nairobi (☎ (02) 822348), Moi International Airport in Mombasa (☎ (011) 433780), Diani Sea Lodge at Diani Beach (☎ (0127 2114) and at the Blue Dolphin Hotel in Malindi.

Europcar manages an excellent choice of good, reliable companies with well-maintained vehicles and similar rates. What they don't have is large fleets of vehicles, so it's important to book in advance if you want to be sure of getting what you want – particularly a 4WD vehicle. Companies in this category include:

Central Rent-a-Car
      Fedha Towers, Standard St, Nairobi (☎ (02) 222888)
Glory Car Hire
      Nairobi (☎ (02) 224428)
      Mombasa (☎ (011) 221159)
      Malindi (☎ (0123) 20065)
      Diani (☎ (0127) 2276)
Habib's
      Agip House, Haile Selassie Ave, Nairobi (☎ (02) 220463)
Market Car Hire
      Market Service Station, on the corner of Koinange & Banda Sts, Nairobi (☎ (02) 225797)
Payless Car Hire
      Olympic House, Koinange St, Nairobi (☎ (02) 338400)
      Saroya House, Moi Ave, Mombasa (☎ (011) 222629)

The Car Hire Company
      New Stanley Hotel, Standard St, Nairobi (☎ (02) 225255)

Central is certainly the best in this category with a well-maintained fleet of fairly new vehicles and a good back-up service. Their excess liability on CDW is also one of the lowest (US$28.50). Glory has some decent cars but also has some real bombs – the car I hired between Mombasa and Malindi to update this book was in a diabolical state – almost unroadworthy. A complaint only elicited a 'take it or leave it' response from the staff in Malindi. Market and Payless are owned by the same people and their excess liability on CDW would leave you penniless if you did have an accident (US$570).

For cheap car hire exclusively in and around Nairobi, go to Rent a Beetle (☎ 33-8041/5), 7th Floor, Finance House, Loita St (PO Box 60517), Nairobi. Here you can hire a VW Beetle for just US$24 per day which includes 250 km free. Insurance is optional provided that the hirer signs a waiver accepting liability in the event of an accident. Comprehensive insurance is available for an extra US$5. (When you telephone, ask for Don Cornes or Margaret.) It's the cheapest car rental you'll find anywhere in Nairobi.

BICYCLE
Bicycles are basically only in use in cities and there's not many of them. Virtually everybody travels by matatu. Anyone foolish enough to risk cycling along main roads in Kenya must be taking suicide seriously.

HITCHING
Hitching is usually good on the main roads and may well be preferable to travelling by matatu, but if you are picked up by an African driver and are expecting a free lift then make this clear from the outset. Most will expect a contribution at least. Hitching to the national parks, on the other hand, can be very difficult since most people either go on a tour or hire their own vehicle. Apart

from that, once you get to the park lodges or camping areas, you will be entirely dependent on persuading other tourists with their own vehicles to take you out with them to view game since walking in the parks is generally forbidden.

Although many travellers hitchhike, it is not a totally safe way of getting around. Just because we explain how hitching works does not mean we recommend it.

BOAT

Lake Victoria Ferry

Ferries connect Kisumu with Kendu Bay, Homa Bay, Mbita, Mfangano and Asembo Bay but there are no international services connecting these Kenyan ports with those of Tanzania or Uganda.

The schedule for the lake ferries can be found in the Kisumu section.

Dhow

Sailing on a dhow along the East African coast is one of Kenya's most worthwhile and memorable experiences. There's nothing quite like drifting along the ocean in the middle of the night with the moon up high, the only sounds the lapping of the waves against the side of the boat and subdued conversation. It's enjoyable at any time of day, even when the breeze drops and the boat virtually comes to a standstill.

There are no creature comforts aboard these dhows so when night comes you simply bed down wherever there is space. You'll probably get off these boats smelling of fish since fish oil is used to condition the timbers of the boat – nothing that a shower won't remove! Take drinking water and food with you although fish is often caught on the way and cooked up on deck over charcoal. Dhows can be picked up in Mombasa, Malindi and Lamu.

Many of the smaller dhows these days have been fitted with outboard motors so that progress can be made when there's no wind. The larger dhows are all motorised and most of them don't even have sails.

Safaris

ORGANISED VEHICLE SAFARIS

There are essentially two types of organised safaris – those where you camp at night and those where you stay in game lodges or luxury tented camps at night. Whichever you choose, safaris typically start and end in either Nairobi or Mombasa, though there are a number of exceptions to this. Apart from transfer to and from Nairobi or Mombasa and driving from one park to another, once you're in a park you'll be taken on a number of game drives – usually two and sometimes three per day. Each drive typically lasts two to 2½ hours and the best (in terms of sighting animals) are those in the early morning and late afternoon when the animals are at their most active. The vehicles used for these drives are six to eight-seater minibuses with roof hatches, Land Rovers, or open-sided trucks.

As a general rule, you'll be left to your own devices between late morning and around 3 pm (except for lunch) though, if you're on a camping safari, you may well be taken to a lodge in the early afternoon to relax over a cold beer or have a swim in the pool (though at some lodges the pool is for guests only). You may also be taken to a lodge after the late-afternoon game drive for the same thing before returning to camp for dinner.

Camping Safaris

Camping safaris cater for budget travellers, for the young (or young at heart) and for those who are prepared to put up with discomfort. They are no-frills safaris, with none of life's little luxuries such as flush toilets, running water or iced drinks. Such safaris can be quite demanding depending on where you go, and you'll be expected to lend a hand. You'll end up sweaty and dusty and there may well be no showers available – even cold ones. On the other hand, you're in for an authentic adventure in the African bush with nothing between you and the animals at night except a sheet of canvas and the embers of a dying fire. It's not at all unusual for elephants or hippos to trundle through the camp at night, or even the occasional lion, and so far no-one has been eaten or trampled on.

Another plus for these safaris is that you'll probably find yourself with travellers from the four corners of the earth. Truck safaris may have as many as half a dozen people of different nationalities on board.

The price of your safari will include three meals a day cooked by the camp cook(s) though on some safaris you'll be expected to lend a hand in the preparation and clean up. Food is of the 'plain but plenty' variety.

The price will also include all the necessary camping gear except a sleeping bag which you must provide or hire locally. The tents provided sleep two people as a rule and you'll be expected to erect and dismantle it yourself though there are some safaris where the camp is taken on ahead of you and the tents erected by the staff. Tents are invariably of the type which sleep two people and, if you're a single traveller, you'll be expected to share with someone else. If you don't want to do that then you'll be up for a 'single supplement' of between 20 to 25% on the price of the safari which will allow you to have a tent of your own. Mosquito nets are generally not provided so you'll have to hire one yourself or bring along insect repellent either in the form of coils or a skin cream.

You'll need to bring clothing and footwear sufficient to cover you for hot days and cold nights but the amount of baggage which you'll be allowed to bring is limited. Excess gear can usually be stored at the safari company's offices. Don't forget to bring along a torch (flashlight) and pocket-knife – the company will provide kerosene lanterns for the camp but they won't be left on all night.

There are also a number of somewhat more expensive camping safaris available which utilise permanent camp sites with pre- erected tents fitted with mosquito nets, beds and sheets and which have showers (though there's sometimes not enough water for everyone to have a shower).

Remember that at the end of one of these safaris your driver/guide and the cooks will expect a reasonable tip. This is only fair since wages are low and these people will have made a lot of effort to make your trip a memorable one. Be generous here. Other travellers are going to follow you and the last thing anyone wants to find themselves closeted with is a disgruntled driver/guide who couldn't care less whether you see game or not.

Lodge Safaris

The other type of safari is for those who want luxury at night and in between game drives. On these the accommodation is in game lodges or luxury tented camps. There are plenty of beautifully conceived and superbly sited lodges in the main national parks where you can expect a fully self-contained room or cottage, cuisine of an international standard, a terrace bar with ice-cold drinks, a swimming pool and videos and plenty of staff to cater for all your requirements. Many of these lodges overlook a watering hole or salt lick so you can sit on the viewing terrace and watch the animals from there. The watering hole or salt lick will usually be floodlit at night. Some of the lodges put out bait or salt to encourage certain animals to visit the spot and while this is often very contrived, it usually guarantees you a sighting of animals which you'd be very lucky to see otherwise.

There's obviously a considerable difference in price for these safaris as opposed to camping and most of the people who go on them are package tourists with expectations and attitudes of mind quite dissimilar to those who opt for a camping safari. For them it's essentially a holiday rather than in-depth involvement in Africa, its people and wildlife. It's the African bush at arm's length. On the other hand, if you have the money, it's worth staying at the occasional lodge just for the contrast.

Lodge safaris will cost you at least four times what a camping safari costs – and often considerably more. Luxury tented camps are no less expensive than lodges and the more exclusive ones cost up to four times the price of a lodge. They're for people to whom money is no object and who want to experience what it must have been like in the days of the big-game hunters, except that they'll be stalking with cameras rather than guns.

Routes

Whether you take a camping safari or a lodge safari, there's a whole plethora of options available ranging from two days to 15 days and sometimes 25 days. If possible, it's best to go on a safari which lasts at least five days and preferably longer since otherwise a good deal of your time will be taken up driving to and from the national parks and Nairobi. You'll also see a great deal more on a longer safari and have a much better chance of catching sight of all the major animals. Remember that sightings of any particular animal cannot be guaranteed but the longer you spend looking, the better your chances are. A longer safari will also give you the opportunity of having some involvement with the local tribespeople.

A three-day safari typically takes you either to Amboseli or Masai Mara. A four-day safari would take you to Amboseli and Tsavo, to Masai Mara or to Samburu and Buffalo Springs. A five-day safari would take you to Amboseli and Tsavo, or to Masai Mara and Lake Nakuru; whereas a six-day safari would take you to lakes Nakuru, Bogoria and Baringo plus Masai Mara, or to Lake Nakuru, Masai Mara and Amboseli. On a seven-day safari, you could expect to visit at least two of the rift valley lakes plus Masai Mara and Amboseli, whereas on an 11-day safari you would take in one or more of the rift valley lakes plus Masai Mara, Amboseli and Tsavo; or Mt Kenya, Samburu and Buffalo Springs, Meru, Lake Nakuru and Masai Mara.

Most of the safari companies cover the above standard routes but some also specialise in different routings designed to take you off the beaten track. There are, for instance, safaris which take in Masai Mara, Lake Victoria, Mt Elgon, Saiwa Swamp and Nakuru,

and others which take in Mt Kenya, Samburu and Buffalo Springs, Nyahururu, Lake Nakuru and Masai Mara. Other safaris visit Shaba, rather than Samburu and Buffalo Springs, where you'll hardly see another vehicle.

Most companies also offer safaris to Lake Turkana which range from seven to 12 days. The shorter trips take one or other of the standard routes – Nairobi, Nakuru, Nyahururu, Maralal, Baragoi, South Horr and Loyangalani or Nairobi, Isiolo, Maralal, Baragoi, South Horr and Loyangalani. The longer trips detour from this route and take you to either or both the Matthews Range and the Ndoto Mountains. A full description of the options available can be found in the East of Turkana section in the Northern Kenya chapter.

Costs

There's a lot of competition for the tourist dollar among the safari companies and prices for the same tour are very similar. The trouble is, there are now so many safaris to choose from which offer similar itineraries and options that it's not that easy to compare prices. It depends what you want, though it's still generally true that the longer you go for, the less it costs per day.

For camping safaris with no frills you are looking at an all-inclusive price of around US$65 to US$70 per day on a reducing scale up to 10 days (plus or minus 15%). The price includes transport, food (three meals per day), park entry and camping fees, tents and cooking equipment. The price per day for safaris over 11 days tends to rise somewhat since there's a lot more organisation involved and you'll be going to remote areas where there are no services available so everything has to be trucked in.

Unfortunately, the situation is not as simple as the above suggests. While it may be OK to use the above figure as a benchmark, prices vary widely. A three-day safari to Amboseli and Masai Mara or Amboseli and Tsavo varies from US$180 to US$570. A five-day safari to Amboseli and Masai Mara or to the rift valley and Amboseli varies from US$300 to US$800; and a seven-day safari to Amboseli, Masai Mara and the rift valley or to Amboseli, Masai Mara and Samburu varies from US$385 to US$1050. In other words, you must do your legwork. Collect as many leaflets as you can (about a morning's work), decide where you want to go, compare prices, work out what's included and what isn't, and then make your choice. Remember that, generally, what you pay for is what you get. A high degree of personal involvement in camp chores and a willingness to eschew creature comforts usually guarantees a low price. If you want the opposite, it will cost you more. No-one works for nothing.

The prices for safaris which involve staying in lodges or tented camps are considerably higher. Here you're looking at a minimum of US$120 to US$150 per person per night in the lodges and up to US$350 in the luxury tented camps.

The above prices are based on the assumption that you will share accommodation (a tent or room) with one other person. If you don't want to do this then you'll have to pay what's called a 'single room supplement'. This is generally around 20 to 25% extra.

Departure Frequency

This varies a lot from company to company and depends on the season. In the high season, many companies have daily or every second day departures to the most popular game parks – Amboseli, Masai Mara and Tsavo – since there's high demand. To the less frequented parks such as Samburu and Buffalo Springs, Shaba and Meru, they generally leave only once or twice per week. Safaris to Lake Turkana are usually only once weekly. In addition, most companies will leave for any of the most popular game parks at any time so long as you have a minimum number of people wanting to go – sometimes four, sometimes six. In the low season, there are fewer departures.

It obviously makes a lot of sense to either book ahead or to get a group together rather than just turn up and expect to leave the very next morning. Advance booking is essential for the Lake Turkana safaris since they're heavily subscribed. It's also essential for any of the more exotic options described in the Other Safaris section.

Choosing a Company

There is no doubt that some safari companies are better than others. The main factors which make for the difference are the quality and type of vehicles used, the standard of the food, and the skills and knowledge of the drivers/guides. It's equally true that any company can take a bunch of people on safari one week and bring them back fully satisfied, and yet the following week take a different set of people on the same safari and end up with a virtual mutiny. That's an extreme example, but whether a company gets praised or condemned can hinge on something as simple as a puncture which takes half a day to fix and for which there are no tools on board, or a broken spring which involves having to wait around for most of the day whilst a replacement vehicle is sent out from Nairobi. There's obviously a lot which companies can do to head off breakdowns but a broken spring, for example, isn't reasonably one of them on a short safari though you would expect such spares to be on board for longer journeys and certainly on a safari to Lake Turkana.

The other major factor to take into consideration before you decide to go with any particular company is whether they actually operate their own safaris with their own vehicles or whether they are just agents for other safari companies. If they're just agents then obviously part of what you pay is their commission but the most important thing here is, if anything goes wrong or the itinerary is changed without your agreement, you have very little comeback and you'll be pushing shit uphill to get a refund. We get letters about this all the time from travellers to whom this happened.

Unfortunately, the situation isn't that easy to avoid. It's a minefield working out which are genuine safari companies and which are just agencies. Go into any office in Nairobi and, naturally, they all have their own vehicles and, of course, they'll compensate you at the end of the safari if anything goes seriously wrong. Not so if they're just agents. They will already have paid the lion's share of what you gave them to the company which actually provided the vehicles and staff so that gives them very little room for manoeuvre. Likewise, there's no way that the actual safari company is going to provide the agency with a refund.

It's perfectly obvious that quite a few so-called safari companies are merely agencies. Simply pick up half a dozen leaflets from various companies and compare the wording – you'll find that quite a few are identical!

Another aspect of Kenya's safari business is that there's a good deal of client swapping between companies whose vehicles are full and those which aren't. This isn't philanthropy; it's pure business. In other words, you may find yourself on a certain company's safari which is not the one you booked through. The reputable companies won't do this without informing you but the agents certainly will. Getting swapped onto another company's safari isn't necessarily a bad thing but make sure they are members of the Kenyan Association of Tour Operators (KATO). That way, they will be answerable to the association's ethics committee in the event of a dispute.

Despite the pitfalls mentioned here, there are a number of reliable companies offering camping safaris which have their own vehicles and an excellent track record. Most of the people who run them paid their dues driving overland trucks around Africa for years so you can be sure they know the business back to front. The following companies have been listed alphabetically, and are not in any order of preference or reliability:

Best Camping Tours
2nd Floor, Nanak House, corner of Kimathi and Banda Sts, PO Box 40223, Nairobi (☎ 29667, 29675).
This is a popular company which offers budget camping safaris on all the main routes ranging from Amboseli or Masai Mara (three to four days) to Amboseli and Tsavo (four days) right through to Amboseli, Tsavo, the rift valley lakes and Masai Mara (eight days) to Turkana (eight days).

Blackwing Safaris
PO Box 42532, Nairobi (☎ 891241; fax 882160).
This small company, run by Dave Mascall, caters for discerning clients who want flexibility and quality and who don't want to be crammed into the usual safari minibus. Dave takes only three clients or less at a time and can arrange safaris of any duration within Kenya or Tanzania. He has excellent equipment and his own private camp site in Masai Mara. His safaris cost a standard US$150 (three clients), US$200 (two clients) and US$250 (one client) per person per day which includes all transport, transfer to and from Nairobi airport, first and last nights at the Boulevard Hotel in Nairobi, all food and drink (including wine and beer), all park entry and camping fees, and the full range of camping and safari equipment.

Bushbuck Adventures
Barclays Bank Bldg, Kenyatta Ave, PO Box 67449, Nairobi (☎ 212975/6/7; fax 218735).
To quote the company's leaflet, 'We do not offer safaris for those requiring all the comforts of home, nor do we offer rock-bottom prices and comparable facilities. We specialise in safaris for (those) who want reasonable comfort while still feeling close to nature'. As a result, they're relatively expensive. Bushbuck has its own camp sites and offers Amboseli (three days, US$570), Masai Mara (five days, US$756), Western Kenya (Masai Mara to Mt Elgon; 12 days, US$1650) as well as a number of more exotic safari options (see later in this chapter).

Eagle Camping & Lodges Safaris
4th Floor, Uganda House, Kenyatta Ave (PO Box 22432), Nairobi (☎ 226192; fax 331276).
This new outfit, run by Charles Ngigi, has received good reports. Charles offers low-budget camping safaris to all the major parks and areas of natural beauty and is an excellent guide and driver. Eagle is worth checking out.

Exotic Safaris
1st Floor, South Wing, Uniafric House, Koinange St, PO Box 54483, Nairobi (☎ 338811; fax 211701).
We have received good reports of this company, which offers a full range of safaris along the standard routes from Amboseli (three days) through lakes Nakuru, Bogoria and Baringo and Masai Mara (six days) to Mt Kenya, Samburu and Masai Mara (eight days) to a 'Turkana Special' which also takes in Samburu (seven days).

Gametrackers Camping Safaris
1st Floor, Kenya Cinema Plaza, Moi Ave, PO Box 62042, Nairobi (☎ 338927, 222703; fax 330903).

Also long-established and reliable, this company offers a whole range of safaris ranging from Amboseli (three days, US$180), to Masai Mara (four days, US$235), Masai Mara and the rift valley lakes (six days, US$310), to Turkana (eight days, US$330, two route options), as well as more exotic options (see the Other Safaris section later in this chapter).

Jomima Tours

4th Floor, Spikes Bldg, Kenyatta Lane, PO Box 2215, Nakuru (☎ 212956; fax 42694).

This company could well be useful if you're in Nakuru but not on an organised safari. It offers daily tours to Lake Nakuru, Lake Baringo and the Aberdares plus it also has cars for hire.

Ketty Tours

Moi Ave (PO Box 82391), Mombasa (☎ 315178; fax 311355).

This company specialises in short tours of the coastal region (Wasini, Shimba Hills, etc) but also offers camping safaris to all the usual parks (Tsavo, Amboseli, Masai Mara, the rift valley lakes, and Samburu) ranging from two to 10 days. The average cost per person is US$70 a day.

Safari-Camp Services

On the corner of Koinange and Moktar Daddah Sts, PO Box 44801, Nairobi (☎ 330130, 328936; fax 212160).

This company is one of the first in Kenya and has been operating for almost two decades. It is the originator of the legendary 'Turkana Bus' which recently celebrated its 600th departure. (As described in the company's leaflet: 'If you want a hot bath and iced cocktails every night and are prepared to be part of a Leo-Centric-Kombi-Ring by day we advise you to take a tour of Kenya's excellent luxury lodges...Our clients require a sleeping bag, they travel in the back of a dusty truck...We offer authenticity and value rather than luxury, we promise you an involvement with the real Africa and an affinity with the new generation of fellow travellers'.

Its Turkana Bus is one of the best (seven days, US$265) and its Wildlife Bus is just as good (seven days, US$385) but there are also 'lodge-equivalent' camping safaris for those who prefer somewhat better facilities. These include the 'Hemingway' (seven days, US$979) and the 'Hemingway Plus' (10 days, US$1320) which take in Samburu, Nyahururu, Lake Nakuru and Masai Mara using the company's own private camp sites, and 'Vanishing Africa' (14 days, US$2420) which takes in the rift valley lakes, Masai Mara and a whole swathe of northern Kenya including Lake Turkana.

Safari Seekers

5th Floor, Jubilee Insurance Exchange Bldg, Kaunda St, PO Box 9165, Nairobi (☎ 226206; fax 334585).

Ground Floor, Diamond Trust Arcade, Moi Ave, PO Box 40126, Mombasa (☎ 228276; fax 228277).

This company has come a long way in the last few years and is well recommended. It offers two three-day safaris (one to Masai Mara and the other to Amboseli), two four-day safaris (one to Amboseli and Tsavo and the other to Masai Mara and Lake Nakuru), a five-day safari to Masai Mara and the rift valley lakes, and a seven-day 'special' to Amboseli, Lake Nakuru and Masai Mara. These camping safaris are all priced on the basis of US$65 per person per day.

Special Camping Safaris Ltd

Gilfillan House, Kenyatta Ave, PO Box 51512, Nairobi (☎ 338325, 220072; fax 211828).

This is a small company operated by two people and their Kenyan staff who pride themselves on personal service. They offer Amboseli and Tsavo (four days, US$225), Masai Mara (four days, US$225), Masai Mara and the rift valley lakes or Samburu, Shaba and Mt Kenya (both six days, US$350), plus Turkana (10 days, US$370) and a 'game safari special' which takes in Masai Mara, the rift valley lakes, Maralal and Samburu (10 days, US$570).

Savuka Tours & Safaris

3rd Floor, Pan Africa House, Kenyatta Ave, PO Box 20433, Nairobi (☎ 725907, 725108).

This outfit is not a member of KATO but we've had good reports of it from those who have taken a safari with them.

Yare Safaris Ltd

1st Floor, Union Towers, Mama Ngina St, PO Box 63006, Nairobi (☎ 214099; fax 213445).

This company specialises in camel safaris but also runs regular safaris, usually on a weekly basis, to Amboseli (four days, US$300), Masai Mara (four/six days for US$350/345), Amboseli and Masai Mara (seven days, US$685), Samburu Game Reserve (seven days, US$520) and Turkana (10 days, US$360).

In addition, Yare Safaris operates an excellent hostel and camp site at Maralal which is used by many other safari companies for overnight accommodation. The hostel is also host to the annual Maralal International Camel Derby in October (see the Maralal section in the Northern Kenya chapter for details).

This is by no means an exhaustive list of companies which offer camping safaris nor is there necessarily any implication that others are unreliable – though some are. On the other hand, we do get hundreds of letters from travellers every year describing their experiences with various safari companies.

Top Left: Market stall, Naivasha (RA)
Top Right: Kenyan woman (GC)
Bottom Left: Kikuyu woman married into Maasai tribe (GH)
Bottom Right: AIDS poster, Nairobi (GP)

Tea Plantations

Tea workers, Kericho (HF)

Kenya is the world's third largest producer of tea and typically it accounts for 20% to 30% of the country's export income. Tea picking is obviously one of the main jobs in the area. A top tea picker can pick up to 100 kg per day, and they are paid at the rate of KSh 0.80 per kg. The bushes are picked every 17 days, and the same picker picks the same patches of the plantation each time. If you look closely at one of the fields of bushes you can see how one stalk of a bush is left to grow here and there; these are the markers by which workers identify their patch. The bushes are cut right back to about 50 cm high in January-March every four years, and after 90 days are ready for picking again. ■

Tea plantation, Kericho (HF)

Some get consistently good reports and others get variable reports but there are some which get consistently bad reports. If you do choose a company not listed here don't blame us if you get into strife but do tell us what the problem was and what was done about it (if anything).

If you don't want to camp but prefer to stay in a lodge each night then check out:

African Tours & Hotels
  Utalii House, Uhuru Highway, PO Box 30471, Nairobi (☎ 336858, fax 218109) and Nkrumah Rd, PO Box 90604, Mombasa (☎ 223509; fax 311022)
Pollman's Tours & Safaris
  Koinange St, PO Box 45895, Nairobi (☎ 337998; fax 337171)
  Moi Ave, PO Box 84198, Nairobi (fax 314502)
  It also has an office in London.
United Touring Company
  Fedha Towers, on the corner of Muindi Mbingu and Kaunda Sts, PO Box 42196, Nairobi (☎ 331960; fax 216871)
  Moi Ave, PO Box 84782, Mombasa (☎ 31-6333/4; fax 314549)
  It also has offices in Europe (London, Munich and Paris), North America (Philadelphia) and the Far East (Tokyo and Singapore).
Vacational Tours & Travel Ltd
  Nairobi Hilton, PO Box 44401, Nairobi (☎ 33-7392; fax 210530).

OTHER SAFARIS
Camel Safaris

This is a superb way of getting right off the beaten track and into areas where vehicle safaris don't or cannot go. Camel safaris offer maximum involvement in areas of

Kenya which the 20th century has hardly touched, if at all. Most of them take place in the Samburu and Turkana tribal areas between Isiolo and Lake Turkana and you'll have plenty of opportunity to become accustomed to the pace of nomadic life as well as to mingle with the indigenous people. You'll also encounter wildlife though, naturally, sightings of any particular animal and in what numbers cannot be guaranteed.

You have the choice of riding the camels or walking alongside them (except in a few spots where you will be forced to dismount). The camels are led by experienced Samburu *morani* (warriors) and accompanied by English-speaking guides of the same tribe who are well-versed in bush lore, botany, ornithology and local customs. Most travelling is done as early as possible in the cool of the day and a camp site established around noon. Following lunch, you are free to relax during the heat of the day and, in the evening, while the sleeping arrangements and dinner are being organised by the staff, take a walk (along with a guide if you choose). Hot showers are normally available before drinks and dinner are served around a camp fire.

All the companies provide a full range of camping equipment (two-person tents, as a rule) and ablution facilities but they vary in what they require you to bring along. Some even provide alcoholic drinks, though normally you pay extra for this. The typical distance covered each day is between 15 and 18 km so you don't have to be super fit. Far more important is flexibility and a good positive attitude, since no two safaris are exactly alike. Itineraries and routes also change depending on the weather and other factors.

Yare Safaris also host the annual Maralal International Camel Derby from their lodge and camp site at Maralal. The derby includes a full day of races in Maralal on the Saturday of the third week of October, plus a longer 18-day endurance race. For full details see the Maralal section in the Northern Kenya chapter.

The following list of recommended companies which offer camel safaris has been listed alphabetically, and not in any order of preference or reliability:

Desert Rose Camels

PO Box 44801, Nairobi (☎ 228936, 330130; fax 212160).

This company is run by Yoav & Emma Chen and Helen Douglas-Dufresne, and their safaris cover the Matthews Range, Ndoto Mountains and Ol Doinyo Nyiru between Wamba and South Horr. They have no hard-and-fast itineraries; the route depends on the season, the number of days you have available and personal interests – so they can tailor a safari to your requirements. If, for instance, you wish to make Lake Turkana your final destination, it can be arranged.

As with Yare's safari, you will be accompanied by experienced Samburu cameleers and guides but, unlike Yare, they do not use a support vehicle. All baggage, camping equipment and food and drink are transported by camels. There are, of course, camels for riding, too.

A seven-day safari costs US$350 per person (one to two people), US$260 (three to five people) and US$210 (six to eight people) and includes all food and drink (even wine and beer), camping equipment (except sleeping bags) and ablution facilities. Specially tailored or longer safaris cost correspondingly more.

Gametrackers

1st Floor, Kenya Cinema Plaza, Moi Ave (PO Box 62042), Nairobi (☎ 338927, 222703; fax 330903).

This company offers a 10-day combined camel safari and vehicle safari which starts and finishes in Nairobi but the camels are used exclusively for transporting baggage. You have to walk alongside them.

The camel trek starts at Laisamis on the Isiolo to Marsabit road and uses local Rendille guides. For the next four days you trek south of the Ndoto Mountains along the Malgis lugga (dry riverbed) and then up to the top of the Ndotos. On the seventh day, you are met by a vehicle and taken to Loyangalani on Lake Turkana. The next day is spent at the lake after which you are driven to Maralal and the final day is spent driving back to Nairobi via Nyahururu and Naivasha.

There are departures twice a month on Monday and the cost is US$430 per person which includes all transport, food and camping equipment (except sleeping bags).

Yare Safaris Ltd

1st Floor, Union Towers, Mama Ngina St, PO Box 63006, Nairobi (☎ 214099; fax 213445).

Its seven-day safari begins and ends at Yare's Maralal hostel. The trek starts at Barsalinga Bridge on the Ewaso Nyiro River (which flows through Samburu and Buffalo Springs game reserves) and it leaves every Saturday.

On the first day of the trek you are transferred by vehicle to the starting point and for the next five days you trek through the bush with your camels and Samburu morani cameleers and guides. Your excess baggage and the camp is moved on ahead of you each day by support vehicle. The camps are equipped with two-person tents, mattresses and showers.

The cost per person is US$360 and includes all transport, food, camping equipment (except sleeping bags), ablution facilities and transfer to and from Nairobi and Maralal. Alcoholic drinks are your responsibility.

Yare also hosts the annual Maralal International Camel Derby from its hostel just outside of town in the last week of October. It's well worth attending if you're anywhere in the area at the time. Full details can be found in the Maralal section of the Northern Kenya chapter.

Walking & Cycling Safaris

For the keen walker and those who don't want to spend all their time in a safari minibus, there are a number of options.

Bushbuck Adventures

Barclays Bank Bldg, PO Box 67449, Nairobi (☎ 212975/6/7; fax 218735).

This company also offers what is essentially a 14-day walking safari which takes in the Aberdare and Mt Kenya national parks including an ascent of Mt Kenya. The last few days are spent touring Shaba National Reserve in a Land Rover. The cost is US$2270 per person all-inclusive.

Gametrackers

1st Floor, Kenya Cinema Plaza, Moi Ave (PO Box 62042), Nairobi (☎ 338927; fax 330903).

This company offers a four-day walking safari into the Aberdare National Park. The first day is spent getting to Mweiga where you meet your guide after which you head up the forested eastern slopes of the Aberdare Range and make camp. The next two days are spent walking in the area and going on a short game drive if weather permits. The last day is spent driving back to Nairobi. There are two departures each month and the cost is US$265 per person (minimum five people).

Hiking & Cycling Kenya

4th Floor, Arrow House, Koinange St, PO Box 39439, Nairobi (☎ 218336/8; fax 228107).

This company specialises in hiking and cycling safaris although they all involve some transport by road and/or boat. All are camping safaris.

Its shortest safari (eight days) involves climbing Mt Longonot and walking through Hell's Gate National Park (Naivasha), walking along the Mara River into Kipsigis country, through Saiwa Swamp, and the slopes of Mt Elgon. The walks are interspersed with game drives through Masai Mara, a drive through the tea plantations of Kericho and a game drive through Nakuru National Park.

The nine-day safari takes you to Lake Turkana in the footsteps of Count Teleki. It involves a visit to Lake Baringo followed by a hike down into the Suguta Valley and Lake Loigipi in the rift valley. Next comes a climb over Teleki's Volcano to the Jade Sea. Here you are met by a boat which takes you to South Island (where you spend the night) followed by another boat to Loyangalani the following day. On the way back to Nairobi, by vehicle, you call off at Maralal and Samburu National Reserve.

This company also runs a 10-day cycling and vehicle safari which begins in the Ngong Hills and ends up in Nairobi taking in Suswa Volcano, Masai Mara, Lake Nakuru and Lake Bogoria.

There's also a 13-day walking and boating safari which takes in Mt Longonot, Hell's Gate National Park, the Mara River, Saiwa Swamp, Mt Elgon, the Cherangani Hills and Lake Turkana. It also includes game drives through Masai Mara and a visit to the remote Sibiloi National Park (by boat) at the north-eastern end of Lake Turkana. This is a very interesting package and one of the few opportunities you will have to visit Sibiloi (hardly any other safari company includes this park on their itineraries).

Hiking & Cycling Kenya can also arrange a six-day mountain trek up Mt Kenya (Sirimon route) topped off by a visit to Samburu National Reserve.

You're not expected to be an experienced hiker or super fit but you need to be in reasonable shape. Also, you won't be required to carry your luggage on your back – this is taken care of by camels, donkeys, a boat, a vehicle or local porters. You will, on the other hand, be required to share daily camp chores.

The prices include all transport, food, porters, park and camping fees, camping equipment and guides.

Kitich Camp

PO Box 14869, Nairobi (☎ 444288)

PO Box 51, Wamba.

This is a relatively new outfit operated by Toby Stark. The camp is at Ngalia village, north of Wamba (which itself is north of Isiolo). Here you can arrange to go walking in the Matthews Range along with a guide (and cooks and porters if you wish). There are no fixed departures or itineraries and you can go walking for any number of days, but you must bring your own tent. Guide fees are

US$2.20 per day and a cook can be provided at extra cost (otherwise do your own cooking). The camp site fee at Kitich is US$3.55 per day or you can stay at their permanent tented site for US$68.85 with full board. To get to the camp, there is at least one matatu daily from Isiolo to Wamba around noon and from there you'll have to hitch (very little traffic) or walk (six hours). If this doesn't appeal, pick-up can be arranged in Isiolo or Wamba.

Sirikwa Safaris

PO Box 332, Kitale.

This outfit is run by Jane & Julia Barnley from their farmhouse/guesthouse and camping site about 20 km outside Kitale on the Lodwar road. They can arrange bird-watching trips to the Cherangani Hills along with a guide (US$5.35 per day for a guide plus US$2.65 if you spend the night out) as well as trips to Saiwa Swamp National Park, Marich Pass, Mt Elgon and the Kongelai Escarpment.

White-Water Rafting

Savage Wilderness Safaris Ltd

PO Box 44827, Nairobi (☎ 521590; fax 501754). This outfit is run by Mark Savage and is the only one of its kind in Kenya. Depending on water levels, rafting trips of up to 600 km in length and of two weeks or more duration can be arranged, though most trips last between one and four days during which you cover up to 80 km.

One of the most popular short trips (one day's duration) is on the Tana River, north-east of Nairobi. You are picked up from the Norfolk Hotel at 8 am and taken to the put-in point near Sagana where you'll be briefed on safety and other procedures and issued with life jackets and helmets. Then it's off into the water. The first of the rapids is only class (or grade) 3 followed by three km of class 2 and 3 (ideal for learning some of the basic skills needed to tackle the larger rapids further on). That's followed by six km of calm scenic water where birdlife abounds. The last six km are the most exciting, consisting of class 3, 4 and, at certain water levels, class 5 rapids interspersed with short sections of calmer water where the boat can be bailed out. A hearty picnic lunch is included and you should be back in Nairobi by around 5 pm.

This trip departs every Tuesday and Saturday (advance bookings required) or by request any day if there are four or more of you.

Another of the popular short trips is the three-day adventure on the Athi River, south-east of Nairobi between Tsavo East and West national parks. The first day is spent driving to Cottar's Luxury Camp at Kibwezi on the Nairobi to Mombasa road. Here you spend the night. The following morning you leave at about 7 am for the put-in point where you are briefed and issued with life jackets and helmets. After that, it's six to eight hours rafting on both calm and white water after which you return to Cottar's Camp for the night. On the third day, you make a pre-dawn start with a picnic breakfast and tackle the much larger and faster rapids which include small waterfalls and gushing shutes interspersed with short lengths of calmer water. These are followed by a picnic lunch and the drive back to Nairobi.

These trips leave any day of the week subject to a minimum of four passengers.

The most exciting times to go on these white-water rafts are from late October to mid-January and from early April to late July when water levels are at their highest. The Tana River generally maintains a higher water level longer than the Athi.

Balloon Safaris

Viewing a game park from the vantage point of a hot-air balloon is a magnificent experience which you won't ever forget – but it is expensive! The experience of floating silently above the plains with a 360° view of everything beneath you, without safari buses

Ballooning over Masai Mara grasslands

competing for the best photo opportunity, is incomparable. It's definitely worth saving up for!

The flights typically set off at dawn and go for about 1½ hours after which they put down and you tuck into a champagne breakfast. After that, you'll be taken on a game drive in a support vehicle and returned to your lodge. At present, these flights are only available in the Masai Mara and they cost around US$300. There are two outfits:

Adventures Aloft
　Eagle House, Kimathi St, PO Box 40683, Nairobi (☎ 221439).
　This company operates out of Mara Fig Tree Lodge (Radiocall 3725) and you can either book in Nairobi or at the Fig Tree Lodge. The flights also depart from this lodge.
Balloon Safaris Ltd
　Wilson Airport, PO Box 43747, Nairobi (☎ 502850).
　This company operates out of Keekorok Lodge so you can either book through Block Hotels, Rehema House, Standard St (PO Box 47557), Nairobi (☎ 335807) or at Keekorok Lodge. The flights also depart from this lodge.

Flying Safaris

These safaris essentially cater only for the rich and those interested in big-game fishing. They centre around Rusinga Island in Lake Victoria. A light aircraft collects you from your nearest airstrip in the early morning and returns you in time for lunch or an afternoon game drive. In the meantime a motorboat takes you out on Lake Victoria where you can feed and photograph fish eagles and go fishing for Nile perch – the largest freshwater fish in the world. Angling gear is provided. Bookings can be made through Lonrho Hotels Kenya (☎ 723776), PO Box 58581, Nairobi.

SAFARIS FURTHER AFIELD

A few companies in Nairobi offer safaris to the Tanzanian game parks of Lake Manyara, Ngorongoro Crater, Serengeti and Tarangire but most of them are just agencies for Tanzanian safari companies based in Arusha so you might as well go there yourself and organise things from there. It would certainly cost less than doing it in Kenya since you won't be paying the agency's commission.

If your time and budget is limited, however, and you want to take in all or most of the major sights of Tanzania (Serengeti, Ngorongoro Crater, Lake Manyara), Burundi (Lake Tanganyika), eastern Zaïre (the gorillas of Kahuzi-Biéga National Park or Virunga National Park, the chimpanzees of Tongo, and Lake Kivu), and Uganda (Queen Elizabeth National Park, and the chimpanzees of the Kitale Forest), then it's worth thinking about booking an extended safari with one of the companies which offers these kind of safaris in Nairobi. It would certainly save on the time and expense of having to do all the legwork and organisation yourself plus the uncertainties of knowing whether you'll be able to join a gorilla or chimpanzee-viewing walk the day after you turn up (this cannot be guaranteed without prior booking).

There are several reliable companies which offer such safaris ranging from 10 to 25 days though, once again, these have been listed alphabetically and not in any order of preference:

Gametrackers
1st Floor, Kenya Cinema Plaza, Moi Ave (PO Box 62042), Nairobi (☎ 338927; fax 330903).
This company offers a longer 19-day version of Yare's and Worldwide's 10-day safaris which not only takes in the gorillas at Djomba (Zaïre) and the Queen Elizabeth National Park (Uganda) but also includes the Semliki Valley (pygmies and hot springs) and Kibale Forest (Uganda), Lake Naivasha, Mt Longonot and Hell's Gate National Park as well as Masai Mara. The safaris begin and end in Nairobi and depart once a month.

The cost is US$790 (or US$660 if you don't want to go to Masai Mara) plus US$75 for food. The price includes everything except visa fees, gorilla-viewing fees, the boat trip on the Kazinga Channel and entry to Kibale Forest. The latter three items amount to US$136.

Kumuka Africa
PO Box 70559, Nairobi (☎ 213123, fax 228107).
This UK-based company, which has a subsidiary headquarters in Nairobi, also offers a four-week 'Gorilla Safari' although the gorillas actually only occupy a small proportion of the total. Most of the trip is spent elsewhere in Tanzania, Uganda and Kenya. Kumuka takes you to virtually every

interesting place, has good trucks and good drivers, cooks and guides but it does tend to appeal to punters with an 'overland everywhere' attitude which may, or may not, be what you are looking for. The cost of this safari is US$1232 plus US$124 which includes everything except visas.

Worldwide Adventure Ltd
1st Floor, Nginyo House, on the corner of Koinange and Moktar Daddah Sts (PO Box 76637), Nairobi (☎ /fax 332407).
This company also offers a 10-day safari in 110 Land Rovers which is almost identical to Yare's safari of the same duration. The only difference is that Worldwide takes in Lake Naivasha and involves no camping at all (accommodation is entirely in budget hotels, except at Kericho on the way out and the way back where you stay at the mid-range Tea Hotel). It costs US$990 which includes everything except lunches, visas and compulsory travel insurance. There are departures every two weeks.

Yare Safaris
1st floor, Union Towers, Mama Ngina St, PO Box 63006, Nairobi (☎ 214099; fax 213445)
Yare pioneered these types of safari back in 1984 and is still the leader. The shorter trips (10 and 14 days) are done in 110 Land Rovers (converted to allow maximum viewing), and accommodation is mostly in budget hotels with occasional camping (in the national parks). Both begin and end in Nairobi. The longer trips (15, 20, 21 and 25 days) are done in trucks with group sizes ranging from 10 to 20 passengers. Accommodation is a mixture of budget hotels and camping.

The 10-day trip takes in Lake Naivasha, the tea plantations of Kericho and on into Uganda. Next it's on to the Zaïre border at Kisoro and the gorilla sanctuary at Djomba, just over the border. After seeing the gorillas, you return to Uganda and visit the Queen Elizabeth National Park including a launch ride up the Kazinga Channel. After that, it's back to Nairobi. The 14-day trip includes all the above but is followed by visits to Serengeti National Park, Ngorongoro Conservation Area and Lake Manyara National Park after which it's back to Nairobi.

The cost of the 10-day trip is US$1075 and for the 14-day trip US$1425, which includes all transport, accommodation, breakfast and dinner each day and all park entry fees. It does not include the cost of visas, lunches and compulsory travel insurance.

The 15-day truck safari is essentially for those who are principally interested in visiting the gorilla sanctuaries of Zaïre and it takes in both the Kahuzi-Biéga National Park (eastern lowland gorillas) and the Virunga National Park (mountain gorillas). The safari begins and ends in

Kampala (Uganda) and follows a route which takes you first into Tanzania, then Burundi, on into Zaïre and back to Uganda. It costs US$975 (plus a food kitty contribution of US$85) which includes all transport, camping and cooking equipment, and national park fees. It does not include the cost of visas, compulsory travel insurance or transport between Nairobi and Kampala.

The 21-day safari, starting in Kampala and ending in Nairobi takes a different route so as to include the Queen Elizabeth National Park (Uganda), the chimpanzee sanctuary at Tongo (Zaïre), the gorillas at Kahuzi-Biéga National Park (Zaïre), Burundi, Serengeti National Park (Tanzania) and Lake Naivasha (Kenya). It costs US$1275 plus US$125 for food and the price includes the same things as the 15-day safari, excluding transport between Nairobi and Kampala.

The 20-day safari is essentially a shorter version of the above but it starts from Bujumbura (Burundi), takes in both Kahuzi-Biéga and Tongo (Zaïre), Queen Elizabeth National Park (Uganda) and ends up in Nairobi. The cost is US$1135 plus US$120 for food.

The 25-day safari is, again, a Land Rover safari but, since this involves only a small group, it allows you a certain flexibility about where you decide to go and what you do. These safaris start and end in Nairobi. The route basically takes in Lake Naivasha and Kisumu in Kenya; Jinja, Kampala, the Semliki Valley (pygmies and hot springs), Kibale Forest (chimpanzees), the Ruwenzori Mountains and Queen Elizabeth National Park, all in Uganda; Virunga National Park (mountain gorillas), Tongo chimpanzee sanctuary, Mt Nyiragongo (volcano), Kahuzi-Biéga National Park (lowland gorillas), all in Zaïre; the Jane Goodall Chimpanzee Sanctuary (Burundi), Serengeti National Park, Ngorongoro Conservation Area and Lake Manyara National Park, all in Tanzania. The cost is US$1495 plus US$280 for food. All the above safaris have regular departures – contact the company for details.

DO-IT-YOURSELF SAFARIS

This is a viable proposition in Kenya if you can get a group together to share the costs since you will have to rent a vehicle and camping equipment. The costs of renting a suitable vehicle can be found under the earlier Car & 4WD section in this chapter.

Doing it yourself has several advantages over organised safaris. The main one is flexibility – you can go where you want, stop whenever you like and stay as long as you like. You don't have to follow the standard tourist routes. Another is that you can choose your travelling companions.

The main disadvantage is the extra effort you have to put in to organise the safari – hiring equipment, buying food and drink, cooking and agreeing among yourselves where you want to go and which route to take. It can also be a worry if none of you have mechanical skills and/or no tools and the vehicle breaks down. There's also the security of the vehicle and contents to think about if you want to leave it somewhere and go off walking. If you do this then you'll have to pay someone to guard it. Lastly, there's the question of maps especially if you intend to get right off the beaten track. Reasonably good large-scale maps are readily available in Kenya but the detailed ones are unavailable without going through a great deal of red tape. This means you could find yourself out in the middle of nowhere with not a clue where you're going and have to backtrack.

As far as costs go, it's probably true to say that organising your own safari is going to cost at least as much and usually more than going on a company organised safari. By how much more depends on a lot of factors but mainly the cost of hiring a vehicle and buying fuel. You'll have to sit down and work this out yourself.

Nairobi

Mark Knopfler could almost have been singing about Nairobi when he wrote *Telegraph Road*. Until the late 1800s there was nothing there. It was just a watering hole for the Maasai. Then came the Mombasa to Uganda railway, with its 32,000 indentured Indian labourers from Gujarat and the Punjab, along with their British colonial overlords intent on beating the German colonial push for the Ugandan heartland. Being approximately halfway between Mombasa and Uganda and a convenient place to pause before the arduous climb into the highlands, it quickly became tent city.

Much of the area was still a foul-smelling swamp at this time and game roamed freely over the surrounding plains, yet by 1900 it had become a town of substantial buildings and five years later succeeded Mombasa as the capital of the British East Africa protectorate. Since then it has gone from strength to strength and is now the largest city between Cairo and Johannesburg. The tower blocks of Nairobi can be seen for miles as you crest the hills which surround the plain on which it sits. Yet, in terms of the world's largest cities, Nairobi is still small with a population of about one million. You can walk from one end of the central business district to the other in 20 minutes. And where else in the world would you be able to see lions, cheetahs, rhinos and giraffes roaming free with the tower blocks of a city as a backdrop?

It's a very cosmopolitan place – lively, interesting, pleasantly landscaped and a good place to get essential business and bureaucratic matters sewn up. This is no Third World capital city though there are some very overcrowded slums on the outskirts and even across the other side of the Nairobi River from Kirinyaga Rd. The latter are periodically bulldozed away and burnt down by the city council in the interests of hygiene but it takes only days for them to regenerate!

Like most cities, Nairobi has its crowded market and trading areas, its middle class/office workers' suburbs and its spacious mansions and flower-decked gardens for the rich and powerful. The first is an area full of energy, aspiration and opportunism where manual workers, exhausted matatu drivers, the unemployed, the devious, the down-and-out and the disoriented mingle with budget travellers, whores, shopkeepers, high school students, food-stall vendors, drowsy security guards and those with life's little illicit goodies for sale. It's called River Rd – though, of course, it spans more than just this road itself. One of the funniest yet most poignant yarns I have ever read about an area such as this is to be found in a novel by Kenyan author Meja Mwangi called *Going Down River Road* (Heinemann, African Writers Series). I'd recommend this book to anyone and especially travellers passing through Nairobi. Even if you are not staying in this area you should make a point of getting down there one day just to see how the other half lives on the wrong side of Tom Mboya St.

Elsewhere in Nairobi are all the things you won't have seen for months if you've been hacking your way across the Central African Republic and Zaïre from West Africa or making do with the shortages in Zambia and Tanzania. Things like the latest films on big screens, bookshops, restaurants, cafés and bars full of travellers from all over the world, offices where you can get things done with the minimum of fuss, banks where you can change travellers' cheques in less than five minutes and a poste restante where you sort out your own letters from the pile so you don't end up with that feeling that letters have been put in the wrong pigeonhole. It's a great place to stay for a week or so but if you stay too long it can get expensive because almost everyone you meet wants to do the same as you did when

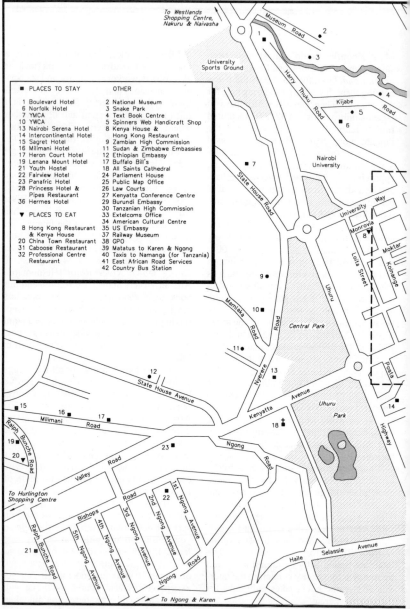

PLACES TO STAY

1 Boulevard Hotel
6 Norfolk Hotel
7 YWCA
10 YWCA
13 Nairobi Serena Hotel
14 Intercontinental Hotel
15 Sagret Hotel
16 Milimani Hotel
19 Heron Court Hotel
19 Lenana Mount Hotel
21 Youth Hostel
22 Fairview Hotel
23 Panafric Hotel
28 Princess Hotel &
   Pipes Restaurant
36 Hermes Hotel

PLACES TO EAT

8 Hong Kong Restaurant
   & Kenya House
20 China Town Restaurant
31 Caboose Restaurant
32 Professional Centre
   Restaurant

OTHER

2 National Museum
3 Snake Park
4 Text Book Centre
5 Spinners Web Handicraft Shop
8 Kenya House &
   Hong Kong Restaurant
9 Zambian High Commission
11 Sudan & Zimbabwe Embassies
12 Ethiopian Embassy
17 Buffalo Bill's
18 All Saints Cathedral
24 Parliament House
25 Public Map Office
26 Law Courts
27 Kenyatta Conference Centre
29 Burundi Embassy
30 Tanzanian High Commission
33 Extelcoms Office
34 American Cultural Centre
35 US Embassy
37 Railway Museum
38 GPO
39 Matatus to Karen & Ngong
40 Taxis to Namanga (for Tanzania)
41 East African Road Services
42 Country Bus Station

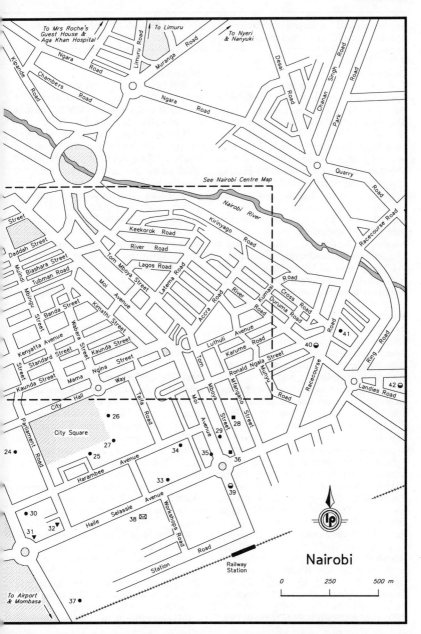

Nairobi

you first arrived – splurge at the restaurants and drink their fill in the bars and rage in the discos.

Orientation

The compact city centre is in the area bounded by Uhuru Highway, Haile Selassie Ave, Tom Mboya St and University Way. The main bus and train stations are within a few minutes' walk of this area, while the main budget travellers' accommodation area is centred around Latema Rd, just east of Tom Mboya St on the fringe of the bustling and somewhat sleazy River Rd area.

To the west of the centre is one of the more enlightened bits of Nairobi town planning – Uhuru Park. It's a much needed lung for this increasingly crowded city and is a pleasant place in the daytime. At night it becomes a mugger's paradise and should be avoided.

Directly west of Uhuru Park, and still within walking distance of the centre (but *don't* walk at night!), are some of the city's better middle and top-range hotels, the popular youth hostel, a number of government ministries and the hospitals. Beyond here are the sprawling upper middle class suburbs of Ngong and Hurlingham with their large detached houses and carefully tended gardens surrounded by high fences, and guarded by askaris (police) along with prominent signs warning that the premises are patrolled by 'Ultimate Security', 'Total Security', 'Securicor' and the like. These signs are surely one of the most enduring impressions of suburban Nairobi!

North of the centre is the university, the national museum, the International Casino and one of Nairobi's original colonial hotels, the Norfolk. Beyond here is Westlands, another of Nairobi's upper middle class suburbs. North-east of the centre is Parklands, which is home to many of Nairobi's Asian minority and where the Aga Khan Hospital is to be found. Close to the hospital is the popular Mrs Roche's guesthouse. Going east, there are the bustling and predominantly African suburbs of Eastleigh and Pangani along with the country bus station.

South of the city is Nairobi National Park,

and to the park's north-east is Jomo Kenyatta International Airport which is connected to the city by an excellent dual carriageway.

Information

Tourist Office In a city the size of Nairobi, and in a country which relies so heavily on tourism, it seems inconceivable that there is no tourist office, but there isn't.

There is a 50-page booklet called *Kenya Tourist Guide* which is published once a month and the quarterly *What's On* both of which are free and can be found at the better class hotels. There also used to be an 80-page leaflet called *Tourist's Kenya* which was published fortnightly and though publication was suspended in early February 1992, the staff are still working and the owners intend to resume publication soon. Its main outlet was the Thorn Tree Café in the New Stanley Hotel. Like the other publications, it's free.

Money At Jomo Kenyatta International Airport the branch of Barclays Bank is open 24 hours a day, seven days a week. In Nairobi, the bank's branch on the corner of Kenyatta Ave and Wabera St is open Monday to Saturday from 9 am to 4.30 pm.

Post The GPO is on Haile Selassie Ave, although a new post office on Kenyatta Ave is nearing completion and may in fact be open by now. The office on Haile Selassie is open Monday to Friday from 8 am to 5 pm and Saturdays from 9 am to noon. The poste restante is well organised and you are allowed to look through as many piles as you like, plus there's no charge for letters collected. The only trouble is that the counter which deals with it is also one of the few which sells stamps, so the queues are often long.

With the huge volume of poste restante mail here it's not surprising that some letters get misfiled but, surprisingly, it doesn't happen too often. As a favour to other travellers you should pull out any letters you come across which are misfiled so the clerk can get them into the right pile.

This post office is also the best one from

which to post parcels. The contents of all parcels sent overseas have to be inspected by the post office staff before being sealed so don't arrive with a sealed parcel or you'll have to pull it apart again. Bring all packing materials with you as there are none for sale at the post office. One of the cheapest places to buy good packing materials is at the supermarket on Koinange St opposite the new post office. Otherwise, try Biba on Kenyatta Ave at the Muindi Mbingu St intersection.

Telephone The Extelcoms office is on Haile Selassie Ave, almost opposite the post office. It is open from 8 am to midnight and you can make direct-dial calls yourself from here with a phonecard or go through the operator. There are also telex and fax facilities here.

The best place to make a call during normal business hours if you have to go through the operator is at the telephone exchange on the ground floor of the Kenyatta Conference Centre. If there is no conference in progress this office is much quieter than the Extelcoms office.

The STD area code for calls to Nairobi from anywhere in Kenya, Uganda and Tanzania is (02).

Foreign Embassies The following countries have diplomatic representation in Nairobi:

Australia
  Riverside Drive, PO Box 39341; open Monday to Thursday 7.45 am to 4.30 pm and Friday 7.45 am to 12.30 pm (☎ 445034)
Belgium
  Silopark House, Mama Ngina St, PO Box 30461; open Monday to Friday 8.30 am to 12.30 pm (☎ 220501)
Burundi
  Development House, Moi Ave, PO Box 44439; open Monday to Friday 8.30 am to 12.30 pm and 2 to 5 pm (☎ 338721)
Canada
  Comcraft House, Haile Selassie Ave, PO Box 30481; open 7.30 to 11 am (☎ 334033)
Denmark
  HFCK Bldg, Koinange St, PO Box 40412; open Monday to Friday 7.45 am to 3 pm (☎ 331088)

Egypt
  Harambee Plaza, Haile Selassie Ave, PO Box 30285; open 9.30 am to 12.30 pm and 2 to 3.30 pm (☎ 225991)
Ethiopia
  State House Ave, PO Box 45198; open 8.30 am to 12.30 pm and 2 to 5 pm (☎ 723027)
France
  Embassy House, Harambee Ave, PO Box 41784; open 9 am to noon (☎ 339783)
Germany
  Embassy House, Harambee Ave, PO Box 30180; open 8.30 am to 12.30 pm (☎ (02) 226661)
Greece
  IPS Bldg, Kimathi St, PO Box 30543; open 10 am to noon (☎ 340722)
India
  Jeevan Bharati Bldg, Harambee Ave, PO Box 30074; open 9 am to 1 pm and 2 to 5 pm (☎ 222566)
Israel
  Bishops Rd, PO Box 30107; open 8.30 am to 12.30 pm and 2 to 4.30 pm (☎ 722182)
Italy
  International House, Mama Ngina St, PO Box 30107; open 8 am to 2 pm (☎ 337356)
Japan
  ICEA Bldg, Kenyatta Ave, PO Box 60202; open 8.30 am to 12.30 pm and 2 to 4.30 pm (☎ 332955)
Madagascar
  Hilton Hotel, Mama Ngina St, PO Box 41723; open 8.30 am to 1 pm and 2 to 5 pm (☎ 226294)
Malawi
  Waiyaki Way, Westlands, PO Box 30453; open 8 am to 12.30 pm and 2 to 4.30 pm (☎ 440569)
Mauritius
  Union Towers, Moi Ave; open 8.30 am to 12.30 pm and 2 to 5 pm; this is also the Air Mauritius office (☎ 330215)
Netherlands
  Uchumi House, Nkrumah Ave, PO Box 41537; open 9 am to 12.30 pm (☎ 227111)
New Zealand
  Mr N G Wall, 3rd Floor, Minet-ICDC House, Mamlaka Rd (☎ 722467)
Pakistan
  St Michael's Rd, Westlands, PO Box 30045; open 9 am to 3.30 pm (☎ 61666)
Portugal
  Re-Insurance Plaza, Taifa Rd, PO Box 34020; open 9 am to noon (☎ 338990)
Republic of Ireland
  Mr J O'Brien, Owashika Rd, Lavington, PO Box 30659 (☎ 562615)
Rwanda
  International Life House, Mama Ngina St, PO Box 48579; open 8.30 am to 12.30 pm and 2 to 5 pm (☎ 334341)

Seychelles
> Agip House, Waiyaki Way, Westlands (☎ 74-8545)

Somalia
> International House, Mama Ngina St, PO Box 30769; open 9 am to 1 pm. This embassy does not presently function and, in fact, anyone can get into Somalia at present without a visa (☎ 224301).

Spain
> Bruce House, Standard St, PO Box 45503; open 10 am to 1 pm (☎ 335711)

Sudan
> Minet-ICDC House, Mamlaka Rd, PO Box 74059; open 8.30 am to noon, closed Wednesdays (☎ 720883)

Sweden
> International House, Mama Ngina St, PO Box 7694; open 8.30 am to 4 pm (☎ 229042)

Tanzania
> Continental House, corner of Uhuru Highway and Harambee Ave, PO Box 47790; open 8.30 am to 12.30 pm and 2 to 5 pm (☎ 331056)

Uganda
> Uganda House, Baring Arcade, Kenyatta Ave, PO Box 60853; open 9.30 am to 12.30 pm and 2 to 4.30 pm (☎ 220801)

UK
> Bruce House, Standard St, PO Box 30465; open 8.30 to 11.30 am and 1.30 to 3.30 pm (☎ 335944)

USA
> Moi Ave, PO Box 30137; open 8.30 am to 3 pm (☎ 334141)

Zaïre
> Electricity House, Harambee Ave, PO Box 48106; open 8.30 am to 12.45 pm and 2 to 5 pm (☎ 229771)

Zambia
> Nyerere Rd, PO Box 48741; open 8.30 am to 12.30 pm and 2 to 4.30 pm (☎ 724796)

Zimbabwe
> Minet-ICDC Bldg, Mamlaka Rd, PO Box 30806; open 8.30 am to 12.30 pm and 2 to 4.30 pm (☎ 721045)

Cultural Centres All the foreign cultural organisations have libraries which are open to the public and are free of charge except for the American Cultural Center which is for members only. Both the French and German cultural centres welcome travellers. The addresses are:

Alliance Française
> ICEA Bldg, Ground Floor, Kenyatta Ave. Open Monday to Friday from 10 am to 1 pm and 2 to 5.15 pm; also Saturdays from 9.30 am to noon (☎ 340054).

American Cultural Center
> National Bank Bldg, Harambee Ave. Open Monday, Tuesday and Thursday from 10 am to 6 pm, Wednesday from 10 am to noon and Friday from 10 am to 4 pm (☎ 337877).

British Council
> ICEA Bldg, Mezzanine Floor, Kenyatta Ave. Open Monday to Friday from 10 am to 5 pm and Saturday from 9 am to noon (☎ 334855).

French Cultural Centre
> Maison Française, on the corner Monrovia and Loita Sts. Open Monday to Friday from 10 am to 6 pm and Saturday from 10 am to 1 pm (☎ 336263).

Goethe Institut
> Maendeleo House, on the corner Monrovia and Loita Sts. Open Monday to Friday from 10 am to 6 pm (☎ 224640).

Italian Cultural Institute
> Prudential Bldg, Wabera St. Open Monday to Wednesday from 8 am to 2 pm, and Thursday and Friday from 8 am to 1 pm and 2.30 to 5.30 pm (☎ 220278).

Japan Information Centre
> Postbank House, on the corner of Market and Banda Sts. Open Monday to Friday from 8.30 am to 12.30 pm and 2 to 4.30 pm (☎ 340520).

Travel Agencies To get the best possible deal on an international airline ticket, first make the rounds of the airline offices to ascertain the standard price and then make the rounds of the travel agencies. Always get several quotes as things change constantly. It's sometimes, but not usually, possible to get as good a deal from the actual airline offices as it is from the agencies. European and Asian destinations are the ones to which you'll find the best discounts. This is less so in the case of North American destinations and virtually impossible for Australasian destinations.

Most of the heavily discounted tickets will involve stopovers between connections – on Aeroflot, EgyptAir, Ethiopian Airlines and Sudan Airways, for example. (See the section on Leaving Kenya in the Getting There & Away chapter for examples of fares.)

One popular agency that gets good reports from many travellers is Bankco Tours & Travel (☎ (02) 336144) on Latema Rd near the New Kenya Lodge. Just as good is Worldwide Adventures (☎ (02) 332407), 1st Floor, Nginyo House, on the corner of Koinange and Moktar Daddar Sts (above Safari Camp Services). This is run by the tall, bearded, bespectacled, Yorkshireman, Philip Jackson. If there's a good deal going, he'll know about it. Worldwide also offers a visa service and can advise you about safari companies, plus it runs some of its own.

Also recommended is Let's Go Travel (☎ (02) 340331) on Standard St close to the Koinange St intersection.

Bookshops There is a good selection of bookshops in the city centre. The Nation Bookshop is on the corner of Kimathi St and Kenyatta Ave, next door to the New Stanley Hotel, and beside it on Kenyatta Ave is the Westland Sundries Bookshop – both are excellent.

On Mama Ngina St there's Prestige Books, next to the 20th Century Cinema. There are others but they don't carry the same range.

Maps There are many maps of Nairobi available in the bookshops but probably the best is the *City of Nairobi: Map & Guide* (Survey of Kenya) in English, French and German which has a red front cover with partially coloured photographs on the back cover. It covers the suburbs as well as having a detailed map of the central area. If you're going to be staying for a long time, however, the *A to Z: Guide to Nairobi* (Kenway Publications), by D T Dobie, is worth buying.

Photography For passport-size photographs, the cheapest place to go is the machine under the yellow and black sign 'Photo Me', a few doors up Kenyatta Ave from the Nation Bookshop on the corner of Kimathi St. It costs US$1.50 for four prints and takes about three minutes. There's another machine on the corner of Tom Mboya St and Accra Rd. You can also get passport photos from the photography shop in Kimathi House opposite the New Stanley

Hotel but here they are marginally more expensive.

For camera repairs or equipment rental the best place is Expo Camera Centre (☎ 22-1797), Jubilee Exchange, Mama Ngina St. Mo Hussein, who runs this place, is a very helpful man and has a well-equipped repair workshop. Expo Camera is also very reliable for developing and printing. Alternatively, try Camera Experts, also on Mama Ngina St, or the Camera Maintenance Centre in the Hilton Arcade.

Medical Services If you need medical treatment try Dr Sheth on the 3rd floor of Bruce House on Standard St. This doctor has his own pathology laboratory if you need blood or stool tests. He charges US$11 per consultation plus laboratory fees. There is also a dentist on the same floor.

Otherwise go to the Nairobi Hospital which has the same scale of charges as Dr Seth. Avoid the Kenyatta Hospital, because although it's free, treatment here is possibly worse than the ailment, according to local residents. The Aga Khan Hospital in Parklands, opposite Mrs Roche's guesthouse, is very good.

For chiropractic treatment the best place to go is the medical centre on Rose Ave, off Argwings Kodhek Rd, just above the Hurlingham shopping centre and before you get to the Hurlingham Hotel. There are several practitioners here and you're looking at around US$7 a session.

For acupuncture there's no better practitioner than Professor Dr Abdul H Mohamed (☎ 744028, 749748), at the Africa (Laser) Acupuncture Centre, 3rd Parklands Ave (diagonally opposite the Aga Khan Hospital), Parklands. He's a little eccentric but has practised acupuncture all over the world and is well regarded by the medical doctors at both the Aga Khan and Nairobi hospitals. He practices Monday to Friday from 11 am to 2 pm and 5 to 6 pm, and on Saturday, Sunday and public holidays from 11.30 am to 1 pm. A session costs US$15.50.

You can get vaccinations at City Hall Clinic, Mama Ngina St. It is open for jabs from 8.30 am to noon and 2.30 to 4 pm Monday to Friday. Yellow fever shots cost US$7.50, cholera US$3, meningitis US$3, typhoid US$7.50 and tetanus US$0.30.

If you want a gamma globulin shot (for hepatitis A) go to Dr Sheth, 3rd Floor, Bruce House, Standard St. The charge is US$12.

Dangers & Annoyances You may hear rumours about Nairobi being a dangerous city at night as far as robberies go. We've certainly had enough letters from people to whom this has happened but never once on any occasion that I've been to Nairobi have I felt uneasy or threatened walking back to my hotel. Perhaps I just look like I know where I'm going or perhaps it's because I pull out my wallet when someone asks me for a few shillings down a dark alley. And I don't walk across Uhuru Park at night.

The best thing that can be said is to be vigilant. It's no worse than many other cities around the world and there are plenty worse. You should definitely not walk from the centre to the youth hostel or through Uhuru Park or along Uhuru Highway/Waiyaki Way (anywhere between Westlands and the roundabout with Haile Selassie Ave) at night. The area to the north and east of River Rd is also a no-go area late at night. You are asking for trouble. That taxi home may cost you US$2 but could save you a lot of money.

While we're on this subject, don't forget to read the stories in the Dangers & Annoyances section of the Facts for the Visitor chapter.

National Museum

The Kenya National Museum is on Museum Rd off Museum Hill which itself is off Uhuru Highway. The museum has a good exhibition on prehistoric people, an incredible collection of native birds, mammals and tribal crafts and a new section on the culture, history and crafts of the coastal Swahili people. It's just unfortunate that many of the displays are moth-eaten and tatty these days.

Opening hours are 9.30 am to 6 pm daily and admission is US$2.

Snake Park

The Snake Park, opposite the museum, has living examples of most of the snake species found in East Africa – some of them are in glass cages, others in open pits. There are also tortoises and crocodiles. Hours and entry charges are the same as for the museum.

National Archives

Right opposite the Hilton Hotel on Moi Ave is the National Archives. It is regarded by many as better value than the National Museum and entry is free. It contains more than the usual documents you'd expect to find in such a building, including photographs of Mzee Kenyatta and Moi visiting different countries, and exhibitions of handicrafts and paintings.

Railway Museum

The Railway Museum is on Station Rd – follow the railway tracks until you are almost at the bridge under Uhuru Highway or walk across the small piece of vacant land next to the Haile Selassie Ave roundabout on Uhuru Highway.

In addition to displays of old steam engines and rolling stock, the museum will give you a good idea of Kenya's history since the beginning of the colonial period. There's also a scale model of the venerable MV *Liemba* which plies the waters of Lake Tanganyika between Mpulungu (Zambia) and Bujumbura (Burundi).

It's open daily from 8 am to 4.45 pm; entry is US$1.50.

Parliament House

Like to take a look at how democracy works in Kenya? If so, you can get a permit for a seat in the public gallery at parliament house on Parliament Rd or, if parliament is out of session, you can tour the buildings by arrangement with the Sergeant-at-Arms.

Art Galleries

There's not much in Nairobi in the way of art galleries but this is gradually changing. The Gallery Watatu on Standard St close to

Lonrho House is the oldest established gallery and has fairly regular exhibitions as well as a permanent display. Another more recently established gallery is the Kenya Arts Museum (☎ 214801), PO Box 34464, which has displays of Kenyan art and artefacts plus top examples of carvings, jewellery and photography. There's also a shop where you can buy superior examples of this type of work. The Kiwi and Kenyan team which runs this venture is currently negotiating to borrow large private collections for permanent display.

Kenyatta Conference Centre

There is a viewing level on the 28th floor of the centre but the revolving restaurant no longer operates. If you'd like to go up there,

you must request a guide at the information desk on the ground floor. He'll expect a tip, but otherwise it's free. You're allowed to take photographs from the viewing level. Access is sometimes restricted when there's a conference in progress.

Activities

Clubs & Societies There are lots of specialist clubs and societies in Nairobi, many of which welcome visitors. Most of the foreign cultural organisations have film and lecture evenings (usually free of charge) at least once or twice a week. Give them a ring and see what they have organised. In addition to these, some local clubs you may be interested in contacting include:

The Kima Killer

Early this century when the railway line was being pushed through from Mombasa to Kampala and beyond, a remarkable incident occurred at Kima, a small siding on the line, about 110 km along the track south-west of Nairobi.

A rogue lion had been terrorising the track gangs and had in fact claimed a few victims. In an attempt to eradicate this menace, a superintendent of the Uganda Railways stationed in Mombasa, Charles Ryall, decided to mount a night vigil in a railway carriage specially positioned at the Kima siding. The station staff wanted nothing to do with the escapade and had locked themselves firmly in the station buildings.

Ryall left the carriage door open, in the hope that the lion would be lured in, and sat back with rifle at the ready and waited. Inevitably he fell asleep and just as inevitably the lion showed up. The struggle that ensued caused the sliding door on the compartment to shut and the lion was trapped inside with a firm grip on Ryall's neck. Accompanying Ryall in the carriage were two European merchants who were travelling to Nairobi and had hitched a ride with Ryall, agreeing to the overnight stop in Kima. So petrified were they that one of them ducked into the toilet and bolted the door, while the other watched transfixed as the lion wrested the body out the train window!

A reward was offered by Ryall's mother for the capture of the offending lion but it was only after a trap, baited with a live calf, was devised that the human-eater was snared. It seems there was no reason for the lion to have turned human-eater as it was a healthy beast and there was abundant herds of game animals in the vicinity – it seems it just developed a liking for human flesh.

The railway carriage involved in this incident is today preserved in the Nairobi Railway Museum, while the tombstone of Ryall, which bears the inscription 'He was attacked whilst sleeping and killed by a man-eating lion at Kima', is in the Hill Cemetery, also in Nairobi. ■

East African Wildlife Society
Nairobi Hilton, PO Box 20110, Nairobi
(☎ 748170).
This society is in the forefront of conservation efforts in East Africa and it publishes an interesting bimonthly magazine. Membership costs US$35 (US$70 if you want the magazine sent by airmail rather than surface mail) but entitles you to certain reductions in the national parks.

Mountain Club of Kenya (MCK)
PO Box 45741, Nairobi (☎ 501747).
The club meets every Tuesday at 8 pm at the clubhouse at Wilson Airport. Members frequently organise climbing weekends at various sites around the country. Information on climbing Mt Kenya and Kilimanjaro is available on the same evening.

Nairobi Chess Club
PO Box 50443, Nairobi (☎ 225007).
The club meets every Wednesday to Sunday at 5 pm at St John's Ambulance Headquarters, top floor, Parliament Rd.

Nairobi Photographic Society
PO Box 49879, Nairobi (☎ 891075).
Members meet at 8.30 pm on the first and third Thursdays of each month at St John Ambulance Headquarters.

Sports The following clubs all offer facilities for tennis, squash and cricket, and some also cater for football and hockey:

Impala Club
Ngong Rd, Nairobi (☎ 568684)
Nairobi Club
Ngong Rd (☎ 725726)
Nairobi Gymkhana
corner of Rwathia and Forest Rds (☎ 742804)
Parklands Sports Club
Ojijo Rd (☎ 742938)

Swimming Pools Most of the international tourist hotels have swimming pools which can be used by nonguests for a daily fee of around US$3. The YMCA on State House Rd also has a large pool with springboard which you can use for US$1.50.

Places to Stay – bottom end
There is a very good selection of budget hotels in Nairobi and the majority of them, except for two very popular places outside the city centre, are between Tom Mboya St and River Rd so if you find that one is full it's only a short walk to another. Virtually all

Kenyatta Conference Centre

the hotels in the city centre suffer from pretty chronic water shortages. Often there is only water for a couple of hours a day, so getting a shower at some of these places can be a bit of an ordeal.

On the other hand, many of the cheaper hotels, such as the Iqbal, the New Kenya Lodge and Mrs Roche's will store baggage for you, usually for a small daily charge. However, you're advised not to leave anything valuable in your left luggage.

Central Nairobi The *New Kenya Lodge* (☎ 222022), on River Rd at the Latema Rd intersection, is a legend among budget travellers and still one of the cheapest places, though many people feel it's a bit past it these days. There's always an interesting bunch of people from all over the world staying there. Accommodation is basic but clean and there's supposedly hot water in the evenings. A bed in a cramped four-bed room costs US$2.35.

The same people who own this also have the *New Kenya Lodge Annex* (☎ 338348) just around the corner on Duruma Rd. Prices here are the same as the old place but it lacks the atmosphere of the former, some of the rooms don't even have windows and security is not what it could be. All the same, it's still quite popular, the staff are friendly, baggage is safe, and the notice board makes interesting reading.

Sharing the legend is the *Iqbal Hotel* (☎ 220914), on Latema Rd, which has also been popular for years and is still a pretty good place. There's supposedly hot water available in the morning but you have to be up early to get it. A night in a three-bed room costs US$3.10, while double/triple rooms cost US$6.15/9.25, all with shared facilities. Baggage is safe here and there's a storeroom where you can leave excess gear if you are going away for a while. The Iqbal's notice board is always a good place to look for just about anything.

If the above two places are full there are three others on Dubois Rd, just off Latema Rd. The *Bujumbura Lodge* (☎ 228078) is very basic and a bit rough around the edges, but it's clean and quiet and very secure. The toilets and showers are clean and there is erratic hot water. It's good value at US$2.10/ 3.30 for singles/doubles with shared facilities. The *New Safe Life Lodging* (☎ 221578) is very similar and the staff are cheerful. The rooms are somewhat overpriced at US$6 but security is good. The *Nyandarua Lodging* is very clean, quiet and comfortable and you can get a large double room for US$4.25. It also has single rooms but they're just glorified cupboards and not such good value for money at US$2.70. The only problem here is that the checkout time is a very uncivilised 8.30 am.

Back on Latema Rd, the *Sunrise Lodge* is clean, secure and friendly and there's usually hot water in the mornings and evenings. Dorm beds cost US$2.30, while singles/doubles go for US$3.50/4.60, all with shared bathroom facilities. The front two rooms overlooking the street are the largest and have a balcony but they are right next door to the Modern Green Day & Night Bar which rages 24 hours a day, 365 days a year, so if you want a quiet room take one of those at the back of the hotel. If you're looking for material for a novel, on the other hand, then take one of these rooms.

Naseem's Lodging on River Rd is a small and friendly place with just a few rooms. Security is good and the place is kept very clean. The price of US$4.30/6.60 is relatively expensive but does include breakfast.

Right at the bottom of the scale is the *Al Mansura Hotel* on Munyu Rd. It's basic and the rooms are clean enough but it's really only good for a night if you can't get in elsewhere. Women are likely to feel uncomfortable in this place as it operates as a brothel. A bed in a shared room costs US$1.60, doubles are US$3.10, and there are no single rooms.

Moving up the scale, there are several hotels in the same area. One of the cheapest is the *Gloria Hotel* (☎ 228916), on Ronald Ngala St almost at the Tom Mboya St intersection. Rooms here are good value at US$5.40/5.80 for a single/double. All rooms have bath and hot water, and the price includes breakfast. The only problem here is that some of the rooms cop the noise from the street below.

A couple of doors along from the Gloria is the *Terrace Hotel* (☎ 221636) which has rooms with bath and hot water for US$4.30/4.60 including breakfast. It doesn't win any prizes for friendliness and some of the rooms are noisy, but overall it's not a bad place.

One of the best places in the budget category is the *Dolat Hotel* (☎ 22797), on Mfangano St, which is very quiet and costs US$5.60/7 for singles/doubles with bath and hot water. The sheets are changed daily, the rooms kept spotless and there's 24-hour water. It's a good, secure place with friendly management and quite a few travellers stay here.

Outside the Centre There are two very popular places away from the city centre. *Mrs Roche's*, on 3rd Parklands Ave opposite the Aga Khan Hospital, is, like the New Kenya and the Iqbal, a legend. Mrs Roche has been making travellers welcome for over 20 years and her guesthouse is a favourite with campers and those with their own vehicles as well as those who want a room away from the city centre. There's always an amazing band of people here and the whole place has the general atmosphere of a gypsy camp – there's never a dull moment.

It's situated in a very pleasant area amongst trees and flowering shrubs and is a very mellow place to stay. It's just a pity that some travellers with vehicles seem to disembowel them here and leave the discarded parts lying around for other travellers to camp amongst. Camping costs US$1.20 per night while a bed in a shared room costs US$1.60. Because it's so popular you may have to sleep on the floor for the first night until a bed is available. This is another place with a good notice board, and you can store baggage safely for a small fee.

To get to Mrs Roche's, take a matatu from the junction of Latema Rd and Tom Mboya St right outside the Odeon Cinema. There'll be a sign 'Aga Khan' in the front windscreen. Tell the driver you're heading for Mrs Roche's guesthouse. It's well known. There are several places to eat cheaply in the immediate vicinity and the nearest bar (which also has an excellent barbecue) is the Everest Hotel just up the road. It's a lively place and I've met Mrs Roche there on several occasions!

The other very popular place is the *Nairobi Youth Hostel* (☎ 221789), on Ralph Bunche Rd between Valley and Ngong Rds. Although it was being refurbished and extended when this edition was researched it's reportedly open again. The hostel is often very crowded so is a good place to meet other travellers.

It's very clean, well run, stays open all day and there's always hot water in the showers. The wardens here are very friendly and will lock up gear safely for you for up to two weeks for US$0.30, then it's US$0.50 per day after that. On a day-to-day basis there are lockers to keep your gear in when you go out, but you must supply your own lock. The notice board here (for messages, things for sale, etc) is one of the best in Africa.

A bed in a shared room costs US$2 but you must have a YHA membership card to stay. If not, you'll have to pay a temporary membership fee of US$0.90 per night or join the association for US$4.90 for a year. Any matatu or bus which goes down either Valley or Ngong Rds will drop you at Ralph Bunche Rd. The No 8 matatu which goes down Ngong Rd is probably the most convenient. You can pick it up either outside the Hilton Hotel or on the corner of Kenyatta Ave and Uhuru Highway. If you're returning to the youth hostel after dark don't be tempted to walk back from the centre of the city. Many people have been robbed. Always take a matatu or taxi.

There is both a *YMCA* (☎ 724066) and *YWCA* (☎ 724699) in Nairobi. The former is on State House Rd and the latter on Mamlaka Rd off Nyerere Rd. The YMCA costs US$5.60 for a dorm bed and US$5.80/10.50 for singles/doubles with shared facilities. Self-contained rooms are US$9.80/14. All the above rates include breakfast. Other meals are available for US$2. You must buy temporary membership to stay here which costs US$1.

The YWCA has dorm beds for US$5.40 (US$29 per month) and double rooms with shared facilities for US$6.70 (US$38 per month). It also has singles/doubles with a washbasin in the new wing for US$9.40/11 (US$51/58 per month) and doubles/family rooms with private bath in the annexe for around US$16/22 (US$89/122 per month). You also have to pay a membership fee of US$1. It take couples as well as single women.

There's also the very quiet and secure *West End Lodgings* (☎ 750524) on Kijabe Rd, which is clean and has helpful staff. It's only a few cents more than the Iqbal for a double room, yet is far removed from the noise of Latema Rd.

Camping Mrs Roche's is the only place to go if you want to camp. In the high season the limited garden space gets pretty cramped, not only with tents but also with vehicles. It costs US$1.20 per person to put up your tent.

If you want to hire camping equipment

(anything from a sleeping bag to a folding toilet seat, tent or mosquito net) the best place to go to is Atul's (☎ 225935), Biashara St. It has the lot and is open Monday to Friday from 8.30 am to noon and 2 to 5 pm and on Saturday from 8.30 am to noon and 2.30 to 4 pm. Hire charges have to be paid in full before commencement of hire as well as a deposit for each item. The deposits are refunded when hired items are returned in good condition. Identification, such as a passport, is required.

The items for hire are far too numerous to mention here, but there is a list which you can pick up for US$0.60. Advance booking is highly recommended and saves a lot of time. If you'd like a list before going to Kenya, write to PO Box 43202, Nairobi.

Places to Stay – middle
Central Nairobi The *Solace Hotel* (☎ 33-1277), is on the horrendously noisy Tom Mboya St – the matatu drivers here honk and rev their engines to drum up business, and it goes on nonstop from early morning until late at night. Rates are US$12/18 for small, self-contained single/double rooms including breakfast. It's somewhat overpriced and the extra money seems to be mainly for a carpet and phone in the room. If you do stay here make sure you get a room away from the street.

The *Sirikwa Lodge* (☎ 226687) on the corner of Munyu and Accra Rds is a good place in the middle bracket. For US$10/13 you get a clean room with bath, hot water, a phone and breakfast. Accra Rd is somewhat quieter than Tom Mboya St so this place is not a bad bet. Another quiet place is the *Africana Hotel* (☎ 220654) on Dubois Rd between Accra and Latema Rds. The rates are US$8/11 for rooms with bath, hot water and breakfast. It's good value and secure.

Further away from this area, on Tom Mboya St down towards Haile Selassie Ave, is the *Princess Hotel* (☎ 214640), which is popular with VSO volunteers. The rooms are self-contained and cost US$9/12 including a good breakfast. Like all places on Tom Mboya St, the quietest rooms are at the back,

though the street is nowhere near as noisy here as further up near Accra Rd. The hotel has its own bar and restaurant. The food is good and the staff friendly.

The *Oakwood Hotel* (☎ 220592), PO Box 40683, is on Kimathi St, right opposite the New Stanley Hotel. It's a very pleasant place to stay and there are 23 self-contained rooms which cost US$34/48 a single/double, and US$55 a triple including breakfast and all taxes. There's constant hot water, a telephone and TV with in-house movies in every room and an overnight laundry service. Other hotel facilities include a bar and restaurant.

The new *Orient Palace Hotel* (☎ 217600) on Taveta Rd is an up-market hotel in a downmarket part of town, but it represents good value at US$44/55 for self-contained air-con rooms. The hotel has a bar and a good Indian restaurant.

The *Ambassadeur Hotel* (☎ 336803), PO Box 30399, is right in the city centre on Moi Ave and is part of the Sarova Hotels chain. It has self-contained singles/doubles for US$34/44 excluding breakfast (US$4.80 extra). The hotel has a bar and, on the ground floor, a good restaurant with lunch/dinner for around US$7.

There's another group of mid-range hotels near Jeevanjee Gardens which we feel are generally better value than those on the River Rd side of Moi Ave, if only for the noise factor and the vehicle fumes, but not everyone agrees.

The *New Garden Hotel* (☎ 33445) and the *Parkside Hotel* (☎ 224033) are both on Monrovia St which runs alongside Jeevanjee Gardens. The New Garden is excellent value at US$5.80 a single with shared bath and US$8.20/9.50 for singles/doubles with private bath. Prices include breakfast. The Parkside has rooms for US$12/15 with bath, hot water and breakfast. The staff are very friendly and the hotel has its own restaurant.

Opposite the Kenya Airways terminal on Moktar Daddah St is the *Terminal Hotel* (☎ 28817), which is also popular with travellers. It offers rooms with clean sheets, hot-water bath, soap and towel for US$8.70

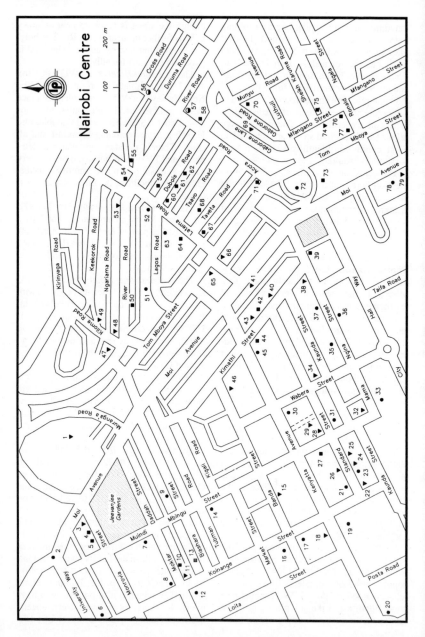

Nairobi Centre

■ PLACES TO STAY

4	Parkside Hotel
5	New Garden Hotel
10	Terminal Hotel
13	Embassy Hotel
27	Sixeighty Hotel
39	Hilton Hotel
42	Oakwood Hotel
44	New Stanley Hotel & Thorn Tree Café
50	Naseem's Lodging
54	New Kenya Lodge
55	New Kenya Lodge Annexe
58	Sirikwa Lodge
59	New Safe Life Lodging
60	Nyandarua Lodging
61	Africana Hotel
62	Bujumbura Lodge
64	Sunrise Lodge & Modern Green Day & Night Bar
67	Iqbal Hotel
68	Orient Palace Hotel
70	Al Mansura Hotel
71	Solace Hotel
73	Ambassadeur Hotel
75	Dolat Hotel
76	Terrace Hotel
77	Gloria Hotel

▼ PLACES TO EAT

1	Khyber Restaurant
3	Curry Pot
11	Goldstar Restaurant
15	African Heritage Café
18	Harvest Restaurant
22	Beneva Coffee House
24	Dragon Pearl Restaurant
25	Calypso Restaurant, Bruce House & British High Commission
26	The Pub & Akasaka Restaurant
28	Rickshaw Chinese Restaurant
29	Jacaranda Café
32	Café Helena & the Coffee Bar
34	Trattoria Restaurant
38	Foresta Magnetica
40	Jax Restaurant
41	Honey Pot
43	Supermac
44	Thorn Tree Café & New Stanley Hotel

46	Minar Restaurant
47	Dhaba Restaurant & Nyama Choma Terrace & Bar
48	Supreme & Mayur Restaurants
49	Zam Zam Restaurant
53	Bull Café
65	Growers Café
66	Nairobi Burgers
69	Malindi Dishes
74	New Bedona Café
79	Zanze Bar & Pagoda Restaurant

OTHER

2	Police Station
6	Safari Club
7	Afro Unity Bar
8	Safari Camp Services & Worldwide Adventures
9	Atul's Camping Equipment Hire
12	Kenya Airways
14	City Market
16	New Florida Nightclub
17	Air Tanzania & Air Zimbabwe (Chester House)
19	Post Office (Under Construction)
20	Immigration (Nyayo House)
21	Let's Go Travel
23	Express Kenya (American Express)
25	Bruce House & British High Commission & Calypso Restaurant
30	Barclays Bank & Ugandan High Commission
31	Central Car Hire
33	City Hall
35	Prestige Books
36	Rwandan & Somali Embassies
37	Expo Camera Centre
45	Westland Sundries Bookshop & Nation Bookshop
51	Akamba Buses
52	Bankco Tours & Travel
56	Coast Bus, Goldline, Mawingo, Malaika & Arusha Express Bus Offices
57	Matatus for Embu, Nanyuki, Isiolo
63	Nairobi Bus Union
64	Modern Green Day & Night Bar & Sunrise Lodge
72	National Archives
78	Florida 2000 Nightclub

a single, US$10.70 a double and US$11 for a twin (two single beds). There are also triples for around US$15. Breakfast is not included. Some of the rooms are getting a little tatty these days but the staff are friendly and honest, and valuables left in the rooms are safe. There's a same-day laundry service on weekdays (but not at weekends).

Close by is the *Embassy Hotel* (☎ 24087), on Biashara St between Koinange and Muindi Mbingu Sts. Rooms with bath, hot water, soap and towel, cost much the same as at the Terminal but there are also a number of cheaper, smaller singles.

Outside the Centre Most of the other mid-range hotels are along Milimani, Ralph Bunche and Bishops Rds.

Very popular indeed with travellers and expatriates on contract work is the *Heron Court Hotel* (☎ 720740), on Milimani Rd, PO Box 41848. It's a large place and excellent value at US$12/15 for singles/doubles with bathroom, hot water, soap and towels. There are also self-contained apartments with a double bedroom, separate lounge with balcony, bathroom and fully equipped kitchen for US$15/17 a single/double. Breakfast is not included in the room rates. Monthly rates come at a considerable discount. The sheets and towels are changed daily in both types of room, and the hotel facilities include a swimming pool, sauna, massage, guarded car park, shop and 24-hour laundry service. The staff here are friendly and helpful and security is excellent. At the front of the hotel is one of Nairobi's most popular bar/restaurants, Buffalo Bill's, which is open daily from early morning until around 11 pm.

Right at the top of Milimani Rd at the Ralph Bunche Rd intersection is the *Sagret Hotel* (☎ 720933), PO Box 18324, which is of a somewhat higher standard than the Heron Court and offers singles/doubles with bath for US$15/21 including breakfast. The hotel has its own bar and restaurant and accepts Visa and MasterCard.

In between the Sagret and the Heron Court

is the *Milimani Hotel* (☎ 720760), PO Box 30715. This is a huge, rambling place popular with expatriates on contract and charges US$25/33 for singles/doubles including breakfast and taxes. There are also more expensive self-contained apartments complete with fully-equipped kitchens. Facilities at the hotel include a swimming pool, bar, beer garden, restaurant and guarded parking.

On Bishops Rd at the back of the Panafric Hotel is the *Fairview Hotel* (☎ 723211), PO Box 40842. Billed as 'the country hotel in the city' (with some justification due to its pleasant garden and quiet location), it offers singles/doubles with shared bath for US$28/48 or US$34/56 with private bath. There are also family units for US$56 and balcony doubles for US$63. All the rooms have a telephone, TV and video service, and prices include breakfast. Other meals average around US$4.70 (set menu) and there's an authentic African buffet every Tuesday and Friday for the same price. The bar has draught Tusker. Guests are entitled to use the swimming pool at the Panafric Hotel.

Further afield, close to Nairobi Hospital, is the *Silver Springs Hotel* (☎ 722451), PO Box 61362, with reasonable singles/doubles at US$26/30.

The *Hurlingham Hotel* (☎ 721920), PO Box 43158, on Argwings Kodhek Rd, west of the Hurlingham shopping centre, is also a popular place to stay. Long-established, it exudes a rustic charm and is set in its own grounds but it's small and often full. Many of the people who stay here return time and time again, so it's best to ring in advance and make sure a room is available. There's a bar and restaurant and it costs much the same as the Silver Springs Hotel.

Places to Stay – top end
In a city the size of Nairobi there are naturally many top-range hotels, some of them in the city centre and others outside this immediate area. If you are planning on staying in one it is worth booking through one of the travel agencies in town instead of

paying the so-called 'rack rates' as an agency can often get you a considerable discount. At the Serena, for example, it's possible to get a discount of nearly 40% by booking through United Touring Company.

Central Nairobi In the centre of town, on Muindi Mbingu St between Standard St and Kenyatta Ave, is the *Sixeighty Hotel* (☎ 332680), PO Box 43436. This is a large modern hotel and good value at US$44/67 for singles/doubles without breakfast. Better value and with considerably better facilities is the *Boulevard Hotel* (☎ 227567), on Harry Thuku Rd (PO Box 42831). It offers rooms with bathroom, balcony, telephone and radio for US$54/63 a single/double, US$70 a triple including taxes but excluding breakfast. Facilities include a swimming pool, tennis court, restaurant, barbecue, bar, and beer garden.

Also in the centre is the *New Stanley Hotel* (☎ 333233), PO Box 30680, on the corner of Kimathi St and Kenyatta Ave. It was built in 1907 and despite numerous subsequent renovations still has a touch of colonial charm. Singles/doubles (including breakfast and taxes) cost US$79/94 plus there are suites ranging from US$100 to US$180. Facilities include a rooftop swimming pool and, at street level, the popular Thorn Tree Café, though the food is mediocre and service can be agonisingly slow.

The *Hilton Hotel*, PO Box 30624, (☎ 33-4000), on Mama Ngina St near Moi Ave, has all the usual Hilton facilities including a rooftop swimming pool yet, despite the relatively high price, some of the rooms are surprisingly gloomy and tatty. Singles here go for US$98 to US$131 and doubles for US$121 to US$168 plus taxes (30% in total). The nearby *Intercontinental Hotel* (☎ 33-5550), PO Box 30353, on City Hall Way, is similarly priced and was recently refurbished.

Outside the Centre A little outside of the city centre where Kenyatta Ave turns into Valley Rd is the *Panafric Hotel* (☎ 720822),

PO Box 30486. Part of the Sarova Hotels chain, it's a huge, multistorey modern hotel with all the facilities you'd expect. Rooms here cost US$60/80 a single/double, plus there are more expensive suites. Prices include breakfast and all taxes.

Not far from here is the much smaller, more intimate *Lenana Mount Hotel* (☎ 71-7044), on Ralph Bunche Rd between Milimani and Lenana Rds (PO Box 40943). It's a brand new place and has singles/doubles for US$58/75, as well as superior rooms for US$63/81 including all taxes. Breakfast costs extra.

Also outside the centre in Westlands off Waiyaki Way is the *Jacaranda Hotel* (☎ 448713), PO Box 47557, which is part of the Block Hotels chain. (For reservations, contact Rehema House (☎ 335807; fax 340541), PO Box 47667, Nairobi.) It's a pleasant place to stay and offers singles/doubles for US$50/72 with breakfast, plus there are more expensive triples and suites. Facilities include an imaginative bar, restaurant and a free shuttle bus service into the centre.

At the top of the line are two hotels: the *Norfolk Hotel* (☎ 3355422), PO Box 40064, on Harry Thuku Rd, and the *Nairobi Serena Hotel* (☎ 725111), PO Box 46302, on the edge of Central Park between Kenyatta Ave and Nyerere Rd. The Norfolk is the oldest of Nairobi's hotels – it was built in 1904 – and was *the* place to stay in the old days. It's still extremely popular among those with a taste for nostalgia and the money to spend. All the olde worlde charm has been retained despite facilities having been brought up to international standards. Singles/doubles in the main block cost US$150/160 plus there are suites for US$195 and luxury double cottages for US$290. Breakfast is not included. Meals range from US$9 (breakfast) to US$13 (lunch/dinner). The Norfolk, which is owned by Lonrho Hotels, has a popular terrace bar and restaurant.

The Nairobi Serena is a much more recent hotel and imaginatively designed. It's owned by the Serena Lodges group and has singles/doubles for US$143/175. It has all the facilities you'd expect from a five-star hotel. Even Jimmy Carter stays here.

Places to Eat

For most people with limited means, lunch is the main meal of the day and this is what the cheaper restaurants cater for. That doesn't mean that they're all closed in the evening (though quite a few are). It does mean, however, that what is available in the early evening is often what is left over from lunch time and the choice is limited. If you want a full meal in the evening it generally involves a splurge or eating from a barbecue attached to a bar.

Nairobi is replete with restaurants offering cuisines from all over the world – Italian, Spanish, Japanese, Chinese, Korean, Indian, Lebanese, and Thai. There are also steak houses, seafood specialists, etc and at many places the prices are surprisingly reasonable. For around US$8 per person you can eat well at quite a few of them. For US$10 to US$15 per person you could eat very well at almost all of them and if you spent that much at some of them you'd hardly need to eat anything the next day.

While there is a good selection of restaurants in the city centre, increasing numbers of restaurants are opening up in the suburbs, which makes it difficult if you don't have transport. The two main eating centres away from the downtown area are the Westlands shopping centre, just a km or so north of the centre along Uhuru Highway, and the new Yaya Centre, about three km from the centre on Argwings Kodhek Rd in Hurlingham.

Cheap Restaurants There are a lot of very cheap cafés and restaurants in the Latema Rd/River Rd area and at the top end of Tom Mboya St where you can pick up a very cheap, traditional African breakfast of mandazi (a semisweet doughnut) and tea or coffee. Most of these places would also be able to fix you up with eggs and the like. Since many of them are Indian-run, they also have traditional Indian breakfast foods like samosa and idli (rice dumplings) with a sauce.

For good local food the restaurant in the *Iqbal Hotel* is very popular and is something of a meeting place for travellers. The mkate mayai (minced meat pancake) is excellent, although it does come served with a curious side plate of shredded lettuce with tomato sauce! One gets the feeling that the animals and birds used in the stews here died of plain old age, but the cabbage and potato stew is very good.

The *Malindi Dishes* restaurant in Gaborone Rd is well worth trying at least once. As the name suggests, the food here has the Swahili influence of the coast, and so coconut and spices are used to rev up what is otherwise pretty ordinary cuisine. Main dishes are around US$2, and the usual snacks and burgers are also available.

Also in this area is the *New Bedona Café* opposite the Dolat Hotel on Mfangano St. The food here is mostly fried, but it's cheap and the place is kept very clean. Another ultra-cheap café which is fairly popular is the *Bull Café* around the corner from the New Kenya Lodge on Ngariama Rd.

For a good solid meal (mixing Western and local cuisine) such as steak and matoke (mashed plantains and maize) or maharagwe (kidney beans), try the *Café Helena* on Mama Ngina St opposite the City Hall. It's only open at lunch time and is popular with businesspeople. Meals are priced at around US$2 and are excellent value. The *Coffee Bar* next door is similar although more expensive. Another place at this end of town is the *Beneve Coffee House* on the corner of Standard and Koinange Sts. It has a tasty selection of instant food ranging from stews to curries, fish & chips, sambusa, pasties and a host of other choices. It's self-service and good value.

Very popular with the lunch-time business crowd and said to be one of the cheapest places in Nairobi for the quality of food it offers is the *Jacaranda Café* in the Phoenix House Arcade between Kenyatta Ave and Standard St. A hamburger, chips and salad costs just US$1.50! Similar are the ramshackle wooden eateries between the Railway Museum and Haile Selassie Ave which are jammed with local office workers in three-piece suits at lunch time. It's quite a sight!

If you're staying at Mrs Roche's up in Parklands, the *Stop 'n' Eat* tin shed just up the road offers ugali (maize meal) and ngombe (beef) at very modest prices.

Kenya is the home of all-you-can-eat lunches at a set price and Nairobi has a wide choice of them, most offering Indian food. One of the best is the *Supreme Restaurant* on River Rd, which offers excellent Indian vegetarian food for US$2.50 depending on whether you want the ordinary or the 'delux' lunch and whether you want dessert. It also has superb fruit juices.

In the Harambee Plaza building on the corner of Uhuru Highway and Haile Selassie Ave, the *Caboose Restaurant* does an 'African buffet' on Wednesday from 12.30 to 3 pm for US$4, while on other weekdays the usual 'businessman's buffet' costs US$3.

The *African Heritage Café*, which you reach through the African Heritage shop on Kenyatta Ave or through a separate entrance on Banda St, is also highly recommended for lunch. There are actually two parts to the restaurant – the main room adjoining Banda St which tends to be somewhat gloomy and is more expensive and the much lighter barbecue grill in the centre of the building. The food in the barbecue section is excellent and there's a choice of meat, fish or chicken which comes complete with chips and salad. Reckon on spending around US$3 for a meal. Get here early if you don't want to wait for a table as it's a popular place to eat.

The restaurant at *The Pub* underneath the Sixeighty Hotel, on Standard St between Muindi Mbingu and Koinange Sts, offers Western dishes such as steak and chicken, but at US$5 and up, these are not particularly good value. Lunch is served from noon to 2 pm and dinner from 6 to 11 pm. You can get much better value across the road at *Calypso* in the basement of Bruce House. Here you can choose from a limited set menu (including meat and seafood) and it won't cost you more than US$2.50. It's a popular

place to eat at lunch times. Try the fish pili pili–it's delicious.

Another good place to go for lunch and well cooked, straightforward food is the *Harvest* on Kenyatta Ave between Koinange and Loita Sts. It's a very pleasant spot to eat.

Jax Restaurant on the 1st floor of the Old Mutual building, Kimathi St, is a very popular place for lunch. It offers a wide selection of beautifully prepared hot meals, a salad buffet and Goan specialities in various dining areas, including an open-air section. There's a licensed bar and you can eat well for US$2.50 and up. It's open from 8 am to 5 pm Monday to Friday, 8 am to 5 pm on Saturday but closed on Sunday and public holidays.

Any of the *Minar* chain of up-market Indian restaurants are a great place to head for on Sunday at lunch time as they do a US$4.50 all-you-can-eat buffet. The food is excellent, the service attentive and there's a good range of both Indian and continental dishes. There are branches on Tom Mboya and Banda Sts in the centre of town, and in the Yaya Centre (1st floor) on Argwings Kodhek Rd, Hurlingham.

Fast Food That well known English staple, fish & chips, has caught on in a big way in Nairobi and there are scores of places offering it. They're all cheap but the quality varies from grease ad nauseam to excellent.

Very popular at lunch time for fish & chips is *Supermac* on Kimathi St, directly opposite the Thorn Tree Café on the mezzanine floor of the shopping centre there. It not only offers some of the best fish & chips in Nairobi, but also serves sausages, salads and fruit juices. Get there early if you don't want to queue.

Also recommended for this type of fast food is the *Prestige Restaurant*, in Tsavo Lane off Latema Rd, which offers large servings of sausage, chips and salad for US$2. It's popular with local people.

The hamburger is all-conquering in Nairobi too, though, surprisingly, none of the US chains have got a foothold in Kenya yet. Too much competition from Indian entrepreneurs perhaps? What has got a solid foothold is the *Wimpy* chain which has branches on Kenyatta Ave, Tom Mboya St and Mondlane St. These places have the usual range of snacks and meals (burgers, sausages, eggs, fish, chicken, milkshakes, etc) costing up to US$4 and are open from 7.30 am to 9.30 pm. Another good café for a meal of burgers, fish or chicken with a mountain of chips and salad for around US$2.50 is *Nairobi Burgers* on Tom Mboya St right opposite the end of Latema Rd. Sweets, soups and ice cream are also served – it's a very popular place.

Also on Tom Mboya St, down near the Princess Hotel, is the fairly new *Pipes Restaurant*. This is a US-style fast-food place with all the usual junk-food snacks.

Breakfast The *Growers Café* on Tom Mboya St is deservedly popular with both local people and travellers and the prices are reasonable. Food on offer includes eggs (boiled or fried), sausages and other hot foods, fruit salads (with or without yoghurt) and good coffee. Another popular breakfast place is the *Honey Pot* on Moi Ave. Here a breakfast of eggs, sausages, juice, toast, jam and tea or coffee is US$1.40.

If you're staying in the Koinange St area, the *Goldstar Restaurant* on the corner of Koinange and Moktar Daddah Sts is a good place for breakfast. For US$1.40 you get juice, cornflakes, eggs, toast, jam and tea or coffee. For a little extra, you can also get bacon and a sausage. Very similar is *Calypso* in the basement of Bruce House on Standard St where you can get an English-style breakfast for the same price.

For a breakfast splurge, try one of the buffets at a major hotel. The *Illiki Café* on the ground floor of the Ambassadeur Hotel on Moi Ave is excellent value. Here you can make a total pig of yourself for US$5. It offers the works – a variety of juices, milk, yoghurt, cereals, porridge, eggs, bacon, beans, sausages, toast, fruits, cakes, you name it.

Most of the other top-end hotels also do buffet breakfasts, although they are more expensive. The best value is offered by the *New Stanley Hotel* where a buffet brekky costs US$7.20. At the *Hilton* you're looking at US$7.50 while the *Intercontinental* charges US$8 and is probably the poorest value among these places.

Mid-Range Restaurants The choice here is legion and spans just about every cuisine in the world. Most of them are mentioned in the *Kenya Tourist Guide* and *Tourists' Kenya* though there's no indication of prices.

Most of the more expensive restaurants are licensed and offer beer, wine and spirits but the major exceptions are the Indian vegetarian restaurants which usually offer only fruit juices and tea or coffee.

Virtually all these restaurants accept one or more international credit cards.

Indian One of the best places in Nairobi for North Indian tucker is the *Dhaba Restaurant* at the top end of Tom Mboya St. A lot of work and thought has gone into the décor here with some fine watercolour murals of Punjabi rural life and ceilings made of mangrove poles and plaster. It's very popular among Indian families, which is a good indication of the quality of the food. The house specialities are the taka-taka meat dishes, which take their name from the noise which comes from the tandoori kitchen as the chef prepares the meat with huge cleavers. Main dishes are in the range of US$3.80 to US$4.50, so expect a full meal to come to around US$7 per person with drinks.

The *Mayur Restaurant* (☎ 331586), above the Supreme Restaurant (see Cheap Restaurants) has been famous for superb Indian vegetarian food for years. It's not bad value at US$4.30 but the hushed atmosphere is a bit daunting. Also excellent is the *Minar Restaurant* (☎ 229999), in Banda St, which specialises in Mughlai dishes and offers buffet lunches and à la carte dinners. Expect to pay around US$8 for a three-course dinner including coffee. The restaurant is licensed, the service friendly and the restaurant is open from noon to 2 pm and 7 to 10.30 pm daily. It also has branches in Tom Mboya St and the Yaya Centre (1st floor) in Hurlingham.

The *Zam Zam Restaurant* (☎ 212128), just off Kilome Rd near the top end of River Rd, is a new place with pleasing décor and good service. The food is good, and remarkably cheap, yet this place remains relatively poorly patronised, perhaps because of its location close to River Rd. Main dishes are all under US$3 and the servings are generous.

Another good and cheap place is the *Safeer Restaurant* in the Ambassadeur Hotel. Despite appearances, this place is not expensive and two people can eat well here for US$6 including a couple of beers. The food is mainly north Indian, and there are complimentary salads, chutney and pickle.

At the Meridien Court Hotel on Muranga'a Rd near the top end of Moi Ave, the *Khyber Restaurant* (☎ 225585) also specialises in Mughlai dishes and offers a buffet lunch. Dinner choices include tandoori chicken, lamb or fish, other special lamb or chicken dishes, seafood, vegetarian dishes and the usual range of Indian breads and sweets. It's licensed and open from 12.30 to 2.30 pm and 7 to 10.30 pm daily including holidays.

West African The *West African Paradise Restaurant* (☎ 741396) is in Rank Xerox House in Westlands. It offers a wide range of food from a number of West African countries and dishes include poulet yassa (chicken with onions and garlic sauce), jollof (rice with onions), and fufu (maize). It's quite different food and is well worth a try if you haven't been to West Africa. The restaurant is open daily from 9.30 am to 9.30 pm.

Chinese Nairobi has a reasonable selection of Chinese restaurants although none of them are cheap. One of the best is the *Hong Kong Restaurant* (☎ 228612) in Kenya House on Koinange St. The soups here at US$2.50 make a meal in themselves, but if you have room for more, main dishes cost around US$2.50 to US$3. This is a surprisingly popular place, especially at lunch time and on Sunday nights.

In Shankardas House, on Moi Ave near the Kenya Cinema, is the recently renovated *Pagoda Restaurant* (☎ 227936). Again, the food here is mainly Szechuan, and you can expect a complete meal to come to around US$8 with drinks.

The *Dragon Pearl* (☎ 340451), in Bruce House on Standard St, also has good Chinese food at prices comparable to the other more expensive restaurants.

Rated as the best Chinese restaurant in town by residents is the *Rickshaw Chinese Restaurant* (☎ 223604), in Fedha Towers, Standard St. It has an extensive menu and the food is delicious. Prices are comparable with the other Chinese restaurants.

Mongolian The only place you'll find this cuisine at the *Manchurian Restaurant* (☎ 444263), Brick Court, on the corner of Mpak Rd and Brookside Drive in Westlands. Here you choose from a range of marinated meats, vegetables, condiments and spices and have your meal cooked in front of you on giant hot-plates. Leaving out drinks, the price is standard and you can go back as many times as you like for more of the same or something else so don't pile everything onto the first plate!

Thai Nairobi's first Thai restaurant is in the Westlands shopping centre, just a few minutes' north of the city centre along Uhuru Highway. The *Bangkok Restaurant* (☎ 75-1311), Rank Xerox House, Parklands Rd, has a good reputation and is open daily from 12.30 to 2.30 pm and 6 to 10.30 pm.

Italian For Italian food there is the long-running and very popular *Trattoria* (☎ 34-0855) on the corner of Wabera and Kaunda Sts. It is open daily from 8.30 am to 11.30 pm and both the atmosphere and the food are excellent. There's a wide choice on the menu and à la carte is available at lunch time. In the evening, it's all à la carte. A soup, main course, salad, dessert and a carafe or two of house chianti will relieve you of around US$10 per person. As you might expect, the ice cream here is superb.

Also good is the *Capolinea* in The Mall

shopping centre at Westlands. This is more of a café-style place, and this is reflected in the prices – around US$1.50 to US$3 for snacks and sandwiches. Another excellent place away from the centre is the *La Cucina* (☎ 562871) in the Yaya Centre in Hurlingham. It has everything from pasta to steak, home delivery is available, and there's an attached wine bar.

Also worth a try is the *Marino Restaurant* (☎ 227150), 1st Floor, National Housing Corporation Bldg, Aga Khan Walk, just off Haile Selassie Ave. It has a spacious interior dining area as well as an open-air patio and is open from 9 am to 2 pm and 7 to 10 pm Monday to Saturday; closed on Sunday. There's a wide range of Italian and continental dishes available with main courses priced from US$3 to US$5.

The best of the lot by far, and marginally the most expensive, is the *Foresta Magnetica* (☎ 728009) on the 1st floor of Corner House, at the junction of Mama Ngina and Kimathi Sts. The food here is delicious and beautifully presented plus there's a live band each evening which plays a mixture of Western and African music and, when the majority of people have finished eating, you are free to dance. Check it out by having a drink at the Picino Bar (in the centre of the restaurant) first. A meal will set you back US$10 to US$20 per person depending on whether you have wine. It's open daily until 2 am except on Sunday.

Greek The *Spyros Wine Bar & Taverna* (☎ 750202) is out of the centre in Brick Court, Mpaka Rd, Westlands. It's not cheap, but there's often live entertainment, and plenty of authentic touches, including retsina – at US$15 a bottle!

At the Yaya Centre in Hurlingham there's the *Sugar & Spice (Zorba the Treat)* (☎ 562876), which is a much more modest place serving a wide variety of snacks.

Japanese There's one Japanese restaurant in the city centre, the *Akasaka* (☎ 333948), which you'll find next to The Pub on Standard St between Koinange and Muindi

Mbingu Sts. As you might expect, it's done out in traditional Japanese style and there's even a tatami room which you can reserve in advance though mostly it's table and chairs. It offers the full range of Japanese cuisine including tempura, teriyaki and sukiyaki as well as soups and appetisers. A full meal will cost US$6 to US$10 per person. It's licensed and open daily from 12.30 to 2 pm for box lunches, and from 6 to 9 pm for dinner.

Korean The only Korean restaurant in Nairobi is the *Restaurant Koreana* in the Yaya Centre, Hurlingham. A full meal costs around US$12 and the restaurant is licensed. It's open from noon to 2.30 pm and 6 to 10.30 pm Monday to Saturday and closed Sunday.

Ethiopian The *Daas* Ethiopian restaurant is in an old house, some distance from the centre off Ngong Rd (signposted) and not far from the Adams Arcade shopping centre. The décor includes many Ethiopian artefacts and there's often live music in the evenings. Meals are based around excellent unleavened bread and are eaten with the fingers. Expect to pay around US$6 per person for a full meal including drinks.

Seafood The best seafood restaurant in Nairobi is the *Tamarind* (☎ 338959) in the National Bank building on Aga Khan Walk, between Harambee and Haile Selassie Aves. It offers a wide selection of exotic seafood dishes, and culinary influences range from European to Asian to coastal Swahili. The cuisine is superb as are the surroundings which are decorated in a sumptuous Arabic-Moorish style. Eating here is definitely a major night out as most main courses are priced well over US$7.50 with crab and prawn dishes up to US$15. There's also a special vegetarian menu. It's open for lunch Monday to Saturday from 12.30 to 1.45 pm and daily for dinner from 6.30 to 9.45 pm.

Western The best restaurant for plain meat and vegie dishes (eg sausages and mashed potato) is the *Zanze Bar* (☎ 222532) on the top floor of the Kenya Cinema Plaza, Moi

Ave, though a range of other dishes are also available. It's open for lunch and dinner daily but is not strictly a restaurant alone – more a combination of bar, wine bar, live music venue and restaurant. You can also play chess, darts and backgammon here. The food is good, reasonably priced (around US$3 per person), but you must pay an extra US$2.20 entry in the evenings (free during the day).

Nyama Choma For steak eaters who haven't seen a decent doorstep since they left Argentina, Australia, Uruguay or the USA and are looking for a gut-busting extravaganza then there's no better place than the *Carnivore* (☎ 501709), out at Langata just past Wilson Airport. To get there take bus Nos 14, 24 or 124 and tell the conductor where you are going; the restaurant is a one-km signposted walk from where you are dropped off. It's easy to hitch back into the centre when you're ready to go. Otherwise, negotiate for a taxi. Whether it's lunch or dinner you take there's always beef, pork, lamb, ham, chicken, sausages and at least one game meat (often wildebeest or zebra). The roasts are barbecued on Maasai spears and the waiters carve off hunks onto your plate until you tell them that you have enough. Prices include salads, bread, desserts and coffee. Meals here can be surprisingly cheap given the amount you receive and you're looking at US$11 for lunch from Monday to Saturday and US$13 on Sunday; dinner is priced at US$13 daily. This is a very popular tourist restaurant and the car park is usually overflowing with tourist buses.

For something a little less extravagant there's the *Nyama Choma Terrace & Bar*, above the Dhaba Restaurant at the top end of

Jamia Mosque

Tom Mboya St. This is a great little place which has nyama choma as well as a number of other Kenyan dishes, and it's dirt cheap.

Highly rated by residents, particularly Africans, is the nyama choma at the *Sagret Hotel*, Milimani Rd. Any day of the week you pass here, you'll see clouds of delicious-smelling smoke rising from the restaurant. The food is OK, relatively cheap and there's usually a good crowd.

For authentic, no-frills Nairobi nyama choma the only place to go is the suburb of Kilmichael, some distance from the centre out past Pangani and Eastleigh. It's certainly not for the squeamish as the goats are slaughtered only a few metres away from where you eat and are then barbecued right in front of you, but there's no doubting the freshness of the meat! This is not a place to go to alone, however, as the people here are not used to seeing *wazungu* and while it's not threatening, it's best to be in the company of a reliable Kenyan. You probably wouldn't find it on your own anyway. There are African prices, as you might expect.

Entertainment

Cinema Nairobi is a good place to take in a few films and at a price substantially lower than what you'd pay back home, but if you don't want scratched films then go to one of the better cinemas such as *The Kenya* on Moi Ave, or *The Nairobi* or *20th Century* on Mama Ngina St. The cheaper ones are on Latema Rd and include the *Odeon* and *Embassy*. There are also two good drive-ins if you have the transport, both have snack bars and bars. Nairobi is also a good place to see an Indian film. If you've never seen one of these then treat yourself one evening. If you have seen them before, you won't need persuading! Check with local papers to see what's on.

Discos There's a good selection of discos in the centre of Nairobi. Single men may or may not find the attention of the many unattached women found in most of them to be exactly what they're looking for but there's

never any pressure other than the occasional request for a drink.

Perhaps the most popular disco in the centre of town is the *Florida 2000* on Moi Ave near City Hall Way. Entry costs US$2.20 for men (US$2.70 on Saturday) and half that for women and it's open until 6 am. Also very popular is the *New Florida* (known to resident expatriates as the 'Mad House'), on the corner of Koinange and Banda Sts, which is a most unusually shaped building above a petrol station! Entry charges are the same as the Florida 2000 and it stays open until 5 am. There are floor shows at about 1 am at both discos but they're pretty kitsch and the dancers are obviously bored. Both discos have bars separate from the main disco areas where you can sit down, escape the noise and order a quiet drink, a snack or a meal.

Another popular disco in the centre is *Visions* on Kimathi St which is open daily except Monday from 9 pm. Less popular but probably just as good is the *Hollywood* on Moktar Daddah St between Koinange and Muindi Mbingu Sts where the entry charges are the same as the above. Further out of town is *Bubbles* at the International Casino, Westlands Rd, just off Uhuru Highway.

There's a live band/disco every Wednesday night at the *Carnivore* in Langata but entry costs US$3 per person. There's usually a good crowd and it makes a refreshing change from the more enclosed and crowded space of the New Florida or the Florida 2000 in town.

Beer in all these places is reasonably priced but other drinks, especially imported liquors, are more expensive. Snacks are available at all of them.

There don't appear to be any rigid dress regulations at any of the discos. Joggers and jeans are quite acceptable as are clean T-shirts, though it's probably true to say that most men wear open-necked shirts and trousers and the local women are always well turned out. Don't turn up wearing grubby clothes – you will not be well received.

Live Music The *African Heritage Café* on Banda St is a popular place to hear live bands on Saturday and Sunday afternoons between 2 and 5 pm. There's a small cover charge.

Also in town, in the next block to the Florida 2000 on Moi Ave and on the top floor of the Kenya Cinema Plaza, is the *Zanze Bar*, which has live music most nights. This bar was extremely popular when it first opened, but with a change of management and the introduction of a US$2.20 cover charge its popularity plummeted. To get the most out of this place, go in a group. Drinks are reasonably priced and the toilets (extremely clean) still have a blackboard on which you can scrawl jokes or obscenities.

Much further out of town, just below the roundabout at Dagoretti Corner on Ngong Rd, is the *Bombax Club* which has live bands every Thursday, Friday, Saturday and Sunday night. Unlike many of the other discos and bars mentioned in this section, this one is frequented mainly by local Kenyans with only a sprinkling of Whites, but the atmosphere is very friendly and convivial. Again, there's a small cover charge. To get there, take a minibus or matatu to Dagoretti Corner from Kenyatta Ave outside Nyayo House, or share a taxi (about US$4).

Bars The *Thorn Tree Café* in the New Stanley Hotel on the corner of Kimathi St and Kenyatta Ave is a bit passé these days but is still something of a meeting place for travellers. The service is generally supercilious and snail-like in pace. Perhaps this is just a ploy by the management to discourage 'shabby' travellers who might lower the tone of the place. Whatever the case, if you sit down between 11 am and 2 pm and 5 and 7 pm for a drink you'll have to order something to eat as well. The best thing about the Thorn Tree is the notice board where you can leave personal messages (but not advertisements of any kind, such as things for sale, or a request for people to join a safari).

Another popular bar (where you don't have to buy a meal in order to have a beer) is *The Pub* on Standard St between Koinange and Muindi Mbingu Sts. It's designed to resemble an English pub (in which it fails miserably) and the beer fridge is a museum piece which rarely has the full range of Kenya Breweries products. Nevertheless, it attracts a remarkable cross section of the population, including people from the British High Commission opposite. It's open from 11 am to 11 pm daily. If you're a single man looking for some action, there are usually plenty of unattached women but it does vary from day to day. That doesn't mean it's solely a pick-up joint – you'll see quite a few businessmen downing a quick beer or three at lunch time. The Pub is part of the Sixeighty Hotel which has another open-air bar, the *Terrace Bar*, on the 1st floor above the entrance lobby.

The liveliest bar in Nairobi by far, however, is *Buffalo Bill's* at the Heron Court Hotel, Milimani Rd. It even got a three-paragraph mention in the National Geographic magazine in May 1990 in an article describing the rift valley. Decked out with mock, denim-covered wagons surrounding a central bar and recently taken over by a resilient Frenchman (Fabrice), it's extremely popular with a wide variety of resident expatriates (who are engaged in all manner of professions), tourists, and locals. It's *the* place to go if you're single, but just as much fun for a couple. While it's open all day, every day, until around 11 pm, it only livens up from about 5.30 pm onwards. Most of the women you see here migrate to the Florida 2000 once the bar closes. Meals and snacks are available throughout the day up until around 11 pm. (It's also here that the familiar Nairobi refrain, 'Just imagine! No problem!' originated. You'll undoubtedly meet the originators: Margaret Zemei, 'Cutie' and Gladys.) This is also one of the favourite bars of safari operators in Nairobi.

For an unparalleled spit-and-sawdust binge, put aside a whole evening to join the beer-swilling, garrulous hordes at the *Modern Green Day & Night Bar*, on Latema Rd next to the Sunrise Lodge. This place rages 24 hours a day, 365 days a year and the front door has never been closed since 1968 – except for one day in 1989 during a national census. All human life is here and you need stamina to survive it – teenage girls chewing *miraa* (stimulating leafy twigs and shoots), hustlers, whores, dope dealers and what one traveller once described as 'lowlife Whites'. The jukebox is always on full blast with screaming Indian vocalists or African reggae and the bar is completely encased in heavy duty wire mesh with a tiny hole through which money goes first and beer comes out afterwards. It's a great night out but is definitely not for the squeamish. The back bar is quieter and you're more likely to meet someone whose brains are intact, but this cannot be guaranteed. Beers are always warm.

There are plenty of other African bars which are not quite so wearing on the average person's sensibilities but are still African bars where you're unlikely to see another White. People here are generally very friendly but, in terms of getting back home, it's probably best you go along with a Kenyan friend. Try *Disneys* or the *Heathrow* along Juja Rd, Pangani.

Those looking for more genteel surroundings in which to sip their beer could try the *Ngong Hills Hotel* on Ngong Rd, the beer gardens at the *Boulevard* or *Jacaranda* hotels, or the terrace bar at the *Norfolk Hotel*. Be wary of going for a drink at either the *Big Five* (Intercontinental Hotel) or the *Jockey Club* (Hilton Hotel) unless you have money to burn. At the former, a beer costs US$2.80 (3½ times the normal price).

Theatre At the *Phoenix Theatre*, Parliament Rd, the auditorium is small and the acting professionally competent but it's quite expensive. Check with local papers to see what's on.

Things to Buy

Nairobi is a good place to pick up souvenirs although you do need to shop around. The City Market on Muindi Mbingu St has a good range of items, particularly kiondo baskets, and there's a whole gaggle of stalls in Kigali St behind the Jamia Mosque. It's all a bit of a tourist trap and you need to bargain fiercely.

Even though they originated in Tanzania (and they're still much cheaper there), makonde woodcarvings have caught on in a big way in Nairobi and the shops are full of them. At the cheaper end of the market, however, it's worth looking at the examples which hawkers bring around to the bars where tourists congregate. Buffalo Bill's at the Heron Court Hotel is one of the best places. The quality of the carving varies a lot, but if you're not in a hurry then you can find some really fine examples at bargain-basement prices. Expect to pay around half to two-thirds of the price first asked.

If you're not into bargaining, or want top-quality stuff, there are plenty of 'fixed-price' souvenir shops around, although even at these they'll usually give you a 'special price' if you are obviously not a Hilton hopper. One of the better shops is on the corner of Kaunda and Wabera Sts, and another on Tubman Rd near the corner of Muindi Mbingu St.

If you want to get kitted out in the latest designer 'White hunter' safari gear, there are literally dozens of shops selling all the requisite stuff at outrageous prices.

The Spinners Web describes itself as a 'consignment handicraft shop' which sells goods made in workshops and by self-help groups around the country. They have some superb items, including hand-knitted jumpers, all sorts of fabrics and the huge Turkana baskets. The shop is on Kijabe Rd, around the corner from the Norfolk Hotel.

The gift shop of the East African Wildlife Society in the arcade of the Hilton Hotel has a range of souvenirs and interesting knick-knacks, many of them with an animal theme. It's well worth shopping here as the proceeds go towards conserving Kenya's wildlife rather than to conserving the lifestyle of rich Kenyans.

For a much less touristy atmosphere try the Kariokor Market east of the centre on Racecourse Rd in Eastleigh. It's a few minutes' ride by bus.

a	b
c	d	e
f	g

a GC   e GC
b TW   f GC
c GC   g TW
d GC

Nairobi (TW)

Getting There & Away

Air Airlines with offices in Nairobi include:

Aeroflot
    Corner House, Mama Ngina St (☎ 220746)
Air Botswana
    Hilton Hotel (☎ 331648)
Air France
    Fedha Towers, Muindi Mbingu (☎ 217512)
Air India
    Bharati House, Harambee Ave (☎ 334788)
Air Madagascar
    Hilton Hotel (☎ 225286)
Air Malawi
    Sixeighty Hotel, Muindi Mbingu St (☎ 333683)
Air Mauritius
    Union Towers, Moi Ave (☎ 229166/7)
Air Rwanda
    Mama Ngina St (☎ 332225)
Air Tanzania
    Chester House, Koinange St (☎ 336224)
Air Zaïre
    Arrow Motors, Monrovia St (☎ 222271)
Air Zimbabwe
    Chester House, Koinange St (☎ 339522)
Alitalia
    Hilton Hotel (☎ 224362)
British Airways
    International House, Mama Ngina St (☎ 334362)
EgyptAir
    Hilton Arcade (☎ 227887)
El-Al Airlines
    KCS House, Mama Ngina St (☎ 228123)
Ethiopian Airlines
    Bruce House, Standard St (☎ 330837)
Gulf Air
    International House, Mama Ngina St (☎ 214444)
Iberia Airlines
    Hilton Hotel (☎ 331648)
Japan Airlines (JAL)
    International House, Mama Ngina St (☎ 220591)
Kenya Airways
    Nationwide House, Koinange St (☎ 229271)
KLM
    Fedha Towers, Muindi Mbingu St (☎ 332673)
Lignes Aerienne (Seychelles)
    Rehema House (☎ 340481)
Lufthansa
    IPS Bldg, Kimathi St (☎ 335819)
Olympic Airways
    Hilton Hotel (☎ 338026)
Pakistan International Airlines (PIA)
    ICEA Bldg, Banda St (☎ 333900)
Qantas Airways
    Rehema House, Kaunda St (☎ 213221)
Sabena
    International House, Mama Ngina St (☎ 222185)

South African Airways
    Lonrho House, Standard St (☎ 229663)
Sudan Airlines
    UTC Bldg, General Kago St (☎ 225129)
Swissair
    Corner House, Kimathi St (☎ 331012)
Uganda Airlines
    Uganda House, Kenyatta Ave (☎ 221354)
Zambia Airways
    Lonrho House, Standard St (☎ 224722)

Kenya Airways is the main domestic carrier and operates from Nairobi's Jomo Kenyatta International Airport. There are 10 flights weekly to Kisumu (USS$44 one way), 14 flights weekly to Malindi (US$65 one way) and 55 flights weekly to Mombasa (US$65 one way). Fares and can be paid either in US dollars or in local currency (it makes them considerably cheaper if you pay in the latter).

Make sure you reconfirm flights 48 hours before departure and remember that delays are frequent on Kenya Airways.

There are several private aviation companies operating light aircraft which also connect Nairobi with Mombasa, Malindi, Lamu, Nanyuki, Nyeri, Kisumu and the national parks/reserves of Amboscli, Masai Mara, Samburu and Kiwayu (north of Lamu). These airlines also normally connect Nairobi with Eldoret and Turkana but these services are temporarily suspended. The companies include Eagle Aviation, Prestige Air Services and Air Kenya Aviation. They all operate out of Wilson Airport. There's generally at least one flight a day to each of the above destinations (except to Kiwayu which depends on demand) by each one of these companies. The services to the national parks would, of course, depend on you having a pre-booked safari (and accommodation) which included being picked up from the airstrip at an agreed time.

Let's Go Travel (☎ 340331) prints a leaflet with most of the options and prices and though it's not totally comprehensive it's worth getting hold of a copy. One-way fares to the various destinations from Nairobi are: Mombasa or Malindi (US$45), Lamu (US$112), Kiwayu (US$150), Nanyuki or Nyeri (US$63), Amboseli (US$65), Masai

Mara (US$83) and Samburu (US$97). Baggage allowance is 15 kg and excess is charged at the rate of approximately US$1 per kg.

Bus In Nairobi most long-distance bus offices are along Accra Rd near the River Rd junction. For Mombasa there are numerous companies (such as Coast Bus, Akamba, Mawingo, Goldline and Malaika) doing the run, both by day and night. They all cost around US$5, give or take US$0.50 or so, and the trip takes around eight hours with a meal break on the way.

Akamba is probably the biggest company in the country and also has the most extensive network. If you must travel by bus, it's probably the safest and most reliable company. The office is conveniently located on Lagos Rd, just off Latema Rd and very close to Tom Mboya St. Apart from the Mombasa service, it also has daily connections to Isiolo, Nyeri, Nanyuki, Chogoria, Embu and Kisumu. If you're heading for Uganda there is a daily Akamba bus direct to Kampala. It leaves Nairobi at 7.30 pm and arrives in Kampala at 10 am; the fare is US$15.

The main country bus station is just off Landies Rd, about 15 minutes' walk from the budget hotel area around Latema Rd. It's a huge but reasonably well-organised place, and all the buses have their destinations displayed in the window so it's just a matter of wandering around and finding the one you want. There is at least one daily departure and often more to virtually every main town in the country, and the buses leave when full. For more details see Getting There & Away for each place.

Train Trains run from Nairobi to Mombasa every day in both directions at 5 and 7 pm and the journey takes about 13 hours. The fares on the 7 pm train are US$40 in 1st class and US$26 in 2nd class. The 5 pm train fares are slightly less.

The 7 pm train prices are for nonresidents and include dinner, breakfast and bedding (whether you want them or not – no discount if you don't want them). The corresponding fares for residents are US$28 (1st class), US$19 (2nd class) but these do not include meals and bedding. (Meals cost an extra US$3 for dinner, US$1.80 for breakfast and bedding is US$0.70.)

This is a popular run so book your tickets as far in advance as possible, although you shouldn't have any trouble a day or two before. There's also a 'deluxe' day train on Saturday at 7 am arriving in Mombasa at 8.15 pm. On Sunday it does the return from Mombasa. The fares are the same as on the 7 pm night train.

From Nairobi to the Ugandan border at Malaba there are trains on Tuesday, Friday and Saturday at 3 pm arriving at 8.30 am the next day. In the opposite direction they depart Malaba on Wednesday, Saturday and Sunday at 4 pm and arrive at 9.30 am the next day. The fares are US$22 in 1st class, US$12.50 in 2nd class and US$4.80 in 3rd class. En route to Malaba these trains go through Naivasha, Nakuru (US$7.50/4.30 in 1st/2nd class, US$1.50 3rd class), Eldoret (US$14.50/8.40) and Bungoma.

The Nairobi to Kisumu trains depart daily at 6 pm arriving at Kisumu at 8 am the next day. In the opposite direction they depart daily at 6.30 pm arriving at Nairobi at 7.35 am the next day. Depending on demand there is usually an additional train ('express') at 5.30 pm from Nairobi daily for the first week of every month (and sometimes for the second week too) which arrives at Kisumu at 6.40 am the next day. The fares are US$15 in 1st class, US$8.70 in 2nd class and US$3.10 in 3rd class. This is also a popular route and the train is often booked out weeks in advance. If that's the case you may have to rely on the extra coach which is added on the day of departure if demand warrants. Many of the carriages used on the Kisumu run are older than those used on the Nairobi to Mombasa run and are not as comfortable.

The booking office at Nairobi railway station (☎ 335160) is open from 8 am to 7 pm daily. Meals and bedding must be ordered and paid for at the time of buying your ticket, not on the train. See the Getting

Around chapter for full details of meal prices.

Nairobi railway station also has a left-luggage office which is open daily from 8 am to noon and 1 to 6.30 pm. It costs US$1 per item per day.

Share-Taxi The share-taxi is a good alternative to that dangerous and heart-stopping mode of transport – the matatu. Although you're still likely to be whisked along at breakneck speed, at least it will be in a vehicle that is not carrying twice its rated capacity and has at least a sporting chance of stopping in a hurry if the need arises. Share-taxis are usually Peugeot 504 station wagons which take seven passengers and leave when full. They are much quicker than the matatus as they go from point to point without stopping, and of course are more expensive. Like matatus, most of the share-taxi companies have their offices around the Accra and River Rds area.

DPS on Dubois Rd has daily Peugeots to Kisumu (US$8, four hours), Busia (US$11.50), Kakamega (US$9.50), Nakuru (US$7.50, two hours), Malaba on the Ugandan border (US$12), Kitale (US$11.50), and Kericho (US$7.50). On any of these services you pay an extra US$0.60 for the front seat. These departures are only in the mornings so you need to be at the office by around 7 am, and it's a good idea to book one day in advance.

Taxis for the Tanzanian border at Namanga leave from the top side of the service station on the corner of Ronald Ngala St and River Rd. They run throughout the day, take about two hours and cost US$6. (A matatu along the same route is cheaper but takes about three hours.) These days, however, most people prefer to take either a bus direct from Nairobi to Arusha, or a shuttle minibus. The Arusha Express bus leaves daily at 8.30 am and 2 pm (US$5.70) from its office on Accra Rd. The DHL shuttle minibus leaves daily at 8.30 am (US$17) and can be booked through a travel agency. Both of these take about five hours and save a lot of messing about at the border.

Car All the major companies, and many smaller ones, have offices in the city centre, and the bigger ones such as Avis and Hertz have desks at the airport. A comprehensive description of car hire, and a list of companies, can be found in the Getting Around chapter.

If you just want to hire a car for use in Nairobi and the immediate environs, try Rent a Beetle, 7th Floor, Finance House, Loita St, PO Box 60157, Nairobi (☎ 338041/5). Ask for Don Cornes or Margaret. Here you can rent a VW Beetle for just US$24 per day

---

Creative Parking
Though the wildlife parks may be Kenya's premier tourist attraction, it's worth strolling around Kenya's other park – Nairobi's kerbsides – to observe the imaginative and often unbelievable way in which drivers utilise every inch of space to park their frequently scratched and battered vehicles. It's virtually impossible to find a spot to park in central Nairobi any day during business hours except Sunday so if there's the slightest possibility of parking another vehicle between two others in any way whatsoever then someone is going to do it! This is often at 90° to the adjoining cars with no thought about what happens to either the front or back ends. Neither pavements nor parking meters are any impediment to these people or the danger of having either end wiped out by either harrassed pedestrians or kamikaze KBS bus drivers. If there's simply not an inch to spare that's just too bad and double parking becomes the order of the day. How you get a car out of this miasma is your problem – not that of the people who've boxed you in.

Parking wardens there certainly are, as well as fines for 'illegal' parking but the deterrent effect of them is minimal and, in any case, always negotiable to a degree.

The best areas to view this spectacle are between Kenyatta Ave and University Way and anywhere between Tom Mboya St and the Nairobi River. ■

with 250 km free. Insurance is optional provided the hirer signs a waiver accepting liability in the event of an accident. It's the cheapest you'll find.

Hitching For Mombasa, take bus Nos 13 or 109 as far as the airport turn-off and hitch from there. For Nakuru and Kisumu, take bus No 23 from the Hilton to the end of its route and hitch from there. Otherwise start from the junction of Chiromo Rd and Waiyaki Way (the extension of Uhuru Highway) in Westlands.

For Nanyuki and Nyeri take bus Nos 45 or 145 from the central bus station up Thika Rd to the entrance to Kenyatta College and hitch from there. Make sure you get off the bus at the college entrance and not the exit. It's very difficult to hitch from the latter. Otherwise, start from the roundabout where Thika Rd meets Forest and Muranga'a Rds.

Getting Around
To/From the Airport The Jomo Kenyatta International Airport is 15 km out of town off the road to Mombasa. The cheapest way of getting into town is on the city bus No 34 *but* (and this is a big but) you must keep your wits about you! The number of people who get ripped off on this bus doesn't bear thinking about. The usual story is that an 'instant crowd' forms, you are jostled and before you know it your bag or money pouch has been slashed or ripped off. It's not much of an introduction to Kenya to lose your valuables on the first day so take the airlines bus if you are at all hesitant. There is generally no problem catching the No 34 city bus to the airport. The fare is US$0.30 and the trip takes about 45 minutes, more in peak periods.

A safer and far more pleasant way of getting into town is the Kenya Airways bus. This leaves the airline's city terminus on Koinange St at 7, 8, 9, 10 and 11.30 am, and 12.45, 2.30, 4.45, 6.30 and 8 pm. The trip takes about 30 minutes and costs US$1.40. When coming in from the airport this bus will drop you at any of the hotels in the centre, which is great if you're jetlagged.

The third way to or from the airport is by taxi, and this is really the only option if you have a dawn or late-night flight. The standard fare is US$9. If you want to share a taxi to the airport, check out the notice boards at the Iqbal and the New Kenya Lodge.

To Wilson Airport (for light aircraft services to Malindi, Lamu, etc) take bus Nos 14, 24 or 124 from in front of Development House, Moi Ave, and elsewhere. The fare is US$0.10.

Bus Buses are the cheapest way of getting around Nairobi, but there is no great need to use them. The only ones you are likely to need are the No 34 to the airport and those mentioned in the Around Nairobi section. Forget about them in rush hours if you have a backpack – you'll never get on and if by some Herculean feat you manage to do that, you'll never get off!

Taxi Other than the fleet of brand new London cabs (which belong to the son of the most prominent politician in the country), Nairobi taxis rate as some of the most dilapidated and generally unroadworthy buckets of bolts that ever graced a city street. Taxis cannot usually be hailed on the street (because they don't cruise for passengers) but there are taxi ranks at the railway station, the National Museum, the City Market and outside most of the main hotels. At night, you'll find them outside bars and the nightclubs.

The cabs are not metered but the fares charged are remarkably standard and few cabbies attempt to overcharge, though they're reluctant to give change if it's KSh 10 or less; US$2 gets you just about anywhere within the city centre. The same would be true from Ralph Bunche or Milimani Rd to the main post office though they sometimes ask for a bit more as it involves backtracking down the other side of Haile Selassie Ave.

Outside this immediate area, the fare generally goes up to US$3.50.

Around Nairobi

NAIROBI NATIONAL PARK

This park is the most accessible of all Kenya's game parks, being only a few km from the city centre. You should set aside a morning or an afternoon to see it. As in all the game parks, you must visit it in a vehicle; walking is prohibited. This means you will either have to arrange a lift at the entrance gate with other tourists, go on a tour, or hire a car. Entry to the park costs the usual US$12 per person plus US$1.50 for a vehicle.

Nairobi National Park is the oldest park in the country, having been created in 1946. For a park so close to the city centre you can see an amazing variety of animals – with a backdrop of jumbo jets coming in to land at Jomo Kenyatta International Airport which is adjacent to the park! Gazelle, oryx, lions, zebras, giraffes, buffaloes, cheetahs and leopards are all seen regularly. Elephants are not found in this park as the habitat is unsuitable. However, it's in this park that you have one of the best chances for spotting a rhino – they are doing quite well here because poachers prefer more remote areas.

The concentrations of game are higher in the dry season when water sources outside the park have dried up. Water is more plentiful inside the park as small dams have been built on the Mbagathi River which forms the southern boundary of the park.

The **Animal Orphanage** by the main gate has a sign inside the gate which reads 'this is not a zoo' – it is. From time to time there are young abandoned animals which are nursed through to good health and then released, but basically it is just a zoo; entry is US$2.40, and US$0.60 for children.

Getting There & Away

If you want to hitch a ride through the park from the main gate, city bus No 24 from Moi Ave will get you there.

There are many companies offering tours of Nairobi National Park and there's probably not much between them. The four-hour tours usually depart twice a day at 9.30 am and 2 pm and cost from US$33 to US$40. If you hang around in front of the Hilton Hotel at around 2 pm it is often possible to get a discounted seat on a tour at the last minute as the operators try to fill the van.

Most of the tour companies also offer a daylong combined tour of the national park with a visit to the Bomas of Kenya (or the Karen Blixen Museum) and including a gargantuan lunch at the Carnivore, but it's an expensive day out at US$75.

THE BOMAS OF KENYA

The Bomas of Kenya is a cultural centre at Langata – a short way past the entrance to the national park on the right-hand side as you head south-west from Nairobi. Here you can see traditional dances and hear songs from the country's 16 ethnic groups amid authentically recreated surroundings, though the dances are all done by one group of professionals rather than representatives of the tribes themselves. There is a daily performance at 2.30 pm (4 pm at weekends). Entry costs US$4.50 for adults and US$2.10 for children. There's the usual clutter of souvenir shops around the site. If you are not on a tour, matatu No 24 from outside Development House, Moi Ave, will get you there in about half an hour.

LANGATA GIRAFFE CENTRE

The Langata Giraffe Centre is on Gogo Falls Rd about one km from the Hardy Estate shopping centre in Langata, about 18 km from central Nairobi. Here you can observe and handfeed Rothschild giraffes from a raised circular wooden structure which also houses a display of information about giraffes. It's open during school terms from 9.30 am to 5.30 pm daily. Admission costs US$1 (free to children). To get there from the centre take matatu No 24 to the shopping centre in Langata and walk from there.

KAREN BLIXEN MUSEUM

This is the farmhouse which was formerly the residence of Karen Blixen, author of *Out of Africa*, and was presented to the Kenyan

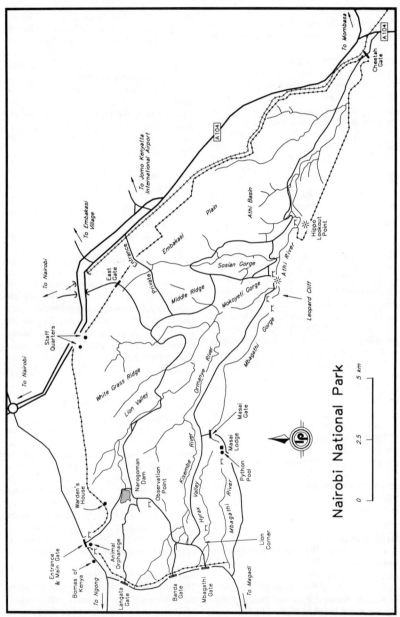

Nairobi National Park

government at independence by the Danish government along with the adjacent agricultural college. It's open daily from 9.30 am to 6 pm and entry costs US$3. It's right next door to the Karen College on Karen Rd about one km past the Karen Club as you come from Nairobi along Ngong Rd.

Getting There & Away
A No 24 matatu from Mfangano St near Hakati St will get you there in about 40 minutes at a cost of US$0.30. Alternatively, take public bus No 27 from Kenyatta Ave or from the corner of Ralph Bunche and Ngong Rds to Karen village (the shopping centre) and change to a No 24 matatu there.

NGONG HILLS
Ngong and Karen, to the west of Nairobi, along with Limuru, to the north, were the sites where many White settlers set up farms and built their houses in the early colonial days. The transformation they wrought was quite remarkable so that, even today, as you catch a glimpse of a half-timbered house through woodland or landscaped gardens full of flowering trees, you could imagine yourself to be in the Home Counties of England or some other European location. And, yes, the eucalypts which you see growing everywhere were an Australian import.

There are some excellent views over Nairobi and down into the rift valley from various points in the Ngong Hills, but it's unwise to go wandering around alone as people have been mugged here, especially at weekends. What you really need to get a feel for these areas is your own car or, alternatively, that of a resident who is willing to drive you around the place.

Horse riding is also available at Karen at a cost of US$30. Contact Let's Go Travel (☎ 340331) in Nairobi for details.

Ngong Races
Every second Sunday for most of the year there's horse racing at the Ngong Racecourse. It's a very genteel day out, and with an entry fee of US$1.10 for the members'

enclosure or just US$0.30 in the public enclosure, it's hardly going to break the bank. There's betting with the bookies or the tote, and while the odds you get are hardly going to set the world on fire, it's great fun to have a punt. You can bet as little as US$0.30 so even the most impecunious should be able to afford a flutter.

Local cynics will tell you that, like everything else in the country, all the races are rigged. It may well be true, but it hardly seems to matter. There's a good restaurant on the ground floor of the grandstand and two bars with beer at regular bar prices. If you don't have transport back to town it's easy enough to find a lift if you talk to people in the members' enclosure. Bus or matatu No 24 from the city centre goes right past the racecourse to the Karen shopping centre.

Places to Stay
There's nowhere to stay in this area of Nairobi but there is an excellent place to eat and drink. This is the *Horseman* (☎ 882033) at Karen village on Langata Rd. Here you have a choice of three restaurants (two open air and one indoors) and a very popular bar (with draught beer) all set in a leafy compound complete with its own pond and croaking frogs. It's straight out of rural Surrey, England. The food in the restaurants (one of which offers barbecued game meats) is excellent though it is relatively expensive. The bar is often packed in the evenings and usually stays open until early morning, though this cannot be guaranteed – sometimes it closes up shop when business is booming.

LIMURU
Limuru possibly has even more of a 'European' feel than the Ngong Hills, except that there are vast coffee and tea plantations blanketing the rolling hills cut by swathes of conifer and eucalypt forest. It's up here that you'll find the *Kentmere Club* (☎ (0154) 41053), Limuru Rd, Tigoni. This is the quintessential White settlers' club – even more so than the Norfolk Hotel in Nairobi.

The club consists of a series of low, intimate wooden cottages with shingle roofs connected to each other by quaint walkways and bridges. The main block is built in the same style and houses a restaurant and a superb recreation of an English country pub with low ceilings, exposed beams and log-burning fireplaces. If you'd like to rent a cottage the cost is US$30/40 for singles/doubles with shared facilities; breakfast is included in the price. It's a very peaceful place, and the restaurant is excellent.

Not far from the Kentmere Club is the *Waterfalls Inn* (☎ (0154) 40672) with its picnic site, waterfall, viewing point, restaurant and disco. Admission costs US$4.50 per car (with up to six passengers). Pony, horse and camel riding is available.

Another thing you can do in the area is to visit a tea farm. If you've never done this before then it's worth a day out. Visits are organised by Mitchell's *Kiambethu Tea Farm* (☎ (0154) 40756) at Tigoni, about 35 km north-east of Nairobi. Here you'll be shown the whole process of tea production as well as taken on an accompanied walk into the forest to see the colobus monkeys. Visits here come in a package which includes pre-lunch drinks and a three-course lunch, all for around US$15 per person. Groups are preferred and visits are by prior arrangement only.

Getting There & Away

KBS public bus No 116 will take you fairly close to the farm. If you have your own transport then take Limuru Rd (C62) past City Park and turn left at Muthaiga roundabout. Seven km further on you reach Ruaka

Fourteen Falls on the Mbagathi River

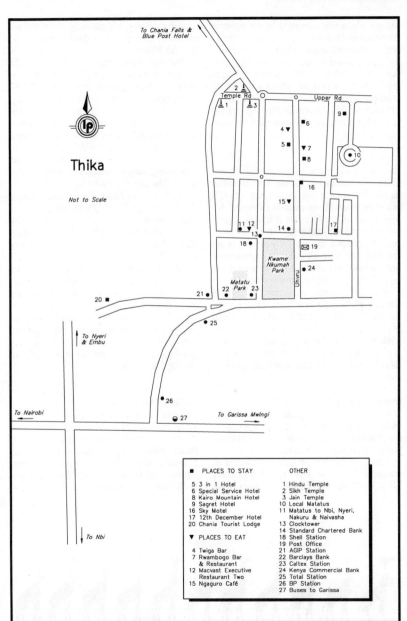

Thika

Not to Scale

To Chania Falls &
Blue Post Hotel

Temple Rd

Upper Rd

Kwame
Nkumah
Park

Matatu
Park

Uhuru

To Nyeri
& Embu

To Nairobi

To Garissa Mwingi

To Nbi

■ PLACES TO STAY	OTHER
5 3 in 1 Hotel	1 Hindu Temple
6 Special Service Hotel	2 Sikh Temple
8 Kairo Mountain Hotel	3 Jain Temple
9 Sagret Hotel	10 Local Matatus
16 Sky Motel	11 Matatus to Nbi, Nyeri,
17 12th December Hotel	Nakuru & Naivasha
20 Chania Tourist Lodge	13 Clocktower
	14 Standard Chartered Bank
▼ PLACES TO EAT	18 Shell Station
	19 Post Office
4 Twiga Bar	21 AGIP Station
7 Rwambogo Bar	22 Barclays Bank
& Restaurant	23 Caltex Station
12 Macvast Executive	24 Kenya Commercial Bank
Restaurant Two	25 Total Station
15 Ngaguro Café	26 BP Station
	27 Buses to Garissa

village where you turn right by the signpost for Nazareth Hospital and onto D407 Limuru Rd (otherwise known as Banana Rd). Some 14½ km down this road you'll see a signpost for Limuru Girls' School where you turn right. Go down past the school and take the entrance on the left-hand side signposted 'L G Mitchell'. The Waterfalls Inn (signposted) is 2½ km down the dirt road from the turn-off.

THIKA

Despite its fame due to the popular *Flame Trees of Thika* novel, the town itself comes as something of a disappointment – there's not even many flame trees in evidence! It's appeal lies in the fact that it makes a great escape from the madness of urban Nairobi just 38 km down the road. If you want to get the feel for a small Kenyan agricultural service town, yet still be in commuting range of Nairobi, it could be just the place.

The town's only 'attraction' as such is **Chania Falls**, one km from the centre of town and on the edge of the busy Nairobi to Nyeri road (which thankfully bypasses Thika). The falls are quite small but there's a good view of them from the up-market Blue Post Hotel, which is a pleasant place to stop for a beer.

Places to Stay & Eat

If you decide to stay, there's a good choice of accommodation, particularly in the mid-range area as it seems Thika is also a popular weekend conference venue.

There's a number of similar boarding & lodgings. The *3 in 1* is typical, and costs US$1.80/3.60 for singles/doubles with shared facilities. It's passably clean and not too noisy. Others include the *Rwambogo* and the *Sky Motel*.

The best value rooms in town are at the *12th December Hotel* (☎ (0151) 22140) near the post office. Large doubles cost US$7.50, and singles US$6.30, though these are tiny. Also a good place is the *Sagret Hotel* (☎ (0151) 21786) where the rooms are a little smaller but all have private bath and balcony, and the price includes breakfast. Small vehicles can be parked securely in the hotel courtyard; larger vehicles remain on the street. The cost for rooms here is US$11/17.

Further up the range is the *Chania Tourist Lodge* (☎ (0151) 22547), though it is poor value compared with the Sagret. Rooms here are way overpriced at US$13/15. At the *Blue Post Hotel* (☎ (0151) 22241) you'll pay US$13/19.

All the mid-range hotels have their own restaurants. For a good meal in a regular restaurant try the amazingly named *Macvast Executive Restaurant Two*! Here the waiters are all done up with pink pinstriped shirts and bow ties, but the prices are low and the menu extensive. It's a popular place with the local youths – the TV and the bar at the back are the big drawcards.

Getting There & Away

Matatus leave from a number of places around town. The main matatu stand, used mostly by local matatus, is near the Sagret Hotel. Most long-distance matatus – to Nairobi, Nakuru, Naivasha, Nyeri and Embu – leave from behind Barclays Bank. The trip to Nairobi only takes 45 minutes.

The Rift Valley

In Kenya the rift valley comes down through Lake Turkana, the Cherangani Hills, lakes Baringo, Bogoria, Nakuru and Naivasha then exits south through the plains to Tanzania. Together these areas make up some of Kenya's most interesting places to visit. Lake Turkana (dealt with in the Northern Kenya chapter) is a huge lake in the semidesert north, home to nomadic pastoralists and a world away from the tourist minibuses and

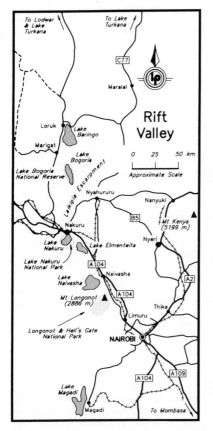

fancy hotels of the south. The Cherangani Hills provide some excellent walking opportunities and brilliant scenery – and hair-raising roads. More accessible are the central lakes which attract literally hundreds of bird and mammal species – they're a naturalist's dream and a visit to at least one of them is a must.

Volcanic activity is usually an accompaniment to rift valleys, and Kenya has both Mt Longonot and Mt Kenya. Longonot is accessible, easy to climb and certainly the most dominant feature of the landscape as you enter the rift valley from Nairobi. Mt Kenya, at 5200 metres, is a challenging climb, although Point Lenana, at 4985 metres, can be reached without specialist equipment. Further south are the vast plains, home of the Maasai, and also home to a profusion of wildlife that you're not likely to come across anywhere else in the world – an area not to be missed.

What is known as the rift valley in Kenya is in fact part of the Afro-Arabian rift system which stretches some 6000 km from the Dead Sea in the Middle East, south through the Red Sea, Ethiopia, Kenya, Tanzania and Malawi to Mozambique. There's a western branch of the system which forms the string of lakes in the centre of the African continent: Mobutu Sese Seko (formerly Albert) and Rutanzige (formerly Edward) which make up part of the Uganda-Zaïre border; Kivu on the Zaïre-Rwanda border; and Tanganyika on the Tanzania-Zaïre border. This western arm joins up with the main system at the northern tip of Lake Malawi.

Soda Lakes

Because the shoulders of the rift (see diagram) slope directly away from the valley, the drainage system in the valley is generally poor, and this has resulted in the shallow lakes along the valley floor in Kenya, some of which have no outlet. Due to high evaporation, the waters have become

Rift Valley

The rift valley system consists of a series of troughs and areas of uplift known as swells. The troughs, generally 40 to 55 km wide, are along parallel fault lines and are formed by blocks dropping down in relation to the rest of the land. They account for most of the lakes and escarpments in East Africa. The swells are the land on either side of the troughs, and it's on these that you find two of Africa's mightiest peaks – Kilimanjaro (5895 metres) and Mt Kenya (5199 metres) – and lesser peaks such as Mt Elgon (4321 metres) – all extinct volcanoes. The floor of the rift valley is still dropping, although at the rate of a few mm per year you are hardly likely to notice anything!

The rift valley is certainly not one long well formed valley with huge escarpments either side, although this does occur in places (the Rift Valley Province is one such place). Sometimes there is just a single scarp on one side (such as the Nkuruman Escarpment east of Masai Mara) or just a series of small scarps. In some cases uplift has occurred between parallel fault lines and this has led to the formation of often spectacular mountain ranges, such as the Ruwenzoris on the Uganda-Zaïre border. ■

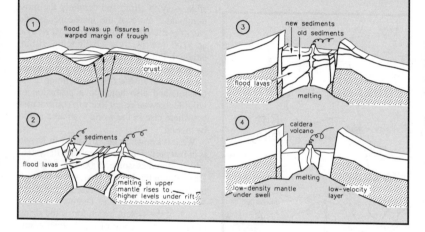

extremely concentrated and the high alkalinity from the area's volcanic deposits makes the perfect environment for microscopic blue-green algae and diatoms, which in turn provide food for tiny crustaceans and insect larvae. These in turn are eaten by certain species of soda-resistant fish.

The water of these soda lakes (Nakuru, Bogoria and Magadi in Kenya, and Lake Natron in Tanzania) may feel a little strange to the touch (it's soapy) and often doesn't smell too pleasant (though this is mostly due to the bird shit). However, the abundant insects and fish are heaven to many species of water bird and they flock here in their millions – it's a twitcher's paradise!

Foremost among the birds is the deep-pink lesser flamingo (*Phoenicopterus minor*), which feeds on the blue-green algae, and the pale-pink greater flamingo (*Phoenicopterus ruber*), which feeds on the tiny crustaceans and insect larvae. Also numerous are various species of duck, pelican, cormorant and stork. The highest concentrations of these birds are found where food is most abundant and this can vary from year to year and lake to lake.

Another curious feature of the uplifting of the valley shoulders is the effect it has had on existing drainage patterns, although this of course happened in the last couple of millions years. In Uganda it caused the

White Nile to form a pond (Lake Nyoga) after it left Lake Victoria, flow up what was previously a tributary, and into the northern end of Lake Albert via a circuitous route. Prior to the uplift the river had flowed direct from Lake Victoria into the southern end of Lake Albert.

Viewpoints

The best place to view the escarpments of the rift valley is from the viewpoints which are signposted along the Nairobi to Naivasha road, just past Limuru. Here the road descends into the valley and the views are stunning. Mt Longonot is directly in front while the plains of the Maasai sweep away to the south. Predictably there are souvenir stalls at the viewpoints, but the stuff for sale is some of the worst I've seen in the whole country.

The old road to Naivasha also descends into the rift in this area, and it's the route to take if you are heading for Mt Longonot or Masai Mara, as the new road runs direct to Naivasha. It's also the road used by heavy vehicles and is often in a diabolical state of repair. This road was originally built by Italian POWs in WW II, and there is a chapel at the bottom of the scarp.

Getting There & Around

Lakes Naivasha, Nakuru, Elmenteita and, to a lesser extent, Baringo are readily accessible to independent travellers without their own vehicle. There are plenty of buses and matatus and a rail link between Nairobi, Naivasha and Nakuru, and less frequent buses and matatus between Nakuru and Marigat (for Lake Baringo). The other lakes, however, are more remote and there's no public transport. Hitching is very difficult and can be impossible. There's also the problem that lakes Nakuru and Bogoria are both in national parks/reserves, which you are not allowed to walk in – you must tour them in a vehicle.

Renting a vehicle may be expensive for budget travellers but it would certainly work out cheaper for four people to hire a vehicle to visit Naivasha, Nakuru, Bogoria and

Baringo than for them all to pay individually for safari company tours. A one-day tour of Lake Nakuru starting from Nairobi goes for around US$40. A two-day tour of lakes Nakuru, Bogoria and Baringo costs about US$150 per person. A car hired for several days and shared between four people would cost considerably less than the total cost of a two-day tour for four people.

MT LONGONOT NATIONAL PARK

Hill climbers and view seekers should not miss the opportunity of climbing to the rim of dormant Longonot (2886 metres), a fairly young volcano which still retains the typical shape of these mountains, although it's far from being a perfect conical shape.

As this is a national park there is an entrance fee of US$12. The scramble up to the rim takes about 45 minutes from the parking area, and to do the circuit of the rim a further 2½ to three hours is needed. If you're feeling game there's a track leading down inside the crater to the bottom, though it's worth hiring a local guide before you set off.

Places to Stay

There's no accommodation in the park or immediate vicinity, but it is possible to camp at the ranger station at the foot of the mountain. If you are just on a day trip you can leave your gear at the Longonot railway station or the police station.

Getting There & Away

If you don't have your own transport it's a long walk from Longonot railway station on the old road to Naivasha. It's about seven km to the trail head, and even if you have your own car it's wise to pay someone to keep an eye on it, or leave it at the Longonot railway station.

NAIVASHA

There's very little of interest in the town of Naivasha itself. It's just a small service centre for the surrounding agricultural district. Most travellers just pass through here on the way to or from Mt Longonot, Lake

Naivasha, Hell's Gate National Park and Nakuru. The main road actually skirts the town so if you're going directly from Nairobi to Nakuru you don't actually pass through Naivasha. It's a good place to stock up with supplies if you're planning a sojourn by the lake as there are very limited stocks in the dukas dotted along the lake-shore road.

The area around Naivasha was actually one of the first settled by wazungu, and the Delamere Estates, originally owned by Lord Delamere, surround the town and stretch away to the west towards Nakuru. Many of the plots around Naivasha are still European-owned, which is hardly surprising given that this was one of the stamping grounds of the Happy Valley set of the 1930s.

The town basically consists of two main roads and a couple of other streets, and everything is within walking distance.

Information

There are branches of both Barclays Bank and the Kenya Commercial Bank on Moi Ave which are open during normal banking hours.

Places to Stay – bottom end

If you need to stay overnight in Naivasha there's a good range of budget hotels. The *Naivasha Super Lodge* has no doubles but the single beds are large enough for a couple; at US$1.80 these are not bad value.

For something a little less cosy try the *Olenkipai Boarding & Lodging* or the *Heshima Bar Boarding & Lodging*, both of which are adequate and charge around US$2.20 for a double.

There are plenty of other cheap places along Kariuki Chotara Rd.

Places to Stay – middle

For more salubrious lodgings the *Naivasha Silver Hotel* on Kenyatta Ave has self-contained rooms with hot water for US$4.50/6 a single/double. There's an upstairs bar and restaurant.

Very good value if you're alone is the *Othaya Annexe Hotel*, in Station Lane, which is very clean and has self-contained

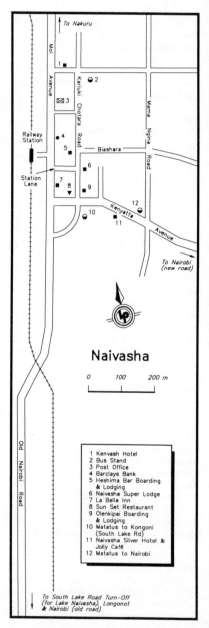

Naivasha

0   100   200 m

1 Kenvash Hotel
2 Bus Stand
3 Post Office
4 Barclays Bank
5 Heshima Bar Boarding
  & Lodging
6 Naivasha Super Lodge
7 La Belle Inn
8 Sun Set Restaurant
9 Olenkipai Boarding
  & Lodging
10 Matatus to Kongoni
   (South Lake Rd)
11 Naivasha Silver Hotel &
   Jolly Café
12 Matatus to Nairobi

singles (no doubles) for US$6.70. The hotel has its own bar and restaurant.

The best accommodation in town is the rustic *La Belle Inn* (☎ (0311) 20116) on Moi Ave, which is a popular rendezvous for local residents and a watering hole and meal stop for safari companies. The staff is friendly and rates are good value at US$12/15 for singles/doubles with shared bathroom facilities, or US$22/23 with private bath. Prices include breakfast. There's a guarded car park, and all credit cards are accepted.

The new, modern *Kenvash Hotel*, beyond the post office, is not yet complete but may well be by the time you read this.

Places to Eat

If you appreciate good food, there's essentially only one place to eat in Naivasha, *La Belle Inn*. While not 'cheap', it's not too expensive either, and the food is some of the best in Kenya. Soups cost around US$1 and main meals between US$2 and US$3. It's open daily (all day) except Tuesday. The outdoor terrace is also an excellent place to have a beer or a meal despite the occasional clouds of dust raised by trucks on their way further west.

The *Jolly Café* next to the Silver Hotel on Kenyatta Ave is slightly less extravagant and has decent food. For good old no-frills African stodge try the *Sun Set Restaurant* on the corner of Kenyatta Ave and Kariuki Chotara Rd.

Getting There & Away

Bus & Matatu The main bus and matatu station is on Kariuki Chotara Rd. There are frequent buses and matatus to Nairobi, Nakuru and all points further west. There are also departures for Nyahururu and Narok. Note that matatus to Nairobi leave from the matatu stand on Kenyatta Ave.

Train Travel from Naivasha to Nairobi by train is inconvenient as all the trains pass through in the early hours of the morning. The trains to Kisumu and Malaba pass through in the late afternoon. Unless you are prepared to travel 3rd class, make a booking in Nairobi before arriving in Naivasha.

Hitching It's useless trying to hitch out of Naivasha town to Nairobi without first getting onto the main road. The accepted point for hitching, and where the main road passes closest to the town, is about 500 metres east of the bus station. It's about one km to the main road in either the Nakuru or Nairobi direction.

LAKE NAIVASHA

Naivasha is one of the rift valley's freshwater lakes and its ecology is quite different from that of the soda lakes. It's home to an incredible variety of bird species and a focus of conservation efforts in Kenya. Not everyone supports these efforts, however, and the ecology of the lake has been interfered with on a number of occasions, the most notable introductions being sport fish, commercial fish (such as Nile perch), the North American red swamp crayfish, the South American coypu (an aquatic rodent, also called a nutria, which escaped from a fur farm) and various aquatic plants including *salvinia*, which is a menace on Lake Kariba in southern Africa.

The lake has ebbed and flowed over the years as half-submerged fencing posts indicate. Early in the 1890s it dried up almost completely but then it rose a phenomenal 15 metres and inundated a far larger area than it presently occupies. It has receded since then and currently covers about 170 sq km.

Since it's a freshwater lake which can be used for irrigation purposes, the surrounding countryside is a major production area of fresh fruit and vegetables as well as beef cattle both for domestic consumption and export. There's even a vineyard on the eastern shore.

On the western side of Lake Naivasha, past the village of Kongoni, there is a **crater lake** with lush vegetation at the bottom of a beautiful but small volcanic crater. If you have transport it's worth visiting. You have to cross private land for about 500 metres in order to get there, so close all gates behind you or ask permission if necessary.

South of the lake is the Hell's Gate National Park which is well worth exploring and one of the few national parks in which you're allowed to walk. (See later in this chapter.) On the eastern side of the lake is **Crescent Island**, a bird sanctuary which you can visit by boat (see the later Getting Around section).

Between 1937 and 1950 Lake Naivasha was Nairobi's airport! Imperial Airways and then BOAC flew Empire and Solent flying boats here on the four-day journey from Southampton. Passengers came ashore at the Lake Naivasha Hotel where buses would be waiting to shuttle them to Nairobi. The lake also featured strongly with the decadent Happy Valley settler crowd in the '30s. The mansion known as Oserian (or the Djinn Palace) which features in the book (and the dreadful movie) *White Mischief* is on the southern shore of the lake. It's privately owned and is not open to the public. For a full account of the history of European activity in the area, get hold of a copy of *Naivasha & the Lake Hotel* by Jan Hemsing, available from the Lake Naivasha Hotel.

Elsamere

Almost opposite Hippo Point, a couple of km past Fisherman's Camp, is Elsamere, the former home of the late Joy Adamson of *Born Free* fame. She bought the house in 1967 with the view that she and her husband, George might retire there. She did much of her writing from Elsamere right up until her murder in 1980. It seems George never spent much time there. It is now a conservation centre and open to the public daily from 3 to 6 pm. The entrance fee of US$2.20 includes afternoon tea on the lawn, a visit to the memorial room, and a film-viewing, *The Joy Adamson Story*.

Subject to 24 hours' notice, you can also visit here in the early afternoon for US$4.40 which includes lunch, the same film and a visit to the memorial room. Bookings can be made through the Elsamere Conservation Centre (☎ (0311) 30079), Moi South Lake Rd, PO Box 1497, Naivasha.

Places to Stay – bottom end

There are a couple of budget accommodation possibilities on the lake shore. The most popular place is *Fisherman's Camp* on the southern shore of the lake. You can camp here for US$1.80 per person (children US$1.40) with your own tent plus there are tents for hire at US$0.90 per night. There are also four fully self-contained *bandas* (round, concrete or mud-brick huts with makuti roofs) with four beds in each for US$6.70 per person (children US$4.50) and what is known as the *Top Camp* (up the hill across the other side of the road). Here they have a range of bandas which cost US$3.40 per person (two beds) and US$4.50 per person (four beds) as well as the *Kongoni Cottage* for US$18. Firewood is for sale at both camps plus, at the main camp, there's a store selling beers, soft drinks and ice cream at reasonable prices, but nothing else.

You can also rent boats from the store between 8 am and 5 pm (see Getting Around). It's a very pleasant site with grass and shady acacia trees. Make sure you camp well away from overland trucks unless you want to party all night, though finding a quiet spot isn't a problem as it's a huge site.

The other choice is the *YMCA*, three km back towards Naivasha town close to the turn-off for Hell's Gate National Park. Although it's difficult to get down to the lake shore from the YMCA, it's still a good camp site, especially if you intend to walk into Hell's Gate. Camping costs US$1.70 per person per night (children are half-price) plus there are a number of somewhat run-down bandas for US$2.20 per person (children half-price). Firewood can be provided for a small charge. It gets busy here with school groups during school holidays. Bring all your own food and drink with you (the nearest dukas are about one km down the road towards Naivasha).

For those without tents and with a desire for more creature comforts, there's the *Elsamere Conservation Centre* (☎ (0311) 30079; PO Box 1497, Naivasha), beyond Fisherman's Camp. Here you can get a room in Joy Adamson's former house with full

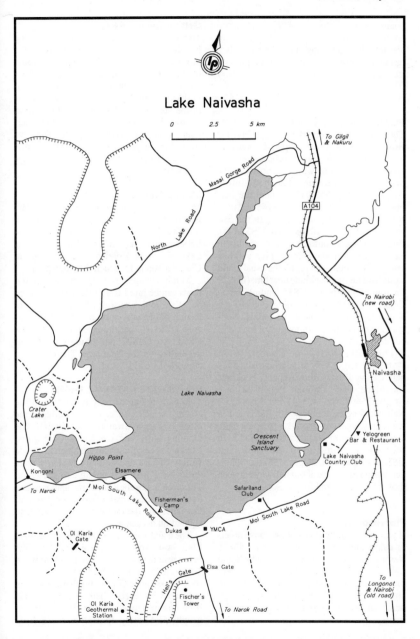

Lake Naivasha

0   2.5   5 km

board (the only choice) for US$29 per person per night. Children under seven years of age are not allowed to stay since it's basically a research centre. It's a very pleasant place to stay and the warden, Tony Bates, is very friendly.

Places to Stay – top end

The *Safariland Club* (☎ (0311) 20241; PO Box 72, Naivasha), is a top-end hotel with all the facilities you might expect. A single/double room with full board in the high season (December to March and July to August) costs US$90/130. There are also one-bedroom cottages for US$165 and two-bedroom cottages for US$270. In the low season, singles/doubles cost US$55/80. Prices in the shoulder season are about halfway between those in the high and low seasons. The club accepts all the usual credit cards, and facilities include boat hire (US$27 for four people plus a US$5 landing fee on Crescent Island), horse riding (US$10 per hour), lawn tennis and table tennis. Non-guests can use the swimming pool for US$3 per day.

The *Lake Naivasha Country Club* (☎ (0311) 13) is very similar and since it's part of the Block Hotels chain, bookings should be made through Rehema House (☎ (2) 335807; fax 340541), PO Box 47557, Nairobi. Singles/doubles with full board in the high season cost US$112/155 plus there are two-bedroom cottages for US$413. In the low season singles/doubles cost US$68/99 and the cottages US$262. Shoulder-season prices are about halfway between those in the high and low seasons.

Places to Eat

If you're not eating at any of the above hotels or camp sites, there's the *Yelogreen Bar & Restaurant* near the eastern end of Moi South Lake Rd. It's a pleasant place for a cold beer plus the food is good and reasonably priced. However, you need your own transport to get here as it's so far from the lake accommodation.

Getting There & Away

The usual access to Lake Naivasha is along Moi South Lake Rd. This also goes past the turn-off to Hell's Gate National Park (both the Elsa and Ol Karia gate entrances). There are fairly frequent matatus between Naivasha town and Kongoni on the western side of the lake. It's 17 km from the turn-off on the old Naivasha to Nairobi road to Fisherman's Camp and costs US$0.20. The road from the turn-off to Kongoni was recently resurfaced and is a beautiful length of tarmac highway.

Getting Around

Motorboats for game-viewing on Crescent Island can be hired from the Safariland Club for US$27 per person for four people, plus a US$5 landing fee on Crescent Island. The Lake Naivasha Hotel also offers trips to Crescent Island for much the same price.

Much cheaper rowing and motorised boats can be hired from Fisherman's Camp, but it's a long way from there to Crescent Island. Rowboats (four people maximum) cost US$1.10 per hour, and motorboats US$11 to US$22 per hour with driver, depending on the boat size. There's also a deposit of US$11.

HELL'S GATE NATIONAL PARK

This park is one of only two parks in the country which you can walk through (the other is Saiwa Swamp near Kitale). The looming cliffs and the Hell's Gate gorge itself are spectacular, and are home to a wide variety of bird and animal life. On a walk through the park it is possible to see zebra, Thomson's gazelle, antelope, baboon and even the occasional cheetah or leopard. Ostriches and the rare lammergeier are also sighted on occasion.

The usual access point is through the main **Elsa Gate**, two km from Moi South Lake Rd. From here the road takes you past **Fischer's Tower**, a 25-metre-high column of volcanic rock named after Gustav Fischer, a German explorer who reached here in 1883. He had been commissioned by the Hamburg Geographical Society to find a route from

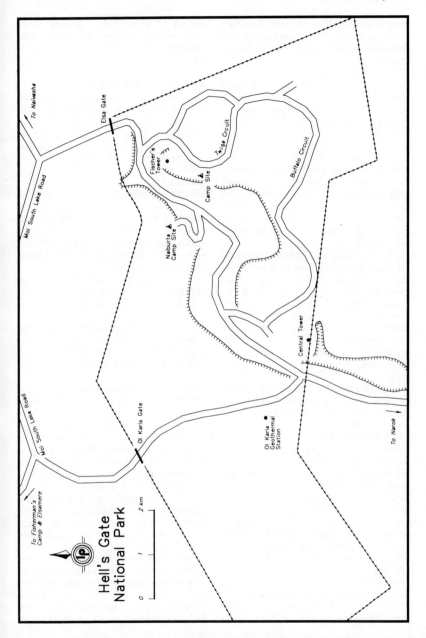

Hell's Gate National Park

Mombasa to Lake Victoria but this was about as far as he got, largely because he was unable to get on good terms with hostile Maasai.

The road then continues through the steep-sided gorge and emerges at the **Ol Karia Geothermal Station** – a power project which utilises one of the hottest sources in the world. You can see the plumes of steam rising into the air from many of the view-points in the park. Left of here, you'll see Central Tower, another column of volcanic rock similar to Fischer's Tower but much larger. From the geothermal plant the track heads back to the lake shore via the Ol Karia Gate, and emerges in the vicinity of Oserian farm (now a large supplier of cut flowers, fruit and vegetables to the European market) and Elsamere.

The entire walk from the lake road turn-off via Elsa Gate and Ol Karia Gate to the lake shore is 22 km. The distance between the two gates via the lake road is nine km. If you intend walking the whole way through the park (and it's well worth doing so), allow a full day, and take along some drinking water and something to eat. The only drinking water available in the park is at the camp sites. The usual park entry and camping fees apply.

If you don't want to walk through the park it may be possible to arrange a trip by car if you ask around at Fisherman's Camp.

LAKE ELMENTEITA
Like Lake Nakuru, Elmenteita is a shallow, soda lake with a similar ecology. Flamingos live here too, but in nowhere near the same numbers as at Nakuru. Elmenteita is not a national park, so you can walk around it and there are no entry fees. However, there are few tracks and, as most of the shoreline is privately owned, there's a lot of fencing. We recently had a letter from a woman traveller who attempted to walk around the lake alone and she was not at all impressed by the absence of a warning about how difficult it was. Think twice before attempting it!

The easiest way to get there is to take a matatu along the Naivasha to Nakuru road

and get off at one of the signposted view-points on the escarpment above the lake. You can either walk down from there or hitch a ride.

KARIANDUSI PREHISTORIC SITE
The Kariandusi site is signposted off to the right of the main road on the way from Naivasha to Nakuru. There's not much to see as the only excavation was carried out by Louis Leakey in the 1920s, although the small museum is worth a look.

NAKURU
Kenya's fourth-largest town is the centre of a rich farming area about halfway between Nairobi and Kisumu on the main road and railway line to Uganda. It's here that the railway forks, one branch going to Kisumu on Lake Victoria and the other to Malaba on the Ugandan border.

It's a pleasant town with a population of 75,000 but is of interest mainly to those who work and farm in the area. The big draw for travellers is the nearby Lake Nakuru National Park with its prolific birdlife. The Menengai Crater and Hyrax Hill Prehistoric Site in the immediate area are both worth a visit (see later in this chapter).

Places to Stay – bottom end
The *Amigos Guest House* on Gusil Rd is a very friendly place to stay and the best value in this range. David, the man who runs it even remembered my face after seven years! The rooms and bathroom facilities are spotlessly clean, towels are provided and there's hot water. Singles/doubles with shared facilities cost US$1.60/3.10, triples are US$4.50. Don't confuse this place with the other Amigos at the junction of Kenyatta Ave and Bondoni Rd. The other one isn't anywhere near as good and can be very noisy because of the upstairs bar.

Around the corner from Amigos are the *City Inn* and the *Gamel Guest House*, though they're more basic than the above. Another good place is the *Tropical Valley Lodge* (☎ 42608) on Moi Rd which has singles/doubles with shared bath for US$2/3.10.

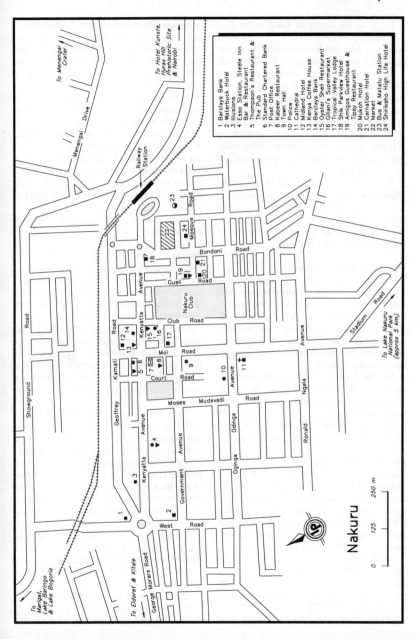

Nakuru

1 Barclays Bank
2 Waterbuck Hotel
3 Illusions
4 Esso Station, Steele Inn
5 Thompson's Restaurant &
  Bar & Restaurant
  The Pub
6 Standard Chartered Bank
7 Post Office
8 Kabeer Restaurant
9 Town Hall
10 Police
11 Cathedral
12 Midland Hotel
13 Kenya Coffee House
14 Barclays Bank
15 Oyster-Shell Restaurant
16 Gillani's Supermarket
17 Tropical Valley Lodge
18 Shik Parkview Hotel
19 Amigos Guesthouse &
   Tipsy Restaurant
20 Mukoh Hotel
21 Carnation Hotel
22 Market
23 Bus & Matatu Station
24 Shiriksho High Life Hotel

Right in the centre of town is the *Shik Parkview Hotel* (☎ 212345) on the corner of Kenyatta Ave and Bondoni Rd. It's a large place, but whoever designed it surely made a basic mistake since although the single rooms are self-contained (ie have private bathrooms), the doubles are not! The beds are comfortable but what other furniture you get varies. Singles/doubles cost US$4/6.20 with breakfast. The rooms overlooking Kenyatta Ave are noisy. The best thing about this place is its proximity to the bus and railway stations.

You could also check out the *Shiriksho High Life Hotel* on Mosque Rd which is conveniently close to the bus and matatu station but is not a great bargain. It's similar in price to the Shik Parkview, but none of the rooms have private bathrooms.

Places to Stay – middle

Going up in price, an excellent choice is the *Mukoh Hotel*, on the corner of Mosque and Gusil Rds, which is clean and comfortable. Singles/doubles cost US$5.60/7.80 with private bath. Soap and towels are provided and there is erratic hot water. The hotel has its own bar and restaurant, and the management is very friendly.

Not far from the Mukoh and similar in quality is the *Carnation Hotel* (☎ 43522) which has singles/doubles for US$5.80/8.90 with shared bath, or US$7.80/11.10 with private bath. There's hot water in the bathrooms and the hotel has its own restaurant.

Places to Stay – top end

There's a choice of two top-end places in Nakuru. The *Midland Hotel* (☎ 212123) on Kamati Rd is a rambling old place with self-contained rooms and hot water for US$8.40/14 including breakfast. It has three bars (including the Long Bar) and two restaurants (one outdoor and one indoor).

More expensive but very pleasant is the *Waterbuck Hotel* (☎ 211516/46) on the corner of Government Ave and West Rd, which offers self-contained rooms with balcony for US$21/27 a single/double, and US$33 a triple. The price includes a good breakfast. There are substantial reductions in the low and shoulder seasons. The hotel has its own bar, restaurant and barbecue bar, and the staff are very friendly. Vehicles can be parked safely in the hotel compound which is guarded 24 hours a day.

Further away from the centre on the road to Nairobi and close to the turn-off for Hyrax Hill is the modern *Hotel Kunste* (☎ 212140, 245612) which is a conference centre/hotel. Rates in self-contained rooms are US$10/17 for a single/double, US$26 a triple, including breakfast. Lunch or dinner costs US$3.80.

Further out, several km down the road towards Nairobi, is the *Stem Hotel* which has rooms for US$17 a double with half board. It's only really of interest to those with their own transport.

Places to Eat

For price and quality, the best place to eat is the *Tipsy Restaurant* on Gusil Rd. It's very popular with local people, especially at lunch time. Dishes include Indian curries, Western food and lake fish. The food is very tasty.

The restaurant on the ground floor of the *Mukoh Hotel* is a good place for breakfast and also serves good meals and snacks. For just a coffee and a snack try the *Kenya Coffee House* on the corner of Moi Rd and Kenyatta Ave. You can also buy roasted coffee beans there.

The open-air bar at the *Midland Hotel*, which offers barbecued chicken and a Sunday curry buffet (chicken or beef), is a popular place to eat especially at lunch time. It's very reasonably priced at around US$1.20 for main courses. The outside bar of the *Waterbuck Hotel* is also very similar. You might also like to check out the *Thompson's Restaurant* between Kenyatta Ave and Kamati Rd.

The *Steele Inn Bar & Restaurant*, next to the Esso station on Kenyatta Ave, is also a pleasant place to eat. It's a little cottage with verandahs in a garden setting and offers chicken or red meat with chips.

Going up somewhat in price, one of the town's best restaurants is the *Oyster Shell Restaurant* (☎ 40946), upstairs on Kenyatta

Ave near the Club Rd corner. The menu is extensive and includes Western, Indian, Mughlai and Indonesian dishes. It's open daily for lunch and dinner and is very reasonably priced. Soups are US$0.80 and main courses US$2.70.

Similar in price and quality is the *Kabeer Restaurant* which offers indoor and al fresco dining. It's open daily until 10 pm and offers Indian food (including tandoori), Chinese dishes, seafood and grills. Main courses are priced between US$2.40 and US$2.80 (prawns cost US$5). You can also get a good Indian-style breakfast here, as well as fruit juices and takeaways at lunch time.

Entertainment
Apart from the bars mentioned earlier, there are two discos in Nakuru. The best is *Illusions* on Kenyatta Ave which is open Wednesday, Friday, Saturday and Sunday evenings until early morning. It's quieter than the discos in Nairobi but it has excellent equipment and a good mixture of music. Entry costs US$1.10 and beers sell for normal bar prices.

The other disco is upstairs from the Oyster Shell Restaurant and is open daily until 4 am. Entry costs US$0.55 for women and double that for men.

Getting There & Away
Bus & Matatu The bus and matatu station is right in the thick of things at the eastern edge of town, near the railway station. It's a pretty chaotic place though generally it doesn't take too long to locate the bus, matatu or Peugeot you want. There are regular departures for Naivasha, Nairobi, Nyahururu and all points west.

Train As is the case with Naivasha, trains often come through here in the middle of the night so you're better off going by road, as the buses and matatus arrive in the daytime only. The daily Kisumu and Nairobi trains come through at 12.30 am and 2.25 am respectively, while the Malaba trains are on Tuesday, Friday and Saturday at 8.45 pm. As for travel to Naivasha, you need to make an advance reservation in Nairobi if you're heading west and want to travel in 1st or 2nd class.

LAKE NAKURU NATIONAL PARK
Created in 1961, the park has since been considerably increased in size and now covers an area of some 200 sq km. Like most of the other rift valley lakes, it is a shallow soda lake. Some years ago the level of the lake rose and this resulted in a mass migration of the flamingos to other rift valley lakes, principally Bogoria, Magadi and Natron. What had been dubbed 'the world's greatest ornithological spectacle' suddenly wasn't anywhere near as spectacular. Since then the lake has receded and the flamingos have returned, once again giving you the opportunity of seeing up to two million flamingos along with tens of thousands of other birds. It's an ornithologists' paradise and one of the world's most magnificent sights. Those of you who have seen the film, *Out of*

Africa, and remember the footage of the flight over the vast flocks of flamingos, are in for a very similar treat. Simply go up to the lookout on the top of **Baboon Cliffs** on the western side of the lake and feast your eyes on the endless pink masses which fringe the lake.

Don't blame us, though, if the birds are not there in such profusion or even if the lake dries up! The flamingos migrate from time to time if food gets scarce and there's a better supply elsewhere – usually to Lake Bogoria further north or to lakes Magadi and Natron further south.

The lake is very shallow and the level fluctuates by up to four metres annually. When the water is low the soda crystallises out along the shoreline as a blinding white band of powder which is going to severely test your skills as a photographer. Lake Nakuru last dried up in the late 1950s and, at that time, soda dust storms and dust devils whipped up by high winds made life unbearable for people in the town and surrounding area. In the dry season you'll see these dust devils (like tiny tornadoes) whipping up soda into the air as they course along the shoreline.

Since the park also has areas of grassland, bush, forest and rocky cliffs there are many other animals to be seen apart from birds. One species you'll see plenty of are wart hogs with their amusing way of running with their tails erect. Right by the water you'll come across waterbuck and buffalo, while further into the bush are Thomson's gazelle and reedbuck – there's even the occasional leopard. Around the cliffs you may catch sight of hyrax and birds of prey. There's even a small herd of hippos which generally lives along the northern shore of the lake.

The national park entrance is about six km from the centre of Nakuru. Entry costs US$12 per person plus US$1.50 per vehicle. As in most national parks, you must be in a vehicle. Walking is not permitted so you will either have to hitch a ride with other tourists, rent your own vehicle or go on a tour.

You can only get out of your vehicle on the lake shore and at certain viewpoints. It's

a memorable experience being in the proximity of several hundred thousand flamingos feeding, preening, grunting and honking and even more memorable when several thousand of them decide that you're a little too close for comfort and they take off to find a more congenial spot.

Warning Don't drive too close to the water's edge, the mud is very soft! Take your cue from the tracks of other vehicles.

Places to Stay – bottom end
There is a good camping site, known as the *Backpackers' Camp Site* just inside the park gate. Fresh water is available and there are a couple of pit toilets, but you need to bring all your own food. Make sure tents are securely zipped up when you're away from them otherwise the vervet monkeys or baboons will steal everything inside them. If you are backpacking and trying to hitch a ride, the rangers at the gate will let you camp here without paying the park entry until you are successful.

If you have no camping equipment there's the very basic *Florida Day & Night Club* about half a km before the entrance gate.

A km or so further into the park is the *Njoro Camp Site* and this is the one to head for if you have a vehicle. It's a beautiful grassy site under acacia trees and there's firewood, water on tap and the usual pit toilets.

Places to Stay – top end
The first place you come to down the eastern access road of the park is Sarova Hotels' *Sarova Lion Hill Lodge* (☎ (2) 333248; fax (2) 211472). It has all the usual facilities including a swimming pool and open-air bar/restaurant area. High-season prices with full board are US$112/132 for singles/doubles and drop to US$47/94 in the low season. There are also more expensive suites. It's a well thought-out site but there are only occasional views of the lake through the thorn trees.

Almost three km beyond the southern end of the lake is the *Lake Nakuru Lodge*, PO

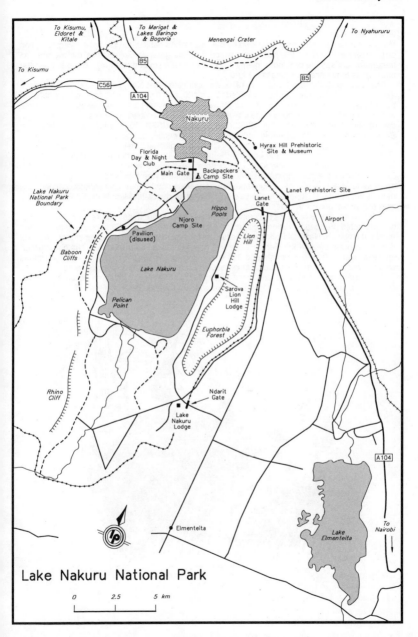

To Kisumu, Eldoret & Kitale

To Marigat & Lakes Baringo & Bogoria

Menengai Crater

To Nyahururu

To Kisumu

B5

C56

A104

Nakuru

B5

Hyrax Hill Prehistoric Site & Museum

Florida Day & Night Club

Main Gate

Backpackers' Camp Site

Lanet Prehistoric Site

Lake Nakuru National Park Boundary

Hippo Pools

Lanet Gate

Airport

Njoro Camp Site

Pavilion (disused)

Lion Hill

Baboon Cliffs

Lake Nakuru

Sarova Lion Hill Lodge

Pelican Point

Euphorbia Forest

Rhino Cliff

Ndarit Gate

Lake Nakuru Lodge

A104

To Nairobi

Elmenteita

Lake Elmenteita

Lake Nakuru National Park

0   2.5   5 km

Rhino Rescue

Many of Africa's animals are threatened by the loss of their habitat due to human overpopulation or by poachers, and it's the poor rhino which is in the greatest danger. The rhino's horn, its trademark, causes the problem – plenty of people covet them and this only serves to push the price up as they become increasingly rare.

The stark statistics are horrific. In 1970, it is estimated that Kenya had about 20,000 black rhinos. By 1985, that number had dwindled to just 425, and rhinos were so few and so scattered that it was becoming increasingly difficult for a lady rhino to meet a compatible gentleman rhino, with the object of creating baby rhinos. With this huge fall in numbers, the price of rhino horns on the black market had soared from US$35 per kg to over US$30,000 per kg – and is still rising. Elsewhere in Africa, the fall in rhino numbers has been equally dramatic.

Rhino horn is a popular ingredient in many Chinese traditional medicines and we have all heard of the supposed effects of rhino horn on the libido. But the major market for rhino horn is the Yemen, where Djambia daggers with rhino horn handles are worth over US$15,000. These fantastic prices are inspiring ruthless tactics from poachers who tote modern weapons and are as likely to shoot as run when confronted by rangers. In 1990, their brazenness reached new heights when they shot not only Kenya's only five white rhinos (in Meru National Park) but first shot the armed guards in order to do so.

The only solution is felt to be the creation of small parks where rhinos can be carefully watched and protected. Funded by Rhino Rescue, an organisation set up in 1986 specifically to save the rhinos, the Nakuru National Park was selected as the first manageable rhino sanctuary. The park is now protected by a 74-km electric fence with guard posts at 15-km intervals. The construction involved over 11,000 fence posts and 880 km of high-tensile wire. An initial group of 19 rhinos was established and there are plans to increase this number, possibly to as many as 60.

Additional sanctuaries are planned but saving the rhino isn't going to come cheap. Donations can be sent to Rhino Rescue, PO Box 1, Saxmundham, Suffolk, IP17 3JT, UK. ■

Box 561, Nakuru (also 2nd Floor, Arrow House, Koinange St, PO Box 70559, Nairobi ☎ 2249998; fax 230962). Like the Sarova Lion Hill, it has all the usual facilities and consists of a series of shingle-roofed cottages; prices are also similar.

Getting There & Away

If you don't have your own vehicle, the only way into the park from Nakuru is by taxi (unless you can persuade a tourist with a car to take you in). A taxi costs between US$12 and US$15 for three hours, though you'll have to bargain hard for this. Alternatively, contact Jomina Tours & Travel Ltd (☎ 21-2956/7), 4th Floor, Spikes Bldg, Kenyatta Lane, Nakuru. This company runs daily tours to Lake Nakuru.

If you're driving, there's access from three points: the main gate; Lanet, just a few km along the Nairobi road; and Ndari Gate near the southern end of Lake Elmenteita.

MENENGAI CRATER

Rising up on the northern side of Nakuru is the Menengai Crater, an extinct 2490-metre high volcano. The crater itself descends to a maximum depth of 483 metres below the rim. You can drive right up to the edge, where there's one of those totally trivial signs telling you that you're five million km from some city halfway across the world.

To walk up to the crater takes a solid couple of hours, and it really is *up*, but still a very pleasant walk. The views back over Lake Nakuru are excellent, as are the views north to Lake Bogoria once you reach the top. About three-quarters of the way along there is a small group of dukas where you can get basic meals, soft drinks and, of course, the amber fluid.

HYRAX HILL PREHISTORIC SITE

Just outside Nakuru on the Nairobi road, this prehistoric site is open daily from 9 am to 6 pm and admission is US$1.60. The small booklet, *Visitor's Guide to the Hyrax Hill Site*, is available from the museum there.

Archeological excavations were first conducted here in 1937 although the significance of the site had been suspected by Louis Leakey since 1926. Further excavations have been conducted periodically, right up into the 1980s.

The finds at the site indicate three settlements were made here, the earliest possibly 3000 years ago, the most recent only 200 to 300 years ago. From the museum at the northern end you can take a short stroll around the site, starting with the North-East Village where 13 enclosures or pits were excavated. Only Pit D, investigated in 1965, is still open; the others have grown over. The North-East Village is believed to be about 400 years old, dated by comparison with the nearby Lanet site. A great number of pottery fragments were found at the site, some of which have been pieced together into complete jars and are displayed in the museum.

From the village the trail climbs to the scant remains of the stone-walled hill fort near the top of Hyrax Hill, which gave the site its name. You can continue up to the peak from where there is a fine view of the flamingo-lined Lake Nakuru.

Descending from the hill on the other side you come to the Iron Age settlement where the position of Hut B and Hut C is clearly visible. Just north of these huts, a series of burial pits containing 19 skeletons was found. Since they were mostly male, and a number of them had been decapitated, it's possible they were killed in sort sort of fighting. Unfortunately, souvenir seekers have stolen the bones that were displayed.

Virtually underneath the Iron Age site, a Neolithic site was discovered. The Iron Age burial pits actually topped a Neolithic burial mound and a second Neolithic burial mound was found nearby. This mound is fenced off as a display. Between the burial mound and the Nairobi road are more Iron Age pits, excavated in 1974. The large collection of items found in these pits included a real puzzle – six Indian coins, one of them 500 years old, two of them dating from 1918 and 1919!

Finally, following the path back to the museum, there's a *bau* board in a large rock.

This popular game is played throughout East Africa.

You are free to walk around the site yourself but a guide is useful. He'll expect a small tip at the end.

LAKE BOGORIA

The two completely dissimilar lakes of Bogoria and Baringo are north of Nakuru off the B4 highway to Marigat and Lodwar. Lake Bogoria is a shallow soda lake while Lake Baringo is a deeper freshwater lake. They're connected to Nakuru by the B4 road which is a superb, sealed highway the whole way.

Lake Bogoria covers an area of 30 sq km and has a maximum depth of nine metres. As with the other soda lakes in Kenya, Bogoria has no outlet and so the intense evaporation has led to high levels of salts and minerals. The result is that the lake supports no fish at all, but is ideal for blue-green algae, which is a favourite of the flamingos. Bogoria is a national park so there's an entry fee of US$12 per person plus US$1.50 per vehicle.

Most of the birdlife on Bogoria has migrated to the (presently) richer pastures of Lake Nakuru, but the stalwarts (of all species) remain. It's a very peaceful area but it doesn't currently compare with the ornithological spectacle of Nakuru. There are, however, the **hot springs** and **geysers** about three-quarters of the way along the lake going south. They're not comparable with those at Rotorua in New Zealand but if you've never seen geysers before then this is the place. The springs are boiling hot so don't put your bare foot or hand into them unless you want to nurse scalds for the next week.

The land to the west of the lake is a hot and relatively barren wilderness of rocks and scrub, and animals are rare though you may be lucky to catch sight of a greater kudu, impala or klipspringer. The eastern side of the lake is dominated by the sheer face of the northern extremities of the Aberdares.

Places to Stay

There are two camp sites at the southern end of the lake: *Acacia* and *Riverside*, but there are no facilities and the lake water is totally unpalatable. Bring all water and food with you if you are intending to stay at either site. Otherwise, the camp sites are shady and very pleasant.

There's another camp site just outside the northern entrance gate (Loboi). Drinking water is available here and there's a small shop nearby which sells basic supplies (canned food, jam, biscuits, washing powder, soft drinks, etc).

The *Lake Bogoria Lodge* (☎ (037) 42696) is a top-range lodge two km from the northern entrance. It's a very pleasant place set in a well-tended garden, but few people seem to stay here. Rooms cost US$46/71 a single/double, while cottages are US$150. Prices include breakfast but not service charges. With full board, charges rise to US$71/121 plus taxes.

Getting There & Away

There are two entrance gates to Lake Bogoria – one from the south (Mogotio) and another from the north (Loboi). You'll see the signpost for the Mogotio Gate on the B4 about 38 km past Nakuru heading north but, if you take it, you'll probably regret it! Most of this road is good smooth dust or gravel but there is about five km of it which leads down to the southern park entrance which will certainly rip apart any tyres and destroy any vehicle driven at more than a few km per hour. Without 4WD you'd be wasting your time. These razor-sharp lava beds don't end once you reach the park gate but continue for at least as far on the other side. In addition, signposting along the route from the turn-off is almost nonexistent.

A far better entry to the park is from the Loboi Gate just a few km before you reach Marigat on the B4. It's also signposted. From the turn-off, it's 20 km to the actual park entry gate and, although the road was once sealed, these days the bitumen is breaking up badly and you need to drive carefully.

Whichever gate you use, you're going to need your own vehicle since hitching is well-nigh impossible. Very few people visit Bogoria and those who do are usually in tourist minibuses which won't pick you up unless you're booked with them. It *may* be possible to walk into the park since there are no large predators living here (with the possible exception of the occasional leopard) but don't count on it. Officially, you're supposed to tour the park in a vehicle.

LAKE BARINGO

Some 15 km north of the town of Marigat you come to the village of Kampi-ya-Samaki which is the centre for exploring Lake Baringo. This lake, like Naivasha, is freshwater. It covers around 170 sq km and has a maximum depth of just 12 metres. The lake supports many different species of aquatic animals and birdlife as well as crocodiles and herds of hippos which invade the grassy shore every evening to browse on the vegetation. You'll hear their characteristic grunt as you walk back to your tent or banda after dark or settle down for the night. They might even decide to crop the grass right next to your tent. If they do, stay where you are. They're not aggressive animals (they don't need to be with their bulk and jaws!) but if you frighten or annoy them they might go for you. And, despite all appearances, they can *move*!

Crocodiles and hippos apart, Lake Baringo's main attraction is the birdlife and the lake is the bird-watching centre of Kenya. People come here to engage in this activity from all over the world. Kenya has over 1200 different species of birds and more than 450 of them have been sighted at Lake Baringo. Some bird-watchers are so keen they're known as 'twitchers' since their primary concern seems to be to rack up sightings of as many different bird species as possible. It's a serious business and the Lake Baringo Club even has a 'resident ornithologist' who leads bird-watching walks and gives advice to guests. A few years ago he set a world record for the number of species seen in one 24-hour period – over 300!

There's a constant twittering, chirping and cooing of birds in the trees around the lake, in the rushes on the lake and even on the steep face of the nearby escarpment. Even if you've had no previous interest in bird-watching, it's hard to resist setting off on the dawn bird walk and the highlight of the morning is likely to be a sighting of hornbills or the magnificent eagles which live almost exclusively on rock hyrax.

Places to Stay – bottom end

There's a superb place to stay just before the village called *Robert's Camp* (☎ Kampi-ya-Samaki 3 – through the operator) where you can camp for around US$2 per person per night; bundles of firewood cost US$0.80. Facilities include clean showers and toilets. There are also three double bandas available with cooking facilities for US$4.50 per person plus 18% tax. I'd strongly recommend the bandas if there is one available but demand is heavy at times and it would be wise to book one in advance (through David Roberts Wildlife, PO Box 1051, Nakuru). The bandas are beautiful, circular, grass-thatched traditional-style houses which are as clean as a new pin and furnished with comfortable beds, table and chairs and mosquito netting at the windows. Showers and toilets are separate and cooking facilities are available for US$4.50. The people here are very friendly and there's a huge land tortoise which ambles around the grounds and appears to be used to the attention it receives.

If you're camping here then you need to exercise some common sense regarding the hippos. Although hippos may graze within just a metre of your tent at night, you should not approach nearer than 20 metres, especially if they have young ones. Don't frighten them in any way with headlights, torches (flashlights) or loud noises and don't use flash photography. No-one's ever been hurt by a hippo in over 10 years but they are wild animals and should be treated with respect.

If Robert's Camp is full or you have no camping equipment then try one of the basic lodges in Kampi-ya-Samaki. The *Hippo Lodge* at the entrance to the village is way overpriced at around US$2 per person for a bed in a basic grubby room. Cheaper but equally basic is the *Lake View Lodge* on the lake side of the town. Rooms here cost around US$1 per person.

There is also a hotel in Marigat if you prefer, though it's quite a way from the lake shore and it's not the world's most interesting place. The *Marigat Inn* is about 1½ km from the signposted main road turn-off. Singles/doubles with breakfast cost US$4.50/8, and it's very pleasant with its own bar and restaurant.

Places to Stay – top end

Right next door to Robert's Camp is the *Lake Baringo Club*, one of the Block Hotels chain (☎ 335807 in Nairobi for reservations or write c/o PO Box 47557). Singles/doubles with full board are US$39/78 in the low season and rise to US$74/116 in the high season (July and August). Children under 12 years sharing a room with adults stay for free, and pay only for meals (50% of adult meal prices). Facilities at the club include a swimming pool, dart boards, table tennis table, badminton court, a library and a whole range of local excursions including boat trips and bird-watching trips accompanied by an expert.

One-hour boat trips cost US$40 (with a minimum of seven people), bird walks US$4 per person (plus US$2 if you need transport) and camel rides US$2 per half-hour. The club also offers trips to Lake Bogoria for US$38 per person (minimum three people) and to a nearby Njemps village for US$5.50 per person (minimum three people). The Njemps are the local tribespeople who live in villages around the lake shore and practice a mixture of pastoralism and fishing. The club has an arrangement with the headman of the village which you visit so you're allowed to walk around freely and take photographs, though you'll probably be hassled to buy some of the handicrafts produced by the villagers.

The facilities at the club are open to non-guests on payment of a US$2 per person per day temporary membership on weekdays

and US$3.30 on weekends, although this fee is waived if you're eating either lunch or dinner there. Use of the swimming pool costs about US$2 per person per day on top of the daily membership fee. If you arrive at the club by vehicle you probably won't be asked for the fee. At 7 pm each evening there's a slide show and commentary featuring some of the more common birds sighted in the area.

Another top-end hotel is the *Island Camp* (☎ (02) 502491, 225941 in Nairobi), which is a luxury tented lodge sited on Ol Kokwa Island in the lake. It is rated highly by those who have stayed there, and is also expensive at US$85/130 for full board. There are 25 double tents each with their own shower and toilet, two bars, a swimming pool and water sports facilities. Activities here include water-skiing (US$45 per hour) and boat trips (US$22 per hour). Boat transfers from the mainland to the island cost US$6.70 return, and the boats leave from a poorly signposted landing on the north side of Kampi-ya-Samaki village. The locals can all point you in the right direction.

Also on the island is the *Saruni Camp* (☎ (02) 333285 in Nairobi), which has eight self-contained double tents, each with views of the lake. Meals are taken in the main mess tent, and the cost of a visit is US$63/102.

Places to Eat

If you're camping at Robert's Camp and want to keep costs down then you'll have to bring your own food with you as well as cooking facilities and equipment (unless you want to cook over a wood fire). Only very basic foodstuffs are available in the village of Kampi-ya-Samaki, and a slightly better choice in Marigat, so bring what you will need from Nakuru.

Those who want to splurge can eat at the *Lake Baringo Club*. As you might expect, the meals here are very good but will cost you around US$6 for breakfast and US$11 for either lunch or dinner. The club is also the only place where you will be able to find a cold beer, and the only place where you can buy petrol and diesel between Marigat and Maralal.

Getting There & Away

There are frequent matatus between Nakuru and Marigat but they don't all continue on to Kampi-ya-Samaki, so you may have to hitch from Marigat or take another of the infrequent matatus which go to the village. In the opposite direction, there's a minibus from Kampi-ya-Samaki at about 7 am which goes to Nakuru and another which comes through later from Loruk at the top end of the lake.

It's an interesting journey between Nakuru and Baringo since the country remains relatively lush and green until you pass the equator where it almost immediately becomes drier and dustier and continues to get more barren and forbidding the further north you go. As you near Marigat there are spectacular mountains, ridges and escarpments.

A gravel track connects Loruk at the top end of the lake with the Nyahururu to Maralal road. It's in good shape if you have your own transport and are contemplating doing the trip. There's no public transport along this road and hitching is extremely difficult.

LAKE MAGADI

Lake Magadi is the most southerly of the rift valley lakes in Kenya and is very rarely visited by tourists because of its remoteness. Like most of the rift valley lakes, it is a soda lake and supports many flamingos and other water birds. It also has a soda extraction factory, hence the railway line there. A few years ago it was the site of a major rescue operation of young flamingos when drought threatened hundreds of thousands of them because of soda encrustation on their feathers – this doesn't affect the adults.

Magadi is quite different from the lakes to the north as it is in a semidesert area. Temperatures hover around the 38°C mark during the day and much of the lake is a semisolid sludge of water and soda salts. There is a series of hot springs around the periphery of the lake.

Getting There & Away

There is a rail link to the lake shore which branches off from the main Nairobi to Mombasa line but there are no passenger services along it. There's also a minor road from Nairobi (the C58) but there's no public transport along it so you will either have to hitch or have your own vehicle.

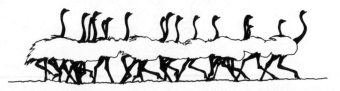

The Central Highlands

The Kenyan central highlands comprise the Aberdares, which begin around Limuru just north-west of Nairobi and continue on up to Maralal, plus the massif of Mt Kenya itself. They form the eastern wall of the rift valley and are the heartland of the Kikuyu people. Within the main area are two national parks, Aberdare and Mt Kenya.

It's a very fertile region, well watered, intensively cultivated and thickly forested.

The climate, likewise, is excellent. Given these qualities, it's not surprising that the land was coveted by the White settlers who began arriving in ever increasing numbers once the Mombasa-Uganda railway was completed. Here they could grow anything year-round, particularly cash crops which were in demand in Europe. It's also not surprising that the Kikuyu eventually became so disenchanted with the alienation of their

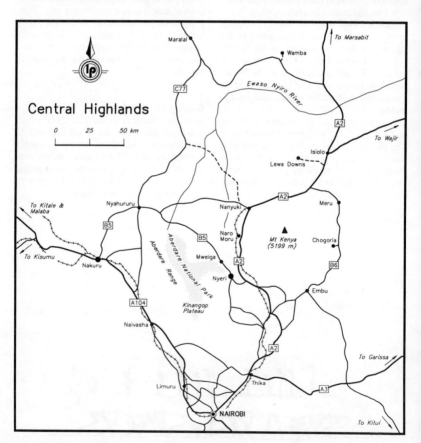

Top: Hot springs, Lake Bogoria National Park (GC)
Bottom: Flamingos & pelicans, Lake Nakuru National Park (HF)

Top: Aloes on rock outcrop (DE)
Bottom: Flora detail (GC)

Top: Cliffs around Lake Baringo (TW)
Bottom Left: Thomson's Falls, Nyahururu (TW)
Bottom Right: Sisal plantation, Nakuru (GC)

Top: Voi bus station (TW)
Bottom Left: Mount Kenya (GC)
Bottom Right: Masai Mara Game Reserve (HF)

best land that war erupted between the two groups in the form of the Mau Mau Rebellion. It is probable that this event, more than any other, forced the British colonial authorities to reassess their position and ultimately to grant independence to the country.

While White Kenyan farmers still exist in considerable numbers in the area, their holdings have been reduced and much of the land parcelled out among the Kikuyu. Given the current level of population growth, it's anyone's guess how much longer this subdivision and further encroachment on the forest can continue before the environment is seriously threatened. Soil erosion is a major problem and many plots are too small to support a family. It's true there's still a great deal of forest remaining but with pressure on it for use as construction material and firewood (the most common form of fuel for cooking and heating) there are limits to the expansion of agricultural land. It's important to remember that much of Kenya is scrub and desert.

The Aberdares

Known to the Kikuyu as *Nyandarua*, 'drying hide', the Aberdares were named after the president of the Royal Geographical Society by the explorer Thomson in 1884. The lower eastern slopes were long cultivated by the Kikuyu while the higher regions, with peaks of up to 4000 metres and covered in dense forests and bamboo thickets, were left to the leopard, buffalo, lion and elephant. The arrival of the Europeans saw the establishment of coffee and tea plantations on the eastern side and wheat and pyrethrum farms on the western slopes. Most of this land has now been returned to the Kikuyu. Not all of the higher reaches of the Aberdares, however, are dense forest. There are also extensive areas of mist-covered moors along the ridges and a good swathe of forest out of which the Aberdare National Park was created in 1950.

ABERDARE NATIONAL PARK

This park essentially encloses the moorland and high forest of the 60-km long Kinangop plateau along with an eastern salient reaching down to the lower slopes in the vicinity of Nyeri. Only rarely does this park feature in the itineraries of safari companies and it's even less visited by individual travellers. There are various reasons for this. The main one is perhaps the weather. As on Mt Kenya, rain can be expected at any time and when it arrives, it's heavy. Roads turn into mud slides and 4WD is absolutely essential. The park is often closed during the wet season as a result.

Another drawback (though the wild game would no doubt describe it as a plus) is the difficulty of seeing animals because of the dense forest. This is not savannah like Amboseli and Masai Mara so you have to take your time and stay a few nights, which brings us to the third drawback – finding a place to stay. Though there are three camp sites within the park, facilities are minimal and you're going to need a good tent and warm sleeping gear. Add to this the fact that there's no public transport whatsoever, hitching is virtually impossible and that, as elsewhere, walking isn't permitted without special permission. That essentially puts the Aberdares out of reach of anyone without their own transport. The only other accommodation possibilities are two very expensive lodges, The Ark and Treetops, which you are not allowed to drive to in your own vehicle. You must make advance reservations for both and be driven there in the lodges' transport.

In the dry season it may be possible to walk over the high moorland between the four main peaks if the weather is favourable but you can't do this without the express permission of the game warden at Mweiga north of Nyeri (☎ 24 in Mweiga). If this is what you want to do then it's best to first contact the Kenya Mountain Club in Nairobi before setting out, as they may be planning such a trip.

These sorts of difficulties and/or the expense involved put off most independent travellers but if you're determined to go then the rewards can well justify the effort.

The park does offer a variety of fauna, flora and scenery which you won't find elsewhere except, perhaps, on Mt Kenya. There are also the dramatic **Gura Falls** which drop a full 300 metres, thick forest, alpine moorland and a slim chance of seeing a bongo, black leopard, elephant or rhino. There are also hundreds of species of birds. The major plus about this park is that you'll never feel part of the safari-bus gravy train as you can often do in Masai Mara, Amboseli or Nairobi national parks.

Game Drives

If you can't afford the overnight charges at the lodges there is a somewhat cheaper way of visiting the park and that is to go on a game drive organised by the Outspan Hotel in Nyeri. You can do this into the eastern park area for US$30 per person (minimum two people) for the day excluding park entry fees. You can also rent self-drive vehicles from the Outspan to explore the whole park for US$78 per day.

Game drives organised by the Aberdare Country Club are yet another option, although these aren't particularly cheap either. A game drive in the salient costs US$162 for the whole vehicle for half a day, or US$312 for a full day. A surcharge of 20% is made if you're not staying at either the Country Club or The Ark.

Places to Stay

If you wish to camp in the park, reservations have to be made at the park headquarters at Mweiga (☎ 24 in Mweiga), about 12 km north of Nyeri. The charges are standard.

Both of the lodges are built beside water holes, and animals – especially elephant and buffalo – are lured to them by salt which is spread below the viewing platforms each day. This is obviously a contrived way of getting the animals to turn up but it pulls in the well-heeled punters and they, in turn, keep Lonrho, Block Hotels, Kodak and Nikon in business. What it doesn't do is anything positive to the immediate environ-

ment. Elephants eat a prodigious amount of herbage each day and trample down even more. Buffaloes aren't exactly light on the hoof either. The two combined make sure that the area in front of the viewing platforms resembles a matatu stand which, in turn, makes the smaller and more timid animals reluctant to approach because of lack of cover. I suppose if you pay big bucks, the video has to be good even if it's thin on authenticity.

On the other hand, *Treetops* isn't exactly a 'luxury' lodge with its trestle tables, creaking floorboards, shoe-box sized rooms and shared bathroom facilities, though it does have that yuppie appeal of knowing that you've stayed under the same roof as various crowned heads of Europe and presidents of state – there are even faded mug-shots of the *nomenclatura* on the walls.

Full board (including transfer from Nyeri but excluding park entry fees) at Treetops costs US$134 (ordinary room) and US$266 (suite) per person between 1 September and 31 March, US$165 and US$201 during July and August, and US$84 and US$114 the rest of the year. Children under seven years old are not admitted. You must book in advance through Block Hotels (☎ (02) 335807), Central Reservation Office, Rehema House, Standard St, PO Box 47557, Nairobi. Having booked, you then turn up at the Outspan Hotel in Nyeri by 11.30 am for lunch (included) and transfer to the park at 2.30 pm. It isn't necessary to stay at the Outspan the previous night unless you particularly want to.

The Ark is somewhat better appointed than Treetops and is further into the park but it costs much more, too. Full board here, including transfer from Mweiga but excluding park entry fees, costs US$207/242 from April to June and November to mid-December, and US$377/448 the rest of the year. As at Treetops, children under seven years old are not admitted; children over seven years pay the full adult rate.

You must book in advance through Lonrho Hotels Kenya (☎ (02) 216940), Bruce House, Standard St, PO Box 58581,

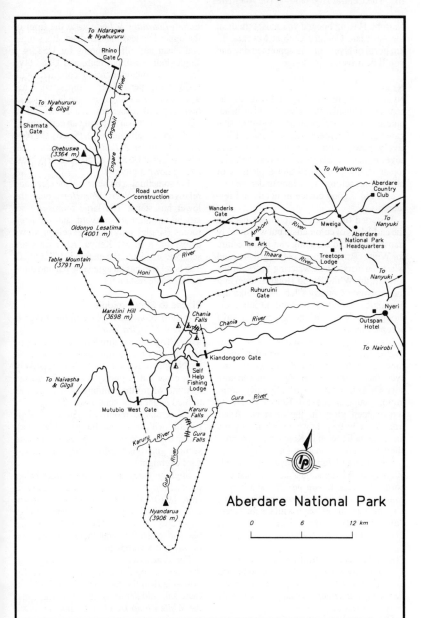

Aberdare National Park

Nairobi. Having booked you must turn up at the Aberdare Country Club at Mweiga, 12 km north of Nyeri, on the appointed day and you'll be driven to the lodge.

NYERI

Nyeri is one of the largest towns in the central highlands, the administrative headquarters of Central province, and the usual gateway to Aberdare National Park. It's a lively place with an extensive market, several banks, hardware stores, vehicle-repair shops, bookshops and a plethora of other stores selling everything under the sun. It also has a good choice of hotels and restaurants.

It started life as a garrison town back in the early days of colonialism but was quickly transformed into a trading and social centre for White cattle ranchers, coffee growers and wheat farmers. Their watering holes, in the form of the White Rhino Hotel in town and the Aberdare Country Club at Mweiga are nostalgic reminders of their proclivities, though the White Rhino appears to have accepted inevitable decline.

It's a very green area and intensively cultivated for all manner of vegetables, sugar cane, citrus fruits, bananas, tea, coffee and even that Australian import – macadamia nuts! On a clear day, too (usually early mornings), you can see Mt Kenya in all its snowcapped glory in the distance. Apart from these virtues, however, it's hardly the most magnetic town in Kenya and few travellers stay more than a couple of nights.

The Gliding Club of Kenya has its headquarters at Mweiga, just a short distance north of Nyeri. If you are into soaring, or would like to take a glide over the Aberdares, it's worth getting in touch with the managers Peter & Petra Allmendinger (☎ (0171) 2748), PO Box 926, Nyeri.

Places to Stay – bottom end

If you're down and out, there are some real dives here such as the *New Alaska Hotel* and the *South Tetu Hotel* but they can't seriously be recommended.

One of the best in the budget range is the *Bahati Boarding & Lodging* at the front of the upper bus and matatu stand. It's simple and clean and offers rooms for US$3/4 a single/double without bath, and US$4.60/6 for a self-contained room complete with lurid wallpaper. There's supposedly hot water in the mornings, and the hotel has its own bar and restaurant. It's a convenient place to stay if you're taking an early bus. If the Bahati is full (unlikely), then try the *New 7 Star Boarding & Lodging* across the road. It's cheaper at US$2.70/5.50 but is very basic and somewhat gloomy.

For something a bit better try the clean and relatively new *Nyeri Star Hotel* near the lower bus stand. The large rooms are set around an internal courtyard, and the front rooms (singles only) have excellent views across town to Mt Kenya. All rooms are self-contained and the charge is US$6/9.70. The hotel also has an agreeable bar and quite a reasonable restaurant.

Places to Stay – middle

The most economical place in this range is the *New Thingira Guest House* (☎ (0171) 4769). To get there, turn left and head downhill just after the mosque as you come in on the Nairobi to Karatina road. It's a relatively new place but is poorly managed, and the institute where the building's architect was trained ought to be shut down! The cost for a self-contained room is US$8.50/14, supposedly with breakfast, but you'll be lucky if this ever materialises. An askari (private security guard) is employed to guard the car park overnight.

Slightly more expensive but a much better proposition is the equally modern *Central Hotel* (☎ (0171) 2906) at the top end of town. Self-contained singles/doubles here with hot water cost US$12/16. The hotel has its own bar and restaurant and there's a disco on Friday and Saturday nights.

For a touch of olde-worlde charm at about the same price (though you pay more for nostalgia than the facilities which it offers) there's the old White settlers' watering hole, the *White Rhino Hotel*. It's a popular place to stay, has a terrace bar, lounge, garden and

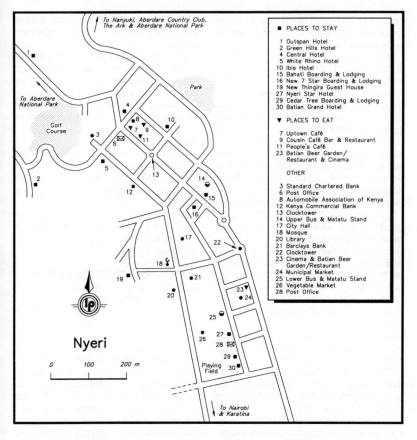

To Nanyuki, Aberdare Country Club,
The Ark & Aberdare National Park

To Aberdare
National Park

Park

Golf
Course

Nyeri

0   100   200 m

Playing
Field

To Nairobi
& Karatina

■ PLACES TO STAY

1 Outspan Hotel
2 Green Hills Hotel
4 Central Hotel
5 White Rhino Hotel
10 Ibis Hotel
15 Bahati Boarding & Lodging
16 New 7 Star Boarding & Lodging
19 New Thingira Guest House
27 Nyeri Star Hotel
29 Cedar Tree Boarding & Lodging
30 Batian Grand Hotel

▼ PLACES TO EAT

7 Uptown Café
9 Cousin Café Bar & Restaurant
11 People's Café
23 Batian Beer Garden/
Restaurant & Cinema

OTHER

3 Standard Chartered Bank
6 Post Office
8 Automobile Association of Kenya
12 Kenya Commercial Bank
13 Clocktower
14 Upper Bus & Matatu Stand
17 City Hall
18 Mosque
20 Library
21 Barclays Bank
22 Clocktower
23 Cinema & Batian Beer
Garden/Restaurant
24 Municipal Market
25 Lower Bus & Matatu Stand
26 Vegetable Market
28 Post Office

quite a cheap restaurant and offers rooms for US$11/18.50 including breakfast.

At the top of the range is the *Green Hills Hotel* (☎ (0171) 2017) which sits on the crest of the hill across the narrow valley opposite the White Rhino. Unless you have transport the location is inconvenient and you'll be much better off in one of the hotels in the town centre. The hotel is set amongst rolling lawns and though it has 124 double rooms it's not high-rise. Rooms cost US$21/33 a single/double including breakfast and taxes. There's no charge for children up to 12 years old occupying the same room as their parents. There are two restaurants, a bar,

sauna, massage facilities, children's playground, swimming pool and guarded parking facilities. Checkout time is 10 am. The staff are friendly and the rooms very pleasantly decorated and furnished.

Places to Stay – top end

In the town centre, not far from the lower bus stand, is the modern *Batian Grand Hotel* (☎ (0171) 4141). Although it's clean, comfortable and well furnished, some of the rooms (particularly the singles) are uncomfortably small, especially considering the sort of money you have to part with to stay here: US$31/58 for a single/double with breakfast. The hotel accepts most major credit cards, has its own bar and restaurant, and a guarded car park.

About a km out of town is the *Outspan Hotel* (☎ (0171) 2424), one of the Block Hotels chain (☎ (02) 335807 in Nairobi). This is the check-in place for guests of the Treetops lodge in the Aberdare National Park. It's sited in beautifully landscaped gardens opposite the golf course and has all the facilities you would expect from a top-end country hotel except that the Mt Kenya Bar has, in fact, no view of Mt Kenya at all – surely a major planning balls-up. Prices depend on the season and the type of accommodation which you take. In the high season (July and August) Singles/doubles with breakfast cost US$84/117 in a standard room, or US$95/123 in one of the very pleasant cottages. In the low season (from 1 April to 30 June and early December) the prices are US$38/75 and US$91/107 respectively. For the rest of the year the prices are US$53/81 and US$98/112. Children under 12 years old are free if sharing the same room with adults.

Self-drive cars can be hired from the hotel to visit Aberdare National Park (see the earlier Game Drives section).

The only other place in this price range is the *Aberdare Country Club* about 12 km north of Nyeri, which is part of the Lonrho Hotels Kenya group (☎ (02) 216940), Bruce House, Standard St, PO Box 58581, Nairobi. Like the Kentmere Club at Limuru and the Norfolk Hotel in Nairobi (also owned by Lonrho), this was once one of the quintessential White planters' watering holes and social foci except that these days it caters for the international leisure set and those with the money to burn on a night or two at The Ark. Full board (including temporary membership) costs US$79/133 for singles/doubles from April to June and November to mid-December, and US$129/168 the rest of the year. Children aged from two to 12 years are charged US$52.

Places to Eat
The most reliable places for a meal are the *White Rhino Hotel* and the *Central Hotel* where you can eat well and relatively cheaply.

The very popular *Uptown Café* is worth a visit if you want cheap, tasty no-frills food. It offers a good range of food such as burgers, various curries and steaks.

Another cheap place for snacks and coffee is the *People's Café* near the main post office.

Getting There & Away
From the upper bus stand there are regular matatus to Nyahururu, Nakuru, Thika, Nairobi and Nanyuki, and less frequently to places further afield such as Meru and Eldoret.

Between Nyeri and Nairobi there are also less frequent and cheaper buses, and if you really want a thrill, Peugeot 504s do the trip at breakneck speeds.

NYAHURURU & THOMSON'S FALLS
Nyahururu, or 'T Falls' as virtually everyone calls it, was one of the last White settler towns to be established in the colonial era and didn't really take off until the arrival of the railway spur from Gilgil (on the main Nairobi to Kisumu line) in 1929. The railway still operates but these days carries only freight. Nyahururu is one of the highest towns in Kenya (at 2360 metres) and the climate is cool and invigorating. The surrounding undulating plateau is intensively cultivated with maize, beans and sweet potatoes and well forested, mainly with conifers. The most interesting approach to the town is probably along the excellent road from Nakuru which snakes up and down through farmlands and forests and offers some spectacular views over the Aberdares.

The falls, on the outskirts of town, are named after Joseph Thomson who was the first European to walk from Mombasa to Lake Victoria in the early 1880s. They're a popular stopover for safari companies en route to Maralal and points further north and are well worth a visit. Formed by the waters of the Ewaso Narok River, the falls plummet over 72 metres into a ravine and the resulting spray bathes the dense forest below in a

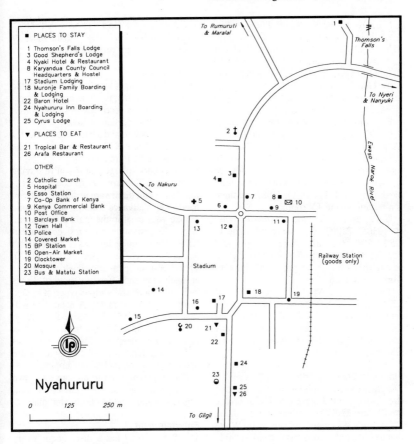

PLACES TO STAY

1 Thomson's Falls Lodge
3 Good Shepherd's Lodge
4 Nyaki Hotel & Restaurant
8 Karyandua County Council
  Headquarters & Hostel
17 Stadium Lodging
18 Muronje Family Boarding
  & Lodging
22 Baron Hotel
24 Nyahururu Inn Boarding
  & Lodging
25 Cyrus Lodge

PLACES TO EAT

21 Tropical Bar & Restaurant
26 Arafa Restaurant

OTHER

2 Catholic Church
5 Hospital
6 Esso Station
7 Co-Op Bank of Kenya
9 Kenya Commercial Bank
10 Post Office
11 Barclays Bank
12 Town Hall
13 Police
14 Covered Market
15 BP Station
16 Open-Air Market
19 Clocktower
20 Mosque
23 Bus & Matatu Station

To Rumuruti & Maralal

Thomson's Falls

To Nyeri & Nanyuki

Ewaso Narok River

To Nakuru

Railway Station (goods only)

Stadium

Nyahururu

0   125   250 m

To Gilgil

perpetual mist. A series of stone steps leads down to the bottom of the ravine and is the only safe access. Don't attempt to go down any other way as the rocks on the side of the ravine are often very loose. Up above the falls and partially overlooking them (though the view is obscured by a row of ugly souvenir shacks) is the old colonial watering hole, Thomson's Falls Lodge, which has retained much of its quaint atmosphere and is still the most interesting place to stay. The hotel grounds are a popular place for a Sunday picnic with local families. There's supposedly a US$0.60 charge for using the hotel grounds if you're not staying there, but this is rarely enforced.

Places to Stay – bottom end

The best place to stay if you have camping equipment is the camp site at *Thomson's Falls Lodge* which is very pleasant and costs US$2 per person per night with as much firewood as you need. Campers have access to all the facilities at the lodge including hot showers and toilets.

For those without camping equipment there are several budget hotels in town. Cheapest are the *Muronje Family Boarding*

& *Lodging* and the *Nyahururu Inn Boarding & Lodging* where you can get a room with shared cold-water bath for around US$3, but both these places are very basic and you shouldn't expect too much. Far better value is the *Good Shepherd's Lodge* which offers self-contained rooms with towel and soap provided for US$4 per person.

For solo male travellers the best bet is probably the quiet *Karyandua County Council Hostel*, behind the post office and provincial headquarters. It only has single rooms (sharing not permitted), but they are all self-contained (soap, towel and toilet paper provided). The cost is US$3 and there is a restaurant and TV room.

Going up in price, the *Stadium Lodging* (☎ (0365) 22002) is quite good value at US$3.50/7 for self-contained singles/doubles with hot water. There's a large grille across the entrance so you don't have to worry about theft.

The modern *Nyaki Hotel* (☎ (0365) 22313) is set back from the main road in the centre of town. Curiously, all the rooms are singles, but they are all self-contained and cost US$6. The hotel has its own bar and a reasonable restaurant.

Places to Stay – middle
The place to stay in this category if you have the money is *Thomson's Falls Lodge* (☎ (0365) 22006) overlooking the falls. Though it's no longer frequented by White planters, it exudes nostalgia and olde-worlde charm with its polished wooden floorboards and log fires. Accommodation is available either in the main building with its bar, lounge and dining room or in separate cottages scattered over the well-maintained lawns. Rooms here are self-contained with hot water and your own log fire, and cost US$30/42 a single/double though there is scope for negotiation.

If you prefer modernity and a place in the centre then the *Baron Hotel* (☎ (0365) 32751) is the choice. It's clean, well-organised and self-contained rooms with hot water go for US$9.70/14 a single/double including breakfast. The hotel has its own

restaurant and the food is good with a choice of three dishes each day – fish, meat or chicken. Prices are very reasonable.

Places to Eat
Most of the budget hotels and many of the bars have a restaurant where you can get standard African food. Meals at the *Baron Hotel* are also excellent value.

For local colour and a barbecued meal, try the *Tropical Bar & Restaurant* around the corner from the Baron Hotel.

For a minor splurge – or if you're staying there – eat at *Thomson's Falls Lodge*. Breakfast, lunch and dinner are available, but you need to give advance warning if you intend to take your meal in the main dining room. A full English-style breakfast costs about US$6. Three-course lunches or dinners with dessert and tea or coffee cost US$9.70. There's also an open-air grill which operates at lunch time and offers a variety of dishes including soups and various types of nyama choma (barbecued meat). A meat dish will cost you about US$3. The lodge also has the most interesting and one of the liveliest bars in town with deep comfortable armchairs and blazing log fires. All the facilities are open to nonguests including campers.

For those who want to prepare their own meals, there's an excellent choice of fruit, vegetables and meat in the covered market.

Entertainment
The *Baron Hotel* has a discotheque every Friday and Saturday night.

Getting There & Away
There are plenty of buses and matatus throughout the day until late afternoon in either direction between Nakuru and Nyeri and Nyahururu. Other destinations served by regular matatus and buses include Nairobi, Nanyuki, Thika, Kericho and Isiolo.

There's also at least one minibus per day in either direction between Maralal and Nyahururu which leaves early in the morning and costs US$4. Get there early if you want a seat. For the rest of the day, hitching is feasible but not easy. The road is surfaced as far as Rumuruti after which it's gravel or *murram* (dirt). Parts of this gravel road are in bad shape but it improves considerably the nearer you get to Maralal.

Mt Kenya Area

Although a distinctly separate massif from the Aberdares, Mt Kenya also forms part of the central highlands. Africa's second-highest mountain at 5199 metres, its gleaming and eroded snow-covered peaks can be seen for miles until the late-morning clouds obscure the view. Its lower slopes, like those of the Aberdares, are intensively cultivated by the Kikuyu and the closely related Embu and Meru peoples, along with the descendants of the White settlers who grow mainly wheat on the grassy and largely treeless plains on the northern side. So vast is this mountain that it's not hard to understand why the Kikuyu deified it, why their houses are built with the doors facing the peak and why it was probably never scaled until the arrival of European explorers.

These days it's every traveller's dream to get to the top and take home with them a memory which money cannot buy.

The mountain is circled by an excellent tarmac road along which are the area's main towns – Naro Moru, Nanyuki, Meru and Embu, along with Isiolo at the extreme north-eastern end. We deal first with the towns along this road and then with Mt Kenya itself since the towns are the jumping-off points for climbing the mountain.

NARO MORU

The village of Naro Moru on the western side of the mountain consists of little more than a string of small shops and houses, a couple of very basic hotels, agricultural warehouses and the famous Naro Moru River Lodge, but it's the most popular starting point for climbing Mt Kenya. There's a post office here but no banks (the nearest are at Nanyuki and Nyeri).

The other important thing to bear in mind

is that the Naro Moru River Lodge has an exclusive franchise on the mountain huts along the Naro Moru route including those at the meteorological ('Met') station so you have to go to this lodge to make bookings. It's all been carefully calculated to sew up the market on this route but that doesn't prevent you from climbing independently so long as you're willing to camp and have the appropriate equipment.

Places to Stay

There are a couple of basic lodges in the village, the *Naro Moru 82 Bar & Restaurant* and the *Mountain View Lodge*, but hardly anyone stays there. Most people head off to the *Naro Moru River Lodge* (☎ (0176) 62622) which is about 1½ km off to the left down a gravel track from the main Nairobi to Nanyuki road. It's essentially a top-range hotel set in landscaped gardens alongside the Naro Moru River but it does have a well-equipped camp site with hot showers and toilets for US$4.50 per person per night. Also at the camp site are dormitory bunkhouses where a bed costs US$6.50. Campers are entitled to use all the hotel facilities.

Those seeking a degree of luxury either before or after climbing the mountain have the option of self-contained 'standard' or 'superior' rooms or cottages. In the low season (24 April to 11 June and 18 September to 17 December) the rooms cost US$36/66 and US$47/81 for half board, while the cottages range from US$36 to US$71. For the rest of the year the prices are US$85/110 and US$98/138 for the rooms, and from US$55 to US$120 for the cottages. The hotel has a swimming pool and a restaurant. There's also a cosy bar complete with log-burning fireplace and decked out with autographed T-shirts of various groups from all over the world who have climbed the mountain at one time or another. American Express and Visa cards are accepted.

The main reason for coming to this lodge if you're an independent traveller is that it's here you must book and pay for any of the mountain huts which you want to stay at along the Naro Moru route. Those at the Met

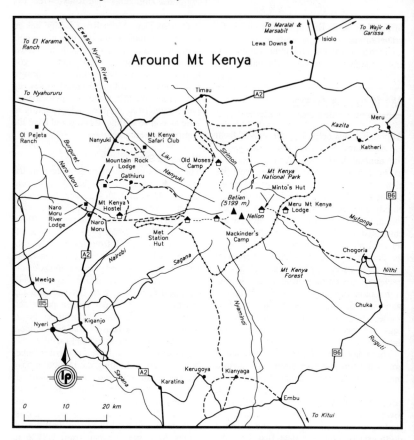

Around Mt Kenya

Station cost US$7.50 and the ones at Mackinder's Camp US$11. You can also pay for the camp sites here which cost US$0.60 (no charge for guides or porters). Members of the Mountain Club of Kenya are entitled to a 25% discount on these prices and the accommodation charges at the lodge.

The other reason for coming to this lodge if you don't have a tent, cooking equipment or appropriate clothing is that it runs a comprehensive hire service which is open daily from 7 am to 1 pm and 2 to 8 pm. The charges are similar to those at Atul's in Nairobi and are detailed under the description of climbing the mountain.

There's also an excess baggage store which costs US$0.80 per piece. You can use this service whether you're a guest or not.

The only cheap place to stay in the vicinity is the *Mt Kenya Hostel*, about 12 km up the road towards the mountain, off the main road to the right. This is a very popular place with budget travellers and campers and it's run by a very friendly and helpful man named Joseph. Accommodation is available in either the main building or in a rustic hut, facilities include hot-water showers and cooking facilities. The hostel is signposted on the main road up to the mountain. The advantage of staying here

The Kikuyu

The Kikuyu number more than three million and their heartland is the area around Mt Kenya. The original Kikuyu are thought to have migrated to the area from the east and north-east over a period of a couple of hundred years from the 16th century, and were actually part of the group known as Meru. Basically they overran the original occupants of the area such as the Athi and the Gumba, although intermarriage and trading did take place.

The Kikuyu's new land was bordered by the Maasai and although there were periods of calm between the two groups, there were also times when raids were carried out against each other's property and cattle. Both groups placed a high value on cattle. Intermarriage was not uncommon between them and there are a number of similarities – particularly in dress, weaponry, and dancing – shared by both as a result of their intermingling.

The administration of the clans *(mwaki)*, made up of many family groups *(nyumba)*, was originally taken care of by a council of elders with a good deal of importance being placed on the role of the witch doctor, medicine man and the blacksmith. Traditionally the Kikuyu god (Ngai) is believed to reside on Mt Kenya *(Kirinyaga* – the 'mountain of brightness', 'mountain of whiteness' or 'black and white peak spotted like ostrich feathers') which accounts for the practice of orientating Kikuyu homes with the door facing Mt Kenya.

Initiation rites for both boys and girls are important ceremonies and consist of circumcision in boys and cliterodectomy in girls (the latter now rarely practiced), accompanied by elaborate preparations and rituals. Each group of youths of the same age belong to an 'age-set' *(riika)* and pass through the various stages of life (with associated rituals) together.

Subgroups of the Kikuyu include Embu, Ndia and Mbeere. ∎

---

is that it's only about four km to the park entrance gate.

Seven km north of Naro Moru on the Nanyuki road is the *Mountain Rock Lodge* (☎ (0176) 62625), tucked away in wooded surroundings less than a km from the main road. It offers pleasant self-contained cottages with hot showers and fireplaces for US$26/29 a single/double. Rates including breakfast are US$34/44, or with full board, US$53/85. 'Superior' rooms are also available and these cost US$32/39, US$39/52 and US$60/95 respectively. There's also a well-equipped camp site with hot and cold water, toilets, cooking facilities, electricity and ample firewood for US$5 per person per

night. Meals in the restaurant cost US$6.50 for breakfast, US$9 for lunch and US$10.40 for dinner. All prices include taxes and service charges. The main block consists of a spacious dining room, bar, lounge and a terrace with a *makuti* (straw or reed) roof. The hotel accepts credit cards.

Horse riding (US$13 per hour), trout fishing (US$6.50 per hour including fishing rod and licence) and bird-watching are some of the activities which the lodge caters for, plus there are traditional dances performed when demand warrants it (US$5 per person with a minimum of six people, or US$104 on demand).

The main reason for coming here,

however, is to take one of the hotel's guided treks to the summit of Mt Kenya via the Naro Moru, Burguret or Sirimon routes. There is a whole range of these to choose from depending on where you want to go and how long you wish to take. The full range of possibilities is outlined in the section dealing with climbing Mt Kenya later in this chapter.

Places to Eat

There are no restaurants at Naro Moru so you'll either have to cook your own food or eat at the *Naro Moru River Lodge*. There's very little choice of food available at the shops in Naro Moru so bring your own or, if you have transport, go to Nanyuki to buy it.

Getting There & Away

There are plenty of buses and matatus from Nairobi and Nyeri to Nanyuki and Isiolo which will drop you off in Naro Moru.

The Naro Moru River Lodge also operates a shuttle bus between the lodge and Nairobi on a daily basis. It departs from the lodge at 9 am and from Nairobi at 2.30 pm and costs US$40 one way and US$73 return (not cheap!). In Nairobi you have to book the bus on the 1st floor of College House (☎ 337-501), University Way – ask for Stanley Matiba. In Naro Moru, book at the lodge. The lodge also does transfers to Nanyuki airstrip (US$20 per person) and to the meteorological station for US$78, the park gate for US$39 or the trailhead on the Sirimon route for US$137.

NANYUKI

Nanyuki is a typical small country town about halfway along the northern section of the Mt Kenya ring road and a popular base from which to trek up the mountain via either the Burguret or Sirimon routes. It was founded by White settlers in 1907 in the days when game roamed freely and in large numbers over the surrounding grassy plains. The game has almost disappeared – shot by the settlers for meat and to protect their crops from damage by foragers – but the descendants of the settlers remain and the town has also become a Kenyan air force base as well

as a British army base for the joint manoeuvres conducted by the two armies each year. It's a fairly pleasant town and still has a faint ring of the colonial era to it. There's all the usual facilities here including banks, a post office and a good range of well-stocked stores.

Places to Stay – bottom end

The cheapest place is the *Nanyuki Youth Hostel* (☎ (0176) 2112) at the Emmanuel Parish Centre, Market Rd, but it's pretty basic, even dismal. The showers have only cold water. There are also some simple lodges, including the *Silent Guest House* and the *Juba Boarding & Lodging*.

More expensive but a popular place to stay is the *Josaki Hotel* (☎ (0176) 2181) which has large, clean, self-contained singles/doubles with hot water for US$4 per person. There's a bar and restaurant on the 1st floor. Secure parking is available. Also popular, but not as good, is the *Sirimon Guest House* fronting the park.

Places to Stay – middle

A short distance from the centre of town along the Isiolo road is the *Simba Lodge*, not far from the Catholic church. Self-contained rooms in this comfortable and quiet hotel cost around US$14/18 including breakfast. Vehicles can be parked in the hotel compound and are guarded by an askari.

Probably the nicest place in this range is the *Sportsman's Arms Hotel* (☎ (0176) 22598), south-east of the town centre and across the river. Run by an Asian lady, Mrs Dia, this was once the White settlers' watering hole as the style of the building and the extensive surrounding lawns indicate. It's certainly a bit rough around the edges these days, but is excellent value at US$12/19. The self-contained rooms are huge and musty, the plumbing antediluvian and the whole place has an air of gradual and inevitable decay. The restaurant serves some of the best meals in town at moderate prices, and the bar is lively in the evenings with the British army lads.

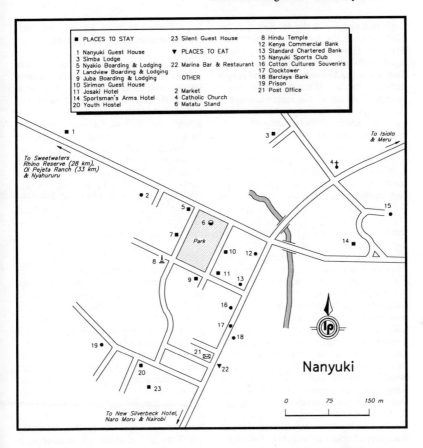

PLACES TO STAY

1 Nanyuki Guest House
3 Simba Lodge
5 Nyakio Boarding & Lodging
7 Landview Boarding & Lodging
9 Juba Boarding & Lodging
10 Sirimon Guest House
11 Josaki Hotel
14 Sportsman's Arms Hotel
20 Youth Hostel
23 Silent Guest House

PLACES TO EAT

22 Marina Bar & Restaurant

OTHER

2 Market
4 Catholic Church
6 Matatu Stand
8 Hindu Temple
12 Kenya Commercial Bank
13 Standard Chartered Bank
15 Nanyuki Sports Club
16 Cotton Cultures Souvenirs
17 Clocktower
18 Barclays Bank
19 Prison
21 Post Office

Nanyuki

Places to Eat

There are very few restaurants in Nanyuki which are not attached to hotels, so take your pick. The *Marina Bar & Restaurant* is a reasonable place to eat in the centre of town and an expats' watering hole. For something a bit more sophisticated, try a meal at the *Sportsman's Arms*.

Things to Buy

There are a number of souvenir stalls and shops set up around town, catering mostly to the British army. The Cotton Culture store on the main street has some interesting items,

including beautiful woollen jumpers (US$52) hand-knitted by a local women's cooperative.

Getting There & Away

There are daily buses from Nairobi and Isiolo to Nanyuki as well as minibuses and matatus from Nyeri and Nyahururu which run throughout the day.

AROUND NANYUKI

There are a number of accommodation possibilities in the vicinity of Nanyuki, although only one of them could be called cheap.

Closest to town is the *Mt Kenya Safari Club*, one of the Lonrho group (☎ (02) 216940). This hotel, originally the homestead of a White Kenyan settler family, was founded in the 1950s by a group of people including the late William Holden, and is now possibly one of the most exclusive in the country. The views up to Mt Kenya are excellent, and facilities include golf, tennis, croquet, snooker, swimming (heated pool), fishing and bowls.

The tariff for all this luxury starts at US$244/317 for full board in a standard room, and there are more expensive suites and studios. There are also a number of two-bedroom cottages (US$770) and three-bedroom villas (US$1148). Children aged from two to 12 years are charged US$57. The turn-off for the hotel is a couple of km from Nanyuki along the Naro Moru road, and from there it's nine km along a dirt road which becomes treacherous in the wet.

More luxury options exist on the *Ol Pejeta Ranch* (☎ (02) 216940 in Nairobi), west of Nanyuki along the Nyahururu road. This 9000-hectare ranch has been converted into a private rhino sanctuary and is accessible only to those who can afford the accommodation. The Ol Pejeta homestead, also belonging to the Lonrho group, was the former vacation getaway of the now-bankrupt international financier Adnan Kashoggi. As he was not one to spare any expense, the hotel is lavishly decorated, and still features Kashoggi's four-metre-wide bed! Full-board rates are US$78/130 in the low season (April to June, and November to mid-December) and US$163/208 the rest of the year. More expensive suites are also available. Children under 16 years are *personae non gratae* here.

Also on the Ol Pejeta Ranch is the *Sweetwaters Tented Camp*, where a number of luxury permanent tents (though they are tents in name only) have been constructed beside a water hole (floodlit at night). With the water hole as a focus, game-viewing is the main activity, although there are other diversions such as swimming in the pool, and camel rides. The cost of full-board accommodation is US$63/117 in the low season,

and US$144/192 in the high season. Children aged from two to 12 years are charged US$52.

Yet another option, and a much more affordable one, is the *El Karama Ranch* (☎ (02) 340331 in Nairobi), 42 km northwest of Nanyuki on the Ewaso Nyiro River. Billed as a 'self-service camp', El Karama is a family-run ranch with a number of bandas for guests. The accommodation is basic but comfortable, and costs just US$1.30 per person per night but if you need extras such as bedding (US$3 per person per night), cooking utensils (US$3 per night), crockery (US$3), firewood (US$3) and kerosene lamps (US$3), the cost can go up somewhat. You need to bring supplies from Nanyuki as meals are not available.

ISIOLO

Isiolo, where the tarmac ends, is the frontier town for north-eastern Kenya – a vast area of both forested and barren mountains, deserts, scrub, Lake Turkana and home to the Samburu, Rendille, Boran and Turkana peoples. It's a lively town with a good market and all the usual facilities including petrol stations, a bank, a post office and a good choice of hotels and restaurants. There are also bus connections to places north, east and south of here.

The resident population of Isiolo is largely Somali in origin as a result of the resettlement here of Somali ex-soldiers following WW I. It ought, in addition, to be famous for the number of formidable speed bumps which force traffic to a snail's pace on the way into town from the south. There are no less than 21 of these and more still at the northern edge of town!

Information

Isiolo is the last place going north which has a bank (Barclays) until you get to either Maralal or Marsabit. There are no banks on the way to or at Lake Turkana (assuming you bypass Maralal).

Likewise, there are no petrol stations north of here until you reach Maralal or Marsabit except at the Samburu Lodge (in Samburu

National Park). This doesn't mean that petrol or diesel is totally unobtainable since you can buy it in Baragoi (with ease) and possibly at Christian mission stations elsewhere (with difficulty or not at all if they're low on stock) but you will pay well over the odds for it due to transport costs and irregularity of supply. Stock up in Isiolo.

Travellers about to go to the national parks north of here or to Lake Turkana and who intend to do their own cooking should stock up on food and drink in Isiolo as there's very little available beyond here except at Maralal, Marsabit and (less so) Wamba. There's a very good market in Isiolo adjacent to the mosque for fresh fruit, vegetables and meat. The general stores, too, have a good range of canned food and other items.

Places to Stay – bottom end
There are a number of fairly basic lodging houses available for those tight on funds which include the *Maendeleo Hotel, Farmers Boarding & Lodging, Savannah Inn, Frontier Lodge, Coffee Tree Hotel* and the *National Hotel*, all offering rooms with shared bathroom facilities (cold water only) from US$3.30/4.50 a single/double. The downstairs area of the Frontier Lodge is taken up by a lively bar which sometimes hosts live bands.

The best place to stay, however, is the *Jamhuri Guest House* which is excellent value and has been popular with travellers for a number of years. It's run by Ibrahim and Arden who are both very friendly and will go out of their way to be helpful. The rooms are very clean and pleasant, mosquito nets are provided and the communal showers have hot water in the mornings. Rooms cost US$3/4 a single/double. Belongings left in the rooms are quite safe. Next door to it and similar in price and quality is the *Silent Inn*.

Another possibility is the *Talent Lodge* near the post office. It offers rooms with shared bath for US$1.80/3.50 a single/double. There is supposedly hot water all day in the showers but this is wishful thinking. The centre of the hotel and the terrace over-

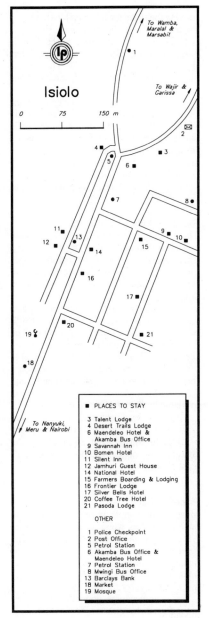

looking the street are taken up by a bar so it's not as quiet as the Jamhuri Guest House.

Going up in price, there is the *Pasoda Lodge* which is clean and quiet and offers doubles with bath for US$5.80. There are no singles. The hotel has its own restaurant and bar.

At the top of the budget category is the brand new *Desert Trails Lodge*, clearly visible behind the BP station on the main street. The design of this place is perhaps a little claustrophobic given all the wide open spaces close by, but it does mean the security is good. Rooms are good value at US$4.50/8 with a bathroom shared between two rooms.

Places to Stay – middle

There's only one mid-range hotel in Isiolo and that is the *Bomen Hotel* (☎ (0165) 2225). This three-storey hotel has a total of 40 spacious rooms, tastefully decorated and furnished. Rates are US$16/23 for singles/doubles with hot-water bath, and prices include breakfast, taxes and service charges. Children under 12 years old are charged 30% of the single rate when sharing a room. The hotel has its own bar and restaurant which serves excellent food at very reasonable prices. Meal times are from 7 to 9.30 am (breakfast), noon to 2.30 pm (lunch) and 7.30 to 10 pm (dinner). Guarded parking is available in the hotel compound.

This is an excellent place to stay if you want to visit the nearby reserves of Samburu or Buffalo Springs but can't afford the charges at the lodges inside the parks or don't want to camp.

Places to Eat

Most of the simple boarding houses also have restaurants where you can eat typical African-style meals for less than US$3. The *Frontier Lodge* has a good café, the restaurant at the *Pasoda Lodge* is one of the better ones, and the *Silver Bells Hotel* does excellent chicken curry for US$1.60.

For a minor splurge, go for lunch or dinner at the *Bomen Hotel*.

Things to Buy

A good proportion of the young men who hang around on the main street of Isiolo are salespeople for the brass, copper and aluminium/steel bracelets which you'll already have come across elsewhere except that the craft here is particularly fine. If you're one of those people who like decking out your forearms with as many of these bracelets as you can get on them, then this is the place to buy them. They're much cheaper here than anywhere else though haggling is, of course, obligatory. The same people also sell daggers in leather scabbards but the craft in these is generally unremarkable.

If you're simply walking around Isiolo then these salespeople will hardly ever bother you but if you're driving around and especially if you're filling up with petrol at a station then expect a real hassle. Their wares will be thrust in front of your face from both sides and you'll be hard-pressed to drive away.

Getting There & Away

Akamba operates three buses daily to Nairobi at 7.30 and 9 am and 8 pm. The journey takes about seven hours and costs US$6. The buses travel via Nanyuki (US$2), Naro Moru (US$2) and Thika (US$5.50), and it's not a bad idea to book one day in advance.

Mwingi Buses operates buses to Marsabit (US$7), supposedly a couple of times a week, but this is very flexible. It also operates less frequent buses to Moyale on the Ethiopian border (US$7 from Marsabit). For either of these services it's just a matter of enquiring at the office several times to try and pin down a departure time or day. There's no alternative except to simply hang around and wait, or either negotiate a ride on a truck (relatively easy and usually somewhat less than the bus fare) or walk out to the police checkpoint north of town where the tarmac ends and hitch a ride with tourists (not so easy). The Mwingi office is an anonymous shopfront at the rear of the Bomen Hotel; just look for the derelict buses out the front.

ranching activities are still maintained. The entire area has been enclosed by a solar-powered electric fence to keep out stock from neighbouring properties.

Black rhinos from other parts of the country have been relocated here and are now breeding. The ranch also has a small group of the more placid white rhinos, and these are a big attraction, especially since those in Meru National Park were slaughtered a few years ago. Other wildlife abounds, and visitors can expect to see elephants, giraffes, eland, oryx, buffaloes, lions and leopards.

The Craig family run the *Wilderness Trails Lodge* on the ranch, and this is a small, superbly sited stone and makuti thatch set-up with stunning views across to Isiolo and the northern plains. It's a top-end place, so you can expect to part with about US$260 per person per day for full board, but the level of service is excellent and the setting perfect. The lodge is closed during April and May, and from 1 November to 15 December. Bookings must be made in advance through Chris Flatt in Nairobi (☎ (02) 502491).

Mwingi also operates buses to Maralal a few times a week (depending on demand) which cost US$6.50. Again, the departure times are uncertain.

There's no scheduled transport to Wajir and Mandera, north-east of Isiolo, and besides, this area is the domain of the shifta (Somali bandits, usually armed) and only those people with a specific reason (or a suicide wish) should contemplate travelling here. Every morning at 8 am a convoy of vehicles headed for Wajir, Mandera or Garissa leaves the police checkpost. They are mostly trucks and many will take passengers for a fee. If you are heading for Garissa a stop is made overnight in the beautiful little village of **Mado Gashi**. Here the *New Mount Kenya Lodge* is good value at US$2.70 for a large double room.

AROUND ISIOLO
Lewa Downs

Lewa Downs is a privately owned ranch of some 16,000 hectares which has been turned into a rhino and wildlife sanctuary, although

MERU

Up at the north-eastern end of the ring road around the southern side of Mt Kenya, Meru is an important town which services the intensively cultivated and forested highlands in this part of Central Province. It's quite a climb up to Meru from either Isiolo or Embu and, in the rainy season, you'll find yourself in the clouds up here along with dense forest which frequently reaches right down to the roadside. When the weather is clear there are superb views for miles over the surrounding lowlands. Views of the peaks of Mt Kenya, on the other hand, are hard to come by due mostly to the forest cover.

Although there's a small centre of sorts, Meru is essentially just a built-up area along the main road and, as far as travellers' interests go, there's precious little reason to stay the night there. It's certainly much too far away from any of the route heads leading to the peaks of Mt Kenya to be a suitable base to take off from. The nearest of these begins at Chogoria, about halfway between Meru and Embu.

Meru's main claim to fame is the quality of its miraa. These are the bundles of leafy twigs and shoots which you'll see people all over Kenya (and particularly Somalia and Ethiopia) chewing for its stimulant and appetite-suppressant properties. While it still grows wild here, much of it is now cultivated and it's become a major source of (legal) income for the cultivators and harvesters who supply both the internal market and also export it to neighbouring countries. No doubt the marijuana growers are green with envy!

Meru National Museum

This small museum just off the main road is worth visiting if you're staying here or passing through. It has the usual display detailing the progress of evolution, along with exhibits of stuffed birds, animals and mounted insects, but there's also a small and informative section concerning the agricultural and initiation practices of the Meru people and their clothing and weapons. Out at the back of the building are a number of appallingly small and sordid cages containing obviously neurotic and pathetically bored specimens of baboon, vervet monkeys and a caracal cat which someone ought to liberate immediately as an act of sheer pity if not humaneness. There's also a reptile pit with a notice advising visitors that 'Trespassers will be bitten'.

The museum is open daily from 9.30 am to 6 pm except on Sundays and holidays when it's open from 11 am to 6 pm and 1 to 6 pm respectively. Entry costs US$0.40 (US$0.20 for children) and US$0.20 for Kenyan residents.

Places to Stay

Two of the cheapest places to stay in Meru are the *Castella Bar & Hotel* and the *Continental Hotel* in the town 'centre'. They're basic and neither is particularly special. The Castella has a noisy bar downstairs, and a curious sign at reception warns that: 'Combing of the hair in the room is not allowed'. Somewhat better value is the *Stansted Hotel* (☎ (0164) 20360) on the main road past the post office. It is clean, quiet and offers self-contained rooms at US$4 per person including breakfast. The hotel has its own bar and restaurant.

Also good value is the *Milimani Hotel*, further up the hill from the Stansted. It

Meru

The Meru arrived in the area north-east of Mt Kenya from the coast sometime around the 14th century following invasions of that area by Somalis from the north. The group was led by a chief known as the *mogwe* up until 1974 when the incumbent converted to Christianity and denied his son inheriting the role. A group of tribal elders *(njuuri)* were all powerful and along with the mogwe and witch doctor would administer justice as they saw fit – which often consisted of giving poison laced beer to an accused person. Other curious practices included holding a newly born child to face Mt Kenya and then blessing it by spitting on it, while witch doctors might eliminate one of their rival's sons by putting poison on the circumcision blade.

Subgroups of the Meru include the Chuka, Igembe, Igoji, Tharaka, Muthambi, Tigania and Imenti. ■

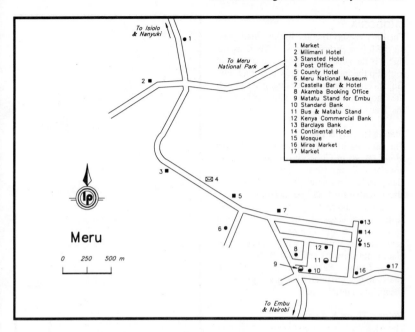

1 Market
2 Milimani Hotel
3 Stansted Hotel
4 Post Office
5 County Hotel
6 Meru National Museum
7 Castella Bar & Hotel
8 Akamba Booking Office
9 Matatu Stand for Embu
10 Standard Bank
11 Bus & Matatu Stand
12 Kenya Commercial Bank
13 Barclays Bank
14 Continental Hotel
15 Mosque
16 Miraa Market
17 Market

Meru

0 250 500 m

offers good self-contained rooms with hot water for US$7/9.40 a single/double. Vehicles can be parked safely in the hotel compound and at weekends there's a disco. If you don't have transport, this hotel is probably too far from the centre – it's about two km uphill.

The best mid-range hotel is probably the *County Hotel*, again on the main road and close to the turn-off for the museum. It's clean, comfortable, has its own restaurant and lively bar and secure parking. Self-contained rooms cost US$18/31 a single/double with breakfast.

Those with their own transport might like to check out the *Rocky Hill Inn*, about eight km out of town to the north, which is essentially a barbecue and bar but has basic chalets for rent. There's also the *Forest Lodge*, even further from town, which has a swimming pool and pretensions to being a sort of country club with expensive chalets.

Places to Eat

For a good, cheap meal of curried fish (US$1.30) or chicken (US$2.60), try the *Copper Coin* restaurant near the bus stand. Another good bet is the snack bar at the *County Hotel*. Meals cost from around US$1.30 to US$2.60, or there's a three-course set meal which is great value at US$3. The food is unexciting, but it's filling and you can have a beer with your meal. The hotel also has a more up-market restaurant.

Getting There & Away

Meru is served by Akamba buses to and from Nairobi (US$5) with departures from Meru at 7.30 and 9 am, and 8 pm. The buses travel via Chogoria (US$1.30), Embu (US$3) and Thika (US$4.50). The buses can be booked in advance, and the office is in the town centre, just off the main road.

From the matatu park there are regular departures for Isiolo, Embu and Nairobi.

CHOGORIA

The only reason to come to this small town on the lower eastern slopes of Mt Kenya is that it is the access point for the most scenic route up the mountain – the Chogoria route. Guides and porters can be engaged through the Chogoria Guides Club, which is based at the Transit Motel.

Places to Stay & Eat

The choices here are limited. The *Transit Motel* (☎ 96 in Chogoria) is about half an hour's walk up from Chogoria, and has cheap and clean singles/doubles. Camping is also possible for US$2 per person.

The other alternative is the *Forest Station*, at the barrier across the track about five km up the route from Chogoria. The 15 cabins here are fully equipped with kitchens, fireplaces, hot showers and three beds.

The *Lenana Restaurant*, just inside the gates of the hospital, is a good place for cheap, substantial meals.

Getting There & Away

The Akamba buses running between Nairobi and Meru pass through Chogoria, or there are regular matatus to Embu and Meru. The bus trip between Nairobi and Chogoria takes about 3½ hours.

EMBU

On the south-eastern slopes of Mt Kenya, Embu is an important provincial centre but spread out over many km along the main road. It has a famous school and hotel and is set in a very hilly area which is intensively cultivated. It's also the provincial headquarters of the Eastern province though it's on the extreme eastern edge of this and can only have been chosen because of its agreeable climate. Not many travellers stay here overnight, and with good reason since there's nothing much to see or do and it's a long way from the only feasible eastern route up Mt Kenya (the Chogoria route).

Places to Stay

There are quite a few cheap hotels spread out along the main road but most of them are

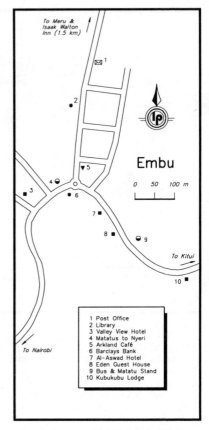

very basic and can't be recommended. Behind a row of shops almost opposite the bus and matatu park is the *Eden Guest House*. While hardly paradise, it offers clean, quiet rooms with shared facilities for US$3/5.

The *Al-Aswad Hotel*, just a little further up the road, has no single rooms, but the doubles are quite good value at US$6. The hotel also has a good restaurant where you can eat for just US$1.30. The *Kubukubu Lodge*, further down the hill from the Eden Guest House, is another reasonable choice.

The *Valley View Hotel* (☎ (0161) 20147), also in this range, has self-contained rooms with hot water for US$7/12 with breakfast. It's clean and tidy and soap and towel are provided, plus the staff are friendly and helpful. The hotel has its own bar and restaurant, and it's much quieter than the hotels around the bus stand.

If you'd like to splurge then consider a night at the *Isaak Walton Inn* (☎ (0161) 20128), about two km up the main road towards Meru from the town centre. It's right out of the colonial era and set in extensive lawns and gardens with a good restaurant and cosy bar – both with log-burning fireplaces. Originally a farmhouse and set on 3.4 hectares, it has 42 double rooms (described as 'specious' in the promotional leaflet though they no doubt meant 'spacious'!), each with bathroom and hot water plus a balcony. Rates are US$18/23 for singles/doubles including breakfast. The staff are friendly and helpful and it's definitely *the* place to stay if you have the money. Even if you don't stay here it's definitely worth turning up for a beer or a meal.

Places to Eat
The *Arkland Café*, near the main roundabout in the centre of town, is a good place for a meal or snack at lunch time. If you want the full treatment, head for the restaurant at the *Izaak Walton*.

Getting There & Away
There are daily Akamba buses between Nairobi and Embu and this is the safest way to travel between the two places. The booking office is on the top side of the bus and matatu stand.

Matatus also offer the same service but they are invariably overcrowded – often dangerously so – and the drivers drive like maniacs. 'Accidents' are frequent and often result in everyone on board being killed. This happens on average about once a fortnight so, if you value your life, *don't do this trip by matatu*. It's not that the road is in bad shape – it's an excellent road – but its sweeping curves, high bridges and constant up-hill-down-dale progression seems to encourage total recklessness among drivers.

The fare to Nairobi on the matatus is US$4.50 and they terminate on Accra Rd (if you're fortunate to get that far).

The alternative to a bus or matatu is a shared Peugeot taxi, although, if anything, these are more dangerous because they travel faster.

The matatus to Meru are not quite the same hair-raising and dangerous prospect since there's not the same pressure on the drivers, but they're no joy ride either. Take the Akamba bus or a Peugeot taxi in preference.

TREKKING ON MT KENYA
Mt Kenya's highest peaks, Batian and Nelion, can only be reached by mountaineers with technical skills. However, Point Lenana, the third-highest peak, can be reached by trekkers and this is the usual goal for most people. As you might imagine, there are superb views over the surrounding country from Point Lenana and other high points around the main peaks, though the summit is often clothed in mist from late morning until late afternoon.

Safety
It's not surprising that trekking on this mountain is high on many travellers' priority list. However, because Mt Kenya is so easy to reach, and because Point Lenana is not technically difficult, this can create its own set of problems. Many people do the ascent much too quickly and end up suffering from headaches, nausea and other (sometimes more serious) effects of altitude sickness (see the Health section in the Facts for the Visitor chapter for more details). Another problem can be the weather; even though they end up seeing the glaciers on the summits, many visitors go up the mountain without proper gear, completely unprepared for the cold and wet conditions often encountered.

This situation is made worse by some tour companies (and some guidebooks) billing the trek to Point Lenana as an easy hike. It's not unknown for ill-prepared independent trekkers to get hopelessly lost on Mt Kenya, sometimes with fatal results. Most years there are reports of people simply disappearing on the mountain.

So, when planning your trek up Mt Kenya, it is important to realise that this is no small mountain: Point Lenana is just under 5000 metres – not much lower than the Everest Base Camp in Nepal. If you spend at least three nights on the ascent before going to the summit of Lenana, you stand a much better

chance of enjoying yourself, and with proper clothes and equipment, you stand a much better chance of surviving too!

If you're not a regular mountain walker, and don't know how to use a map and compass, going up and down anything other than the Naro Moru route, without a competent companion or a local guide, is simply asking for trouble.

Mt Kenya – Geology, Flora & Fauna

Africa's second-highest mountain at 5199 metres, Mt Kenya was formed between 2½ and three million years ago as a result of successive eruptions of the volcano. Its base diameter is about 120 km, and it is probable that when first formed it was over 6000 metres in height and had a summit crater much like that on Kilimanjaro. Intensive erosion, however, principally by glacial ice, has worn away the cone and left a series of jagged peaks, U-shaped valleys and depressions containing glacial lakes or tarns.

In many of these valleys you will come across terminal moraines (curved ridges of boulders and stones carried down by the glaciers) whose position – some as low as 3000 metres – indicates that during the Ice Ages the glaciers must have been far more extensive than they are today. They began retreating rapidly about 150,000 years ago as the climate changed and the process is still going on today. Since records were first kept back in 1893, seven of the glaciers have already disappeared leaving only the current 11, yet even these are getting quite thin. It's estimated that if the present trend continues, there might be no permanent ice left on the mountain in 25 years.

The volcanic soil and the many rivers which radiate out from the central cone have created a very fertile environment, especially on the southern and eastern sides which receive the most rain. Human agricultural activity currently extends up to around 1900 metres in what used to be rainforest, yet which today is still well wooded in many parts. Above this zone, except where logging takes place, stretches the untouched rainforest characterised by an abundance of different species, particularly the giant camphors, along with vines, ferns, orchids and other epiphytes. This forest zone is not quite so dense on the northern and eastern sides since the climate here is drier and the predominant tree species are conifers. Vines, likewise, are absent.

The forest supports a rich variety of wildlife and it's quite common to come across elephants, buffaloes and various species of monkey on the forest tracks. Rhinos, numerous varieties of antelope, giant forest hogs, and lions also live here but are usually only seen in the clearings around lodges.

On the southern and western slopes the forest gradually merges into a belt of dense bamboo which often grows to 12 metres or more. This eventually gives way to more open woodland consisting of hagena and hypericum trees along with an undergrowth of flowering shrubs and herbs.

Further up still is a belt of giant heather which forms dense clumps up to four metres high interspersed with tall grasses. Open moorland forms the next zone and can often be very colourful because of the profusion of small flowering plants which thrive there. The only large plants to be found in this region – and then only in the drier, sandier parts such as the valley sides and the ridges – are those bizarre specimens of the plant kingdom, the giant lobelias and senecios. This moorland zone stretches right up to the snow line at between 4500 metres and 4700 metres though the vegetation gets more and more sparse the higher you go. Beyond the snow line, the only plants you will find are mosses and lichens.

The open woodland and moorland support various species of antelope, such as the duiker and eland, as well as zebras, but the most common mammal is the rock hyrax. Leopards also live in this region and have occasionally been observed as high as 4500 metres! Of the larger birds which you'll undoubtedly see up here are the verreaux eagles (which prey on hyrax), auger buzzards and the lammergeier (or bearded vulture). Smaller birds include the scarlet-tufted malachite sunbird, which feeds on nectar and small flies, and the friendly cliff chat which often appears in search of scraps. ■

The best times to go, as far as fair weather is concerned, is from mid-January to late February or from late August to September.

Here is a letter from a traveller who had a less than ideal trip:

I'm sure thousands of people agree that your books are extremely useful but the travel survival kit is very aptly named.

I went missing for five days on my own on the descent from Point Lenana. I lost my rucksack, sleeping bag and food. I managed to keep an army surplus bag with my camera, purse belt, hypothermia foil and guide book.

By the end of the fourth day the foil was ripped to shreds and gaining inspiration from the street dwellers in London I ripped out pages from the travel survival kit to cover myself with. I also ate some of the pages on Uganda!

Thanks for helping me survive!

Gillian Tree, UK

Books & Maps

Before you leave Nairobi we strongly recommend that you buy a copy of *Mt Kenya 1:50,000 Map & Guide* (1993) by Mark Savage & Andrew Wielochowski. It has a detailed topographical map on one side and a full description of the various routes, mountain medicine, flora & fauna, accommodation, etc on the reverse. This is money well spent and contains everything which most trekkers will need to know. It's stocked by all the main bookshops.

For keen trekkers looking for more information, or for details on wilder routes and some of the more esoteric variations that are possible on Mt Kenya, get hold of Lonely Planet's *Trekking in East Africa* by David Else. This book covers not only Mt Kenya but also a selection of treks and long-distance walks in Kenya, Tanzania, Uganda and Malawi.

Those who intend to do some technical climbing or mountaineering (as opposed to walking) should think seriously about getting a copy of the Mountain Club of Kenya's *Guide to Mt Kenya & Kilimanjaro*, edited by Iain Allan. This is a much more substantial and comprehensive guide, and is also available in all the main bookshops, or contact the Mountain Club of Kenya, PO

Box 45741, Nairobi. It may also be available from West Col Productions, Goring-on-Thames, Reading, Berks RG8 9AA, UK, and from Stanford's Map Centre, 12/14 Long Acre, Covent Garden, London WC2E 9LP, UK.

Clothing & Equipment

The summits of Mt Kenya are covered in glaciers and snow, and the temperature at night often drops to below -10°C so you are going to need a good sleeping bag. A closed-cell foam mat is also advisable if you are going to sleep on the ground as it provides the necessary insulation under your body and is far more comfortable than sleeping without one. A good set of warm clothes is equally important and that should include some sort of headgear and gloves. As it can rain at any time of year – and heavily – you will also need waterproof clothing. A decent pair of boots is an advantage but not strictly necessary. A pair of joggers is quite adequate most of the time though it's a good idea to have a pair of thongs, sandals or canvas tennis shoes to wear in the evening if your main shoes get wet.

Remember that it's not a good idea to sleep in clothes which you have worn during the day because the sweat which your day clothes absorb from your skin keep them moist at night and so reduce their heat-retention capabilities.

If you don't intend to stay in the huts along the way you'll need a tent and associated equipment.

Unless you intend to eat only canned and dried food along the way (not recommended) then you'll also need a stove, basic cooking equipment and a water container with a capacity of at least one litre per person as well as water-purifying tablets for use on the lower levels of the mountain. Stove fuel in the form of petrol and kerosene (paraffin) is fairly easily found in towns, and methylated spirits is available in Nairobi, as are gas cartridges although the supply of these is not guaranteed. Except in an emergency, using wood gathered from the vicinity of camp sites to light open fires is prohibited within

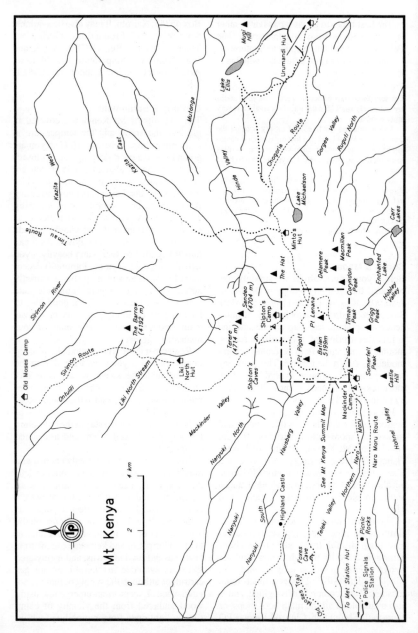

the confines of the national park and for good reason. If you intend to engage porters then you'll also have to supply each of them with a rucksack to carry your gear and theirs.

Equipment Hire All the gear you need for the trek can be hired in Nairobi at Atul's (☎ (02) 225935), Biashara St, PO Box 43202, or from the Natural Action Mountain Centre (☎ (02) 740214), in the Museum Hill Shopping Mall, PO Box 12516. Atul's also sells some second-hand and locally made trekking and camping equipment.

Natural Action claims to be the only specialist outdoor shop on the African continent (outside South Africa) and has a good range of equipment. The guys who run the shop are off-duty guides from Mt Kenya and are helpful with information and advice. Advance booking of gear (from Atul's) is a good idea if you want to be absolutely sure, but is not normally necessary.

Rental gear is also available at the Naro Moru River Lodge (☎ (0176) 22018), PO Box 18, Naro Moru, and is mostly in good condition and well maintained. Gear cannot be booked in advance at the Naro Moru River Lodge. Here it's first come, first served. Both places carry plenty of stock. The Mountain Rock Lodge near Naro Moru also has equipment for hire, but the range is less extensive.

Examples of the sort of daily hire charges and deposits (in US dollars) which you'll have to pay at Atul's are:

Item	Hire Cost	Deposit
sleeping bag	$1.60-$2.30	$20-$39
air mattress	$1.40	$20
air-mattress pump	$0.40	$9.75
dome tent		
(two-person)	$6	$78
dome tent		
(three-person)	$9.40	$117
gas stove	$1.20	$31
kerosene stove	$0.60	$7.80
water container		
(one litre)	$0.20	$1.60
water container		
(10 litre)	$0.30	$1.60
mess kit		
(one person)	$0.60	$2.30
cooking pot	$0.25-$1.70	$2.30-$7.80
gas lamp	$1.60	$39
kerosene lamp	$0.20	$7
rucksack	$4.60	$71-$130
woollen socks	$0.80	$7.80
woollen gloves	$0.80	$7.80
climbing boots	$2.70	$31
raincoat	$1.20	$23

These charges apply for the first 10 days of hire; longer term rentals are quite a bit cheaper. The hire charges at the Naro Moru River Lodge are consistently higher than those at Atul's.

Food

In an attempt to cut down on baggage, quite a few people forgo taking a stove and cooking equipment and exist entirely on canned and dried foods. You can certainly do it so long as you keep up your fluid intake but it's not a good idea. That cup of hot soup in the evening and pot of tea or coffee in the morning can make all the difference between enjoying the trek and hating it or, at least, feeling irritable.

There are, however, a few things to bear in mind about cooking at high altitudes. The major consideration is that the boiling point of water is considerably reduced. At 4500 metres, for example, water boils at 85°C. This is too low to sufficiently cook rice or lentils (pasta is better) and you won't be able to brew a good cup of tea from it either (instant coffee is the answer). Cooking times are also considerably increased as a result (with consequent increased use of fuel).

The best range of suitable foods for the mountain is, of course, to be found in the supermarkets of Nairobi. If you're going straight to the mountain from Nairobi by bus or share-taxi, it's no problem to bring all your supplies from there. Otherwise there's a good range of food in the towns around the mountain (Nyeri, Nanyuki, Embu and Meru) although precious little at Naro Moru. Dehydrated foods are not all that easy to find and given the low boiling point of water at high altitudes you really need the precooked variety. Fresh fruit and vegetables are available in all reasonably sized towns and villages.

Take plenty of citrus fruits and/or citrus drinks with you as well as chocolate, sweets or dried fruit to keep your blood sugar levels high on the trek.

One last thing – and this is important to avoid severe headaches caused by dehydration – is to drink at least three litres of fluid per day. It may also help to avoid the effects of altitude sickness.

Park Fees

Entry fees to the national park are US$12 plus US$1.50 for a vehicle. If you take a guide and/or porters then you'll have to pay their entry fees too, and these are US$1 per person per night. Camping fees are an additional US$3.20 per person per night.

Guides & Porters

The charges for guides, porters and cooks vary according to the route taken. On the Naro Moru route they are US$4.75, on the Chogoria route they are US$4, and on the Sirimon route a guide or cook is US$10, while a porter is US$6.

Porters will carry up to 18 kg for a three-day trip or 16 kg for a longer trip, excluding the weight of their own food and equipment. If you want them to carry more then you'll have to negotiate a price for the extra weight. A normal day's work is regarded as one stage of the journey – from the Met Station to Mackinder's Camp on the Naro Moru route or from the Chogoria road head to Minto's Hut on the Chogoria route, for example. If you want to go further than this then you'll have to pay them two days' wages even if they don't do anything the following day.

Guides, porters and cooks can be engaged at the Naro Moru River Lodge, the Mountain Rock Lodge or through one of the hotels in Chogoria village and possibly at the park entry gates (though this isn't as reliable). They can also be found by contacting the Naro Moru Porters & Guides Association (☎ (0176) 6205), PO Naro Moru, Naro Moru; or the Chogoria Porters (☎ 88 in Chogoria), PO Box 96, Chogoria, who are based at the Transit Motel in Chogoria. If you're staying at the Mt Kenya Hostel near Naro Moru, Joseph will fix you up if you ask him.

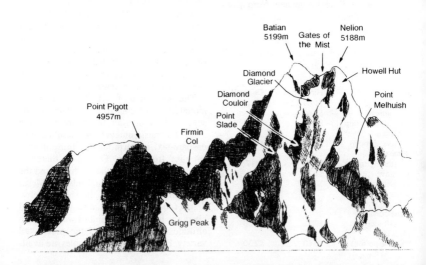

Accommodation

There are quite a lot of huts on the mountain but not all of them are available to the general public. Several are owned by the Mountain Club of Kenya (MCK). A few of these huts are reserved exclusively for use by members, others can be used by the public, although these are all basic and most are in very bad condition.

There are also some larger bunkhouses with more facilities on the mountain. These are owned by lodges outside the park and are mainly for people going on treks organised by these lodges, but they can also be used by independent trekkers. Beds in the large bunkhouses have to be booked and paid for, but there is no reservation system.

On the Naro Moru route, the bunkhouses are at the meteorological station (always called the Met Station), and Teleki Lodge (more usually called Mackinder's Camp), and both can be booked through the Naro Moru River Lodge, or Let's Go Travel in Nairobi.

On the Sirimon route, the bunkhouses are at Old Moses Camp and Shipton's Camp, and both can be booked through the Mountain Rock Lodge.

On the Chogoria route, there are some comfortable bandas at the Meru Mt Kenya Lodge, near the park gate. It costs around US$26 to stay there. Reservations are not always necessary but it's possible to book through Let's Go Travel in Nairobi.

The small MCK huts can be booked and paid for in Nairobi at the MCK clubhouse, or at Let's Go Travel, or at the Naro Moru River Lodge. They cost around US$3, but are generally in such bad condition that very few trekkers use them. If you are going independently and not planning to use the bunkhouses, it's much better to camp than to use these MCK huts.

Officially you can camp anywhere on the mountain but it is usual to camp near one of the huts or bunkhouses as there is often a water supply nearby.

Getting to the Trekking Routes

There are at least seven different routes up the mountain, but only the three main routes are covered here – Naro Moru, Sirimon and Chogoria. The other routes are much harder to follow and there's a real chance you can get lost without decent maps and the ability to read them, and if you have no experience with a compass.

If you intend to do the trek independently then public transport (bus or matatu) along the Mt Kenya ring road is the first step towards getting to the mountain. For the Naro Moru route it's Naro Moru village where there's a prominent signpost on the

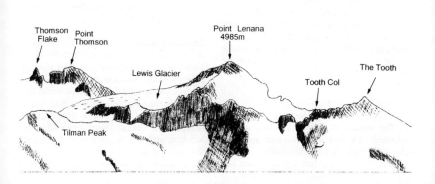

right-hand side just outside the village on the way to Nanyuki. For the Sirimon route, first go to Nanyuki and then take another matatu about 13 km up the main road towards Isiolo where the route is signposted off to the right. For the Chogoria route all matatus and buses between Embu and Meru stop at Chogoria village, just off the main road.

From where the buses or matatus drop you it's quite a walk to any of the park entry gates but it's possible to find private (though relatively expensive) transport from the main roads to the park entry gates. See the individual routes for details.

If you have your own transport, you can get up to all three of the national park entry gates in 2WD but to get to the road heads beyond that you will need 4WD. Don't attempt these last sections in anything other than that. And don't even expect a small Suzuki 4WD to make it up to the meteorological station on the Naro Moru route in wet weather. The road up there from the park entry gate is diabolical in wet weather. On the Chogoria route, 4WD is essential to get from Chogoria village to the national park entry gate. The top section of the track up through the forest is totally impassable in wet weather, even for 4WDs fitted with snow chains!

Mt Kenya Routes

The normal weather pattern is for clear mornings with the mist closing in from 10 am though this sometimes clears again in the early evening. This means that if you want to make the most of the trek you should set off early every morning and, for the final assault on Point Lenana (the highest point that can be reached by trekkers), you need to make an early start if you want to see the sunrise from the top.

Naro Moru Route

This is the most straightforward and popular of the routes. It's also the least scenic, although it's still a spectacular and very enjoyable trail. You should allow a minimum of four days for the trek up and down this

route, or three if you have transport between Naro Moru and the meteorological station, although doing it this quickly if you're not acclimatised is asking for altitude sickness.

Naro Moru to the Met Station Your starting point here is the village of Naro Moru on the Nairobi to Nanyuki road where the turn-off for the mountain is well signposted. To get there, take one of the daily Akamba buses from Nairobi to Naro Moru. The depot is on Lagos Rd in Nairobi and the buses can be booked in advance. You can also get to Naro Moru from Nyeri by matatu though these are often crowded.

The first part of the route takes you along a relatively good gravel road through farmlands for some 12 km (all the junctions are signposted) to the start of the forest where there's a wooden bridge across a small river. A further five km brings you to the park entry gate at 2400 metres. Having paid your fees, you continue on another eight km to the road head and *Met Station Hut* (3000 metres) where you stay for the night.

If your time is limited you can cut out this part of the trek by taking the Naro Moru River Lodge's Land Rover all the way to the meteorological station. This costs US$78 per person, plus the driver's park entry fee and US$3 for the vehicle shared by up to eight people. It's also possible to take this vehicle just as far as the park entry gate for US$39 per person. You don't have to be on one of the lodge's organised treks to use this vehicle. Hitching is also possible but the chances of a lift *up* the mountain are limited – it's easier to get a ride on the way down.

The Met Station to Mackinder's Camp On the second day you set off up the Teleki Valley along a well-marked path past the police signals station and up to the edge of the forest at around 3200 metres. From here you scale the so-called Vertical Bog and up onto a ridge from where you can see Mackinder's Camp. The route divides into two here and you have the choice of taking the higher path, which gives the best views but is often wet, or the lower path which

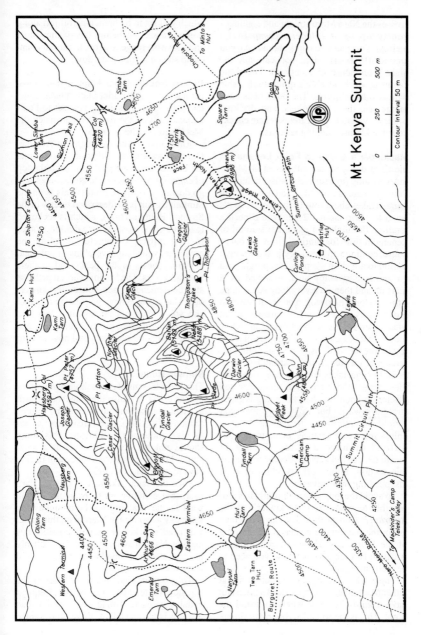

Mt Kenya Summit

Contour Interval 50 m

0   250   500 m

crosses the Naro Moru stream and continues gently up to *Mackinder's Camp* (4160 metres). This part of the trek should take you around 4½ hours. Here you can stay the night (bunkhouse or camping). The stone cabins at Mackinder's are quite comfortable with two large dorms. The bunk beds have mattresses, there are toilets, and drinking water is available. The caretaker here checks your bunkhouse booking receipts.

Mackinder's Camp to Point Lenana On the third day you can either rest at Mackinder's Camp (to help acclimatise) or aim for Point Lenana. From Mackinder's to Point Lenana takes about four to five hours, so it's usual to leave around 2 am (you'll need a torch or flashlight) to reach the summit of Lenana in time for sunrise. From the bunkhouse, continue up the valley past the ranger station to a fork in the path. Keep right, and go across a swampy area, followed by a morrain and then up a very long scree slope – this is a long, hard slog. You reach Austrian Hut about three to four hours from Mackinder's. This is about one hour below the summit of Lenana, so it's a good place to rest before the final push for the summit. This section of the trek, from Austrian Hut up to Point Lenana, takes you up a steep ridge and then across the edge of a snow-covered glacier. In good weather, the going is fairly straightforward, but in bad weather you should not attempt to reach the summit unless you are experienced in mountain conditions or have a guide. Plenty of inexperienced trekkers have come to grief on this section, falling off icy cliffs or even disappearing into crevasses.

To avoid the long slog in the dark, it is also possible to walk from Mackinder's to the *Austrian Hut* on the third day, stay there, then go for the summit of Lenana on the morning of the fourth day. However, conditions at Austrian Hut are very basic, so you need to be well equipped.

Those who are camping and not staying at either Mackinder's Camp or the Austrian Hut have a third choice of where to spend the night. This is the so-called *American Camp*,

which you get to by branching off left along a minor track just before the swampy area and above the ranger station. It's an excellent camp site on a grassy meadow.

Return Routes From Point Lenana most people return to the Met Station back down the same route. Assuming you get to Point Lenana early in the day, you can reach the Met Station on the same day.

Alternatively, you can return to Austrian Hut then walk north and north-west around the base of the main peaks to reach the top of either the Sirimon or Chogoria routes, and go down one of those routes. This is on the Summit Circuit path (described briefly in the Sirimon Route section), which is reckoned to be one of the most exciting trekking routes in East Africa. Completely circling the mountain, you cross several major cols, and get great views of the peaks and glaciers from all angles. The Summit Circuit path can also be demanding and potentially dangerous. Many people have got lost on this trail and you should not attempt it unless you have plenty of time, proper equipment, and a map and compass that you know how to use.

Sirimon Route

This is the least used of the three main routes but the driest. It is also the longest approach to Point Lenana, and involves some serious sections of trekking. If you are inexperienced in high mountain conditions, this route should not be attempted without a local guide. You should allow a minimum of five days to undertake this trek.

Take the same Akamba bus as to Naro Moru but continue on to Nanyuki. If you want to start walking up the mountain the same day as you leave Nairobi on this route, you need to take the earliest possible bus leaving Nairobi otherwise you'll probably have to stay in Nanyuki for the night and leave the following day.

To get from Nanyuki to the start of the Sirimon route, take one of the frequent matatus going to Timau on the main road towards Isiolo and tell the driver you want to be dropped off at the start of the Sirimon track (signposted). If you go over a fairly large river (the Sirimon River) then you've gone too far. The start of the route is about 13 km from Nanyuki.

Turn-Off to Old Moses Camp On the first day you walk from the main road to the park entrance gate (about 10 km) and on from there to the road head at 3150 metres (a further nine km). The going is straightforward to this point. At the road head there's a good camp site and a bunkhouse called *Old Moses Camp*. If you have your own vehicle then you'll need 4WD for the last five km as the road is in bad shape. Transport to the gate or the road head can also be arranged at the Mountain Rock Lodge.

Old Moses Camp to Shipton's Camp On the second day you leave Old Moses Camp, aiming uphill on a gradually deteriorating track. After about one hour you reach a fork – the left branch goes to the Liki North Hut, although this route is not used much. Take the right branch, which leads to a path over two ridges into the Mackinder Valley. Look out for red and white marker posts. The path leads up the east side of the valley, eventually crossing the Liki Stream and passing Shipton's Caves (in an obvious cliff on the left side of the path) before reaching *Shipton's Camp* bunkhouse and camp site. From the road head at Old Moses Camp to Shipton's Camp takes about seven hours. Shipton's Camp is a good place to spend two nights and have a rest day to help acclimatise. However, if you're feeling OK, one night here is sufficient.

Shipton's Camp to Point Lenana Both of the ways around the Summit Circle path, from Shipton's Camp to Point Lenana, are among the most spectacular trails on the mountain (indeed, in all of East Africa), but either route is strenuous and can be hard to follow – even in good weather. When visibility is poor the trails can be very difficult to follow and many people get lost. It is not uncommon for inexperienced trekkers to head down the wrong valley and then become hopelessly lost in the forest. Use common sense – if you can't use a map or compass, or are inexperienced in mountain conditions, don't go this way without a local guide. Also, if you are camping at American Hut or sleeping at Austrian Hut, make sure you are fully equipped for cold conditions.

Via American Camp From Shipton's Camp you join the Summit Circuit path, so on the third day you can go west or east of the main peaks to reach Point Lenana. If you want to go west, go straight up the valley side from Shipton's, keeping the main peaks to your left, to reach Kami Hut (which is in very bad condition) and then continue up a long scree slope to reach the Hausberg Col. From here you drop down into the next valley to reach Hausberg Tarn and Oblong Tarn. Follow the path between the tarns, then go up again to the col between the summit of Arthur's Seat and the Western Terminal. Aim south from here, passing Nanyuki Tarn to your right, to reach Two Tarn Hut, from where you drop down to American Camp at the head of the Teleki Valley. You can camp here or go down to the nearby Mackinder's Camp bunkhouse. From Shipton's Camp to American Camp by this route takes about four to five hours. On the fourth day you can reach Point Lenana (as described in the Naro Moru Route section).

Via Austrian Hut Your second choice from Shipton's is to go east of the main peaks, up the head of the steep-sided valley to Simba Col, or up the large scree slopes to Harris Tarn. From both of these points you can reach Simba Tarn, then Square Tarn. From Square Tarn you aim south, through Tooth Col (next to a large, jagged pinnacle) and then gradually up to reach Austrian Hut. From Shipton's Camp to Austrian Hut by this route takes about six hours. On the fourth day you can reach Point Lenana (as described in the Naro Moru Route section). If you are going east of the main peaks and don't feel like going for the summit of Lenana, from

Simba Col you can join the Chogoria route and drop down to Minto's Hut.

There is another route from Harris Tarn direct to the summit of Lenana up the north face, which means you can go from Shipton's up to Lenana then down to Austrian Hut in one day. However, this option is very serious (and impassable after snow) and should only be tackled by experienced trekkers, or by groups with competent local guides.

Return Routes From Point Lenana you can retrace your route down to Shipton's and go back down the Sirimon route, or return via the Naro Moru or Chogoria routes.

Chogoria Route

This route, from the eastern side of the mountain, is undoubtedly the most beautiful of the access routes to the summit and certainly the easiest as far as gradients go. This is a good route if you've got a tent and some trekking experience. From Minto's Hut there are breathtaking views of the head of the Gorges Valley and the glaciers beyond.

To get started on this route, take an Akamba bus from Nairobi direct to Chogoria village, or one first to Embu and then a matatu to Chogoria. Unless you get to Chogoria village early in the day, you will probably have to spend the night in Chogoria before setting off up the mountain, as the first day's hike is a long slog. It's about 30 km from the village to the park entry gate up the forest track with nowhere to stay en route.

Chogoria to Park Entry Gate The first day is spent walking up to the park entry gate at 2990 metres through superb rainforest and on into the bamboo zone. You have the choice here of staying at the *Meru Mt Kenya Lodge*, near the park entry gate, or continuing on a further three km to the small MCK's *Urumandi Hut*. At the road head itself (3200 metres), six km from the park entry gate, there's also an excellent camp site.

It's possible to hitch all the way to the park entry gate from Chogoria as at least one official vehicle does the run most days

between the village and the Meru Mt Kenya Lodge, though there's no set timetable. There may also be people staying at the lodge who can help out with lifts. Alternatively, if you want guaranteed transport, this can be arranged at one of the hotels in Chogoria village. Natural Action (see the earlier Equipment Hire section for details) also has a base and transport here.

Park Entry Gate to Minto's Hut The second day is spent walking from either the Meru Mt Kenya Lodge, the Urumandi Hut or the road head camp site to Minto's Hut with spectacular views all the way. The route is well defined and first crosses a stream then climbs to a ridge which it follows all the way to Minto's Hut. You need to bring water with you as there are no sources en route. From the road head to Minto's Hut should take you about 4½ to five hours. You can stay at *Minto's Hut* for the night, although recent reports suggest that it is in a pretty dire state – dirty and rat-infested – or head further up the valley where there are a number of sheltered camp sites.

Minto's Hut to Austrian Hut On the third day you continue to the head of the Gorges Valley, a steep climb across scree slopes, aiming south-west to reach Square Tarn. The last section of this leg of the route is very steep.

From the tarn the route becomes the Summit Circuit path, continuing south through Tooth Col (to the east of Point Lenana), after which it descends briefly and then goes up across a scree slope to the right to reach Austrian Hut. The route is marked with cairns in some places but it is still easy to get lost, especially in mist or snow. The section between Tooth Col and Austrian Hut is where most trekkers get lost. It is essential to realise that there is another huge valley (called Hobley Valley) in between the Gorges and Teleki valleys. The route goes *around* the head of the Hobley, not down into it. From Minto's to Austrian Hut should take about three to four hours.

Top: Turkana camp, Lake Turkana (HF)
Bottom: Heading towards South Horr (GC)

Top: Eliye Springs, Lake Turkana (HF)
Bottom: El-Molo market, Lake Turkana (DT)

Top Left: Baboon investigating Tuskers (beer), Tsavo National Park (GC)
Top Right: Mt Kilimanjaro from Amboseli National Park (GC)
Bottom: Amboseli National Park (GC)

The Samburu

Closely related to the Maasai, and in fact speaking the same language, the Samburu occupy an arid area directly north of Mt Kenya. It seems that when the Maasai migrated to the area from Sudan, some headed east (and became the Samburu) while the bulk of them continued south to the area they occupy today.

As is often the case, age-sets are an integral part of the society and the men pass through various stages before becoming a powerful elder at the top of the ladder. Circumcision is practiced in both sexes; with the girls it is only done on the day of marriage, which is usually when she is around 16 years old. Men are often in their thirties by the time they pass out of warriorhood and become elders qualified to marry. ∎

Samburu women - South Horr (GC)

Austrian Hut to Point Lenana From Austrian Hut you can scale Point Lenana (allow another hour) the same day or stay there for the night and make the ascent the following morning, as described in the Naro Moru Route section.

Return Routes From Point Lenana you can retrace the route back down to Minto's Hut which should take about two hours after which it's a further three to five hours back down to the Meru Mt Kenya Lodge. Alternatively, from Austrian Hut you can descend to Mackinder's Camp, and then return via the Naro Moru route.

Organised Treks

If your time is limited or you'd prefer someone else to make all the arrangements for a trek on Mt Kenya, there are several possibilities.

The Naro Moru River Lodge (☎ (0176) 22018), PO Box 18, Naro Moru, does a range of trips, all of which include a guide/cook, porters, all meals, park entry fees, camping fees, and transport to and from the road heads. The standard five-day trip takes you up and down the Naro Moru route using the lodges' own bunkhouses. The cost is US$480 per person in a group of eight, or US$754 for one person. Shorter trips are available at reduced cost.

The Mountain Rock Lodge (☎ (0176) 62625), between Naro Moru and Nanyuki, also offers a range of organised treks, usually up and down the Sirimon route, taking from three to six days and using its own bunkhouses en route. Costs vary according to the number of days you wish to spend on the mountain and the number of people in the party, though it's cheapest with a group of eight or more people. A three-day direct trip to Point Lenana via the Sirimon route costs US$507 to US$273 per person (one to eight people respectively); a four-day trip along the same route is from US$630 to US$358 per person.

A four-day trip going up the Sirimon and down the Naro Moru routes costs from US$644 to US$370, while a five-day trip going in on the Sirimon trail and out via the Chogoria route costs from US$884 to US$543. All prices include park entry fees, guide and porter fees, food, transport to and from the road heads, accommodation, and a special half-board deal at the lodge itself.

There are several safari companies in Nairobi which offer Mt Kenya treks, but most of these companies just sell the treks operated by Naro Moru and Mountain Rock lodges, charging you an extra commission in the process. However, some companies are running their own treks, and these include:

Kenya Hiking & Cycling
  Arrow House, Koinange St, PO Box 39439, Nairobi.
  This company's Mt Kenya trek goes up the Sirimon route and down the Naro Moru in five days, staying at bunkhouses. The cost is US$520 including transport to and from Nairobi (☎ 218336).

Natural Action Ltd
  Nairobi National Museum, PO Box 12516, Nairobi.
  A standard five-day Mt Kenya trek goes up the Chogoria route and down the Naro Moru, following more unusual paths for some of the way. The cost is around US$754 per person. Even if you don't take one of its treks, Natural Action provides information for trekkers, sells books and maps, and hires out equipment. There's also a trekkers' message board which you can use to find trekking companions, buy and sell gear and so on (☎ 740214).

Western Kenya

Western Kenya is an area with many attractions, but is often overlooked by travellers, and you won't find a single safari minibus out this way either. For this reason alone it's worth spending a bit of time exploring here, just to get the feel of Kenya without the tourists.

The countryside is, for the most part, beautiful rolling hills, often covered with the bright green bushes of vast tea plantations. Further west you have Lake Victoria and the regional capital of Kisumu on its shore. From here there are plenty of possibilities – just a short distance to the north lies the Kakamega Forest with its lush vegetation and abundant wildlife. Further north still, close to the regional town of Kitale, are the national parks of Mt Elgon (well worth exploring) and Saiwa Swamp, where the only way of getting around is on foot and the attraction is the rare sitatunga or marshbuck deer.

If you have your sights set on more distant horizons, head west for Busia or Namanga and Uganda, or south to Isebania and across the border into Tanzania.

This area is the home of Kenya's Luo people. Numbering around two million they make up the third-largest ethnic group in the country. Marginalised politically, you'll nevertheless find them a friendly people. The atmosphere in this part of the country is in sharp contrast to that of the central provinces.

Getting Around

This is the most densely populated part of the country so the road system is good and there are hundreds of matatus of varying shapes and sizes plying the routes. Accidents are unnervingly common, but these seem to happen more amongst the very small matatus which are usually dangerously overloaded. The small-truck sized matatus are a lot safer as they generally travel more slowly and can carry loads with greater ease.

One annoying factor of matatu travel in this region is the way the destination changes suddenly depending on the number of passengers. So if your matatu is supposedly going from, say, Kakamega to Kitale and it gets to Webuye and everyone gets out, it's a fairly safe bet that you will have to as well. When this happens, and you have paid the fare to the final destination, the driver will find you a seat in another vehicle and fix things with its driver. You will get there in the end, but it may take longer than you think. It took me three matatus to get from Kisumu to Kisii, despite being told when I boarded the first two that they were going all the way.

Lake Victoria

With an area approaching 70,000 sq km, Lake Victoria is obviously the major geographical feature in this part of the continent. Unlike the lakes further west, Victoria is not part of the rift valley system, and so is wide and shallow (only 100 metres deep) compared with, say, Lake Tanganyika which is nearly 1½ km deep.

Lake Victoria touches on three countries – Uganda, Tanzania and Kenya – but it's not possible to take a boat between Kenya and Uganda and/or between Kenya and Tanzania. The only possibilities for lake excursions in Kenya are the ferries which run from Kisumu to Kenyan ports further south.

Bilharzia is prevalent in Lake Victoria so don't swim in the water or walk in the grass along its shores – this is the hideout of the snails which are the host for the parasitic flukes which invade your body. (See the Health section in the Facts for the Visitor chapter for more information.) Admittedly, you face only a very small risk of contracting bilharzia if you spend only a short time here.

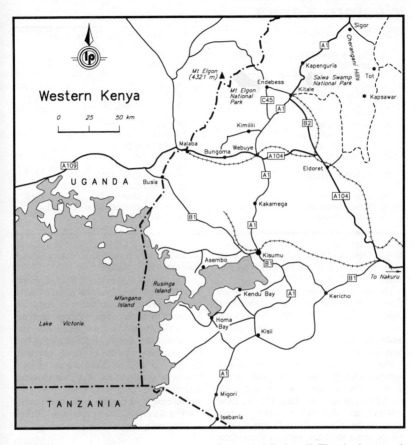

KISUMU

Although it hardly feels like it, Kisumu is Kenya's third-largest town. It has a very easy-going, almost decaying, atmosphere, possibly partly due to the fact that with the cessation of international ferry services on the lake, and the decline in through traffic to Uganda, it's a bit of a dead end these days. It was a busy port from early this century right up until the East African Community split up in 1977, and it seems that from this point on the town has just been marking time.

Don't be put off by that though, as it's the ideal place to head for from the east of the country as the travel connections are excel-

lent, especially by rail. There's also enough to do in the town itself to make it an interesting place to stop for a few days.

If you've arrived from the higher country further east the first thing that you will notice is the heat and humidity. Kisumu is always a good few degrees hotter than say Nairobi and the steamy conditions only add to the general torporific air.

Orientation

Kisumu is sited on the gently sloping shore of Lake Victoria. Although it's a fairly sprawling town, everything you are likely to need is within walking distance. The main

■   PLACES TO STAY

 5   Black & White Boarding & Lodging
 6   New Victoria Hotel
 7   Mirukas Lodge & Nasim's Lodge
 8   New Rozy Lodge
10   Safina Lodge
12   YWCA
14   Hotel Inca
16   Imperial Hotel
17   Razbi Guest House
18   Lake View Hotel
30   Hotel Royale

▼   PLACES TO EAT

 9   Octopus
11   Wimpy Restaurant
15   Chicken Palace

21   Talk of the Town Coffee House
23   Mona Lisa Restaurant

OTHER

 1   Mosque
 2   Hospital
 3   Bus & Matatu Station
 4   Market
13   Kisumu Museum
19   Standard Chartered Bank
20   Barclays Bank
22   Malaika Buses
24   GPO
25   British Council Library
26   Kenya Airways
27   Immigration
28   Wananchi Craft Shop
29   Town Hall

drag is Oginga Odinga Rd and along it are virtually all the shops, the banks and the post office.

The railway station and ferry jetty are close together about five minutes' walk from Oginga Odinga Rd, while the noisy bus and matatu station is on Jomo Kenyatta Highway behind the market, about 10 minutes' walk from the centre.

Most of the cheap hotels are in the area between Oginga Odinga Rd and Otiena Oyoo St. The mid-range and top-end hotels are mostly along Jomo Kenyatta Highway plus there are others further afield. The best access to the lake itself is at Dunga, a small village about three km south of town along Nzola Rd.

Information

The GPO is in the centre of town on Oginga Odinga Rd and is open Monday to Friday from 8 am to 5 pm and Saturday from 9 am to noon. If you need to make international calls there is a cardphone outside and you can dial direct. Phonecards are sold at the post office.

The British Council Library, also on Oginga Odinga Rd, has newspapers and magazines and quite a good library. It's open from 9.30 am to 1 pm and 2 to 5 pm Monday to Friday, and 8.30 am to 12.45 pm on Sat-

urday. Behind it is the UK Voluntary Service Overseas (VSO) office.

Immigration is on the 1st floor, Reinsurance Plaza (behind Deakons Supermarket), on the corner of Oginga Odinga Rd and Jomo Kenyatta Highway. The officials here are friendly and helpful and will renew your visa for up to three months. It all takes just five minutes, there's no fee or photos required, though you will be asked for an onward ticket (tell them you left it in your hotel for safekeeping).

The best bookshop in town is the well-stocked Sarit Bookshop on Oginga Odinga Rd diagonally opposite the post office.

Kisumu Museum

It comes as something of a surprise to find this excellent museum here – it's probably the best in the country and is well worth a visit. It's on Nairobi Rd within easy walking distance of the centre and is open daily from 9.30 am to 6 pm; entry is US$1.10.

The displays are well presented and wide ranging in their variety. There's a very good collection of everyday items from the various peoples of the area, including agricultural implements, bird and insect traps (including a white-ant trap!), food utensils, clothing, furniture, weapons, musical instruments, and a fairly motley collection of

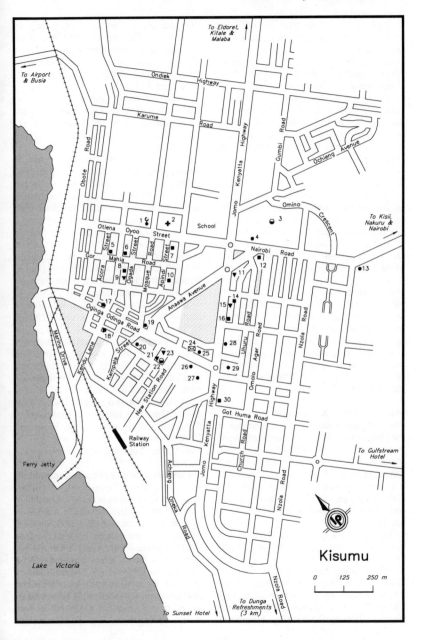

Kisumu

0   125   250 m

stuffed birds and animals including an amazing centrepiece of a lion riding on a wildebeest.

Outside there is a traditional Luo homestead consisting of the husband's mud and thatch house, and separate houses for each wife. There's usually a man near the homestead who will show you around for a few shillings and point out the salient features. Also outside are the inevitable crocodile and tortoise enclosures which are small and a bit depressing.

Market

Kisumu's market is one of the most animated in the country, and certainly one of the largest. Whether you're in the market for a bag of potatoes or are just curious, it's worth a stroll around. You can cut through to the bus station through the hole in the back wall of the market compound.

Hippo Point

Hippo Point is at Dunga, about three km south of town, and the café on the point is a good place to head for. There were no hippos in evidence when I visited but it's a pleasant spot all the same. Known as Dunga Refreshments, it is well signposted once you get out of town along Nzola Rd. This place also has the only camp site in Kisumu.

Places to Stay – bottom end

The cheapest option for accommodation is the *YWCA* (☎ 43192) on the corner of Omolo Agar and Nairobi Rds which has dorm beds (three people per room) for US$1.10 with shared facilities. It also has self-contained double rooms which vary from US$1.80 to US$2.20 per person. The Y takes both men and women and there's a canteen where you can get basic meals.

The best area for a cheap hotel is that between Oginga Odinga Rd and Otiena Oyoo St.

Very popular with expatriate volunteer workers is the *Razbi Guest House* (☎ 42-152), upstairs on the corner of Oginga Odinga Rd and Kendu Lane. It's very secure (there's a locked grille at the top of the stairs),

the rooms are spotless and a towel and soap are provided. The rates are US$1.90/2.90 for singles/doubles with shared cold-water bath. There's certainly no confusion between the showers and toilets here – one of the toilets is labelled 'Urine'!

Somewhat more basic is the *New Rozy Lodge* (☎ 41990) on Ogada St which has singles/doubles with shared bath for US$1.90/2.70. It's hardly 'new' but the staff is friendly.

Two streets east of Ogada St is Apindi St where you'll find a choice of three basic lodges. The first is *Safina Lodge* which has singles/doubles for US$1.80/2.50 and triples for US$3.10, all with shared facilities. Next up is *Mirukas Lodge* which has similar rooms for the same price. Next door is *Nasim's Lodge*, the best of the bunch, which is excellent value (apart from the saggy beds) at US$2.20/2.80 for self-contained singles/doubles with clean sheets and hot water. At this price, you won't find better.

Back on Oginga Odinga Rd, there's another slightly more expensive hotel which is, nevertheless, good value. This is the *Mona Lisa Guest House* (above the restaurant of the same name) which has singles/doubles with shared bath for US$2.20/3.40 or US$3.40/4.50 with private bath. There's hot water supposedly 24 hours a day. Around the corner, the *Talk of the Town Coffee House* has rooms at a similar price. Singles/doubles with shared bath cost US$2.20/3.40 or US$4/5.40 with private bath. There's hot water in the mornings and evenings.

Campers should head for *Dunga Refreshments* (☎ 44023) at Hippo Point, right on the shores of Lake Victoria three km south of town. It takes nearly an hour to walk it, or you can take a taxi for US$2.20. It's a well-run place with good facilities but there's little shade. Camping here costs US$1.80 per person plus there's also a dormitory block which costs US$4.50 per bed with shared facilities. The complex includes a very pleasant restaurant with reasonably priced meals (omelette and chips for US$1.90 or main meals of chicken, fish or mutton for

US$2.50). It also caters for vegetarians, and fruit juices and cold beers are available. It's a mellow place to stay and highly recommended.

Places to Stay – middle

The *Black & White Boarding & Lodging*, in the centre of town, has singles/doubles for US$4/5.90 and triples for US$7.40, all including breakfast. Bathrooms are shared by three rooms and there is hot water. Close by is the *New Victoria Hotel* (☎ 2909) on the corner of Kendu Lane and Gor Mahia Rd. It's good value, especially if you get one of the front rooms with a balcony and views of Lake Victoria. Rates (including breakfast) are US$4.60 a single with shared bath or US$8/12 for a double/triple with private bath. The hotel also has a good restaurant.

The *Lake View Hotel* is aptly named and has spacious rooms as well as a bar and restaurant. Bed and breakfast in self-contained rooms with hot water here costs US$6.70/9.40 a single/double. It's good value for the price and very clean, plus the staff are friendly and helpful.

Opposite the Lake View is the *Western Lodge* (☎ 42586) which only has single, self-contained rooms at US$5.40.

Just off Jomo Kenyatta Highway close to the Imperial Hotel is the *Hotel Inca* (☎ 40158) which is also good value. It's a large place and offers well-furnished, very clean, self-contained rooms with fan and hot water for US$5.60/10. There's a bar and restaurant and the staff are friendly.

Places to Stay – top end

The best hotel in this range is the charming *Hotel Royale* (☎ 44240) on Jomo Kenyatta Highway. It's an old hotel with a gleaming white façade, open-air terrace bar and polished wooden floorboards. It's twin is the Castle Hotel of Mombasa and, like the Castle, has been recently refurbished. If you have the money, and can get one of the rooms on the 1st floor, it's excellent value at US$15/22 for self-contained singles/doubles including breakfast. Some of the rooms on the ground floor are gloomy, so ask to see a

room first before booking in. The hotel has its own very good restaurant, and credit cards are accepted.

The *Imperial Hotel* (☎ 41485), also on Jomo Kenyatta Highway, is a much newer place with five-star facilities. The cheapest rooms with all the facilities you would expect cost US$37/42 a single/double plus there are deluxe rooms for US$42/46. There are also more expensive apartments and suites. There's a rooftop bar, two restaurants (breakfast US$3.40, lunch/dinner US$5.60) and a swimming pool, but the pool is tiny and hemmed in by the building.

On the southern edge of town, the *Sunset Hotel* (☎ 41100/4), in Impala Lane (off Jomo Kenyatta Highway), does indeed have views of the sunset, and of the lake, from each room. There's also a swimming pool and a good, if expensive, restaurant (US$8/10 for lunch/dinner). Bed and breakfast costs US$38/50 for singles/doubles and US$70 for triples throughout the year. All credit cards are accepted. The hotel is part of the African Tours & Hotels group so reservations are also possible in Nairobi.

There's also the *Gulfstream Hotel* (☎ 43927) off to the east of town which is very well appointed but inconvénient if you don't have your own transport. Standard singles/doubles here cost US$13/15, plus there are luxury suites for US$24 without breakfast. The hotel has two bars and a restaurant.

Places to Eat

One of the most popular restaurants for those on a budget as well as expatriate VSO workers is the *Talk of the Town Coffee House* just off Oginga Odinga Rd. It has a wide variety of good cheap meals and is a popular place for breakfast, though is open all day. It's a friendly place and you can meet lots of people here. Similar is the *Mona Lisa Restaurant*, on Oginga Odinga Rd.

The *New Victoria Hotel* also does an excellent breakfast of juice, papaya, eggs, toast, butter and tea or coffee for about US$1. It's open for breakfast from 7 to 9 am and also serves standard dishes such as steak, chicken and chips.

For stand-up-and-eat or takeaway greasy-spoon food there's the *Chicken Palace*, the *Wimpy*, or *Rafiq Refreshments & Fast Burgers* all on Jomo Kenyatta Highway.

For a splurge, go for lunch or dinner (especially the latter) at the *Hotel Royale* and soak in the atmosphere. Both the service and the food are excellent. And talk about service! All you have to do is blink and there'll be a waiter there asking if everything is alright! Food at the *Imperial Hotel* is equally good. A meal at either will cost US$6 to US$10 per person.

If you're out at Hippo Point, don't forget *Dunga Refreshments* which has good food at budget prices plus you can eat outside right on the water's edge.

Entertainment
Everyone in search of action goes to the excellent disco/bar/restaurant complex called *Octopus Night Club* on Ogada St. It's a weird and wonderful place, and has three bars (The Pirate's Den, the Fisherman's Wharf, and the Captain's Wives) where you can also get meals or snacks, as well as the actual disco. Beers are sold at normal prices and the disco is a good rage. You haven't seen Kisumu until you've been here.

Things to Buy
Kisumu is about the best place to buy Kisii soapstone carvings and there are pavement stalls set up on the northern side of Oginga Odinga Rd near the British Council Library.

The Wananchi Craft Shop near the town hall is a cooperative selling crafts made by local women, and there are some interesting items.

Getting There & Away
Air Kenya Airways has 11 flights weekly to Nairobi. The trip takes one hour and costs US$44. You can pay in local currency which makes the flight a good deal cheaper. Kenya Airways (☎ 44055/6) is in the Alpha building on Oginga Odinga Rd.

Bus & Matatu Buses and matatus leave from the large bus station just north of the market for Busia, Kakamega, Homa Bay, Kitale, Nakuru, Kericho and Nairobi.

It's possible to book Nairobi buses in advance at the bus station. Both Coast Bus (US$3.80) and Akamba (US$4.45) have once-daily buses to Nairobi which travel at night. Re-Union Buses (US$3.35) also has a daily departure. These are the best buses to use as they operate on a regular schedule. Nyayo Buses and JA Buses also cover similar routes, but their schedules are unreliable.

Nissan matatus go to Nairobi (US$4.45), Busia (on the Ugandan border, US$1.55), Homa Bay (US$0.90), Isebania (on the Tanzanian border, US$3.35), Kakamega (US$0.90), Kitale (US$2.90), Malaba (on the Ugandan border, US$1.80) and Nakuru (US$2.65).

There are also shared Peugeot taxis to Nairobi (US$8) which leave when full.

Train There are trains to Nairobi daily at 6.30 pm, arriving at 7.35 am the next day. Depending on demand there is often a second daily train. Fares to Nairobi are US$15.10 in 1st class, US$8.70 in 2nd class and US$3.10 in 3rd class. It's advisable to book in advance. The booking office at the station is open daily from 8 am to noon and 2 to 4 pm.

Car For car rental see Kamba Travel (☎ 28-131) on Jomo Kenyatta Highway in the red-roofed building diagonally opposite the Hotel Royale and in front of Reinsurance Plaza.

Boat With the demise of the international services, the Lake Victoria ferries now only go to places close to Kisumu such as Kendu Bay, Homa Bay, Asembo Bay and Mfangano Island. There are three classes on the MV *Reli* and only 2nd and 3rd classes on the MV *Tilapia* and MV *Alestes* but none of them is ever very crowded, so 2nd or 3rd class is quite OK.

The MV *Reli* has the following services from Kisumu on Wednesday and Sunday:

	Arrival	Departure
Kisumu	–	9 am
Kendu Bay	10.50 am	11.05 am
Homa Bay	1.55 pm	2.25 pm
Asembo Bay	5 pm	8 am (next day)
Homa Bay	10.35 am	11.05 am
Kendu Bay	1.55 pm	2.10 pm
Kisumu	4 pm	–

The MV *Alestes* leaves Kisumu on Tuesday (9.30 am) but doesn't return until Saturday (5.30 am). In the meantime it services other lake ports such as Homa Bay and Mfangano Island so it's of limited interest to travellers other than those who want to stay at Homa Bay or Mfangano Island for four nights.

The MV *Tilapia* provides the following service from Kisumu on Tuesday, Friday and Sunday:

	Arrival	Departure
Kisumu	–	9 am
Kendu Bay	10.50 am	11.10 am
Homa Bay	2 pm	2.30 pm
Asembo Bay	5 pm	8 am (next day)
Homa Bay	10.35 am	11.05 am
Kendu Bay	1.55 pm	2.10 pm
Kisumu	4 pm	–

The fares from Kisumu to Kendu Bay are US$0.90/0.65/0.35 in 1st/2nd/3rd class, to Homa Bay US$1.55/1.20/0.55, to Asembo Bay US$2.10/1.65/0.65, and to Mfangano Island US$2.80/2/1.

AROUND THE LAKE
Kendu Bay
This small lakeside village has little to offer apart from a somewhat strange volcanic lake a couple of km from town. There's basic accommodation in the town, and the ferry jetty is about one km away.

Homa Bay
This is a very nondescript yet surprisingly busy town on a small bay in Lake Victoria. Most of the action involves transporting agricultural products from the area to Kisumu. Nearby is the intriguing volcano-shaped **Mt Homa** and the small **Ruma National Park**.

Places to Stay & Eat There are several budget hotels along the main road from the ferry, but none are anything to rave about. They basically service the lust of those who frequent the bars out front. Take your pick.

If, on the other hand, you have money to spare, there's the very pleasant *Homa Bay Hotel* (☎ (0385) 22070) set in its own grounds on the shore of the lake. It's part of the Msafiri Inns group so you can book it in Nairobi. A good room here facing the lake costs US$20/25 a single/double or US$40 a triple including breakfast. Other meals cost US$4.90. It's a mellow place to relax if you want to get away from it all for a few days.

Getting There & Away Most people come here by ferry but there's plenty of transport (bus and matatu) from here to Kisumu, Kisii, Migori and Isebania (Tanzanian border).

Rusinga Island
Mbita is the town on Rusinga Island which is connected by a causeway to the mainland. The only remarkable thing about the island is the mausoleum of Tom Mboya on the northern side of the island – he was born here in 1930 and was shot dead by police in 1969 during political unrest. (See the History section in the Facts about the Country chapter for more details.)

There are matatus to Homa Bay, as well as the ferry services to Kisumu, Mfangano Island and Homa Bay.

Mfangano Island
There's little to see here and very little in the way of facilities. The small fishing community is about as far off the beaten track as you can get in Kenya.

There is one cheap hotel and the island is connected to the mainland by the ferry mentioned in the earlier Kisumu Getting There & Away section.

Western Highlands

The western highlands are the agricultural heartland of Kenya and they separate Kisumu and Lake Victoria from the rest of the country. In the south around Kisii and Kericho lie the vast tea plantations, while further north around Kitale and Eldoret it's all fertile farming land.

The towns of the highlands are really just small agricultural service towns, much the same as you'd find in similar areas in Australia or the USA – and they're about as interesting. For visitors, the attractions of the area lie outside these towns – the tea plantations around Kericho, Kakamega Forest near Kakamega, Mt Elgon and Saiwa Swamp national parks both near Kitale, and the Cherangani Hills which lie north-east of Kitale and Eldoret.

KISII

As you might expect, this is where Kisii soapstone comes from but it's not on sale here at all, the simple reason being that Kisii sees very few tourists and those that do come this way tend to just keep moving. You can, however, visit the quarries if you like. Not much happens in Kisii, and even the locals will tell you that it's 'a remote place'. On the other hand people are friendly, and as so few tourists come here you'll be regarded with curiosity.

Kisii is the main centre of the region known as the **Gusii Highlands**, home of the Gusii people. The Gusii, numbering around one million, are a Bantu-speaking people in the middle of a non-Bantu area; the Maasai to the south, Luo to the west and north and Kipsigis to the east all speak unrelated languages.

The town centre is compact and, as usual, the market is the liveliest place in the town during the day.

Whilst you're here, it's worth making the four-hour round trip to the top of nearby Manga Ridge from which the views – especially over Lake Victoria – are magnificent.

You can also see Kisumu in the distance and the tea plantations of Kericho behind you.

Places to Stay – bottom end

There are two excellent places to stay in Kisii. The cheaper one is the relatively new *Sabrina Lodge*, just around the corner from the matatu park. It's a very friendly place and has rooms with shared facilities for US$2.60/4 a single/double. The hotel also has a bar and restaurant.

Somewhat more expensive is the *Safe Lodge* (☎ 202950), opposite the BATA shop, which has friendly staff and costs US$3.40/4.50 for singles/doubles with hot-water bath. Soap and towels are provided, and breakfast is included in the price. The single rooms have double beds so a couple could get away with a single. It also has an excellent restaurant and a rough and ready bar as well as an upstairs balcony overlooking the street. The hotel is also the main social focus of the town – at least the video machine in the restaurant is.

On the Kisumu road out of town are two other budget hotels, the *Kianbu Lodge* and the *Highway Lodge* (☎ 213), right next door to each other. Both offer self-contained singles/doubles for US$2.20/3.80. There's a bar and restaurant upstairs at the Kianbu. On the other side of the road is the *Ngaŭ Guest House* which also offers self-contained rooms.

Places to Stay – middle

The modern high-rise building on the north-eastern side of the market is the *Sakawa Towers Hotel* (☎ 21218). Self-contained rooms here with balcony and hot water in the mornings cost US$5/7.20 including breakfast. The staff are friendly and it's a clean place to stay. Towels are provided and there's a bar and restaurant on the 1st floor.

At the eastern end of town is the modern *Mwalimu Hotel* in its own compound. Self-contained singles/doubles cost US$5/7.60 including breakfast. The hotel has a popular bar, terrace, beer garden and restaurant. There's also guarded parking.

The most pleasant place to stay in this

range is the *Kisii Hotel* which is set in its own gardens (complete with turkeys) on the western side of town. It's a single-storey building with a popular bar and restaurant and has self-contained doubles (no singles) for US$8.70.

Places to Eat

For breakfast try the restaurant in the *Safe Lodge*. For less than US$1 you get juice, fruit, cereals, eggs, sausage, toast and tea or coffee – good value – and there are also good meals. The fact that there is a video and that beer is served makes this a gregarious and lively place, especially in the evenings.

For somewhat more expensive meals, go to the *Kisii Hotel* or the *Mwalimu Hotel*.

Getting There & Away

To make life confusing, matatus leave from two separate locations. Matatus for Kisumu (US$1.35, three hours) leave from in front of the market, while those for everywhere else (Migori, Kericho, Tabaka) leave from the station up past the Standard Chartered Bank.

Akamba has two direct buses daily to Nairobi (US$4.10) at 9 am and 9 pm via Kericho (US$1.55) and Nakuru (US$2.80). Tickets should be booked one day in advance. Gusii Deluxe Buses, across the road, also has daily departures for Nairobi (US$4) at 6.45 am and 5 and 8 pm which go via Kericho (US$2.20) and Nakuru (US$3.35). The trip to Nairobi takes around 8½ hours.

TABAKA

This is the village where the soapstone is quarried and carved, and on arrival it's easy enough to locate someone who can show you one of the workshops. It's basically just a cottage industry and there are few people who actually work the stone for a living – to most people it's just a handy way to supple-

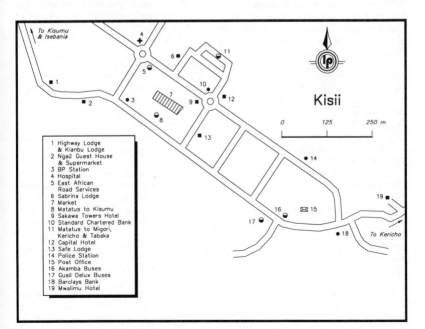

1 Highway Lodge & Kianbu Lodge
2 Ngaū Guest House & Supermarket
3 BP Station
4 Hospital
5 East African Road Services
6 Sabrina Lodge
7 Market
8 Matatus to Kisumu
9 Sakawa Towers Hotel
10 Standard Chartered Bank
11 Matatus to Migori, Kericho & Tabaka
12 Capital Hotel
13 Safe Lodge
14 Police Station
15 Post Office
16 Akamba Buses
17 Gusii Delux Buses
18 Barclays Bank
19 Mwalimu Hotel

Kisii

To Kisumu & Isebania

To Kericho

0   125   250 m

ment a meagre income made from agriculture.

To get there, take one of the fairly infrequent matatus from Kisii.

KERICHO

Tea – it's everywhere! This is the heart of western Kenya's tea plantation area and the rolling hills are a uniform bright green. Kericho's climate is perfect for growing tea, mainly because of the afternoon showers which fall every day of the year. Yes, Kericho is a wet place, but the showers are generally only brief and, apart from benefiting the tea bushes, they make the area green and pleasant.

The town takes its name from the Maasai chief, Ole Kericho, who was killed by the Gusii in the 18th century in a battle over land – the Maasai had been in the area for years and didn't appreciate the Gusii moving in, though the Gusii themselves were being pushed out by the advancing Luo. The area today is the home of the Kipsigis people, who are part of the greater Kalenjin group. The name *Kalenjin* (literally 'I tell you') was given in the '50s to the group of Nandi-speaking tribes, including the Pokot, Nandi, Kipsigis and Marakwet.

There's not a great deal to the town itself but it's not a bad place to stop for the night.

Information

The post office and the two main banks are all on Moi Highway. The banks are open Monday to Friday from 8 am to 1 pm and on Saturday from 8.30 to 11 am.

Tea Plantations

The closest plantation to town is behind the Tea Hotel, itself once owned by the Brooke Bond company. If you walk through the hotel grounds behind what was the service station and out through the back gate, the path leads through the tea bushes to the hotel workers' huts. If you're lucky there may be picking in progress.

It may be possible to organise a tour of a plantation and processing plant through the Tea Hotel.

Places to Stay – bottom end

There's not a lot of budget hotel accommodation available in Kericho but check out the *Sugutek Hotel* on Tengecha Rd and the *Njekimi Bar & Restaurant* on John Kericho Rd. At either you'll get a basic single/double room for US$1.60/2.40 with shared facilities.

There are also a few more boarding & lodging places on the road below the matatu station but they're really basic.

Campers should head for the *Tas Lodge* where you can camp in the pleasant grounds for around US$1 per person per night.

Places to Stay – middle

The *Tas Lodge* (☎ 21112) on the Nakuru road (Moi Highway) is about the best in this range. The hotel has a pleasant garden setting including an open-air bar under makuti roofs. Self-contained singles/doubles with hot-water shower cost US$3.40/5.60 including breakfast. In the centre of town there's the more modern *Mwalimu Hotel* which has a popular bar and restaurant. Singles/doubles with private bath cost US$8/10.20 including breakfast.

Places to Stay – top end

The cheapest of the top-range hotels is the modern *Mid-West Hotel* (☎ 20611) which has standard singles/doubles with private bath for US$14/18 and deluxe singles/doubles for US$16/19, plus there are more expensive suites. Prices include a substantial breakfast and all taxes. The hotel has its own bar and restaurant.

At the top of the line is the grand old *Tea Hotel* (☎ 30004/5) which was originally built by the Brooke Bond company in the 1950s for its managers but which is now managed by African Tours & Hotels (☎ (2) 336858). It's set in its own well-tended grounds and exudes an atmosphere of days gone by. The rooms are spacious in the extreme, especially the two suites at the back overlooking the tea plantations. All the rooms are self-contained with hot-water showers. Rates (inlcuding breakfast) are US$18/21 for singles/doubles, US$38 for triples, plus there are suites with two double beds for US$44. Other meals cost US$3.40 (lunch) and US$4 (dinner). There's a popular bar/lounge area which sprawls over much of the ground floor and out onto the terrace. The staff is friendly and there's guarded parking.

Places to Eat

For basic African stodge and stews the *Mother Hotel* on Uhuru Rd does as good a job as any, as does the restaurant in the *Sugutek Hotel* on Tengecha Rd, which has chips, chicken, ugali, etc.

The restaurant in the *Mwalimu Hotel* is a little more sophisticated, while the US$3.10/4 set lunch/dinner in the *Mid-West Hotel* is good value. The buffet lunches and dinners at the *Tea Hotel* are also good but somewhat more expensive. On the other hand, there is a grand piano which you are welcome to use if you feel like playing some Mozart or Elton John.

For a real spit and sawdust experience, call in for a beer at the *Snow Day & Night Club* on Isaac Salat Rd.

Getting There & Away

The matatu station is fairly well organised,

■ PLACES TO STAY

1 Cheap Hotels
5 Tea Hotel
6 Tas Lodge
9 Mid-West Hotel
10 Njekimi Bar & Restaurant
11 Mwalimu Hotel
12 Mother Hotel
16 Sugutek Hotel

OTHER

2 Bus & Matatu Stand
3 Market
4 Police
7 Kobil Station
8 Shell Station
13 Law Courts
14 Snow Day & Night Club
15 Post Office
17 Standard Chartered Bank
18 Barclays Bank
19 Town Hall
20 Caltex Station
21 Hindu Temple
22 Hospital

To Nakuru

Harambee Road

John Kericho Road

Moi Road

Isaac Salat Road

Lane

Tengecha

Uhuru Road

Kenyatta Road

Tengecha Road

Temple Road

Moi Highway

Hospital Road

To Kisii & Kisumu

Kericho

0   100   200 m

The Gusii

The Gusii number around one million and inhabit an area in the western highlands east of Lake Victoria. The area is dominated by Nilotic speaking groups with just this pocket of the Bantu-speaking Gusii.

Being a relatively small group, the Gusii were always on the move following influxes of other groups into their existing lands. After migrating to the Mt Elgon area sometime before the 15th century, the Gusii were gradually pushed south by the advancing Luo, and over the next couple of centuries came into conflict with the Maasai and the Kipsigis. They finally settled in the hills here as the high ridges were easier to defend. Having fought hard for their autonomy the Gusii were unwilling to give it up to the British and suffered heavy losses in conflicts early this century. Following these the men were conscripted in large numbers into the British army.

The Gusii family typically consists of a man, his wives and their married sons, all living together in a single compound. Large families served two purposes: with high infant mortality rates the survival of the family was assured, and the large numbers facilitated defence of the family enclosure. Initiation ceremonies are performed for both boys and girls, and rituals accompany all important events. Death is considered not to be natural but the work of 'witchcraft'. The Gusii were primarily cattle keepers but also practiced some crop cultivation and millet beer was often an important ingredient at big occasions.

As is the case with many of Kenya's ethnic groups, medicine men *(abanyamorigo)* had a

Gusii in traditional dress

highly privileged and respected position. Their duty was to maintain the physical and mental wellbeing of the group – doctor and social worker combined. One of the more bizarre practices was (and still is) the removal of sections of the skull or spine to aid maladies such as backache or concussion. ■

with matatus on the upper level and minibuses and buses on the lower level.

As is the case throughout the west, there is plenty of transport in any direction. Nissan minibuses and matatus leave regularly for Kisumu. The companies running buses to Nairobi have small offices at the matatu station.

If you are hitching, the turn-off to Kisumu is about two km south of town along the Kisii road, so you need to get there first, either on foot or by matatu.

KAKAMEGA FOREST RESERVE

The Kakamega Forest Reserve is a superb slab of virgin tropical rainforest in the heart of an intensively cultivated agricultural area. It is home to a huge variety of birds and animals and is well worth the minimal effort required to get to it.

The Forest Department maintains a beautiful four-room rest house here, as well as a large nursery for propagating trees and shrubs used for ceremonial occasions around the country and for planting in the area. The

The Luo

The Luo people live in the west of the country on the shores of Lake Victoria. Along with the Maasai, they migrated south from the Nile region of Sudan around the 15th century. Although they clashed heavily with the existing Bantu-speaking people of the area, intermarriage and cultural mixing took place readily.

The Luo are unusual amongst Kenya's ethnic groups in that circumcision is not practiced in either sex. This practice was instead replaced by something that one can imagine being almost as painful – the extraction of four or six teeth from the bottom jaw. Although it is not done that much these days, you still see many middle-aged and older people of the region who are minus a few bottom pegs.

Although originally cattle herders, the Luo have adopted fishing and subsistence agriculture. The family group consists of the man, his wife (or wives) and their sons and daughters-in-law. The house compound is enclosed by a fence, and includes separate huts for the man and for each wife and son. (There is a good reconstruction of a Luo village in the grounds of the Kisumu Museum.)

The family group is member of a larger grouping of families *(dhoot)*, several of which in turn make up a group of geographically related people *(ogandi)* each led by a chief *(ruoth)*. Collectively the ogandi constitute the Luo tribe. As is the case with many tribes, great importance is placed on the role of the medicine man and the spirits. ■

Luo chief

workers are very friendly and it's no problem to get shown around.

The forest near the rest house is very dense and there are paths leading all over the place. For that reason, and certainly for a greater appreciation of the forest flora & fauna, it's worth engaging one of the staff to guide you around. Leonard is the most well-known guide. He is friendly and his knowledge of the trees and birds is extensive. Binoculars and wet-weather gear are essential (it usually rains heavily every afternoon for a couple of hours). For that reason it's best to arrive in the morning as you usually have to walk a few km to reach the rest house. The driest period here is from December to April, but even then it rains daily.

Places to Stay & Eat

The *Forest Rest House* is a superb place to put your feet up for a few days. It's an elevated wooden building with a verandah which looks directly on to the seemingly impenetrable Kakamega Forest. There are only four double rooms but they all have a bathroom and toilet. Blankets are supplied but you need to have your own sleeping bag or sheet. The rooms cost US$1.50 per person plus you can also camp for a few cents. If the rest house is full when you arrive, and you have your own sleeping gear, it is usually possible to sleep on the verandah for next to nothing. If you want to be sure of a room, book in advance through the Forest Ranger, PO Box 88, Kakamega.

The only problem here is food. Basically you need to bring your own and preferably something to cook it on, although it is possible to cook on a fire. There's a small kiosk which sells beer, tea and soft drinks (sodas) and also cooks basic meals at lunch time. Evening meals are cooked on request (beans or corn and rice is about the limit), but you need to make sure they know you are coming as the kiosk closes at 6.30 pm. You can get basic meals and supplies from a small group of dukas about two km back towards Shinyalu.

Getting There & Away

The Forest Rest House lies about 12 km east of the A1 Kisumu to Kitale road, about 30 km north of Kisumu. Access is possible either from Kakamega village on the main road when coming from the north, or from Khayaga also on the main road when coming from the south. From both places dirt roads lead east to the small market village of Shinyalu, from where it's a further five km to the rest house, signposted to the left. There are matatus from Kakamega to Shinyalu, and even the occasional one from Khayaga to Shinyalu.

If you want to walk – and it is beautiful walking country – it's about seven km from Khayaga to Shinyalu, or about 10 km from Kakamega to Shinyalu. These roads become extremely treacherous after rain and you may prefer to walk when you see how the vehicles slip all over the road. There's very little traffic along either of the roads but you may get a lift with the occasional tractor or Forest Department vehicle. Whatever means you employ to get there, allow half a day from Kitale or Kisumu. From the turn-off to the rest house the dirt road continues on to Kapsabet so you could also come from that direction but it is a long walk if you can't get a lift.

KAKAMEGA

The town of Kakamega is on the A1 route, 50 km north of Kisumu and 115 km south of Kitale. About the only reason to stay here is if you are heading for the Kakamega Forest and arrive too late in the day to walk or get a vehicle. It's also the last place to stock up with supplies if you're heading for a forest sojourn.

The town has the usual facilities – a couple of banks, a post office, market and the ubiquitous boardings & lodgings.

Places to Stay & Eat

There's a limited range of hotels here. At the bottom end of the scale is the *New Garden View Lodge*, which is conveniently close to the matatu station and offers singles/doubles with shared facilities for US$1.80/2.60. It's basically a brothel. Much better is the *Franca Hotel* which has two-bed rooms with hot-water bath for US$3.40 a room. The beds are larger than a single, but not quite a double.

At the opposite end of the scale is the *Golf Hotel* set in its own grounds with very comfortable, self-contained rooms for US$35/40 a single/double or US$65 a triple including breakfast. There's a bar, restaurant (lunch/dinner for US$6/7) and barbecue area. It's also a great place to relax with a cold beer even if you're not staying here.

Getting There & Away

The matatu station is at the northern edge of town. There are buses, matatus or Peugeots to Kisumu, Webuye, Kitale, Nairobi and Busia. Hitching is not too difficult.

ELDORET

There is little to see or do in Eldoret but it may make a convenient stop for the night in your peregrinations around the western highlands, particularly if you are heading to or from the Cherangani Hills which lie to the north of Eldoret.

The town has benefited hugely from the university here and that has led to a lot of new development.

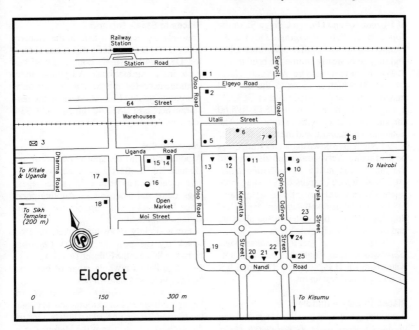

Eldoret

	PLACES TO STAY		24	Spark Milk Bar
1	Eldoret Wagon Hotel			OTHER
2	Sirikwa Hotel		3	Post Office
9	New Paradise Bar & Lodging		4	Police
14	White Castle Motel		5	National Bank of Kenya
15	Mahindi Hotel		6	Town Hall
17	New Miyako Hotel		7	Library
18	Sosani View Hotel		8	New Church
19	New Lincoln Hotel		10	Midnite Cave
25	Top Lodge		11	Standard Chartered Bank
			12	Barclays Bank
▼	PLACES TO EAT		16	Bus & Matatu Station
			20	Eldoret Travel Agency
13	Otto Café		23	Akamba Bus
21	Sizzlers Café			
22	Gilma's Restaurant			

Information

The post office is on the main street, Uganda Rd, and is open Monday to Friday from 8 am to 5 pm and Saturday from 9 am to noon. Also on the main street are branches of Barclays and Standard Chartered banks.

For car rental, check out the Eldoret Travel Agency (☎ 33351) on Kenyatta St.

Places to Stay – bottom end

For a rock-bottom hotel, check out either the *New Paradise Bar & Lodging* on the corner of Uganda Rd and Oginga Odinga St, or the *Top Lodge*, also on Oginga Odinga St. Neither has much to offer other than a bed and they're basically short-time brothels.

Much better is the *Mahindi Hotel* (☎ 31520) which is close to the bus and matatu station and is good value at US$2.70 a single with shared bath or US$3.40/5.60 for singles/doubles with private bath. The hotel has a restaurant, and the noise from the Silent Night Bar downstairs can sometimes be distracting. Very similar and also close to the bus station is the *New Miyako Hotel* (☎ 22954) which charges US$2.70 a single with shared bathroom facilities and US$3.40/4.50 for self-contained singles/doubles. There's hot water in the showers and the hotel has an upstairs bar.

Also in this same area is the *Sosani View Hotel* which offers singles/doubles with hot-water bath for US$2.70/4.50. The hotel has its own bar and restaurant.

Places to Stay – middle

A popular place to stay in this range and one of the cheapest is the *New Lincoln Hotel* (☎ 22093) which is quiet and has guarded parking if you're driving. Self-contained rooms are good value at US$5.70/8.10 including breakfast. The staff are friendly, there's hot water in the showers and the hotel has its own bar and restaurant.

Up in price, the somewhat characterless *White Castle Motel* (☎ 33095) on Uganda Rd offers bed and breakfast for US$10/19 a single/double. There's a bar and restaurant on the ground floor.

The pick of the hotels in this range is the recently refurbished *Eldoret Wagon Hotel* (☎ 62270/1/2) on Oloo Rd. This hotel was built years ago in the colonial era and was once a watering hole for White settlers. It still exudes a certain charm but the open veran-dah where you used to be able to sit and drink a cold beer has now been entirely enclosed. The bar memorabilia, however, is still intact. Self-contained singles/doubles including breakfast cost US$10/17. Credit cards are accepted. The bar keeps 'English' hours: 11 am to 2 pm and 5 to 11 pm.

Places to Stay – top end

The only top-end hotel here is the modern *Sirikwa Hotel* (☎ 31655) which has rooms for US$30/40 a single/double, US$54 a triple including breakfast. All major credit cards are accepted and the hotel has the only swimming pool in Eldoret. Meals in the restaurant here cost US$3.40 (lunch) and US$4 (dinner).

Places to Eat

A popular lunch-time spot is *Otto Café* on Uganda Rd. It offers good cheap Western-style meals such as steak, chicken, sausages, eggs, chips and other snacks. Another good place for snacks is the *Spark Milk Bar* on Oginga Odinga St.

For a slightly more up-market meal or snack try the popular *Sizzlers Café* on Kenyatta St, near the Eldoret Travel Agency. Here you'll find a whole range of burgers, curries, steak and sandwiches.

Also good is *Gilma's Restaurant* on Oginga Odinga St. For a splurge, eat at either the *Eldoret Wagon* or *Sirikwa* hotels. One of the liveliest bars in town is the *Midnite Cave* near the top of Oginga Odinga St.

Getting There & Away

Air Light aircraft flights between Nairobi and Eldoret are temporarily suspended.

Bus & Matatu The bus and matatu station is in the centre of town, just off Uganda Rd. Buses, minibuses, Peugeots and matatus depart throughout the day for Kisumu, Nakuru, Naivasha, Nairobi, Kericho and Kitale.

Train There are services three times a week to Nairobi on Wednesday, Saturday and Sunday at 9 pm, arriving the next day at 9.30 am. Trains to the Ugandan border at Malaba depart on Wednesday, Saturday and Sunday at around 4 am.

CHERANGANI HILLS

The beautiful Cherangani Hills are part of the rift valley system and extend for about 60 km from the north-east of Eldoret. They form the

The Akamba

The traditional homeland of the Akamba people *(Ukumbani)* is the region east of Nairobi towards Tsavo National Park. They migrated here from the south several centuries ago in search of food, mainly the fruit of the baobab tree which was accorded great nutritional value.

The Akamba were great traders and ranged all the way from the coast to Lake Victoria and up to Lake Turkana. Ivory was one of the main barter items but locally made products such as beer, honey, iron weapons and ornaments were also traded. From the neighbouring Maasai and Kikuyu they used to obtain food stocks as their own low-altitude land was relatively poor and couldn't sustain the increasing population which followed their arrival in the area.

In colonial times the Akamba were highly regarded by the British for their intelligence and fighting ability and were drafted in large numbers into the British army. Thousands lost their lives in WW I. When it came to land, however, the British were not quite as respectful and tried to limit the number of cattle the Akamba could own (by confiscating them) and also settle more Europeans in Ukumbani. The Akamba response was the formation of the Ukamba Members Association, whose members marched en masse to Nairobi and squatted peacefully at Kariokor market in protest. After three weeks the administration gave way and the cattle were eventually returned to the people.

All adolescents go through initiation rites to adulthood at around the age of 12, and have the same age-set groups common to many of Kenya's peoples. The various age-set rituals involve the men, and the women to a lesser extent, gaining seniority as they get older.

Young parents were known as 'junior elders' *(mwanake* for men, *mwiitu* for women) and were responsible for the maintenance and upkeep of the village. Once his children were old enough to become junior elders themselves, the mwanake went through a ceremony to become a 'medium elder' *(nthele)*, and later in life a 'full elder' *(atumia ma kivalo)* with the responsibility for death ceremonies and administering the law. The last stage of a person's life is that of 'senior elder' *(atumia ma kisuka)* who is responsible for the holy places.

The Akamba subgroups include Kitui, Masaku and Mumoni. ■

A *kiinga* basket, used for storing grain

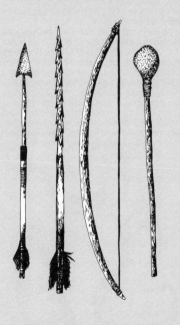

Traditional weapons of the Akamba

The Kalenjin

Kalenjin is a name formulated in the 1950s to describe the group of peoples previously called the Nandi by the British. The Nandi tag was erroneous as the people were all Nandi speakers (one of many dialects) but were not all Nandis; the other groups included Kipsigis, Marakwet, Pokot and Tugen (arap Moi's people). The word *kalenjin* means 'I say to you' in Nandi.

The Kalenjin people occupy the western edge of the central Rift Valley area which includes Kericho, Eldoret, Kitale, Baringo and the Mt Elgon area. They first migrated to the area west of Lake Turkana from southern Sudan around 2000 years ago and gradually filtered south as the climate changed and the forests dwindled.

Although originally pastoralists, most Kalenjin groups took up agriculture. Some, however, such as the Okiek, stuck to the forests and to a hunter-gatherer existence. Beekeeping was a common practice and the honey was used not only in trade but also for brewing beer.

As with most tribes, Kalenjin have age-sets into which a man is initiated after circumcision and remains for the rest of his life. Polygamy was widely practiced. Administration of the law is carried out at the *kok* – an informal gathering of the clan's elders and other interested parties in the dispute. Unusually, the doctors were usually women and they used herbal remedies in their work. Other specialist doctors practiced trepanning – taking out pieces of the skull to cure certain ailments – which is also practiced by the Bantu-speaking Gusii of the Kisii district. ■

Kalenjin in traditional dress

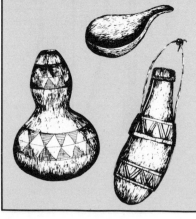

western wall of the spectacular **Elgeyo Escarpment**. You could easily spend weeks exploring here, and never come across another mzungu.

The area is best explored on foot as the roads are rough and some of those which scale the Elgeyo Escarpment are incredibly steep. In wet conditions the roads in this area become treacherous. For serious exploration you would need to get copies of the relevant Survey of Kenya maps to the area, which are almost impossible to get (see the Maps section in the Facts for the Visitor chapter). Otherwise contact Jane or Julia Barnley of Sirikwa Safaris, PO Box 332, Kitale, who can organise ornithological tours of the hills along with a guide at a very reasonable price. Jane and Julia also run an excellent guesthouse and camp site 23 km north of Kitale (see the Kitale section later in this chapter for full details).

The hills are dotted with small towns and although none of them have any recognised accommodation, it should be possible to arrange something with the local people (ask the village chief or ask in the bars). If you have a tent it's just a matter of finding a good spot and asking permission.

From Eldoret it should be possible to hitch, or even find a matatu, as far as **Kapsowar**, 70 km to the north-east in the **Kerio Valley** and right in the heart of the hills. Coming from the north there is a road which starts from Sigor at the Marich Pass and finds its way to Kapsowar via Tot and the impossibly steep escarpment road, but don't expect much in the way of transport along it.

The hills are the home of the Marakwet or Markweta people (part of the greater Kalenjin grouping) who migrated here from the north. They found the area provided good safety, and that the streams were ideal for agriculture as the rainfall was low. To this end they have made good use of, and extended, the water-distribution channels which were already in existence when the Marakwet first migrated to the area. The channels distribute the water to all the small shambas in the hills.

For further details on these hills, see the Marich Pass section in the Northern Kenya chapter.

KITALE

Kitale is another in the string of agricultural service towns which dot the western highlands. It does have an interesting museum but its main function for travellers is as a base for explorations further afield – Mt Elgon, Saiwa Swamp National Park – and a take-off point for the trip up to the western side of Lake Turkana. As such it's a pleasant enough town and can make an enjoyable stopover for a couple of days.

Information

The post office is on Post Office Rd (surprise, surprise) and is open the usual hours. It's possible to make international calls but these have to be made through the operator in Nairobi, and this takes time.

Kitale has the usual banks and a busy market.

Kitale Museum

The museum has a variety of indoor exhibits, including good ethnographic displays of the Turkana people. The outdoor exhibits include traditional homesteads of a number of different tribal groups, the inevitable tortoise enclosure and an interesting biogas display.

Probably most interesting is the small **nature trail** which leads through some virgin forest at the back of the museum. There are numbered points along the way; the small guidebook available from the craft shop in the museum explains the points of interest.

The museum is open Monday to Friday from 7.30 am to 6 pm, Saturday from 8 am to 6 pm and Sunday from 9 am to 6 pm; entry is US$1.10.

Places to Stay – bottom end

Best of the usual bunch of cheapies/brothels is the *Star Lodge*. Good-sized rooms upstairs cost US$2.20 a double with shared bath, but cop a bit of noise from the road below.

Very similar is the *Kahuroko Boarding &*

Lodging where self-contained singles cost US$2.70 and doubles with shared bath US$2.20. It's getting run-down these days but is still OK for a night. Another cheapie is the *New Mombasa Hotel* which offers clean singles with shared facilities for US$1.80 though there's a very noisy bar on the 1st floor. The *Hotel Mamboleo* is much quieter, though the rooms are somewhat gloomy. Self-contained singles/doubles here cost US$2.20/3.40 plus there's hot water in the showers.

Other travellers have recommended the *New Kitale House* next door to the Mamboleo which offers beds with clean sheets and shared bath for just US$1.40. The *Executive Lodge*, on Kenyatta St, has self-contained singles for US$3.40, but no doubles.

If you want to camp, the only place in the area is *Sirikwa Safaris,* about 23 km north of Kitale on the Kapenguria road. It's run by Jane and Julia Barnley at their farmhouse and is a beautiful place to stay. Jane and Julia are very friendly and know the western highlands like the back of their hand, plus they're great conversationalists. Stay here and feel right at home! You won't regret the little effort it takes to get here. Camping with your own tent costs US$2.70 including the use of firewood, hot showers, flush toilets and electricity. If you don't have your own tent, that's no problem as there are also 'permanent' furnished tents for US$6.70 per person.

To find Sirikwa Safaris, look for the green concrete posts and the sign on a rise on the right-hand side of the road several km past the entrance to Saiwa Swamp National Park.

Places to Stay – middle

The *New Kitale Hotel* is the town's old colonial place but, these days, it wears a garb of total neglect bordering on dereliction. Despite this, and the feeling that everytime you open a wardrobe in one of the rooms that a skeleton dressed ready for a June ball will fall out, the rooms are spacious, self-contained and have a balcony. Rates are US$3.40/6.70 for singles/doubles without towels, soap or toilet paper. It's a shame that

it has not been looked after – it could be beautiful.

The most popular place to stay in this range is the *Bongo Hotel* (☎ 20593) on Moi Ave which has singles/doubles with shared bath (no breakfast) for US$6/6.70, or US$7.80/10 with private bath and an excellent breakfast. There's hot water in the showers, clean sheets, and towel, soap and toilet paper are provided.

Also excellent value is the *Alakara Hotel* (☎ 20395) on Kenyatta St which offers spacious singles/doubles with shared bath for US$5.60/7.80. Twin-bed rooms with private bath cost US$8.90, and double-bed rooms with bath US$11.10. Single-occupancy rates are less. Prices include breakfast. Facilities include a good bar/restaurant, a car park and a residents' video room. The staff are friendly and helpful.

Outside of town, Jane and Julia Barnley's farmhouse is the place to head for (see Sirikwa Safaris earlier for directions). Apart from tents there are two very comfortable rooms with double beds for US$16/24 a single/double including breakfast. Half-board/full-board rates are US$20/32 and US$24/40 respectively. Children are half-price and babies stay free of charge. It's a very quiet and homely place and Jane and Julia are the perfect hosts.

Places to Eat & Entertainment

The *Wandi Café* on Kenyatta St is a popular place at lunch time. Meals are basic but tasty, and include dishes such as beef stew with rice, and chicken and chips. Another good place is the *Delicious Restaurant* on the same street.

The *Bongo Hotel* on the corner of Moi Ave and Bank St has a slightly more up-market restaurant which is a good place for an evening meal. It also serves alcohol. Right next door is the lively Bongo Bar and there's also a takeaway food section. Even better, though slightly more expensive, are the meals at the *Alakara Hotel* on Kenyatta St. You can either eat in the restaurant section or have meals brought to you in the popular bar.

Another lively bar here with loud music is

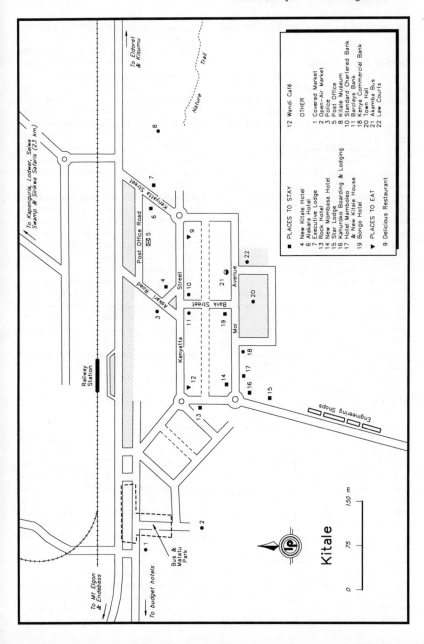

■ PLACES TO STAY

4 New Kitale Hotel
6 Alakara Hotel
13 Executive Lodge
    Rock Hotel
14 New Mombasa Hotel
15 Star Lodge
16 Kahuroko Boarding & Lodging
17 Hotel Mamboleo
    & New Kitale House
19 Bongo Hotel

▼ PLACES TO EAT

9 Delicious Restaurant

12 Wandi Café

OTHER

1 Covered Market
2 Open-Air Market
3 Police
5 Post Office
8 Kitale Museum
10 Standard Chartered Bank
11 Barclays Bank
18 Kenya Commercial Bank
20 Town Hall
21 Akamba Bus
22 Law Courts

Kitale

the one on the 1st floor of the *New Mombasa Hotel.*

Getting There & Away

The bus and matatu park is fairly chaotic – it's just a matter of wandering around and finding a vehicle going your way. Competition for passengers is usually keen and you'll soon be spotted and pointed in the right direction.

For Lodwar and Kalekol in the Turkana district, Githiora and Trans Nzoia usually operate a daily bus leaving around 10 am but these don't always run so you need to make enquiries the day before. The Nissan matatus are more reliable and leave about five times daily (five hours, US$4.45). From Lodwar to Kalekol there's usually a daily matatu but you'll have to make enquiries as the service depends on demand. Turkana tribespeople in traditional gear get on and off, seemingly in the middle of nowhere.

On the Nairobi route there is a variety of transport – bus, matatu, Peugeot – so it's a matter of finding which suits you. Akamba runs daily buses to Nairobi at 9 am and 9 pm (US$4.80). There's also the Eldoret Express which runs daily to Nairobi at 6 pm and costs US$4. The bus companies have their offices mainly around the bus station area. The exception is Akamba which has its office on Moi Ave.

For Eldoret, you have a choice of bus (US$0.90 to US$1.10), Nissan matatu (US$1.10) or Peugeot (US$1.35).

For Kisumu, Jamhuri Express has one daily departure at 7.15 am which costs US$2.

For the village of Enderbess (the nearest place to Mt Elgon National Park), Nissan matatus cost US1.10. (See the Mt Elgon section for more details on getting to this national park.)

SAIWA SWAMP NATIONAL PARK

This small park north of Kitale is a real delight. The swamp area is the habitat of the sitatunga antelope *(Tragelaphus spekii),* known in Swahili as the *nzohe,* and this park has been set aside to protect it.

What makes this park unique is that it is only accessible on foot. There are marked walking trails which skirt the swamp, duckboards right across the swamp in places, and some extremely rickety observation towers. The sitatunga is fairly elusive and really the only way to spot one is to sit atop one of these towers armed with a pair of binoculars and a hefty dose of patience. As is the case in most of the parks, the best time for animal-spotting is in the early morning or late afternoon.

This shy antelope is not unlike a bushbuck in appearance, although larger, and has elongated hooves which are supposed to make it easier for it to get around in swampy conditions – it's hard to see how, but no doubt nature has it all worked out. The colouring is basically grey-brown, with more red noticeable in the females, and both sexes have white spots or stripes on the upper body. The males have long twisted horns which grow up to a metre in length.

The park is also home to the impressive black-and-white colobus monkey *(Colobus polykomos).* It inhabits the higher levels of the trees and, not having the gregarious nature of many primates, is easy to miss as it sits quietly in the heights. When they do move, however, the flowing 'cape' of white hair is very distinctive. Birdlife within the park is also prolific.

With all this on offer it's surprising how few people visit Saiwa Swamp.

Places to Stay

It is possible to camp at the ranger station inside the park but there is nothing in the way of facilities. A much better option is to camp or stay at the *Sirikwa Safaris* farmhouse about four km away. For the cost of camping or staying in a room here see the Kitale section. The owners can also arrange a field guide who is well versed in the birdlife of the park for US$2.65 (half day) or US$5.35 (full day) as well as transport to the park entrance.

Getting There & Away

Saiwa Swamp National Park lies five km east of the main A1 road, 18 km north of Kitale. Any of the matatus running between Kitale and Kapenguria will let you off at the signposted turn-off, from where you'll probably have to walk to the park as there is little traffic along the dirt road.

MT ELGON NATIONAL PARK

Mt Elgon sits astride the Kenya-Uganda border and, while it offers similar trekking possibilities to Mt Kenya, its location makes it a far less popular goal. The lower altitude also means that the weather on the upper slopes is not quite as severe.

The mountain is an extinct volcano and the national park extends from the lower slopes right up to the border. The highest peak is Wagagai (4321 metres) which is actually on the far side of the crater in Uganda. The highest peak on the Kenyan side is Koitoboss. The Mt Elgon range is the fourth-highest in East Africa after Mt Kilimanjaro

Mt Kenya and the Ruwenzoris. There are warm springs in the crater itself, the floor of which is around 3500 metres above sea level.

Access to the 170 sq-km national park is only officially allowed with a vehicle, but this may change when the hiking trails and huts being set up by the Mt Elgon Conservation & Development Project in Uganda are open to the public. The project is based in Mbale. The plan is to link up the Ugandan trails with those on the Kenyan side.

The mountain's biggest attraction is the elephants, renowned the world over for their predilection for salt, the major source of which is in the caves on the mountain slopes. The elephants are such keen excavators that some have gone so far as to claim that the elephants are totally responsible for the caves! Sadly, the numbers of these saline-

loving creatures has declined over the years, mainly due to incursions by poachers from the Ugandan side. There are three caves open to visitors – Kitum, Chepnyali and Mackingeny. Kitum is the one which you are most likely to see elephants in, while Mackingeny is the most spectacular. Obviously a good torch (flashlight) is essential if you want to explore the caves.

A less obvious attraction is the range of vegetation found on the mountain. Starting with rainforest at the base, the vegetation changes as you ascend to bamboo jungle and finally alpine moorland with the bizarre giant groundsel and giant lobelia plants. The lower forests are the habitat of the impressive black and white colobus monkey along with many other species of birds and animals. Those most commonly sighted include buffalo, bushbuck, giant forest hog and Sykes monkey.

Elgon can be a wet place at any time of the year, but the driest months seem to be December, January and February. As well as waterproof gear you are going to need warm clothes as it gets cold up here at night.

Walks

If you want to walk in the park, the most popular route is from **Kimilili**, a small village 36 km south of Kitale on the main A1 road to Webuye and Kisumu. There's basic accommodation here, and matatus run the

seven km to **Kapsakwany**, from where you start walking. The Kimilili Forest Station is about five km past Kapsakwany and from there it's a further 20 km to the Chepkitale Forest Station, and another seven km past this station to the mountain hut. Obviously it's a long day's walk from Kapsakwany to the hut (32 km for those of you who can't add up) but the rangers at either of the forest stations shouldn't mind if you camp there.

From the hut it takes around four hours to reach the lake known as Lower Elgon Tarn, and from here it's a further one hour walk along a marked trail (cairns and white blazes) to Lower Elgon peak. The pass at the foot of Koitoboss peak and the **Suam hot springs** are around the crater rim to the right (northeast) and once here you are in the national park. If you reach this point and descend via the park entrance (Chorlim Gate), which is in fact illegal as you're not supposed to walk in the park, expect some difficult questions and be prepared to pay the park entry fee. The options are to return the same way, or via the third route, known as the Masara route, which goes to the small village of **Masara** on the northern slopes of the mountain, a trek of about 25 km.

Places to Stay

There are no lodges in the park itself but there is a beautiful camp site with good facilities close to the Chorlim Gate which you'll

be allowed to walk to. You need to bring all your own food, camping and cooking equipment with you as there's none for hire and there are no shops.

About one km before the Chorlim Gate is the *Mt Elgon Lodge* (PO Box 7 Enderbess, Kitale), one of the Msafiri Inns chain of hotels. Comfortable rooms with full board cost US$25/45/60 a single/double/triple in the low season, US$40/65/85 in the high season. The hotel has a bar and restaurant.

Getting There & Away
To get to the village of Enderbess (the nearest place to Mt Elgon National Park), there are normal matatus for US$0.55 or Nissan matatus for US$1.10 from Kitale. Part of this road is good tarmac but there are also some horrific sections with huge potholes. The turn-off for Mt Elgon National Park (Chorlim Gate) is several km before Enderbess on the left-hand side (clearly signposted). If you're hitching, you'll need to get to the turn-off but it's still a long way into the park from there and there's very little transport. Rangers' vehicles and support trucks do come along the road at least once a day but you could be waiting half the day. Although the road into the park is a good gravel road, in the wet season the only way in is to have your own 4WD.

Northern Kenya

This vast area, covering thousands of sq km to the borders with Sudan, Ethiopia and Somalia, is an explorer's paradise hardly touched by the 20th century. The tribes which live here – the Samburu, Turkana, Rendille, Boran, Gabra, Merille and El-Molo – are some of the most fascinating people in the world. The whole area is a living ethnology museum. Like the Maasai, most of them have little contact with the modern world, preferring their own centuries-old traditional lifestyles and customs which bind members of a tribe together and ensure that each individual has a part to play. Many have strong warrior traditions and, in the past, it was the balance of power between the tribes which defined their respective areas.

As late as 1980 there was a clash between the Samburu and the Turkana over grazing land near South Horr which required army intervention. Since most of the tribes are nomadic pastoralists these sort of conflicts have a long history. Nevertheless, the settlement of disputes between the tribes is based on compensation rather than retribution so wholesale violence is a rare occurrence.

Change is slowly coming to these people as a result of missionary activity (there is an incredible number of different Christian missions, schools and aid agencies, many of them in very remote areas), their employment as rangers and anti-poaching patrollers in national parks and game reserves, the construction of dams and roads, and the tourist trade. You may well be surprised, for example, to see a young man dressed smartly in Western-style clothes doing some business in a small town and then later on the same day meet him again out in the bush dressed in traditional regalia. It might even turn out that he's a college student in Nairobi for much of the year. Pride in their heritage is one thing these people are very unlikely to lose.

Yet, such examples of sophistication aside, not only are the people another world away from Nairobi and the more developed areas of the country but the landscapes are tremendous. Perhaps no other country in Africa offers such diversity.

Geography

Much of northern Kenya is scrub desert dissected by luggas (dry river beds which burst into a brief but violent life whenever there is a cloud burst) and peppered with acacia thorn trees which are often festooned with weaver birds' nests. But there are also extinct and dormant volcanoes; barren, shattered lava beds; canyons through which cool, clear streams flow; oases of lush vegetation hemmed in by craggy mountains and huge islands of forested mountains surrounded by sand deserts. And, of course, the legendary 'Jade Sea' (Lake Turkana) – Kenya's largest lake and, as a result of the Leakeys' archaeological digs, regarded by many as the birthplace of humanity.

A long narrow body of water, Lake Turkana stretches south from the Ethiopian border for some 250 km, yet is never more than 50 km wide. While it looks fairly placid most of the time, it is notorious for the vicious squalls which whip up seemingly out of nowhere and are largely responsible for the fatalities among the local Turkana and El-Molo people who live along the lake shores.

The lake was first reached by Europeans in the late 19th century in the form of two Austrian explorers, von Hehnel and Teleki, who named it Lake Rudolf and it wasn't until the early 1970s that the name was changed to Turkana. The fossil hominid skulls discovered here by the Leakeys in the 1960s are thought to be around 2½ million years old. At that time it is believed that the lake was far more extensive than it is today and supported a richer plant and animal life. Around 10,000 years ago the water level was high enough for the lake to be one of the sources

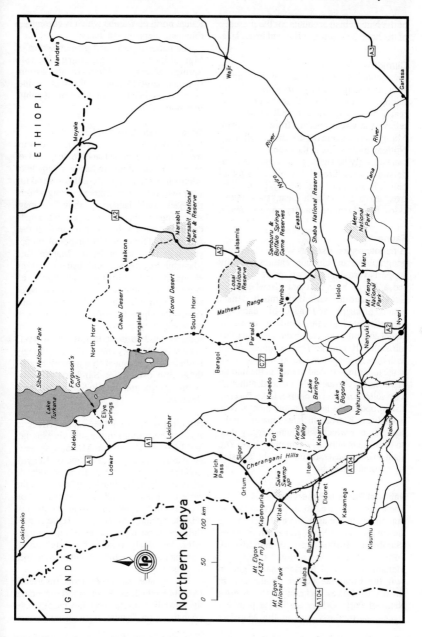

Northern Kenya

of the Nile, which accounts for the presence of the huge Nile perch still found in the lake.

Climate

The contrasts are incredible in this part of Kenya and the climate mirrors this. By midday on the plains the temperature can reach 50°C without a breath of wind to relieve the sweat pouring from your brow. Mirages shimmer in the distance on all sides. Nothing moves. Yet in the evening, the calm can suddenly be shattered as a violent thunderstorm tears through the place taking all before it. And, just as suddenly, it can all be over leaving you with clear, star-studded skies. It's adventure country *par excellence*.

Fauna

A remote region like this with such diverse geographical and climatic features naturally supports varied fauna. Two species you will see a lot of here (but not elsewhere) are Grevy's zebra, with their much denser pattern of stripes and saucer-like ears, and the reticulated giraffe. Herds of domestic camel are commonplace in the area and often miraculously emerge from a mirage along with their owner when you are bogged down to the axles in soft sand or mud in the middle of the desert. A rope is all you need, although it's a seller's market of course. Lake Turkana also supports the largest population of Nile crocodile in Kenya which feed mainly on the lake fish but which will quite happily dine on incautious humans swimming there. The giant eland finds sanctuary in the forested hills around Marsabit.

National Parks & Reserves

There are several national parks and game sanctuaries in the area, three of them along the Ewaso Nyiro River just north of Isiolo (Samburu, Buffalo Springs and Shaba). Further north are the national reserves of Maralal, Losai and Marsabit and right up near the Ethiopian border on the eastern shores of Lake Turkana is the Sibiloi National Park. Others are in the planning stages, particularly one in the Mathews

Range north of Wamba which is currently a rhino and elephant sanctuary.

The national parks and game reserves of Marsabit, Maralal, Samburu, Buffalo Springs, Shaba and Meru, on the eastern side, and Saiwa Swamp, on the western side, are all accessible by a combination of public transport and hitching.

Getting There & Around

Car & 4WD For most travellers who want freedom of movement and to see a lot of places it comes down to hiring a vehicle or going on an organised safari. If you're taking your own vehicle remember to bring a high-rise jack, sand ladders, a shovel, a long, strong rope or chain (that you can hitch up to camels or other vehicles) plus enough fuel and water. The only regular petrol pumps you will find are at Isiolo, Maralal and Marsabit. Elsewhere there's usually nothing except missions, which will reluctantly sell you limited amounts of fuel for up to three times the price in Nairobi. You can't blame them – they have to transport it in barrels in the back of their Land Rovers or pay for someone else to do it in a truck. A 4WD vehicle is obligatory and you'd be extremely foolhardy to attempt such a journey in anything else except for Samburu National Game Reserve and Buffalo Springs National Reserve.

Hitching Apart from three routes (Kitale to Lodwar, Nyahururu to Baragoi via Maralal, and Isiolo to Moyale via Marsabit, there is no public transport in this area of Kenya). You can certainly hitch as far as Maralal or Marsabit (from Nyahururu or Isiolo) on the eastern side and to Lodwar (from Kitale) on the western side but that's about the limit of reliable hitching possibilities. There is *very* little traffic on any other routes though travellers regularly report that hitching to Loyangalani is not difficult although it does take time.

The mission stations/schools invariably have their own Land Rovers (and some have their own light aircraft) but they usually only go in to regional centres once a week or once a fortnight. Although most will try to help you out if you're stuck, you cannot be guaranteed a lift. The vehicle might be full of people who need urgent medical assistance or (on the return journey) full of supplies. Hitching is possible, of course, but you must have no deadlines to meet and you must be the sort of person who is quite happy to wait around for days for a ride. In some ways, this could be a very interesting way of getting around and you'd certainly meet a lot of local people but if it is lifts you want you can only hitch along the main routes.

You could, of course, buy a camel and do a John Hillaby but this isn't something to approach lightly. It is, however, a distinct possibility especially if you are part of a small group. You'd have the adventure of your life!

Safaris Most organised safaris last from seven to 10 days, though there are others which last 14 days, and they all seem to follow much the same route. Starting from Nairobi, they head up the rift valley to Lake Baringo, over to Maralal and then up the main route to Loyangalani on Lake Turkana via Baragoi and South Horr. On the return journey, again via Maralal, they take in Samburu National Game Reserve and Buffalo Springs National Reserve. Only one or two of them take in Marsabit National Park & Reserve since the only way of getting there from Loyangalani is directly across the Koroli Desert (hazardous after rain) or via the long loop north through North Horr and Maikona. Even this involves crossing the Chalbi Desert which, like the Koroli, is hazardous after rain.

The cost of safaris varies between US$265 and US$1650 depending on the number of days and the standard of accommodation. The price includes transport, all meals, park and camping fees, and camping equipment. Since the terrain is rough beyond Isiolo or Maralal, open-sided 4WD trucks are used for these safaris and it's a dusty journey. Don't expect any of life's little luxuries on these safaris (such as hot showers or cold beers), though these can be found with determina-

tion! The following companies all offer Turkana tours, usually once a week but sometimes once a fortnight (see also the Safari section of the Getting Around chapter). Note also that these have been listed alphabetically, not in any order of preference:

Best Camping
  Nanak House, 2nd Floor, on the corner of Kimathi and Banda Sts, PO Box 40223, Nairobi (☎ 28091, 27203).
  Like the others, Best takes the usual route but its safari lasts eight days.
Bushbuck Adventures
  Barclays Bank Bldg, Kenyatta Ave, PO Box 67449, Nairobi (☎ 212975/6/7; fax 218735).
  Bushbuck offers a 12-day safari to Lake Turkana but it keeps well away from the usual route taking in the Mathews Range, the Ndoto Mountains and Shaba National Game Reserve. It leaves once a month in the dry season and costs US$1650. There's also an 18-day 'Northern Frontier Expedition' which takes in Samburu, the Ndoto Mountains, Lake Turkana and North Horr and, like the previous tour, keeps well away from the usual route. It costs US$1480 and includes a return flight from Loyangalani to Nairobi.
Exotic Safaris & Travel
  1st Floor, Uniafric House, Koinange St, PO Box 54483, Nairobi (☎ 338811; fax 211701).
  This company also offers a seven-day safari to Lake Turkana.
Gametrackers
  1st Floor, Kenya Cinema Plaza, Moi Ave, PO Box 62042, Nairobi (☎ 338927; fax 330903).
  This company is the only one which takes in Marsabit National Park and then crosses the Chalbi Desert to Lake Turkana. It takes eight days, costs US$330 and departs twice a month on Fridays. It also has an eight-day safari to Lake Turkana which takes the normal route, departs twice a month on Fridays and costs the same.
Safari Camp Services
  PO Box 44801, on the corner of Koinange and Moktar Daddah Sts, Nairobi (☎ 28936, 330130; fax 212160).
  This is the group which blazed the trail 17 years ago and recently celebrated its 600th departure. You won't find better. There's a seven-day safari (US$265) which leaves every second Saturday year-round (every Saturday in the high season).
Special Camping Safaris
  Gilfillan House, Kenyatta Ave, PO Box 51512, Nairobi (☎ 338325; fax 211828).
  This company takes the usual route but its safari

lasts 10 days. The cost is US$370 and there are departures twice per month.

Yare Safaris

1st Floor, Union Towers, Mama Ngina St, PO Box 63006, Nairobi (☎ 214099; fax 213445).

Yare's 10-day safari covers the usual route and includes a night at its Maralal hostel and camp site. The cost is US$360 and there are departures twice (sometimes three times) a month on Saturdays.

West of Turkana

From Kitale the road north winds through the fertile highlands, passing the turn-off for the tiny Saiwa Swamp National Park (well worth a visit) before reaching **Kapenguria**, the town most famous for being the place where Jomo Kenyatta and five associates were held and tried in 1953 for their part in the Mau Mau Rebellion.

The road then snakes its way up along a forested ridge and through the narrow northern gorges of the Cherangani Hills, emerging on to the desert plains through the Marich Pass. The change in scenery is dramatic and there are some fantastic views of the plains. The only town in this part of the hills is **Ortum**, just off the road. If you want to stop and explore the area, there is basic accommodation in the town but the best place to stay is the Marich Pass Field Studies Centre further north (see the following Marich Pass section).

Shortly after Marich Pass is a turn-off to the left (west) to the Turkwel Gorge. It's here that you'll find the huge hydroelectric project which is destined to supply electricity to a large area of the densely populated highlands – the northern areas will still have to rely on generators.

After km of endless plains and dry creek beds the town of **Lokichar** is little more than a collection of dismal dukas by the side of the road. The heat here is oppressive and the settlement seems to be gripped by a permanent torpor. The one redeeming feature of the place is that it is possible to buy basketware

and other Turkana trinkets cheaper than you'll find them further north.

MARICH PASS AREA

The main reason for visiting this area is to stay at the Marich Pass Field Studies Centre (see Places to Stay & Eat) and use this as a base for a number of excursions in the area.

Those with their own vehicles should bring sufficient supplies of petrol as there are no service stations between Kapenguria and Lodwar. If you intend walking in the vicinity then you need to be adequately prepared for a variety of weather conditions.

A few km to the north-west, **Mt Sekerr** (3326 metres) can be climbed comfortably in a three-day round trip via the agricultural plots of the Pokot tribe, passing through forest and open moors. The views from the top are magnificent when the weather is clear.

To the south are the **Cherangani Hills**, which offer some of the best hill walks anywhere in Kenya ranging from half-day excursions to week-long safaris by vehicle and on foot. Possibilities include a half-day walk along the old road perched high on the eastern side of the Marich Pass to a local Pokot trading centre; a hard day's slog up the dome of Koh which soars some 1524 metres above the adjacent plains; a safari of several days' duration along the verdant Weiwei Valley to Tamkal and then up to Lelan Forest and the main peaks of the Cherangani.

The **Elgeyo Escarpment** rises to more than 1830 metres in places above the Kerio Valley and offers spectacular views and waterfalls. It's only 1½ hours away from the field studies centre along a road that passes through several local market centres and intensively farmed garden plots.

The **South Turkana National Reserve** in dry and rugged hills north-east of the field studies centre is the domain of Turkana herders and rarely visited by outsiders. The 50-km drive to get there traverses grazing lands of the pastoral Pokot.

Lastly, the **Turkwel Gorge** hydroelectric station is only 30 km away along a fine tarmac road. Much of the gorge, with its

The Turkana

The Turkana are another of Kenya's more colourful (and warlike) people. Originally from the Karamajong district of north-eastern Uganda, the Turkana number around 250,000 and live in the virtual desert country of Kenya's north-west. Due to their isolation, the Turkana are probably the least affected by the 20th century of all Kenya's people.

Like the Samburu and the Maasai (with whom they are linguistically linked), the Turkana are cattle herders first, and more recently they have taken up fishing the waters of Lake Turkana and even growing the occasional crops, weather permitting. But unlike the other two tribes, the Turkana have discontinued the practice of circumcision.

The traditional dress of the Turkana people is amazing, as is the number of people who still wear it – catching a bus up in the north-west is a real eye-opener for a first-time visitor. The men cover part of their hair with mud which is then painted blue and decorated with ostrich and other feathers. The main garment they wear, despite the blast-furnace heat of the region, is a woollen blanket (usually a garish modern checked one) which is worn around one shoulder.

Traditional accessories include a small wooden stool carved out of a single piece of wood (used either as a pillow or a stool), a wooden stick with a distinctive shape, and a wrist knife. Both the men and the women wear with great flourish the lip plug through the lower lip which looks a bit gruesome to tourists. The women wear a variety of beaded and metal adornment, much of it indicating to the trained eye events in the woman's life. A half skirt of animal skins and a piece of black cloth are the only garments worn, although these days pieces of colourful cloth are not uncommon for use as baby slings.

Turkana women (HF)

Tattooing is also surprisingly common and usually has special meaning. Men are tattooed on the shoulders and upper arm each time they kill an enemy – the right shoulder for killing a man, the left for a woman; it's surprising the number of men you still see with these markings. Witch doctors and prophets are held in high regard and tattooing on someone's lower stomach is usually a sign of witch doctors' attempts to cast out an undesirable spirit rather than any sort of decoration. ∎

Top: El-Molo girls, Lake Turkana (DT)
Bottom Left: Samburu woman, Lake Turkana (DT)
Bottom Right: Billboard (& bored Bill?) (HF)

towering rock walls, has not been affected by the construction, while the dam itself (the highest of its type in Africa) is spectacular. The 35 km-long lake will eventually be available for fishing, sailing and other water sports.

Places to Stay & Eat

The best place to stay in this area is the *Marich Pass Field Studies Centre* (☎ (0321) 31541), PO Box 2454, Eldoret. This is essentially a residential facility for groups pursuing field courses in geography, botany, zoology, ecology, conservation, geology and rural development, but it's also open to independent travellers who want to spend a day, a week or a month in a little-known corner of Kenya.

The centre occupies a beautiful site alongside the Weiwei River and is surrounded by

Heron

dense bush and woodland. The birdlife is prolific, monkeys and baboons are 'in residence', while antelope, buffaloes, wart hogs and elephants are regular visitors. Facilities include a secure camp site (US$1.80 per person per night) with drinking water, toilets, showers and firewood, as well as dorm beds for US$2.20 and simple but comfortable bandas for US$6.20 (two people) and US$9.40 (three people).

English-speaking Pokot and Turkana guides are available on request. There's also a restaurant where you can get breakfast for US$1.50, lunch for US$1.10 and dinner from US$1.70 (vegetarian) to US$2.10 (meat). Meals should ideally be ordered in advance since the very friendly manager often has to walk into the nearest village to buy the food. You can, of course, bring your own food with you and cook it at the centre. There's little available in the villages of this area.

Getting There & Away

To reach the field studies centre, take the main Kitale to Lodwar road and watch out for the centre's signpost two km north of the Sigor to Tot road junction (signposted) at Marich Pass. The centre is about one km down a clearly marked track.

There are three approaches to Marich Pass. The first and easiest is through Kitale and Kapenguria and then a further 67 km down a tarmac road (described as 'possibly Kenya's most spectacular tarmac road'). There are daily bus services from Nairobi to Kapenguria, and matatus (US$0.80 or US$0.90 in a Nissan) from Kitale to Kapenguria. There are also a few daily matatus which cover the stretch from Kitale to Lokichar via Marich Pass.

The second approach is through Iten either from Eldoret or via Kabarnet using the scenic road across the upper Kerio Valley from Kabarnet. The all-weather Cherangani Highway can be picked up from Iten to cross the main pass of the Cherangani Hills and join up with the Kitale to Lodwar road near Kapenguria.

The roughest of the three approaches is the

road from Lake Baringo through the Kito Pass and across the Kerio Valley to Tot but its main advantage is that it gives you the chance to visit the hot waterfalls at **Kapedo**. From Tot, the track skirts the northern face of the Cherangani Hills and involves fording numerous streams which may be impassable after heavy rain, although an Italian-funded road project should soon make this an all-weather road.

LODWAR

The hot and dusty administrative town of Lodwar is the only town of any significance in the north-west. With a bitumen road connecting it with the highlands, and air connections with Nairobi, it is no longer the isolated outpost of the Northern Frontier District as the area was known during colonial days but is certainly lagging a few steps behind the rest of the country.

Lodwar is also the base for any excursions to the lake from the western side and you will probably find it convenient to stay here for a night at least. There's little to do in the town itself but it has an outback atmosphere which is not altogether unpleasant and just watching the garrulous locals is entertainment in itself. The Turkana have suddenly found that tourists are a good touch when it comes to selling trinkets and they approach with alarming audacity and don't conceal their disgust when you don't want to buy. They are also remarkably persistent. The small market is a good place to watch women weaving the baskets.

Information

The town has a post office and a branch of the Kenya Commercial Bank.

Places to Stay – bottom end

Lodwar is one place where it's worth spending a bit more on accommodation – mainly to get a room with a fan. The rooms in the cheaper places are all hellishly hot and, as the mosquitoes are fierce, you need to cover up or burn coils if you don't have a net. It seems the recently surfaced road from the south has put Lodwar on the map, and there are new hotels springing up all the time.

Best of the cheapies is the *Mombasa Hotel*, almost next door to the JM Bus office which is where you'll be dropped if arriving that way from Kitale. The friendly Muslim owners charge US$1.40/2.10 for singles/doubles. The singles are cooler (it's all relative though) as they have high ceilings. If you have a mosquito net you can sleep in the courtyard.

The *Marira Boarding & Lodging* is a new place and could be worth a try. Another bottom-end cheapie is the *Ngonda Hotel*. Both charge the same as the Mombasa Hotel.

Places to Stay – middle

The *Turkwel Hotel* (☎ 21201) is the town's social focus and also has the best accommodation. Single rooms with fan and shared bath go for US$2.20, while singles/doubles with fan and bath cost US$4/5.40. There are also a few spacious cottages which are very pleasant and cost US$8 for two including breakfast.

It is rumoured that a luxury hotel of the African Tours & Hotels chain is to be built on the southern side of the Turkwel River on the approach into town.

Places to Eat

The restaurant at the *Mombasa Hotel* does reasonable local food and has excellent fresh mandazis (semisweet doughnuts) early in the morning. The *Marira Boarding & Lodging* has little variety but its chips are excellent and freshly cooked to order. For something a bit more sophisticated the *Turkwel Hotel* restaurant does standard Western fare such as steak, chips, etc. Breakfast here consists of a couple of eggs and a sausage, and non-guests are not served until all the hotel guests have finished. The bar here is also a popular place.

Getting There & Away

In theory, there are daily Githiora and Trans Nzoia buses from Kitale to Lodwar which generally leave around 10 am and (sometimes) at 2 pm but sometimes they don't run at all. The matatus are more reliable and there are usually five per day which leave when full. The trip takes around seven hours and costs US$4.50.

Matatus also run from Lodwar to Kalekol near the lake if demand warrants, but you can't count on them. The trip takes one hour. If you want to hitch to Kalekol the place where the locals wait is under the tree about 200 metres north of the Kobil station. To give an indication of how long you can expect to wait, there is a chai (tea) stall here which also sells mandazis.

KALEKOL

Most travellers head on from Lodwar to Kalekol, a fairly dismal little town a few km from the lake shore. The main building in this one-street town is the fish-processing factory built with Scandinavian money and expertise and, although fairly new is currently not operating. There is also an Italian-sponsored plant closer to the lake shore.

Places to Stay & Eat

A good place to stay is the rudimentary but friendly *George Oyavi's Hotel*. It is right next to the bus office and George meets all incoming buses. The rooms are only rough grass constructions and so thankfully get some breeze. There's a rough-and-ready shower rigged up and George and his staff somehow muddle through and cook meals although you need to order in advance. Warm beer and sodas are also available. If you want anything more sophisticated to eat than rice, chapatis or fish you'll need to bring it from Lodwar.

There's a second hotel called *Skyway Bar & Lodge* on the right-hand side as you enter Kalekol from the south. Rooms here cost US$0.80/2.70 a single/double with shared bathroom facilities. Next door is the *Safari Hotel* which has a reasonable restaurant.

Getting There & Away

Assuming one of the buses made it from Kitale the previous day, it generally leaves for the return journey at around 5 am. There

is no danger of missing it as the driver revs the engine and honks the horn well before he leaves. Alternatively, there's usually a matatu which leaves later in the day. Make enquiries the night before if you want to be sure of leaving next day.

To get out to the lake it's a hot 1½ hour walk. Someone at George's will guide you, or just walk to the Italian fishing project and cut across the lake bed from there to the lodge.

FERGUSON'S GULF

This is the most accessible part of the lake shore and while it's not particularly attractive, although the sense of achievement in just getting there usually compensates. The water has receded greatly, mainly due to drought in Ethiopia, so you have to walk a long way over the lake bed to actually get to the water. The birdlife along the shore is prolific. There are also hippos and crocodiles, so seek local advice before having a refreshing dip.

There is a small fishing village of grass huts on the far side of the Turkana Fishing Lodge and that's about the limit of development.

To get out on the lake you can hire the launches from the lodge to take you to **Central Island National Park**, a barren yet scenic volcanic island. By all accounts the trip is worthwhile but it's not cheap. A covered cruiser which takes eight people costs US$52, while the open four-seater long boat costs US$39. Talk to the fishers and they might take you out for a good deal less but make sure their craft is sound – the danger posed by the lake's squalls is not to be taken lightly.

Places to Stay

If you don't mind really roughing it, the local villagers will put you up for a few bob, otherwise you'll have to come here just for a day trip from Kalekol or stay at the lodge.

The *Lake Turkana Fishing Lodge* (☎ (2) 26623), PO Box 41078, Nairobi, is supposedly on an island but the level of the lake has fallen so far in recent years that it's now possible to drive to the lodge, in the dry season at least. It takes around 1½ very hot hours to walk out there from Kalekol – follow the track to the Italian fishing project then head across the lake bed from there. There are children with canoes who will paddle you across the 20 metres or so of channel. By car you just follow the main road through Kalekol and it takes a circuitous route to the far side of the lodge.

Although reportedly busy on weekends, the lodge was deserted when I visited on a weekday and the underworked staff were happy to pass the time playing darts in the bar. The cottages are all self-contained and cost US$48/96 for singles/doubles with full board. Day visitors are catered for in the restaurant if you're not staying the night. Although the water once used to lap at the edge of the bar terrace, it is now more than 100 metres away across a blinding expanse of sand.

ELIYE SPRINGS

This is a far more attractive place than Ferguson's Gulf but is inaccessible without a 4WD. The small village here has an army post, a couple of dozen grass huts, and a lodge which is of marginal status to say the least. The springs however do provide moisture enough for a curious variety of palm tree (the doum palm) to grow here which gives the place a very misplaced tropical island feel. This particular palm tree has an unusually shaped fruit which the locals eat.

If you do make it here you will be greeted by a number of Turkana girls and young women selling trinkets at absurdly cheap prices. With an average of one vehicle a week, it's a real buyer's market. Items for sale might include fossilised hippo teeth and fish backbones threaded into necklaces!

Places to Stay & Eat

The only way you can stay here is to camp and you must bring your own food with you. The lodge fell apart years ago though there are still one or two workers milling around. Rumour has it that it may reopen one day.

Getting There & Away

The turn-off for Eliye Springs is signposted about halfway along the road from Lodwar to Kalekol. There are a few patches of heavy sand so a 4WD is advisable although you'd probably get through in a conventional vehicle. As there are so few vehicles, hitching is not an option and it's 35 long hot km if you plan to walk it.

LOKICHOKIO

This frontier town is the last on the Pan African Highway before the Sudan border. The road has been sealed all the way here and is in excellent condition but you can't get beyond Lokichokio without a police permit. Even if this was forthcoming, the area is not safe as long as the civil war in southern Sudan continues.

Places to Stay

There's a hotel of sorts here with a couple of mud huts out the back, and there's a bar in town. On the other hand, if you get this far, you'll probably find yourself staying with aid/famine relief workers who take care of the refugee camps around here.

East of Turkana

There are two main routes here. The first is the A2 highway from Nairobi to Marsabit, via Isiolo and Laisamis, and north from there to Moyale on the Ethiopian border. The other is from Nairobi to Maralal, via Gilgil and Nyahururu or via Nakuru and Lake Baringo, and north from there to Loyangalani on Lake Turkana, via Baragoi and South Horr. It's also possible to cross from Isiolo to Maralal. From Loyangalani you can make a loop all the way round the top of the Chalbi Desert to Marsabit via North Horr and Maikona.

Getting There & Around

Bus & Matatu Mwingi buses run from Isiolo to Marsabit but there is no real schedule so you could be stuck in either place for a few days waiting for the bus to arrive. The fare is

US$6.80. There's no alternative except to simply hang around and wait or either negotiate a ride on a truck (relatively easy and usually somewhat less than the bus fare) or walk out to the police checkpoint north of Isiolo town where the tarmac ends and hitch a ride with tourists (not so easy). A convoy system is in operation in order to deter shiftas from stopping and robbing trucks, buses and cars.

Mwingi also operates buses from Isiolo to Maralal a few times a week (depending on demand) which cost US$6.50.

North of Maralal, the only public transport is a matatu which plies between Maralal and Baragoi once daily if demand warrants it.

Car & 4WD None of the roads in this region are surfaced and the main A2 route is corrugated *piste* which will shake the guts out of both you and your vehicle depending on your speed. The road connecting Isiolo with Maralal (which branches off the A2 north of Archer's Post) is similarly corrugated but otherwise in good shape. The road from Lake Baringo to Maralal and from Maralal to Loyangalani, however, is surprisingly smooth though there are bad patches here and there including a diabolical section of several km from the plateau down to Lake Turkana.

The main cross route between Isiolo and Maralal the two is via Wamba and Parsaloi (though you don't actually go through Wamba itself). This road leaves the main A2 about 20 km north of Archer's Post and joins the Maralal to Loyangalani road about 15 km south of Baragoi. Though a minor route, this road is very smooth most of the way with the occasional rough patch. Its main drawback is the steep-sided luggas, none of which are bridged. In the dry season you won't have any problems with a 4WD (impossible with a 2WD) but you can forget about it in the wet season. The worst of these luggas is just outside Wamba and there's a way around it by taking the Maralal road from Wamba and turning first right along a dirt road once you've crossed an obvious bridge. You'll

probably only use it if you want to visit the Mathews Range and the Ndoto Mountains.

Forget about the Maralal to Parsaloi road marked on the Survey of Kenya maps. It's all washed out and you won't even make it in 4WD.

NATIONAL PARKS & RESERVES
Just north of Isiolo are three national reserves, **Samburu**, **Buffalo Springs** and **Shaba**, all of them along the banks of the Ewaso Nyiro River and covering an area of some 300 sq km. They are mainly scrub desert and open savannah plain, broken here and there by small rugged hills. The river, however, which is permanent, supports a wide variety of game and you can see elephants, buffaloes, cheetahs, leopards and lions as well as dik-dik, wart hogs, Grevy's zebra and the reticulated giraffe. Crocodiles can also be seen on certain sandy stretches of the river bank. You are guaranteed close-up sightings of elephants, reticulated giraffe and various species of smaller gazelle in both Samburu and Buffalo Springs but other game is remarkably thin on the ground, particularly on the route into Samburu from Archer's Post. The rhino were wiped out years ago by poachers.

If you are driving around these parks in your own vehicle it's useful to have a copy of the Survey of Kenya map, *Samburu & Buffalo Springs Game Reserves* (SK 85).

The roads inside Buffalo Springs and Samburu are well maintained and it's easy to get around, even in 2WD, though you might need a 4WD on some of the minor tracks.

Entry to all three parks or game reserves costs US$12 per person plus US$1.50 per vehicle per day. Even though they're contiguous, if you drive from Buffalo Springs to Samburu (or vice versa) in one day then you'll have to pay two lots of park entry fees. However, if it's very late in the afternoon when you cross the boundary, the guards will generally postdate your ticket for the following day.

These parks are much less touristed than Amboseli or Masai Mara so, once you're out of the immediate vicinity of the lodges and camp sites, you'll frequently have the place to yourself.

Places to Stay

Buffalo Springs In Buffalo Springs National Reserve there are four *public camp sites* close to the Gare Mara entrance gate (the nearest to Isiolo and accessible from the main Isiolo to Marsabit road). However, none of them are particularly safe as far as robberies go so stick with a group and make sure your tent is guarded when you're out on game drives or pack it up and take it with you. There's also a *special camp site* further west. Camping costs US$2.50 per person per night.

For those with adequate finances, there's the *Buffalo Springs Tented Lodge* (☎ (0165) 2234) up at the north-eastern end of the reserve just south of the Ewaso Nyiro River. The lodge consists of 30 tents shielded from the sun by makuti roofs and each with its own bathroom. There are also eight cottages which sleep two to four people. The lodge has a swimming pool and a bar/restaurant overlooking a natural spring where you can sit and observe the wildlife. In the high season, tents or cottages cost US$106/156 for singles/doubles with full board; the price includes a game drive. Advance bookings can be made through African Tours & Hotels Ltd (☎ (02) 221855), PO Box 30471, Nairobi. The best access to the lodge is either from the Gare Mara Gate or the Buffalo Springs Gate just south of Archer's Post.

Samburu In Samburu National Game Reserve, the most convenient places to stay are the *public camp sites* close to the Samburu Lodge and close to the wooden bridge which connects the western extremity of Buffalo Springs to Samburu across the Ewaso Nyiro River. The sites themselves are fairly pleasant and adjacent to the river but the facilities are minimal and the 'toilets' are nothing short of pigsties. If you don't want to cook for yourself their only advantage is that they're very close to the lodge with its restaurant and bar. There are also two *special camp sites* further west. Camping costs US$2.50 per person per night.

For those with money, there's a choice of five top-range lodges/tented camps. The most popular is perhaps the *Samburu Lodge* which is part of the Block Hotels chain (☎ (02) 335807), PO Box 47557, Nairobi. It's built right alongside the river and consists of a main building (stone and makuti roof) which houses the restaurant, bar and reception area, and a series of self-contained cottages strung out along the river bank. The tariff depends on the season. In the high season it's US$123/182, whereas in the low season it's US$66/112 for singles/doubles, all with full board. Rates in the shoulder season are intermediate.

The lodge is the only place in the two parks where petrol can be bought. Game drives through the park can be organised at the lodge.

The supposed 'highlights' of any evening here are the appearance of a leopard across the other side of the river and the crocodiles which crawl up onto a sandy bank adjacent to the bar. The leopard, which is lured by a hunk of meat strung up from a tree by two very blasé employees just before dusk, is extremely contrived but Kodak make a fortune supplying film to fools who think they can get anything but a picture of midnight in the bush with an Instamatic from about 100 metres. The crocodile 'show' is equally contrived but at least it takes place right in front of you even if pieces of dead meat in the sand don't encourage dynamism.

Further east and also alongside the river is *Larsens* which is a luxury tented camp also owned by the Block Hotels chain. The rates depend on the season. In the high season (15 December to 31 March and 1 July to 31 August) full board costs US$166/242 in a tent and US$209/286 for a suite, whereas in the low season (1 April to 30 June) the corresponding rates are US$70/140 and US$83/166. For the rest of the year the costs are intermediate. All these rates include two game drives.

The *Samburu Intrepids Club* (☎ 338084 in Nairobi), further upstream on the northern side of the river, is another luxury tented

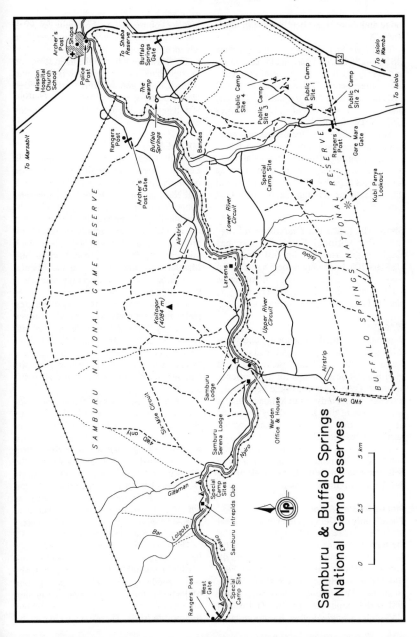

Samburu & Buffalo Springs
National Game Reserves

lodge and more like a beach resort in many ways. A night here costs US$138/208.

The *Samburu Serena Lodge* charges US$124/156 for full board in the high season and US$46/91 in the low season. For bookings contact Serena Lodges & Hotels (☎ (02) 710511), PO Box 48690, Nairobi. The last place is the *Samburu Lodge*, which charges US$138/198 for full board.

You can take any of the park access gates to get to these lodges but remember that if you drive through Buffalo Springs and into Samburu on the same day then you'll be up for two lots of park entry fees. You can avoid this by entering through the Archer's Post gate.

Shaba The spectacular *Shaba Sarova Lodge* in Shaba National Game Reserve has single/double rooms with full board for US$165/208. For campers there's a beautiful camp site about 20 minutes' drive away. There's abundant firewood here but you need to bring water from the lodge.

WAMBA

Wamba is a small, essentially one-street town off the Isiolo to Maralal road north of Samburu National Game Reserve and a sort of provincial headquarters for the surrounding area. There's precious little here for the traveller and its only claim to fame is that it was from here that John Hillaby organised his camel trek to Lake Turkana which resulted in his book, *Journey to the Jade Sea*.

It has quite a few well-stocked dukas, a butchery, a hospital, schools and a large police station but no bank and no electricity despite its proximity to Isiolo.

Places to Stay & Eat

There's only one lodge in the village and that is the *Saudia Lodge* run by Jamal which is at the back of the main street off to the right-hand side coming into town (signposted). Jamal – and indeed his whole family – is very friendly and helpful. You get a pleasant, clean room here (mosquito nets, soap, towel and toilet paper are provided) for just US$4/5.80 a single/double. Bathroom facil-

ities are communal. A wholesome breakfast can be provided for you if you order it in advance.

There's a lively bar on the main street, on the right-hand side as you enter the main part of town, where you can drink your fill though there's no refrigeration. You can't miss it – just listen for the cassette player blaring away!

MARALAL

Maralal is high up in the hills above the Lerochi Plateau (essentially a continuation of the central highlands), north of Nyahururu and Nanyuki and north-west of Isiolo, and connected to all these towns by gravel roads. Surrounding it is the Maralal National Sanctuary which is home to zebras, impala, eland, buffaloes, hyenas and wart hogs, all of which you can see from the road leading into Maralal from the south or at the Maralal Safari Lodge which has the only permanent water hole in the area.

It's an attractive area of grassy undulating plains and coniferous forests which was once coveted by White settlers in the colonial era. However, their designs for taking it over were scotched by the colonial authorities due to anticipated violent opposition from the Samburu for whom it holds a special significance.

The town itself, while a regional headquarters, retains a decidedly frontier atmosphere. There's a sense of excitement blowing in the wind which frequently sweeps the plains and whips up the dust in this somewhat ramshackle, but very lively, township with its wide streets and wild west-type verandahs. It's also the preferred route and overnight centre for the safari companies which take people up to Lake Turkana. People here are very friendly and it's a great place to buy Samburu handicrafts.

There's a post office (with telephones), petrol stations, mechanics, the only bank north of Isiolo other than in Marsabit, shops with a good range of stock, hotels, bars, one of the best camp sites in Kenya, a surprising number of butchers' shops and regular bus transport to Isiolo. There are also matatus to

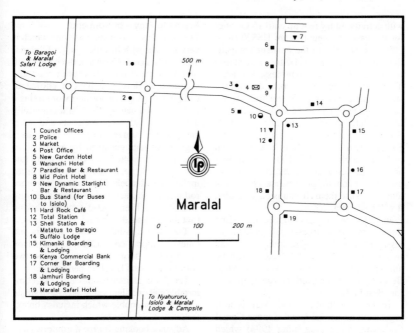

1 Council Offices
2 Police
3 Market
4 Post Office
5 New Garden Hotel
6 Wananchi Hotel
7 Paradise Bar & Restaurant
8 Mid Point Hotel
9 New Dynamic Starlight Bar & Restaurant
10 Bus Stand (for Buses to Isiolo)
11 Hard Rock Café
12 Total Station
13 Shell Station & Matatus to Baragio
14 Buffalo Lodge
15 Kimaniki Boarding & Lodging
16 Kenya Commercial Bank
17 Corner Bar Boarding & Lodging
18 Jamhuri Boarding & Lodging
19 Maralal Safari Hotel

Maralal

0   100   200 m

To Nyahururu,
Isiolo & Maralal
Lodge & Campsite

Baragoi which leave from the Shell station. If you're not travelling with a safari company you may well consider spending a few days here. It's a bizarre but captivating place.

Information

The Kenya Commercial Bank is open during normal banking hours. This is the last bank going north apart from those in Marsabit so stock up on cash.

The post office is open normal hours and the staff are very helpful should you want to make national or international calls.

There are two petrol stations (Shell and Total) in the centre of town where you can be assured of getting what you need at regular prices. North of here you will only find petrol at Baragoi and Loyangalani, and if there is some it is always at a high price.

Safaris

Regular camel safaris depart from Yare Safaris' Maralal Lodge & Campsite and they can also arrange safaris to Lake Turkana by truck (see the Getting Around and Northern Kenya chapters for details).

Maralal International Camel Derby

Inaugurated by Yare Safaris in 1990, this annual event takes place on the Saturday of the third week of October. It's a great time to be here and the three races which are held (amateurs, semiprofessional, and professional) are open to everyone. It attracts riders and spectators from the four corners of the earth, there's substantial prize money to be won (US$10,000), the media is there in force, you can make excellent contacts which will stand you in good stead for the rest of your trip, it's good fun, and, last but not least, it's one hell of a binge! Even George Thesiger attends!

The races start and finish at Yare's Maralal Lodge, a few km outside of town on the Nyahururu to Isiolo road, and there's no chance of missing it as the road will be festooned with flags and bunting and choked with activity. Entry fees up until 15 October for the various categories are US$20 (KSh 200 for residents) in the amateur competition; and US$30 (KSh 300 for residents) in the semiprofessional and professional races. Thereafter, entries are accepted up until the start of the race at a premium of 50%. Applications for entry should be made to either the Maralal International Camel Derby (MICD) Secretariat, PO Box 47874, Nairobi, or Yare Safaris, PO Box 63006, Nairobi. Camels can be hired locally for US$100. The amateur and semiprofessional classes require you to use handlers but the professional class is not allowed to use them. If you need a handler, it will cost extra.

In 1992, the Kenyans scooped up the first three places in the professional and semiprofessional races but an Australian (1st) and two Americans (2nd and 3rd) cleaned up the amateur race and – just imagine! – Mem Bourke (of New Zealand) picked up the cup for 'Best Lady'.

To tie in with this event, Yare is also organising an annual Great Kenyan Camel Endurance Race (beginning 1993) which takes 18 days and covers around 660 km. The race begins at Isiolo and ends in Maralal on the day before the Camel Derby and the entry fee is US$700 per team (four people). The first prize is worth US$50,000. If you're thinking of entering, four camels, saddles and a handler can be hired for US$35 per day plus US$250 per team for camel insurance and US$250 per team for vet coverage.

A substantial amount of the money made on these events goes towards the provision of medical facilities for the Samburu people.

And just in case you're thinking this is a good laugh for the humans but a lousy deal for the animals, International Camel Races Association rules apply so the camels are checked daily by a vet and monitored by a KSPCA officer.

Get yourself up there! This is one of the major events on the Kenyan calendar. Yare Safaris can provide transport to Maralal on the Friday before the race (returning Sunday) for US$45 which includes camping fees and a two-person tent.

Places to Stay – bottom end

The best place to stay here and one which is very popular with travellers is Yare Safaris' *Maralal Lodge & Campsite*, three km south of town on the Isiolo to Nyahururu road, and signposted. Here you have a choice of camping, staying in a dormitory or renting a self-contained banda. It's been thoughtfully constructed with local materials and is set amongst Samburu *manyattas*. (A manyatta is a group of huts occupied by an extended family and protected by a ring of thorn tree cuttings to keep out wildlife.) Facilities include a well-stocked bar/lounge, reference room, and self-service restaurant serving local dishes. There's also guarded parking (not that you need it around here).

The camp site has its own showers and toilets. Camping costs US$1.70 per person per night. A dorm bed in one of the two dormitories costs US$1.95 per person.

The self-contained bandas are clean, comfortable and excellent value at US$8 a single and US$12 a double which includes breakfast.

Advance booking for the dormitories and camp site is not normally necessary but it's a good idea for the bandas. Advance booking is essential for any sort of accommodation here during the week of the camel derby (third week of October). For bookings, contact Yare Safaris (☎ 214099; fax 213445), 1st Floor, Union Towers, Mama Ngina St, PO Box 63006, Nairobi.

In Maralal itself the most popular place to stay is the *Buffalo Lodge* (☎ 2228) which is a fairly modern structure offering rooms with clean sheets, towels and hot water in the mornings for US$6.70 a single or double. It's a lively place and there's a bar/video room at the back. Sammy, the barman here, is a real live wire and very friendly.

Cheaper but excellent value is the *Kimaniki Boarding & Lodging* which is a two-storey wooden building offering good rooms for US$1.10/2.20 a single/double. Clean sheets are provided as well as hot showers (if requested) and vehicles can be parked safely in the hotel compound. There's also the *Mid Point Hotel* (☎ 2221) which offers good lodging for single people at US$1.10 plus hot water in the mornings. Also good value is the *Paradise Bar & Restaurant* which has singles/doubles for US$1.60/3.10 with hot water in the mornings.

Other possibilities include the *Corner Bar Boarding & Lodging, Jamhuri Boarding & Lodging, Maralal Safari Hotel, New Garden Hotel* and *Wananchi Hotel* – all rather basic.

Places to Stay – top end

The only top-range hotel in Maralal is the *Maralal Safari Lodge* (☎ 2060 in Maralal; 225641 in Nairobi), PO Box 70, Maralal and PO Box 42475, Nairobi. It consists of a main building housing a restaurant, bar and souvenir shop and a series of cottages. It costs US$68/90 for singles/doubles with half board and US$72/98 with full board. Children's rates are US$22/24 respectively. Meals are available to nonguests for US$4.60 (breakfast) and US$8.60 (lunch or dinner). The staff here are pleasant and Diners Club cards are accepted. There's a watering hole, which attracts a varied selection of game, right in front of the bar's verandah so you can watch the animals whilst sipping a cold beer. The lodge is quite a way from the centre of Maralal (about three km), off the road to Baragoi (signposted).

Places to Eat & Entertainment

The best place to eat here is the relatively new *Hard Rock Café* opposite the Shell station. The food is good and the staff are friendly and eager to please. As a result, it's the most popular place in town.

The liveliest bar – and one where you can get good, tasty, cheap food – is the improbably named *New Dynamic Starlight Bar & Restaurant* which, nevertheless, lives up to its name. The inside rooms are painted with the most bizarre and florid representations of African flora & fauna and there's even a traditionally dressed Samburu hooker here most evenings who does a roaring trade. Unfortunately, there's no refrigeration so the beers are warm but the company makes up for it and some of the characters who come

in here have walked straight out of a Breugel canvas. It's a great spot to meet local live wires, get completely out of it and have numerous animated conversations.

The Buffalo Lodge also has two good bars but the one out at the back, although the best, is essentially a video lounge.

There's usually a disco on Friday and Saturday nights so, if you're interested, ask around.

Getting There & Away

If you're not coming in on a Yare Safaris' bus, Mwingi operates buses every second day to Isiolo which cost US$6.50. They leave from the dirt patch in front of the New Garden Hotel.

There are also matatus to Nyahururu daily which leave early in the morning, and usually one to Baragoi, though this only runs when there's sufficient demand. Matatus leave from in front of the Shell station.

MATHEWS RANGE

North of Wamba, off the link road between the Isiolo to Marsabit road and the Maralal to Loyangalani road via Parsaloi, is the Mathews Range. Much of this area is thickly forested and supports rhinos, elephants, lions, buffaloes and many other animal species. The highest peak here rises to 2285 metres. The whole area is very undeveloped and populated by Samburu tribespeople but the government is in the process of making it into a game sanctuary especially for the rhino. Some of the tribespeople are already employed to protect the rhino from poachers and there's a game warden's centre.

A few km from this centre (where you have to report on the way in, though there are no charges as yet) is a camp site with no facilities other than river water and firewood. At one time it was a well set-up research centre, as the derelict huts indicate. It's a superb site and a genuine African bush experience. You are miles from the nearest village and elephants are quite likely to trundle through your camp in the middle of the night – lions too. During the day, traditionally dressed Samburu warriors will probably visit you to see if you need a guide (which you will if you want to see game or climb to the top of the range as we did). Agree on a reasonable price beforehand, and remember you'll also have to pay for the one who stays behind to guard your vehicle.

Also, don't forget that the rules of hospitality will oblige you to provide them with a beer, soft drink or cup of tea, a few cigarettes and perhaps a snack when you get back to camp. They're extremely friendly people. One or two will be able to speak English (the nearest school is in Wamba) but most can converse in Swahili as well as Samburu.

Another accommodation possibility is the *Kitich Camp* (☎ (0176) 22053), on the banks of the Ngeng River, off the Wamba to Parsaloi road about 40 km from Wamba. It's mainly set up as a luxury tented camp with all the facilities, and it costs US$90 a double with full board. It's also possible to camp for US$4.50 per person, but the facilities for independent campers are minimal.

Getting There & Away

Getting to the camp site in the Mathews Range is not at all easy, even with 4WD. There are many different tracks going all over the place and you are going to have to stop many times to ask the way. Perhaps the best approach is from the Wamba to Parsaloi road. Just before Wamba you will get to a T-junction. Instead of going into Wamba, continue north and take the first obvious main track off to the right, several km after the junction. If there are tyre tracks in the sand – follow them. There are two missions down this track and both have vehicles. You will be able to ask the way at either.

One of the mission stations is right next to a large river course which generally has some water flowing through it and which you have to ford. If you get lost, ask a local tribesman to come along and guide you but remember that you will have to drive him back to his manyatta after you have found the place. No-one in their right mind walks around in the bush after dark except in large groups – the buffaloes and elephants make it too dangerous. It might sound like a *tour de*

force getting to this place but it's well worth it!

PARSALOI

Further north, Parsaloi (sometimes spelt Barsaloi) is a small scattered settlement with a few very basic shops but no petrol station. It has a large Catholic Mission which may or may not offer to accommodate you or allow you to camp. There are no lodges. The EC recently funded the building of quite a large school.

There are two very rugged and steep-sided luggas at this point on the road, one on either side of the village, and you'll definitely need 4WD to negotiate them.

BARAGOI

Next on is Baragoi, a more substantial settlement full of tribespeople, a couple of very basic lodges, a new and better appointed hotel, and a few shops. There's also a derelict petrol station but petrol can usually be bought here from a barrel – the local people will show you where to find it. If you're White, you'll probably be the only one in town and therefore an object of considerable curiosity. Quite a few people speak English around here. The town seems to get rain when everywhere else is dry so the surroundings are quite green.

Be careful not to take photographs in the town as it's supposedly forbidden and the local police are keen to enforce the rule and are not at all pleasant about it.

Places to Stay & Eat

If you ask at any of the restaurants in town they'll usually come up with accommodation but it will be very basic – just a bed in a bare room with no toilet facilities. Some will also allow you to camp in their back yards.

If you have camping equipment, the best place to stay is the camp site at the water-pumping station about four km to the north of town. To get there, take the road north towards South Horr. After a while you'll go through a small gully and then, a little further on, across a usually dry river bed. Take the next track on the right-hand side and follow this for about one km. It will bring you to a concrete house and a fairly open patch of ground. This is the camp site and there's always someone around. Facilities include toilets and showers and your tent will be guarded by Samburu warriors. It costs about US$2.50 per person per night. Trips can be arranged to nearby manyattas for a small fee and you'll be allowed to take photographs.

There's a large new *hotel* in town which costs US$5.80/12 for a clean single/double with shared bathroom. It's the first building you come to when arriving in Baragoi from the south.

For food in the town itself, the best is the *Wid-Wid Inn* run by Mrs Fatuma. It's on the top side of the main street and you'll know you've got the right place because all the staff wear garishly pink pinafores! She'll cook you up an absolutely delicious meat stew and chapatis for dinner as well as pancakes, omelettes and tea for breakfast.

There are also two bars in the town but only one of them – the *Sam Celia Joy Bar*, at the end of the main street going north – usually has beers. The other, on the back street, usually only has *conyagi* (local firewater) and other spirits.

SOUTH HORR

The next village is South Horr which is set in a beautiful lush canyon between the craggy peaks of Mt Nyiro (2752 metres) and Mt Porale (1990 metres) and Mt Supuko (2066 metres). It's a lively little place with a huge Catholic Mission but there's no petrol available.

There are two small and very basic hotels on the main street – the *Mt Nyiro Hotel* and the *Good Tourist Hotel* – where you can find accommodation of sorts as well as a reasonably tasty meal of meat stew, mandazi and tea for around US$2 per person. The hotels will generally need up to two hours' notice if you want to eat, but tea is usually immediately available.

Skull 1470

In the early 1970s, archaeologist Richard Leakey (now head of the Kenya Wildife Service) made a significant fossil find on the shores of Lake Turkana. It was the discovery of a fossilised skull, which came to be known somewhat prosaically as 1470 (its Kenya Museum index number).

The almost complete, but fragmented, skull was thought to be from an early hominid. It was hoped that it would back up earlier fossil discoveries made by the Leakeys in the Olduvai Gorge in Tanzania in the '60s which suggested that the direct human ancestral line went back further than the 1½ million years that most people thought at the time.

The pieces of the skull were painstakingly fitted together – a demanding task in itself which kept two people fully occupied for over six weeks. The completed jigsaw confirmed what they had suspected: here was an evolutionary sophisticated hominid, named *Homo habilis*, which was a direct ancestor of *Homo sapiens*. It was 2½ million years old.

Since then *homo* fossil finds have been made which push the date back even further, but at the time the 1470 was a very important person'! ∎

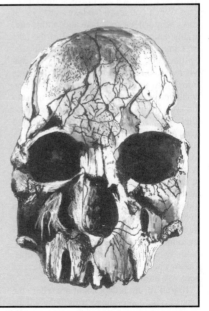

There's a camp site (the signpost reads 'Camping' but it's easy to miss) about 12 km out of town on the right-hand side as you head north. It's a pleasant site owned by Safari Camp Services in Nairobi and facilities include showers and toilets. There's also plenty of firewood. The charge is US$2 per person per night. Guards can be arranged to watch your tent if you want to eat in town.

South Horr also sports a very lively bar – the *Serima Bar* – on the main road heading north out of town. It's only open in the evenings and seems to have a plentiful supply of beer though there's no refrigeration.

LAKE TURKANA (THE JADE SEA)

Further north, the lushness of the Horr Valley gradually peters out until, finally, you reach the totally barren, shattered lava beds at the southern end of Lake Turkana. Top the ridge here and there it is in front of you – the Jade Sea. It's a breathtaking sight – vast and yet apparently totally barren. You'll see nothing living here except a few brave, stunted thorn trees. When you reach the lake shore, you'll know why – it's a soda lake and, at this end, highly saline. The northern end of the lake isn't anywhere near as saline because it's fed by the Omo River from Ethiopia (is that where the name of the washing powder came from!?). At this point, most people abandon whatever vehicle they're in and plunge into the lake. If you do this, watch out for crocodiles. They're quite partial to a meal of red meat as a change from Nile perch.

LOYANGALANI

A little further up the lake shore and you are in Loyangalani – Turkana 'city'. There is an airstrip, post office, fishing station, luxury lodge, two camp sites, a Catholic Mission (which may reluctantly sell petrol at up to three times the price in Nairobi) and all of it surrounded by the yurt-like, stick and doum-palm dwellings of the Turkana tribespeople. Taking photographs of people or their houses here will attract 'fees'.

If you're an independent traveller, the Oasis Lodge can organise trips to the village where the El-Molo live. Otherwise, ask the safari-truck drivers at the camp sites if they have room for you – organised safaris to this part of Kenya usually include a trip to the El-Molo village. They're one of the smallest tribes in Africa and quite different from the Turkana though it seems their days are numbered as a distinct tribe. Tourism has also wrought inevitable changes in their lifestyle and you may feel that the whole thing has been thoroughly commercialised. You'll also pay handsomely for taking photographs. One traveller who felt the tribe had totally prostituted their traditional way of life to make money from tourists has put it this way, 'If they live on fish it must be smoked salmon and caviar'.

Trips to **Mt Kulal** and **Mt Porr** can also be arranged at the Oasis Club but they're expensive. The Mt Kulal trip is a part-drive, part-walking trip up to the forest there, and Mt Porr is a well-known fossicking spot. A better thing to do would be to get in touch with Francis Langachar who is a very friendly young Turkana man and ask him to organise something similar for you. He speaks fluent English, and his father accompanied John Hillaby on his trek to Lake Turkana, recounted in *Journey to the Jade Sea*.

Places to Stay & Eat

Of the two camp sites, it's hard to favour one over the other though only one has a restaurant and bar. Both are staffed by very friendly people and theft doesn't appear to be a problem at either of them. The first you come to is *El-Molo Camp* (☎ (02) 724384), PO Box 34710, Nairobi. It has excellent facilities including good showers and toilets, a swimming pool (US$4.50 for day use), a large dining hall and bar (with cold beers!) and electricity up to 9.30 pm at night (kerosene lanterns after that). Camping costs US$2.70 per person per night. There are also 20 self-contained bandas for rent which cost US$52/83 a single/double with full board. Meals can be ordered at short notice in the dining room here whether you are staying on the site or not, but they take a long time to arrive: 1½ hours is normal. The food, on the other hand, is very good. Cold beers naturally cost more than in Nairobi but are still very reasonably priced.

The other camp site adjacent to El-Molo is *Sunset Strip Camp,* which is also run by Safari Camp Services in Nairobi. It costs US$2.30 per person per night. Facilities include showers and toilets and covered dining areas but you cannot buy food and drink here and there's no electricity.

Neither camp site has firewood so you'll have to bring your own from further south.

Whichever place you camp at, beware of sudden storms which can descend from Mt Kulal. If there is a storm, stay with your tent otherwise it may not be there when you get back because of the wind, and neither will anything else.

Other than the camp sites there is the luxury *Oasis Lodge* (☎ (02) 751190; PO Box 34464, Nairobi) which has 25 self-contained double bungalows with electricity (own generator) at US$105/150 for a single/double with full board. It's a beautiful place with two spring-fed swimming pools, and ice-cold beers and meals are available. The only trouble is, if you are not staying there but want to use the facilities (bar and swimming pools), it's going to cost you a US$15 entrance fee. It's a lot of money to pay for a brush with luxury but you won't wring any concessions out of the owner (Wolfgang) who can be quite belligerent about this. Basically, he doesn't want what he considers to be 'riffraff' marring the tone of the place.

Other than the El-Molo Camp, there are a couple of basic teahouses on the main street of Loyangalani and, if you ask around, you'll meet villagers who will cook up a meal of Nile perch for you in their houses.

Getting There & Away
There is no scheduled transport of any sort in or out of Loyangalani, so you need to be independent.

NORTH HORR
North of Loyangalani the road loops over the lava beds to North Horr. There is a short cut across the desert through the village of Gus.

There are no lodges here and no petrol available but the people at the Catholic Mission are very friendly and will probably offer you somewhere to stay for the night if you are stuck. It's staffed by German and Dutch people.

MAIKONA
Next down the line is Maikona where there is a large village with basic shops (but no lodges) and a very friendly Catholic Mission and school, staffed by Italian people, where you will undoubtedly be offered a place to stay for the night. Please leave a donation before you go if you stay here. The mission usually has electricity and the Father goes into Marsabit once a fortnight in his Land Rover.

MARSABIT
South of Maikona is Marsabit, where you are back in relative civilisation. Here there are three petrol stations, a bank, post office, dry cleaners, shops, bars and lodges, buses and an airport. The main attraction here though is the Marsabit National Park & Reserve centred around Mt Marsabit (1702 metres).

The hills here are thickly forested and in stark contrast to the desert on all sides. Mist often envelopes them in the early morning and mosses hang from tree branches. The views from the telecommunications tower on the summit above town are magnificent in all directions. In fact, they're probably as spectacular as any of the views from Mt Kenya or Kilimanjaro. The whole area is peppered with extinct volcanoes and volcanic craters (called *gofs*), some of which have a lake on the crater floor.

One of the most memorable sights in Marsabit is the tribespeople thronging the streets and roads into town. Most noticeable are the Rendille with their elaborate braided hairstyles and dressed in skins, fantastic multicoloured beaded necklaces and bracelets. These people graze camels and, like the Samburu and Maasai, show little interest in adopting a more sedentary lifestyle, prefer-

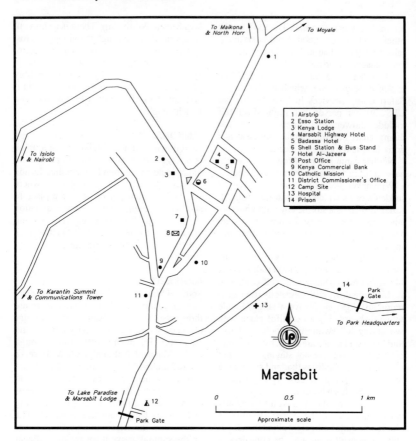

Marsabit

1	Airstrip
2	Esso Station
3	Kenya Lodge
4	Marsabit Highway Hotel
5	Badassa Hotel
6	Shell Station & Bus Stand
7	Hotel Al–Jazeera
8	Post Office
9	Kenya Commercial Bank
10	Catholic Mission
11	District Commissioner's Office
12	Camp Site
13	Hospital
14	Prison

ring to roam the deserts and only visiting the towns when necessary for trade. They are the major non-Muslim people in what is otherwise a largely Muslim area.

The other major tribes are the Boran and the Gabra, both pastoralists who graze cattle rather than camels. They're allied to the Galla peoples of Ethiopia from where they originated several hundred years ago. Many have abandoned their former transient life style and settled down to more sedentary activities. In the process, many have adopted Islam and the modes of dress of the Somalis with whom they trade and who have also migrated into the area. There are also quite a few Ethiopians in town as a result of that country's tragic and turbulent recent past.

Marsabit National Park & Reserve
The Marsabit National Park & Reserve is home to a wide variety of the larger mammals including lions, leopards, cheetahs, elephants, rhinos, buffaloes, wart hogs, Grevy's zebra, the reticulated giraffe, hyena, Grant's gazelle, oryx, dik-dik and greater kudu among others. Because the area is thickly forested, however, you won't see too much game unless you spend quite some time here and, preferably, camp at **Lake Paradise**. The lake, which occupies much of the

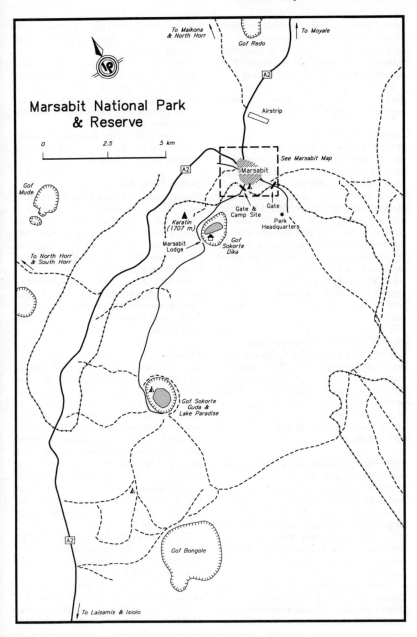

Marsabit National Park & Reserve

crater floor of Gof Sokorte Guda, is appropriately named. It's an enchanting place and right out in the bush. Entry to the park, which is open from 6 am to 7.15 pm, costs US$12 per person plus US$1.50 for a vehicle.

The Survey of Kenya's map, *Marsabit National Park & Reserve* (SK 84) is worth buying if you are touring this park.

Places to Stay & Eat

In the Park Few camp sites in Kenya would rival the one at Lake Paradise. There are no facilities (except lake water and firewood) so bring everything with you. A ranger has to be present when you camp here so it costs more than an ordinary site (US$15 per group and only one group at a time) but you can arrange all this at the park entrance gate.

There's also another good camp site next to the entrance gate (water and plenty of firewood) but the so-called showers are a joke. You could die of thirst waiting for enough water to wet the back of your ears here. Camping at this site costs US$1.90 per person.

More up-market is the *Marsabit Lodge* (☎ (0183) 2044), a luxury safari lodge overlooking a lake in another gof, Sokorte Dika. Singles/doubles cost US$51/79 with full board, except from 1 April to 30 June when the price drops to US$29/57. Bookings can be made either directly with the lodge, or at Msafiri Inns (☎ (02) 229751), 11th Floor, Utalii House, Uhuru Highway, PO Box 42013, Nairobi.

In the Town If you have no camping equipment there's a good choice of lodges available in the town of Marsabit. One of the best is the *Kenya Lodge*. It's very clean and pleasant and rooms cost US$3.30/5.20 a single/double with soap and toilet roll provided. The showers are communal and the hotel has its own bar and restaurant at the front. The restaurant offers excellent Ethiopian food.

Almost as good is the *Marsabit Highway Hotel* which costs US$4.20 for a double with shower and toilet. It's a large place and very clean. The hotel has its own bar/restaurant

which is open from 11 am to 2 pm and 5 pm to midnight. There is a disco on Friday and Saturday nights.

The cheapest place, though not such good value, is the *Hotel Al-Jazeera* which costs US$1.95 per person with communal showers. There's a bar and restaurant at the front. For something vaguely mid-range, try the *Badassa Hotel*.

The best place for tea, mandazi and snacks is the *Bismillah Tea House* in front of the Catholic Technical School.

Getting There & Away

Mwingi buses run from Marsabit south to Isiolo and north to Moyale on the Ethiopian border. They supposedly run a couple of times a week depending on demand and breakdowns – be prepared for a wait. The cost to either place is US$6.80 and the trip to either takes six hours.

All vehicles, including buses travelling between Marsabit and Isiolo or Marsabit and Moyale, must travel in convoy. The reason for this is to minimise the danger of attack from shiftas.

MOYALE

Straddling the Kenyan-Ethiopian border, Moyale lies some 250 km north of Marsabit across the Dida Galgalu Desert. It's a small town of sandy streets with bars, a post office, police station, several shops selling basic commodities, and a small market area. Unlike Marsabit, however, where most of the roofs these days are of corrugated iron, there are still a large number of traditionally built houses here with sturdy pole frames supporting mud and stick roofs which can be up to half a metre thick thus ensuring that the interiors stay cool even when the outside temperature is 30°C and more.

There's not a great deal to do here, though the town attracts the occasional intrepid traveller either just for the hell of it or for the sake of an exotic passport stamp.

There is no bank in Moyale and only derelict petrol stations, so come prepared.

The Ethiopian side of the town is somewhat larger and the facilities are much better, with sealed roads, electricity, a number of bars and small restaurants, a hotel, and a lively market area.

Places to Stay & Eat

There are only three places to stay on the Kenyan side of Moyale and they're all pretty basic. Probably the best of the bunch is the *Barissah Hotel* which also has the town's bar. Out at the back surrounding an earth compound there are several basic cubicles without locks where you can rent a bed for US$1.95 person. There are no showers (though you can order a bucket of water) and the place is far from clean but the staff are friendly. The Barissah is also the preferred place to eat, the usual fare being meat stew and chapatis.

If it's full, head for the *Bismillahi Boarding & Lodging* across from the Barissah and up behind the derelict Esso station. It's a family-run place and you'll find yourself sharing the same roof as the family. A bed here costs US$1.95 and facilities are absolutely minimal.

Boran woman

On the Ethiopian side of Moyale, the best place to stay is the *Bekele Molla Hotel* which is government owned and about two km from the border. It has a very lively bar – especially in the evenings – and the rooms are clean and self-contained.

For somewhere to eat closer to the border, try the *Negussie Hotel*, up on the hill to the left after you've crossed the border. It offers the standard Ethiopian fare of wat (a fierce hot sauce) and injera (bread made of millet flour), and there's also a bar here.

Kenyan shillings are acceptable when paying for meals and drinks.

Getting There & Away

Bus services between Marsabit and Moyale are detailed in the Marsabit section.

CROSSING TO ETHIOPA

Except for Kenyans and Ethiopians, this border was officially closed throughout Mengistu's regime but is now open, though you'll still need an Ethiopian visa to enter. This may well take some effort in Nairobi at the Ethiopian Embassy since you're required to have an airline ticket to Addis Ababa. References with clout obviously increase your chances of being able to enter overland. Otherwise, follow the rules to get your visa and trade in your Addis ticket later.

The North-East

Like the north of Kenya, the north-east up to the border with Somalia covers a vast area of desert and semidesert with very few centres of population and limited public transport possibilities. The main towns are Garissa and Wajir. Most of the area is relatively flat yet it's through here that one of Kenya's major rivers, the Tana, flows. The river enters the ocean about halfway between Malindi and Lamu and is the territory of the Orma, Pokomo and Bajun tribes. Straddling this river just north of Garsen is the Tana River Primate Sanctuary which is included on a few safari companies' itineraries but otherwise difficult to get to. The reserve was set up to protect the red colobus and crested mangabey monkeys both of which are endangered species. The other main river, the Ewaso Nyiro which flows through Samburu and Buffalo Springs national reserves, eventually peters out into the Lorian Swamp, never reaching the ocean.

Few travellers come this way except those taking the back route to Lamu via Garissa and Garsen. The area north and east of Garissa is now the domain of gun-toting 'refugees' from Somalia. When the UN/American troops went into Somalia in late 1992 to help in the distribution of food aid, many of those with guns sought shelter in Kenya where they could rustle cattle and create havoc with relative impunity. It's not a safe area to venture into unless you're with one of the aid agencies, and even then your safety is not guaranteed. Although the Somali border is still open, the country itself is pretty much a no-go area for the average traveller.

Other than a visit to Meru National Park, which would be worth it if security could be guaranteed, and the Tana River area, the north-east isn't a particularly interesting region even for desert fans, though Wajir, with its predominantly Somali population, Beau Geste fort and market, would definitely have the edge over Garissa, itself quite a nondescript town hardly worth stopping for.

Warning You should think twice before driving a vehicle around Meru National Park (or even taking an organised safari) until the poaching situation is resolved because tourists have been robbed at gunpoint and some of them actually shot dead. If you do go there and you're held up, don't mess about! Get your money and cameras out and hand them over. Any prevarication will invite a bullet in the head.

MERU NATIONAL PARK

On the lowland plains east of the town of Meru, the Meru National Park is a complete contrast to the more northerly reserves of Samburu, Buffalo Springs and Shaba where open bush is the norm. In Meru, abundant rainfall and numerous permanent streams flowing down from the Mt Kenya massif support a luxuriant jungle of forest, swamp and tall grasses which, in turn, provide fodder and shelter to a wide variety of herbivores and their predators. As in other parks, such as Marsabit, where the vegetation is dense, the wildlife is not so easily sighted so you need to spend a few days here if you're to fully appreciate what the park has to offer.

Unfortunately this area was one of the worst hit by poachers and shifta, and so there is not the abundance of wildlife that you find in other parks. With some difficulty, elephants, lions and cheetahs can all be seen. Buffaloes and giraffes are more common, and eland and oryx are the main antelope to be seen. Monkeys, crocodiles and a plethora of bird species are common in the dense vegetation alongside the watercourses.

Meru National Park was also the home of Kenya's only herd of white rhinos which were imported from the Umfolozi Game Reserve in South Africa. Jealously guarded 24 hours a day by rangers to protect them from poachers, these huge animals were quite unlike their more cantankerous cousins, the black rhino, in being remarkably docile and willing to allow their keepers to herd them around the camp sites and park headquarters area during the day and pen them up at night. Sadly, that's all gone now. Heavily armed poachers shot the lot of them and, for good measure, killed their keepers too.

The park is also famous for being Joy and George Adamson's former base where they raised orphaned lion and leopard cubs until they were old enough to be returned to the wild. Both paid for their efforts with their lives – Joy several years ago when she was murdered in Meru park by poachers, and George in 1989 when he too met the same fate along with two of his assistants in the nearby Kora National Reserve.

Security in the park has been beefed up since George Adamson was murdered but there is still a small risk of encountering poachers and bandits here so you need to

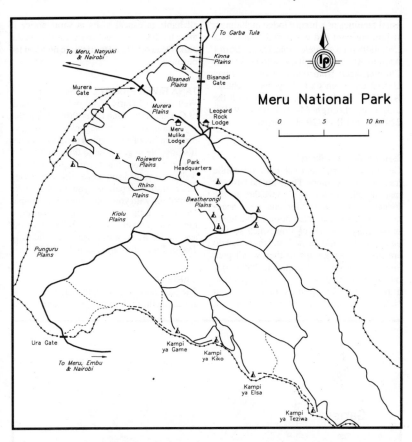

Meru National Park

bear this in mind, especially if you're driving your own vehicle. It's true to say, however, that the chances of running into bandits is just as great in Masai Mara or Tsavo as it is in Meru. The one major plus about Meru National Park is that you're unlikely to come across another safari vehicle anywhere in the park except outside the lodges.

The tracks through the park are well maintained and signposted though it's a good idea to have a copy of the Survey of Kenya's *Meru National Park* map with you.

Places to Stay

There are several public camp sites in the park, but the one at junction 12 is the only one operating. There's running water and an askari in attendance.

More expensive are the 10 self-contained bandas at *Leopard Rock Lodge* which have electricity, hot water, mosquito nets and fully equipped kitchens. These cost US$21 per person per night; children aged from two to 15 years pay US$4. There's a shop at the site which sells basic commodities including canned goods and beer. Bookings can be made through Let's Go Travel (☎ (02) 213033) in Nairobi.

At the top of the range is the *Meru Mulika Lodge* (☎ (0164) 20000) which has all the usual facilities of a luxury lodge including a swimming pool and where full board costs US$70/96 for a single/double, except from 1 April to 30 June when it drops to US$39/70. Children aged from two to five years pay US$19, and from six to 11 years the charge is US$21. Bookings can be made with the lodge, or through Msafiri Inns (☎ (02) 229751), PO Box 42013, Nairobi.

Getting There & Away

Getting to Meru National Park by public transport is a problem. There are no buses or matatus which will take you either to the lodges or the camp sites and park headquarters. Likewise, attempting to hitchhike is basically a waste of time since so few vehicles come into the park and those that do are mainly tour groups so they won't pick you up. It's almost essential to have your own vehicle or be part of a tour group. Quite a few safari companies include Meru National Park on their itineraries but they are all liable to cancel visits at short notice if there has been any trouble with shiftas in the park. Dead or robbed tourists are no good for business.

TANA RIVER PRIMATE SANCTUARY

Well south of Garissa and not too far north of Garsen is the Tana River Primate Sanctuary which, as its name suggests, is a reserve for a number of endangered monkey species. It's possible to get close to the sanctuary by public transport but there's still a lot of walking involved and the facilities have long fallen into disrepair so you need to take everything with you. Very few safari companies include the reserve on their itineraries. Let's Go Travel (☎ (02) 340331) is the agency for a seven-day trip which takes in Tsavo, Tana River and Lamu for US$410.

GARISSA

The only reason to come to Garissa is if you are taking the back route to Lamu direct from

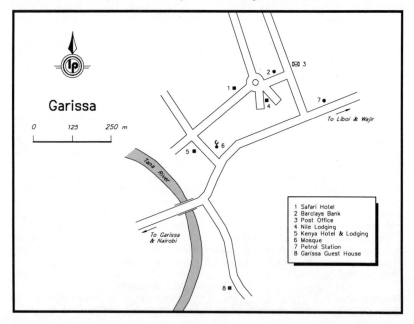

Garissa

0   125   250 m

To Liboi & Wajir

Tana River

To Garissa & Nairobi

1 Safari Hotel
2 Barclays Bank
3 Post Office
4 Nile Lodging
5 Kenya Hotel & Lodging
6 Mosque
7 Petrol Station
8 Garissa Guest House

Nairobi via Garsen. There's nothing much to see or do here and the heat and humidity are unrelenting but there's a bank (open normal hours), petrol stations, bars and a fair choice of places to stay.

Places to Stay & Eat
Perhaps the best place to stay for the night is the *Safari Hotel* which offers clean rooms with running water for US$4/6 a single/double. There's reasonable food in the attached restaurant. The *Garissa Government Guest House*, a short distance out of town, is somewhat more expensive at US$6 per person for rooms with bathroom and breakfast, but is worth the extra money. If both are full then there's the more basic *Nile Lodging* or the *Kenya Hotel & Lodging*.

Getting There & Away
Garissa Express operates a bus from the KBS depot Eastleigh, Nairobi, to Garissa on Monday, Wednesday, Friday and Sunday at 8 am. The depot is a 10-minute matatu ride from Ronald Ngala St (route No 9). The fare is US$5.20 and the journey takes about eight hours.

There's also a daily Garissa Express bus from Lamu (at Mokowe on the mainland) to Garissa which leaves at 7 am, costs US$9.40 and takes 10 hours when the weather is dry.

LIBOI
Liboi, right on the Kenya-Somalia border, is a staging post in the *qat* (drug) trade to Somalia. It has also become a major refugee centre following the civil war and famine in Somalia. It has only one place to stay, the *Cairo Hotel*.

GARSEN
If you're heading towards Lamu from Garissa then you may have to stay here overnight as it's necessary to change buses – the bus from Garissa to Mokowe on the mainland opposite Lamu is not direct. There's nothing at all special about Garsen but there are several basic hotels to choose from. The best is the *3-in-1 Lodging & Restaurant* which is fairly clean and has its own restaurant.

For details of buses passing through Garsen, see either the Malindi or Lamu sections.

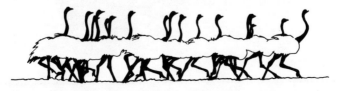

Amboseli, Masai Mara, Tsavo & Taita Hills

AMBOSELI NATIONAL PARK

Amboseli is the next most popular park after Masai Mara, mainly because of the spectacular backdrop of Africa's highest peak, Mt Kilimanjaro, which broods on the southern boundary of the park.

At 392 sq km Amboseli is not a large park, and it certainly doesn't have the profusion of game which you find in Masai Mara but the game here is easy to spot. The western section of the park is the dry bed of Lake Amboseli, and although it is occasionally flooded in the wet season, for the majority of the time it is a dry, dusty, shimmering expanse.

Probably the best reason for visiting Amboseli is that you stand the best chance of spotting a black rhino. Amboseli also has huge herds of elephant, and to see a herd of them making their way sedately across the grassy plains, with Kilimanjaro in the background, may be a real African cliché but is an experience which leaves a lasting impression.

Other animals which you are likely to see here include buffaloes, lions, gazelle, cheetahs, wildebeest, hyenas, jackals, wart hogs, Masai giraffes, zebras and baboons.

Amboseli more than any other park has suffered greatly from the number of minibuses which drive through each day. It has a much drier climate than Masai Mara and so for much of the year is a real dust bowl. If you are driving through the park, stick to the defined tracks, and hopefully others will follow suit.

Outside the town's petrol station there are a couple of shops selling Maasai crafts. The first prices asked are totally ridiculous, so bargain fiercely.

Most visitors approach Amboseli through Namanga, the main border post between

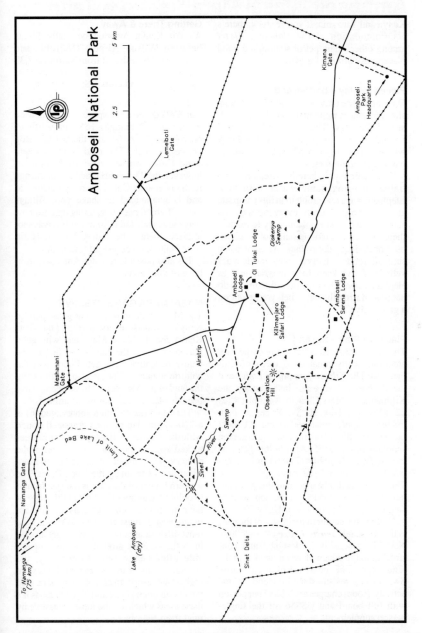

Kenya and Tanzania. If you're stuck, there's accommodation at the *Namanga Hotel* among others. The petrol station is a good place to ask around for lifts.

Places to Stay – bottom end

Once again the only budget option is a camp site. This one is right on the southern boundary of the park. The only facilities are a couple of long-drop toilets, and a kiosk where you can buy warm beer and sodas and pay the camping fees.

The water supply here is extremely unreliable so bring some water with you. Elephants are a real problem in this camp site at night and practically everyone who has stayed here has an elephant story to relate – there are some hilarious (and not so hilarious) ones doing the rounds. At night make sure all food is locked away inside your vehicle. *Don't* keep food in your tent as elephants have a habit of investigating, as do baboons during the day when you're out on a game drive.

Places to Stay – top end

The group of lodges in the centre of the park are strategically situated for views of Kilimanjaro. The *Kilimanjaro Safari Lodge* and the *Amboseli Lodge* are both run by the Kilimanjaro Safari Club in Nairobi (☎ (2) 227136), PO Box 30139. Prices at both lodges are approximately the same at US$92 per person with full board. The single-person supplement is US$55. Also in this group is the *Ol Tukai Lodge* (☎ 334863 in Nairobi) which consists of self-catering cottages. These are much cheaper than the Kilimanjaro lodges at US$13 per person, with a single-person supplement of US$9.20.

Close to the southern perimeter of the park is the *Amboseli Serena Lodge* (☎ 339800 in Nairobi), a sensitively designed and constructed lodge which blends in well with the landscape. The nearby Enkongo Narok Swamp ensures constant bird and animal activity. Room charges are US$87 per person with full board and US$56 for the single-person supplement.

Getting There & Away

Air Air Kenya Aviation has daily flights between Wilson Airport (Nairobi) and Amboseli. These depart from Nairobi at 7.30 am and Amboseli at 8.30 am; the trip takes about an hour and costs US$65 one way.

Car & 4WD The usual approach to Amboseli is through Namanga, 165 km south of Nairobi on the A104, and the last fuel stop before the park. The road is in excellent condition from Nairobi to Namanga, however, the 75-km dirt road from Namanga to the Namanga Gate is fiercely corrugated and is guaranteed to shake your fillings loose. If you'd been wondering up until now why the suspension in your minibus was shot to pieces, here is the answer. The whole trip from Nairobi takes around four hours.

It's also possible to enter Amboseli from the east via Tsavo.

MASAI MARA GAME RESERVE

The Mara is the most popular game park in Kenya. Virtually every person who visits Kenya goes to Masai Mara, and with good reason as this is the Kenyan section of the wildly evocative Serengeti Plains and the wildlife abounds. This is also traditionally the land of the Maasai, but these people have been displaced in favour of the animals.

The Mara (as it's often abbreviated to) is a 320-sq-km slab of open grassland dotted with the distinctive flat-topped acacia trees tucked away in the south-west corner of the country. It is watered by the tree-lined Mara River and its tributary the Talek River. The western border of the park is the spectacular Oloololo Escarpment and it's at this edge of the park that the concentrations of game are the highest. It must also be said that it's the most difficult area of the park to get around in as the swampy ground becomes impassable after heavy rain. Conversely, the concentrations of tourist and minibuses are highest at the eastern end of the park around the Oloolaimutia Gate and Talek Gate as it's these areas which are the most accessible by road from Nairobi.

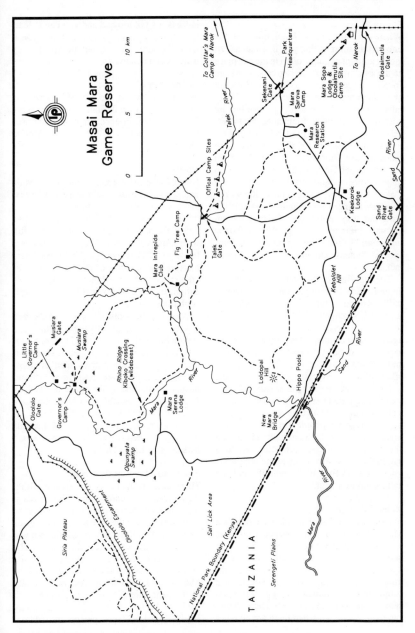

Masai Mara
Game Reserve

Fauna

Wherever you go in the Mara, however, the one certain thing is that you'll see an astonishing amount of game, often in the one place at the one time. Of the big cats, lions are found in large prides everywhere and it's not at all uncommon to see them hunting. Cheetahs and leopards are harder to spot but are still fairly common. Elephants, buffaloes, zebras and hippos also exist in large numbers within the reserve. Of the antelopes, the black-striped Thomson's gazelle (Tommys) and the larger Grant's gazelle are found in huge numbers, while the impala, topi and Coke's hartebeest and of course the wildebeest are also profuse. Rhinos do exist in the park but are rarely seen. Other common animals include Masai giraffes, baboons (especially around the lodges), wart hogs, spotted hyenas and grey (or side-striped) jackals.

The highlight of the Mara is no doubt the annual wildebeest migration when literally millions of these ungainly beasts move north from the Serengeti in July and August in search of the lush grass, before turning south again around October. It is truly a staggering experience to be in the reserve at that time – and one which is likely to have a profound effect on your own feeling of insignificance.

Masai Mara doesn't have national park status. The fundamental difference between a national park and a game reserve is that in a game reserve people (in this case the Maasai) can graze their animals and can also shoot animals if they are attacked. In a national park however, the entire area is set aside exclusively for the wildlife and the natural environment.

Maasai Village

Just outside the Oloolaimutia Gate there's a Maasai village which has opened itself up as a tourist attraction. For around US$3.50 per person you can walk around and take as many pictures as you like. As you might imagine, it's a real zoo when you have a couple of dozen tourists poking their video cameras and long lenses everywhere. *If* you can manage to visit when there are no other tourists it's not too bad and you can at least talk to the villagers. At other times you'll have the crap hassled out of you to buy trinkets and bead work.

Ballooning

If you can afford the US$300 price tag, balloon safaris are definitely the way to go. It's a superb experience. For more details see the Safaris section in the Getting Around chapter.

Narok

Narok is the main access point to the Mara and is a small provincial town a few hours' drive west of Nairobi. As most vehicles stop to refuel here (it's the last place to do so before the park itself) the town is chock-full with souvenir shops and hawkers. There are branches of Barclays and the Kenya Commercial banks, a post office, and a range of budget and mid-range hotels. For accommodation, try the *Spear Hotel* which has self-contained rooms.

A very popular place to grab a snack here is *Kim's Dishes* diagonally opposite the Agip station on the right hand side if you're standing with your back to the petrol station. It offers cheap fast-food items such as chips, sausages, etc. There are also several basic but busy bars on the main street as well as *Pussy's Bar* across the river from the main street about one km from the centre.

There are frequent buses and matatus buzzing between Nairobi and Narok which park outside Kim's Dishes.

Places to Stay – bottom end

There is no budget accommodation within the reserve so it's camp or pay high prices at the lodges and tented camps. It's possible to camp just outside the park at any of the gates for a small fee. There are no facilities but you can usually get water from the rangers. The Maasai run the *Oloolaimutia Campsite* between the gate of the same name and the Mara Sopa Lodge at the western extremity of the park. This place is very popular with the budget safari outfits and is usually pretty lively. For US$2 per person the Maasai provide firewood and an askari at night. The water supply here is very limited and if you need any water you'll have to buy it from the Maasai. The staff canteen of the nearby Mara Sopa Lodge is usually a lively place and you can get meals and warm beer.

There are official camp sites at the usual price along the Talek River by the Talek Gate on the north-eastern border of the park, and just outside the reserve on the banks of the Mara River near the Oloololo Gate. If you want to use any of these sites it's advisable to book them in advance in Nairobi (at the Kenya Wildlife Service) but people who roll up unannounced generally seem to have no problems. The only problem with using these sites is that they are none too secure – baboons and thieves can both take their toll on your gear.

What isn't widely known is that it's possible to camp at *Cottar's Mara Camp* (see the following section) for US$3.40 per person. The owners certainly don't encourage it but won't turn you away.

Places to Stay – top end

The lodges and tented camps are all pitched at the top end of the market and should all be booked in advance. Prices for accommodation with full board vary between US$80 and US$150 per person per night. The lodges generally consist of separate self-contained bandas, while the tented camps are often almost identical, the difference being that the 'rooms' have canvas walls protected from the elements by an open-sided makuti-roofed structure. It's certainly stretching things to call them tents but it seems to satisfy the desire for a token of authenticity among those with money to burn.

The *Mara Sopa Lodge* (☎ (2) 336088; PO Box 72639, Nairobi) by Oloolaimutia Gate is one of the newer ones and has a commanding view plus it's been attractively designed and built. Singles/doubles with full board cost US$135/180. *Keekorok Lodge* is one of the Block Hotels (☎ (2) 335807; PO Box 47557, Nairobi) and is an older but well-maintained lodge on a grassy plain. Singles/doubles with full board cost US$129/187 in

the high season, US$75/109 in the low season. Prices in the shoulder season are about halfway between the two. Keekorok is one of the two lodges which operates balloon flights.

The *Mara Sarova Camp* is part of the Sarova Hotels chain (☎ (2) 333233; PO Box 30680, Nairobi) and is not far from the Sekenani Gate and has the works, including a swimming pool. The room rates here with full board are US$78/157 a single/double in the high season, less in the shoulder and low seasons.

Along the northern banks of the Talek River are the *Fig Tree Camp* (☎ (2) 21439; PO Box 40683, Nairobi), and the *Mara Intrepids Club*. The Fig Tree Camp is attractively designed, has a swimming pool, and is approached across a wooden bridge from the car park on the opposite bank. It's a tented camp and has singles/doubles/triples for US$94/127/174 with full board. This is the other lodge from which you can take a balloon safari. It's wise to book them in advance at the Nairobi office though you can also do this at the camp. The Mara Intrepids Club is considerably more expensive at US$122/244 for singles/doubles with full board but the price does include game drives.

In the centre of the reserve is the *Mara Serena Lodge* (☎ (2) 339800) on a superb site overlooking the Mara River. It blends in beautifully with the surrounding countryside and was built to resemble a modern Maasai village. Singles/doubles with full board cost US$87/175.

Most expensive of all is the *Mara Safari Club* (☎ (2) 216940), part of the Lonrho chain of hotels (PO Box 58581, Nairobi). Singles/doubles with full board cost US$215/290 in the high season and US$155/205 in the low season. Shoulder-season prices are about halfway between the two, and all prices include game drives.

In the northern section of the park is another group of tented camps including the *Governor's Camp* (☎ (2) 331871) and *Little Governor's Camp* (owned by the same people). Singles/doubles with full board plus game drives cost US$150/300.

Other accommodation outside the park north of Oloololo Gate includes the *Kichwa Tembo Camp* (☎ (2) 335887) at US$77/140; the *Mara River Camp* (☎ (2) 331191) at US$56/100, and the *Mara Buffalo Camp*.

About 15 km from Sekenani Gate is another tented lodge, *Cottar's Mara Camp* (☎ (2) 882408). The 'cottages' are dotted around a beautiful green clearing with shady trees, sweeping lawns and flowers. There's an open bar and dining room and a roaring log fire at night. Although it's not actually in the reserve there's a lot of game around the camp itself. There is a baited hide nearby and you have a good chance of seeing leopards. Dawn walks and night-time spotlight game drives are also organised from the camp.

Even if you can't afford to stay in one of these camps, they are usually great places to drop in for a cleansing ale and perhaps a snack although, not surprisingly, prices are relatively high.

The Mara Sarova Camp, Keekorok Lodge and Mara Serena Lodge all sell petrol and will usually part with it to nonguests, though prices are higher than in Narok or Nairobi.

Getting There & Away

Air Air Kenya Aviation has twice-daily flights between Nairobi's Wilson Airport and Masai Mara, departing from Nairobi at 10 am and 3 pm, and from the Mara at 11 am and 4 pm. The one-way fare is US$83, but to these you have to add the cost of chartering a vehicle in the park to collect you from the airstrip.

Car & 4WD The Mara is not a place you come to without transport. There is no public transport to or within the park, and even if there was there's certainly no way you could do a game drive in a matatu! If you are patient and persistent you should be able to hitch a ride with other tourists, but get yourself to Narok first.

From Narok onwards the bitumen runs out and public transport dries up. It's almost 100 km from here to any of the park gates.

It's also possible to approach the reserve from Kisii and the west along reasonably well-maintained dirt roads. You can get closer to the park by public transport but there are far fewer tourist vehicles to hitch a ride with. Matatus run as far as Kilgoris directly south of Kisii, or Suna on the main A1 route close to Isebania on the Tanzanian border.

TSAVO NATIONAL PARK

At just over 20,000 sq km, Tsavo is the largest national park in Kenya, and for administrative purposes it has been split into Tsavo West National Park, with an area of 8500 sq km, and Tsavo East National Park, which covers 11,000 sq km.

The northern area of Tsavo West, west of the Nairobi to Mombasa A109 road, is the most developed and has some excellent scenery. Tsavo East is much less visited and consists of vast rolling plains with scrubby vegetation. The entire area north of the Galana River, and this constitutes the bulk of the park, is off limits to the general public. This is due to the ongoing campaign against poachers, who still find the relative remoteness of Tsavo a good prospect. Happily it seems the authorities are winning the battle, but in the meantime the rhino population has been absolutely decimated – from around 8000 in 1970 to less than 200 today.

When driving around the park, all track junctions have a numbered cairn which makes navigation fairly simple. Don't attempt this park without 4WD if you intend to get off the main routes. You can certainly get to Kilaguni Lodge and Ngulia Lodge on the main service road from Mtito Andei in a 2WD but you'll get into strife and possibly get hopelessly stuck on the minor tracks. You will not make it to the above lodges in a 2WD if you enter through the Tsavo Gate further south unless you're a rally driver and/or willing to risk damaging the car. There are some diabolical sections on this access road; the lava flows along here will rip with underside of any normal car apart.

Tsavo West National Park

The focus here is the watering holes by the Kilaguni and Ngulia lodges. The one at

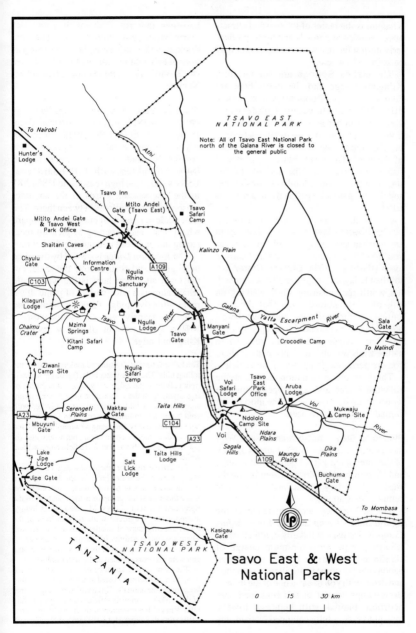

To Nairobi

Hunter's Lodge

Tsavo Inn

Mtito Andei Gate (Tsavo East)

Mitito Andei Gate & Tsavo West Park Office

Shaitani Caves

Chyulu Gate

Information Centre

Ngulia Rhino Sanctuary

Kilaguni Lodge

Mzima Springs

Ngulia Lodge

Tsavo Gate

Kitani Safari Camp

Chaimu Crater

Ziwani Camp Site

Ngulia Safari Camp

Serengeti Plains

Maktau Gate

Taita Hills

Mbuyuni Gate

Lake Jipe Lodge

Jipe Gate

Salt Lick Lodge

Taita Hills Lodge

TSAVO EAST NATIONAL PARK

Note: All of Tsavo East National Park north of the Galana River is closed to the general public

Athi

Tsavo Safari Camp

Kalinzo Plain

Galana

Yatta Escarpment

River

Sala Gate

Manyani Gate

Crocodile Camp

To Malindi

Voi Safari Lodge

Tsavo East Park Office

Aruba Lodge

Voi

Mukwaju Camp Site

River

Ndololo Camp Site

Ndara Plains

Dika Plains

Voi

Sagala Hills

Maungu Plains

Buchuma Gate

To Mombasa

Kasigau Gate

TSAVO WEST NATIONAL PARK

TANZANIA

Tsavo East & West National Parks

0   15   30 km

Kilaguni is the better of the two and attracts huge varieties of animals and birds, particularly during the dry season when water may be scarce elsewhere.

The **Mzima Springs** are not far from Kilaguni Lodge and the pools here are favourite haunts of both hippos and crocodiles. The much vaunted underwater viewing chamber was designed to give you a view of the hippos' submarine activities, but the hippos have retreated to the far end of the pool. There are, however, plenty of fish to be observed. The springs are the source of the bulk of Mombasa's fresh water and there is a direct pipeline from here to the coast.

Also in the area of the lodges is the spectacular **Shetani lava flow** and caves. Both are worth investigating, though for the caves you'll need to exercise caution and carry a torch (flashlight). The **Chaimu Crater** just south of Kilaguni Lodge can also be climbed. It's worth remembering while walking on any of these nature trails that the park animals are far from tame, and while there's little danger, you do need to keep your eyes on what's happening around you. These nature trails are also the only places where you are permitted to get out of the vehicle.

There is an information centre at Kilaguni Lodge and if it's open it may be worth checking to see where the most recent animal sightings have been.

Places to Stay – bottom end Tsavo West has a number of camp sites, namely at each of the three main gates (Tsavo, Mtito Andei and Chyulu) and the *Ziwani Campsite* on the western boundary of the park. The usual camping fees apply.

The self-service accommodation at the *Ngulia Safari Camp* and the *Kitani Safari Camp* is, by park standards, quite cheap at US$19 per person (minimum charge of US$38 per banda) in the fully equipped bandas but you must bring all your own food and drink with you or eat at one of the lodges. Both camps consist of self-contained one-bedroom bandas with bedding, towels, mosquito nets, a fully equipped kitchen, and

kerosene lanterns. Take with you toilet paper, washing-up liquid, soap, matches, drinking water and an ice box. For reservations at either camp, contact Let's Go Travel (☎ (2) 340331), Caxton House, Standard St, Nairobi.

Places to Stay – top end The *Ngulia Lodge* (☎ (2) 336858) is part of the African Tours & Hotels group (PO Box 30471, Nairobi). It's not the most attractive of lodges but it is comfortable and the views are excellent. Singles/doubles with full board cost US$90/120 in the high season and US$42/85 in the low season. Prices in the shoulder season are about halfway between these. The water hole here is small but there's a leopard which visits each evening to pick up meat strung up on a dead tree outside the patio.

The *Kilaguni Lodge* is owned by the same hotel group and costs exactly the same, but the main attraction here is the water hole which attracts a wide variety of game. It's a more attractive lodge than the Ngulia and there are extensive views out to the west.

Here's an account of a day spent at Kilaguni Lodge:

The lodge is beautifully situated looking out over the rolling hills. The large water hole, floodlit at night, is right in front of the lodge and you can sit in the bar or restaurant, or on the verandah in front of your room, and watch the wildlife. You can even lie in bed with your binoculars to hand – every room faces a water hole. All this luxury, including a swimming pool and lush garden, doesn't come cheap, but where else do you need a pair of binoculars and a field guide at hand while you eat?

We arrive in time for lunch and watch the comings and goings at the water hole. To the left there are impala and a couple of waterbuck; back from the water there's a small group of ostrich, and off to the right there's a herd of oryx. Marabou storks lounge around in the foreground while right in front of the restaurant are groups of smaller birds and mongoose. There's so much activity it's hard to concentrate on lunch – and this is just after the wet season when the game are less concentrated at the water holes!

The scene is only spoilt by the idiots who persist, in spite of numerous posted warnings, in throwing bread out to the animals. This has already taught some of the storks (notoriously efficient scavengers) to line up in front of the restaurant wall. It would be all too easy to turn this wonderful scene into a cheap zoo with

The Maasai

It is the Maasai more than anyone who have become the symbol of 'tribal' Kenya. With an (often exaggerated) reputation as fierce warriors and a supercilious demeanour, the Maasai have largely managed to stay outside the mainstream of development in Kenya and still maintain their cattle herds in the area south of Nairobi straddling the Tanzanian border.

They first came to the region from the Sudan and eventually came to dominate a large area of central Kenya until, in the late 19th century, they were decimated by famine and disease, and their cattle herds routed by rindepest. Up until the Masai Mara Game Reserve was created in the early 1960s, the Maasai had plenty of space for cattle grazing, but at a stroke much of this land was put off limits. As their population increased (both the cattle and the Maasai) pressure for land became intense and conflict with the authorities constant. Settlement programmes have only been reluctantly accepted as Maasai traditions scorn agriculture and land ownership is a foreign concept to them.

Another consequence of the competition for land is that many of the ceremonial traditions can no longer be fulfilled. Part of the ceremony where a man becomes a warrior *(moran)* involves a group of young men around the age of 14 going out and building a village *(manyatta)* after their circumcision ceremony. Here they spend as long as eight years alone, and while the tradition and will survives, the land is just not available.

Tourism provides an income to some, either through selling everyday items (gourds, necklaces, clubs and spears), dancing or simply posing for photographs. However, while a few can make a lot of money from tourism the benefits are not widespread. ∎

Maasai men - Tsavo West National Park (TW)

Top: Fort Jesus, Mombasa (GP)
Bottom Left: Malindi market (TW)
Bottom Right: Lamu House (TW)

View from Kilaguni Lodge

animals begging for hand-outs. This is the same Africa of Ethiopia and Mozambique and there's something obscene about dumb tourists hurling whole bread rolls just for amusement and a better shot with the Instamatic.

After lunch we watch from the verandah of our room – some zebras and two more ostriches appear but all the storks have left and gradually the animals wander off as the afternoon wears on. By 4.30 pm there's only the solitary waterbuck left; even the ostriches finally troop off in a stately line.

Down at the northern end of the lodge grounds is a tree full of weaver-bird nests with twittering hordes of these bright yellow birds furiously at work. Some of their nests, mainly older ones, have fallen out of the tree, and on close examination they are amazingly intricate and neatly woven; coconut-sized with a funnel-like entrance underneath. Right in front of our room a small squad of mongoose appears, cavorts around for a few minutes, then wanders away. By 5 pm it's baboon time again and the tribe wanders down to the water hole again for their evening visit. A few of them come up to our room to hassle us but soon give up. Rock hyrax scamper around, one even coming right into our room, and the mongoose come and go. Gradually the impala reappear.

Dinner time, unhappily, is the one blot on the perfect experience. Once again there are the idiotic food hurlers at work and a hyena trots up and waits expectantly for hand-outs, joined by a slender mongoose-like genet. With much shouting, loud conversation and cameras flashing madly there's a distinct theatre-restaurant feel to the whole meal and we're glad to get back to the quiet of our rooms.

The baboons leave soon after dark and by bedtime it's basically the impalas and zebras. I get up several times in the night to check what's up but, apart from bats swooping around, the scene seems static until dawn. The impala keep watch all night long.

At dawn the zebras wander off, the oryx reappear, the whole baboon tribe wanders back and immediately start carousing merrily. A couple of pairs of impala bucks square off for a morning duel and the whole cycle starts again.

Although we didn't see elephants or lions we still enjoyed every minute of it. Now if only they could put those 'don't feed the animals signs' on every table...

Tony Wheeler

In a fairly isolated spot on the western boundary of the park and almost on the Tanzanian border, the *Lake Jipe Lodge* (☎ (2) 27623) is one of the cheaper places but it's a long way from anywhere else.

If you don't have the money to stay at one of the lodges in the park but don't want to camp or go to the trouble of organising your own food, etc for one of the self-catering camps, then you have options though they involve staying just outside the park boundaries alongside the main Nairobi to Mombasa road. Even here, you're not looking at budget hotel options.

Right opposite the Mtito Andei Gate is the *Tsavo Inn* (PO Box 20, Mtito Andei) which is fairly pleasant but otherwise unremarkable. Doubles with breakfast cost US$52 (no singles) plus there are slightly more expensive half-board and full-board rates. For Kenyan residents it's considerably less expensive at US$16/19 for singles/doubles with breakfast.

Better is the *Hunter's Lodge* at Kiboko north of Mtito Andei at the extreme northern end of the park but also on the main Nairobi to Mombasa main road. Rooms here cost around US$13 per person per night including breakfast.

Getting There & Away The main access to Tsavo West is through the Mtito Andei Gate on the Mombasa to Nairobi road near the northern end of the park. The park headquarters is here and there's a camp site. From the gate it's 31 km to the Kilaguni Lodge.

A further 48 km along the main road away from Nairobi is the Tsavo Gate, where there's another camp site. This gate is 75 km from the Kilaguni area, so if you're hitching the Mtito Andei Gate is much closer and far busier. It's also worth taking into consideration the diabolical state of certain sections of the road between the Tsavo Gate and the lodges.

From Voi there is access past the Hilton-owned Taita Hills and Salt Lick lodges via the Maktau Gate. This road cuts clear across the park, exiting at the Mbuyuni Gate, to Taveta from where it's possible to cross into Tanzania and the town of Moshi at the foot of Kilimanjaro.

Tsavo East National Park

The southern third of this park is open to the public and the rolling scrub-covered hills are home to large herds of elephants, usually covered in red dust.

The **Kanderi Swamp**, not far into the park from the main Voi Gate and park headquarters, is home to a profusion of wildlife and there's a camp site here. Further into the park, 30 km from the gate, is the main attraction in this part of the park, the **Aruba Dam** built across the Voi River. Here too you'll encounter a wide variety of game without the usual hordes of tourists – very few people visit Tsavo East.

Places to Stay – bottom end There are camp sites at the Voi Gate, Kanderi Swamp *(Ndololo Campsite)*, Aruba Lodge and the *Mukwaju Campsite* on the Voi River 50 km in from the main gate.

Places to Stay – top end The *Voi Safari Lodge* (clearly signposted in the town of Voi) is part of the African Tours & Hotels group (☎ (2) 336858; PO Box 30471, Nairobi) and is five km inside the park from the Voi Gate. As you might imagine, things are a good deal more peaceful here than at the lodges in Tsavo West. Singles/doubles with full board cost US98/120 in the high season. In the low season they are US$41/81 and somewhere between the two in the shoulder season. The *Crocodile Camp* is somewhat cheaper at US$46 per person per night with full board.

The *Aruba Lodge* (☎ 340331 in Nairobi) is in a good shady location by the dam but considerably more expensive, as is the *Tsavo Safari Camp*. Both cost US$80 per person with full board.

Getting There & Away The main access point and the park headquarters is Voi Gate near Voi off the Nairobi to Mombasa road. Further north near the Tsavo Gate entrance of Tsavo West is the Manyani Gate. The murram (dirt) road from here cuts straight across to the Galana River and follows the river clear across the park, exiting at Sala Gate on the eastern side, a distance of 100 km. From Sala Gate it's a further 110 km to Malindi.

TAITA HILLS & VOI

The Taita Hills to the west of the main Nairobi to Mombasa road cover a vast area and are scenically spectacular. They have the status of a game reserve despite the fact that the main Voi to Taveta road passes through it on the southern side. Game is prolific in this area and you can even see plenty of it along the road to Taveta. There are also two lodges on the south-western side – the Taita Hills Lodge and the Salt Lick Lodge.

Taita Hills

The cheapest of the lodges is the *Taita Hills Lodge* which has rooms with full board for US$102 per person per night. More expensive is the *Salt Lick Lodge* which has the same for US$136 per person per night.

There are matatus from Voi to Wundanyi (in the heart of the Taita Hills) for US$0.90, and both trains (five hours) and matatus (2½ hours) from Voi to Taveta for US$2.60. The trains and matatus from Voi to Taveta will get you close to the lodges but, if you can afford to stay there, you'll probably be in your own vehicle anyway.

Voi

The town of Voi was described recently by a Peace Corps volunteer who works there as, 'an attractive spaghetti western-like setting surrounded by hills that are good for hiking and catching expansive views of the surrounding plains'. That's close to the truth but it's not Maralal and a lot of development is going on. Nevertheless, it's a pleasant, small town and worth considering as a base for exploring the Taita Hills and Tsavo National

Park or even as an overnight stop between Mombasa and Nairobi.

The cheapest place to stay with decent facilities is *Johari's Guest House* (☎ 2079) where singles/doubles go for US$2.20/4 with shared bath. The *Voi Restpoint Hotel* (☎ 2079) is the only budget hotel with self-contained rooms including fan and telephone. Singles/doubles with breakfast cost US$5.40/7.60. There are three restaurants in the hotel, including one on the rooftop.

Slightly more expensive is the *Kahn Silent Guest House* (☎ 2058), on Moi Hospital Rd opposite the Kenya Commercial Bank. It has singles/doubles for US$2.70/4 and is working on budget tours of Tsavo National Park.

Up in price is *Vuria's Bar & Lodging*, opposite the town hall, which offers self-contained rooms for US$3.40/5.60 including breakfast.

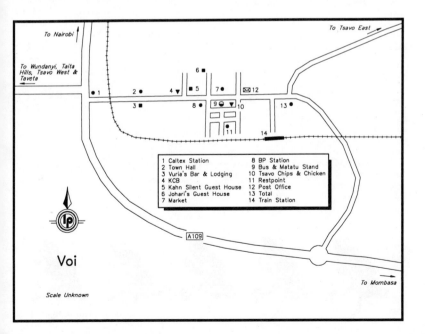

All the guesthouses have reasonable restaurants plus there's *Tsavo Chips & Chicken* at the matatu stand. Out on the main Nairobi to Mombasa road at the roundabout is the Caltex petrol station which has a whole complex of shops, fast-food outlets and a bar. The food here is OK and very reasonably priced, plus beers in the bar are ice-cold.

The Coast

This cannot be less than natural beauty, the endless sand, the reefs, the lot, are completely unmatched in the world.

Ernest Hemingway

The coast of Kenya is one of the country's main attractions. It offers a combination of historical sites, trading ports with a strong Arab-Muslim influence, superb beaches and diving opportunities – an area not to be missed.

Mombasa is the coast capital, if you like, and is the first port of call for most people after leaving Nairobi. It is an old trading port with a history going back at least to the 12th century, and the old city here shows heavy influence of the town's previous rulers – the mosques and the Portuguese fort in particular. It has a steamy humid climate but is a pleasant place nonetheless. Unfortunately, many people are in such a rush to get to the beach that they really only transit Mombasa, which is a pity as the city, particularly the old part, is well worth exploring.

To the north it's much the same story, with Malindi being the big coastal resort centre, but there's a couple of interesting attractions here as well – the historical site of Gedi just a short bus ride to the south, and the excellent diving on the coral reef in the offshore Malindi and Watamu marine national parks.

Head further north and you come to the island of Lamu – a beautiful Arab-influenced town which has been something of a travellers' Mecca for years and still draws visitors by the thousands. Despite this it retains the very distinctive personality which attracted people to it in the first place – an easy-going unhurried pace, traditional architecture, and a unique culture which owes a great deal to its Muslim roots.

The people of the coast are the Swahili, and it's here that KiSwahili (Swahili) – the lingua franca of the modern nation – evolved as a means of communication between the local inhabitants and the Arab traders who first began plying their dhows up and down this coast sometime before the 7th century. Other influences also shaped the language and there is a smattering of not only Arabic but also Portuguese, Hindi and English words.

History

The first traders here appear to have been Arabs from the Persian Gulf who sailed south along the coast during the north-east monsoon, sailing home north with the south-west monsoon. By the 12th century some substantial settlements had developed, mainly on islands such as Lamu, Mandu, Pemba and Zanzibar, as these provided greater security than the coast itself. The main export trade in this early part was in ivory, tortoiseshell and leopard skins, while items such as glass beads from India and porcelain from as far afield as China were finding their way here.

From the 12th to the 15th centuries settlements grew and a dynasty was established at Kilwa (in present-day Tanzania). By the end of this period Mombasa, Malindi and Paté (in the Lamu archipelago) were all substantial towns. The inhabitants were largely Arab but there were also significant numbers of African labourers. Intermarriage was common and, culturally, the settlements were more closely connected with the Islamic Persian Gulf than they were with inland Kenya. Although all these city-states had this common heritage and cultural link, they were all virtually independent and were often vying with one another for power.

So preoccupied were they with their own internal struggles that the coastal centres were quite unprepared for the arrival of the Portuguese in 1498. Before long they were paying tribute to the Portuguese and by 1506 the Portuguese had sacked and gained control of the entire coast. In the century which followed, the Portuguese had raided

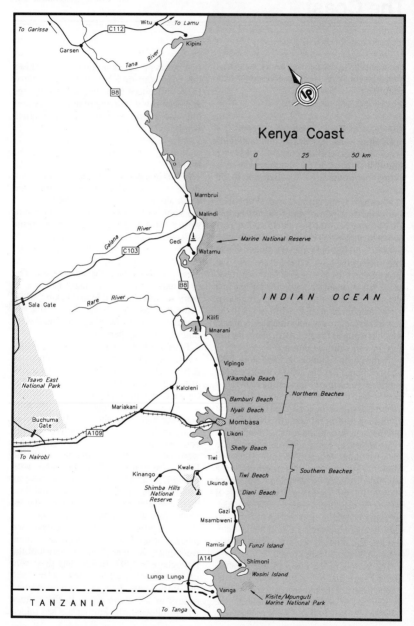

Kenya Coast

To Garissa
Witu
To Lamu
C112
Garsen
Kipini
Tana River
B8

0   25   50 km

Marnbrui
Malindi
Galana River
C103
Gedi
Watamu
Marine National Reserve

B8

Rare River
Sala Gate

INDIAN OCEAN

Kilifi
Mnarani

Vipingo

Tsavo East National Park
Kaloleni
Kikambala Beach

Bamburi Beach
Nyali Beach
Northern Beaches

Mariakani
Buchuma Gate
A109
Mombasa
Likoni

To Nairobi
Shelly Beach

Tiwi
Kwale
Kinango
Tiwi Beach
Southern Beaches
Ukunda
Shimba Hills National Reserve
Diani Beach

Gazi
Msambweni

Ramisi
Funzi Island
A14
Shimoni
Lunga Lunga
Wasini Island
Vanga
TANZANIA
To Tanga
Kisite/Mpunguti Marine National Park

Mombasa on two further occasions and built the beautiful defensive Fort Jesus in that city.

Trade was the main interest of the Portuguese and they concentrated their activities in that area. They did not exercise direct control over the administration of the coastal cities – just kept them in line and dependent.

Not all the locals were happy with this arrangement and trouble started for the Portuguese with local uprisings in the 17th century. They were mainly inspired by the disaffected Sheikh Yusuf of Mombasa, who spent most of his time in conflict with the Portuguese, and in fact occupied Fort Jesus in Mombasa after murdering the Portuguese commandant there in 1631. With the help of the sultans of Oman, the Portuguese were defeated and Fort Jesus occupied by 1698.

The Omani dynasties flourished and Mombasa and Paté became the pre-eminent spots on the coast, although both were defeated by Lamu in 1810. The internecine struggles of the various Omani factions led to Zanzibar coming into ascendancy, which in turn led the rulers of Mombasa to seek British assistance. The British, however, were reluctant to intervene and jeopardise their alliance with Seyyid Said, the Omani ruler, as their route to India passed close to Muscat. Before long the whole coast was under the control of the Omani ruler.

It was in this period of Omani rule that the slave trade flourished. Up until this time it had been carried out only on a small scale, but soon the newly established clove plantations on Zanzibar required labourers, and from there slaves were shipped to the Persian Gulf and beyond. It was also this increase in economic activity that brought the first Indian and European traders into the area. Trade agreements were made with the Americans (1833), the British (1839) and the French (1844), and exports to India also flourished – ivory, cloves, hides and coconut oil were all important. This increase in trade led Seyyid Said to transfer his capital from Muscat to Zanzibar in 1840, and decreased his reliance on the slave trade for revenue. He was thus able to sign a treaty banning the export of slaves to the Middle East.

Despite the fact that the British East Africa Company took over administration of the interior of the country, a 10-mile-wide coastal strip was recognised as the sultan's patch and it was leased from him in 1887, first for a 50-year period and then permanently. In 1920 the coastal strip became the British protectorate, the rest of the country having become a fully fledged British colony.

Mombasa

Mombasa is the largest port on the coast of East Africa. It has a population of nearly half a million of which about 70% are African, the rest being mainly Asian with a small minority of Europeans. Its docks not only serve Kenya, but also Uganda, Rwanda, Burundi and eastern Zaïre. The bulk of the town sprawls over Mombasa Island which is connected to the mainland by an artificial causeway which carries the rail and road links. In recent years Mombasa has spread onto the mainland both north and south of the island.

Large Mombasa may be but, like Dar es Salaam to the south, it has retained its low-level traditional character and there are few high-rise buildings. The Old Town between the massive, Portuguese-built Fort Jesus and the old dhow careening dock remains much the same as it was in the mid-19th century, asphalt streets and craft shops apart. It's a hot and steamy town, as you might expect being so close to the equator, but an interesting place to visit.

History
Mombasa's history goes back to at least the 12th century when it was described by Arab chroniclers as being a small town and the residence of the King of the Zenj – Arabic for Black Africans. It later became an important settlement for the Shirazis and remained so until the arrival of the Portuguese in the early 16th century. Determined to destroy the Arab monopoly over maritime

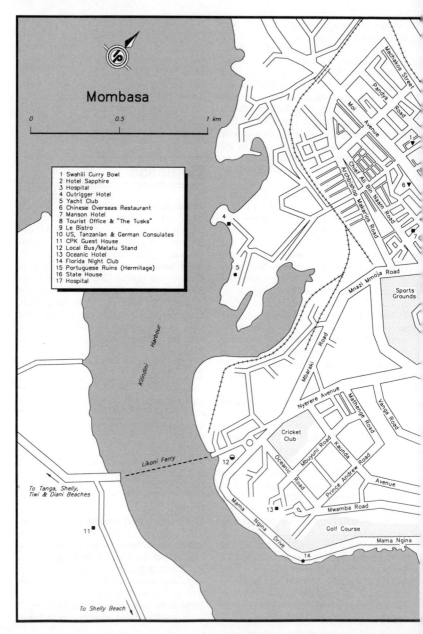

Mombasa

0   0.5   1 km

1 Swahili Curry Bowl
2 Hotel Sapphire
3 Hospital
4 Outrigger Hotel
5 Yacht Club
6 Chinese Overseas Restaurant
7 Manson Hotel
8 Tourist Office & "The Tusks"
9 Le Bistro
10 US, Tanzanian & German Consulates
11 CPK Guest House
12 Local Bus/Matatu Stand
13 Oceanic Hotel
14 Florida Night Club
15 Portuguese Ruins (Hermitage)
16 State House
17 Hospital

Machakos Street

Pandya Road

Moi Avenue

Archbishop Makarios Road

Chai Ali Bin Naam Road

Mnazi Mmoja Road

Sports Grounds

Kilindini Harbour

Mbaraki Road

Nyerere Avenue

Mathenge Road

Vanga Road

Cricket Club

Oceanic Road

Mbuyuni Road

Kaunda Road

Prince Andrew Avenue

Likoni Ferry

To Tanga, Shelly,
Tiwi & Diani Beaches

Mama Ngina Drive

Mwamba Road

Golf Course

Mama Ngina

To Shelly Beach

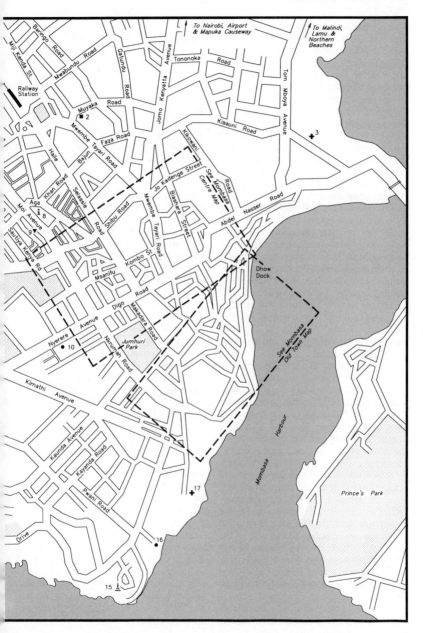

trade in the Indian Ocean, especially with regard to spices, the Portuguese, under Dom Francisco de Almeida, attacked Mombasa with a fleet of 23 ships in 1505. After a day and a half it was all over and the town was burnt to the ground. So great was the quantity of loot that much of it had to be left behind, for fear of overloading the ships, when the fleet sailed for India.

The town was quickly rebuilt and it wasn't long before it regained its commanding position over trade in the area, but peace didn't last long. In 1528, another Portuguese fleet under Nuña da Cunha arrived on the East African coast too late to catch the south-western monsoon which would take them to India, so they were forced to look around for temporary quarters. Naturally, Mombasa was in no mood to welcome them but, unfortunately, Mombasa was at that time engaged in bitter disputes with the kings of Malindi, Pemba and Zanzibar. An alliance was patched together and the Portuguese were again able to take Mombasa, but sickness and constant skirmishing over many months eventually decided the outcome. The city was again burnt to the ground and the Portuguese sailed for India.

The Portuguese finally made a bid for permanency in 1593 with the construction of Fort Jesus, but in 1631 they were massacred to the last person in an uprising by the towns-people. The following year a Portuguese fleet was sent from Goa and Muscat to avenge the killings but was unable to retake the town. By this time, however, the Mombasan ruler had decided that further resistance was useless and, having reduced the town to rubble and cut down all the fruit trees and palms, he withdrew to the mainland. It was reoccupied without a fight by the Portuguese the following year. Portuguese hegemony in the Indian Ocean was on the wane by this time, not only because of corruption and nepotism within Portuguese ranks, but because of Dutch, French and English activity in India and South-East Asia.

The 17th century also saw the rise of Oman as a naval power and it was the Omanis who, in 1698, were the next to drive the Portuguese from Mombasa, after a 33-month siege in which all the defenders were slaughtered. Even this disaster wasn't enough to convince the Portuguese that their days were over and Mombasa was reoccupied. However, the end finally came in 1729 following an invasion by an Arab fleet, a general uprising of the population in which Portuguese settlers were slaughtered, and an abortive counteroffensive which involved the entire military resources of the viceroyalty of Goa.

In 1832 the Sultan of Oman moved his capital from Muscat to Zanzibar and from then until Kenya's independence in 1963 the red flag of Zanzibar fluttered over Fort Jesus. Meanwhile, the British became active along the East African coast. In their attempts to suppress the slave trade, they interfered increasingly in the affairs of Zanzibar until, in 1895, the British East Africa protectorate was set up with Mombasa as the capital (until it was moved to Nairobi) and the Sultan of Oman's possessions were administered as a part of it. When independence came, the Sultan's coastal possessions were attached to the new republic.

During the protectorate years the British confirmed Mombasa's status as East Africa's most important port by constructing a railway from Mombasa to Uganda. It was completed in 1901 using indentured labourers from Gujarat and Punjab in India – hence the origin of Kenya's (and Uganda's and Tanzania's) Asian population.

Information

Tourist Office The regional tourist office (☎ 311231) is just past the famous tusks on Moi Ave and is open Monday to Friday from 8 am to noon and 2 to 4.30 pm, and on Saturdays from 8 am to noon. It has a reasonable map of south-east Kenya and the Kenyan coast for sale but is otherwise geared to big spenders – mainly those who want to stay at a beach resort hotel – so is of little help to budget travellers. You can also buy the local guide books to Fort Jesus and Mombasa Old Town here.

Money The branch of Barclays Bank on Moi Ave, 200 metres west of the Castle Hotel, is open Monday to Friday from 9 am to 3 pm and on the first and last Saturday of the month from 9 to 11 am. Outside these hours you may be able to change travellers' cheques at the Castle Hotel, or at any of the beach resort hotels north and south of Mombasa, although their exchange rates are relatively poor.

American Express is represented by Express Kenya (☎ 312461), PO Box 90631, Nkrumah Rd.

Post The GPO is on Digo Rd and is open Monday to Friday from 8 am to 4.30 pm and on Saturday from 8 am to noon.

Embassies As Mombasa is an important port and tourism town, a number of countries also have consulates here:

Austria
    Raili House, Nyerere Ave (☎ 313386)
Belgium
    Mitchell Cotts Bldg, Moi Ave (☎ 20231)
Denmark
    Liwatoni Bay (☎ 311826)
France
    Southern House, Moi Ave (☎ 20501)
Germany
    Palli House, Nyerere Ave
India
    Bank of India Bldg, Nkrumah Rd (☎ 24433)
Netherlands
    ABN Bank Bldg, Nkrumah Rd (☎ 311043)
Sweden
    Southern House, Moi Ave (☎ 20501)
Tanzania
    Palli House, Nyerere Ave (☎ 228596); open Monday to Friday from 8.30 am to 12.30 pm and 2.30 to 4 pm.
UK
    The Missions to Seamen, Mogadishu Rd (☎ 316502, 316331)
USA
    Palli House, Nyerere Ave (☎ 315101)

Books If you'd like more details about Mombasa's stirring history, the best account is to be found in *The Portuguese Period in East Africa* (East African Literature Bureau, 1971), by Justus Strandes, which can be bought in most good bookshops in Nairobi and Mombasa.

Before you set off on a tour of the Old Town of Mombasa get a copy of the booklet *The Old Town Mombasa: A Historical Guide* (Friends of Fort Jesus), by Judy Aldrick & Rosemary Macdonald. It can be bought from the tourist office, Fort Jesus, or one of the bookshops on Moi Ave. This excellent guide is an essential companion for an exploration of this part of town and has photographs, drawings and a map.

Also well worth buying is *Fort Jesus* by James Kirkman, which gives a detailed account of the history of the Fort, as well as pointing out the salient features. It is available from the fort, the bookshops and sometimes the tourist office.

Maps The best map you can buy of Mombasa is the Survey of Kenya's *Mombasa Island & Environs*, last published in 1977. Many of the street names have changed, but little else. The craft shop on the terrace of the Castle Hotel usually stocks it.

Fort Jesus

The Old Town's biggest attraction dominates the harbour entrance. Begun in 1593 by the Portuguese, it changed hands nine times between 1631 and 1875. These days it's a museum and is open daily from 8.30 am to 6 pm. Entry costs US$2.20 (US$0.45 for Kenyan residents). There are no student reductions.

It's well worth a visit and it's easy to pass a couple of hours here. Early morning is the best time as the air is still cool and the rest of the tourists are still in bed. The guidebook, *Fort Jesus*, by James Kirkman is useful for a full description of the history and finer points of the fort.

The fort was designed by an Italian architect, Joao Batista Cairato, who had done a lot of work for the Portuguese in Goa. He incorporated some ingenious elements into the design, such as the angular configuration of the walls, making it impossible for would-be invaders to lay siege to one wall without being sitting ducks for soldiers in one of the other walls.

The most interesting features today include the **Omani house** in the San Felipe bastion in the north-western corner of the fort. Built in the late 18th century it has served different functions as the purpose of the fort changed – it was the chief warder's house when the fort was a prison in the early 20th century. The view of the Old Town from the roof here is excellent.

The **museum** along the southern wall is built over what was the barracks rooms for the garrison. The exhibits are mostly ceramics but include other interesting odds and ends and have either been donated from private collections or dug up from various sites along the coast. The origins of many of the pieces are a reflection of the variety of cultures which has influenced the coastal culture – Chinese, Indian, Portuguese and Persian. Also displayed in the museum are finds from the Portuguese frigate *Santo António de Tanná* which sank off the fort during the siege in 1697.

The **western wall** of the fort is probably the most interesting and includes an Omani audience hall (now covered by a second storey but still complete with official inscriptions – and unofficial graffiti) and the Passage of the Arches – a passage cut through the coral giving access to the outer part of the fort, although it was later blocked off.

The Old Town

The Old Town isn't as immediately interesting as the fort, but it's still a fascinating area

Fort Jesus

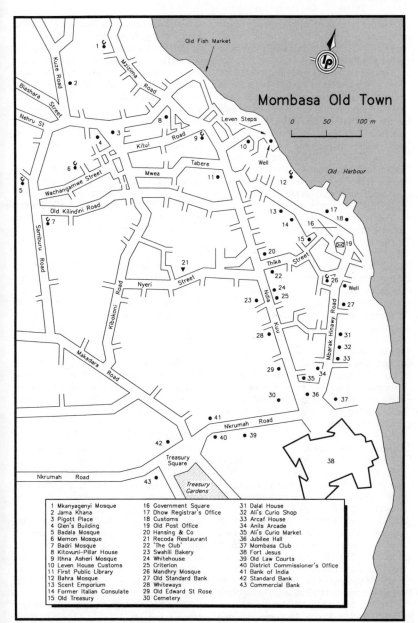

Mombasa Old Town

0   50   100 m

Old Fish Market

Old Harbour

Leven Steps

Well

Well

Old Harbour

Treasury Square

Treasury Gardens

Nkrumah Road

1 Mkanyagenyi Mosque
2 Jama Khana
3 Pigott Place
4 Glen's Building
5 Badala Mosque
6 Memon Mosque
7 Badri Mosque
8 Kitovuni-Pillar House
9 Ithna Asheri Mosque
10 Leven House Customs
11 First Public Library
12 Bahra Mosque
13 Scent Emporium
14 Former Italian Consulate
15 Old Treasury

16 Government Square
17 Dhow Registrar's Office
18 Customs
19 Old Post Office
20 Hansing & Co
21 Recoda Restaurant
22 'The Club'
23 Swahili Bakery
24 Whitehouse
25 Criterion
26 Mandhry Mosque
27 Old Standard Bank
28 Whiteways
29 Old Edward St Rose
30 Cemetery

31 Dalal House
32 Ali's Curio Shop
33 Arcaf House
34 Anils Arcade
35 Ali's Curio Market
36 Jubilee Hall
37 Mombasa Club
38 Fort Jesus
39 Old Law Courts
40 District Commissioner's Office
41 Bank of India
42 Standard Bank
43 Commercial Bank

to wander around in. Early morning or late afternoon is the best time to walk around; there's more activity then, and it's very quiet in the middle of the day.

Though its history goes back centuries, most of the houses in the Old Town are no more than 100 years old but you'll come across the occasional one which dates back to the first half of the 19th century. They represent a combination of styles and traditions which include the long-established coastal Swahili architecture commonly found in Lamu, various late-19th century Indian styles and British colonial architecture with its broad, shady verandahs and glazed and shuttered windows.

There are very few houses constructed entirely of coral rag, however. Most are of wattle and daub though they may include coral here and there. Most of the old palm thatch or tile roofing has been replaced with corrugated iron as well. What does remain are many examples of the massive, intricately carved doors and door frames characteristic of Swahili houses in Lamu and Zanzibar. It seems that when anyone of importance moved from these towns to Mombasa they brought their doors with them or had them newly made up to reflect their financial status. Of course, they're not as numerous as they used to be, either because of the ravages of time, or because they have been bought by collectors and shipped abroad. There is now a preservation order on those remaining so further losses should hopefully be prevented.

It's not just carved doors that you should look out for, though. Almost as much effort was put into the construction of balconies, their support brackets and enclosures. Fine fretwork and lattice work are a feature of the enclosures, reflecting the Muslim need for women's privacy. Sadly, quite a few of these were damaged or destroyed along Mbarak Hinawy Rd in the days when oversized trucks used the road for access to the old port.

By 1900, most of the houses in the main streets were owned by Indian businesspeople and traders whilst Mbarak Hinawy Rd (previously called Vasco da Gama St) and

Government Square had become the centre for colonial government offices, banks, consulates and business or living quarters for colonial officials. Ndia Kuu housed immigrant entrepreneurs from India, Goa and Europe. The colonial headquarters at this time were situated in Leven House on the waterfront overlooking the old harbour, but shortly afterwards they were moved to Government Square and, in 1910, moved again up the hill to Treasury Square above Fort Jesus.

In later years, as Mombasa expanded along what are today the main roads, many of the businesses which had shops and offices in the Old Town gradually moved out, leaving behind ornate signs, etched glass windows and other relics of former times. Their exact location is described in *The Old Town Mombasa: A Historical Guide*.

You can start your exploration of the Old Town anywhere you like but the main points of interest are marked on the street map. There is a notice in Government Square saying that photography of the old harbour area (but not the buildings) is prohibited. I don't know how serious the authorities are about this since I can't imagine what is so sensitive about the place, but if you want pictures of it there are plenty of narrow streets leading off to the waterfront between the square and the Leven Steps where no-one will bother you.

Harbour Cruises

Those looking for a luxury dhow cruise around the harbour should book a trip with Tamarind Dhow Safaris (☎ 20990, 315569) but be warned that they're not cheap at US$43 for the lunch cruise and US$51 for the evening cruise. The price includes a four-hour cruise around the harbour, a gourmet lunch or dinner (seafood or steak) cooked on board, an on-board live band and transport to/from your hotel. The dhow has its own fully stocked bar. The lunch cruise begins at 10.30 am and the evening cruise starts at 6.30 pm.

There's also another outfit called *Jahazi Marine Ltd* (☎ 472213, 471895) which offers night-time dhow cruises on Monday and Thursday for US$65. The price includes a sundowner cruise with a cocktail past Mombasa Old Town and the fort, a barbecue at Bamburi Nature Park, a torchlit safari through the park, a visit to the casino and the Bora Bora Nightclub and transfers from your hotel.

You can book either of the above cruises direct or at any travel agency or top-end hotel.

Places to Stay

There's a lot of choice for budget travellers and for those who want something slightly better, both in the centre of the city and on the mainland to the north and south. Accommodation up and down the coast from Mombasa Island itself is dealt with separately.

Places to Stay – bottom end

One of the best value places in this category is the *Mvita Hotel*, on the corner of Hospital and Turkana Sts. The entrance is on the first alley on the left-hand side on Turkana St or through the bar on the ground floor on Hospital St. It's Indian-run, clean, quiet and secure, all the rooms have fans and a washbasin and the beds are comfortable. The showers and toilets are scrubbed out daily. Rooms cost US$3.30 a double, but the hotel is often full as it's only a small place. There's a lively bar downstairs (which you can't hear in the rooms upstairs) and at lunch and dinner times barbecued meat and other snacks are available in the back yard.

Equally good value and popular with travellers is the *Cosy Guest House* (☎ 313064), on Haile Selassie Rd, though we have had reports that Salim, the owner, hassles women. It costs US$2.70/4 for singles/doubles, US$6 for triples, all with shared facilities. All the rooms have fans but due to chronic water problems the toilets can stink. The guesthouse will most likely be full if you get there late in the day.

On the opposite side of the road from the Cosy Guest House is the *Midnight Guest House* (☎ 26275) which is a bit scruffy, and

the management is not all that friendly, but it would do if you're stuck. There are no singles, and a double with shared facilities costs US$3.60.

Just around the corner on Shibu Rd is the friendly *New Al Jazira Hotel* which has doubles with balcony and shared bath (no fans) for US$3.10. As is the case with many Mombasa hotels, there are no single rooms.

If all these places are full then you could try the *Balgis Lodge* (☎ 313358), on Digo Rd, which is very friendly. It has singles/ doubles for US$2.70/4 and triples for US$5.40, all with shared facilities. The rooms only have internal windows which makes them pretty hot, but there's also a dorm which has windows overlooking noisy Digo Rd. Another real cheapie which is habitable though very scruffy is the *Down Town Lodge* on Hospital St for US$2.50 per room. Most of the rooms don't have fans.

Heading towards the northern end of town, the *Al Nasser Lodging* (☎ 313032) on Abdel Nasser Rd is good value at US$4.90 for a double with shower.

Another budget hotel in this area, and one which has been popular for years, is the *New People's Lodge* (☎ 312831), on Abdel Nasser Rd right next to where the buses leave for Malindi and Lamu. Some travellers rate this place very highly and it certainly compares very well in price with the others but it is a little tatty and the rooms which face onto the main road are very noisy. The air also stinks of diesel fumes because bus drivers always rev their engines for up to an hour before they actually leave. The management is friendly, and gear left in the rooms is safe. Rooms cost US$1.70/3.40 a single/double with shared showers and toilets, and US$2.80/5.60/8.40 a single/double/triple with private facilities. There are also four-bed and five-bed rooms with shared facilities for US$4.50/5.60. All the rooms have fans, the sheets are clean and the water in the showers is generally lukewarm. It's a large place and is rarely full. There's a good, cheap restaurant downstairs.

Another place which was once a popular budget hotel is the *Hydro Hotel* (☎ 23784),

■ PLACES TO STAY

1	New People's Lodge
3	Al Nasser Lodging
11	Hydro Hotel
12	Unity Guest House
13	Down Town Lodge
15	Mvita Hotel
16	Balgis Lodge
17	New Al Jazira Hotel
18	Midnight Guest House
19	Visitor's Inn
20	Cosy Guest House
22	Continental Guest House
23	Hotel Fortuna
25	Hotel Hermes
29	New Britania Boarding & Lodging
31	Glory Guest House & ABC Lodge
33	Hotel Splendid
37	Kilindini Guest House
41	Castle Hotel
44	Manor Hotel
49	New Palm Tree Hotel

▼ PLACES TO EAT

14	Geetanjali Restaurant
20	New Chetna Restaurant
21	Indo African Restaurant
24	Blue Room Restaurant

26	Splendid View Restaurant
28	Masumin Restaurant
32	Pistacchio Ice Cream & Coffee Bar
34	Blue Fin Restaurant
36	Mombasa Coffee House
42	Fontanella Restaurant
45	Hard Rock Café
47	Capri Restaurant

OTHER

2	Buses & Matatus to Malindi & Lamu
4	Coast Bus
5	Bus Station
6	Cat Bus
7	Mawingo Buses
8	Akamba Bus
9	Malindi Taxi Bus
10	Market
27	Sheik Jundoni Mosque
30	GPO
35	Bahati Book Centre
38	Bahari Bookshop
39	Barclays Bank
40	Istanbul Bar
43	Fort Supermarket
46	Kenya Airways
47	Executive Air Services
48	American Express

on Digo Rd at the Kenyatta Ave junction, but it's barely habitable these days and you'd have to be desperate to stay there. In better shape is the *New Britania Boarding & Lodging* on Gusii St. The hotel entrance is through the downstairs bar and then up the stairs. The rooms are clean and good value at US$2.90.

Not far from the tourist office and similar in price to the other budget hotels is the quiet *Kilindini Guest House* off Shibu Rd.

Somewhat more expensive than the above (but not necessarily better value) is the *Hotel Fortuna*, on Haile Selassie Rd, which costs US$4/5.10 for singles/doubles with private showers and toilets. The *Hotel Fortuna Annex* across the road shares the same reception but is cheaper since the rooms are not self-contained.

Better value is the *Continental Guest House* (☎ 315916) on Haile Selassie Rd near the Hotel Fortuna. Double rooms (no

singles) go for US$5.40 with bath and breakfast. It's run by a very friendly guy, but you need to get there early as it fills up quickly. Close by is the similarly priced *Visitor's Inn* on the corner of Shibu Rd. The rooms are self-contained and the price includes breakfast. However, some of the rooms overlook Haile Selassie Rd and so cop the noise. The entrance is on Shibu Rd and is easy to miss.

Places to Stay – middle
One of the cheapest in this range is the new *Unity Guest House* (☎ 221298) just off Msanifu Kombo St. It has self-contained singles/doubles with fan for US$5.60/10 and doubles with air-con for US$17.

Also on Msanifu Kombo St is the *Hotel Splendid* (☎ 220967), a huge place which is rarely full. It has singles with shared facilities for US$6.40, and self-contained doubles/triples for US$12/19. The prices include breakfast. It's an old place but very

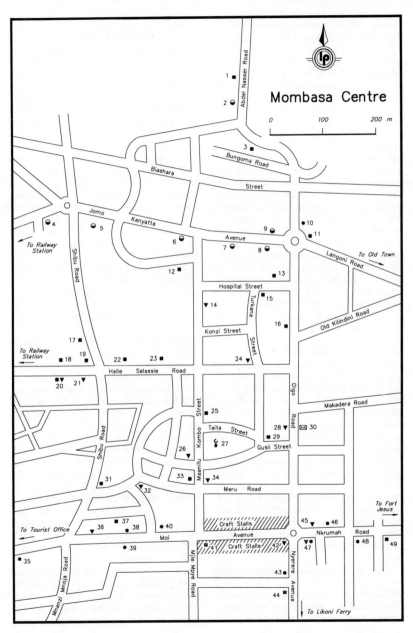

Mombasa Centre

0   100   200 m

To Railway Station

To Railway Station

To Tourist Office

To Old Town

To Fort Jesus

To Likoni Ferry

Abdel Nasser Road

Bungoma Road

Biashara Street

Jomo Kenyatta Avenue

Shibu Road

Langoni Road

Old Kilindini Road

Hospital Street

Konzi Street

Turkana Street

Digo Road

Makadera Road

Haile Selassie Road

Kombo Street

Taita Street

Gusii Street

Msanifu Street

Meru Road

Craft Stalls

Craft Stalls

Moi Avenue

Nkrumah Road

Nyerere Avenue

Mwanzi Mnoja Road

Mijie Mye Road

Shibu Road

clean and there's a popular rooftop restaurant which gets sea breezes in the evenings.

Another well-maintained hotel in this category is the *Hotel Hermes* (☎ 313599) on Msanifu Kombo St near the Sheik Jundoni Mosque. The rooms are pleasant, if a little dingy, and self-contained doubles (no singles) with air-con cost US$14 including breakfast.

Not far from here is the *Glory Guest House* (☎ 313204) on Shibu Rd. The rooms are a bit on the small side but are spotlessly clean and well maintained. Self-contained singles/doubles with fan cost US$11/16 plus there are doubles with air-con for US$18. Breakfast is included in the price. There is also an annexe with cheaper rooms and shared facilities. Singles/doubles here cost US$8.90/13.40.

An excellent-value mid-range place is the *New Palm Tree Hotel* (☎ 312169), on Nkrumah Rd. A comfortable self-contained room with fan here costs US$11/15 a single/double including breakfast. The staff are friendly and helpful, and the hotel has its own bar and restaurant.

Places to Stay – top end

One of the cheaper top-end hotels is the brand new *Manson Hotel* (☎ 222356), on Kisumu Rd. It has 84 self-contained rooms which cost US$16/20 a single/double without air-con, US$20/24 with air-con. Prices include breakfast. The hotel has a restaurant (exclusively vegetarian food) but no bar.

Similar in price and also some distance from the centre but close to the railway station, is the brand new *Hotel Sapphire* (☎ 491657) on Mwembe Tayari Rd. All the rooms are self-contained with air-con and cost US$18/27 including breakfast. Children under 12 years of age sharing with parents cost US$4.50 extra. Diners Club cards are accepted.

The most popular hotel and the one with most character is the central *Castle Hotel* (☎ 223403, 221683) on Moi Ave. Originally constructed in 1908, it was Mombasa's premier hotel throughout the colonial period

when it was run by a Mr Schwentafsky, otherwise known as 'Champagne Charlie' on account of his notoriously keen interest in female guests. Following WW II, it was allowed to run down but was recently restored to its former glory by Alliance Hotels which has retained the original snow-white façade, the balcony balustrades and the polished wooden floors and grand staircases.

All the rooms have air-con, private bathrooms and colour TV. Singles/doubles cost US$29/40, and children aged between two and 12 years sharing with adults cost an extra US$7.80. The price includes an excellent US-style buffet breakfast. All major credit cards are accepted and there's guarded parking. Amenities include a restaurant and three bars, one of which is the popular open-air Terrace overlooking Moi Ave; virtually every visitor to Mombasa comes to the Terrace at one time or another for a cold beer.

Not quite as old, but another colonial landmark, is the nearby *Manor Hotel* (☎ 314643), on Nyerere Ave, with a wide verandah and surrounding garden. Like the Castle, it's been renovated since it was first built in the 1920s, but is cheaper at US$17 a single with shared facilities. Self-contained singles/doubles with fan are US$19/31, US$25/33 with air-con. Children under 12 years sharing a room with their parents cost US$5.60 extra. Prices include breakfast and there's guarded parking at the rear. Amenities include a restaurant and bars.

Superbly located overlooking the Indian Ocean and with a range of amenities which includes Indian, Chinese and Italian restaurants, a swimming pool and an open-air bar in a garden setting, is the relatively modern *Oceanic Hotel* (☎ 311191/2/3), off Oceanic Rd, not far from the Likoni ferry. Self-contained, air-con rooms in this high-rise hotel cost US$22/31 a single/double and triples US$40 including breakfast. All major credit cards are accepted.

Top of the range is the *New Outrigger Hotel* (☎ 220822) set in landscaped gardens leading down to Kilindini Harbour on the western side of Mombasa Island. All the rooms are self-contained with air-con and have a balcony facing the harbour. Singles/doubles cost US$55/65 including breakfast. The hotel is under Belgian management, the cuisine is French, there's a swimming pool and all credit cards are accepted.

Places to Eat

Mombasa has a good range of restaurants. If you are putting your own food together, or want to stock up with goodies to take down the coast, the Fort Supermarket on Nyerere Ave is well stocked, and there's a wide variety of fruit and vegies in the market on Digo Rd next to the Hydro Hotel.

Places to Eat – cheap

If you are just looking for fish or chicken with chips try the *Blue Fin Restaurant*, on the corner of Meru Rd and Msanifu Kombo St. There's very little variety but it's not a bad place. There's a better choice at the *Blue Room Restaurant* on Haile Selassie Rd. It serves excellent burgers for US$0.60 to US$1, depending on what you have with them, and the fish & chips and Indian snacks are also worth a try.

The *Masumin Restaurant*, opposite the GPO on Digo Rd, does a good full breakfast for US$1.20, and at other times has various curries with rice for US$1, as well as steaks and cheap juices.

The *Mombasa Coffee House* on Moi Ave is a good place for fresh coffee and snacks, and you can also buy coffee beans here.

Indian Food Since many of the restaurants in Mombasa are Indian-owned you can find excellent curries and thalis and at lunch time (from 12.30 to around 3 pm) there is often a cheap, substantial set meal available. One which you'll hear nothing but praise for is the *Geetanjali*, on Msanifu Kombo St, which offers a 'deluxe' thali for US$1.50. Both the food and service are excellent.

Similar is the popular *New Chetna Restaurant*, on Haile Selassie Rd directly under the Cosy Guest House. The food here is South Indian vegetarian (with dishes such as masala dosa and idli) and sweets. An all-you-can-eat set vegetarian lunch costs US$1.50.

Excellent tandoori specialities can be found at the very popular *Splendid View Restaurant*, which is opposite, but not part of, the Hotel Splendid. Food on offer includes chicken, lamb, fruit juices and lassis and you can eat well here for around US$1.80. There are tables outside and inside.

Swahili Food For coastal Swahili dishes made with coconut and coconut milk, the *Swahili Curry Bowl*, on Tangana Rd off Moi Ave, is recommended. Prices are reasonable. It's also one of *the* places for coffee and ice cream. Don't bother trekking out here on a Sunday as it's closed then.

Another excellent place, and one you should try at least once, is the *Recoda Restaurant* on Nyeri St in the Old Town. It's a hugely popular place amongst the locals and the tables are set up along the footpath. The atmosphere is great and the waiters are keen to explain what is available that day – usually dishes such as beans in coconut, grilled fish, meat, superb chapatis and salad. You may well find yourself coming back here each night (it's not open at lunch time).

Places to Eat – more expensive

Going up in price, the rooftop restaurant in the *Hotel Splendid* catches the breeze in the evenings and has surprisingly moderate prices (from US$1.40 to US$2 for a main meal), though the food is only mediocre. Don't come here with any ideas of having a quick meal, as the service is far from lightning fast.

The new Hotel Sapphire also has the *Mehfil Restaurant* which serves Mughlai and continental dishes.

The *Pistacchio Ice Cream & Coffee Bar* is a small café near the Hotel Splendid. Not only does it have excellent ice cream, but the fruit shakes are great. The buffet lunch or dinner for US$2.20 is not bad value although the selection is limited. À la carte dishes such as spaghetti are also served. It's open daily from 9 am to 10 pm.

For Chinese tucker you could try the *Chinese Overseas Restaurant* on Moi Ave, just north of the tusks. Main dishes are priced around US$3.40.

The *Fontanella Restaurant* is in a shady courtyard on the corner of Digo Rd and Moi Ave. The extensive menu runs the whole gamut from fish & chips (US$1.40) through steaks (US$2.20) to lobster thermidor (US$8.90). It's great for a minor splurge or just a quiet beer or snack.

For a real splurge, head for *Le Bistro*, on Moi Avenue, close to the tusks. This recently opened restaurant and cocktail bar is owned and run by the same Swiss Germans who own the Pistacchio and it's open daily from breakfast to late at night. Both the atmosphere and the food, which includes pizza, pasta, steak and seafood, are excellent. Expect to pay from US$4.50 to US$5.60 for a full meal and a drink, though there are considerably cheaper meals such as toasted sandwiches from US$1.50, hamburgers from US$1.90 and lunch-time specials.

Those keen to dine in an atmosphere as far removed from Kenya as anyone could imagine, and to choose from a range of dishes named after famous musicians, should try the *Hard Rock Café*, Nkrumah Rd, next door to Kenya Airways. It's all somewhat contrived, but popular with Mombasa yuppies (young, 'upwardly mobile' professionals). Before you go for a meal here you need to be absolutely certain that a constant bombardment of heavy rap music will be conducive to the digestive process. A main course plus a drink will set you back around US$6.

Mombasa's best restaurant by far is the *Capri Restaurant* (☎ 311156), in Ambalal House, Nkrumah Rd, opposite Kenya Airways. French-run with a range of continental and seafood dishes, and a well-stocked cellar of European wines, the food here is superb. Nowhere else compares. It's open daily for lunch and dinner but closed on Sunday and public holidays. Expect to pay around US$11 for a full meal. Attached to this restaurant is the *Hunters Snack Bar* which is a good place for an ice-cold beer in air-con surroundings. Down on the ground floor of the same building is a branch of the restaurant called the *Arcade Café* open from 8.30 am to 5.30 pm which serves coffee, fruit juices, milk shakes, pizza, hot dogs, meat pies, sandwiches and ice cream.

Entertainment

For an ice-cold beer in the heat of the day many people go to the terrace of the *Castle Hotel* which overlooks Moi Ave. It's the nearest thing you'll find to the Thorn Tree Café in Nairobi but the comparison isn't really valid. If you're on a strict budget, don't come here between 11 am and 3 pm as the price of beer is double the usual charge.

If you prefer cheaper beer and a livelier place then go to the *Istanbul Bar* also on Moi Ave, on the opposite side of the road from the Castle Hotel towards the tusks. Though primarily a pick-up joint and delightfully degenerate, it's very popular and attractively set under makuti roofs in the open air. It's undoubtedly one of Mombasa's landmarks with an atmosphere not unlike that of the Modern Green Day & Night Bar in Nairobi. Here you'll find every nutcase in town along with everyone else with a few 'bob' in their pockets to spend on what are remarkably cold beers (given the refrigeration facilities). If you're looking for someone in Mombasa, you'll find them here.

The best night club/disco in town is the *Florida* on Mama Ngina Drive. Built right on the seashore and enclosing its own swimming pool, it's owned by the same people who run the Florida 2000 and New Florida clubs in Nairobi. The atmosphere is much the same but here there are three open-air bars as well as an enclosed dancing area. Entry costs US$1.10 for women and US$2.20 for men (US$1.40/2.70 on Friday and Saturday nights).

Things to Buy

While Mombasa isn't the craft entrepôt you might expect it to be, it's still not too bad. The trouble is that there are a lot of tourists and sailors who pass through this port with lots of dollars to shed in a hurry. Bargains, therefore, can take a long time to negotiate.

The main craft stall area is along Moi Ave from the Castle Hotel down to the roundabout with Nyerere Ave. Many specialist craft shops have sprung up in recent years in the Old Town close to Fort Jesus, especially along Mbarak Hinawy Rd and Ndia Kuu.

Along Moi Ave it's mainly makonde woodcarvings, soapstone chess sets and animal or human figurines, basketwork, drums and other musical instruments, and paintings.

Biashara St, which runs west of the Digo Rd intersection, is the centre for fabrics and *kangas* or *kikoi*, those colourful, beautifully patterned, wraparound skirts complete with Swahili proverbs, which most East African women (who aren't Hindus) wear even if they wear it under a buibui (black wraparound skirt). You may need to bargain a little over the price (but not too much). What you get is generally what you pay for and, as a rule, they cost around US$4.50 a pair (they are not sold singly). Assuming you are willing to bargain, the price you pay for one will reflect the quality of the cloth. Buy them in Mombasa if possible. You can sometimes get them as cheaply in Nairobi but elsewhere prices escalate rapidly.

Getting There & Away

Air Three companies operate flights from Mombasa to Malindi and Lamu. They are Eagle Aviation Ltd (☎ Mombasa 316054/5), Prestige Air Services Ltd (☎ Mombasa 21443), and Skyways Airlines (☎ Mombasa 221964).

Each company has two flights per day in either direction between Mombasa and Malindi and between Mombasa and Lamu. Flights from Mombasa depart at 8.30 am and 2.15 pm and arrive in Malindi 30 minutes later and in Lamu 70 minutes later. The fare to Malindi is US$14.50 one way and US$29 return. Between Mombasa and Lamu the fares are US$68 one way and US$124 return. Children over two years old pay the full fare; those from three to 12 years pay 50%. Check-in time is 30 minutes before departure and the baggage allowance is 10 kg per person. Most of the time you won't be hassled if your baggage weighs over 10 kg but, even if you are, excess charges are minimal (US$0.20 per kg). The airport departure tax is US$1.50 at Malindi and Mombasa but there's no charge at Lamu.

Kenya Airways also flies from Mombasa to Nairobi via Malindi in either direction at least once daily except on Sunday, using F50 propeller planes. If you're relying on these flights to get back to Nairobi to connect with an international flight, then make absolutely sure you have a confirmed booking or, preferably, go back a day before. Don't join the legion of people who are left on the tarmac tearing out their hair because they didn't reconfirm and the flight was full.

Bus & Matatu In Mombasa bus offices are mainly along Jomo Kenyatta Ave. For Nairobi, there are many departures daily in either direction (mostly in the early morning and late evening) by, among others, Coast, Cat, Mawingo, Malaika and Akamba. The fare ranges from US$3.65 to US$4.20 and the trip takes from seven to eight hours including a meal break about halfway.

To Malindi there are also many departures daily in either direction from early morning until late afternoon by several bus companies and matatus. Buses take up to three hours; matatus about two hours. In Mombasa they all depart from outside the New People's Hotel, Abdel Nasser Rd. See the Malindi section for more details, and for the alternative of hiring a share-taxi.

It's possible to go straight through from Mombasa to Lamu but most travellers stop en route at Malindi.

For Tanga and Dar es Salaam in Tanzania, Cat Bus has departures on Monday, Wednesday and Friday at 4 pm. The journey to Tanga takes about eight hours (US$3.20) and all the way to Dar es Salaam about 20 hours (US$8).

For buses and matatus to the south of Mombasa you first need to get off the island via the Likoni ferry (see the later Getting Around section).

Train Trains to or from Nairobi operate in either direction at 5 and 7 pm, arriving at 8 and 8.30 am respectively. The 7 pm train (the so-called 'deluxe service') is the better of the two but costs more. On the 5 pm train you get to see a bit more of the countryside before it gets dark. The fares on the deluxe service are US$40 in 1st class and US$26 in 2nd class, including dinner, breakfast and bedding (whether you want them or not). You should make a reservation as far in advance as possible as demand sometimes exceeds supply. The booking office at the station in Mombasa is open daily from 8 am to noon and 2 to 6.30 pm.

The left-luggage service at the railway station costs KSh 12 per item per day. It's open from 8 am to noon and 2 to 6.30 pm Monday to Saturday, and from 7.30 to 10 am and 2 to 6.30 pm on Sunday.

Boat Depending on the season, it's possible to get a ride on a dhow to Pemba, Zanzibar or Dar es Salaam in Tanzania. Departure times used to be haphazard, and there were periods when foreigners were prohibited from travelling in this manner. However, this has all changed now and there's a standardised procedure you have to go through. First go down to the dhow registrar's office on Government Square in the Old Town (entry to the compound will cost you KSh 5 which is payable at an office on the right-hand side of the entrance gate) and find out when the next dhow is going.

The next step is to write or type a declaration which reads:

I .... (full name) of .... (country) born on .... (birth date) travelling on passport number .... (number) intend to travel by dhow from Mombasa to .... (destination) on .... (date) at my own risk.

In no way shall I hold the boat captain or the Kenyan government responsible for my safety.

.... (name & address)

Take this to be stamped at the district commissioner's office on Treasury Square (just up from the fort on the left-hand side) and then return to the dhow registrar's office. Here you pay KSh 350 (which is your fare

on the dhow), get a receipt and you'll be told which dhow you're going on. Make sure you are well stocked as the trip takes anything up to 36 hours and you get zilch in the way of food or facilities. The toilet is a long-drop perched out over the back of the boat.

If you want something more reliable (but not necessarily frequent), there's now an aircon catamaran, the MV *Flying Horse* which does the run from Mombasa to Zanzibar and Dar es Salaam on a fairly regular basis taking 7½ hours to Zanzibar and 11 hours to Dar es Salaam. It costs US$50 (1st class), US$40 (business class) and US$30 (deck class) one way. For bookings in Mombasa contact Ketty Tours Ltd (☎ 315178), Eagle Travel Ltd (☎ 316416), Noor Travel Ltd (☎ 31-3276) or Friendly Travels Ltd (☎ 312493). In Nairobi contact A H Khimji (☎ 765993).

If you're interested in yachts or boats to India or the Seychelles it's worth getting out to Kilibi Creek. Most of the people with yachts moor at Kilibi Creek because mooring berths at the Mombasa Yacht Club are very expensive. If you want to make enquiries you can get to Kilibi by going to Tom's Beach, about 1½ km out of Mombasa centre, near the Seahorse Hotel.

Getting Around

To/From the Airport Kenya Airways operates a shuttle bus from its Nkrumah Rd office at 10.20 am, and 2.20 and 5.40 pm. There's a regular public bus which goes to the airport and costs a few cents. Any 'Port Reitz' matatu will take you past the airport turn-off (ask to be dropped off) from where it's about a 10-minute walk. The standard taxi fare is US$4.45.

Taxi Mombasa's superbly beaten up old taxis are not metered so make sure you agree on a fare before stepping in.

Car All the major companies and many of the smaller outfits have offices in Mombasa as well as in Nairobi. Details can be found under Rental Agencies in the Getting Around chapter.

The Automobile Association of Kenya or

AAA (☎ 26778) has its office just north of the tourist office on the road which connects Aga Khan Rd with the railway station. It has a few road maps and may be of use if you have specific questions about road or traffic conditions.

Boat The Likoni ferry connects Mombasa Island with the southern mainland and runs at frequent intervals throughout the night and day. There's a crossing every 20 minutes on average between 5 am and 12.30 pm; less frequently between 12.30 and 5 am. It's free to pedestrians; KSh 17 for a car. To get to the ferry from the centre of town take a Likoni matatu from outside the GPO on Digo Rd.

South of Mombasa

The real attractions of the coast south of Mombasa are the beaches, and although it is basically all resort hotels, there are a few options for the budget traveller – at Tiwi and Diani beaches.

All the beaches are white coral sand and are protected by a coral reef so there is no danger from sharks when you go swimming. Tiwi is probably the best beach since it's less developed though, like Shelly, it suffers from large amounts of floating seaweed, depending on the season. Diani doesn't have this to anywhere near the same extent but in some places much of the sand has been washed away leaving just a coral bed.

SHELLY BEACH
Shelly Beach is the closest beach to Mombasa and as such, is not a bad place to swim if you just want to day-trip from Mombasa, though, at times, it's like pea soup because of the seaweed problem. There is no budget accommodation available here so forget it for a long stay unless you have plenty of money.

Places to Stay
The cheapest place to stay, but some distance from the beach, is the *CPK Guest House*

(☎ 451619) not far from the Likoni ferry. It's a pleasant place, and costs US$5.60 per person with breakfast, full board US$9.40.

One of the few places to stay on the beach itself (other than renting a holiday let) is the *Shelly Beach Hotel* (☎ 451001/2), about three km from the Likoni ferry. As far as resort hotels go it's not a bad place, and seems to be popular with British tour groups. Most people seem to prefer swimming in the pool rather than in the sea just a few metres away. Half-board rates are US$21/33 for singles/doubles, or US$27/47 with air-con. In the off season it may be possible to get a reduction on these rates, but don't expect too much.

Further south are *Savannah Cottages* (☎ 23456) which are self-contained, air-con holiday lets with fully equipped kitchens, bathrooms, lounge and dining areas, and double bedrooms with twin-bunk beds.

Getting There & Away
From the Likoni ferry, take the first turn to the left after the bus stand. From here it's a 30-minute walk and there are occasional matatus and enough traffic to make hitching possible. The Shelly Beach Hotel has its own transport into town, but you pay extra for this.

TIWI BEACH
Next along the coast is Tiwi Beach, also about two or three km off the main coast road, along either one of two gravel tracks (only one of which is signposted 'Tiwi') which wind their way through the coastal scrub. This is the best beach to head for if you're on a budget and/or have your own camping gear. It's also the least developed, though there's not much in the way of beachfront which isn't already spoken for. The good thing here is that the hotels are all low key, consist mainly of individual, largely self-contained, cottages with a central bar and restaurant appealing to independent travellers. It's a totally different world from the package tourist ghetto of Diani Beach. The prices also reflect this difference.

The thing which you must do at this beach

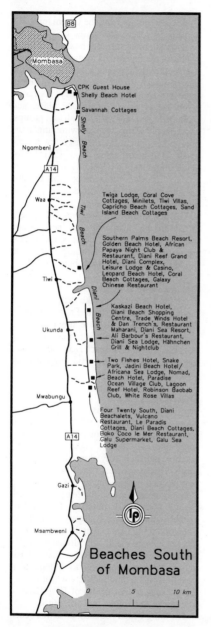

Beaches South of Mombasa

is book in advance if you intend to stay during the high season (January, April to early July, August to early September and Christmas/New Year), otherwise you'll probably find them full. It's essential to book ahead for the self-catering lodges at *any* time of year otherwise you probably won't find anyone around who can deal with you. (If the lodges are full, the owners often head off to Mombasa and the 'managers' are not empowered to rent anything out.)

The last thing you need to know is that you'll have to bring all your own food and drink if you're staying at a self-catering lodge, though you could, of course, arrange to eat at a lodge which has a restaurant and bar.

Coming from the north, the hotels are: Sand Island Beach Cottages, Capricho Beach Cottages, Maweni Beach Cottages, Tiwi Villas, Coral Cove Cottages, Twiga Lodge, Minilets and Tiwi Beachlets. Most of these are signposted on the main road.

Places to Stay & Eat

Cheapest of the lot (but only by a small margin) is the very popular *Twiga Lodge* (☎ (0127) 2457). It is certainly *the* place to camp along the coast as you can pitch your tent just a few metres from the water plus there's plenty of shade. Camping charges are minimal. Single/double rooms go for US$6.70/13 with breakfast plus there are cottages accommodating four people for US$12 (plus US$3.40 for each extra bed if there are more than four people). There's a restaurant, bar and shop. It's a good place to stay as there's usually an interesting mix of people here.

Right next door to the Twiga Lodge are the *Coral Cove Cottages* (☎ (0127) 4164). The cottages here are similar in price to those at Twiga Lodge and range from those with no facilities to others which are fully self-contained (complete with cooking equipment). It's a very pleasant place to stay and popular with young expatriate workers.

South of Twiga Lodge are the *Minilets* (☎ (0127) 2551), a collection of small, self-contained, cliff-top chalets connected to the beach by a series of paved walkways. Singles/doubles cost US$11/15, and there's a bar and restaurant.

Going further north, *Tiwi Villas* (☎ (0127) 2362) is an attractive complex, again on top of a cliff, with a swimming pool, bar and restaurant. A double cottage here costs US$11, one which sleeps four people US$20, and a more spacious triple US$26.

Further up the coast, the *Capricho Beach Cottages* (☎ (0127) 24630) are a collection of self-contained one, two and three-bedroom cottages with lounge/dining room, verandah and a full range of cooking equipment. You must provide your own bed linen and mosquito nets, though these can be hired with advance notice. In the low season the cottages cost US$15 (up to two people), US$25 (up to five people) and US$30 (up to six people), plus 20% tax. Prices are US$17/35/41 in the high season. The complex has its own swimming pool.

Beyond here, the *Sand Island Beach Cottages* (☎ (0127) 2461) is another group of self-catering and self-contained cottages similar to those at Capricho which range in price between US$15 (up to two people) and US$30 (up to six people) in the low season and US$17 to US$41 in the high season plus 20% tax. There are also campers available with outside toilets and showers which sleep two people for US$4 and US$8 in the low season and US$6 and US$11 in the high season plus 20% tax. Bed linen and mosquito nets must be brought with you unless arranged in advance.

Getting There & Away
The buses and matatus drop you at the start of the gravel access road, from where it's a three-km (45-minute) walk. This road is notorious for muggings so, unless you're part of a group (in which case you can assume you're safe), wait for a lift. There are no buses or matatus but quite a few cars so you shouldn't have to wait long.

DIANI BEACH
Diani is a package-tourist hotel/resort complex. If you're an independent traveller looking for a patch of authentic Kenyan coast and a mellow atmosphere, you'll hate it here. The promotional literature looks very alluring and the architecture can be very imaginative but the clientele is dreadful. Lobotomised European wage slaves on day release wouldn't be too far from the truth.

At least, that's the story as far as the tarmac stretches at the back of this beachfront development. Further south, it does change and you get back into something resembling the Kenyan coast before the 'developers' decided to recreate the Costa Lotta. It's in this area that you'll find Dan Trench's, the only budget accommodation on this part of the coast.

As at Tiwi beach, you need to make advance booking for any of the cheaper places at Diani during the high season otherwise you'll find them full, though some sort of accommodation can usually be found at any time at Dan Trench's.

Information
The village of Ukunda on the main Mombasa to Tanzania highway is the turn-off point for Diani Beach. It's here that you'll find the nearest post office plus a number of basic lodging houses. From here a tarmac road runs about two km down to a T-junction with the beach road which runs several km in either direction north and south. Along this beach road is everything which Diani has to offer.

Do not walk along the road from Ukunda to the beach road. It's notorious for muggings. Avoiding walking is no problem as there are plenty of matatus (and KBS buses) running backwards and forwards all day on their way to or from Likoni.

Places to Stay – bottom end
The only cheap place is *Dan Trench's* (PO Box 8, Ukunda), behind the Trade Winds Hotel. It's not signposted, but if you turn off when you see the sign for the Trade Winds, it's on the right before you get to the Trade Winds entrance gate. Dan unfortunately died some time ago but the place has been taken over by Tony Partridge who is doing a lot of

work to improve the facilities. These now include new water tanks, a security wall, laundry service, lighting, and breakfast on request. Camping costs US$1.70 per person per night (no tents for hire) plus there are eight double rooms and one single at US$3.40 per person per night and four self-contained apartments with kitchen, lounge and verandah at US$8.90 per day. It's a mellow place, and there are no security problems. If you're staying here you can use the beach and bar at the Trade Winds Hotel.

Places to Stay – middle

The only places in this category, and even these are not cheap, are the lodges and cottages south of the tarmac on the beach road.

At the southern end, after two km of pot-holed dirt road, is the *Galu Sea Lodge*, a pleasant two-storey building with a swimming pool. Next up, heading north, you come to the *Galu Supermarket* then the *Boko Boko Coco le Mer Restaurant* followed by the *Diani Beach Cottages* (☎ 3348) which cost US$50/69 for singles/doubles with half board. All major credit cards are accepted.

Next up are *Le Paradis Cottages*, the *Vulcano Restaurant* and *Diani Beachalets* (☎ 2180). At the latter, there's a range of self-contained rooms ranging from US$12 to US$14 in the high season (US$7.80/9.10 in the low season) for one bedroom, US$21.35 in the high season (US$14.20 in the low season) for two bedrooms, and US$27 in the high season (US$18 in the low season) for four bedrooms all plus 20% tax.

Further north still, at the beginning of the tarmac, is the popular *Four Twenty South* (☎ 2034). Here there are a number of different cottages which cost between US$17 and US$21 a double in the high season (US$17 and US$13 in the low season) plus US$4 for each extra person. Bookings can be made through Mrs M Martin, PO Box 42, Ukunda, Kenya; Let's Go Travel in Nairobi; or by ringing Nairobi ☎ 744815.

Unless indicated, all the above places to stay are self-catering and kitchen facilities are provided.

Beyond this point you're looking at major expense and the sort of ennui that only major resort complexes can offer.

Places to Stay – top end

The other hotels along this beach cost mega-bucks and are basically for those with money to burn. They range from US$35/45 a single/double to US$44/65 in the low season to *double* and *triple* that in the high season with full board. They all offer much the same – air-con rooms, swimming pool, bars, restaurant, usually a disco, and some have water sports equipment for hire. The better ones (and there are quite a few) have been designed with the environment and local architectural styles in mind; others are not so special.

From north to south along the strip the hotels are:

Southern Palms Beach Resort – US$51/65 a single/double with half board (low season); US$74/93 in the high season (☎ 3721)

Golden Beach Hotel – US$50/100 a single/double with half board (low season); US$105/210 in the high season (☎ 2625)

Diani Reef Grand Hotel – US$72/103 a single/double with half board (low season); US$110/146 in the high season. There are also more expensive deluxe rooms (☎ 2723).

Leisure Lodge & Casino – US$93/121 a single/double with full board (low season); US$136/183 in the high season. There are also more expensive suites (☎ 2011).

Leopard Beach Hotel – US$44/65 with full board (low season); US$104/152 in the high season. There are also more expensive suites and cottages (☎ 2111).

Coral Beach Cottages – US$20/34 for two/three-bedroom cottages (low season) or US$56/66 (high season), but these cottages can only be rented for a minimum period of one year (☎ 2206)

Kaskazi Beach Hotel – US$55/90 for singles/doubles including breakfast (low season); US$125/180 in the high season (☎ 3170)

Trade Winds Hotel – US$42/85 a single/double with full board (low season); US$90/120 (high season)

Diani Sea Resort – under construction.

Diani Sea Lodge – US$74/99 with full board in the high season (☎ 2114)

Two Fishes Hotel – US$47/96 a single/double with full board (low season); US$98/129 in the high season (☎ 2101)

Jadini Beach Hotel/Africana Sea Lodge – US$77/115 a single/double with full board (low season); US$120/185 in the high season (☎ 2726)

Nomad Beach Hotel – US$35/45 a single/double including breakfast (low season); US$100/135 in the high season. This hotel is closed throughout May (☎ 2155).

Safari Beach Hotel – US$85/125 a single/double with full board (low season); US$135/205 in the high season (☎ 2726)

Paradise Ocean Village Club – a private French-owned club not open to the general public

Lagoon Reef Hotel – US$43/72 a single/double with half board (low season); US$76/114 in the high season (☎ 2627)

Robinson Baobab Hotel – US$144/240 a single/double in the high season with full board (☎ 2026)

The Trade Winds Hotel and the Golden Beach Hotel are part of the African Tours & Hotels group. Bookings can be made through them at PO Box 30471, Nairobi (☎ 336858) or at PO Box 90604, Mombasa (☎ 223509).

The Diani Sea Lodge is part of the Welcome Inns Ltd Kenya. Bookings can be made through them at PO Box 86779, Mombasa (☎ 314732).

The Lagoon Reef Hotel is part of the Reef Hotels group. Bookings can be made through PO Box 82234, Mombasa (☎ 47-1771).

The Safari Beach Hotel, Jadini Beach Hotel and the Africana Sea Lodge are all part of the Alliance Hotels group.

Places to Eat

Diani beach is well supplied with shopping centres so you needn't bring everything with you from Ukunda village if you are self-catering, though the fruit and vegetables are naturally more expensive on the beach road than they are in Ukunda.

One of the largest complexes is the *Diani Beach Shopping Centre*, not far from the Trade Winds Hotel/Dan Trench's. It has a supermarket, bank, doctor's surgery, boutiques and a branch of Glory Car Hire. Further north there is *Quinnsworth Supermarket* and, further north again, is *Diani Complex* which has a supermarket, a branch

of the Kenya Commercial Bank, a boutique and an Indian restaurant. Way down south beyond the tarmac and not far from the Galu Sea Lodge, is the *Galu Supermarket* which is OK for basics but carries only a limited range of goods.

If you're staying at the southern end of the beach off the tarmac, there's the *Vulcano Restaurant da Lina* (☎ 2004) which is an excellent place to eat, though a bit of a splurge. It's open every night from 7 pm until late and offers a range of classic Italian dishes as well as seafood (lobster, prawns, crabs, calamari and fish). Table reservations are recommended.

Back on the tarmac about halfway towards the T-junction are a cluster of restaurants and nightclubs. Here you'll find the *Hähnchen Grill & Nightclub* (which, as the name suggests, is a German restaurant), *Temura's Restaurant* and the *Restaurant Maharani*. The latter is an Indian restaurant and is open daily from 7 to 11 pm as well as for lunch on Saturday and Sunday from 12.30 to 3 pm. In the same area but down a track on the opposite side of the road is *Ali Barbour's* which is an expensive seafood restaurant set in a coral cave between the Trade Winds Hotel and the Diani Sea Lodge.

North of the T-junction are the *Galaxy Chinese Restaurant* (next to the Quinnsworth supermarket) and the *Shan-e-Punjab* Indian restaurant in the Diani Complex. Beyond here, not far from the Diani Reef Grand Hotel, is the *African Papaya Nightclub & Restaurant*.

Apart from the above, many of the beach hotels offer buffet lunches and dinners at the weekends which are open for nonguests. Make enquiries as to which currently offer the best deals and/or the best food. Most are priced in the US$10 to US$15 range.

Entertainment

Apart from the discos in the hotels (which you may have difficulty getting into if you're not a guest), there are now four discos independent of the hotels. Because the clientele is more mixed in these discos they're more lively and worth checking out.

Opposite the Two Fishes Hotel is the *Bush Baby Nightclub*, an open-air restaurant and nightclub which is not a bad place for a bop. Not too far from here is the nightclub at the Hähnchen Grill (see Places to Eat). Almost next door to this is the *Shakatak Disco*. It's probably the best of the lot and entry is free but the price of drinks is outrageous (around three times what you would pay in a reasonable bar!).

Lastly, way up near the northern end of the tarmac, is the *African Papaya Nightclub & Restaurant* (see the earlier Places to Eat section).

Getting There & Away

Diani is the most accessible beach if you are dependent on public transport. From the Likoni ferry there are KBS buses (No 32) every 20 minutes or so from early morning until around 7 pm. The fare is minimal and the trip takes about 30 minutes.

Plenty of matatus make the trip from Likoni to Diani. They do the journey slightly faster and cost a little more.

When the buses and matatus get to Diani they first head north along the Diani beach road then turn around and go to the southern end of the bitumen where they turn again and head for Likoni. Just tell the driver where you want to get off.

SOUTH OF DIANI

Going south of Diani, you first come to the village of **Msambweni** where you'll see a sign for a now-defunct hotel (the Black Marlin – which is being redeveloped as a semi-private hotel resort). A little further on is another sign for the *Beachcomber Hotel* alongside a surfboard on the left-hand side. This English-run place set on a cliff above a small cove has to be one of the most mellow places on the coast. Unfortunately, because it has a steady flow of regular clients throughout the year, it's not really open to walk-ins but you could try. It's about five km from the main road past the old Black Marlin.

Continuing on south (70 km from the Likoni ferry) you'll come to **Ramisi** and just

beyond it is a sign (easy to miss) on the left-hand side of the road indicating 'Lazy Lagoon'. This is the turn-off for Tony Duckworth's camp site at **Bodo** which is 2½ km down the gravel road on the right-hand side.

SHIMONI & WASINI ISLAND

Shimoni is right out at the end of a small peninsula 76 km south of Likoni, and not far from the Tanzanian border. There's not a great deal here apart from the Shimoni Reef Lodge, but it's the headquarters of the Kisite National Marine Park.

Wasini Island itself is just off the coast of the Shimoni Peninsula. It's well wooded and unspoilt and is the perfect place to relax and experience a Swahili culture virtually untouched by the 20th century and tourism. There are no cars, roads or running water and the only electricity comes from generators.

On a wander around you can come across Muslim ruins, local women weaving mats, men preparing for fishing by mending nets and making fish traps, huge old baobab trees and the extensive 'coral gardens' with its odd-shaped stands of old coral that you can walk through (except at certain times of year when the sea floods it).

Kisite National Marine Park

To visit this park, which is offshore to the south-east of Wasini Island, you'll need to go by boat. See the park headquarters in Shimoni to make arrangements. Entry to the park costs US$4 for nonresidents and US$0.65 for residents. Boats to take you there cost US$4.90 per person (less than 12 people) or US$1.90 per person (12 or more people). If the sea is rough, the boats don't sail so keep an eye on the weather and tides.

Snorkelling & Diving

In addition to the boats which can be hired from the Kisite park headquarters in Shimoni, Masood Abdullah (who runs the Mpunguti Restaurant on Wasini Island) can arrange trips to the marine park. He has his own dhow as well as masks and snorkels.

There's also another outfit which can

arrange all this for you known as Kisite Dhow Tours (☎ 2331 in Diani) which operates out of Jadini Beach Hotel on Diani Beach. It offers full-day tours from Shimoni jetty for US$49 (US$65 with transport from Diani Beach) which include a morning's dhow tour and snorkelling in Kisite marine park, a traditional seafood lunch and a guided walk through Wasini Island village. With a little effort, you can arrange all this for much less.

Diving safaris off the Pemba channel (spectacular!) and dhow trips to Kisite National Marine Park can also be arranged from the Shimoni Reef Hotel, but are expensive.

The Swahili People

Although the people of the coast do not have a common heritage, they do have a linguistic link – Kiswahili (commonly referred to as Swahili), a Bantu-based language which evolved as a means of communication between Africans and foreign traders such as Arabs, Persians and the Portuguese. As might be expected with such diverse input, the Swahili language borrows words from Arabic, Hindi, Portuguese and even English. The word *swahili* is a derivative of the Arabic word for coast – *sahel*.

Arab traders first started plying the coast in their sailing dhows sometime before the 7th century, arriving with the north-east monsoon and sailing home on the south-west monsoon. The main exports were ivory, tortoiseshell and leopard skins, while items such as glass beads from India and porcelain from as far afield as China found their way here.

After the 7th century Islam became a strong influence as traders began settling along the coast. Today the majority of the coastal people are Muslims, although it's a world away from the puritanical forms of Islam which prevail in some places in the Middle East.

Swahili subgroups include Bajun, Siyu, Pate, Mvita, Fundi, Shela, Ozi, Vumba and Amu (residents of Lamu). ■

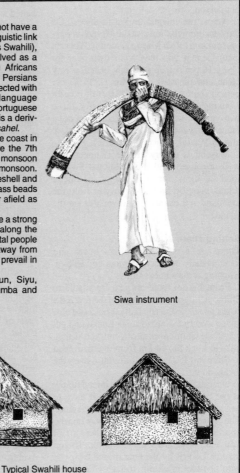

Siwa instrument

Typical Swahili house

Places to Stay & Eat

The only place to stay at Shimoni is the *Shimoni Reef Hotel* (☎ 471771 in Mombasa; 9 in Shimoni), which is beautifully situated on a bluff overlooking the channel to Wasini Island. The facilities are excellent and it's a very mellow place to stay. The price for singles/doubles with half board is US$43/76 in the low season, US$72/114 in the high season. The full-board supplement is US$10 per person.

Across the channel on Wasini Island, the only accommodation is at the *Mpunguti Restaurant*, run by Mr Masood Adullah. You can camp here if you have your own gear for US$1.10 per person per night or rent a very clean and pleasant room for US$6.70 per person (half board) or US$10 (full board). Cooking facilities are available for those who prefer self-catering (fish, coconuts, maize flour and rice are for sale in Shimoni and on Wasini, but very little else).

Masood is a very affable character and well organised, and the traditional Swahili food he turns out is delicious. Alcoholic drinks must be brought with you from the mainland – there are none available on the island.

Getting There & Away

There are a couple of direct buses and matatus daily between Shimoni and Likoni. Hitching is also a possibility.

From Likoni there are taxis available to Shimoni, or you can take one of the few KBS buses which do the trip daily. You could also take a matatu towards Lunga Lunga and get off at the Shimoni turn-off, but you'd then have to hitch the 14 km from the main road to Shimoni. It's not that difficult – even the locals do it.

Once at Shimoni (unless you intend to stay at the Shimoni Reef Hotel) you'll have to negotiate a dhow ride across the channel. The price for this depends to a degree on who you meet on arrival, how many there are of you and how affluent you look. If you assume US$18 for the boat (round trip) you won't be too far wrong, though you can get it cheaper.

The same people who run the dhows will also take you to the reefs for snorkelling for much the same price but you'll have to negotiate a price for the hire of snorkelling gear.

SHIMBA HILLS NATIONAL RESERVE

This national reserve is in the hills behind the coast south of Mombasa, directly inland from Diani Beach. The forest setting is beautiful but the game is not prolific. There is a baited water hole at the Shimba Hills Lodge, and so it's possible you'll see leopards and plenty of elephants but not much else. Other animals which frequent the reserve include the rare sable antelope – a tall and compact animal with beautifully curved horns on both the male and female. The adult bull is a dark brown on the upper body and white below, while the female is a lighter brown. The animals are, unfortunately, often killed by poachers for meat, and this is the only reserve where they are found.

Places to Stay

The camp site has a superb location on the edge of the range with views right down to Diani Beach. It's about three km from the main gate, which itself is about three km from the village of Kwale.

The only alternative to camping is Block Hotels' *Shimba Hills Lodge* (☎ 335807 in Nairobi) where singles/doubles with half board cost US$97/124 in the low season (1 April to 30 June) and US$162/206 in the high season. There is an additional supplement of US$19 per person at Christmas and Easter. Note that children under seven years old are not admitted to this lodge. The water hole here is baited to attract a few animals and is floodlit at night.

Getting There & Away

There are KBS buses to Kwale, from where it shouldn't be too difficult to hitch to the park entrance. Once there, however, you may have a long wait for a vehicle back. The road from Kwale to Kinango, the next inland town, actually passes through the northern part of the park and there's a chance of seeing animals from the KBS buses. The No 34 bus runs from Likoni to Kwale.

North of Mombasa

MOMBASA TO KILIFI

Like the coast south of Mombasa, the north coast has been well developed almost two-thirds of the way up to Kilifi with resort complexes which take up much of the beach frontage. Most of them cater to package tourists on two to three-week holidays from Europe but there is scope for individual initiative here and there, though only the Jauss Farm at Vipingo and the 'youth hostel' at Kimabala genuinely fall into the budget accommodation bracket.

As with Shelly and much of Tiwi beaches south of Mombasa, the northern beaches are plagued with seaweed which clogs them and makes swimming an often unpleasant experience. Only at the expensive resort hotels are people employed to minimise this inconvenience by raking it into piles and either burning it or burying it. Elsewhere you literally have to jump into the soup.

Going north from Mombasa the names of the beaches are Nyali, Bamburi, Shanzu, Kikambala and Vipingo.

Mamba Crocodile Village

Mamba Village (☎ (011) 472709) is north of Mombasa on the mainland opposite Nyali Golf Club in the Nyali Estate. It's a crocodile farm set amongst streams, waterfalls and wooden bridges. If you've never seen a crocodile farm with reptiles ranging from the newly born to the full grown, here's your chance. Personally, I've seen a lot of these farms in the past and I don't find them very interesting. They're often just a collection of concrete and wire-mesh cages with thousands of young crocodiles up to five years old, and a few token, fully grown adults to pull in the punters. You pay through the nose to see them, too, even though the owners of the farms are making megabucks selling skins to Gucci and the like.

Bamburi Quarry Nature Trail

Further up the coast, this nature trail (☎ (011) 485729) has been created on reclaimed and reforested areas damaged by cement production activities which ceased in 1971. Once the forest was established, the area was restocked with plants and animals in an attempt to create a mini replica of the wildlife parks of Kenya. At present, animal species represented include eland, oryx, waterbuck, buffaloes, wart hogs, bush pigs, various monkeys and many different varieties of birds. There's also what the owners claim to be an 'orphan' hippo which was introduced as a baby from Naivasha and which has remained bottle-fed ever since. A likely story!

The complex also includes a fish farm, crocodile farm, reptile pit and plant nursery. The centre is open daily from 2 to 5.30 pm. Feeding time is at 4 pm. To get there take a public bus to Bamburi Quarry Nature Trail stop (signposted) on the main Mombasa to Malindi road.

Places to Stay – bottom end

There are very few cheap places to stay on the beaches north of Mombasa. Even places way back from the beach with nothing special going for them can be remarkably expensive.

One of the few genuine cheapies is the *Kanamai Conference Centre* (☎ (0125) 32046) at Kikambala Beach which was previously a youth hostel but is no longer affiliated to the IYHF. Dormitory beds are US$3.90 in either two, six or 10-bed rooms, while self-contained one-bedroom cottages are US$16, two-bedroom US$31, and three-bedroom US$48. Meals are available for US$2.50 for breakfast, US$3.50 for lunch and US$3.90 for dinner – expensive for what is basically ugali and chicken stew. There's also a laundry service.

The trouble with this place is getting there! First you have to take a matatu to Majengo on the Mombasa to Kilifi road (from near the New People's Hotel in Mombasa). Get off when you see a yellow sign saying 'Camping Kanamai'. Go down

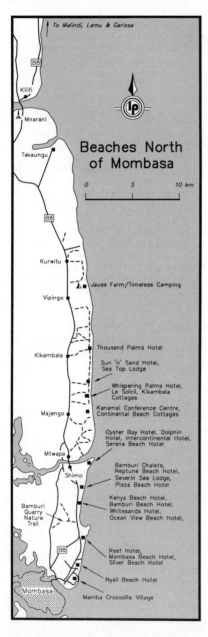

To Malindi, Lamu & Garissa

B8

Kilifi

Mnarani

**Beaches North
of Mombasa**

Takaungu

0   5   10 km

B8

Kurwitu

Jauss Farm/Timeless Camping

Vipingo

Thousand Palms Hotel

Kikambala

Sun 'n' Sand Hotel,
Sea Top Lodge

Whispering Palms Hotel,
Le Solcil, Kikambala
Cottages

Kanamai Conference Centre,
Continental Beach Cottages

Majengo

Oyster Bay Hotel, Dolphin
Hotel, Intercontinental Hotel,
Serena Beach Hotel

Mtwapa

Shimo

Bamburi Chalets,
Neptune Beach Hotel,
Severin Sea Lodge,
Plaza Beach Hotel

Kenya Beach Hotel,
Bamburi Beach Hotel,
Whitesands Hotel,
Ocean View Beach Hotel,

Bamburi
Quarry
Nature
Trail

B8

Reef Hotel,
Mombasa Beach Hotel,
Silver Beach Hotel

Nyali Beach Hotel

Mombasa

Mamba Crocodile Village

the dirt track by this sign for about 300 metres and then turn left at the fork. Continue for about three km and you'll find it on the left-hand side by the beach. It's a long, hot walk and lifts are few and far between. With a backpack it's a major effort.

Close by, a little further to the north along the track which runs parallel to the beach, are the *Continental Beach Cottages* (☎ (0125) 32077) which are good value at US$19.50 per person in the high season (US$21 with breakfast), dropping to US$14 in the low season. Accommodation is in one and two-bedroom self-contained cottages each with lounge, kitchen, bathroom and air-con. It's rarely full and there's a good swimming pool, bar and restaurant and a pleasant beach. Cheap meals (omelette & chips and curries) are available for around US$3. As with the Conference Centre, the only problem about this place is getting there; taxis are expensive.

Right next door to the Continental is *Kikambala Cottages* (☎ (0125) 32032), a very basic place with no pool or restaurant. However, the self-contained cottages are comfortable enough, and cheap at US$35 with two bedrooms, lounge, and kitchen with fridge. You need to be fairly self-sufficient here as there are no shops or cheap restaurants nearby.

If you're staying at either of the above places and want a change of scene or a cold beer, the Whispering Palms Hotel is about 15 minutes' walk north along the beach. Breakfasts here cost US$5.80 and you can use the swimming pool for US$3.90 per day.

A little further north, just behind the Sun 'n' Sand Hotel and about three km off the main coast road, is the *Sea Top Lodge* (☎ (0125) 32184), a small hotel which seems to be a bar first and a hotel second. The cost is US$9.70 for a small but clean double room. There are a few small dukas nearby and the beach is a short walk away. With a little discretion you could probably use the facilities at the Sun 'n' Sand.

Further up the coast at Vipingo, about 40 km north of Mombasa, there is *Timeless Camping* (☎ (0125) 32218) on the Jauss

Top: Mosque, Lamu (GP)
Bottom Left: Palace ruins, Gedi (TW)
Bottom Right: Lamu market (TW)

Dhows

Dhows have been sailing along the coast of East Africa for centuries and, until fairly recently, were the principal trading vessels used between the eastern coast of the continent and the Persian Gulf and India. They once numbered in the thousands but, since the turn of the century, they have declined rapidly in the face of competition from steamships. These days only a few make the journey to the Gulf. Those that remain confine themselves to sailing between the mainland and the offshore islands and between the islands themselves, and even then only in certain areas. Their romantic appeal, nevertheless, remains and a dhow trip around the Lamu archipelago is an extremely popular activity amongst travellers.

Essentially, all dhows are wooden vessels, either planked or dug out, along with a rudder, mast and lateen (triangular) sail. Like all sail boats unless motorised, they're completely dependent on the wind but, unlike boats with only square sails, they're capable of tacking into the wind.

Dhows are differentiated by size and shape. The largest are known as *jahazi*, which are planked, ocean-going vessels with broad hulls and ruggedly designed to be capable of withstanding constant bumping along rocky shores and submerged coral reefs. They can have either one or two lateen sails. Most have woven coconut fibre matting fixed to their sides to reduce splash and a wooden 'eye' attached to each side of the bow below a decorated or carved tailboard. Dhows of this type built in the Lamu archipelago often have a perpendicular bow whereas those from Zanzibar have sloping bows. A jahazi often has a toilet hanging off the stern of the boat.

Motorised versions of the jahazi are known as *mtaboti* or *mchaboti*. The only difference is that these have an inboard motor instead of a sail.

Smaller craft go under the generic name of *mashua* and there are many different types. Around Lamu they're usually known as *kijahazi*. These dhows differ from the jahazi in being smaller, much narrower in the hull and having only one sail. They can be remarkably fast given a favourable wind and are the ones you're most likely to utilise for trips around Lamu.

Another common type of dhow, smaller still, is the *dau la mwao* – a sort of dugout canoe with a narrow hull, small mast and no keel which sits low in the water and is frequently used for transporting soil, sand and coral-rag building blocks. Most do not have a square stern. A variation of this type from the Kizingitini area is the *mtori* which is somewhat smaller and faster and fitted with a keel. Decoration on the mwao and the mtori is restrained. It's interesting to note that the mwao is the nearest surviving relative to the *dau la utango* which was the most common type of dhow found along the coast during the 19th century.

There are excellent models of the various types of dhow in the Lamu Museum. ■

Dhows (TW)

family farm. It consists of a camp site, budget chalets, and two self-contained bungalows on an 85-hectare dairy and tropical-fruit farm with its own quiet and unspoilt silver-sand beach. The camp site is equipped with showers and toilets and costs US$1.95 per person per night. The budget chalets are fairly basic twin rooms with clean beds and mattresses, and toilets and showers have to be shared with those occupying the camp site. The cost for these is US$5.90 per person. The bungalows are fully equipped and cost US$58 for the four-bed one, and US$78 for the large bungalow which sleeps 10 people. Excellent and filling meals are available, no matter which accommodation you are using, and these are very good value at US$2.30 for a half breakfast, US$4.50 with the works, and US$6.10 for lunch or dinner. The bar has the coldest beers on the coast, and there's a well-stocked library. This very laid-back place has a wonderfully informal atmosphere and is the perfect place to drop out for a few days – or weeks. If arriving by public transport, get off at Vipingo village and ring from there; someone will come and collect you. If you have your own transport, take the signposted turn-off to Timeless Camping, on the main road 1.6 km north of Vipingo.

Places to Stay – top end

Virtually all the other hotels along this stretch of the East African coast before you arrive at Kilifi are resort complexes and cater largely for package tourists from Europe. Most of them are so self-contained that many of those staying there hardly ever see anything of Africa other than Mombasa airport, the inside of minibuses, the hotel itself and Black Kenyan waiters. As at the hotels south of Mombasa and at Malindi, many cater almost exclusively for one specific European nationality whether they be British, German or Italian (French people don't feature prominently in East African tourism). There's precious little intermingling.

All the hotels compete furiously with each other to provide the utmost in creature comforts, mellow surroundings, day trips and

sports facilities and there's little to choose between them though it's generally true to say that the further you get from Mombasa, the cheaper and less ritzy they become.

Down at Nyali Beach – the closest to Mombasa – even places which don't face the sea and are in no way hotel resorts, and which you might imagine should be fairly cheap given the facilities they offer, can be surprisingly expensive. *Bamburi Chalets* (☎ (011) 485706), for example, which offers self-contained cottages with two bunk beds, two normal beds, shower, cooking facilities, gas stove, refrigerator, and use of a swimming pool cost US$78 per night or US$117 with sea views. The *Cowrie Shell Apartments* (☎ (011) 485971) all have two bedrooms and face the sea, and cost US$58 to US$117 depending on the season. The *Baharini Chalets* (☎ (011) 486302) have only one bedroom and are much cheaper at US$23, but are not great value as there are no cooking facilities.

It's unlikely that if you intend to stay at any of the genuine resort complexes that you'll be reading this book since you'd have reserved your hotel via an agent and your air fares would be included in a package deal. Should you wish to make your own arrangements for staying at any of the resort complexes, however, here's a selection of the hotels.

Nyali Beach The following resorts are at Nyali Beach:

Mombasa Beach Hotel – singles/doubles cost US$114/151 with breakfast (☎ (011) 471861)
Nyali Beach Hotel – US$159/190 with breakfast, US$137/229 with half board, US$195/263 with full board (☎ (011) 471551)
Reef Hotel – singles/doubles for US$99/148 with half board (☎ (011) 471771)

Kenyatta-Bamburi Beach Further north are the following hotels:

Bamburi Beach Hotel – singles/doubles with breakfast cost US$35/46 (low season), US$58/73 (high season); add US$6 for full board (☎ (011) 485611)

Neptune Beach Hotel – US$39/55 with breakfast (low season), US$55/74 (mid-season) and US$105/144 (high season); children aged from three to 12 years pay 50% (☎ (011) 485701)

Ocean View Beach Hotel – US$70/109 with half board (☎ (011) 485601)

Plaza Beach Hotel – US$62/70 with breakfast (low season), US$195/211 with full board in the high season (☎ (011) 485321)

Severin Sea Lodge – US$39/78 for singles/doubles with breakfast (low season), US$94/129 (mid-season) and US$97/136 (high season); children pay 50% (☎ (011) 485001)

Whitesands Hotel – US$55/109 for singles/doubles with half board (low season), US$234/434 for a one-bedroom/two-bedroom apartment (high season). Children pay 75% of the full price and meals cost US$9 for breakfast, US$14 for lunch and US$16 for dinner (☎ (011) 485926).

Shanzu Beach At Shanzu Beach are the following resorts:

Dolphin Hotel – US$58/104 for singles/doubles with full board (☎ (011) 485801)

Intercontinental Hotel – singles/doubles with breakfast cost US$118/150 (low season), US$138/175 (mid-season), and US$152/191 in the high season (☎ (011) 485811)

Oyster Bay Hotel – singles/doubles with breakfast cost US$27/55 (low season), US$35/70 (mid-season), US$39/78 (high season) (☎ (011) 485061)

Serena Beach Hotel – singles/doubles cost US$45/91 with breakfast (low season), US$91/117 (mid-season), US$117/156 (high season). Other meals cost US$12, and children aged three to 12 years pay 50% (☎ (011) 485721).

Kikambala Beach Finally, Kikambala Beach offers the following:

Whispering Palms Hotel – singles/doubles with full board cost US$94/122 (low season), and US$120/165 in the high season (☎ (0125) 32004)

Sun 'n' Sand Beach Hotel – singles/doubles with half board cost US$52/104 in the low season, and US$110/130 in the high season; children are charged 50% of the adult rate (☎ (0125) 32133)

Takaungu Right up at the top end of this long line of beaches close to Kilifi is the village of Takaungu. It's supposedly the oldest slave port on the Kenyan coast – Zanzibar is the oldest. It's worth a visit if you have the time. The local people are very superstitious and no-one goes down to the beach at night except the fishers. If you can speak Swahili you'll hear many weird stories going around which date back to the time of slavery. It's an interesting place right off the beaten track where you won't meet any other travellers.

Rooms can be rented in private houses in Takaungu for around US$2.60 per night. Ask at the teashops.

For those with slightly less limited resources there's *Takaungu House* (☎ (02) 502491), a luxury house privately owned and run. There are just three bedrooms, but other features include a swimming pool, beach frontage, snorkelling, water-skiing and deep-sea fishing on request. The charge for full board is US$116 per person.

KILIFI

Other than Mtwapa Creek, just north of Mombasa, Kilifi is the first major break in the coastline between Mombasa and Malindi. It has been a backwater for many years, ignored by developers yet coveted by discerning White Kenyans, artists, writers and adventurers from various parts of the world who have gradually bought up most of the land overlooking the wide creek and the ocean and built, in many cases, some quite stunning and imaginative houses. They form a sort of society within a society and keep largely to themselves. Without an introduction, it's unlikely you'll meet them though sailing a yacht into the creek would probably secure you an invitation! Kilifi Creek is a popular anchorage spot for yachties in this part of the world and you can meet them in the evening at the Seahorse Hotel off to the left of the main road on the northern side of the creek.

So why stop off in Kilifi? The answer to this is mainly for the contrast it offers to Mombasa and Malindi, and for the Mnarani ruins on a bluff overlooking the creek on the Mombasa side. Very few travellers ever see these ruins yet they're well preserved and just as interesting as those at Gedi though not as extensive. The beach, too, on either side of the creek is very pleasant and doesn't

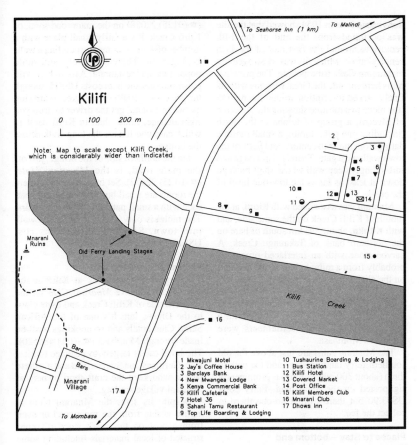

Kilifi

0   100   200 m

Note: Map to scale except Kilifi Creek, which is considerably wider than indicated

To Seahorse Inn (1 km)

To Malindi

Mnarani Ruins

Old Ferry Landing Stages

Kilifi Creek

Bars

Bars

Mnarani Village

To Mombasa

1 Mkwajuni Motel	10 Tushaurine Boarding & Lodging
2 Jay's Coffee House	11 Bus Station
3 Barclays Bank	12 Kilifi Hotel
4 New Mwangea Lodge	13 Covered Market
5 Kenya Commercial Bank	14 Post Office
6 Kilifi Cafeteria	15 Kilifi Members Club
7 Hotel 36	16 Mnarani Club
8 Sahani Tamu Restaurant	17 Dhows Inn
9 Top Life Boarding & Lodging	

suffer from the seaweed problem which plagues the beaches further south. The only problem is access, which is mostly through private property, though you can walk along it from the ferry landing at low tide.

The present district centre of Kilifi is on the northern bank of the creek.

Information

Kilifi consists of the small village of Mnarani (or Manarani) on the southern bank of the creek and Kilifi itself on the northern bank. It's a small town which you can walk around within minutes.

There's a good variety of shops (including a small bookshop), a lively open-air market and an enclosed fruit and vegetable market, a post office, a number of basic hotels and two banks. Barclays Bank is open Monday to Friday from 8.30 am to 1 pm and on Saturday from 8.30 to 11 am. The Kenya Commercial Bank keeps the same hours.

Mnarani Ruins

Mnarani, on the southern bank of Kilifi Creek overlooking the ferry landing, was once one of the string of Swahili city-states which dotted the East African coast. Excavations carried out in 1954 showed that the site was occupied from the end of the 14th century to around the first half of the 17th century after which it was destroyed by marauding Galla tribespeople. The principal ruins here include the Great Mosque with its finely carved inscription around the mihrab (the niche in a mosque showing the direction of Mecca), a group of tombs to the north (including one pillar tomb), a small mosque dating from the 16th century, and parts of the town wall and a gate. There's also a large and forbiddingly deep well whose shaft must go down at least as far as the low-tide level of the creek.

Mnarani was associated with **Kioni**, at the mouth of Kilifi Creek on the same side, and with **Kitoka**, about 3½ km south of here on the northern bank of Takaungu Creek. A carved stone with an interlaced ornament, probably from a mihrab, was found at Kioni on the cliff above the creek and is presently in the Fort Jesus museum at Mombasa. The ruins at Kitoka include a mosque similar to the small mosque at Mnarani along with a few houses. All these settlements were subject to Mombasa.

The Mnarani ruins are just above the old southern ferry landing stage and the path to them (about 300 metres long) is prominently signposted on the main road. Entry costs US$3.90 but there's often no-one there to collect the fee.

Places to Stay – bottom end

There are a number of cheap places to stay in Kilifi including the *Top Life Boarding & Lodging* (hardboard cubicles), the *Kilifi Hotel*, the *Hotel 36* and the *New Mwangea Lodge* but probably the best place to stay is the *Tushaurine Boarding & Lodging* (☎ (0125) 22486) near the bus station. This is a recently constructed hotel, several storeys high, which offers good, clean, simple rooms with mosquito nets and shared bathroom facilities for US$3.90/5.80 a single/double.

Places to Stay – middle

The best place in this range is the *Dhows Inn*

(☎ (0125) 22028) on the main road south of Kilifi Creek. It's a fairly small place with a number of double rooms surrounding a well-kept garden. There's a lively and quite popular bar and restaurant. A room here with mosquito nets and bath costs US$15, though the price is negotiable to a degree. If arriving by bus or matatu, get the driver to drop you right outside, rather than in Kilifi itself in which case you'll have the long walk across the bridge.

On the northern side of the bridge, just off the main road, is the *Mkwajuni Motel* (☎ (0125) 22472). Set in a spacious garden, the rooms are small but very clean and neat, each with a small patio and table and chairs. The motel is only about 10 minutes' walk into town. Single/double rooms cost US$12/16 including breakfast.

Places to Stay – top end

The large resort complex at Kilifi is the somewhat exclusive *Mnarani Club* on the southern side of Kilifi Creek and quite close to the Dhows Inn. It's one of the African Safari Club hotels and so bookings must be made through Mombasa (☎ (011) 485520). The hotel caters largely to package tourists from Germany and Switzerland and it's these people who keep the craft-shop owners of Mnarani village smiling.

Despite its size, the Mnarani Club is hardly visible from the main road or even from a boat on the creek since it's constructed of local materials (including some enormous makuti roofs) and surrounded by beautifully landscaped gardens full of flowering trees.

The other top-range hotel is the *Seahorse Inn* (☎ (0125) 22813), about 1½ km off to the left of the main Mombasa to Malindi road on the northern side of the creek. It's a very pleasant place with individual bandas set in a coconut grove right on the banks of Kilifi Creek, which at this point is a couple of km wide. To stay here will set you back US$51/78 for full board. Like the Mnarani Club, the Seahorse is run by the African Safari Club, so the same applies with bookings.

Places to Eat

A cheap and very popular place to eat both for lunch and dinner is the *Kilifi Hotel* at the bus station. Standard Indo-African fare is on offer, and you can eat well here for around US$2.60. Another popular place, especially at lunch time, is the *Kilifi Cafeteria* though prices here are somewhat higher.

Across on the southern side of the creek, you can eat at the *Dhows Inn* which has a limited menu of meat and seafood dishes. The only trouble with eating here is that food takes forever to arrive and the quality is variable: sometimes it's good, sometimes it's almost inedible. The average price of a main course is around US$3.

For a splurge, go for a meal at the *Mnarani Club* or the *Seahorse Hotel*. At both places you can partake in the buffet lunch spread for US$6.50, which is excellent value. In the evenings à la carte meals are available for the same price.

Even more up-market is the very agreeable *Sahani Tamu Restaurant* on the northern side of the creek, opposite the Mnarani Club. The food here is mainly Italian and seafood and is very well prepared and presented. Main dishes such as spaghetti are in the US$3 to US$4 range, steaks are around US$6, and seafood dishes from US$9 to US$15. It's well worth the expense and makes a very pleasant evening out. The restaurant is open daily, except Tuesday, from 11 am to 2 pm and 6 to 10 pm.

Entertainment

For a spit-and-sawdust evening on Tusker or White Cap you can't beat the bars in Mnarani village of which there are several, but the amount of action depends largely on how many tourists brave the 200 metres or so of dirt road between the Mnarani Club and the village. Don't expect cold beers at any of these bars.

The bar at the *Dhows Inn* on the other hand is usually pretty lively and you can be assured of cold beer.

The *Mnarani Club* has a nightly floor show – usually of tribal dancing – followed by a live African band which plays until late.

Entry to the show and dance costs US$3.90. Nonguests can rent windsurfing equipment from this hotel during the day for US$3.90 per hour.

For a far more informal evening pay a visit to the *Kilifi Members Club* on the northern side of the creek.

Getting There & Away

All the buses and matatus which ply between Mombasa and Malindi stop at Kilifi but getting on a bus at Kilifi to go to either Mombasa or Malindi can be problematical since they're often full. Matatus are a much better bet.

WATAMU

About 24 km south of Malindi, Watamu is a smaller beach resort development with its own marine national park – part of the Marine National Reserve which stretches south from Malindi. The coral reef here is even more spectacular than at Malindi since it has been much less exploited and poached by shell hunters. In addition, underwater visibility is not affected by silt brought down into the sea by the Galana River.

The coast at Watamu is broken up into three separate coves divided by craggy and eroded headlands and there are a number of similarly eroded islands just offshore. The coral sand is a dazzling white and although there is some shade from coconut palms, you'll probably have to retreat to the cooler confines of a hotel bar or restaurant in the middle of the day. The most southerly cove is fronted entirely by beach resorts and exclusive private houses. The central cove also has many resorts, though they are not as extensive. The northern cove and part of the headland is covered by the rambling Watamu Beach Hotel at the back of which is the actual village of Watamu.

Before tourist development got underway here, Watamu was a mellow little fishing village of makuti-roofed cottages nestled beneath coconut palms and it still retains much of that atmosphere despite the intrusion of souvenir shops, bars and restaurants catering for the tourist hordes. In fact the contrasts are quite bizarre – it's the only place I've seen package tourists in beach wear wandering down the dusty streets of an African village! A lot of development has taken place on the outskirts of the village and seems destined to continue.

Information
There is a branch of Barclays Bank in the village of Watamu which is open from 9 am to noon on Monday, Wednesday and Friday.

Watamu National Marine Park
The actual coral reef lies between one and two km offshore and to get to it you'll have to hire a glass-bottomed boat. These can be arranged at any of the large hotels or, alternatively, ask at any of the souvenir stalls that line the main road in Watamu. Expect to pay US$15.60 per person. It's worth every cent!

There are also boat trips to a group of **caves** at the entrance to **Mida Creek** which are home to a school of giant rock cod many of which are up to two metres long. Diving equipment is usually necessary to get down to their level since, most of the time, they remain stationary on the bottom.

Places to Stay – bottom end
Budget accommodation has always been something of a problem in Watamu. There are a couple of cheap lodges in the village but they can't seriously be recommended. The *Blue Lodge* charges US$5.90 for a scruffy, stuffy and gloomy double room illuminated by only the feeblest of globes – only for the desperate. The other alternative, *Sam's Lodge*, is no better, though it is marginally cheaper at US$4.60 for a double. Neither place has fans or mosquito nets – which are absolutely essential on the coast.

Another possibility in the village is a private house known as the *Maasai House*. It has one double room for US$9, and another self-contained room for US$9.80. There's a kitchen, big verandah, a garden with a well, and a housekeeper who will cook meals at a reasonable charge. It's a good place to meet the Samburu performers from the Watamu Beach Hotel.

Of the regular lodges, the best value is the family-run *Villa Veronica/Mwikali Lodge* (☎ (0122) 32083), opposite the Hotel Dante Bar & Restaurant. This is a very friendly and secure place which offers spotlessly clean rooms with fan, mosquito nets, shower and toilet for US$16/19 a single/double including breakfast.

The *Hotel Dante* itself is about the cheapest habitable place, and self-contained doubles (no singles) go for US$14. The price does not include breakfast, but there is a small swimming pool.

The only other place that fits this price bracket is *Watamu Cottages* (☎ (0122) 32211), on the main access road to the village and about 15 minutes' hot walk. These are a good deal at US$15 for a self-contained double including breakfast. The rooms are set in a pleasant garden which also has a swimming pool.

It may occasionally be possible to get a cheap room at the *Seventh Day Adventist Youth Camp* if there's no group there but don't count on it. You can also camp here if you have your own tent. The facilities are minimal though there is a gas cooker which you can use.

Places to Stay – middle
Peponi Cottages (☎ (0122) 32246) consists of a two-storey, makuti-roofed block of rooms which are quite pleasant, if a little small. Each has mosquito netting on the windows, and a balcony runs the length of the building. There's also a small pool. A double costs US$19, which does not include breakfast.

On the main road leaving the village is the *Watamu Paradise Restaurant & Cottages* (☎ (0122) 32062) which has a number of cottages each containing three double bedrooms with fan, mosquito nets and bathroom. A double here costs from US$19 to US$28, depending on the facilities. It's a very pleasant place to stay and there's a swimming pool in the complex.

Places to Stay – top end
Top-end hotels take up much of the beach

1   Watamu Beach Hotel
2   Sam's Lodge
3   Blue Lodge
4   Bank
5   Bicycle Hire
6   Peponi Cottages
7   Watamu Paradise Restaurant
    & Cottages
8   Come Back Club Tim's Restaurant
9   Villa Veronica
10 Barclays Bank
11 Hotel Dante Bar & Restaurant
12 Happy Night Bar & Restaurant
13 Barracuda Inn
14 Seventh Day Adventist Youth Camp
15 Watamu Cottages
16 Blue Bay Village
17 Ocean Sports Hotel
18 Hemingways Hotel
19 Turtle Bay Beach Hotel

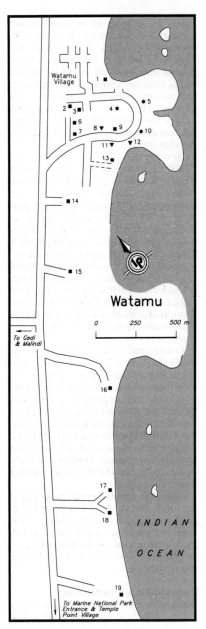

frontage along each of the three coves. As at Malindi, they're mostly resort-type hotels which cater to package tourists' every need and are quite specific as to the European nationality which they appeal to – German, British or Italian.

At the northern end and next to Watamu village is the rambling *Watamu Beach Hotel* (☎ (0122) 32001), where most of the German tourists stay. It's one of the many hotels operated by the African Safari Club, a German-based organisation, and casual bookings are not encouraged – they don't even know at the reception desk what the tariff is! If you want to stay, bookings can be made at the African Safari Club office in Mombasa (☎ (011) 485520). Room rates start at US$70/90 for full board. The hotel has a swimming pool, and with a little discretion nonguests can use it.

At the northern end of the central cove is the *Barracuda Inn* (☎ (0122) 617074). This is another foreign-owned place and bookings can only be made in Italy! They will let you stay if there's a vacancy, but expect to pay at least US$47 for a double. It has a very pleasant makuti-roofed bar and restaurant area, while the air-con cottages are set back from the beach.

The southern cove sports at least five

hotels, all of them of the resort variety. Closest to Watamu village is the *Blue Bay Village* (☎ (0122) 323626), which caters mostly to Italians. Full-board singles/doubles vary from US$78/140 for standard rooms in the low season to US$94/168 in the high season, including all taxes and service charges. There are also more expensive deluxe rooms and suites. Children aged between three and 12 years are charged half the adult rate.

Next along is *Ocean Sports* (☎ (0122) 320008), where the clientele is mainly British. It's much smaller than the other places and the facilities are fairly modest. It does, however, have excellent diving equipment and for US$19 will take experienced divers out for a dive on the reef. Singles/doubles cost US$104/136 for half board in the high season; low-season rates are less.

Hemingways, right next to Ocean Sports, is a much bigger place. The rates here start at US$53/70 for half board in the low season and go up to US$139/186 in the high season. There is also an off-season special deal of US$294/387 for seven days including half board.

At the far end of the cove is the *Turtle Bay Beach Hotel* (☎ (0122) 32622) which caters to a mixture of nationalities – mainly British and German. Like the Watamu Beach Hotel, it's a huge, rambling place with all the usual facilities and water-sports equipment. Prices vary according to the standard of the rooms. Full board in a twin room costs US$58/74 a single/double. For a room with an ocean view the cost rises to US$66/90, while new air-con rooms cost US$86/113, all with full board.

Right at the entrance to the marine park is the lavish *Temple Point Village* (☎ (0122) 32057) which caters to young Italians. This is another brand new place complete with soaring makuti roofs; to stay here you'll have to part with US$113/164 for full-board accommodation.

Places to Eat & Entertainment
Budget eating facilities are at a premium in Watamu though it is possible to get simple meals at one or other of the local bars in the village – the *Ujamaa Restaurant*, attached to the bar of the same name, is one possibility. *Friend's Corner* is a small duka on the road between the Come Back Club and Villa Veronica. It has about the best cheap food in town, although the variety is limited.

The *Hotel Dante* is probably the best of the non-resort restaurants. The service is slow but there's warm beer and a juke box to distract you while you're waiting. Almost opposite is *Come Back Club Tim's Restaurant*, but the food is not up to much and it's hard to think of a good reason to come back, except perhaps to dance in the disco which operates some nights.

The *Happy Night Bar & Restaurant* has ice-cold beers and European-style food, all at Kenyan (rather than lodge) prices, but its opening hours are erratic. It sometimes has live music or disco nights.

For a splurge, the lunch-time buffet meals at the *Watamu Beach Hotel* are a real bargain. For US$6.50 you can dip into the buffet as many times as you like, and the range of dishes is very good. This is one of the few places on the coast where outside guests are openly welcome to use the restaurant – even if they do greet you with 'Guten tag'!

Getting There & Away
Matatus leave from the bus station in Malindi throughout the day. They cost US$0.50 to Watamu and take about 30 minutes. Most of these first go down to the Turtle Bay Beach Hotel after which they turn around and go to Watamu village. On the return journey they generally go direct from Watamu village to Malindi without first going down to the Turtle Bay Beach Hotel.

Getting Around
Bicycles can be hired for US$0.50 per hour or US$2 per day from a place next door to the Nyambene Lodge in Watamu village.

GEDI
Some three to four km from Watamu, just off the main Malindi to Mombasa road, are the famous Gedi ruins, one of the principal his-

torical monuments on the coast. Though the ruins are extensive, this Arab-Swahili town is something of a mystery since it's not mentioned in any of the Portuguese or Arab chronicles of the time.

Excavations, which have uncovered such things as Ming Chinese porcelain and glass and glazed earthenware from Persia, have indicated the 13th century as the time of its foundation, but it was inexplicably abandoned in the 17th or 18th century, possibly because the sea receded and left the town high and dry, or because of marauding Galla tribespeople from the north. The forest took over and the site was not rediscovered until the 1920s. Even if you have only a passing interest in archaeology it's worth a visit.

Entry costs US$3.90 (US$0.75 for students and children) and the site is open daily from 7 am to 6 pm. A good guidebook with map is for sale at the entrance.

The site is surprisingly large and surrounded by two walls, the inner one of which was possibly built to enclose a smaller area after the city was temporarily abandoned in the 15th to 16th centuries. In places it actually incorporates earlier houses into its structure. The site is lush and green with numerous baobab trees. Monkeys chatter in the tree tops, lizards rustle in the undergrowth and large, colourful butterflies flutter among the ruins.

The buildings were constructed of coral rag, coral lime and earth and some have pictures incised into the plaster finish of their walls, though many of these have deteriorated in recent years. The toilet facilities in the houses are particularly impressive, generally in a double-cubicle style with a squat toilet in one and a wash stand in the other where a bowl would have been used. Fancier versions even have double washbasins with a bidet between them.

The other notable feature of the site is the great number of wells, many them remarkably deep.

Most of the interesting excavated buildings are concentrated in a dense cluster near the entrance gate. There are several others scattered around the site within the inner wall

and even between the inner and outer walls. Outside the site, by the car park, there's a small museum with some items found on the site. Other items are exhibited in Fort Jesus in Mombasa.

The Tombs

On your right as you enter the site is the Dated Tomb, so-called because the Muslim date corresponding to 1399 has been deciphered. This tomb has provided a reference point for dating other buildings within the complex. Next to it is the Tomb of the Fluted Pillar which is characteristic of such pillar designs found up and down the East African coast. There's another good example of this kind of pillar in Lamu.

The Great Mosque

The Great Mosque originally dates from the mid-15th century but was rebuilt a century later, possibly as a result of damage sustained at the time of Gedi's first abandonment. The mosque is of typical East African design with a mihrab facing towards Mecca. You can see where porcelain bowls were once mounted in the walls flanking the mihrab.

The Palace

Behind the mosque are the ruins of the extensive palace which is entered through an arched door. Once through the doorway, you enter a reception court and then a large audience hall while to the left of this are numerous smaller rooms. Look for the many 'bathrooms' and the room flanking the audience hall with its square niches in the walls intended for lamps. Behind that room is another one with no doorway at all which would probably have been used to store valuables. Entry was by ladder through a small hatch high up in the wall. Beyond this is a kitchen area with a small but still very deep well.

The Palace also has a particularly fine pillar tomb, while to the right is the Annexe with four individual apartments, each with its own courtyard.

The Houses
In all, 14 houses have been excavated at Gedi, 10 of which are in a compact group beside the Great Mosque and the Palace. They're named after particular features of their design or after objects found in them by archaeologists. They include the House of the Cowrie, House of the Cistern and House of the Porcelain Bowl.

Other Buildings
Follow the signposted path from the Tomb of the Fluted Pillar to the adjoining House of the Dhow and House of the Double Court with a nearby tomb. There are pictures in the wall plaster in these houses.

A path follows close to the inner city wall from the houses to the Mosque of the Three Aisles where you will also find the largest well in Gedi. Beside it is the inner wall of the East Gate from where a path leads to the Mosque Between the Walls; a path cuts back to the car park from here.

Alternatively, from the East Gate you can follow another path right around the inner circuit of the inner wall or divert to the Mosque on the Wall at the southern extremity of the outer wall. The House on the West Wall actually comprises several adjoining houses of typical design while at the northern end of the town there is the more complex North Gate.

Just outside the North Gate is a 'traditional' **Giriama tribal village**, and here the package tourists are entertained with 'traditional' Giriama dances. Unfortunately it's *very* contrived and the dancing girls' costumes look something like a cross between a Hawaiian skirt and a tennis outfit!

Getting There & Away
Take the same matatu as you would to go to Watamu but get off at Gedi village where the matatu turns off from the main Malindi to Mombasa road. From there it's about a one-km signposted walk to the ruins along a gravel road.

It's also possible to get a taxi to take you on a round trip from Malindi for about US$19 with an hour or more to look around

the site. This could be worth it if your time is limited and there's a small group to share costs.

MALINDI
Malindi was an important Swahili settlement as far back as the 14th century and often rivalled Mombasa and Paté for control of this part of the East African coast. It was also one of the very few places where the early Portuguese mariners found a sympathetic welcome, and today you can still see the cross which Vasco da Gama erected as a navigational aid.

These days, on account of its beaches, it has experienced a tourist boom similar to that north and south of Mombasa, and resort hotels are strung out all the way along the coast. On the other hand, it still retains a recognisable African centre where commerce, business and everyday activities, which aren't necessarily connected with the tourist trade, continue. Cotton growing and processing, sisal production and fishing are still major income earners. It isn't, however, a Lamu or Zanzibar. The streets here are relatively wide and straight and there are few buildings more than a century old.

It's a popular port of call for travellers heading north from Mombasa although the beach here is nothing special and is often choked with seaweed – as are many of the beaches along the coast. The only drawback to Malindi is the brown silt which flows down the Galana River at the northern end of the bay during the rainy season which makes the sea very muddy. For the rest of the year it's perfect and even during the rainy season you can largely avoid the muddy waters by going to the beaches south of town.

Information
Tourist Office There is a tourist office next door to Kenya Airways opposite the shopping centre on the Lamu road. The staff are helpful but have little useful information.

Money Barclays Bank is open Monday to Friday from 8.30 am to 1 pm and 2.30 to 5 pm and on Saturday from 8.30 am to noon.

In the low season it's often closed on Saturdays. The Standard Chartered Bank has much the same hours.

Post & Telecommunications The post office is open for international telephone calls from 7 am to 7 pm Monday to Friday and 8 am to 2.30 pm on Saturdays. There is also a cardphone here but, as usual, the supply of cards is erratic.

Immigration There is an office next to the Juma Mosque and pillar tombs on the waterfront (see street map for location).

Warning Don't walk back to your hotel along the beach at night. In past years many people have been mugged at knife-point, although these days the beach appears to be safer. Go back along the main road (which has street lighting) or take a taxi. You also need to exercise caution if returning to the youth hostel late at night.

Town Buildings
Malindi has a pedigree going back to the 12th century and was one of the ports visited by the Chinese junks of Cheng Ho between 1417 and 1419, before the Chinese emperor prohibited further overseas voyages. It was one of the few places on the coast to offer a friendly welcome to the early Portuguese mariners and to this day the pillar erected by Vasco da Gama as a navigational aid still stands on the promontory at the southern end of the bay. The cross which surmounts this pillar is of Lisbon stone (and therefore original) but the supporting pillar is of local coral.

There's also the partial remains of a Portuguese church, which is undoubtedly the one which St Francis Xavier visited on his way to India. A painting of the crucifixion is still faintly visible. Not far to the north are a number of pillar tombs and the remains of a mosque and a palace. Other than this, however, little remains of the old town. The nearest substantial ruins from pre-Portuguese days are at Gedi, south of Malindi.

Malindi National Marine Park
The most popular excursion from Malindi is to the Malindi National Marine Park to the south of town past Silver Sands. Here you can rent a glass-bottomed boat to take you out to the coral reef. Masks and snorkels are provided though they're usually pretty well used and the quality is not what it might be. Fins can be rented for US$1.60 from the kiosk on the beach inside the marine park gate.

The variety and colours of the coral and the fish are simply amazing and you'll be surprised how close you can get to the fish without alarming them. On the other hand, the area is getting a little overused and there's been quite a lot of damage to the coral. Shell collectors have also degraded the area. During the rainy season visibility is severely reduced by the silt in the water which gets washed in from the Galana River.

You can arrange these trips in Malindi – people come around the hotels to ask if you are interested in going. The usual price is US$18 per person which includes a taxi to take you to and from your hotel, hire of the boat and the park entry fee. You may be able to get it for less if you bargain hard but you won't be able to knock too much off this price. The marine park is open daily from 7 am to 7 pm, but the boats only go out at low tide.

Snake Park
Yes, Malindi has the inevitable snake park. It's behind the Sabaki shopping centre on the Lamu road and is open from 9 am to 5 pm daily. Entry is US$4.50 for adults and US$2.35 for children.

Falconry
The falconry has a number of caged birds of prey, as well as a huge tortoise which roams the grounds, and a chimp on a rope – fine if you like that sort of thing. The opening hours and entry fees are the same as for the snake park.

Scuba Diving
If you'd like to go scuba diving you can do

■ PLACES TO STAY

1   Sultan Cottages
2   Eddie's
3   African Pearl Hotel
4   Malindi Cottages
5   Eden Roc Hotel
6   Lutheran Guest House
11 African Dream Cottages
16 Glory Guest House
18 Blue Marlin Hotel, Europcar,
    Eagle Aviation
23 Fondo Wehu Guest House
27 Lawford's Hotel
28 New Lamu Lodge
29 New Safari Hotel & Garissa
    Express Bus
30 Wananchi Day & Night Club
31 Salama Lodge
32 Tana Hotel
36 Ozi's Guest House
37 Metro Hotel, I Love Pizza Restaurant
    & Malindi Fishing Club
39 Travellers' Inn
40 Da Gama's Bed & Breakfast
    & Baobab Café
44 Scorpio Villas
45 Youth Hostel
46 El Pescatori Restaurant &
    Sailfish Club
47 Silver Sands Camp Site
48 Driftwood Club
49 Coconut Village
50 Tropical Village

▼ PLACES TO EAT

2   Eddie's Restaurant
12 Malindi Fruit Juice Garden
13 Hermann's Beer Garden,
    Putipu Restaurant & Stardust Club

14 Trattoria Restaurant
19 Slot Machines Bar & Restaurant
22 Palm Garden Restaurant
24 Urafiki Bar
34 Bahari Restaurant
37 I Love Pizza Restaurant, Metro Hotel
    & Malindi Fishing Club
40 Baobab Café &
    Da Gama's Bed & Breakfast
42 Travellers' Café
46 El Pescatori Restaurant &
    Sailfish Club

OTHER

7   Falconry
8   Snake Park
9   Sabaki Shopping Centre
10 Casino
13 Stardust Club, Hermann's Beer
    Garden & Putipu Restaurant
15 Tourist Office & Kenya Airways
17 Barclays Bank & Avis
18 Europcar, Eagle Aviation &
    Blue Marlin Hotel
20 Glory Car Hire
21 Police
25 Post Office
26 Standard Chartered Bank &
    Prestige Air Services
29 Garissa Express Bus &
    New Safari Hotel
33 Malindi & Tana River Bus Offices
35 Souvenir Market Stalls
37 Malindi Fishing Club, Metro Hotel &
    I Love Pizza Restaurant
38 Matatu Stand, Bus Stand &
    Vegetable Market
41 Vasco da Gama's Pillar
43 Portuguese Church

this from the Driftwood Club at the Silver Sands resort. A dive costs US$39 plus the park entry fee (US$7.15). There is also a diving school here for those who wish to learn, but it's not cheap at US$455 for a course.

Deep-Sea Fishing
Kenya is famous for the game-fishing opportunities off the coast. The Malindi Fishing Club can organise trips at a cost of US$468 per boat for four people including all equipment. Most of the resort hotels can also arrange these trips.

Places to Stay – bottom end
There are a number of cheap, basic lodges in the centre of town, but they're usually fairly noisy at night and you don't get the benefit of sea breezes or instant access to the beach. Most travellers prefer to stay in one of the hotels closer to the beach, although it is not

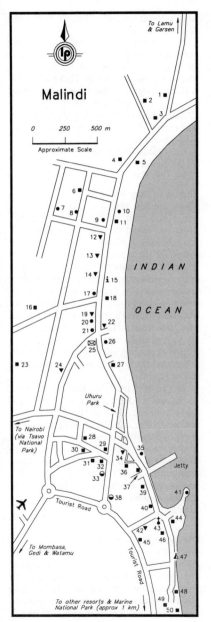

Malindi

0   250   500 m

Approximate Scale

To Lamu
& Garsen

INDIAN

OCEAN

Uhuru
Park

To Nairobi
(via Tsavo
National
Park)

Jetty

Tourist Road

To Mombasa,
Gedi & Watamu

Tourist Road

To other resorts & Marine
National Park (approx 1 km)

really a swimming beach in the town – you have to go a couple of km south before the beaches improve.

By far the best place is the *Fondo Wehu Guest House* (☎ (0123) 30017) in the western part of town. It's about 10 minutes' walk from the bus station, and you may need to ask directions as it can be a little hard to find the first time. It's run by an English-woman and her Kenyan husband and is a very popular place to stay. Dorm beds in the airy upstairs dorm cost US$3.90, and comfortable single/double rooms cost US$10/14. The price includes an excellent breakfast and free laundry service. Tasty snacks are also available.

Next best is probably *Ozi's Guest House* (☎ (0123) 20318) on the foreshore road. It's kept spotlessly clean, and safe lockers are available for US$0.40 per day. The rooms, all with fans and mosquito nets, cost US$7.80/15 with breakfast in the low season, up to US$12/23 in the high season. Bathrooms and toilets are shared between four rooms. The only problem here is that rooms on one side face the mosque, while those on the other side overlook the Malindi Bus depot – either way you'll be woken early.

Another popular place is the *Silver Sands Camp Site* (☎ (0123) 20412), two km south of town along the coast road. It costs US$1.95 per person to camp here (less in the low season) and there are good toilets, salt-water showers, and freshwater taps but very little shade.

There are also three types of banda for rent. The so-called *Mzuri Huts* are self-contained and cost US$12 for a double. The *White Huts* have two single beds, mosquito nets, screened windows, electric lights and lockable doors but shared showers and toilets for US$7.80 a double. The *Green Huts*, of which there are three, are actually tents under a makuti roof and cost US$6.50 a double. They have mosquito nets, private bathroom facilities and electric lights. There is no single-occupancy tariff, and prices are negotiable if you plan to stay for a while.

Bicycles can be rented for US$3.10 per

day or US$0.60 by the hour. The main drawback here is that there is nowhere to eat or buy provisions, although at the time of writing it seemed a shop/café was under construction which may now be open.

If you are happy with dormitory accommodation, the very friendly *Malindi Youth Hostel* is not a bad choice. It's a fairly relaxed place and there are no silly restrictions – dorms are only segregated if you request it, alcohol is permitted and there is no curfew. The dorms hold four to five people, and the cost of a bed is US$3.10. The kitchen is reasonably well equipped and there's access to a fridge and washing facilities. The hostel is in the southern part of the town, about 10 minutes' walk from the bus and matatu stands.

Also popular in the past has been the *Travellers' Inn*, on the beachfront road just south of the main part of town. It's hard to see the attraction of this place as the rooms are basic and somewhat gloomy, but it is kept immaculately clean and the owner is very friendly. Rooms cost US$9.70 for a double including breakfast, and there's no single tariff.

Da Gamas Bed & Breakfast (☎ (0123) 30295) is a new place just south of the Travellers' Inn. It has received favourable reports from a number of travellers, and the owner, James, is friendly and helpful. The cost of rooms varies from US$7.80/15 to US$12/23 depending on the season.

Also cheap is the *Lutheran Guest House* (☎ (0123) 21098) at the opposite end of town off the Lamu road. This is excellent value and very popular. The rooms are set around a quiet courtyard – very reminiscent of an Indonesian *losmen* – and are clean and well maintained. The cost is a very reasonable US$12 for a double with breakfast (US$16 with private bath). Once again there is no reduction for single occupancy.

Further north again is *Eddie's* (☎ (0123) 20283) which is basically a restaurant with a pool, but there are a few very pleasant rooms. These are all self-contained and have a small patio with table and chairs. It's excellent value at US$13 per person with breakfast,

although you are quite a distance from town if you are on foot.

If you want to stay in the noisy town centre there are several places where you can get a double room for around US$5.20 with shared bathroom facilities. They include the *Salama Lodge* and the *New Lamu Lodge*. Also here is the *Tana Hotel* (☎ (0123) 20234) which is very clean and comfortable and costs US$5.90/7.80 for singles/doubles with shared bath or US$12 for a self-contained double. The rooms are all at the back of the building and so are fairly quiet.

Places to Stay – middle
There are few places to stay in this price range and their tariffs vary considerably from one month to another. *Malindi Cottages/Robinson Island* (☎ (0123) 20304) is out on the Lamu road, close to the Eden Roc Hotel, and consists of several fully furnished, self-contained cottages surrounding a swimming pool. Each cottage has two bedrooms, a sitting room, kitchen and verandah. Facilities include a refrigerator, gas cooker, mosquito nets and fans. Each cottage sleeps up to five adults and costs from US$32 to US$47 depending on the season. It's a pretty rough-and-ready place much in need of a major facelift.

Just beyond the Eden Roc Hotel on the Lamu road are *Sea View Cottages* (☎ (0123) 20439) which consists of a number of round, makuti-roofed cottages divided in half to form two double rooms each with its own shower and toilet. The prices here are US$35/43 with breakfast in the low season, rising to US$51/70 in the high season. It's another place which is in need of renovation but it is reasonably close to the centre of the action.

Places to Stay – top end
Malindi's top-range hotels are strung out along the beachfront both north and south of the town centre and more are being built each year. Some are very imaginatively designed and consist of clusters of makuti-roofed cottages in beautifully landscaped gardens full

of flowering trees. Others are fairly standard beach hotels. All of them have swimming pools and other sporting facilities and many have a discotheque. They cater mostly, but not exclusively, to package tourists from Europe on two to three-week holidays and they all seem to pitch their business at a specific nationality – British, German or Italian. Very little intermingling seems to take place and you can definitely feel you've come to the wrong spot in some hotels if you don't belong to the dominant nationality. It's a common trait with package tourism anywhere in the world.

Most of the hotels impose a supplement over the Christmas and New Year periods which can be quite considerable (US$19, for example), so bear this in mind if you intend to stay at this time of the year.

If being by the beach is important, it's also worth bearing in mind that the hotels north of town do not have a beach frontage as there is a wide swathe of sand dunes here; those to the south of town don't have this problem.

Right in the town itself are *Lawford's Hotel* and the *Blue Marlin Hotel*, which are managed by the same people (☎ (0123) 20440). Lawford's is the cheaper of the two and in the low season it offers bungalows at the rear for US$47/62, bungalows with a sea view for US$52/70 and air-con rooms with a view for US$55/74, all with half board. In the high season the rates jump to US$55/70, US$66/82 and US$70/86 respectively.

The Blue Marlin offers a somewhat higher class of accommodation with superb facilities and costs US$61/82 for singles/doubles in the low season and US$78/94 in the high season. All prices are for half board and include taxes.

North of town on the Lamu road is the *Eden Roc Hotel* (☎ (0123) 20480), one of the few hotels which seems to have a mixed clientele. It's also one of the few places with tennis courts, though these are not open to nonguests. The hotel is one of the older resorts in Malindi, and certainly not much imagination has gone into its design. The rates are US$45 per person in a bungalow, US$52 per person in a deluxe double, and

US$58 per person for a deluxe suite. All prices include breakfast and taxes.

South of town, the top-range hotels stretch all the way from the path leading to the Vasco da Gama monument down to Casuarina Beach and the Malindi National Marine Park.

First is the *Sailfish Club* (☎ (0123) 20-016), which is a very intimate hotel with only 10 rooms, all of them self-contained and air-con. It's essentially for those interested in big-game fishing and caters largely for private prebooked groups. The cost is US$43 per person including breakfast.

Almost opposite is *Scorpio Villas* (☎ (0123) 20194) which has 17 cottages spread over some 1½ hectares of beautiful tropical gardens, with three swimming pools and just 50 metres from Silver Sands Beach. All the cottages are fully furnished in Lamu style and come complete with your own cook/house steward. There's an excellent restaurant and bar within the complex. It's Italian-owned and Italians form the bulk of the clientele. Full-board charges are US$117/169 to US$156/208 depending on the season.

Further down the beach beyond the Silver Sands Camp Site is the *Driftwood Club* (☎ (0123) 20155). This was one of the first beach resorts to be built at Malindi and it's different from the other hotels as it's used more by individual travellers rather than package groups. Although it gets more of a mixture of nationalities, the clientele is mainly British and White Kenyan. The club offers a variety of rooms from US$23/32 to US$52/68 depending on the season and facilities. The cheaper rooms have shared bathrooms while the more expensive are self-contained and have air-con. All prices include breakfast and taxes. The bar, restaurant and other facilities are open to nonguests on payment of a temporary membership fee of US$1.55 per day, so there's often an interesting mix of budget travellers hanging out by the pool.

Next down the beach is *Coconut Village* (☎ (0123) 20928), where the clientele is mainly Italian. Double rooms with full board cost between US$74/97 and US$136/156 depending on the time of year (and there are no less than six 'seasons'!). Children under two years old are free of charge and those under 12 years old pay 50% of the above rates. All prices include taxes and service charges. The hotel has a popular open-air, makuti-roofed discotheque which overlooks the beach.

Next door is the *Tropical Village* (☎ (0123) 20256) where, again, the clientele is mainly Italian. Rooms cost US$51/66 including breakfast and US$65/94 for full board. This is one of the most imaginatively conceived places with two huge soaring makuti-roofed areas for the bar and restaurant.

Further south is the *African Dream Village* (☎ (0123) 20119) which is owned by the same people who run the African Dream Cottages on the Lamu road. Unlike the cottages, this is a fully fledged beach resort which has double rooms with shower, toilet, verandah, air-con and telephone, and a range of facilities including a swimming pool, sports centre, bars and restaurant. Full-board rates are US$140/203 while singles/doubles with breakfast cost US$117/156. Meals taken separately are charged at the rate of US$16 for lunch and US$19 for dinner.

Next is the *Silver Sands Villas* (☎ (0123) 20842) which consists of a main building with single and double rooms and a number of two and four-person self-contained villas. Rooms with half board range from US$53/74 to US$84/125, while four-bed villas cost from US163 to US$263 and six-bed villas from US$248 to US$387. All prices include taxes and service charges.

The *White Elephant* (☎ (0123) 20223), further down the beach, has two-storey apartment-type accommodation set in a lush garden complete with swimming pool and games room. The charges range from US$110/169 to US$175/299 for full board depending on the season. There's a temporary membership charge of US$7.80 for nonguests to use the facilities.

Further still are two more resorts – the *Jambo Club* and *Kivolini Hotel*.

Places to Eat – cheap
There's not a lot of choice in this range. The *Travellers' Cafe* in the shopping complex near the Portuguese Church has been popular for years and is a convenient place if you're staying at the youth hostel. It offers Western and African-style meals for between US$2.30 and US$5.20.

Other cheap meals can be found in the restaurants at the hotels in the centre of town. The fare is standard Indo-African. The *Bahari Restaurant* offers much the same sort of thing plus seafood and very good milk shakes. The *New Safari Hotel* is a very popular place with the locals at lunch time. Also worth visiting for its excellent milk shakes and fruit juices is the *Malindi Fruit Juice Garden* on the Lamu road near the casino.

Slightly more expensive but excellent value is the *Palm Garden* on Lamu road opposite the petrol station. Food here is very tasty, and the place is usually packed with escapees from the resorts. The menu is mainly seafoods and curries. The front part of the restaurant serves snacks and light meals, while the makuti-roofed back section (entered from the side street) does full meals. Meals in the snack area include burgers & chips for US$2.70, weiner schnitzel (US$5.50), steaks (US$4.80) and curries (US$2.90).

Ozi's Guest House is also worth checking out for reasonably priced curries (around US$3) though they do have more expensive seafood dishes such as prawns and lobster.

Places to Eat – more expensive
For a splurge, it's worth trying the *Driftwood Club* where you have to pay US$1.55 for temporary membership. This entitles you to the use of the swimming pool, hot showers, bar and restaurant. The prices are very reasonable – lunch for US$7.50, dinner for US$10, good snacks (such as smoked sailfish and prawn sandwiches) from US$1.95, and à la carte seafood main dishes for US$3.30 to US$6.50. It's especially convenient if you are staying at the Silver Sands Camp Site.

I Love Pizza in front of the fishing jetty and close to the Metro Hotel is a popular place for a splurge. As you might expect, it serves Italian food (pizza and pasta for around US$6) and also more expensive meals such as chicken casserole and seafood dishes from US$7.80. It's open from noon to midnight daily. Further south towards the Driftwood Club is the open-air *El Pescatori* restaurant, which is open in the evenings and serves up-market seafood meals.

In the northern part of town near the disco and casino are a couple of places which also cater largely to the resort crowds. At *Hermann's Beer Garden* you can eat German and other continental dishes for US$7.80 and up. It's hardly the place for a quiet meal as the music is always loud. Right next door at the Stardust Club is the open-air *Putipu Restaurant,* where the emphasis is on Italian food. Main dishes are in the US$6 to US$12 range, while pizzas cost US$7.80.

Further north, just off the Lamu road is *Eddie's,* which is probably one of the best seafood restaurants in Malindi as well as having a tastefully intimate atmosphere. It's open from 12 to 2.30 pm and 7.30 to 10.30 pm and there's a swimming pool which you can cool off in before eating your meal. Expect to pay US$4.50 for fish dishes and up to US$16 for lobster.

For superb gelati ice cream, the *Gelateria Bar* in the Sabaki shopping centre has a range of flavours, but it's not cheap. There's a similar place in the courtyard of this complex.

Entertainment

Because Malindi is a holiday resort there are a number bars and discos to visit in the evening, some of which rock away until dawn. The most famous of them is the *Stardust Club* which generally doesn't get started until late (10 or 11 pm) and costs US$3.90 entry (US$7.80 on Saturday night).

There's also a disco at least once a week – usually on Wednesday – at *Coconut Village* past the Driftwood Club and, if you get there early enough, you won't have to pay the entry charge. It's a pleasant place to dance away the evening and you won't drown in perspiration as it's open-air under makuti roofs right on the beach. The bar is incredible and is worth a visit just to see it. It's built around a living tree with one of the branches as the bar top!

Another place which is worth checking out if you want to catch a film is the *Malindi Fishing Club,* right next to the Metro Hotel. It's a very attractive, traditionally constructed building with a makuti roof. There's a bar and snacks are available. The clientele, mainly British, are friendly, although some of the videos they show are decidedly daggy and there's a membership charge of US$0.75.

The liveliest tourist bar is the makuti-roofed *Hermann's Beer Garden,* where the music is loud, the lighting subdued and the girls ever present. One of the liveliest African bars is the *Urafiki Bar & Restaurant* with its deafening jukebox that seems to be playing nonstop. It closes by 11.30 pm and the beers are often lukewarm but, somehow, you don't miss the Arctic fetish for ice-cold beers.

The *Malindi Golf & Country Club,* a couple of km north of town, is open to all comers on payment of a temporary membership fee. Apart from golf, there is tennis, a bar/restaurant, and a library.

Malindi's newest drawcard is the *Casino* on the Lamu road. It has all the usual international games and you can bet as little as US$0.75 on most games. If you happen to be around at midnight, free spaghetti is served! It's open daily from noon until 5 am.

Things to Buy

There's a collection of at least 30 craft shops (tin shacks) on the beachfront near the mosque. Prices are reasonable, though you must, of course, bargain, and the quality is also reasonable. Crafts on offer include makonde carvings, wooden animal carvings, soapstone and wooden chess sets, basketware and the like. If you have unwanted or excess gear (T-shirts, jeans, cameras) you can often do a part-exchange deal with these people.

Getting There & Away

Air Three companies operate flights to Malindi from Mombasa and Lamu. They are Eagle Aviation Ltd (☎ Malindi (0123) 21258, Mombasa (011) 316054, Lamu (0121) 3119), Prestige Air Services Ltd (☎ Malindi (0123) 20860, Mombasa (011) 21443, Lamu (0121) 3055), and Skyways Airlines (☎ Malindi (0123) 20951, Mombasa (011) 221964, Lamu (0121) 3226).

All the above companies have their offices on the Lamu road in Malindi, and all have two flights per day in either direction between Mombasa and Malindi and between Lamu and Malindi. Flights from Mombasa depart at 8.30 am and 2.15 pm and arrive in Malindi 30 minutes later. From Lamu they depart at 10 am and 4 pm and arrive in Malindi 40 minutes later. The fare from Lamu to Malindi is US$49 one way and US$83 return. Children over two years old pay full fare. Check-in time is 30 minutes before departure and the baggage allowance is 10 kg per person. Most of time you won't be hassled if your baggage is over 10 kg but, even if you are, excess charges are minimal. The airport departure tax is US$1.50 at Malindi and Mombasa but there's no charge at Lamu.

Air Kenya Aviation (☎ Mombasa (011) 433982) also operates between Malindi and Mombasa with one flight per day four times a week. The fare is US$56.

Kenya Airways (☎ (0123) 20237) also flies from Nairobi to Mombasa via Malindi in either direction twice daily. If you're relying on these flights to get back to Mombasa or Nairobi to connect with an international flight then make absolutely sure you have a confirmed booking or, preferably, go back a day before.

Bus & Matatu Three bus companies operate between Mombasa, Malindi and Lamu on a daily basis. They are Malindi Bus service, Tana River Bus Service and Garissa Express

and they all have offices in Mombasa, Malindi and Lamu. There are several departures daily in either direction between Mombasa and Malindi which take about 2½ hours and cost US$1.50. There are also matatus which do this run taking about two hours and costing US$3. There's no need to book in advance from Mombasa if you turn up early enough in the morning. In Mombasa the buses leave from outside the New People's Hotel early in the morning. Matatus leave from the same place all day until late afternoon and go when full.

Both the buses and matatus *fly* up and down this coast road as though they were being pursued by a marauding army of shifta (bandits) in high-speed Land Cruisers, and they pack in as many punters as they possibly can. I counted 138 people on one such bus and that didn't include the driver and his mate!
Geoff Crowther

Buses from Lamu to Malindi leave from the mainland between 7 and 7.30 am. The fare from Lamu to Malindi is US$4.50 and the journey takes about five hours. You must book in advance for this journey as there's a heavy demand for tickets.

Tana River Buses also have direct buses to Nairobi at 7 am and 7 pm (around US$7, eight hours), and to Hola at 9.30 am (US$4, six hours).

Garissa Express buses for Garissa leave from outside the New Safari Hotel at 11.30 am daily. The trip costs US$5.75 and as there's no advance booking you need to turn up at 11 am to grab a seat when the bus pulls in.

Share-Taxi It's also possible to find Peugeot 504 station wagons which do the journey between Mombasa and Malindi. They leave when full (seven passengers) and cost US$3 per person. You'll find them at the bus station in Malindi but only in the mornings. Commissioning a normal taxi to take you between Mombasa and Malindi will obviously cost you far more.

Train You can make advance reservations for Kenyan Railways at most of the large hotels in Malindi and at travel agencies, but you'll be charged US$2.60 for the service. All they do for this is make a telephone call to Mombasa railway station. You can do it yourself (☎ (011) 312221) for a fraction of the cost. See the Mombasa Getting There & Away section for information on train fares and timetables.

Getting Around

Glory Car Hire (☎ (0123) 20065), Hertz (☎ (0123) 20069), Avis, and Europcar all have offices on the main street near the Blue Marlin Hotel.

You can rent bicycles from the Silver Sands Camp Site or from Ozi's Guest House. This is probably the best way to get around town unless you prefer to walk.

Lamu

In the early 1970s Lamu acquired a reputation as the Kathmandu of Africa – a place of fantasy and other-worldliness wrapped in a cloak of medieval romance. It drew all self-respecting seekers of the miraculous, the globetrotters, and that much maligned bunch of people called hippies. The attraction was obvious. Both Kathmandu and Lamu were remote, unique and fascinating self-contained societies which had somehow escaped the depredations of the 20th century with their culture, their centuries-old way of life and their architecture intact.

Though Kathmandu is now overrun with well-heeled tourists and the hippies have retired to their rural communes or into business as purveyors of the world's handicrafts, Lamu remains much the same as it has always been – to a degree.

With an almost exclusively Muslim population, it is Kenya's oldest living town and has changed little in appearance or character over the centuries. Access is still by diesel-powered launch from the mainland (though there's an airstrip on Manda Island) and the only motor-powered vehicle on the island is that owned by the district commissioner. The

streets are far too narrow and winding to accommodate anything other than pedestrians or donkeys. Men still wear the full length white robes known as *khanzus* and the *kofia* caps, and women cover themselves with the black wraparound buibui as they do in other Islamic cultures, although here it's a liberalised version which often hugs their bodies, falls short of the ankles and dispenses completely with the dehumanising veil in front of the face.

There are probably more dhows to be seen here than anywhere else along the East African coast and local festivals still take place with complete disregard for camera-toting tourists. The beach at Shela is still magnificent and uncluttered and nothing happens in a hurry. It's one of the most relaxing places you'll ever have the pleasure to visit.

At least, that was the story until the late 1980s. Since then a number of pressures have been threatening to undermine the fabric of this unique Swahili settlement. The most important is tourism. In the high season several hundred tourists visit Lamu every day, either by air or overland by bus and launch. One of the spin-offs of this influx is that many of the houses at Shela have been bought up by foreigners. As a result, local newspapers (particularly *Mvita*, published in Mombasa) have begun running scare articles with headlines such as 'Lamu Under Siege', and suggesting that tourism is gradually destroying the culture and even physical fabric of Lamu. It's a moot point but neither entirely right or wrong.

The other major pressure is population increase. It's expected that the town's current population of around 12,000 will increase to 30,000 by the end of the century. To accommodate and provide services for all those extra people is going to take some very sensitive planning.

Tourism certainly distorts centuries-old cultural values and economic patterns and can even destroy them but Lamu urgently needs an injection of cash for preservation, restoration, creation of employment, schools and for a cleanup – particularly of the open

■ PLACES TO STAY	▼ PLACES TO EAT
1 Peace Guest House	13 Coral Rock Restaurant
2 Kishuna Guest House	19 Ghai's Restaurant
3 Jannat House	27 Kenya Cold Drinks
4 Sanctuary Guest House	33 Bush Gardens Restaurant &
5 Jambo Guest House	Bush Lodge
6 Karibuni Guest House	36 Hapa Hapa Restaurant &
8 Saiga Guest House	Lodge
10 Starehe Guest House	40 Mid-Town Nyama Chroma
11 Pool Guest House	51 New Star Restaurant
12 Pole Pole Guest House	54 Swahili Dishis
14 Buhari Hotel	56 Labanda Restaurant
15 Salama Lodge	58 Olympic Restaurant
16 Yumbe House	60 Coconut Juice Garden
18 Shuweri Guest House	
21 Haludy Guest House	OTHER
22 Sanaa Guest House	
23 New Kenya Lodge	7 Jamaa Mosque
24 Casuarina Rest House	9 Door Carving Workshops
25 Lamu Guest House	17 Swahili House Museum
28 Petley's Inn	20 Donkey Sanctuary
30 Sunrise Guest House	26 Lamu Museum
31 Paradise Guest House & Amu House	29 Prestige Air Services
33 Bush Lodge &	32 Standard Chartered Bank
Bush Gardens Restaurant	35 Eagle Aviation &
34 Bahati Lodge	Full Moon Guest House
35 Full Moon Guest House & Eagle	41 Fort
Aviation	42 Customs
36 Hapa Hapa Lodge & Restaurant	43 Post Office
37 Lamu Sea Shore Lodging	45 Market
38 New Century Lodge	47 Hospital
39 New Maharus Hotel	49 Riyadha Mosque
44 New Castle Lodge	50 Malindi Bus Office
46 Dhow Lodge	52 Tana River Bus Office
48 Rainbow Guest House	53 Gypsies Gallery
57 Lamu Palace Hotel	55 Garissa Express Office &
59 Bahawaba Lodge	Lamu Book Centre

drainage system. Tourism could be the source of that cash and, to a large extent, is already. And it's hardly fair to blame tourism for corrugated iron replacing traditional wall and roofing materials. Most tourists would much prefer to see traditional materials used.

History

The 20th century may have brought Lamu a measure of peace and tranquillity but it has not always been that way. The town was only of minor importance in the string of Swahili settlements which stretched from Somalia to Mozambique. Although it was a thriving port by the early 1500s, it surrendered without a fight to the early Portuguese mariners and

was generally politically dependent on the more important sultanate of Paté which, at the time, was the most important island port in the archipelago. Until the late 1700s it did manage to avoid the frequent wars between the sultanates of Paté, Mombasa and Malindi following the decline of Portuguese influence in the area.

After that there followed many years of internecine strife between the various island city-states of Lamu, Paté, Faza and Siyu, which only ended in 1813 when Lamu defeated the forces of Paté in a battle at Shela. Shortly afterwards Lamu became subject to the sultanate of Zanzibar which nominally controlled the whole of the coastal

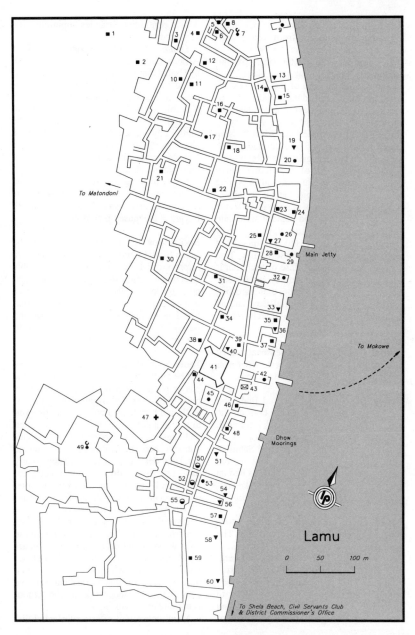

To Matondoni

To Mokowe

Main Jetty

Dhow
Moorings

Lamu

0   50   100 m

To Shela Beach, Civil Servants Club
& District Commissioner's Office

strip from Kilwa to the Somali border (under a British protectorate from 1890) until Kenya became independent in 1963.

In common with all the other Swahili coastal city-states, Lamu had a slave-based economy until the turn of the 20th century when the British forced the Sultan of Zanzibar to sign an anti-slavery agreement and subsequently intercepted dhows carrying slaves north from that island. All that cheap labour fuelled a period of economic growth for Lamu and traders grew rich by exporting ivory, cowries, tortoiseshell, mangrove poles, oil seeds and grains, and importing oriental linen, silks, spices and porcelain.

With the abolition of slavery in 1907, the economy of the island rapidly went into decline and stayed that way until very recently when increased receipts from tourism gave it a new lease of life. That decline, and its strong sense of tradition, is what has preserved the Lamu you see today. No other Swahili town, other than Zanzibar, can offer you such a cultural feast and an undisturbed traditional style of architecture.

Information

Tourist Office There's a seasonal tourist information counter on the waterfront near the dhow jetty, but it's of limited use.

Money The Standard Chartered Bank and the Kenya Commercial Bank, both on the harbour front, are the only banks in Lamu. Standard Chartered is open Monday to Friday from 8.30 am to 1 pm and Saturday from 8.30 to 11 am. In the low season, cashing a cheque can take as little as half an hour but in the high season it can take considerably longer. Get there early.

Books There are some excellent books about Lamu and the Swahili civilisation. The best general account is *The Portuguese Period in East Africa* (East African Literature Bureau, Nairobi, 1971) by Justus Strandes. This is a translation of a book originally published in German in 1899 with up-to-date notes and appendices detailing recent archaeological findings, some of

which contradict Strandes' opinions. It's very readable.

Lamu: A Study of the Swahili Town (East African Literature Bureau, Nairobi, 1975), by Usam Ghaidan, is a very detailed study of Lamu by an Iraqi who was formerly a lecturer in architecture at the University of Nairobi and has since devoted his time to research into the Swahili architecture of the north Kenyan coast. You can find both of the above books in most good bookshops in Nairobi or Mombasa and the latter at the museum in Lamu.

If you're going to stay long in Lamu the leaflet-map *Lamu: Map & Guide to the Archipelago, the Island & the Town* is worth buying at the museum bookshop.

Bookshops Apart from the museum, the Lamu Book Centre, next door to the Garissa Express office, has a small but reasonable selection of English-language novels and other books. It's also the only place where you can buy local newspapers, and international news magazines such as *Time* and *Newsweek*. It's open from 6.30 am to 12.30 pm and 2.30 to 9 pm.

Touts Your first introduction to Lamu may not be all that pleasant. As you step off the bus or plane you will be approached by a number of touts (known all along the coast as 'beach boys') who will try to entice you to stay at a particular hotel. They will often make rash promises (bordering on straight-out lies) about the facilities provided by the hotel in order to get you to stay. They usually have nothing to do with the hotels, but receive a hefty commission from the hotel owners. This commission is of course built into the price you pay for the room.

If you don't want any assistance in finding a room, be polite but firm in telling these guys where to get off – they can be amazingly persistent. When you do get to the hotel you want, if a tout is still clinging to you, make it clear to the hotel owner that you have come to the hotel independently and the tout is nothing to do with you.

Many hotels will offer a substantial discount for a longer stay, particularly if things are quiet. If you are planning on staying for a while (and many people do, despite earlier intentions!) it's not a bad idea to pay the full price the first night and then spend a bit of time checking out other places before committing yourself to a place for any length of time – many travellers find somewhere they'd rather stay after paying for a week at the first place.

Town Buildings

Lamu town dates back to at least the late 14th century when the Pwani Mosque was built. Most buildings date from the 18th century, but the lower parts and basements are often considerably older. The streets are narrow, cool and quiet and there are many small courtyards and intimate spaces enclosed by high walls. Traditionally, buildings were constructed entirely out of local materials – faced coral-rag blocks for the walls, wooden floors supported by mangrove poles, makuti roofs and intricately carved shutters for windows. This is changing gradually with the increasing use of imported materials and is one of the factors of great concern to conservationists.

One of the most outstanding features of the houses here, as in old Zanzibar, is the intricately carved doors and lintels which have kept generations of carpenters busy. Sadly, many of them have disappeared in recent years but the skill has not been lost. Walk down to the far end of the harbour front in the opposite direction to Shela and you'll see them being made.

Only a few of the mosques have minarets and even these are small affairs. This, combined with the fact that there's little outward decoration and few doors and windows opening onto the street, makes them hard to distinguish from domestic buildings.

Both in Lamu and in Shela, private developers have recently been allowed to build ugly, modern hotels despite local pressure, but fortunately there is only one in each place. There has been quite an increase in the number of hotels and guesthouses, but as most of them have used existing buildings the fabric and atmosphere of the old town has, by and large, been retained.

Lamu Museum

A couple of hours spent in the Lamu Museum, on the waterfront next to Petley's Inn, is an excellent introduction to the culture and history of Lamu. It's one of the most interesting small museums in Kenya. There's a reconstruction of a traditional Swahili house, charts, maps, ethnological displays, models of the various types of dhow and two examples of the remarkable and ornately carved ivory *siwa* – a wind instrument peculiar to the coastal region which is often used as a fanfare at weddings. There's a good slide show available at the museum – ask to see it. Entry costs US$1.50 (US$0.30 for residents) and the museum is open daily from 8 am to 6 pm.

The museum has a good bookshop specialising in books on Lamu and the Swahili culture.

Swahili House Museum

If the museum stokes your interest in Swahili culture then you should also visit this museum tucked away off to the side of Yumbe House (a hotel). It's a beautifully restored traditional house with furniture and other house wares as well as a pleasant courtyard. Entry charges and opening hours are the same as the main museum.

Lamu Fort

The building of this massive structure was begun by the Sultan of Paté in 1810 and completed in 1823. From 1910 right up to 1984 it was used as a prison. It has recently undergone complete restoration and now houses an impressive walk-through aquarium and natural history museum, as well as the island's library.

Donkey Sanctuary

One of the most unexpected sights on Lamu is the Donkey Sanctuary which is run by the International Donkey Protection Trust of Sidmouth, Devon, UK. Injured, sick or

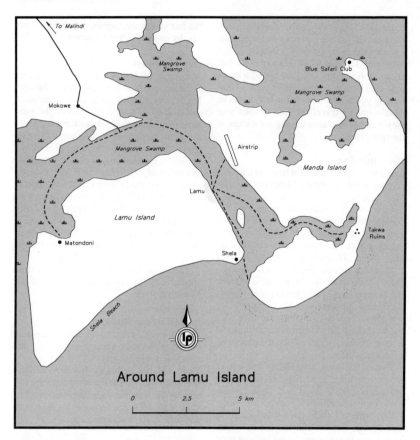

Around Lamu Island

0   2.5   5 km

worn-out donkeys are brought here to find rest and protection. As in most societies where they're used as beasts of burden, donkeys are regularly abused or get injured so it's good to see something positive being done for their welfare. The sanctuary is right on the waterfront.

The Beach

The best part of the beach if you want waves is well past Peponi's Hotel at Shela – there's no surf at Peponi's because you're still in the channel between Lamu and Manda islands. There was also a spate of robberies and a couple of rapes way out along this beach

several years ago but there's been no repeat of that following a big police crackdown at the time, so it's probably safe to go as far along the beach as you like. It's possible to hire windsurfing equipment at Peponi's.

Matondoni Village

You'll see many dhows anchored in the harbour at the southern end of town but if you want to see them being built or repaired the best place to do this is at the village of Matondoni.

To get there you have a choice of walking (about two hours), hiring a donkey, or hiring a dhow. If you choose the dhow it will cost about US$13 for the boat (so you need a small group together to share the cost) but it usually includes a barbecue fish lunch.

To walk there, leave the main street of Lamu up the alleyway by the side of Kenya Cold Drinks and continue in as straight a line as possible to the back end of town. From here a well-defined track leads out across the island. You pass a football pitch on the right-hand side after 100 metres. Follow the touch line of the pitch and continue in the same direction past the paddock/garden on the left-hand side and then turn left onto another track. This is the one to Matondoni. The football pitch has telephone wires running above it which go to Matondoni and they're almost always visible from the track so if you follow them you can't go wrong. If you don't cut across the football pitch you'll head off into the middle of nowhere and probably get lost – although this can be interesting (old houses, wells goats, etc).

Set off early if you are walking. It gets very hot later in the day. There's a small café in the village where you can get fish and rice for around US$1.30 as well as fruit juice. There are no guesthouses in the village but a bed or floor space can usually be arranged in a private house if you ask around. An impromptu group of travellers generally collects later in the afternoon so you can all share a dhow ride back to Lamu.

One traveller also recommended a visit to **Kipongani village** where local people make straw mats, baskets and hats. It's a friendly place, and tea and snacks can be arranged plus there's a beautiful empty beach nearby with waves.

Shela Village

Shela village, a 40-minute walk from Lamu, is a pleasant little village well worth a wander around. The ancestors of the people here came from Takwa when that settlement was abandoned in the late 17th century and they still speak a dialect of Swahili which is distinct from that of Lamu. Many have migrated to Malindi in recent years. Don't miss the famous mosque with its characteristic minaret at the back of Peponi's. Many of the houses in this village have been bought up and restored by foreigners in the last few years, so while it has a surprising air of affluence, the languorous atmosphere remains unspoiled. Quite a few travellers prefer to stay in Shela rather than in Lamu town.

To get to Shela, follow the harbour-front road till it ends and then follow the shore line. You will pass the new hospital built by the Saudi Arabian government and a ginning factory before you get to Shela. If the tide is out, you can walk along the beach most of the way. When it's in, you may well have to do a considerable amount of wading up to your thighs and deeper. If that doesn't appeal, there is a track all the way from Lamu to Shela but there are many turn-offs so stay with the ones which run closest to the shore (you may find yourself in a few cul-de-sacs doing this as a number of turn-offs to the left run to private houses and end there). A popular alternative to walking there is to take one of the frequent motorised dhows which shuttle back and forth between the two villages. This costs US$0.75 per person. In the past few years a number of people have been mugged, and one British tourist was killed, while walking between Lamu and Shela. Although it is safe at the moment, it may be an idea to check locally before setting out.

Dhow Trips

Taking a dhow trip is almost obligatory, and it is a very relaxing way to pass a day. You'll constantly be approached while walking along the waterfront by people wanting to take you out for a trip. The cost is around US$4 per person for four or more people, US$7.80 for less than four people. Five is a comfortable number as the boats are not that big. The price includes fishing and snorkelling, although both are largely fruitless exercises because it's virtually impossible to catch fish at midday, and the best snorkelling is a couple of hours away. A barbecue fish lunch on the beach at Manda is provided, supposedly with the fish you have caught but usually with fish provided by the captain. Make sure you take a hat and some sunblock as there is rarely any shade on the dhows, despite assurances to the contrary.

See the Islands Around Lamu section later in this chapter for details about longer dhow trips.

Places to Stay – bottom end

Lamu has been catering for budget travellers for well over a decade but, in the last few years, budget hotels have mushroomed to cater for the hordes of travellers who come to stay here. As a result, there's a bewildering choice of simple, rustic lodges, rooftops and whole houses to rent. Don't believe a word anyone tells you about there being running water 24 hours a day at any of these places. There often isn't. Water is not an abundant commodity on Lamu and restrictions are in force most of the year. It's usually only available early in the morning and early in the evening which, in most cases, means bucket showers only and somewhat smelly toilets.

Prices are remarkably consistent because there's a lot of competition though you obviously get what you pay for both in terms of facilities and position. A dormitory bed or space on the floor of a rooftop costs around US$2, a single room between US$2 and US$5.80, and a double room US$3.10 to US$7.80. Almost all of these would involve sharing bathroom facilities but some of the higher priced doubles might have their own bathroom. Prices rise in the high season (August to September) by a factor of up to 50%; at other times there's room for negotiation, particularly if you plan to stay for more than just a day or two. If a lodge is full when you arrive but you like it a lot and want to be first in line for a room, they'll usually let you sleep on the roof or elsewhere until the following morning.

Where you stay initially will probably depend largely on what sort of room you are offered, what's available and who meets you getting off the ferry from the mainland.

If you plan on staying in Lamu for a while it's worth making enquiries about renting a house, so long as there's a group of you to share the cost. On a daily basis it won't be much cheaper (if at all) than staying at a lodge but on a monthly basis you're looking at a considerable saving. You can share them with as many people as you feel comfortable with or have space for and prices usually include a house steward. Some of the simpler houses can be very cheap indeed and include a refrigerator and cooking facilities. They're available in Lamu town itself but also at Shela and between Lamu and Shela. Some of them can be excellent value and very spacious. You need to ask around and see what is available. It's possible to find some remarkably luxurious places, especially around Shela.

Lamu Town It's virtually impossible to arrange budget hotels in any order of preference since there are so many and conditions and facilities vary so much. This selection has been done on the basis of the cheapest available beds or rooms but implies no preference.

There's a couple of choices right on the waterfront. The *Full Moon Guest House* is a friendly place with an excellent 1st-floor balcony overlooking the water. It costs US$5.80 per room (single or double) and there's one triple room for US$9.80, all with shared facilities. Close by is the spotlessly clean *Lamu Sea Shore Lodging*. It's run by a friendly old Muslim man who has very little time for the 'beach boys', so chances are you won't be brought here by them. Security is good and items left in the rooms are safe. The charge here is US$5.80 for a single or double room.

On the first street back from the waterfront there are a number of other places, most of them pretty basic. Right at the bottom of the pile is the *Badhawaba Lodge* at the southern end of the street. It's clean enough, although about as basic as you can get on Lamu. It's also as cheap as you'll find anywhere, with rooms for US$2.40/3.50. Also on this same street and of a similar standard are the *Dhow Lodge* and the *Rainbow Guest House*.

A definite notch up the scale is the *New Kenya Lodge*, behind the Kenya Commercial Bank. It's fairly clean and has mosquito nets and cold bucket showers. The rooms cost US$4.60/5.50.

Further north again is the *Salama Lodge*, which is run by a friendly Englishwoman. It's basic but clean and there's a small kitchen for guests to use. In the high season double rooms with shared facilities cost US$12, but in the off season the price drops to US$3.90/5.90. All beds have mosquito nets.

Very good value, clean and simple, is the *Lamu Guest House* at the back of the Lamu Museum. There's a choice of different rooms here but the best are probably those on the top floor, which cost US$9.80. There are no fans but the sea breezes and sea views adequately compensate for this. Lower down there are doubles with bathroom and fan for US$18 and smaller doubles with the same facilities for US$13.

Next to the fort is the *New Castle Lodge* which overlooks the main square and picks up sea breezes since it's fairly high up. It has a rooftop dormitory for US$3.50 per bed and doubles with shared bathroom facilities for US$7.80.

At the northern end of town there's the *Saiga Guest House*, which costs US$9.80/12 for self-contained singles/doubles in the high season, dropping to a more reasonable US$4.90/5.90 in the low season. It's not great value. The *Karibuni Guest House* close by is similar.

Further west of town (15 minutes' walk) is the *Peace Guest House* (☎ (0121) 3020) which is clean, provides mosquito nets and morning tea and charges US$2.40 for a bed in a four-bed dormitory, and US$8.50 for a self-contained double. It's a wooden building surrounded by gardens, and there's a modern addition which contains the double rooms. You can also camp here for US$1.95. Facilities include two showers and access to the kitchen. This place has been popular for a number of years and still gets high praise from most travellers who stay here. It's well signposted from the northern part of town near the Buhari Hotel.

Moving further back from the waterfront there are a number of places in the maze of small streets that make up Lamu town. The *Paradise Guest House* is a large, unrestored three-storey Lamu house. It's very rough and ready but has heaps of atmosphere and is cheap at US$9.80 for a double with attached bath. A cheaper option close by is the *Bahati Lodge*. The rooms are small and somewhat gloomy, but all the beds have mosquito nets. The rooms on the upper floors have the advantage of catching views and the sea breezes. It's certainly a fairly basic place, but is popular and cheap at around US$2/4 for a single/double with shared bath.

Also further away from the waterfront is the *Sunrise Guest House* which is a very friendly place. The rooms however, are extremely basic and have just hardboard partitions. At US$5.80 a double, it's quite a popular place to stay.

Shela Quite a few travellers, especially beach lovers, prefer to stay at Shela village rather than in Lamu itself. There is no real budget accommodation here apart from a few rooms which are let out by the owner of the *Bahari Restaurant*, and these are no great bargain at US$16 for a double.

If you're going to stay here for a while – and it seems most of the people who stay here do – then it's best to ask around for a house to rent and have a small group together to share the cost. Many of the houses here are owned by expatriate foreigners (especially Italians) who have poured vast amounts of money into them but only live here for part of the year. Most of them have been very sensitively upgraded and some are stunning. Quite a lot of them can be rented out so ask around in the restaurants.

Places to Stay – middle
Lamu Town The best value in this range is undoubtedly the *Casuarina Rest House* (☎ (0121) 3123) which was formerly the police headquarters. It offers large, airy rooms with good views and is clean and well maintained. It's good value at US$18/27 a double depending on how long you intend to stay, but like all places it's negotiable to an extent, and prices are much lower in the off

season. There's access to a large, flat, roof area.

A slightly cheaper option is the *Hapa Hapa Lodge* behind the restaurant of the same name on the waterfront. The rooms are clean, huge and simply furnished, and good value at US$27 for a self-contained double, or US$16 with shared bath. Almost next door is the *Bush Lodge*, behind the Bush Gardens Restaurant. There are just three double rooms (US$9.80) and one large triple (US$14), as well as a kitchen for guests' use.

Close to the main square is the *New Maharus Guest House* which has variable prices depending on which floor you stay on. There are no single rooms, and the doubles cost US$12 on the 3rd floor, US$16 on the 2nd floor and US$19 on the 1st floor; all rooms on the 1st and 2nd floors are self-contained, while those on the 3rd floor have shared facilities. It's not great value.

A better bet is the *Haludy Guest House* away from the village. Self-contained rooms in this spacious and airy place cost US$23/31 in the high season, dropping to US$12/16 in the low season. There's a fridge and cooking facilities for those who want to put their own meals together.

One of the most beautiful places in this range is *Yumbe House* (☎ (0121) 3101), close to the Swahili House Museum. It's a four-storey traditional house surrounding a central courtyard which has been superbly and sensitively converted into a hotel with airy terraces and makuti roofs. All rooms are self-contained (towels and soap are provided), spotlessly clean, and there are mosquito nets. It's excellent value at US$19/33, including breakfast.

Another good place in this range is the *Pool Guest House*, so-called because it has a (very small) swimming pool, though this is not always filled. It's a maze of a place and the rooms vary quite a bit, some having sea views and breezes. All are excellent value at US$17/23; half that in the low season.

Also worth trying is *Jannat House*, away from the village. The rates are US$16 for a self-contained room with two traditional single beds, US$14 for a double with shared

bath, and there's one enormous family room with four beds at US$31.

The *Buhari Hotel* (☎ (0121) 3172) is a new place with a very pleasant terrace, but variable rooms. The downstairs rooms are small, gloomy and poor value at US$12/23, but the upstairs rooms, particularly those at the front, are very good and cost US$17/29. All rooms are self-contained and have mosquito nets.

Right away from town is the *Kishuna Guest House* (☎ (0121) 3125) but as it is a new building it lacks the character of most of the other places. The rooms are large, self-contained, well furnished and cost US$16/23 a single/double.

Shela The only mid-range places in Shela are whole villas which, as previously described, are available for longer term rental (a couple of weeks or more). Typical is the *Bustani Square*, close to the Stop Over Restaurant on the foreshore. It's a five-bedroom place which can sleep eight people comfortably but more if necessary. The cost is US$58 per night, but this is open to negotiation, depending on how long you want to stay and what time of year it is.

Places to Stay – top end

Lamu Town The best top-range hotel in Lamu itself is *Petley's Inn* (☎ (0121) 3107) right on the harbour front next to the Lamu Museum. It was originally set up in the late 19th century by Percy Petley – a somewhat eccentric English colonist who ran plantations on the mainland at Witu until he retired to Lamu. At the time of writing it is undergoing a major renovation but should be open once again by the time you read this. Facilities include a swimming pool and excellent rooftop terrace (open to nonguests). Expect to pay at least US$39 per person for a self-contained room including breakfast.

Lamu's latest blot on the landscape is the *Lamu Palace Hotel* (☎ (0121) 3272) right on the foreshore. It's the only hotel on the island which has air-con rooms; singles/doubles cost US$39/71 with private bath.

An excellent place in this category is *Amu*

House (☎ (0121) 3246) next to the Paradise Guest House in the heart of town. The hotel is a restored 16-century Swahili dwelling and is very comfortably furnished. The price is a very reasonable US$27 including breakfast.

Shela At the far end of Shela village and right on the beach is *Peponi's Hotel* (☎ (0121) 3029) which is *the* place to stay if you want a top-range hotel on Lamu. It consists of self-contained, whitewashed cottages with their own verandahs facing the channel between Lamu and Manda islands and is reckoned to be one of the best hotels in the country, both in terms of its position and the quality of the cuisine. It's run by young Danish people and up-market informality is the name of the game here. The rates for full board are US$195/286 a single/double, while singles/doubles with breakfast cost a mere US$169/221. Children sharing the same accommodation are charged US$19 to US$84 depending on age and meal requirements. There's a full range of water sports facilities. Advance booking is essential and the hotel is closed during May and June.

Also on the channel is *Kijani House* (☎ (0121) 3235), which has beautifully furnished rooms arranged around a lush and colourful garden. Facilities include a swimming pool, and like Peponi's, it is also closed in May and June. The cost here is US$91/117 for self-contained rooms with breakfast and US$123/175 for full board. Children aged from two to seven years are charged US$39 and US$52 respectively.

In the same area is the *White Rock Pool Guest House* (☎ (0121) 3234). It's fairly sparsely furnished and somewhat tatty, despite being quite new. It too has a swimming pool, and there's also a kitchen for guests to use. Self contained doubles with breakfast cost US$58 in the high season, dropping to US$39 in the low season. It's not particularly good value.

Much more pleasant is the *Island Hotel* (☎ (0121) 3290), another new place but further back from the water. It was built using traditional methods and the upper rooms with makuti roofs and sea views are superb. The lower rooms are a bit cramped. To stay it'll cost you US$52/80 with breakfast, and US$78/117 for full board. Children aged between two and 12 years are charged US$13 for bed and breakfast, and US$25 for full board. The hotel has its own excellent restaurant (open to nonguests), but there is no swimming pool.

A good deal cheaper, and the place to stay if you want to do your own catering, is the *Shela Rest House* (☎ (0121) 3091) not far from the Island Hotel. It too has open makuti-roofed areas and sea views. Two-bedroom apartments with kitchen and fridge cost US$39 for three people and US$52 for four. It's a friendly place and the management can arrange for a cook to prepare your meals if you want a rest from doing it yourself.

Lastly there's the ugly three-storey blot on the foreshore that should never have got past the planning stage – the *Shela Beach Hotel*. This brand new place is unnecessarily large for Shela and could easily have been made smaller to make less of a visual impact. It was still under construction at the time of writing but should be open by now.

Places to Eat – cheap

One of the cheapest places to eat in Lamu is the *New Star Restaurant*. You certainly won't beat the prices and some people recommend it highly, but others visit once and never return. Service is sometimes painfully slow (depending on what you order and the time of day) and the menu is often an unbridled act of creativity, though I thought the food was average. Fish & chips or rice costs US$2.70.

Cheaper still is the very basic *Swahili Dishis* (sic) just off the waterfront. This tiny place caters purely for the locals and serves no-frills African food at rock-bottom prices. Another local eatery is the *Mid-Town Nyama Choma* café on the main square by the fort. There are no prizes here for culinary excellence, but for a cheap meat meal it's the place to go.

For snacks and shakes there's *Kenya Cold Drinks*, a popular little place on the road which runs parallel to the foreshore. It also serves more substantial dishes such as steak or fish from US$3.10 to US$3.90 and lobster for US$7.10. The service here is very haphazard. The *Bantu Café* in the New Castle Lodge also does basic snacks but on Tuesday and Friday evenings it serves a seven-course meal of local Lamu dishes for US$3.10. This is a good way to sample some local food and, unless you get invited to eat with a family or can hire someone to cook for you, this café is probably the only way to taste coastal cooking in Lamu. You need to book by 3 pm on the day so they know how many to cater for.

On the verandah of the old fort is the *Mazangira Café*, which is another great place for people watching. It serves good juices, as well as snacks and main dishes in the range of US$2.30 to US$3.70.

For consistently good food at a reasonable price there are a handful of very popular restaurants. The menus at all are pretty standard, with fish, seafood, steaks and curries. All do excellent juices and shakes. Despite the excellent seafood available, the seafood meals in Lamu are really very basic

The first is the *Olympic (Sindbad) Restaurant* on the waterfront overlooking the dhow moorings. Here you can get pancakes with various fillings, grilled fish and salad or a full lunch or dinner of soup, main course and fruit juice. Close by is the *Labanda Restaurant*, which apart from the standard dishes also does poulet yassa, a delicious Senegalese chicken dish for US$5.20. It also serves some vegetarian dishes, which are hard to find on Lamu.

The *Coral Rock* has also been popular for years, although not always under that name. It offers all the usuals including banana pancakes with honey, grilled fish, crab, and lassi. The food is generally OK but the service is careless and I really got the feeling that customers were seen as something of a nuisance. It's open daily, except for Tuesday during the off season.

Somewhat more expensive but very popular is the *Bush Gardens* on the waterfront, next door to the Hapa Hapa Restaurant. It's run by the very personable and energetic 'Bush Baby' who personally supervises the cooking which sometimes makes for slow service but guarantees you an excellent meal. Fish dishes (barracuda, tuna, snapper or shark) cost US$3.50, crab US$7.80, prawns US$6.80 and lobster US$13, all served with chips or coconut rice and salad. Fruit juices are also available. It's arguably the best seafood restaurant in Lamu.

Next door is the *Hapa Hapa Restaurant* which is also very good, and offers a similar range of dishes, including seafood and possibly the best fruit juices and milkshakes in town. Prices are similar to those at Bush Gardens, and it's also a very popular place, especially at breakfast time.

Another place on the waterfront, at the northern end of town, is *Ghai's*. This place gets very mixed reviews, some people think the food is excellent while others come away dissatisfied. The set meal – juice, crab toast with cheese, chips and salad – is good value at US$3.90, while à la carte dishes are much the same price as the other places. It's open daily from 10.30 am to 10 pm.

The rooftop terrace at *Petley's* serves surprisingly cheap food and it's open to nonguests of the hotel. A fixed-price, three-course seafood lunch or dinner is a bargain at US$5.80, and the cheese samosas are excellent.

Many travellers come across a man popularly called 'Ali Hippy' who, for several years, has been offering travellers meals at his house. The meal usually includes lobster, crab, fish, coconut rice and vegetable stew and the whole family entertains you while you eat. Some people come away quite satisfied (it's definitely an unusual evening out) but the majority these days feel it is not worth the US$3 per person.

At Shela, the *Stop Over Restaurant* right on the beach is a popular place to eat or drink and prices are very reasonable though they only offer simple meals. Steaks are US$2.90, fish dishes US$3.30 and lobster US$9.80.

Similar and offering a slightly wider range is the *Bahari Restaurant* on the foreshore near Peponi's.

Places to Eat – more expensive

For an up-market snack or coffee, the café in the *Gypsies Gallery* on the street parallel to the waterfront is worth a try.

For a splurge meal the range is strictly limited. The restaurant at the *Lamu Palace Hotel* is far from cheap and the food is patchy – some nights it's excellent, other times it's practically inedible.

A meal at the *Petley's Inn* outdoor barbecue used to be a pleasant night out, but was being renovated at the time of writing. It should be open by now.

The rooftop restaurant at the *New Mahrus Hotel* touts itself as a classy restaurant but the food is only average and the hygiene suspect.

For a splurge at Shela the *Barbecue Grill* at Peponi's offers delicious food and is open to nonguests. There's a choice of both barbecued fish and meat and a superb range of salads. Also worth trying is the *Barracuda Restaurant* at the Island Hotel. Main dishes cost around US$5.20, while crab and lobster are available for US$14.

Entertainment

Bars There are four places where you can get a beer in Lamu itself but only two of them have cold beers. One of them is the makuti-roofed terrace bar *Petley's Inn* which is a very pleasant place to relax and catch the sea breeze. It's the most popular watering hole on the island and is open to nonguests. On the ground floor of the hotel there's an 'African' bar which serves warm beer at cheap prices. It's a bar with character, though I suspect that once renovation of the rooms is complete, the character will change.

The other place with cold beer is the bar at the *Lamu Palace Hotel* on the waterfront. It's also a good place to catch the breezes, and as you're on ground level it's interesting to watch the passing parade of pedestrians.

The *Police Club* by the police station serves warm beer. It's open in the evenings

until fairly late and you don't have to be in the police force to get in. Ask directions from the Garissa Express bus office.

There's another bar at the *Civil Servants' Club* which has a disco on some Friday and Saturday nights. Keep an eye out for advertising posters around the town. Entry costs US$2 and it's a good night out.

Out at Shela, *Peponi's* is a mandatory watering hole and the beer here is always ice-cold. The bar is on the verandah overlooking the channel and beach. It's open all day until late at night.

Getting There & Away

Air Three companies operate flights to Lamu from Mombasa and Malindi. They are Eagle Aviation Ltd (☎ Mombasa (011) 316054, Malindi (0123) 21258, Lamu (0121) 3119), Prestige Air Services Ltd (☎ Mombasa (011) 21443, Malindi (0123) 20860, Lamu (0121) 3055), and Skyways Airlines (☎ Mombasa (011) 221964, Malindi (0123) 20951, Lamu (0121) 3226).

Each has two flights per day in either direction between Mombasa and Lamu, and Malindi and Lamu. Flights from Mombasa depart at 8.30 am and 2.15 pm and arrive in Lamu an hour and 10 minutes later. From Malindi they depart at 9 am and 3 pm and arrive 40 minutes later. In the opposite direction, they depart Lamu at 10 am and 4 pm for both Mombasa and Malindi. The fares are US$68 (Mombasa to Lamu) and US$49 (Malindi to Lamu) one way. Return fares are US$124 and US$83 respectively. Children over two years old pay full fare. Check-in time is 30 minutes before departure and the baggage allowance is 10 kg per person. Most of the time you won't be hassled if your baggage is over 10 kg but, even if you are, excess charges are minimal. The airport departure tax is US$1.50 at Mombasa and Malindi but there's no charge at Lamu.

The airport at Lamu is on Manda Island and the ferry across the channel to Lamu costs US$0.60. Hotel touts will be waiting for you at the airport and will pursue you all the way. They're very persistent and hard to shake off.

Air Kenya Aviation (☎ (02) 501421 in Nairobi) operates daily flights in either direction between Lamu and Nairobi's Wilson Airport. The fare is US$112 one way and Petley's Hotel is the Lamu agent.

Bus Three bus companies operate between Mombasa, Malindi and Lamu on a daily basis. They are Malindi Bus service, Tana River Bus service and Garissa Express and they all have offices in Mombasa, Malindi and Lamu. The fare from Malindi to Lamu is around US$4.50 and the journey takes about five hours. Buses leave in either direction at 7 or 8 am depending on the company. The fare to Mombasa is US$4.50. The buses from Mombasa to Lamu arrive in Malindi around 8.30 am and leave around 9.30 am so there's a choice of departure times from Malindi if seats are available. It's wise to book in advance as there's a heavy demand for tickets. Garissa Express also operate a daily service between Garissa and Lamu which costs US$9.40 and takes around 10 hours.

The buses terminate at the ferry jetty on the mainland not far from Mokowe. From here you take a motorised ferry to Lamu which costs US$0.60.

Dhow Other than trips around the Lamu archipelago, you can also find dhows sailing to Mombasa. The journey takes two days on average and prices are negotiable. Before you set off you need to get permission from the district commissioner. His office on the harbour front close to the post office and opposite the main quay. It's best if you can persuade the captain of the dhow to take you along here and guide you through the formalities. It shouldn't take more than 1½ hours in that case. Usually they will do this without charging you money but be prepared to pay if the captain is unwilling.

Getting Around

Boat There are frequent ferries between Lamu and the bus terminus on the mainland (near Mokowe). The fare is US$0.60. Ferries between the airstrip on Manda Island and Lamu also cost US$0.60. Between lamu village and Shela there are regular motorised dhows and these too cost US$0.60.

There are also regular ferries between Lamu and Paté Island – see the following section for details.

Islands Around Lamu

A popular activity while you're in Lamu is to take a dhow trip to one of the neighbouring islands. You need a small group (six to eight people) to share costs if you're going to do this but it's very easy to put a group like that together in Lamu. Just ask around in the restaurants or the budget hotels.

Since taking tourists around the archipelago is one of the easiest ways of making money for dhow owners in Lamu, there's a lot of competition and you'll be asked constantly by different people if you want to go on a trip. Negotiation over the price and what is included is essential both to avoid misunderstandings and being overcharged. The price of day trips is usually settled quickly because a lot of travellers will have been on them and the cost will be well known.

Dhow trips are usually superb whoever you go with so it's unfair to recommend any particular dhow or captain but, if you're going on a long trip – say, three days – then it's a very good idea to check out both the dhow and the crew before committing yourself. Don't hand over any money until the day of departure except, perhaps, a small advance (say US$4) for food for a long trip. Also, on long trips, it's probably best to organise your own beer, soft drink and bottled water supplies. And remember that the person who touts for your business is often not the captain of the boat but an intermediary who takes a commission for finding you.

Dhows without an outboard motor are naturally entirely dependent on wind to get them anywhere, though poling – or even pushing – the boat is fairly common along narrow creeks and channels. If you have to

Lamu Archipelago

0   7.5   15 km

INDIAN OCEAN

pole the boat or you get becalmed out in the channels between the islands, there's no point in remonstrating with the captain. He's not God and there's nothing he can do about it, yet it's surprising how many people imagine otherwise. With that in mind, never go on a long trip if you have a deadline to meet. A three-day trip can occasionally turn into five-day one, although this is unusual.

Likewise, dhows are dependent on the tides. You can't sail up creeks if the tide is out and there's not enough depth of water to float the boat. This will be the main factor determining departure and return times.

To give you some idea of what a longer

dhow trip involves, here's a brief description of one which Geoff took with five others:

After discussions with three different intermediaries in Lamu about trips to Kiwayu we made our choice and arranged to meet outside the Kisiwani Lodge at 6 am the next morning. The price was fixed at US$120 for a three-day trip, or around US$6 per person per day including food. Meanwhile we purchased beers and soft drinks from the Kenya Breweries depot and dropped them off at the Kisiwani (the crews will generally do this for you but it will cost more).

Next morning the dhow finally turned up at 7.30 am along with a crew of four and we set off in the direction of the channel between Manda Island and the mainland. Since the wind wasn't in the right direction, the dhow had to tack all the way to the channel by which time it was low tide. There was sufficient water in the channel to just keep the boat afloat – but the wind had dropped completely. There was no alternative but to pole and push the dhow all the way to the end of the channel and naturally we all lent a hand. It took hours.

Once out in the open sea again, the wind picked up and we were able to get close to Paté Island but again the wind dropped and the clouds burst. It looked very much like we and all our gear were about to get a soaking so it was with considerable relief that we discovered the crew had brought along an enormous sheet of plastic.

After the storm, the wind picked up again and we reached Mtangawanda by about 3.30 pm where we got off the boat and had a late lunch cooked by the crew. Despite only having one charcoal burner, they did an excellent job of this and the food was delicious.

We set off again about 4.30 pm and headed for Faza with a stiff side wind which enabled us to make good progress for the next two hours. After that it died completely and darkness fell. By 10 pm, it was obvious we were going nowhere that night so the anchor was dropped and a meal prepared (by torchlight!). By now we were all getting to know each other very well and there was a good rapport between crew and passengers. The tranquillity and beauty of a becalmed night at sea added immensely to this. After the meal, we all bedded down as best we could for a night of 14th-century discomfort.

By first light we discovered that seepage through the hull of the boat had brought the water level to well above the toe-boards so it was all hands on deck and bail out with anything to hand. Shortly after this, the wind picked up and we sped our way across the channel between Paté Island and Kiwayu, arriving at about 11 am off the tip of the island. At this point, all the passengers and one of the crew got off the dhow and went snorkelling among the reefs on the eastern side. The dhow, meanwhile, sailed on to Kiwayu village.

We caught up with the dhow again around 3 pm

after walking along the beach and climbing over the ridge. Lunch was prepared by the crew (again delicious) and we settled down to an afternoon and evening of relaxation – sunbathing, fishing and exploring the village. Those with tents camped on the beach and the others took a banda at the camp site.

Next morning brought heavy rain but by 11 am we were on our way back to Lamu with a strong tailwind and making excellent progress. Just off Faza, however, the wind died again and the captain (rightly) predicted there'd be no more that day so it was Faza for the night at his family's house. But it wasn't that simple getting off the boat! The tide was out and we couldn't sail up the creek to the town. It didn't look like a particularly feasible idea from the relative 'comfort' of the boat but, after some persuasion, we all jumped overboard with our packs on our heads and headed for the shore in thigh-deep water. There were no mishaps but a lot of jokes and laughter. Half an hour later we reached Faza.

The dhow was brought up at high tide and we were given three bedrooms to share at the family house. That evening a superb meal was prepared for us by the captain's family which we ate in the company of what must have been a good proportion of the town's younger children, all fascinated by this strange collection of wazungu that had turned up in town. Though we did offer, the family refused to take any money for the meal and the accommodation.

After the meal, the captain gave us his prediction about the winds next day – pretty pessimistic – and advised us to take the motor launch back to Lamu. The food was at an end, the last beers had been consumed with the meal that night and so, in the end, we all opted for the motor launch rather than another possible two days and a night back to Lamu. He did, on the other hand, firmly offer to take any or all of us back to Lamu on the dhow at no further cost if that's what we preferred.

All things considered, an excellent trip, superb value, great company, quite an adventure and I'd do it again.

MANDA ISLAND

This is the easiest of the islands to get to since it's just across the channel from Lamu and almost everyone takes a half-day trip to the Takwa ruins at the head of the creek which almost bisects the island. The average cost of a dhow to this place is around US$19 shared by however many people you can put together. Sometimes (but not always) this includes a barbecued fresh-fish lunch so settle this issue before you leave.

The extensive Takwa ruins are what remains of an old Swahili city which flourished between the 15th and 17th centuries and which attained a peak population of some 2500. It was abandoned for reasons unknown when the townspeople moved to Shela. The ruins consist of the remains of about 100 limestone and coral houses, all aligned towards Mecca as well as a mosque and tomb dating from 1683 (1094 by the Islamic calendar). The settlement is surrounded by the remains of a wall and huge baobab trees dot the site. It's maintained by the National Museums of Kenya and entry costs KSh 100.

Just off the north-east coast of Manda is **Manda Toto Island** which offers some of the best snorkelling possibilities in the archipelago. The reefs here are excellent and there are also good beaches. The only way to get here is by dhow.

Places to Stay

Apart from the *camp site* adjacent to the ruins, the only other accommodation option on the island is the very expensive Italian-run and owned *Blue Safari Club* (☎ (01) 338838 in Nairobi) at the northern tip of the island. Accommodation consists of 15 bandas and a separate restaurant and bar. The cost is a mere US$432 per person per day for full board, including drinks and transfers from the airstrip.

Getting There & Away

The trip across to Manda takes about 1½ hours and can only be done at high tide as it's reached by a long mangrove-fringed inlet which is too shallow at low tide. You may well have to wade up the final stretch, so wear shorts. Since you have to catch the outgoing tide, your time at the site will probably not be more than 45 minutes.

It's possible to walk to the Takwa ruins from either the airstrip or the village of Ras Kitau but it's quite a long way and the paths are not too clear.

PATÉ ISLAND

There are a number of historical sites on Paté Island including Paté the town, Siyu, Mtangawanda and Faza. All are still inhabited – mainly by fishers and mangrove-pole cutters – but very little effort has been put into preserving or clearing the remains of the once powerful Swahili city-states and that's not likely to happen until tourist receipts warrant the expense. Indeed, the only foreigners who come to this island are those on dhow trips and the occasional archaeologist so you can expect to be a novelty and treated with friendly curiosity especially by the children.

Accommodation and food on the island is easy to arrange with local families. The cost is negotiable but very reasonable. There are no guesthouses as such except at Faza but there are generally one or two simple restaurants which offer basic meals like bean or meat stews and tea.

Partly because the island is so flat, mosquitoes are a real pest and you're going to need insect repellent. Mosquito coils are for sale in the island's shops.

Paté

The origins of Paté are disputed. There are claims that it was founded in the 8th century by immigrants from Arabia, but recent excavations have produced nothing earlier than the 13th century when another group of Arabs, the Nabahani, arrived and gradually came to exert considerable influence over the other semiautonomous settlements along the coast.

By the time the Portuguese arrived in the early 16th century, Paté's fortunes were on the decline but were given a shot in the arm by the European mariners' interest in the silk cloth for which the town was famous and the introduction by the Portuguese of gunpowder. A number of Portuguese merchants reputedly settled here but their welcome was relatively short-lived, and by the mid-17th century their descendants had withdrawn to Mombasa following a series of uprisings by the Patéans against taxes imposed by the Portuguese authorities.

For the next half century or so, Paté regained some of its former importance and successfully fought off attempts by the Omani Arabs to take it over. Paté's harbour, however, had long been silting up and the city-state was eventually forced into using that of Lamu. The dependency created frequent tensions, particularly as Paté claimed sovereignty over Lamu, and the two were frequently at war. The final crunch came in 1812 when a Patéan army was soundly defeated at Shela. Thereafter, Paté faded into insignificance and lost all importance after the ruling family was driven out by Seyyid Majid in 1865 and was forced to set up the short-lived sultanate of Witu on the mainland.

Today, Paté resembles a down-at-heel Lamu. The narrow, winding streets and high-walled houses are there but the streets are earthen and the coral-rag walls unplastered. Its one redeeming feature is the Nabahani ruins just outside of town. These are quite extensive and include walls, tombs, mosques and houses. They're worth exploring but they've never been seriously excavated or cleared so it can be difficult to get around because of the tangle of vegetation. In addition, local farmers plant their tobacco crops among the ruins and have demolished substantial sections of the walls.

Getting There & Away There is a motor launch which usually leaves Lamu for Mtangawanda (about two hours) and Faza (about four hours) three times a week on Monday, Wednesday and Friday (Tuesday, Thursday and Saturday in the opposite direction). The fare is US$2.60.

From Mtangawanda it's about an hour's walk to Paté town along a narrow footpath through thick bush and across tidal flats but you're unlikely to get lost as the path is easy to follow and you'll probably be walking it together with local people who get off the launch.

The launch doesn't always call at Mtangawanda on the return trip from Faza to Lamu, so it's best to walk across to Faza and take it from there, paying a visit to Siyu on the way.

Siyu

Founded in the 15th century, Siyu was famous not for commerce or military opportunism but as a centre of Islamic scholarship and crafts. In its heyday (between the 17th and 19th centuries) it boasted some 30,000 inhabitants and was the largest settlement on the island though, today, less than 4000 people live here and there are few signs of its former cultural and religious influence.

Though one of the last upholders of coastal independence, Siyu's demise came in 1847 when it was occupied by the Sultan of Zanzibar's troops. The huge fort outside town dates from this period and is one of the largest buildings on the island. It's well worth a visit, as unlike many other Swahili relics, it has undergone considerable renovation.

The modern village displays little of Siyu's former glory and consists essentially of a sprawl of simple mud-walled and makuti-roofed houses.

Getting There & Away The mangrove-lined channel leading up to Siyu is too shallow and silted up to allow the passage of anything but the smallest boats and so cannot be reached directly from the sea by dhow or motor launch. The only feasible access is on foot either from Paté or Faza.

From Paté it's about eight km to Siyu along an earth track through the bush. The first part is tricky since there are turn-offs which are easy to miss so it's a good idea to take a guide with you as far as the tidal inlet. From here on it's easy as the path bears left and then continues straight through to Siyu. This last leg should take you about one hour.

Faza

Faza has had a chequered history. It was destroyed by Paté in the 13th century and rebuilt in the 16th century only to be destroyed again by the Portuguese in 1586 as a result of its collaboration with the Turkish fleet of Amir Ali Bey. It was subsequently re-established and switched its allegiances to the Portuguese during their attempts to subdue Paté in the 17th century but declined into insignificance during the 18th and 19th centuries. These days it has regained some of its former importance after being chosen as the district headquarters for Paté Island which includes part of the Kenya mainland to the north.

Faza has very little to offer in the way of interesting ruins. About the only thing there is in the town itself are the remains of the **Kunjanja Mosque** right on the creek front next to the district headquarters where the ferries anchor. Even so, most of it is just a roofless pile of rubble though there's a beautifully carved mihrab and some fine Arabic inscriptions above the doorway. Outside town is the tomb of Amir Hamad, commander of the Sultan of Zanzibar's forces, who was killed here in 1844 whilst campaigning against Siyu and Paté.

The modern town is quite extensive and includes a post office, telephone exchange, the district headquarters, a simple restaurant, two general stores and two guesthouses.

It's an interesting place to wander around and easy to strike up conversations with just about anyone – men, women or children. Most of the houses here are mud-walled or coral-rag walled with makuti roofs though concrete and corrugated iron make an occasional appearance.

Places to Stay & Eat The two guesthouses – *Lamu House* and *Shela House* – are essentially family residences but they're more than willing to turn over one or more bedrooms for your use and cook you a delicious evening meal if you need somewhere to stay. The price is negotiable but the family is very friendly.

The simple restaurant mentioned earlier offers bean stews, tea and mandazi for just a few cents and is a popular meeting place for the men of the town.

Getting There & Away The inlet leading up to Faza from the main channel is deep enough at high tide to allow the passage of dhows and motor launches (though at low tide you'll have to walk in over the mud and sand banks from the main channel).

There's a regular motor launch which connects Lamu with Faza via Mtangawanda three times a week on Monday, Wednesday and Friday (Tuesday, Thursday and Saturday in the opposite direction). The fare is US$2.60 and the journey takes four hours. From Faza to Lamu, the launch leaves at about 6 am but you need to be down by the district headquarters about half an hour before that as you have to ferried out to the launch in small boats.

Getting to Siyu from Faza involves a two-hour walk through shambas and thick bush along an earth track. The first hour's walk as far as the disused airstrip is no problem, and there are generally people you can ask for directions if you're unsure. The second half is more confusing and you may need a guide so it might be best in the long run to take a guide with you all the way from Faza.

KIWAYU ISLAND

Kiwayu Island is at the far north-east of the Lamu archipelago and is included in the Kiunga National Marine Reserve. It acquired a reputation some years ago as an exclusive hideaway for rock stars and various other members of the glitterati, both local and foreign. It's unlikely you'll be rubbing shoulders with these people. The main reason for coming here is to explore the coral reefs off the eastern side of the island which the tourist literature rates as some of the best along the Kenyan coast. Personally, I think it's somewhat overrated (Watamu is better) but the dhow trip there is definitely a highlight of a trip to Lamu and I can highly recommend it.

The village on the western side of the island where the dhows drop anchor is quite small but it does have a general store with a few basics. The place to stay here is the *Kiwayu Camping Site* run by a friendly man named Kasim. There are several beautifully conceived bandas to stay in, all constructed out of wooden poles and makuti including one on stilts and another built over a tree. The cost varies between US$13 and US$26 depending on which one you take, but they'll all sleep up to three people. Clean sheets, pillows and mattresses are provided as well as a kerosene lantern and mosquito coil. There are good toilet and shower facilities. Campers can erect their tents here for US$2.60 including use of showers and toilets. You'll pay the same charge even if you camp on the beach below the site since this is also apparently owned by Kasim. There's a covered dining and cooking area for the use of both campers and banda dwellers.

Further up the coast across from Kiwayu on the mainland is the luxury lodge, *Kiwayu Safari Lodge* (☎ (02) 503030 in Nairobi) which gains a listing in Harper's *100 Best Hotels in the World* (the only hotel in Kenya and one of only a handful in Africa to do so) and where the glitterati stay. The cost of a night here is US$248 with full board. There's a speed launch to it from Lamu which takes less than an hour, or flights by Air Kenya Aviation from Nairobi in six-seater planes for US$195 one way. You can forget about going up there for a cold beer if you're staying at the camp site as there's no transport across the channel between the island and the mainland.

Getting There & Away
Virtually the only way to get to Kiwayu is by dhow and, for most people, this would be part of a longer trip from Lamu with stopovers elsewhere. If there's sufficient wind, the return trip to Kiwayu from Lamu takes three days and two nights.

Thanks

To the following travellers who wrote in after using either *Africa on a shoestring* or *East Africa – a travel survival kit*, I'd like to express my sincere thanks for the time and effort which you put in. The information contained in your letters has been an extremely valuable source of original material and for cross-reference. Please keep it up! It all gets read personally and used.

Beverley Adlawan (USA), Chloe Anderson (C), Dick Anderson (Aus), Alison Armstrong (UK), Rev John H Backus (USA), Jane Bailey (UK), Dr Nia Barak (Isr), Agnes Beal (F), Rachel Benneworth, Stuart Bernstein (USA), A D Bhatt, Marie-Louise Boley, Sylvia Bradley (UK), Sajjad Butt, Marc Cassidy, Ilan Chaitowitz (UK), Ben Chaston (UK), David Chianda (Ken), Daniel Collins (UK), M de P-Brouwer, A J W Dixson, P M Dodhia (Ken), Kathy Duarte (USA), Malcolm Edmunds (UK), Tarek El Gammal (Ken), Malcolm Gascoigne (Ken), Bas Hagoort (NL), Tim & Suzanne Harrison (UK), Chris Hawley (Ken), C C Hawley, Ronnie Heller (UK), Mrs Narinder K Heys (Ken), Petri Hottola (Fin), Caroline Jansson (S), Pete Jones (UK), P K Kohli (Ken), P K Kohli (Ken), John Mwok Komolkat, Dr Athene Lane (UK), A Lane (UK), Douglas Lattey (UK), Lara Letteau (USA), Ram Lior (Isr), Patricia Little, Mr & Mrs D Mahaffey (USA), Robert March (Ken), Mario Bevione (I), Ellen W McBride (USA), Mark McClure, Michael McElman, Alain Melis (B), Gillian Mellors (UK), Susan Miano, Kate Minogue, Pam Moore (USA), Deborah Mwaura (USA), Hemant Nayak (USA), Massimo Nesta, Charles Ngigi (Ken), Martin Nielsen (DK), Mary O'Gorman (IRL), Pierre Oberson, Daniela Oudin (F), Lisa Pitre (C), Susan Puis (USA), Scott Randall (UK), Mark Roth (USA), Maurice Rubia (Ken), Carr Rufa (Ken), Edwin Sadd (Ken), Margaret Sanko, Mark Savage, Nelly Schaefers, Alfred Scoma (USA), Carole Sentein (F), Raf Shah (Ken), George Shah (Ken), Ron Shlomit (Isr), Judy Sierra (USA), Mrs M Smith (USA), Peter Soileau (USA), Raymond Stephens (IRL), Julia Stone (Aus), Susan & Andy Tatam (UK), Howard Taylor (UK), Niels Thomsen (DK), Teresa Timms (UK), Dirk van der Made (NL), Tina Villamajna (UK), John Jenkin Wafula (Ken), Shayna Watson (C), David Waugh (UK), Relinde Weil (NL), Jo White (UK), Naomi Williams, Michelle Wilson, Mike Wylie, and Connie Yung Shan Man (HK).

Aus – Australia, B – Belgium, C – Canada, DK – Denmark, F – France, Fin – Finland, HK – Hong Kong, I – Italy, IRL – Ireland, Isr – Israel, Ken – Kenya, NL – Netherlands, S – Sweden, UK – United Kingdom, USA – United States of America

For the technically minded and those interested in the possibilities of living without another Chernobyl, this book was written on a solar-powered computer using an Arrow microprocessor, 24 Solarex X100 GT solar panels, a Siemens 2000 watt inverter and 24 BP PVSTOR 1000 AH lead-acid batteries.

Index

Maps

Text

Safari
Guide

Safari Guide

ANTELOPES

The large, striped bongo antelope is rarely seen. About your only chance of sighting one is in Aberdare National Park. They live close to water in dense forest, only leaving the forest cover to graze at night in open clearings.

The bongo stands around 120 cm high at the shoulder and measures around 250 cm from head to tail. Mature males are a beautiful dark mahogany-brown colour, while the females are a much lighter reddish-brown. Both sexes have distinctive vertical white stripes on the body, never less than nine, never more than 14. Horns are sported by both males and females, and these are slightly spiralling (lyre shaped) with yellow tips, with those on the male being slightly shorter and sturdier than on the female.

The bongo grazes mainly on leaves and will often stand on its hind legs to increase its reach. It also digs for roots with its horns. Bongos are usually found in small family herds although bulls often lead a solitary existence, meeting up with other animals only to mate.

Bongo
(*Tragelaphus eurycerus*)
Swahili: *bongo*

Although the small bushbuck antelope exists in fairly large numbers in most of Kenya's game parks, it is a shy, solitary animal and is rarely sighted.

Standing at about 80 cm at the shoulder, the bushbuck is chestnut to dark brown in colour with a variable number of white vertical stripes on the body between the neck and rump, as well as (usually) two horizontal white stripes lower down which give the animal a 'harnessed' appearance. There are also a number of white spots on the upper thigh and a white splash on the neck. Females are reddish brown. Horns are usually only grown by males but females have been known to grow them on rare occasions. They are lyre shaped with gentle spirals and average about 30 cm in length.

Bushbuck are rarely found in groups of more than two and prefer to stick to areas with heavy brush cover. When startled they take off and crash loudly through the undergrowth. They are nocturnal animals and browsers yet rarely move far from their chosen spot. Though shy and elusive they can be aggressive and dangerous when cornered. Their main predators are leopards and pythons.

Bushbuck
(*Tragelaphus scriptus*)
Swahili: *pongo*

1

Dik-dik
Kirk's dik-dik
(Madoqua kirki)
Swahili: *dik-dik*

Kirk's dik-dik is the more common of the two dik-diks found in Kenya (the other is Gunther's dik-dik, found only in Marsabit National Park & Reserve) and is commonly seen in Nairobi, Tsavo, Amboseli and Masai Mara reserves. Its name comes from the 'zic-zic' call it makes when alarmed.

The dik-dik is a tiny antelope, standing only around 35 cm at the shoulder. It is a reddish-brown colour on the back, with lighter flanks and white belly. Size is usually the easiest way to identify a dik-dik, but other telltale marks are the almost total lack of a tail and the tuft of dark hair on the forehead. Horns (found on the males only) are so short (around six cm) that they are often lost in the hair tuft.

Dik-diks are usually seen singly or in pairs and are often found in exceedingly dry places – it seems they don't have a great dependence on water. They are territorial creatures, each pair occupying an area of around five hectares. They are mainly nocturnal but can be seen grazing in acacia scrub in the early morning and late afternoon; like so many animals they rest in the heat of the day.

The females bear a single offspring twice a year. After six months the young dik-dik reaches sexual maturity and is then driven out of the home territory.

Duiker
Common or bush duiker
(Sylvicapra grimmia)
Swahili: *nsya*

This is the most common of the duikers, of which there are at least 10 species. Even so, they are not often sighted as they are largely nocturnal, usually only live in pairs and prefer areas with good scrub cover. They are known to exist in Marsabit, Tsavo, Nairobi, Amboseli, Meru and Masai Mara reserves.

The duiker stands only 60 cm at the shoulder, is a greyish light-brown colour with white belly and a dark brown vertical stripe on the face. The horns (males only) are short (around 20 cm), pointed, and grow straight.

Duikers are widely distributed and can be found in a variety of habitats ranging from open bush to semidesert and up to the snow line of the highest mountains except for bamboo forest and rainforest. This ability to survive in many different habitats explains their survival in cultivated areas where other herbivorous species have been exterminated.

They are almost exclusively browsers and only rarely eat grasses though they appear to supplement their diet with insects and guinea fowl chicks. They are capable of doing without water for long periods but will drink it when available.

The eland looks similar to some varieties of cattle seen on the Indian subcontinent, and is found in Nairobi, Marsabit, Tsavo and Masai Mara parks/reserves.

The biggest of the antelopes, the eland stands about 170 cm at the shoulder and a mature bull can weigh up to 1000 kg. Horns are found on both sexes and these are spiralled at the base, swept straight back and grow to about 65 cm. Males have a much hairier head than the females, and their horns are stouter and slightly shorter. They are a light greyish-brown in colour, and bear as many as 15 vertical white stripes on the body, although these are often almost indistinguishable on some animals.

The eland prefers savannah scrub to wide open spaces, but also avoids thick forest. It grazes on grass and tree foliage in the early morning and late afternoon, and is also active on moonlit nights. It needs to drink once a day, but can go for a month or more without water if its diet includes fodder with high water content.

Eland are usually found in groups of around six to 12, but there may be as many as 50 in a herd. A small herd normally consists of several females and one male, but in larger herds there may be several males, and there is a strict hierarchy. Females reach sexual maturity at around two years and can bear up to 12 calves in a lifetime. The young are born in October-November.

Eland
(*Tragelaphus oryx*)
Swahili: *pofu*

The gerenuk is probably the easiest of all antelopes to identify because of its inordinately long neck, which accounts for its Swahili name, *swala tiga*, meaning giraffe-gazelle. Its distribution is limited to Meru, Samburu, Tsavo and Amboseli national parks.

Growing to around 100 cm at the shoulder, the gerenuk is a dark fawn colour on the back which becomes much lighter on the sides and belly. The horns (found on the male only) curve gently backward and grow up to 40 cm long.

The gerenuk's habitat ranges from dry thorn bush country to semidesert and its food consists mainly of the tender leaves and shoots of acacia bushes. It is quite capable – in the same way as a goat – of standing on its hind legs and using one of its forelegs to pull down the higher branches of bushes to get at the leaves and shoots. Also like goats, they are quite capable of doing without water.

Gerenuk
(*Litocranius walleri*)
Swahili: *swala tiga*

Grant's Gazelle
(Gazella granti)
Swahili: *swala granti*

This is one of the most common antelopes and exists in large numbers in Nairobi, Amboseli, Masai Mara, Tsavo and Marsabit reserves.

Grant's gazelle are most easily identified by their colouring and long horns: sandy brown on the back, clearly demarcated from a lighter colour on the flanks and white belly, and white around the tail and hind legs. They are not a large gazelle, standing around 90 cm at the shoulder. Horns are found on both sexes and are heavily ridged with around 25 rings; in the male they grow to around 60 cm (although they often appear longer because of the relatively small body) and curve gracefully and evenly up and back, usually with some outward curving as well; in the female the horns are much shorter but follow the same pattern.

You usually come across herds of Grant's gazelle in open grassy country where there is some forest cover, although they are also occasionally found in heavily wooded savannah country. Herd size is usually between 20 and 30, with one dominant male, does and young. Food consists mainly of leaves and grass. As water is obtained through dietary intake these gazelles do not need to drink.

Greater Kudu
(Tragelaphus strepsiceros)
Swahili: *tandala mkubwa*

The greater kudu is one of the largest of the antelopes but it's a rare sight and only found in any numbers in Marsabit National Park & Reserve. Elsewhere, kudu prefer hilly country with fairly dense bush cover. The kudu stands around 1.5 metres at the shoulder and weighs up to 250 kg, yet it's a very elegant creature, light grey in colour, with broad ears and a long neck. The sides of the body are marked by six to 10 vertical white stripes and there is a white chevron between the eyes. Horns are carried only by the males and are both divergent and spiralling.

Kudu live in small herds of up to four or five females with their young but these often split up during the rainy season. The males are usually solitary though occasionally they band together into small herds.

They are mainly browsers and only seldom eat grasses but are capable of eating many types of leaves which would be poisonous to other animals.

Although somewhat clumsy animals when on the move, they are capable of clearing well over two metres when jumping.

The hartebeest is a medium-sized antelope and is found in Nairobi, Tsavo, Amboseli and Masai Mara parks. It is easy to recognise as it has a long, narrow face and distinctively angular short horns (on both sexes) which are heavily ridged. Colouring is generally light brown on the back, becoming paler towards the rear and under the belly. The back slopes away from the humped shoulders. They prefer grassy plains for grazing but are also found in lightly treed savannah or hills.

The hartebeest feeds exclusively on grass, and usually drinks twice daily, although it can go for months without water if necessary.

They are social beasts and often intermingle with animals such as zebras and wildebeest. Their behaviour is not unlike the wildebeest's, particularly the head tossing and shaking.

Sexual maturity is reached at around 2½ years and calving goes on throughout the year, although there are peak periods in February and August. Predators are mainly the large cats, hyenas and hunting dogs.

Hartebeest
(Alcelaphus buselaphus)
Swahili: *kongoni*

The graceful impala is one of the most common antelopes and is found in virtually all national parks and reserves in large numbers.

A medium-sized antelope, it stands about 80 cm at the shoulder. The coat is a glossy rufous colour though paler on the flanks with the underparts, rump, throat and chin being white. A narrow black line runs along the middle of the rump to about halfway down the tail and there's also a vertical black stripe on the back of the thighs but, unlike in Grant's gazelle, this does not border the white buttocks. It's also distinguishable from Grant's gazelle by having a tuft of long black hair above the heels of the hind legs. Only the males have horns which are long (averaging 75 cm), lyre-shaped and curve upwards as they spread.

Impala are gregarious animals with each male having a 'harem' of up to 100 females, though more usually around 15 to 20. Males without such a 'harem' form bachelor groups. There is fierce fighting between males during the rutting season but otherwise they are fairly placid animals.

One of the most noticeable characteristics of impala is their speed and prodigious ability at jumping. They are quite capable of clearing 10 metres in a single jump lengthwise or three metres in height and this they frequently do even when there are no obstacles in their path.

Impala are both browsers and grazers and are active during the day and by night. They are quite highly dependent on water but are capable of existing on just dew for fairly long periods. Their main predators are leopards, cheetahs and hunting dogs.

Impala
(Aepyceros melampus)
Swahili: *swala pala*

Klipspringer
(Oreotragus oreotragus)
Swahili: *mbuzi mawe*

The distinctive klipspringers inhabit rocky outcrops in Tsavo, Amboseli, Masai Mara, Marsabit and Meru reserves.

Standing about 50 cm at the shoulder, they are easily recognised by their curious 'tip-toe' stance (the hooves are designed for balance and grip on rocky surfaces) and the greenish tinge of their speckled coarse hair. Horns (found on the male only) are short (10 cm) and widely spaced.

Klipspringers are most often seen on rocky outcrops, or in the grassland in the immediate vicinity, and when alarmed they retreat into the rocks for safety. They are amazingly agile and sure-footed creatures and can often be observed bounding up impossibly rough rock faces. These antelope can also go entirely without water if there is none around, getting all they need from the greenery they eat. They are most active just before and after midday, and single males often keep watch from a good vantage point. The klipspringer is usually found in pairs, or a male with two females, and inhabits a clearly defined territory.

Klipspringers reach sexual maturity at around one year, and females bear one calf twice a year. Calves may stay with the adult couple for up to a year, although young males usually seek their own territory earlier than that.

Predators are mainly the leopard and the crowned eagle, but also include jackals and baboons.

Lesser kudu
(Tragelaphus imberbis)
Swahili: *tandala ndogo*

The lesser kudu is a smaller model of the greater kudu, the major differences being the lack of a beard, more numerous and more pronounced vertical white stripes on the body, and two white patches on the underside of the neck. As with the greater kudu, only the males have horns. The coat colour varies from brownish grey to blue-grey. It stands around a metre high at the shoulder.

Kudu usually live in pairs accompanied by their fawns though females occasionally form small herds. They are very shy animals and spend much of the day hiding in dense bush, only moving out of cover to feed in the early morning and at dusk. This makes them difficult to spot.

Kudu are browsers and feed on a mixture of leaves, young shoots and twigs and, though they drink regularly if water is available, are capable of doing without it for relatively long periods – more so than the greater kudu.

The most likely places you will find them are Tsavo and Marsabit national parks where they prefer the drier, more bushy areas.

Not unlike a duiker in appearance, the small oribi is relatively uncommon, and your best chance of spotting one is in the Masai Mara reserve.

The oribi's most distinguishing mark, although you'll need binoculars to spot it, is a circular batch of naked black skin below the ear – it is actually a scent gland. Another useful indicator is the tuft of black hair on the tip of the short tail. Otherwise the oribi is a uniform golden brown with white on the belly and insides of the legs. Short straight horns about 10 cm in length are found on the males only.

Oribi usually graze in grassy plains with good shelter. If water is available they will drink willingly but can also go without it entirely. When alarmed they bolt and then make bouncing jumps with a curious action – all four legs are kept completely stiff. It is thought this helps them to orient themselves in places with poor visibility. After 100 metres or so they stop and assess the danger.

Oribi are usually found in pairs and are territorial. Sexual maturity is reached at around one year, and the females bear one calf twice a year.

Being quite small, the oribi has many predators, including the larger cats.

Oribi
(Ourebia ourebi)
Swahili: *taya*

The fringe-eared or Kilimanjaro oryx *(Oryx gazella callotis)* is found in Kenya's Amboseli and Tsavo national parks and is a large antelope standing around 120 cm at the shoulder. The coat is a sandy fawn with a black spinal stripe which extends to the tip of the tail. The underparts are white and separated from the lower flanks by another black stripe. There are also two black rings just above the knee of the forelegs.

The related galla oryx *(Oryx gazella gallarum)* is reddish-grey and is most commonly seen in the Marsabit reserve and along the Tana River. (Note that the oryx species name may also be referred to as *beisa*.) Both types of oryx have ovate, pointed ears with the main distinguishing feature being, as the name suggests, a tuft of black hair on the ears of the fringe-eared one. Oryx are easy to distinguish from other antelopes due to their straight, very long and heavily ridged horns which are carried almost parallel. Both the males and females have horns. These horns come into their own when the animal is forced to defend itself. Held down between the forelegs, they are formidable weapons and used to impale an enemy.

Oryx are principally grazers but will also browse on thorny shrubs. They are capable of doing without water for long periods but will drink daily if it is available.

Herds vary from five to 40 individuals and sometimes more though the bulls are usually solitary. Oryx are often found in association with zebra and Grant's gazelle.

Oryx
Fringe-eared oryx
(Oryx gazella callotis)
Swahili: *choroa*

Reedbuck

Bohor reedbuck
(Redunca redunca)
Swahili: *tohe*

The best places to spot the dusty brown reedbuck is in Nairobi and Amboseli national parks, and they are occasionally seen in Tsavo National Park.

The reedbuck is a medium-sized antelope, standing around 80 cm high at the shoulder. The most distinctive features are the forward curving horns (found on the males only) and the bushy tail. The underbelly, inside of the thighs, throat and underside of the tail are white.

The reedbuck frequents open grassy plains or hills and is never found more than around eight km from a water supply. It is very territorial and is found in small groups of up to 10 animals. The groups usually consist of an older male and accompanying females and young. Its diet consists almost exclusively of grass but does include some foliage.

At mating time males fight spiritedly. After reaching sexual maturity at around 1½ years, females bear one calf at a time.

The bohor reedbuck's main predators include the big cats, hyenas and hunting dogs.

Roan Antelope

(Hippotragus equinus)
Swahili: *korongo*

The roan antelope is one of Kenya's less common antelope species. The best place to see one these days is in the Shimba Hills National Reserve, where they have been translocated from other parts of the country, although there are still a few small herds in Masai Mara.

The third largest of the antelopes after eland and kudu at up to 150 cm at the shoulder, a roan bears a striking resemblance to a horse. The coat varies from reddish fawn to dark rufous with white underparts and there's a conspicuous mane of stiff, black-tipped hairs which stretches from the nape to the shoulders. Under the neck, there's another mane of sorts consisting of long dark hairs. The ears are long, narrow and pointed with a brown tassel at the tip. The face is a very distinctive black and white pattern. Both sexes have curving backswept horns which can measure up to 70 cm.

Roan are aggressive by nature and fight from a very early age – a characteristic which frequently deters predators. For most of the year they live in small herds of up to 20 and sometimes more, led by a master bull, but in the mating season, the bulls become solitary and take a female out of the herd. The pair stay together until the calf is born after which the females form a herd by themselves. They eventually return to their former herd. Herds congregate during the dry season.

Being principally grazers, roan rarely move far when food is plentiful but they are susceptible to drought and during such periods they may be constantly on the move.

Also found only in the Shimba Hills National Reserve, the sable antelope is slightly smaller than its cousin the roan, but is more solidly built. The colouring is dark brown to black, with white face markings and belly. Both sexes carry long back-swept horns which average around 80 cm, those of the male being longer and more curved.

The sable antelope is active mainly in the early morning and late afternoon, and is found in herds of up to 25 and sometimes more in the dry season. They are territorial and each group occupies a large area, although within this area individual males have demarcated territories of up to 30 hectares. Sables feed mainly off grass but leaves and foliage from trees account for around 10% of their diet.

Females start bearing calves at around three years of age, and the main calving times are January and September.

Like the roan, the sable is a fierce fighter and has been known to kill lions when attacked. Other predators include the leopard, hyena and hunting dog.

Sable Antelope
(Hippotragus niger)
Swahili: *pala hala*

The sitatunga is a swamp antelope with unusual elongated hooves which give it the ability to walk on marshy ground without sinking. It is restricted solely to the Saiwa Swamp National Park near Kitale, and it's well worth a visit to this small, walkers-only park.

Very similar to the bushbuck in appearance, except that the coat of the male is much darker and the hair of both sexes much longer and shaggier, the sitatunga stands something over one metre at the shoulder. The females have a lighter, reddish coat and the males have twisted horns up to 90 cm long. It is a fairly shy antelope and sightings are not all that common. A good swimmer, the sitatunga will often submerge itself almost completely when alarmed.

It feeds largely on papyrus and other reeds and is usually nocturnal though in places where it remains undisturbed it can be diurnal. Animals normally live singly or in pairs but sometimes come together in small herds numbering up to 15.

Sitatunga
(Tragelaphus spekei)
Swahili: *nzohe*

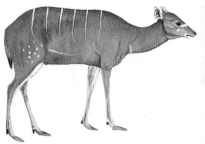

Thomson's Gazelle
(Gazella thomsonii)
Swahili: *swala tomi*

The small and frisky Thomson's gazelle is instantly recognisable by the black slash across the side which separates the brown back from the white underbelly. They are very common in the plains country – Amboseli, Masai Mara and Nairobi reserves, but very rare in different habitats such as Tsavo National Park.

Standing around 60 cm at the shoulders, the 'Tommy' is one of the smaller antelopes. Horns on the male grow to about 30 cm and almost straight with just a gentle curve towards the tips; in the female the horns are straighter and much shorter. Another easy to identify characteristic is the short black tail which seems to be constantly twitching. Along with the oribi, Tommys also do the stiff-legged bouncing jump when alarmed.

Group size varies: one old (largely territorial) male may be accompanied by anything from five to 50 females, or there may be herds of up to 500 young males without territory. When food is plentiful the herds tend to be smaller and more territorial. In times of drought herds of several thousand may gather and roam for food. They are often found in close proximity to other animals, including Grant's gazelles and wildebeest.

Sexual maturity is reached at around one year but males only mate after establishing their own territory, which occurs sometime after two years of age. Calving occurs throughout the year though tends to peak at the end of the rainy season.

Being a small animal, Tommys have many predators, including the big cats, hunting dogs, hyenas and servals.

The topi is not unlike the hartebeest in appearance, but is a dark almost purplish colour and has black patches on the rear thighs, front legs and face. Its horns, which are found on both sexes, also differ in shape from the hartebeest in curving gently up, out and back. Although fairly widely distributed in East Africa, in Kenya it is only found in Masai Mara where it exists in large numbers.

A highly gregarious antelope which lives in herds numbering from 15 up to several hundred individuals, topi congregate at certain times of year in gatherings of up to 10,000 in preparation for a migration to fresh pastures. They are often found mingling with wildebeest, hartebeest and zebra.

In the mating season, bulls select a well-defined patch of ground which is defended against rivals and this is where mating takes place. At this time females are free to wander from one patch to another. After mating, the herds split into single-sex parties.

Topi are exclusively grazers and prefer flood plains which support lush pasture though they are capable of thriving on dry grasses which other antelopes will not eat. When water is available they drink frequently but they are also capable of surviving long periods without water so long as there is sufficient grass available.

Their main predator is the lion.

Topi
(Damaliscus lunatus)
Swahili: *nyamera*

Waterbuck
Defassa or common waterbuck
(*Kobus ellipsiprymnus*)
Swahili: *kuru*

The defassa waterbuck is a fairly solid animal and is easily recognisable by its thick, shaggy, dark brown coat, and white inner thighs. It is fairly common and easily seen in Nairobi and Nakuru national parks, and in Masai Mara. A second variety, the ringed waterbuck (also *Kobus ellipsiprymnus*), so-called because of the white ring around its rump, is also seen in Marsabit, Tsavo and Amboseli parks. Both varieties have white facial and throat markings.

Only the males have horns, and these curve gradually outwards then grow straight up to a length of about 75 cm. As you might expect from the name, waterbuck are good swimmers and readily enter the water to escape from predators. Their habitat is always close to water, and males have marked territories by the water's edge. Females and younger males tend to wander at random through male territories. Herds are small and usually consist of cows, calves and one mature bull – the other bulls live in small groups apart from the herd.

The bulk of the waterbuck's diet is grass but it does eat some of the foliage of trees and bushes.

Sexual maturity is reached at just over one year, although a male will not become the dominant bull in the herd until around five years of age.

Waterbuck are usually only preyed on when other food is scarce. The reason being that when mature the flesh is tough and has a distinct odour. Predators such as lions, leopards and hunting dogs go for the young calves and females.

Wildebeest are to the African savannah what the bison once were to the North American prairies. Numbering in their millions in certain areas, particularly Masai Mara and over the border in Serengeti, they are unmistakable for their prehistoric appearance. Wildebeest (also known as blue wildebeest or brindled gnu) are well known for their eccentric behaviour which includes loud snorting, tossing and shaking of the head, bucking, running around in circles and rolling in the dust (thought to be a reaction to the activity of the botfly larva which manage to find their way right up into their nostrils). They are heavily built with a massive head and wild mane, are somewhat clumsy, and have been described as having the forequarters of an ox, the hind parts of an antelope and the tail of a horse.

Their sheer numbers, nevertheless, are testimony to their superb adaptation to the environment.

Almost entirely grazers, they are constantly on the move in search of good pasture and water, and their annual migration between the Serengeti and Masai Mara (and vice versa) has to be one of the world's most spectacular sights. Thousands lose their lives in this annual event – drowning in rivers, being taken by crocodiles and other predators or just through sheer exhaustion. The migration north from Serengeti takes place in July and the return trip from Masai Mara in October.

They're very gregarious animals and are usually seen in large herds numbering up to tens of thousands in association with zebra, Thomson's gazelle and other herbivores.

During the mating season, groups of up to 150 females and their young are gathered together by one to three bulls which defend a defined territory against rivals even when on the move. There's apparently no hierarchy amongst the bulls and, at the end of the mating season, the breeding herds are reabsorbed into the main herds.

Although they graze in a scattered fashion without any apparent social organisation during the rainy season, they coalesce around water holes and remaining pasture in the dry season. Wildebeest prefer to drink daily and will walk up to 50 km to secure water but are capable of surviving for up to five days without it. They're also a noisy animal when grazing, constantly producing a series of snorts and low-pitched grunts.

Their main predators are lions, cheetahs and hunting dogs though hyenas are also very partial to young calves.

Wildebeest (Gnu)
Blue wildebeest or brindled gnu
(Connochaetes taurinus)
Swahili: *nyumbu*

BIRDS

Flamingo
(Phoenicopterus minor,
Phoenicopterus ruber)
Swahili: *heroe*

Flamingos are found by the million in Kenya. They are attracted by the proliferation of algae and crustaceans which thrive in the soda lakes of Baringo, Bogoria, Nakuru and Magadi in the Rift Valley, and Lake Natron across the border in Tanzania.

There are always some birds at each lake but large concentrations seem to move capriciously from one to another over a period of years. Lake Nakuru is the current hot spot but this may well change. It is thought that the changing water levels may be one reason why they change locations. Whatever lake they are presently at, the best time of the year for flamingo viewing is in January-February when they form huge pink masses around the shores of the lakes.

Flamingos have a complicated and sophisticated system for filtering the foodstuffs out of the water. This is because the highly alkane water would be toxic if consumed in large quantities. The deep-pink lesser flamingo, *Phoenicopterus minor*, filters algae and diatoms out of the water by vigorous suction and expulsion of the water in and out of its beak several times per second. The minute particles are caught on fine hairlike protrusions which line the inside of the mandibles. This is all done with the bill upside down in the water. The suction is created by the movement of the thick and fleshy tongue which lies in a groove in the lower mandible and works to and fro like a piston. Where the *Phoenicopterus minor* obtains its food largely by sweeping its head to and fro and filtering the water, the greater flamingo, or *Phoenicopterus ruber*, is more a bottom feeder and supplements its algae diet with small molluscs, crustaceans and other organic particles from the mud. It has been estimated that one million lesser flamingos consume over 180 tons of algae and diatoms daily!

The very distinct and instantly identifiable ostrich is the largest living bird. It is widely distributed throughout the savannah plains of Kenya, and so is most widely seen in the southern parks and reserves – Masai Mara, Amboseli and Tsavo.

The adult ostrich stands around 2½ metres high and weighs as much as 150 kg. The neck and the legs are bare, and all these areas of bare skin turn bright red in breeding males. The bushy plumage on the males is black, with white feathers in the redundant wings and the tail. The females are a uniform greyish brown and are slightly smaller and lighter than the males. The ostrich's long and strong legs can push it along at up to 50 km/h.

Ostriches tend to be territorial and are rarely seen in groups of more than six individuals. They feed on leaves, flowers and seeds of a variety of plants. When feeding, the food is gradually accumulated in the top of the neck and then passes down to the stomach in small boluses, and it's possible to see these masses of food actually moving down the neck.

The ostrich breeds in the dry season, and the males put on quite an impressive courtship display. Having driven off any possible rival males, the male trots up to the female with tail erect, then squats down and rocks from side to side, simultaneously waving each wing in the air alternately. Just for good measure the neck also waves from side to side. The males may couple with more than one female, in which case the eggs of all the females (up to five) are laid on the same nest, and so it may contain as many as 30 eggs. The eggs are incubated by the major female (the one first mated with) by day, and by the male at night. The other female birds have nothing further to do with the eggs or offspring.

Ostrich
(Struthio camelus)
Swahili: *mbuni*

Vulture
Nubian vulture
(Torgos tracheliotus)
Swahili: *gushu*

Vultures are a large, eagle-like bird belonging to the Accipitridae family, of which hawks and eagles are also members. There are a whole range of different species, the most common ones in Kenya being the Egyptian *(Neophron percnopterus)*, hooded *(Necrosyrtes monachus)* and white-headed vulture *(Trigonoceps occipitalis)*. Others include Rüppell's vulture *(Gyps ruppellii)*, a common nester in Kenya's Hell's Gate National Park, and the white-backed vulture *(Gyps bengalensis)*, found in all East African national parks. Vultures prefer savannah country with high concentrations of game.

These large birds, with a wing span of up to three metres and weighing up to five kg, feed almost exclusively by scavenging. They are fairly inefficient fliers and so rely to a large degree on finding rising hot-air thermals on which to glide and ascend. For this reason you won't see them in the air until well into the morning when the upcurrents have started.

African vultures have no sense of smell and so depend totally on their excellent eyesight, and that of their colleagues, for locating food. Once a kill or a fallen animal has been sighted a vulture will descend rapidly and await its turn at the carcass. Of course other vultures will follow the first downwards and in this chain reaction they may come from as far afield as 50 km. They are very efficient feeders and can rapidly strip flesh from bone, although they are not good at getting a start on a completely intact carcass. A large group of vultures (and they congregate in groups, often of up to 100) can strip an antelope to the bone in half an hour. Because they are poor fliers, however, vultures often cannot fly with a belly full of food and so after gorging will retreat a short distance and digest their meal.

BUFFALO

The buffalo is another animal which appears in great numbers in all the major parks, with the exception of Nairobi National Park.

The massive animal is said to be the most dangerous (to humans) of all African animals and should be treated with caution, although for the most part they will stay out of your way. Females protecting young calves, and solitary rogue bulls, are the most aggressive, and having 800 kg of angry animal thundering towards you is no joke.

Both sexes have the distinctive curving horns which broaden and almost meet over the forehead, although those in the female are usually smaller. The buffalo's colour varies from dark reddish brown to black.

Buffalo are often found in herds of 100 or more and never stray too far from water, especially in the dry season. When food and water are plentiful the herds often disperse. They are territorial in that they have a home range of about 50 km outside of which they don't stray.

Syncerus caffer
Swahili: *mbogo*

CARNIVORES

Cheetah
(Acinonyx jubatus)
Swahili: *duma*

The cheetah is one of the most impressive animals you can hope to see – sleek, streamlined and menacing. It's found in small numbers in all of Kenya's major game reserves – Nairobi, Amboseli, Masai Mara, Tsavo, Samburu, Buffalo Springs, Marsabit and Meru.

Similar in appearance to the leopard, the cheetah is longer and lighter in the body, has a slightly bowed back and a much smaller and rounder face. It stands around 80 cm at the shoulder, measures around 210 cm in length (including the tail) and weighs anything from 40 to 60 kg.

When undisturbed, the cheetah hunts in early morning or late evening, although these days with the number of tourist vehicles around, it is often found hunting at midday when the rubbernecks are back in the lodges stuffing their faces and the poor animal has a chance to stalk some dinner undisturbed. This forced change in habit is particularly stressful for the cheetah as it relies on bursts of tremendous speed for catching its prey, and this speed (up to 110 km/h) is only sustainable for a very short time. Obviously, as the midday heat is much greater than morning or afternoon, hunting for the cheetah becomes much more difficult. During a hunt the cheetah stalks its prey as close as possible and then sprints for 100 metres or so; if by that time it hasn't caught its victim, it will give up and try elsewhere. The prey (usually small antelope) is brought to the ground often with a flick of the paw to trip it up. Other food includes hares, jackals and young wart hogs.

Cheetah cubs reach maturity at around one year but stay with the mother much longer than that as they have to learn hunting and survival skills. Cubs are usually born in litters numbering from two to four, and the main breeding period is from March to December.

The cheetah rarely fights but predators (mainly of cubs) include lions, leopards and hyenas.

Civet
(Viverra civetta or *Civetticus civetta)*
Swahili: *fungo*

The civet is a medium sized omnivore around 40 cm high at the shoulder and 90 cm long (excluding the tail), with some canine features and short, partially retractile claws. Its coat of long coarse hair is basically grey but with a definite and variable pattern of black spots over most of the body, along with two black bands stretching from the ears to the lower neck and two black bands around the upper part of the hind legs. The tail is bushy at the base becoming thinner towards the tip, held out straight when the animal is on the move, and black except for three to four greyish bands near the base. The head is mostly greyish white and the ears are quite small, rounded and tipped with white hairs.

Civets are solitary, nocturnal animals which hide in thickets, tall grass or abandoned burrows during the day and so are rarely sighted. The most likely places to spot one are in Marsabit or Tsavo West reserves, although they are also known to inhabit Nairobi, Amboseli and Masai Mara.

It has a very varied diet consisting of rodents, birds and their eggs, reptiles, amphibians, snails, insects (especially ants and termites) as well as berries, the young shoots of bushes and fruits.

Litters consist of up to four cubs and these have a similar, though slightly darker colouring.

The other conspicuous feature of the civet is the presence of musk glands in the anal region which produce a foul-smelling oily substance used to mark territory. This musk is used in the manufacture of perfumes though in Western countries it is collected from animals held in captivity.

Genet
Small-spotted or common genet
(*Genetta genetta*)
Swahili: *kanu*

Unlike the civet, the genet distinctly resembles the domestic cat though the body is more elongated and the tail longer and bushier. The coat is long and coarse with a prominent crest along the spine. The basic colour varies from grey to fawn and is patterned from the neck to the tail with roundish dark brown to blackish spots. The tail is banded with nine to 10 similarly coloured rings and has a whitish tip. Another species of genet, the large-spotted or rusty-spotted genet (*Genetta tigrina*), is similar in appearance to the common genet, but has a brownish-black spinal stripe and larger spots.

The genet lives in savannah and open country and is a very agile tree climber but not frequently sighted since it is entirely nocturnal. During the day it sleeps in abandoned burrows, rock crevices, hollow trees or up on high branches and seems to return to the same spot each day. The animals live singly or in pairs.

Its prey is generally hunted on the ground though it will climb trees to seek out nesting birds and their eggs. Like the domestic cat, it stalks prey by crouching flat on the ground. Its diet consists of a variety of small animals (mostly rodents), birds, reptiles (including snakes), insects and fruits. It is well known for being a wasteful killer, often eating only a small part of the animals it catches.

Litters typically consist of two to three kittens. Like the domestic cat, the genet spits and growls when angered or in danger.

Hunting Dog
(*Lycaon pictus*)
Swahili: *mbwa mwitu*

The hunting dog is the size of a large domestic dog and is found in all the reserves, or where there is a high concentration of game animals.

The dog's unusual coloration makes it quite an ugly creature – the black and yellowish splotches are different in each animal, ranging from almost all black to almost all yellow. The only constant is the white tail tip. Prominent physical features are the large rounded ears.

Hunting dogs tend to move in packs ranging from four or five up to as many as 40. They are efficient hunters and work well together. Once the prey has been singled out and the chase is on, a couple of dogs will chase hard while the rest pace themselves; once the first two tire another two step in and so on until the quarry is exhausted. Favoured animals for lunch include gazelle, impala and other similar sized antelope. They rarely scavenge, preferring to kill their own.

Hunting dog cubs are usually born in grass-lined burrows in litters averaging seven, although litters of up to 15 are not unheard of. By six months they are competent hunters and have abandoned the burrow. The hunting dog has no predators, although unguarded cubs sometimes fall prey to hyenas and eagles.

The spotted hyena is a fairly common animal throughout most of Kenya and especially where game is plentiful. Bearing a distinct resemblance to dogs, it is a large, powerfully built animal with a very sloping back, broad head and large eyes but with rather weak hindquarters. The sloping back is what gives the animal its characteristic loping gait when running. Its coat is short, dull grey to buff and entirely patterned with rounded blackish spots except on the throat. Its powerful jaws and teeth enable it to crush and swallow the bones of most animals except the elephant.

Hyenas are mainly nocturnal animals but are frequently seen during the day, especially in the vicinity of lion or cheetah kills impatiently waiting for their turn at the carcass along with vultures. Otherwise, the days are spent in long grass, abandoned aardvark holes or in large burrows which they dig out up to a metre below the surface of the soil. It's a very noisy animal and when camping out in the bush at night you'll frequently hear its characteristic and spine-chilling howl which rises quickly to a high-pitched scream. This is only one of the sounds which the spotted hyena emits. Another is the well known 'laugh', though this is generally only produced when the animal finds food or is mating.

The hyena has highly developed senses of smell, sight and sound, all important in locating food (carrion or prey) and for mutual recognition among pack members and mating pairs.

Hyenas are well known as scavengers and can often be seen following hunting lions and hunting dogs, usually at a respectable distance, though they will occasionally force these animals to abandon their kill. On the other hand, although carrion does form an important part of their diet, hyenas are also true predators and are more than capable of bringing down many of the larger herbivores. To do this they often form packs to run down wildebeest, zebra and gazelle, and are able to reach speeds of up to 60 km/h. They also stalk pregnant antelope and, when the female gives birth, snatch and kill the newly born foal and occasionally the mother too. Domestic stock are also preyed on.

In the mating season, hyenas assemble in large numbers especially on moonlit nights. All hell breaks loose on these occasions and the noise is incredible. The gestation period is about 110 days and litters number up to four though usually less. The young are born in the mother's burrow. The pups are weaned at around six weeks old and become independent shortly afterwards.

Humans are the hyena's main enemy, though lions and hunting dogs will occasionally kill or mutilate hyenas if they get too close to a kill. Although they are reputed to be cowardly, you're advised to keep your distance from them as they do occasionally attack humans sleeping in the open.

Hyena
(Crocuta crocuta)
Swahili: *fisi*

Jackal
Common or golden jackal
(Canis aureus)
Swahili: *bweha*

There are two species of jackal found in Kenya: the common or golden jackal, and the black-backed jackal *(Canis mesomelas)*, which is a common sight in the major reserves. The black back which gives it its name is usually more silvery than black, is wide at the neck and tapers to the tail. The golden jackal is similar, though without the back markings. Although the jackal is in fact a dog, its bushy tail and long ears are more like those of a fox than a dog.

The jackal is mostly a scavenger and so is commonly seen in the vicinity of a kill. The jackal will hunt for itself – insects, small mammals and birds, even the occasional small antelope. They are also found on the outskirts of human settlements and will attack sheep, poultry and calves.

Jackals are territorial and a pair will guard an area of around 250 hectares. Cubs are born in litters of five to seven and, although they don't reach maturity until almost a year old, they usually leave the parents when just two months old.

Enemies of the black-backed jackal include the leopard, cheetah and eagle.

Leopard
(Panthera pardus)
Swahili: *chui*

The leopard is perhaps the most graceful and agile of the large cats. A powerfully built animal which uses cunning to catch its prey, it is present in all the major game reserves but is difficult to find as it is nocturnal and spends the day resting on branches of trees, often up to five metres above the ground. It is as agile as a domestic cat in climbing such trees and this is also where it carries its prey so that it's out of the way of other scavengers which might contest the kill.

The leopard's coat is usually short and dense with numerous black spots on a yellowish background. The underparts are white and less densely spotted. In addition, the coats of leopards found in open country are generally lighter than those in wooded country.

Leopards are solitary animals except during the mating season when the male and female live together. The gestation period is three months and a litter usually consists of up to three cubs. They prey on a variety of birds, reptiles and mammals including large rodents, rock hyrax, wart hogs, smaller antelopes and monkeys (especially baboon), though they occasionally take domestic animals such as goats, sheep, poultry and dogs. This wide range of prey explains why they are still able to survive even in areas of dense human settlement long after other large predators have disappeared. But their presence is generally unwelcome since they do occasionally turn human-eater. It also explains why they are found in very varied habitats ranging from semidesert to dense forest and as high as the snow line on Mt Kenya and Kilimanjaro.

Lions are one of the main attractions of the game reserves and are found in all the main ones. They spend most of the day lying under bushes or in other attractive places and when you see a pride stretched out in the sun like this, they seem incredibly docile. It is possible to drive up very close to them in a vehicle – they either don't sense humans or realise that humans in vehicles are not a threat. Whatever the case, don't be tempted to get out of a vehicle at any time in the vicinity of a lion. Loud noises and sudden movement also disturb them. They're at their most active for around four hours in the late afternoon, then spend the rest of the time laying around.

Lions generally hunt in groups, with the males driving the prey towards the concealed females who do most of the actual killing. Although they cooperate well together, lions are not the most efficient hunters – as many as four out of five attacks will be unsuccessful. Their reputation as human-eaters is largely undeserved as in most circumstances they will flee on seeing a human. However, once they have the taste for human flesh, and realise how easy it is to make a meal of one, lions can become habitual killers of people. This mostly occurs among the old lions which no longer have the agility to bring down more fleet-footed animals.

Lions are territorial beasts and a pride of one to three males and accompanying females (up to 15) and young will defend an area of anything from 20 to 400 sq km, depending on the type of country and the amount of game food available.

Lion cubs are born in litters averaging two or three. They become sexually mature by 1½ years and males are driven from the family group shortly after this. Lions reach full maturity at around six years of age. Unguarded cubs are preyed on by hyenas, leopards, pythons and hunting dogs.

Lion
(Panthera leo)
Swahili: *simba*

Mongoose
Banded mongoose
(Mungos mungo)
Swahili: *kicheche*

The banded mongoose (the one most commonly found in Kenya) is usually seen in groups in Tsavo, Amboseli and Masai Mara reserves. It is brown or grey in colour and is easily identifiable by the dark bands across the back which stretch from the shoulder to the tail. The animal is about 40 cm in length and weighs between 1.3 and 2.3 kg.

Mongoose are very sociable animals and live in packs of between 30 and 50 individuals which stay close to one another when foraging for prey. They are often very noisy, having a wide variety of sounds which they use to communicate with each other. When threatened they growl and spit in much the same manner as a domestic cat. Being diurnal animals, they prefer sunny spots during the day but retire to warrens – rock crevices, hollow trees and abandoned anthills – at night. A pack frequently has several warrens within its territory.

The mongoose's most important source of food are insects, grubs and larvae but they also eat small amphibians, reptiles, birds' eggs, fruits, berries and birds. Their main predators are birds of prey though they are also taken by lions, leopards and hunting dogs. Snakes rarely pose a danger since these would-be predators are attacked by the entire pack and the snake is frequently killed.

Mongoose are one of the creatures which have become very habituated to humans in some places and come right up to the game lodges scavenging for scraps.

Serval
(Felis serval)
Swahili: *mondo*

The serval is a wild cat, about the size of a domestic cat but with much longer legs. It is found in all the major game reserves in Kenya.

The serval's colouring is a dirty yellow with large black spots which follow lines along the length of the body. Other prominent features are the large upright ears, the long neck and the relatively short tail. It stands about 50 cm high and measures 130 cm including the tail. Being a largely nocturnal animal, the serval is usually only seen in the early morning or late evening. It lives on birds, hares and rodents and is an adept hunter – it catches birds in mid-flight by leaping into the air.

Serval cat young are born in litters of up to four and although independent at one year, don't reach sexual maturity until two years of age.

ELEPHANT

Everyone knows what an elephant looks like so a description of them is unnecessary except perhaps to mention that African elephants are much larger than their Asian counterparts and that their ears are wider and flatter. A fully grown bull can weigh up to 6½ tonnes and sometimes more. In Kenya they are found in all the major game parks with the exception of Nairobi National Park where they would be too destructive to the environment to make their long term presence viable. They have been encountered as high as 3600 metres on the slopes of Mt Kenya.

The tusks on an old bull can weigh as much as 50 kg each, although 15 kg to 25 kg is more usual. The longest tusks ever found on an elephant in Kenya measured 3½ metres! Both the males and females grow tusks, although in the female they are usually smaller. An elephant's sight is poorly developed but its senses of smell and hearing are excellent.

Elephants are gregarious animals and are usually found in herds of between 10 and 20 individuals consisting of one mature bull, a couple of younger bulls, cows and calves, though herds of up to 50 individuals are sometimes encountered. Old bulls appear to lose the herding instinct and often lead a solitary existence, only rejoining the herd for mating. Herds are often very noisy since elephants communicate with each other by a variety of sounds, the most usual ones being various rumbles produced through the trunk or mouth. The most well known elephant sound, however, is the high-pitched trumpeting which they produce when frightened or in despair and when charging.

Herds are on the move night and day in order to secure sufficient water and fodder, both of which they consume in vast quantities – the average daily food intake of an adult is in the region of 250 kg. They are both grazers and browsers and feed on a wide variety of vegetable matter including grasses, leaves, twigs, bark, roots and fruits and they frequently break quite large trees in order to get at the leaves. Because of this destructive capacity, they can be a serious threat to a fragile environment especially in drought years and are quite capable of turning dense woodland into open grassland over a relatively short period of time. Because of Africa's rapidly increasing human population and the expansion of cultivated land, they also come into conflict with farmers when they destroy crops such as bananas, maize and sugar cane.

The other essential part of an elephant's diet are various mineral salts which they obtain from 'salt licks'. These are dug out of the earth with the aid of their tusks and swallowed in considerable quantities.

Loxodonta africana
Swahili: *ndovu* or *tembo*

Elephants breed year-round and the period of gestation is 22 to 24 months. Expectant mothers leave the herd along with one or two other females and select a secluded spot where birth occurs. They rejoin the herd a few days later. Calves weigh around 130 kg at birth and stand just under a metre high. They're very playful and guarded carefully and fondly by their mothers until weaned at two years old. After that, they continue to grow for a further 23 years or so, reaching puberty at around 10 to 12 years. An elephant's life span is normally 60 to 70 years though some individuals reach the ripe old age of 100 and even longer.

GIRAFFE

Rothschild's Giraffe
(Giraffa camelopardalis rothschildi)
Swahili: *twiga*

Rothschild's giraffe, one of three types of giraffe common to East Africa, is found in western Kenya around Lake Baringo, and Uganda. The Masai giraffe *(Giraffa camelopardalis tippelskirchi)* is more widespread in Kenya and is found in all the parks south and west of Nairobi. Rothschild's is paler and more thickset than the Masai, with less-jagged patches, and is usually unmarked below the knee. The Masai giraffe has irregular, star-shaped patches and is usually buff-coloured below the knee. However, it is often difficult to identify a particular giraffe type because individual and regional variations in colour and pattern are wide.

The average male stands around 5½ metres; females are mere midgets at 4½ metres. Horns are found on both sexes, but are merely short projections of bone covered by skin and hair. These are all that's left of what would once have been antlers. Despite the fact that the giraffe has such a huge neck, it still has only seven vertebrae – the same number as humans.

Reticulated Giraffe
(Giraffa camelopardalis reticulata)
Swahili: *twiga*

The reticulated giraffe differs from the Masai and Rothschild's giraffes in both colouring and pattern. It is a deeper brown and its body has a much more regular 'tortoiseshell' pattern, with white rather than buff-coloured outlines. It is found in the north and north-east of the country – Meru, Marsabit and Samburu reserves. You can easily come across them at the side of the road between Isiolo and Marsabit but probably the biggest herds are to be seen in Samburu and Buffalo Springs reserves.

Giraffes graze mainly on acacia tree foliage in the early morning and afternoon; the rest of the time they rest in the shade. At night they also rest for a couple of hours, either standing or lying down.

HIPPOPOTAMUS

In Kenya the hippo is found in greatest numbers in Masai Mara but can also be observed at Amboseli, Nairobi and Tsavo national parks and at Lake Baringo. At Tsavo there is a submarine viewing tank but the hippos are not very cooperative and seem to have deserted the immediate area.

Hippos are too well known to need description except to note that these huge, fat animals with enormous heads and short legs vary between 1350 kg and 2600 kg when fully grown. Their ears, eyes and nostrils are so placed that they remain above water when the animal is submerged.

Hippos generally spend most of the day wallowing in shallow water, coming out to graze only at night. They are entirely herbivorous and feed on a variety of grasses in pastures up to several km away from their aquatic haunts. They are voracious feeders and can consume up to 60 kg of vegetable matter each night. They urinate and defecate in well-defined areas – often in the water in which case they disperse the excreta with their tails.

Hippos are very gregarious animals and live in schools of 15 to 30 individuals though, in certain places, the schools can be much larger. Each school consists about equally of bulls and cows (with their calves) and, like other herd animals, there's an established hierarchy. Hippos may appear to be placid but they fight frequently among themselves for dominance and this is especially so among the males. The wounds inflicted in such fights are often quite horrific and virtually every hippo you see will bear the scars of such conflicts. They're not normally dangerous to humans unless cornered or frightened but you should definitely keep your distance. They may look sluggish but they are capable of running at considerable speed.

Hippos breed all year and the period of gestation is around 230 days. The cows give birth to a single calf either in the water or on land and suckle it for a period of four to six months after which it begins to graze on a regular basis. Sexual maturity is reached at about four years old and the life span is about 30 years (longer in captivity).

The only natural predators of hippos are lion and crocodile which prey on the young. Though hippos occasionally foul up fishing nets, they're considered to be beneficial since their wallowing stirs up the bottom mud and their excreta is a valuable fertiliser which encourages the growth of aquatic organisms.

Hippopotamus amphibius
Swahili: *kiboko*

HYRAX or DASSIE

Procavia capensis
Swahili: *pimbi*

The species of hyrax you're most likely to encounter (especially on Baboon Cliffs in Nakuru National Park but also in Nairobi, Tsavo, Masai Mara and Marsabit reserves) is the cape rock hyrax *(Procavia capensis)* or cape dassie. It's a small but robust animal about the size of a large rabbit with a short and pointed snout, large ears and thick fur. The tail is either absent or reduced to a stump.

Hyrax are extremely sociable animals and live in colonies of up to 60 individuals, usually in rocky, scrub-covered locations. They're diurnal, feeding mostly in the morning and evening on grass, bulbs and roots, and on insects such as grasshoppers and locusts. During the rest of the day they can be seen sunning themselves on rocks and chasing each other in play. Where habituated to humans, they are often quite tame but in other places, when alarmed, they dash into rock crevices uttering shrill screams. Their senses of hearing and sight are excellent.

Hyrax breed all year and the period of gestation is about seven months – a remarkably long period for an animal of this size. Up to six young are born at a time and the young are cared for by the whole colony. Predators include leopards, hunting dogs, eagles, mongoose and pythons.

Despite being such a small creature, hyrax are more closely related to the elephant than any other living creature by virtue of certain common physical traits.

PRIMATES

Baboon
(Papio cynocephalus)
Swahili: *nyani*

The yellow baboon is just one of at least seven subspecies of baboon and is the one most commonly sighted in Kenya. The other relatively common one is the olive baboon *(Papio anubis),* most often seen in Nairobi National Park. The main difference between the two is that the olive baboon has long facial hair and a mane on the shoulders, especially the males.

Baboons have a dog-like snout which gives them a much more aggressive and less human-like facial appearance than most other primates. They are usually found in large troops (of up to 150 animals, with a dominant male) which will have a territorial area ranging from two to 30 sq km. They spend most of the time on the ground searching for insects, spiders and birds' eggs. The baboons have also found that the lodges in the game parks are easy pickings, especially when idiotic tourists throw food to them so they can get a good snap with the Instamatic.

Baboons are fierce fighters and their only real natural enemy is the leopard, although young cubs are also taken by lions and hunting dogs.

Looking more like an Australian possum, the bush-baby is in fact a small monkey and is about the size of a rabbit. It is found in all major reserves, although being a nocturnal creature it is rarely sighted by day. The head is small with large rounded ears and, as might be expected on a nocturnal animal, relatively large eyes. The thick fur is dark brown and the bushbaby sports a thick bushy tail. Your average bushbaby measures around 80 cm in length, of which the tail is around 45 cm, and weighs less than two kg.

The lesser bushbaby *(Galago senegalensis)* is about half the size of the greater bushbaby. It is a very light grey in colour and has yellowish colouring on the legs.

Greater Bushbaby
(Galago crassicaudatus)
Swahili: *komba*

This forest-dwelling colobus monkey is a hand-some creature found only in the forest parks – Mt Kenya, Mt Elgon, Aberdare and Saiwa Swamp.

The monkey is basically black but has a white face, bushy white tail and a white 'cape' around the back which flows out behind when the monkey moves through the trees – an impressive sight. An average colobus measures about 140 cm, of which about 80 cm is tail, and weighs from 10 kg to 23 kg.

The black and white colobus spends most of its time in the forest canopy and is easily missed unless you keep a sharp eye out. It is unusual for them to leave the trees; they get most of their water from small puddles formed in the hollows of branches and trunks.

Colobus monkeys are usually found in troops of up to 12 animals, consisting of a dominant male, females and young. Newborn monkeys are initially white, gaining their adult coat at around six months.

Eastern Black & White Colobus
(Colobus guereza caudatus)
Swahili: *mbega*

The playful vervet is the most common monkey in Kenya and is seen in parks and reserves through-out the country. It is easily recognisable with its black face fringed by white hair, and yellowish-grey hair elsewhere except for the underparts which are whitish. The males have an extraordi-nary bright blue scrotum.

Vervets are usually found in groups of up to 30 and are extremely cheeky and inquisitive – as you may well find if camping in the game reserves; they are often very habituated to humans and will come right inside tents or minibuses in search of a hand-out. Normally they live in woodland and savannah but never in rainforest or semi-desert areas.

Vervet
Green monkey or grivet
(Cercopithecus aethiops)
Swahili: *tumbili*

RHINOCEROS

Diceros bicornis
Swahili: *kifaru*

One of Africa's most sought-after species by poachers, the numbers of black rhino in Kenya have fallen dramatically in the past, though they are now once again on the increase, thanks to some determined conservation efforts. They are now thought to number around 500, compared with around 20,000 in 1970!

Rhinos are one of the more difficult animals to sight, simply because they're so few in numbers compared to other wildlife. They are seen in Amboseli quite often, and also in Masai Mara, Tsavo East (rarely), Nairobi National Park and Nakuru. Rhinos usually feed in the very early morning or late afternoon; at other times they tend to keep out of sight.

The eyesight of the rhino is extremely poor and it relies more on its keen senses of smell and hearing. Usually when alarmed it will flee from perceived danger, but if it decides to charge it needs to be given a wide berth, though with its poor eyesight chances are it'll miss its target anyway. Rhinos have been known to charge trains and even the carcasses of dead elephants!

A rhino's territory depends on the type of country and the availability of food, and so can be as little as a couple of hectares or as much as 50 sq km. The diet consists mainly of leaves, shoots and buds of a large variety of bushes and trees.

Rhinos reach sexual maturity by five years but females do not usually become pregnant for the first time until around seven years of age. Calves weigh around 40 kg at birth and by three months of age weigh around 140 kg. Adult animals weigh in at anything from 1000 kg to 1600 kg! They are solitary animals, only coming together for some days during mating. Calves stay with the mother for anything up to three years, although suckling generally stops after the first year.

WART HOG

Although there are a number of wild-pig species in Kenya, the one you're most likely to see is the wart hog. It is found in all the major parks – Amboseli, Masai Mara, Nairobi, Tsavo, Meru, Marsabit and Samburu.

The wart hog gets its name from the somewhat grotesque wart-like growths which grow on its face. They are usually found in family groups of a boar, a sow and three or four young. Their most (or perhaps only) endearing habit is the way they turn tail and trot away with their thin tufted tails stuck straight up in the air like some antenna.

The males are usually bigger than the females, measuring up to one metre and weighing as much as 100 kg. They grow upper and lower tusks; the upper ones curve outwards and upwards and grow as long as 60 cm; the lower ones are usually less than 15 cm.

Wart hogs live mainly on grass, but also eat fruit and bark, and, in hard times, will burrow with the snout for roots and bulbs. They rest and give birth in abandoned burrows or sometimes excavate a cavity in abandoned termite mounds. The young are born in litters of up to eight, although two to four is far more usual.

Phacochoerus aethiopicus
Swahili: *ngiri*

ZEBRA

Equus burchelli,
Equus grevyi
Swahili: *punda milia*

Zebras are one of the most common animals in the Kenyan parks and are widely distributed. You'll find them in great numbers in Nairobi, Tsavo, Amboseli, Samburu, Buffalo Springs, Maralal and Marsabit reserves as well as Masai Mara where they are present in the thousands.

Zebras often intermingle with other animals, most commonly the wildebeest but also with topi and hartebeest.

There are two species to be seen in Kenya, the most common being Burchell's zebra which is found in all the western and southern parks all the way up to Samburu and Maralal. In the more arid north-west and north-east, however, the most common species is the Grevy's zebra which differs from Burchell's in having much narrower and more numerous stripes, prominent, broad, rounded ears, and a pure white underbelly.

Some taxonomists classify Burchell's zebra into various 'races' or subspecies but this is a contentious issue since it is impossible to find two zebras exactly alike even in the same herd. What is more certain is that although Burchell's and Grevy's zebra often form mixed herds over much of their range, they do not interbreed in the wild.

Zebras are grazers but will occasionally browse on leaves and scrub. They need water daily and rarely wander far from a water hole, though they appear to have considerably more resistance to drought than antelope.

Reproductive rituals take the form of fierce fights between rival stallions for control of a group of mares. The gestation period is about 12 months and one foal is born at a time.

The most usual predator is the lion, though hyenas and hunting dogs will occasionally take zebras too.